The Dynamics of Mass Communication

MEDIA IN THE DIGITAL AGE

The McGraw-Hill Series in Mass Communication and Journalism

The Dynamics of Mass Communication

MEDIA IN THE DIGITAL AGE,
7th Edition

Joseph R. Dominick
University of Georgia, Athens

Boston   Burr Ridge, IL   Dubuque, IA   Madison, WI   New York
San Francisco   St. Louis   Bangkok   Bogotá   Caracas   Kuala Lumpur
Lisbon   London   Madrid   Mexico City   Milan   Montreal   New Delhi
Santiago   Seoul   Singapore   Sydney   Taipei   Toronto

McGraw-Hill Higher Education

A Division of The McGraw-Hill Companies

The Dynamics of Mass Communication: Media in the Digital Age

Published by McGraw-Hill, an imprint of The McGraw-Hill Companies, Inc., 1221 Avenue of the Americas, New York, NY, 10020. Copyright © 2002, 1999, 1996, 1994, 1993, 1990, 1987, 1983 by The McGraw-Hill Companies, Inc. All rights reserved. No part of this publication may be reproduced or distributed in any form or by any means, or stored in a database or retrieval system, without the prior written consent of The McGraw-Hill Companies, Inc., including, but not limited to, in any network or other electronic storage or transmission, or broadcast for distance learning.

Some ancillaries, including electronic and print components, may not be available to customers outside the United States.

This book is printed on acid-free paper.

International 1 2 3 4 5 6 7 8 9 0 VNH / VNH 0 9 8 7 6 5 4 3 2 1
National   1 2 3 4 5 6 7 8 9 0 VNH / VNH 0 9 8 7 6 5 4 3 2 1

ISBN 0-07-240766-2

Editorial director: *Phillip A. Butcher*
Sponsoring editor: *Valerie Raymond*
Marketing manager: *Kelly M. May*
Project manager: *Christina Thornton-Villagomez*
Director of design: *Keith J. McPherson*
Production supervisor: *Susanne Riedell*
Media producer: *Jessica Bodie*
Photo research coordinator: *David A. Tietz*
Photo research: *Corrine Johns*
Interior/cover design: *Keith J. McPherson*
Cover images: *© Photo Disc 2001, © Corbis 2001*
Supplement producer: *Susan Lombardi*
Printer: *Von Hoffmann Press, Inc.*
Typeface: *10/12 Palatino*
Compositor: *Black Dot Group*

Library of Congress-in-Publication Data

Dominick, Joseph R.
    The dynamics of mass communication : media in the digital age/Joseph R. Dominick—
7th ed.
      p. cm.—(McGraw-Hill series in mass communication)
    ISBN 0-07-240766-2 (alk. paper)
    1. Mass media. I. Title. II. Series.
    P90.D59 2002
    302.23—dc21   2001030392

INTERNATIONAL EDITION
Copyright © 2002. Exclusive rights by The McGraw-Hill Companies, Inc., for manufacture and export. This book cannot be re-exported from the country to which it is consigned by McGraw-Hill. The International Edition is not available in North America.

When ordering this title, use ISBN 0-07-112329-6

www.mhhe.com

For Meaghan and for Carole

About the Author

Joseph R. Dominick received his undergraduate degree from the University of Illinois and his Ph.D. from Michigan State University in 1970. He taught for four years at Queens College of the City University of New York before coming to the College of Journalism and Mass Communication at the University of Georgia where, from 1980 to 1985, he served as head of the Radio-TV-Film Sequence. Dr. Dominick is the author of three books in addition to *The Dynamics of Mass Communication* and has published more than 30 articles in scholarly journals. From 1976 to 1980, Dr. Dominick served as editor of the *Journal of Broadcasting*. He has received research grants from the National Association of Broadcasters and from the American Broadcasting Company and has consulted for such organizations as the Robert Wood Johnson Foundation and the American Chemical Society.

Preface

Previous adopters will notice something different about the seventh edition: It has a subtitle. The timing seemed right to add "Media in the Digital Age" to *The Dynamics of Mass Communication*.

I did a Google search for the term "digital age" and got back 295,000 hits, including such items as privacy in the digital age, art in the digital age, children in the digital age, scholars' information requirements in the digital age (I read that one carefully), archives in the digital age, culture in the digital age, antitrust in the digital age, matte painting in the digital age (?), dentistry in the digital age, Hootie and the Blowfish in the digital age. I could go on with another 294,991 examples, but I think I already made the point: There's something to this digital age thing.

BEING DIGITAL

Sometime between 1998 (when much of the sixth edition was written) and 2001 (when the seventh edition appears), the digital age came of age. Consider just a few of the events that transpired during this period:

- The number of American homes with computers passed the 50 percent mark.
- The number of regular Internet users increased to 100 million.
- Napster's digital music file-sharing program attracted more than 50 million users and shook up an entire industry.
- Stephen King and Elmore Leonard both wrote e-books designed for the online community.
- *Star Wars: The Phantom Menace* was released in digital form.
- Two digital radio satellite companies announced plans to start a service for car radios.
- Digital AOL absorbed traditional Time Warner in a $183 billion deal.
- My cable company went digital, and now I have to pay an extra $4.95 per month for a converter. (Granted, this last event is not on the same level as AOL/Time Warner, but it hit closer to home.)

I have tried to make the seventh edition reflect these changes. Specifically:

- Chapter 1 includes a new model for studying mass communication that reflects the new reality of the Internet as mass communication.
- Chapter 1 also introduces the term "disintermediation," a neologism of the digital age with profound implications for mass communication.
- Chapter 3 has an expanded section describing the digital revolution. I have tried to explain it using Nicholas Negroponte's distinction between "atoms" and "bits."
- The chapters in Parts Two and Three (the "media" chapters) all have new sections detailing how each medium is dealing with the digital age.
- Chapter 8 contains a section on the impact of Napster on the sound-recording business.

- Chapter 11 ("The Internet and the World Wide Web") has been expanded and talks about broadband access, streaming video, Web TV, and e-commerce.
- The chapters in Part Four (the "media professions" chapters) contain extended treatment of how news reporting, advertising, and public relations are adapting to digital media.
- In all chapters I have tried to use examples that stress digital media.

 BOX SCORE

As in past editions, the boxed inserts in each chapter provide background material, present further examples of topics mentioned in the text, and raise issues that students might think about or discuss. The seventh edition contains more than 80 revised or new boxed inserts. Also as in previous editions, I have kept the issue-oriented focus in constructing these inserts. More than 40 spotlight some kind of pertinent ethical, social, or critical/cultural issue. In addition, a new series of "Decision Makers" boxes features profiles of key figures in the various media whose choices have had a significant impact on the development of their industries.

MORE CRITICAL/CULTURAL

The sixth edition introduced the critical/cultural perspective to the *Dynamics of Mass Communication.* The seventh edition expands on this perspective by including four new or revised Critical/Cultural Issues boxes that illustrate the approach.

WHAT ELSE IS NEW?

In addition to the items mentioned above, the following are new to this edition:

- Parts Two and Three (the "media" chapters) contain a new section that briefly describes the defining features of each medium.
- The history sections in Parts Two and Three have been streamlined for easier reading.
- Chapter 15 has an extended discussion about copyright and the Internet.
- Chapter 16 uses the *Los Angeles Times*–Staples Center brouhaha to illustrate the workings of the ethical model presented at the beginning of the chapter.
- Chapter 18 includes a section on research about the social impact of the Internet.
- The questions at the end of each chapter are now divided into two sets. One set of questions reviews material in the chapter, while the other set encourages more critical thinking about topics raised in the chapter.

KEEPING IT CURRENT

As Bill Gates is fond of saying, "The Internet changes everything." That has been especially true for the mass media in the past couple of years. The task of bringing each chapter up to date was much more challenging because of the impact of the net. Nonetheless, all chapters and tables have been revised to reflect the most recent information available at press time. Finally, the book has been given a sparkly new design in keeping with the digital age.

SOMETHING FAMILIAR

Past users of *Dynamics* will notice some continuity from the sixth to the seventh edition. The number of chapters remains the same, as does the book's organization. Further, the emphasis on media economics is maintained in the seventh edition. Media mergers, competition, convergence, and the bottom line are still important factors in understanding digital age media. In addition, the book's emphasis on the social impact of the media has been preserved. The concern over the media's effect on antisocial behavior, the controversy over media coverage of scandals involving public figures, and the media's role in the recent tumult surrounding the 2000 presidential election make this material crucial for students to know.

Once again (and it gets harder every time), I have tried to keep the writing style informal and conversational. As before, I have chosen many examples from popular culture that I hope all students are familiar with. Technical terms are boldfaced and defined in the Glossary. I have also included a number of charts, tables, and figures that I hope will aid understanding.

. . . IN A SUPPORTING ROLE

THE DOMINICK ONLINE LEARNING CENTER

www.mhhe.com/dominick

Including for the instructor:

- A teaching guide, incorporating all text supplements, written by Max V. Grubb, Southern Illinois University–Carbondale
- Detailed chapter summaries, written by Jerry Pinkham, College of Lake County
- PowerPoint slides for each chapter, also written by Professor Pinkham
- Chapter web resources, written by Steven J. Dick, Southern Illinois University–Carbondale

And for the student:

- Interactive web exercises, written by Steven J. Dick
- Practice tests
- Media timelines
- Learning objectives
- Chapter outlines
- Key terms and crossword puzzles
- An Online glossary

POWERWEB: AN ONLINE READER AND RESOURCE SITE

Each new book comes with a PowerWeb passcard to a website made available in partnership with Dushkin/McGraw-Hill, publisher of the popular *Annual Editions* series. The site includes:

- Articles on mass communication issues, refereed by content experts
- Real-time news on mass communication topics
- Weekly course updates
- Interactive exercises and assessment tools
- Student study tips
- Web research tips and exercises
- Refereed and updated research links
- Daily news
- Access to the Northernlight® Special Collection of journals and articles

 COMPUTERIZED TEST BANK

Written by Rebecca Ann Lind, University of Illinois at Chicago, this computerized test bank has all new questions that are now page referenced to the text. It is available in both Windows and Macintosh formats.

 POWERPOINT SLIDES

Created by Jerry Pinkham, College of Lake County, these all new PowerPoint slides can be used by instructors in class presentations and by students for review. They are available in a variety of formats: on disk, on the Instructor's CD-ROM, and on the Online Learning Center.

 INSTRUCTOR'S CD-ROM

This convenient to use CD-ROM was developed to facilitate class presentations. It includes:

- All instructor's resource material from the Online Learning Center
- The entire Test Bank
- Video clips keyed to the chapter outlines

VIDEO

Keyed directly to this text, the McGraw-Hill Mass Communication Video is 14 concept videos compiled onto one videotape. Each segment is approximately 10 minutes in length. The segments are (1) The Newest Mass Communication Medium; (2) Modern Mass Communication: Bringing Us Together or Keeping Us Apart? (3) The Impact of Television; (4) The Global Network; (5) Are Books Going to Become Obsolete? (6) Newspapers: Developing to Compete in a Media-Rich

World; (7) The Movie Business; (8) The Cultural Impact of Film; (9) Radio: A Miraculous New Medium; (10) The Business of Making It in the Recording Industry; (11) Television Broadcasting Takes Off; (12) Advertising: Always with Us; (13) How Free Is the Press? (14) A Right to Know?

Additional videos are available from your McGraw-Hill sales representative.

 ACKNOWLEDGMENTS

Once again, I would like to thank all the students and instructors who have used the first six editions of this book and who were kind enough to suggest improvements. Your feedback was greatly appreciated. Several colleagues deserve special mention: Drs. Carolina Alzura, Vince Benigni, Keisha Hoerrner, and Patrica Priest provided special material for this edition as did doctoral student Rita Van Sant. Dr. Lynn Sallot provided details about public relations and Dr. James Weaver of Virginia Polytechnic was kind enough to help me understand his experiments. An extra special thank you to Dr. Rebecca Ann Lind at the University of Illinois at Chicago for her close reading of the text and her suggestions for improvement. Professor Lind was also kind enough to provide the provocative, insightful, and thoughtful questions that appear in the Critical/Cultural boxed inserts. Her efforts went way beyond the call of duty and I deeply appreciate them. In addition, thanks to graduate student Doowang Lee for his Internet research; thanks to Cheryl Christopher for her help with logistics; thanks to Meaghan Dominick for her knowledge of popular music; and a particular thanks to Carole Dominick for her help with photography, the index, and for putting up with my whining during the revision process.

As always, I would like to thank the reviewers who offered helpful and valuable suggestions for improvement:

Ernest Bereman—Truman State University
Susan L. Brinson—Auburn University
Thomas Draper—University of Nebraska at Kearney
Anthony Georgilas—Pasadena City College
Margaret J. Haefner—Illinois State University
Kirk Hallahan—Colorado State University
Ralph E. Hanson—West Virginia University
Sharon R. Hollenback—Syracuse University
James L. Hoyt—University of Wisconsin at Madison
W. A. Kelly Huff—Miami University
Arnold H. Ismach—University of Oregon—Eugene
Kathy Merlock Jackson—Virginia Wesleyan College
Laurence Jankowski—Bowling Green State University
Jack Keever—Austin Community College
Diane Lamb—University of New Mexico
Michael J. Laney—Lee University
John A. Lent—Temple University
Rebecca A. Lind—University of Illinois at Chicago
Kathleen Matichek—Normandale Community College

Barry Melton—Lee College
Michael D. Murray—University of Missouri, St. Louis
K. R. M. Short—University of Houston
Glenn Sparks—Purdue University
Karon Speckman—Truman State University
Susan M. Stolzfus—Green River Community College
Hazel G. Warlaumont—California State University at Fullerton
Barbara Wilson—Parkland College
David O. Woolverton—Eastern Kentucky University

Finally, at the risk of making this section sound like an Oscar acceptance speech, a big thank you to the talented folks at McGraw-Hill who worked so hard on this project: to Valerie Raymond, for her thorough professionalism, keen insight, intelligent suggestions, unwavering enthusiasm for the project, clever caption writing, and for tolerating my somewhat warped sense of humor; to Phil Butcher, for continuing to support the book; to Kelly May for her marketing efforts; to Christina Thornton-Villagomez for once again flawlessly handling all the details; to Corrine Johns for digging up all the neat photos; to Jennifer Van Hove for capturing all the screen captures; and to Keith McPherson, whose design concept made the book look spiffy.

In closing, I'll repeat what I said in the six prior editions (I can't find anything better to say). The media are a vital force in our society; I hope this book helps us understand them even better.

Joseph R. Dominick

Your Guided Tour

CHAPTER 10 Television

It might be surprising to some to discover that one of the defining moments of modern television occurred on "The Drew Carey Show." The November 17, 1999, episode of the popular sitcom started off with Mimi Bobeck, Drew Carey's nemesis, looking into the camera and saying, "Hey, all you geeks out there. Both hands on the keyboard!" This rather peculiar line inaugurated one of the most enterprising examples of the convergence between television and the Internet: It was the first time a large-scale, streaming video webcast was used to enhance and expand the content of a prime-time, network television show.

Audience members for the segment, entitled "Drew-Cam," were encouraged to put their computers near their television sets. Those that visited the website for the show were treated to material not available to those watching TV. The storyline for the episode involved Carey's agreeing to have webcams installed in his apartment. Although there was some overlap with the tele-

Like "The Drew Carey Show," the quiz show "Who Wants to be a Millionaire" also uses the Internet to enhance the viewing experience. (Newsmakers/Liaison Agency)

vised version, web viewers saw some scenes the TV audience didn't. In one segment, while Drew is at work, the webcams show his dog letting neighborhood mutts into his kitchen for a party. In another, Ed McMahon drops by with a $10 million check but leaves when he finds no one is at home. The experiment was a success. The website received a record 1.9 million clicks.

The "Drew Carey" experiment may have been the most visible example of TV and Internet convergence, but it is certainly not the only one. There is a web counterpart to "Who Wants to Be a Millionaire" in which web surfers play along with the show. ESPN.com synchronizes some of its content with ABC's "Monday Night Football" broadcast. The National Basketball Association (NBA) combines a special satellite-delivered NBA channel with complementary content from the NBA website.

The most important word in the above paragraphs is "convergence." Although people have been talking about

---

- Splashy graphics and color.
- Short, easy-to-read stories.
- Lots of graphs, charts, and tables.
- Factoids (a factoid is a list of boiled-down facts—much like this list).

A somewhat controversial reporting philosophy surfaced in the mid-1990s. **Public journalism** (see Social Issues, "Public Journalism") embraces the view that newspapers should do more than just report the news; they should try to help communities solve problems and encourage participation in the political process. Some reporters think this philosophy exceeds the established tenets of journalism.

With the exception of the early 1990s, when a weak economy and a depressed advertising market caused several big-city papers to fold, the newspaper industry has enjoyed prosperity. By the late 1990s, layoffs, cost-cutting measures, and an increase in advertising revenue helped newspapers increase their profits.

The late 1990s also saw many newspapers start online editions. This trend continued into the new century as newspapers came to grips with the promises and pitfalls of the Internet.

NEWSPAPERS IN THE DIGITAL AGE

The newspaper industry is still experimenting to find the best way to incorporate an online presence with the traditional print editions. Fearful that online companies such as Yahoo! and Excite would use the web to steal away readers and advertising, many newspapers rushed to set up websites. The earliest newspaper sites were simply watered-down versions of the printed paper. They did little to promote the print version, nor did they generate enough revenue to pay for themselves. In short, for most papers, the website was simply a drain on finances and resources.

The Digital Age

All "media" chapters have new sections detailing how each medium is dealing with the digital age.

demand, however, publishers don't have to guess how many books they should print. They simply print one whenever somebody orders it. This eliminates all the expensive production and shipping costs and guarantees that no books will be returned unsold. Eliminating these costs and the guesswork involved in forecasting demand means that publishers can make money on a book that sells only a few hundred copies. This might open up the way for a multitude of special-interest books that would be too expensive to publish with the traditional method.

Moreover, a book title would never go out of print. It would be permanently stored somewhere on some hard drive or disk. Even the most esoteric or obscure titles could be easily accessed.

■ What Is a Book?

Finally, the digital age raises fundamental questions about what exactly constitutes a book. E-books could easily incorporate a sound track that plays while a person reads. Video clips that demonstrate how something works could be inserted into instruction books. Illustrations as lush as those done by monks during the Middle Ages are possible. The creative potential of e-books is still unexplored territory.

Does all this signal the death of the traditional paper-and-ink book? Probably not. People will still be drawn to the feel of books and the unique experience of reading paper pages bound between covers. Dick Brass, the executive in charge of Microsoft's e-book efforts, put it this way in a *Newsweek* article: "[Traditional] books will persist because they're beautiful and useful. They're like horses after the automobile—not gone but transformed into a recreational beast."

The rest of this chapter discusses the more concrete aspects of the book industry—its organization, ownership, production techniques, economics, and audiences. Keep in mind, however, that book publishing is in a state of transition as it quickly enters the digital age.

DEFINING FEATURES OF BOOKS

Books are the least "mass" of the mass media. It took about 40 years to sell 20 million copies of *Gone With the Wind*, but more than 50 million people watched the movie version in a single evening when it came to television. Even a flop TV show might have 10 million people in its audience, whereas a popular hardcover book might make the best-seller list with 125,000 copies sold. Even a mass-market paperback might sell only about 6 million copies.

Books, however, can have a cultural impact that far outweighs their modest audience size. *Uncle Tom's Cabin* is credited with changing a nation's attitude toward slavery. Dr. Spock and his *Baby and Child Care* altered the way parents brought up their children and became the target of critics who blamed him and his methods for the social unrest of the 1960s. *Silent Spring* changed the nation's attitudes toward the environment.

Finally, books are the oldest and most enduring of the m[...] printed a book back in the 15th century. Public libraries have [...] dreds of years. Many individuals have extensive collections [...] home libraries. People throw away newspapers and magazi[...] ing them, but most save their books.

Defining Features

All "media" chapters also have new sections that briefly define features of each medium.

Critical/Cultural Issues

Critical/Cultural boxes carry the critical/cultural perspective, introduced in Chapter 2, throughout the text.

ETHICAL ISSUES Don't Hold Your Breath Waiting for the Prize Patrol

Is it right to intentionally mislead people in an effort to sell them magazines? Should an industry depend on deception to stay profitable? Those are only two of the many ethical and legal questions raised by sweepstakes promotions for magazine subscriptions.

Sweepstakes, such as those run by the Publishers Clearinghouse (the one with the prize patrol and the oversized check) and American Family Publishers (the one with Ed McMahon and Dick Clark), account for about one-third of all the new magazine subscriptions in a given year.

Consumers receive so much junk mail, however, that these companies have resorted to more extravagant and questionable techniques to get consumers to read their mailings. The envelopes are oversized and emblazoned with messages such as "You are scheduled to win the $1 million super prize on August 20th" or "You're our #1 top prize winner in this sweepstakes with a cash prize of $100,000." A letter inside the envelope belatedly points out that these claims are true *if and only if* you hold the winning number. The odds of having the winning number (which happen to be about 150 million to 1) are never mentioned. It is also strongly implied that the more magazines you subscribe to, the better your chances of winning. Once you subscribe, you get more personalized mailings that are even more misleading.

Most people are not taken in by such flimflammery. But some people, particularly the elderly, have fallen for it. A Congressional hearing on the practices of these companies revealed horror stories of elderly people spending thousands of dollars on subscriptions in the hopes of making a prize patrol visit more likely.

Class-action lawsuits against these sweepstakes companies were filed in several states. Both the Publishers Clearinghouse and American Family Publishers agreed to multimillion-dollar settlements but admitted no wrongdoing. They also agreed that all future mailings will include the actual odds of winning, state that subscribing to one or more magazines will not improve the chances of winning, and print their rules in 8-point type (which is this big).

Because of these changes and the bad publicity, the sweepstakes haven't been nearly as effective in generating new subscriptions, and magazine circulation figures are down as a result.

Should the bottom line take precedence over ethical business practices? Is it right to profit from a practice that takes advantage of vulnerable people, who might not fully understand what they read? Maybe the magazine industry will now explore other ways of finding subscribers.

The biggest business development was the merger of the world's largest magazine publisher (Time Warner) with the world's largest Internet company, America OnLine (AOL). The new company offered many opportunities for cross-pollination between the print and digital media. All of Time Warner's magazines, for example, could sell subscriptions on AOL.

Several magazines, such as *Slate* and *Salon*, appeared in an online-only form. Many print magazine publishers viewed these new competitors with some apprehension because they feared that they would take away readers and advertising revenue. As it turned out, they needn't have worried. As a group, online-only magazines were generally money-losing propositions. A few narrowly targeted "e-zines" were successful (see Media Probe, "The Wonderful (and Sometimes Weird) World of E-zines"), but in general, as discussed in more detail below, the Internet turned out to be a friend rather than an enemy to traditional print magazines.

MAGAZINES IN THE DIGITAL AGE

When the Internet was first becoming popular, many publishers feared that it would spell the end for the printed magazine. It was thought that magazines available for free on the net would siphon r[...] from the traditional magazine. Online magazines were [...] would inevitably replace the "old" glossy-paper magazine[...] ever, magazine publishers have come to the conclusion tha[...] a complement to the traditional magazine that a competito[...]

SOCIAL ISSUES: Media Specialization: Gains and Losses

The trend toward more mass media and more specialized content seems irreversible. Several consequences of this movement, however, bear scrutiny. To begin, the traditional media, whatever their shortcomings, did provide a national agenda for society and helped define a national consensus. They focused the attention of the nation and mobilized its resources. The fireside chats of Franklin Roosevelt, for example, were credited with helping the country survive the hardships of the depression. Could such a phenomenon take place in the 21st century? Douglas Cater is a media critic who was among the first to question whether media specialization was beneficial to society. In a 1973 *Wall Street Journal* article, Cater posed the fundamental question: "What happens when each minority group listens to its own prophets? When there are no more Walter Cronkites each evening to reassure us that despite its afflictions the nation still stands?"

Mass communication scholar Wilson Dizard described the traditional mass media as a kind of social "Elmer's glue" that bound people together (see the discussions of "Linkage" and "Transmission of Values" in the next chapter). Communication researcher Gladys Gantley in a 1991 *Washington Quarterly* article speculates that the growth in the number of specialized and personalized media might have political repercussions. Increased access to a greater range of information could serve as a democratizing force, but there might be a downside: "[If] [s]pread to millions of individuals throughout the world, each literally following his or her own agenda, such power could remove the glue of social cohesion . . . Power to the people could mean that nobody is in control."

Neil Postman, in his provocative book *Amusing Ourselves to Death*, suggests another troubling possibility. The proliferation of media and messages could result in a flood of trivialized content that distracts us from the key social issues of the day. We might, as his title suggests, amuse ourselves to death.

Although the following chapters discuss the various media individually, these media do not exist in a vacuum. In the future, we are likely to see more examples of the synergy that exists among all communication media.

Disintermediation

This rather ungraceful, tongue-twisting word refers to the process whereby access to a product or a service is given directly to the consumer, thus eliminating the intermediary, or "middleman," who might typically supply the product or service. The Internet and the World Wide Web have created a ubiquitous and easily accessible network where buyers and sellers make direct contact. The Internet has already provided several examples of **disintermediation**. Travelers bypass travel agents and book airline tickets directly online; traders bypass brokers and purchase stocks directly online; consumers bypass salespeople and buy insurance online. (Some businesses have more to fear from disintermediation than others. It's unlikely that consumers will bypass restaurants because of the Internet.)

Disintermediation is of obvious concern to mass media organizations. Those media that can easily be distributed over the Internet are the first to feel its effects. Take sound recording, for example: An artist can use the web to distribute a CD directly to the consumers via the net. The recording company, distributor, and retailer are no longer needed in the process. Or consider book publishing: An author can put a book directly on a website for readers to download, thereby bypassing publishing companies and bookstores altogether.

Other mass communication organizations, even though they may not have the immediate fears of the recording and publishing industries, will also have to face the implications of this phenomenon. For example, audience members can listen to radio on the web; local stations are no longer necessary. Before long, movie fans will be able to download current full-length films onto DVDs. Will motion picture theaters become obsolete? The chapters in Parts Two and Three of this book will have more to say about disintermediation and its impact on the various media.

27

treatment of certain diseases are another example of this **linkage** function. The needs of those suffering from the disease are matched with the desires of others who wish to see the problem eliminated.

Another type of linkage occurs when geographically separated groups that share a common interest are linked by the media. Publicity about the sickness known as Gulf War Syndrome linked those who claimed to be suffering from the disease, who formed a coalition that eventually prompted government hearings on the issue.

The best examples of linkage, however, are the various websites, newsgroups, and chat rooms on the Internet. The online auction site eBay, for example, links people who have some item to sell with people who are looking for an item to buy. A person in California looking to sell an Alex Rodriguez rookie baseball card might be linked with a buyer in Maine, a linkage that would have been much more difficult without the Internet. Match.com bills itself as the place where "You are just a few clicks away from meeting thousands of interesting, intelligent, and successful singles just like you!" WebMD offers subscribers various "communities" where they can share stories about their medical condition with others in the same situation.

This linkage function is present in other media as well. The magazine *Gambling Times* allows a person interested in games of chance to be linked to others with a similar interest. *The General*, a publication devoted to those who play board war games, contains a classified ad section where readers advertise for opponents. Some firms, with the help of the local phone company, are offering "party lines" or "gab lines." A person dials a number and is linked up with similarly minded folks. Most users of this service are looking for dates, and if two people hit it off, they can ask the operator to transfer them to a private line. One New York–based party line logged about 100,000 minutes in calls a day.

Of course, it is entirely possible that the media can create totally new social groups by linking members of society who have not previously recognized that others have similar interests. Some writers call this function the public-making ability of the mass media. A concrete example occurred in Virginia in 1996. Wal-Mart had proposed to the county board of supervisors that a new store be built near the site of George Washington's boyhood home. T[he board approved the] request with little fanfare. The local newspaper, however, [became involved] and ran a series of articles and cartoons against building th[e store near the his]toric site. The series inspired citizens to unite against the p[roposed board] decision. Eventually, Wal-Mart agreed to move the store to [a new location] away from the original location.

The biggest newspaper group is the Gannett Company with 101 dailies and a combined circulation of about 6 million. Knight-Ridder Newspapers Inc. controls 34 dailies with about a 3.8 million circulation. Other newspaper chains that own dailies with a combined circulation of more than 2 million are Newhouse Newspapers, Tribune/Times Mirror Company, and the New York Times Company (see Table 4.2).

Table 4.2	Five Biggest Newspaper Groups, 2000	
Name	**Number of Papers Owned**	**Leading Papers**
Gannett Company Inc.	101	*USA Today, Nashville Tennessee*
Knight-Ridder Newspapers Inc.	34	*Philadelphia Inquirer, Miami Herald*
Newhouse Newspapers	23	*Cleveland Plain Dealer, Trenton Times*
New York Times Company	11	*Newsday, Los Angeles Times, Chicago Tribune*
Tribune/Times Mirror Company	21	*New York Times*

107

Media Probe

Media Probe boxes introduce business issues.

Decision Makers

New to this edition, Decision Maker boxes profile key media people.

messages simultaneously—one aural, one visual. Both humans and machines can be thought of as decoders. The radio is a decoder; so is a videotape playback unit; so is the telephone (one end encodes and the other end decodes); so is a film projector.

A single communication event can involve many stages of decoding. A reporter sits in on a city council meeting and takes notes (decoding); he or she phones in a story to the rewrite desk where another reporter types the story as it is read (decoding). The story is read by an editor (decoding). Eventually it is printed and read by the audience (decoding). What we said earlier about encoding also applies to decoding: Some people are better at it than others. Many of you will not be able to decode "¿Dónde está el baño?"; others will. Some people are able to read 1,500 words a minute; others struggle along at 200. There are some messages that may never be decoded because the encoder put the message in the wrong channel. A telephone call may not be decoded by someone with impaired hearing. E-mail can only be received by those with access to a computer.

The **receiver** is the target of the message—its ultimate goal. The receiver can be a single person, a group, an institution, or even a large, anonymous collection of people. In today's environment, people are more often the receivers of communication messages than the sources. Most of us see more billboards than we put up and listen to more radio programs than we broadcast. The receivers of the message can be determined by the source, as in a telephone call, or they can self-select themselves into the audience, as with the audience for a TV show. It should also be clear that in some situations the source and receiver can be in each other's immediate presence, while in other situations they can be separated by both space and time.

■ Feedback

Now let us examine the bottom half of Figure 1–1. This portion of the figure represents the potential for **feedback** to occur. Feedback refers to those responses of the receiver that shape and alter the subsequent messages of the source. Feedback represents a reversal of the flow of communication. The original source becomes the receiver; the original receiver becomes the new source. Feedback is useful to the source because it allows the source to answer the question, How am I doing? Feedback is important to the receiver because it allows the receiver to attempt to change some element in the communication process. Communication scholars have traditionally identified two different kinds of feedback—positive and negative. In general terms, positive feedback from the receiver usually encourages the communication behavior in progress; negative feedback usually attempts to change the communication or even to terminate it.

Consider the following telephone call:

"Bambi?"
"Yes."

Soundbyte

Soundbyte boxes enliven the material throughout the text.

and females tend to predominate during the daytime hours from Monday to Friday. On Saturday mornings, most of the audience is under 13. Prime time is dominated by those in the 18- to 49-year-old age group.

Various demographic factors, such as age, sex, social class, and education, affect viewership. For example, teenagers watch the least. People in low-income homes generally watch more television than their middle-income counterparts. People with more education tend to watch less, and women watch more often than men. Cable subscribers are younger, have more children, and are more affluent than the average viewer. They also are dissatisfied with traditional television and want more program variety. Subscribers to the pay-cable channels have younger heads of households, are more affluent, and watch more TV than families in noncable homes.

CAREER OUTLOOK

THE TELEVISION INDUSTRY

Someone hunting for a job in TV quickly discovers that it's a relatively small industry. According to recent figures provided by the FCC, about 110,000 people are employed in commercial TV; 100,000 in CATV; 10,000 in noncommercial television; and about 16,000 at TV networks.

In any given year, probably 5,000 to 10,000 people are hired by the TV industry. Many of these people are replacing employees who have retired or gone on to other careers, while others are filling newly created positions. Also, in any given year, about 15,000 to 20,000 people are looking for TV jobs. Speaking conservatively, we can say that there are at least two people looking for each available position. In some areas of television, especially for the so-called glamour jobs (TV reporter, network page, on-camera host for an interview show, series writer), the competition will be much more intense.

■ Entry-Level Positions

Despite this competition, individuals who are skilled, intelligent, and persistent are likely to be successful in finding jobs. Here are some general hints on job hunting in TV:

1. *Think small.* As in radio, small-market TV stations offer more employment potential than larger-market stations. Moreover, at a small station, you have a chance to do more and learn more than you might at a larger station.

2. *Don't be afraid to start at the bottom.* Once you get in, it is easier to move upward into a position that might be more to your liking. Many successful people in TV started in the mailroom, secretarial pool, or shipping department.

3. *Be prepared to move.* Your first job will probably not be a lifetime commitment. Frequently, the road to advancement in TV consists of moving about and up—from a small station to a large station, from an independent station to a network affiliate, from the station to the network.

■ Upward Mobility

Those interested in producing TV shows might consider looking for jobs as camera operator, floor manager (the person who gives cues to the talent and makes sure everything in the studio goes smoothly during the telecast), or production

Careers

Career Outlook sections offer insights into the working world of each medium.

■ MAIN POINTS

- The motion picture developed in the late 19th century. After being a main attraction in nickelodeons, films moved into bigger theaters and movie stars quickly became the most important part of the new industry. Sound came to the movies in the mid-1920s.
- Big movie studios dominated the industry until the late 1940s, when a court decision weakened their power. Television captured much of the film audience in the 1950s. By the end of the 1960s, however, Hollywood had adapted to television and was an active producer of TV shows. A major trend in modern movies is the rise of big-budget movies.
- The transition to digital moviemaking may transform the film industry.

- The movie industry consists of the production, distribution, and exhibition components. Large conglomerates control the business. Producing a motion picture starts from the concept, proceeds to the production stage, and ends with the postproduction stage.
- Movie revenues have shown small but steady growth over the past 10 years. Videocassette sales and rentals and foreign box-office receipts are important sources of movie income.
- Movie audiences are getting older, but a significant part of the audience is still the 30-and-under age group.
- Motion picture studios are now using the Internet to promote their products.

■ QUESTIONS FOR REVIEW

1. What are the defining features of motion pictures?
2. What caused the rise and fall of the Motion Picture Patents Company?
3. How did the film industry react to TV?
4. What are the three main segments of the motion picture industry?
5. What are the various ways films are financed?

■ QUESTIONS FOR CRITICAL THINKING

1. Suppose the movie industry had never moved to Hollywood, staying instead on the East Coast. How might films be different?
2. What are the potential advantages and disadvantages of big corporations controlling motion picture production?
3. Do filmmakers have an obligation to be socially responsible for what they present on the screen? Why or why not?
4. Will the Internet help or hurt independent filmmakers? In what ways?
5. Someone once said that Hollywood producers don't make films; they make deals. Comment on the validity of this statement and its implications.

■ KEY TERMS

phi phenomenon (p. 227)
persistence of vision (p. 227)
Kinetoscope (p. 228)
Motion Picture Patents Company (MPPC) (p. 230)

block booking (p. 232)
double features (p. 233)
digital videodisk (DVD) (p. 238)
pickup (p. 248)
limited partnership (p. 248)

joint venture (p. 249)
sliding scale (p. 249)
Variety (p. 251)
focus group (p. 252)
pay-per-view (PPV) (p. 253)

Visit our Online Learning Center for additional resources.

Brief Contents

Contents

Part II Print Media 83

Chapter 4
Newspapers 84

Part III   Electronic Media   169
Chapter 7
Radio   170

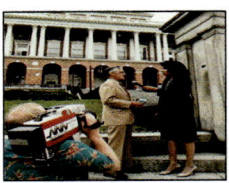

Part IV Specific Media Professions   325

Chapter 12
News Gathering and Reporting   326

Part V   Regulation of the Mass Media 395

Chapter 15
Formal Controls: Laws, Rules, Regulations 396

Part VI   Impact   457

Chapter 17
The Global Village: International and Comparative Media Systems   458

List of Boxes

Chapter 17

Chapter 18

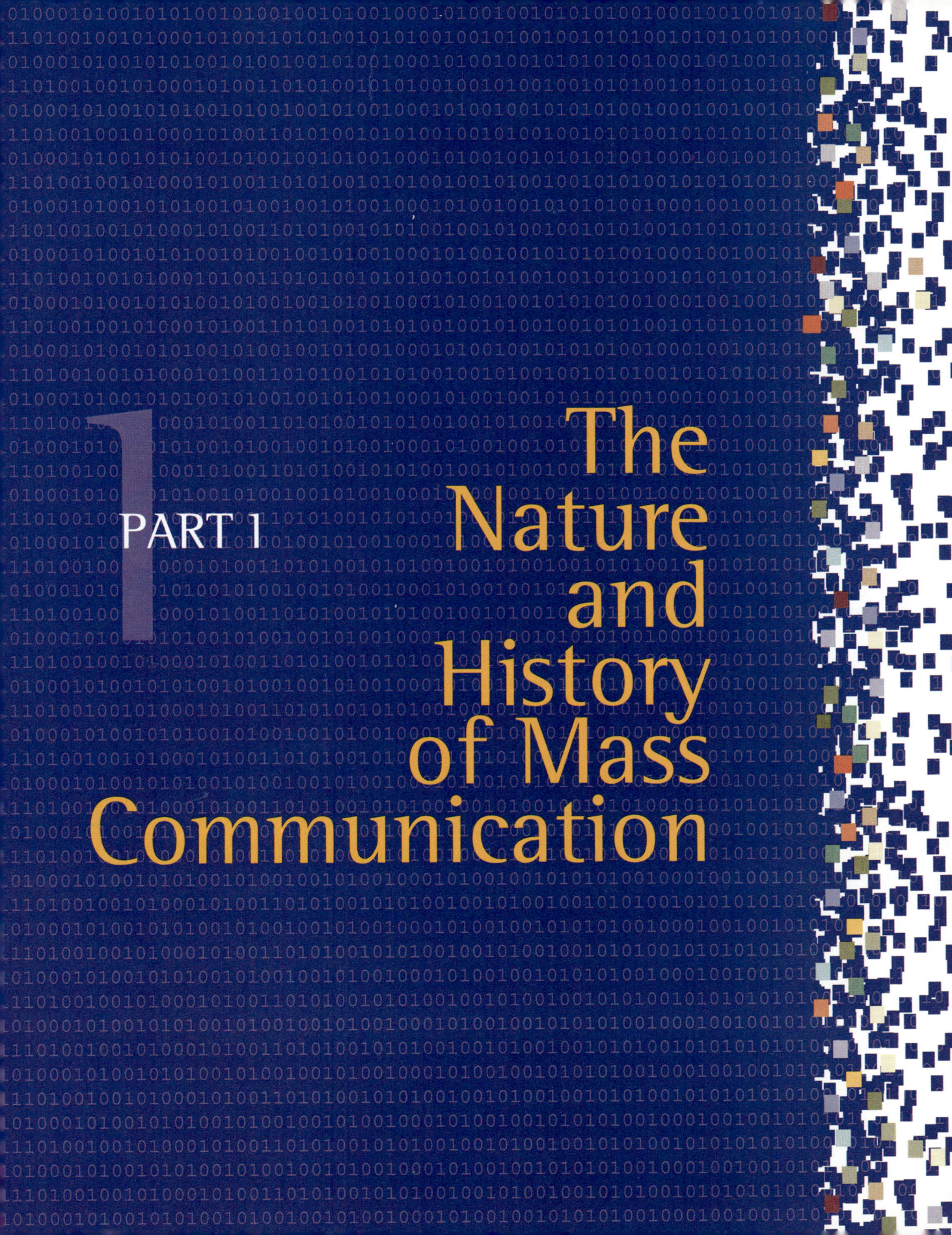

PART 1

The Nature and History of Mass Communication

CHAPTER 1

Communication
Mass and Other Forms

It started off innocently enough. On the afternoon of May 4, 2000, a worker in the Hong Kong office of a U.S. company received an anonymous e-mail with a subject line that read "ILOVEYOU." An attachment to the e-mail was labeled "LOVE-LETTER-FOR-YOU.TXT.VBS." Curious about the identity of the sender, the employee opened the attachment by clicking on it. After that, things were not so innocent.

The attachment contained a virus that infected digital photographs and digital music files stored on the computer's hard drive. It also invaded the computer's Microsoft Outlook address book and sent itself to every listed address, clogging e-mail servers. On a more sinister note, the virus also scanned the hard drive for passwords and tried to e-mail them to a site in the Philippines.

The virus quickly spread from computers in Asia to computers in Europe, doing damage all the way. In Germany, the virus destroyed more than 2,000 digital photographs in the archive of a leading newspaper. ATMs in Belgium were disabled when the virus clogged their systems. The British Parliament had to shut down all its

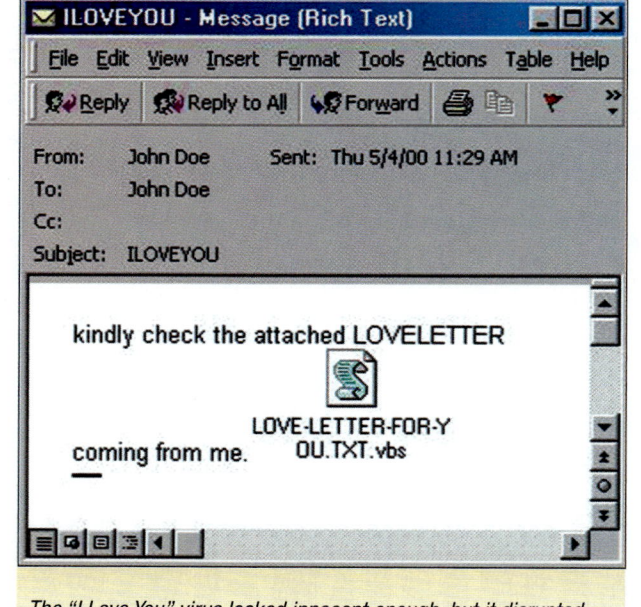

The "I Love You" virus looked innocent enough, but it disrupted computers all over the world.

computers to avoid infection. It was estimated that 70 percent of the computers in Germany, the Netherlands, and Sweden were disabled.

The United States did not escape. Four classified e-mail systems at the Defense Department were infected. Computers at the George W. Bush presidential campaign headquarters had to be shut down. The Georgia secretary of state's office found that 1,000 files had been damaged. E-mail systems at Wall Street financial centers were paralyzed. As systems all over the country were immobilized, workers realized how much they relied on e-mail and struggled to get by without a technology that didn't even exist 10 years earlier. More than 300,000 computers in the United States were infected in just a few hours after the release of the virus.

The virus did most of its damage in just 48 hours. Estimates of the total damage from destroyed files and lost work time for people all over the world ranged from $10 billion to $15 billion.

Authorities traced the virus to the Philippines and arrested a student at a local technical college. Under questioning, the student admitted that he may have released the virus by accident. Although there was some speculation that the student was also the author of the virus, he never admitted to being its creator. (Interestingly, at the time of the student's arrest, the Philippines had no law against computer crimes. The student was charged with fraud and theft, but those charges were dismissed when a Philippine court ruled that the existing laws did not apply.)

Communication between people is a fragile thing. As the new century begins, technological advances have increased the speed and the reach of human communication, but as the above example illustrates, it may be even more fragile than before. Consider the following examples:

- A police computer in Fort Worth, Texas, programmed to make automatic phone calls, switched itself on at 3 A.M. and awoke people in 400 homes with a recorded invitation to a police community forum.
- A computer error by a Sao Paulo, Brazil, phone company caused a customer to get a monthly phone bill for $43 million.
- In the Ukraine, a businessman bought 50 pagers and put them in the backseat of his car. The pager company's computer automatically sends the message "Congratulations on a successful purchase" to each of its pagers a few minutes after they are activated. As you would expect, all 50 pagers in the backseat went off at once and scared the businessman so much he drove his car into a lamppost.
- During the impeachment trial of President Clinton, U.S. Senators signed oaths with a ceremonial pen that was emblazoned with the words "Untied States Senator." Apparently, the designers relied on a spell-check program to find mistakes in their copy, and the program found no misspelled words.
- The student designing the cover for the student directory at a religious college in the South decided to use a mosaic of hundreds of tiny images as background. He downloaded what looked like an appropriate mosaic from a website and slightly blurred the images with a computer. Unfortunately, he didn't look closely at the miniature images he was using. When the directory was released, sharp-eyed students noticed the mosaic featured hundreds of pornographic images.

Even with low-tech devices, communication often goes awry:

- A printing company produced millions of Grand Canyon postage stamps before somebody finally noticed that the stamps incorrectly said the Grand Canyon was in Colorado instead of Arizona.
- In Great Britain, education officials printed 50,000 copies of a poster promoting literacy with the word "vocabulary" spelled "vocablury."
- Headline in a San Diego newspaper: "Poll says that 53% believe media offen make mistakes."
- As part of his criticism of the political views of unsuccessful presidential candidate Pat Buchanan, William Bennett said, "It's a real us-and-them kind of thing." When the *New Yorker* reported the quote, it came out as, "It's a real S&M kind of thing."
- *Newsweek* had to recall several hundred thousand copies of a special issue on "Your Child" because the magazine had said it was OK to feed five-month-olds bits of carrots and zwieback. Feeding those foods to babies of that age could cause choking.
- From the résumé of a graduating senior: "I am a rabid typist."
- From a church bulletin: "Thursday night—potluck supper. Prayer and medication to follow."
- A banner welcoming visiting Philippine dignitaries to the San Jose, California, public library was supposed to say "Welcome" in the visitors' native dialect. Something got lost in translation, and the banner actually read, "You are circumcised."

These seemingly unrelated examples of high-tech and low-tech communication problems illustrate several different types of human communication. They range from the relatively simple—typing a résumé—to the relatively complicated—publishing a magazine. Despite their apparent lack of similarity, these illustrations share certain elements common to communication. A glance at these elements will serve as a starting point for examination of the differences between mass and other forms of communication.

ELEMENTS IN THE COMMUNICATION PROCESS

At a general level, communication events involve the following:

1. A source.
2. A process of encoding.
3. A message.
4. A channel.
5. A process of decoding.
6. A receiver.
7. The potential for feedback.
8. The chance of noise.

Figure 1–1 depicts the communication process. We will refer to this figure as we examine the process more fully.

Transmitting the Message

To begin with, the source initiates the process by having a thought or an idea that he or she wishes to transmit to some other entity. Naturally, sources differ in their communication skills ("Garçon . . . I will have du Boeuf Haché Grillé au Charbon de Bois" versus "Gimmeahamburger"). The source may or may not have knowledge about the receiver of the message. If you are in a conversation with your roommate, you probably know there are some topics that might send him or her up the wall. So you avoid bringing them up (most of the time). Conversely, as I write these lines, I have only a general notion about the kinds of people who will read them, and I have absolutely no idea what you'll be doing while you're reading them (that's probably for the best). Sources can be single individuals, groups, or even organizations. For example, in the *Newsweek* example, the publication was the source. In the police example, the source is harder to pin down. At first glance, it appears that the computer was the source of the errant message. Upon closer examination, since the computer was programmed by human beings, perhaps those persons are the ultimate source.

Encoding refers to the activities that a source goes through to translate thoughts and ideas into a form that may be perceived by the senses. When you have something to say, your brain and your tongue work together (usually) to form words and spoken sentences. When you write a letter, your brain and your fingers cooperate to produce patterns of ink or some other substance that can be seen on paper. If you were trying to communicate with someone who has impaired vision, you might produce a series of pinholes in a piece of paper that can be experienced by touch. If you were a Hollywood director, you would point your camera at a scene that re-creates the image you had in your mind, and you would capture light rays with photosensitive chemicals. Encoding in a communication setting can take place one or more times. In a face-to-face conversation, the speaker encodes thoughts into words. Over the telephone, this phase is repeated, but the phone subsequently encodes sound waves into electrical energy. Some people are better encoders than others; in like manner, some machines are better encoders than others. Music recorded on a $40,000 audio console in a sound studio will probably sound better than that recorded on a pocket cassette recorder.

Elements of the
Communication Process

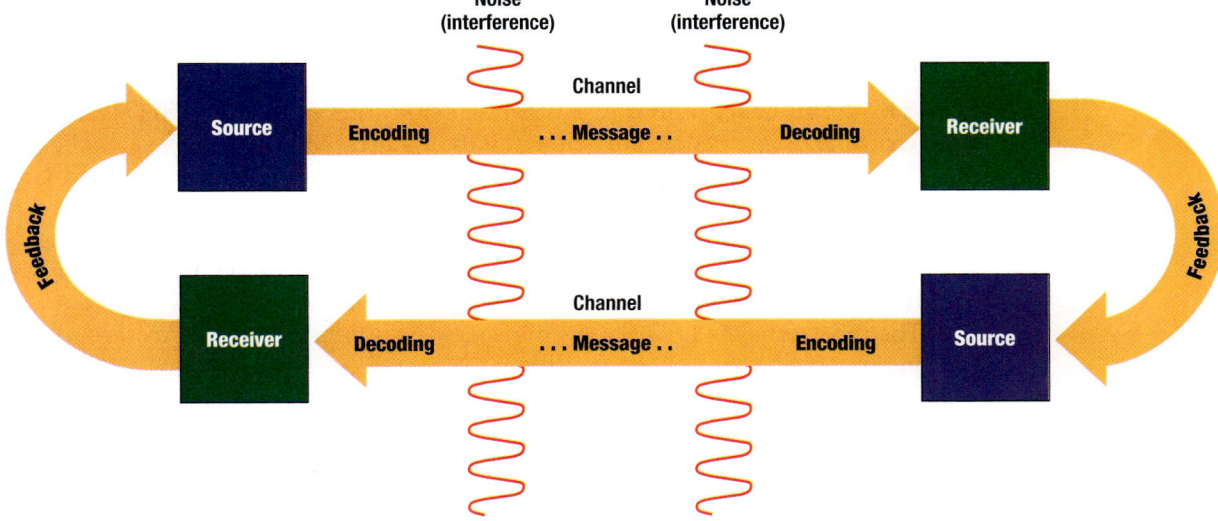

The **message** is the actual physical product that the source encodes. When we talk, our speech is the message. When we write a letter home, what we put on the paper is the message. When a television network presents "Frasier" or "ER", the programs are the message. Human beings usually have a large number of messages at their disposal that they can choose to send, ranging from the simple but effective "No!" to something as complicated as Darwin's *On the Origin of Species*. Messages can be directed at one specific individual ("You turkey!") or at millions (*People* magazine). Messages can be cheap to produce (the spoken word) or very expensive (this book). Some messages are more under the control of the receiver than others. For example, think about how hard or easy it is for you to break off communication (1) in a face-to-face conversation with another person, (2) during a telephone call, and (3) while watching a TV commercial.

Channels are the ways the message travels to the receiver. Sound waves carry spoken words; light waves carry visual messages. Air currents can serve as olfactory channels, carrying messages to our noses—messages that are subtle but nonetheless significant. What kind of message do you get from someone who reeks of Chanel No. 5? Of Brut? Of garlic? Touch is also a channel (e.g., braille). Some messages use more than one channel to travel to the receiver. Radio signals travel by electromagnetic radiation until they are transformed by receiving sets into sound waves that travel through the air to our ears.

Receiving the Message

The **decoding** process is the opposite of the encoding process. It consists of activities that translate or interpret physical messages into a form that has eventual meaning for a receiver. As you read these lines, you are decoding a message. If you are playing the radio while decoding these lines, you are decoding two messages simultaneously—one aural, one visual. Both humans and machines can be thought of as decoders. The radio is a decoder; so is a videotape playback unit; so is the telephone (one end encodes and the other end decodes); so is a film projector.

A single communication event can involve many stages of decoding. A reporter sits in on a city council meeting and takes notes (decoding); he or she phones in a story to the rewrite desk where another reporter types the story as it is read (decoding). The story is read by an editor (decoding). Eventually it is printed and read by the audience (decoding). What we said earlier about encoding also applies to decoding: Some people are better at it than others. Many of you will not be able to decode "¿Dónde está el baño?"; others will. Some people are able to read 1,500 words a minute; others struggle along at 200. There are some messages that may never be decoded because the encoder put the message in the wrong channel. A telephone call may not be decoded by someone with impaired hearing. E-mail can only be received by those with access to a computer.

The **receiver** is the target of the message—its ultimate goal. The receiver can be a single person, a group, an institution, or even a large, anonymous collection of people. In today's environment, people are more often the receivers of communication messages than the sources. Most of us see more billboards than we put up and listen to more radio programs than we broadcast. The receivers of the message can be determined by the source, as in a telephone call, or they can self-select themselves into the audience, as with the audience for a TV show. It should also be clear that in some situations the source and receiver can be in each other's immediate presence, while in other situations they can be separated by both space and time.

■ Feedback

Now let us examine the bottom half of Figure 1–1. This portion of the figure represents the potential for **feedback** to occur. Feedback refers to those responses of the receiver that shape and alter the subsequent messages of the source. Feedback represents a reversal of the flow of communication. The original source becomes the receiver; the original receiver becomes the new source. Feedback is useful to the source because it allows the source to answer the question, How am I doing? Feedback is important to the receiver because it allows the receiver to attempt to change some element in the communication process. Communication scholars have traditionally identified two different kinds of feedback—positive and negative. In general terms, positive feedback from the receiver usually encourages the communication behavior in progress; negative feedback usually attempts to change the communication or even to terminate it.

Consider the following telephone call:

"Bambi?"

"Yes."

"This is Harold. I sit in front of you in econ class."

"Are you the one who keeps scratching your head with a pencil?"

". . . Gee, I never noticed it. I guess I do it unconsciously. Say, I was wondering if you would like to have coffee with me sometime after class."

"Are you kidding?"

Click.

Negative feedback. The original receiver terminated the message. Another conversation:

"Bambi, this is Rod."

"Oh, hi, Rod. Has your leg healed up from the last game yet?"

"Yeah."

"How are your classes going?"

"I can't get econ."

"I'll be over in twenty minutes to give you some help. OK?"

"OK."

Click.

Positive feedback. The original receiver encouraged the communication.

Feedback can be immediate or delayed. Immediate feedback occurs when the reactions of the receiver are directly perceived by the source. A speech maker who hears the audience boo and hiss while he or she is talking is getting immediate feedback. On the other hand, suppose you just listened to the latest CD by a popular group and decided it wasn't very good. To communicate that evaluation to the source, you would first have to find out the company that distributed the CD, find a mailing address, phone number, e-mail address, or website address. You would then have to send your feedback via the appropriate channel. If you got your message through to the company, it would still have to be passed on to the group, a process that might take several days or even longer.

Ricky Martin performing "La Vida Loca." What he and other singers want is *feedback positivo.* (Reuters/Colin Braley/Archive Photos)

Noise

The last factor we will consider is **noise.** Communication scholars define noise as anything that interferes with the delivery of the message. A little noise might pass unnoticed, while too much noise might prevent the message from reaching its destination in the first place. There are at least three different types of noise: semantic, mechanical, and environmental.

Semantic noise occurs when different people have different meanings for different words and phrases. Some examples: If you ask a New Yorker for a "soda" and expect to receive something that has ice cream in it, you'll be disappointed. The New Yorker will give you a bottle of what is called "pop" in the Midwest. An advertising copywriter penned the following slogan for a cough syrup company: "Try our cough syrup. You will never get any better." On the first day of class a professor asked his students to sit in alphabetical order so that, as he put it, "I'll be able to get to know you by looking at your seats."

Noise can also be mechanical. This type of noise occurs when there is a problem with a machine that is being used to assist communication. A TV set with a broken focus knob, a pen running out of ink, a static-filled radio, and a keyboard-withabrokenspacebar are all examples of mechanical noise. In addition, problems that are caused by people encoding messages to machines can also be thought of as a type of mechanical noise. Thus the typographical error in the résumé example (see page 3) and the printing error on the pen are examples of mechanical noise.

A third form of noise can be called environmental. This type refers to sources of noise that are external to the communication process but that nonetheless interfere with it. Some environmental noise might be out of the communicator's control—a noisy restaurant, for example, where the communicator is trying to hold a conversation. Some environmental noise might be introduced by the source or the receiver; for example, you might try to talk to somebody who keeps drumming his or her fingers on the table. A reporter not getting a story right because of a noisy room is an example of someone subjected to environmental noise.

As noise increases, message fidelity (how closely the message that is sent resembles the message that is received) goes down. Clearly, feedback is important in reducing the effects of noise. The greater the potential for immediate feedback—that is, the more interplay between source and receiver—the greater the chance that semantic noise will be overcome ("Don't you mean 'any better' cough syrup?"), that mechanical noise will be corrected (Isn't it "vocabulary?"), and that environmental noise will be brought under control ("Turn down that stereo. I'm trying to talk.").

S O U N D B Y T E

Stumbling across the Language Barrier

Semantic noise is bad enough, but imagine the problems that crop up when messages are translated into a foreign language:

- A sign in a Norwegian cocktail lounge: "Ladies are requested not to have children in the bar."

- A detour sign in Japan: "Stop. Drive Sideways."

- In a hotel in Vienna: "In case of fire, do your utmost to alarm the hotel porter."

- In a Japanese hotel: "You are invited to take advantage of the chambermaid."

- In an elevator in Germany: "Do not enter the lift backwards, and only when lit up."

- In the window of a dry cleaner in Bangkok: "Drop your pants here for best results."

- In China: The "Pepsi Comes Alive" slogan was originally translated as "Pepsi brings your ancestors back from the grave."

 ## COMMUNICATION SETTINGS

Interpersonal Communication

Having looked at the key elements in the communication process, we next examine three common communication settings, or situations, and explore how these elements vary from setting to setting. The first and perhaps the most common situation is **interpersonal communication,** in which one person (or group) is interacting with another person (or group) without the aid of a mechanical device. The source and receiver in this form of communication are within each other's physical presence. Talking to your roommate, participating in a class discussion, and conversing with your professor after class are all examples of interpersonal communication.

The source in this communication setting can be one or more individuals, as can the receiver. Encoding is usually a one-step process as the source transforms thoughts into speech and/or gestures. A variety of channels are available for use. The receiver can see, hear, and perhaps even smell and touch the source. Messages are relatively difficult for the receiver to terminate and are produced at little expense. In addition, interpersonal messages can be private (whassup?) or public (a proclamation that the end of the world is near from a person standing on a street corner). Messages can also be pinpointed to their specific targets. For example, you might ask the following of your English professor: "Excuse me, Dr. Iamb, but I was wondering if you had finished perusing my term paper?" The very same message directed at your roommate might be put another way: "Hey, Space Cadet! Aren't you done with my paper yet?" Decoding is also a one-step process performed by those receivers who can perceive the message. Feedback is immediate and makes use of visual and auditory channels. Noise can be either semantic or environmental. Interpersonal communication is far from simple, but in this classification it represents the least complicated situation.

Machine–Assisted Interpersonal Communication

Machine-assisted interpersonal communication (or technology-assisted communication) combines characteristics of both the interpersonal and mass communication situations. Furthermore, the growth of the Internet and the World Wide Web has further blurred the boundaries between these two types of communication. This section concentrates on those situations that are closer to the interpersonal setting. The next section examines how the computer and the Internet have redefined many of the features of mass communication.

In the machine-assisted setting, one or more people are communicating by means of a mechanical device (or devices) with one or more receivers. One of the important characteristics of machine-assisted interpersonal communication is that it allows the source and receiver to be separated by both time and space. The machine can give a message permanence by storing it on paper, magnetic disk, or some other material. The machine can also extend the range of the message by amplifying it and/or transmitting it over large distances. The telephone allows two people to converse even though they are hundreds, even thousands, of miles apart (Richard Nixon placed a person-to-person call to the *Apollo 11* astronauts while they were on the moon). A letter can be reread several years after it was written and communicate anew.

A tremendous variety of modern communication falls into this category. Here are some diverse examples of machine-assisted communication:

1. E-mail allows people to send messages across the country in a matter of minutes.
2. People get money out of automatic teller machines by inserting a magnetic card and following the machine's instructions.
3. Chat rooms and newsgroups on the Internet allow individuals to communicate by typing messages on their computer for all to see.
4. An inventor in Philadelphia has perfected the Lawn Buddy message machine in which a five-inch tall animal arises from a flowerpot and asks a visitor to leave a message.

Microsoft's Bill Gates uses machine-assisted communication to get his point across at the annual meeting of the World Economic Forum. (*Raymond Reuter/Sygma*)

5. The Sports' Nightmare Reminder Service allows you to torment sports fans you don't like. For a small fee, the service will mail an unmarked envelope to whomever you choose with news clippings of a particular team's biggest loss.

6. Telephone companies offer 900 or 976 lines, where, for a fee, people can hear recorded horoscopes, erotic fantasies, or information regarding the latest Elvis sightings.

Let's examine how each of the eight major elements of communication functions in the machine-assisted interpersonal situation.

The source in the machine-assisted situation is easy to identify in some instances, harder in others. The person on the other end of the phone, the person who wrote the letter, the person at the computer—all of these are fairly easy examples. But what about messages from automatic teller machines? In this example, the source of the message is the human being or beings who actually programmed the device in the first place. To sum up, the source in the machine-assisted setting can be a single person or group of persons. The source may or may not have first-hand knowledge of the receiver.

Encoding can also take several forms in this setting. It might be as complicated as writing a computer program or as simple as speaking into a telephone. There are at least two separate stages of encoding in machine-assisted communication. The first involves the source translating his or her thoughts into words or other appropriate symbols, while the second occurs when the machine encodes the message for transmission or storage. Thus when you are typing a term paper, the first encoding stage occurs when you form your thoughts into words and sentences ("It will be the purpose of this paper to examine the pros and cons of fraternity and sorority membership in today's college world"). The second stage occurs as your fingers fly over the keyboard to produce a permanent message ("It will be the porpoise of this paper to examin the prose and cones of fraternity and sorrity member ship in todays colleg world"). As you can see, some noise might get into the message. In other forms of machine-assisted communication, there may be several stages (e.g., writing a computer program on paper, keying it in, debugging it, testing it, and loading the finished program into the machine).

Channels are more restricted in machine-assisted communication. Whereas interpersonal communication can make use of several channels, machine-assisted settings generally restrict the message to one or two. The telephone relies on sound waves and electrical energy. A written document uses light rays to convey the message. Machine-assisted interpersonal communication has at least one machine interposed between source and receiver.

Messages vary widely in machine-assisted communication. They can range from messages that can be altered and tailor-made for the receiver, as is the case with e-mail, to a small number of predetermined messages that cannot be altered once they are encoded. An automatic teller machine, for example, can send no more than two dozen or so messages. Messages are relatively cheap to send in most forms of machine-assisted communication: A telephone call costs a small amount, and writing a letter is a fairly cheap way to send a message, even when the postage is included.

Messages can be either private or public, depending on the circumstances. A letter, a phone call, or personal e-mail are examples of private machine-assisted messages. A sound truck broadcasting an election-day message, a person handing out pamphlets, a poster nailed to a telephone pole are all examples of public messages. The ease with which the message can be terminated is also variable but, by and large, people need little effort to end communication. Throwing away the pamphlet, hanging up the phone, closing your window to avoid the sound truck are all accomplished with ease. Walking out on a speaker while he or she is at the microphone is a little harder, but the interposition of a machine between source and receiver tends to increase what we might call the psychological distance between these two elements.

Decoding in machine-assisted communication can go through one or more stages, similar to the encoding process. Reading a letter requires a single phase of decoding. Reading e-mail requires two phases: one for the computer to decode the electrical energy into patterns of light and dark, and another for your eye to decode the patterns into words or symbols that have meaning.

The receiver in the machine-assisted setting can be a single person or a small or large group. The receivers can be in the physical presence of the source or out of physical view. The receivers can be selected by the source, as would be the case for a letter or a telephone call, or they can self-select themselves into the audience, as would happen if you took a pamphlet from a person on a street corner.

Feedback can be immediate or delayed. When the source and receiver are in close proximity, feedback will be immediate. The speaker at a political convention will hear the applause immediately. If the source and the receiver are separated by geography, feedback may or may not be immediate. Writing a letter, leaving a message on an answering machine, and inserting your plastic card into an automated teller machine and having it disappear without a sound are examples of

As the text points out, machine-assisted and mass communication use fewer channels than does interpersonal communication. A group of inventors, however, is trying to overcome this shortcoming, particularly with e-mail. "Scentography" will let you see and actually smell your e-mail.

Here's how scentography works. A device hooked to your computer contains an assortment of chemicals. When somebody sends you an e-mail with a picture of an orange or a forest, for example, you slide an adhesive piece of paper into the device, which mixes up the appropriate chemicals and slaps them on the adhesive sheet so that when you sniff the paper, it smells like an orange or a forest.

Think about some of the possibilities. You could test a perfume before buying it over the net. How about an auto ad that is accompanied by that new-car smell? Or the aroma of freshly baked cookies with a cookie ad?

Of course, like all other technologies, scentography has the potential for both good and bad. Suppose somebody really disliked you. What terrible odors might she or he send you?

situations in which feedback would be delayed, if it occurred at all. The person who plays back the tape on the answering machine may not want to call back, the letter might not be answered, and so on. The extent of possible feedback depends on the circumstances. Although some circumstances allow for a great deal of feedback (the speaker at the political rally can see and hear the audience react), it is never as abundant as it is in the interpersonal setting. In an interpersonal setting it might be possible for the speaker to seek out reactions from some or perhaps all of the audience, whereas the speaker in front of an audience of thousands may not have that opportunity. In other situations, feedback is limited. In a telephone conversation, feedback is limited to the audio channel. Feedback in the form of written communication is limited to the visual channel. Sometimes, feedback is difficult or even impossible. If the automatic teller gives you a coded message that says "Insufficient funds," you cannot tell it, "Well, I just made a deposit this morning. Look it up."

Noise in machine-assisted communication can be semantic and environmental, as in interpersonal communication, but it can also be mechanical, since interference with the message might be due in part to difficulties with the machine involved.

Machine-assisted interpersonal communication will continue to grow. New personal communication media, such as cellular telephones, laptop computers, and palm-sized personal digital assistants (minicomputers that store messages, send and receive faxes, schedule appointments, receive e-mail, etc.) are becoming more and more popular, and the computer is being used more and more as a communication device. (See Chapter 11.)

New forms of machine-assisted interpersonal communication have altered some of the functions and customs of interpersonal communication. The new personal media allow for communication that is distanced both physically and psychologically. By faxing your order, you can now have lunch without talking to anybody. Also, despite their giving the illusion of closeness, online computer conversations allow participants to have total control over the amount and kind of information that they disclose. Cellular phones keep people in constant communication but also are a new source of interruptions in face-to-face communication. It's safe to say that the new personal media increase our range of contacts and experience, but they do so at a price.

E-mail is fast and environmentally friendly; it uses no paper and vehicles burn no gasoline delivering the message. It is no wonder then that American businesses send billions of e-mail messages every year. *(Courtesy Lotus Development Corporation)*

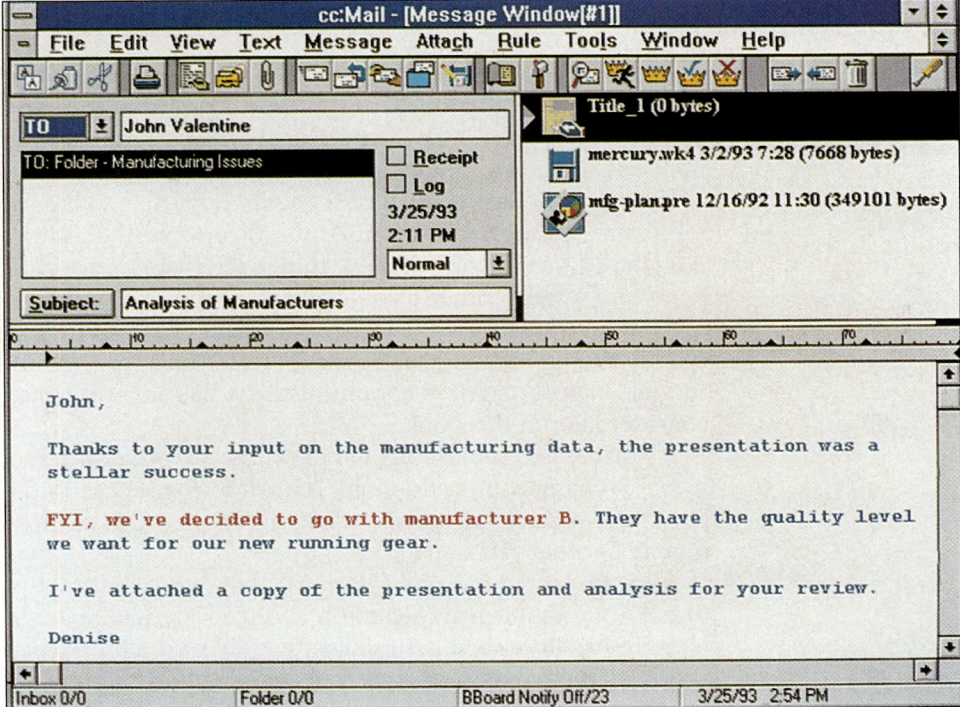

Mass Communication

The third major communication setting is the one that we will be most interested in. The differences between machine-assisted interpersonal communication and mass communication are not that clear. **Mass communication** refers to the process by which a complex organization with the aid of one or more machines produces and transmits public messages that are directed at large, heterogeneous, and scattered audiences. There are, of course, situations that will fall into a gray area. How large does the audience have to be? How scattered? How heterogeneous? How complex must the organization be? For example, a billboard is constructed on a busy street in a small town. Obviously, this would qualify as machine-assisted communication (a machine was used to print the billboard), but is this example better defined as mass communication? An automatic letter-writing device can write thousands of similar letters. Is this mass communication? There are no correct answers to these questions. The dividing line between machine-assisted interpersonal communication and mass communication is not a distinct one.

The line is even less distinct when the Internet and the World Wide Web are considered. Take an e-mail message, for example. It can be addressed to one person, much like machine-assisted interpersonal communication, or it can go to thousands, a situation closer to mass communication. Or take the case of a chat room where one person might be communicating with dozens of others. If two people want more privacy, they can move to a "private" room, a situation that resembles machine-assisted interpersonal communication. On the other hand, feedback in the chat room is limited, a feature of mass communication. The usual clues from personal appearance, tone of voice, and gestures are not present.

Further, much like mass communication, online conversations are easily terminated.

Until the advent of the Internet and the web, the source in the traditional mass communication situation was typically a group of individuals who acted in pre-determined roles in an organizational setting. In other words, mass communication was the end product of more than one person's efforts. For example, think about how a newspaper is put together. Reporters gather news; writers draft editorials; a cartoonist draws an editorial cartoon; the advertising department lays out ads; editors lay out all these things on a sample page; technicians transfer this page to a master; other technicians print the final paper; the finished copies are given to the delivery staff; and, of course, behind all this is a publisher who has the money to pay for a building, presses, staff, trucks, paper, ink, and so on. This institutional nature of mass communication has several consequences that we will consider later in this book.

As discussed in more detail below, the advent of Internet-based mass communication changes this situation. Thanks to the World Wide Web, one person can become a mass communicator. The full implications of this change may take some time to become clear.

For both traditional and Internet-based mass communication, the source usually has little detailed information about its particular audience. The author of a website has little detailed information about the individual people who visit the site. Traditional mass media may have collective data, but these are typically expressed as gross audience characteristics. The newspaper editor, for example, may know that 40 percent of the readers are between 25 and 40 years old and that 30 percent earn between $20,000 and $50,000, but the editor has no idea about the individual tastes, preferences, quirks, or individual identities of these people. They are an anonymous group, known only by summary statistics.

Encoding in mass communication is always a multistage process. A film producer has an idea. He or she explains it to a screenwriter. The writer goes off and produces a script. The script goes to a director, who translates it for the camera. Cinematographers capture the scenes on film. The raw film goes to an editor, who splices together the final version. The film is copied and sent to motion picture theaters, where a projector displays it on the screen, where the audience watches it. How many examples of encoding can you find in that oversimplified version of moviemaking?

Mass communication channels are characterized by the imposition of at least one, and usually more than one, machine in the process of sending the message. These machines translate the message from one channel to another. Television makes use of complicated devices that transform light energy into electrical energy and back again. Radio does the same with sound energy. Unlike interpersonal communication, in which many channels are available, mass communication is usually restricted to one or two.

Messages in mass communication are public. Anyone who can afford the cost of a newspaper or a CD player or a TV set can receive the message. Additionally, the same message is sent to all receivers. In a sense, mass communication is addressed "to whom it may concern." Of all the various settings, message termination is easiest in mass communication. The TV set goes dark at the flick of a switch, an automatic timer can turn off the radio, the newspaper is quickly put aside. There is little the source can do to prevent these sudden terminations, other than bullying the audience ("Don't touch that dial!") or trying to stay interesting at all times ("We'll be back after these important messages").

Encoding in the movies. Eduardo Sanchez and Daniel Myrick wrote and directed *The Blair Witch Project*. A motion picture goes through several stages of encoding before it gets to the receiver: idea, story, script, shooting script, filming, and editing. *(AP/ Wide World Photos)*

Mass communication typically involves multiple decoding before the message is received. The CD player decodes patterns of light waves into sound waves for our hearing mechanism. The TV receiver decodes both sight and sound transmissions.

One of the prime distinguishing characteristics of mass communication is the audience. The mass communication audience is a large one, sometimes numbering in the millions of people. The audience is also heterogeneous; that is, it is made up of dissimilar groups who may differ in age, intelligence, political beliefs, ethnic backgrounds, and so on. Even in situations where the mass communication audience is well defined, heterogeneity is still present. (For example, consider the publication *Turkey Grower's Monthly*. At first glance, the audience for this publication might appear to be pretty homogeneous, but upon closer examination we might discover that members differ in intelligence, social class, income, age, political party, education, place of residence, and so on.) Third, the audience is spread out over a wide geographic area; source and receiver are not in each other's immediate physical presence. The large size of the audience and its geographic separation both contribute to a fourth distinguishing factor: The audience members are anonymous to one another. The person watching the "CBS Evening News" is unaware of the several million others in the audience. Lastly, in keeping with the idea of a public message, the audience in mass communication is self-defined. The receiver chooses which film to see, which paper to read, which website to visit, and which program to watch. If the receiver chooses not to attend to the message, the message is not received. Consequently, the various mass communication sources spend a great deal of time and effort to get your attention so that you will include yourself in the audience.

Feedback is another area where there are differences between interpersonal and mass communication. The message flow in mass communication is typically one-way, from source to receiver, and feedback is more difficult than in the interpersonal setting. The growing popularity of the Internet and the World Wide Web has made feedback somewhat easier, but there are still situations where sending feedback to the source takes a great deal of effort. Suppose, for example, you were offended by the content of a TV program. You might call the station immediately. If you got through, you would probably be referred to the network if what you saw was a network show. You could choose to call the network (a long-distance call for most), in which case you would probably reach a receptionist, who would suggest you put your complaint in writing or send an e-mail message. Alternatively, you could search for the network's website and find a place to post your comments. In any case, you would not be sure how long it would take for your message to be read, and you would never know if it was read by anybody associated with the program. Systematic, large-scale feedback gathered by media companies is even more delayed since it is typically gathered by an outside organization, such as Nielsen Media Research for television and the Audit Bureau of Circulations for newspapers.

Finally, noise in the mass communication setting can be semantic, environmental, or mechanical. In fact, since there may be more than one machine involved in the process, mechanical noise can be compounded (watching a scratchy copy of an old film on a snowy TV set).

Figure 1–2 summarizes some of the differences among the three communication settings that we have talked about.

NATURE OF THE MASS COMMUNICATOR

Since a large portion of this book will examine the institutions that are in the business of mass communication, it will be to our advantage to consider some common characteristics that typify mass communicators. This task has been made more complicated by the emergence of the computer and the Internet as communications media. Internet mass communication is distinctly different from the traditional forms of mass communication. Nonetheless, we will first present the salient characteristics of traditional mass communicators and then examine how communication on the Internet has blurred the established definition of mass communication sources. First, the list of traditional defining features:

1. Mass communication is produced by complex and formal organizations.
2. Mass communication organizations have multiple gatekeepers.
3. Mass communication organizations need a great deal of money to operate.
4. Mass communication organizations exist to make a profit.
5. Mass communication organizations are highly competitive.

Figure 1–2

Differences in
Communication Settings

	Setting		
Element	**Interpersonal**	**Machine-assisted interpersonal**	**Mass**
Source	Single person; has knowledge of receiver	Single person or group; great deal of knowledge or no knowledge of receiver	Organizations or single person; little knowledge of receivers
Encoding	Single stage	Single or multiple stage	Multiple stages
Message	Private or public; cheap; hard to terminate; altered to fit receivers	Private or public; low to moderate expense; relatively easy to terminate; can be altered to fit receivers in some situations	Public; can be expensive; easily terminated; same message to everbody
Channel	Potential for many; no machines interposed	Restricted to one or two; at least one machine interposed	Restricted to one or two; usually more than one machine interposed
Decoding	Single stage	Single or multiple stage	Multiple stages
Receiver	One or a relatively small number; in physical presence of source; selected by source	One person or a small or large group; within or outside physical presence of source; selected by source or self-defined	Large numbers; out of physical presence of source; self-selected
Feedback	Plentiful; immediate	Somewhat limited; immediate or delayed	Highly limited; usually delayed
Noise	Semantic; environmental	Semantic; environmental; mechanical	Semantic; environmental; mechanical

■ Formal Organizations

Publishing a newspaper or operating a TV station requires control of money, management of personnel, coordination of activities, and application of authority. Accomplishing all these tasks requires a well-defined organizational structure characterized by specialization, division of labor, and focused areas of responsibility. Consequently, traditional mass communication will be the product of a bureaucracy. As in most bureaucracies, decision making will take place at several different levels of management, and channels of communication within the organization will be formalized. Thus many of the decisions about what gets included in a newspaper or in a TV program, for instance, will be the result of committee or group decisions. Further, decisions will have to be made by several different individuals in ascending levels of the bureaucracy and communication will follow predetermined and predictable patterns within the organization. This results in end products that seldom resemble the original idea of the creator. For example, TV writer Merle Miller describes one such experience in his book *Only You Dick Daring or How to Write One Television Script and Make $50,000,000.* Miller's idea for a TV show about a Peace Corps worker had to be approved by the vice president of the production company, the vice president of CBS program development, the vice president of CBS programming, the president of CBS, the producer, the director, and the research department. When everything had settled, the show was about a county agent working in the Southwest, and Miller, totally frustrated, quit the project.

Gatekeepers

Another important factor that characterizes the traditional mass communicator is the presence of multiple **gatekeepers.** A gatekeeper is any person (or group) who has control over what material eventually reaches the public. Some are more obvious than others, for example, the editor of a newspaper or the news director at a TV station. Some gatekeepers are less visible. To illustrate, let's imagine that you have the world's greatest idea for a TV series, an idea that will make "ER" and "Friends" look mediocre. You write the script and mail it off to Universal Studios in California. A clerk in the mailroom judges by the envelope that it is a script and sees by the return address that it has come from an amateur writer. The clerk has been instructed to return all such packages unopened with a note saying that Universal does not consider unsolicited material. Gate closed.

Frustrated, you decide to go to Los Angeles in person and hand-deliver your work. You rush to the office of Universal's vice president in charge of production, where a receptionist politely tells you that Universal never looks at scripts that are not submitted through an agent. Gate closed. You rush out to a phone booth and start calling agents. Fourteen secretaries tell you that their agencies are not accepting new writers. Fourteen closed gates. Finally, you find an agent who will see you (gate open!). You rush to the agent's offices where he or she glances through your script and says, "No thanks" (gate closed). By now the point is probably clear. Many people serve as gatekeepers. In our hypothetical example, even if an agent agreed to represent you, the agent would then have to sell your script to a producer who, in turn, might have to sell it to a production company which, in turn, might have to sell it to a network.

In the newsroom, an assignment editor decides whether to send a reporter to cover a certain event. The reporter then decides if anything about the event is worth reporting. An editor may subsequently shorten the story, if submitted, or delete it altogether. Obviously, gatekeepers abound in mass communication. The more complex the organization, the more gatekeepers will be found.

The gang from "Survivor," the surprise hit of the 2000 TV season. The producers capitalized on the program's appeal to young viewers to get the gatekeepers at CBS to air the series. *(Photofest)*

Operating Expenses

It costs a large sum of money to start a mass communication organization and to keep it running. Recently, the Gannett Company bought 21 newspapers from the Thomson Corporation for $1.13 billion. In 1999, Gemstar bought *TV Guide* for about $14 billion. In Los Angeles an FM station was sold for nearly $110 million and a TV station was bought for $510 million.

Once the organization is in operation, expenses are also sizable. In the late 1990s, it cost approximately $4 million to $5 million annually to run a small daily newspaper (one with a circulation of about 35,000 to 40,000). A radio station in a medium-sized urban market might spend $700,000 annually in operating expenses. A TV station in one of the top 10 markets might need more than $10 million to keep it going. Only those organizations that have the money necessary to institute and maintain these levels of support are able to produce mass communication.

Media economics have contributed to another trend that made itself evident at the end of the decade: consolidation of ownership. Companies that have strong financial resources are the likeliest to survive high operating expenses and are better able to compete in the marketplace. Consequently, by 2000 a number of global media giants had emerged to dominate the field. Table 1.1 lists these "megamedia" companies. Note that the names listed in the table will turn up frequently in succeeding chapters.

Competing for Profits

In the United States, mass communication organizations exist to make a profit. Although there are some exceptions (the Public Broadcasting System, for example), most newspapers, magazines, record companies, and TV and radio stations strive to produce a profit for their owners and stockholders. And while radio and television stations are licensed to serve in the public interest and newspapers commonly assume a watchdog role on behalf of their readers, if they do not make money, they go out of business. The consumer is the ultimate source of this profit. When you buy a CD or a movie ticket, part of the price includes the profit. Newspapers, TV, magazines, and radio earn most of their profits by selling their audiences to advertisers. The cost of advertising, in turn, is passed on by the manufacturers to the consumer. The economics of mass communication is an important topic, and we will have more to say about it later in this book.

Table 1.1	Global Media Giants	
	Company (Home Country)	**1999 Revenue (in billions)**
1.	AOL Time Warner (USA)	$34.2
2.	Walt Disney Company (USA)	23.5
3.	Vivendi Universal (USA)	22.6
4.	Viacom/CBS (USA)	20.3
5.	Sony (Japan)	16.9*
6.	News Corporation (Australia)	14.3
7.	Bertelsmann (Germany)	11.2

*Includes media revenue only.

Since the audience is the source of profits, mass communication organizations compete with one another as they attempt to attract an audience. This should come as no surprise to anyone who has ever watched television or passed a magazine stand. The major TV networks compete with one another to get high ratings. Millions of dollars are spent each year in promoting the new fall season. Radio stations compete with other stations that have similar formats. Record companies spend large sums promoting their records, hoping to outsell their competitors. Daily newspapers compete with weeklies and with radio and television. Motion picture companies gamble millions on films to compete successfully. This fierce competition has several consequences, and we will return to this topic time and again.

INTERNET MASS COMMUNICATION

The emergence of the computer and interlinked computer networks, such as the Internet, has created a new channel for machine-assisted and mass communication (Chapter 11 presents a more detailed look at the Internet and mass communication). E-mail is a good example of one-to-one machine-assisted communication, with characteristics similar to both the telephone and written letters. Chat rooms, electronic bulletin boards, listservers, and multiuser domains (MUDs—originally called multiuser dungeons) represent a special case of machine-assisted communication where many are communicating to many. Such arrangements have no parallel among traditional media (conference phone calls and videoconferences come the closest). It is the World Wide Web, however, that brings the computer into the realm of mass communication and reverses the established pattern of one-to-many communication. Websites are a special case of mass communication that creates a different type of mass communicator.

This new mass communication source is possible because the Internet brings the cost of mass communication to a level where many can afford it. Unlike the steep costs that go with starting a new radio station or newspaper, one individual can create his or her own website for an extremely small investment. A computer with access to the Internet is all that is needed. The whole setup could easily be purchased for less than $2,000. Once established, a website can be ridiculously cheap to maintain. Some services, such as Netzero and Blue Light, offer free Internet access. Websites can be maintained for only a few dollars a month. The affordability of this new channel can make a person an instant electronic publisher with access to an audience of millions of Internet users, creating a whole new class of mass communicators.

This wide range of sources present on the net creates some exceptions to the five characteristics of mass communication sources listed on page 16. Specifically, websites can be produced by a single individual. There is little need for a large staff, multiple managers, or organizational structure. Next, many websites bypass gatekeepers. Information posted at a website is directly available to the audience, a circumstance that has both positive and negative consequences. On the one hand, writers and artists have complete freedom to post whatever they choose without fear that some editor will veto or change their copy. Creative freedom is supreme. On the other hand, there are no safeguards that what is made available is accurate or worthwhile. Rumors, fantastic conspiracy theories, and tasteless messages that would never make it in the mainstream media abound on the Internet. There are no fact checkers or editors to sort out the credible from the bizarre or to distinguish merit from trash. Conversely, some innovative and origi-

The World Wide Web has changed the nature of mass communication: Anybody can imitate Milos Radakovich and become a mass communicator. Yahoo! has a listing of more than 40,000 personal pages such as this one. *(Reprinted by permission of Milos Radakovich)*

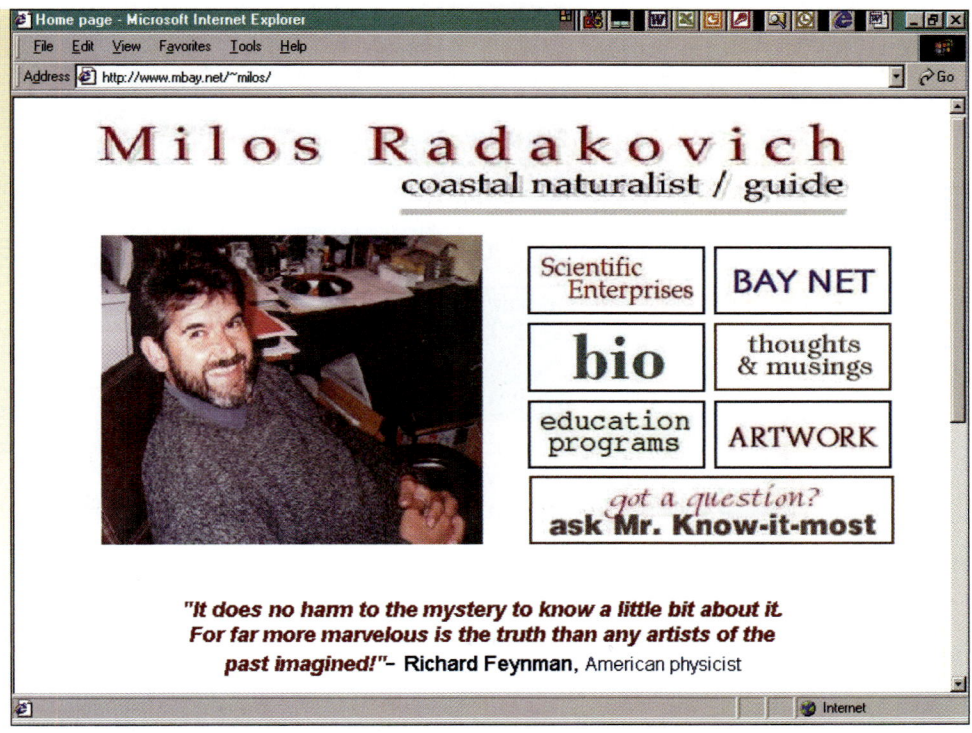

nal content, too cutting-edge for traditional media, might find an audience on the web.

Third, as we have already noted, expensive start-up and operating costs are not typical of all websites. Further, the concentration of ownership that characterizes the established media does not exist on the web. There are literally millions of owners of web pages. Finally, although many companies and individuals have started websites to make a profit, many others have no such motivation. Some websites seem to exist to serve the public or to gain attention and prestige for their owners. By the same token, competing for an audience may typify some of the larger commercially sponsored sites, but there are many other websites where competition is not a crucial factor.

In sum, the Internet and the World Wide Web contain a wide range of communication situations and sources. They have prompted mass communication scholars (and textbook writers) to rethink conventional definitions and categories of mass communication. In that same connection, these new media have also necessitated fresh models to describe the mass communication process.

MODELS FOR STUDYING MASS COMMUNICATION

Figure 1–1 outlined the elements present in the general process of communication. When we want to talk about mass communication, however, we need to construct a new model that adequately represents its distinctive features. The following discussion introduces two models of the process. The first (Figure 1–3) applies to the traditional mass communication situation, while the second (Figure 1–4) is a new model for describing Internet mass communication.

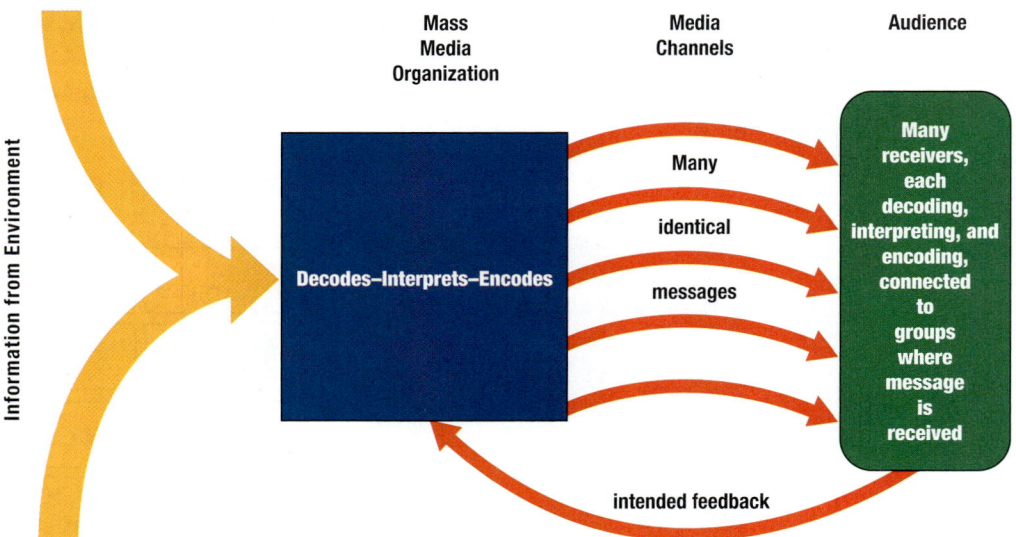

Figure 1–3

Traditional Mass Communication Model

The traditional representation of mass communication represented in Figure 1–3 is adapted from an early model described by Wilbur Schramm.[1] Although nearly a half century old, it still illustrates the main concepts. Let's begin our discussion at the far left of the model and work toward the right. Information from the environment (both news and entertainment) is filtered through a mass media organization (newspaper, TV network, movie studio, recording company, etc.) where it is decoded, interpreted, and encoded. In other words, the media organization serves as a gatekeeper. Of all the possible CDs that a recording company could release, only a few are noted, interpreted as potential hits, and reproduced in large numbers. At a newspaper, reporters cover potentially newsworthy events and then encode a story. In turn, the story is reviewed by editors who decide if it should make it through the gate and into the newspaper.

Once through the gate, the message is reproduced many times over and sent through the appropriate channel. A recording company, for example, produces a large number of CDs that are sent to retail outlets or directly to consumers. Hundreds or thousands of copies of a newspaper are printed and distributed to subscribers.

The far right side of the model represents the receivers, or the audience. The model suggests that these audience members are not just passive recipients of messages. They decode, interpret, and encode messages themselves. In addition, audience members are not isolated from one another. They are connected to groups, such as family, peers, and co-workers, where the messages they receive from the media are talked about, reinterpreted, and often acted upon. Some audience behavior (buying a product, subscribing to a paper, watching a TV show) is

---

[1]Adapted from Wilbur Schramm, *The Process and Effects of Mass Communication* (Urbana: University of Illinois Press, 1954).

observed by the media organization and is used as feedback to help shape future messages. There is little direct interaction between sources and receivers. All in all, the Schramm model represents the traditional few-to-many world, where only those sources that can afford to do so, publish and distribute information to everyone else.

In contrast, Figure 1–4 is a rough attempt to represent Internet mass communication, a new arrangement that makes it possible for many sources to communicate to many receivers. Note that in this simplified model, content is provided not only by organizations but also by individuals. In this circumstance, there are no organizational gatekeepers. A single individual performs the decoding, interpreting, and encoding functions. Also note that Figure 1–4 is not a one-way model. Communication doesn't proceed from left to right, but flows inward. The traditional mass communicator no longer necessarily initiates the process. Instead, it is possible for the receiver to choose the time and manner of the interaction. Suppose you wanted to find out what happened in a game involving your favorite baseball team that went into extra innings and finished late at night. With the traditional media, you would have to wait for a newspaper to be published or wait for your favorite TV station, cable network, or radio station to report the score. With the Internet, you could visit a sports news website and find the information immediately. Furthermore, if you wanted to know more, you could visit your team's website for more details and check message boards for the reactions of others to the outcome. In short, the audience member has more control of the process.

Another area of contrast between the traditional and Internet model is that the messages that flow to each receiver are not identical. For example, you have many different choices about what you can use as your starting page when you access the Internet. In addition, it's possible to customize the information you receive.

Figure 1–4

Internet Mass
Communication Model

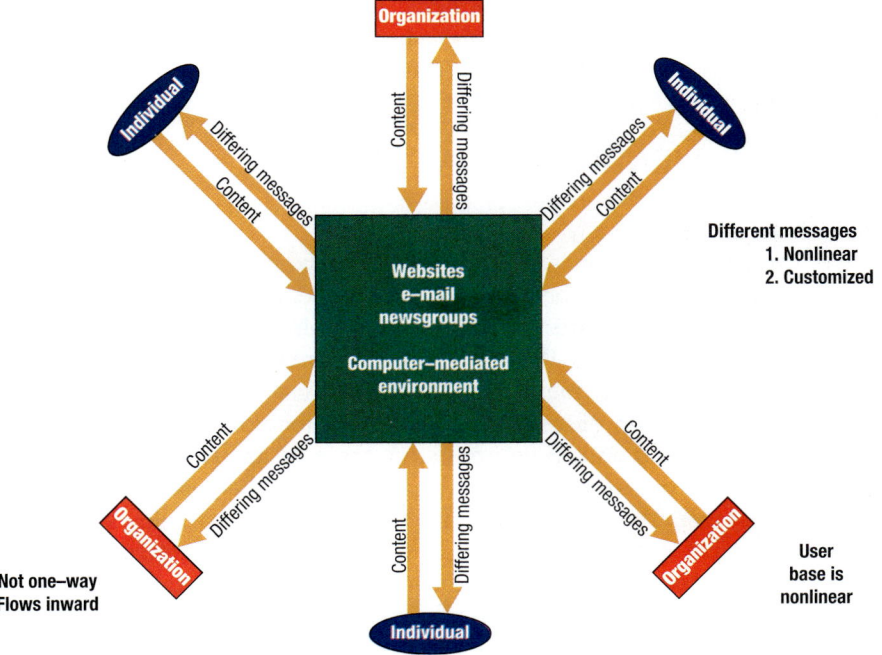

Excite, for example, offers many different configurations that allow you to choose specific sports scores, news headlines, stock market reports, weather forecasts, and entertainment news. Each receiver can customize the information that he or she receives. Some writers have characterized the traditional mass communication model as a "push" model (the sender pushes the information to the receiver) whereas the Internet model is a "pull" model (the receiver pulls only the information that he or she wants).

Moreover, in the traditional model, many messages proceed in a linear manner. A newspaper, for instance, is designed to be read from page 1 to page 2, and so on. A book is designed to be read from chapter 1 to chapter 2. Thanks to **hypertext,** a means of presenting information in which text, sounds, images, and actions are linked in a way that allows you to jump around between them in whatever order you choose, the receiver no longer has to start at the beginning to find the information he or she wants. For example, I was looking for information on the health benefits of the mineral zinc. Before the advent of the web, I would have had to find the appropriate book, look in the contents or index, and then search for what I wanted on the designated pages. Instead, I simply did an Internet search for the words "zinc" and "health," which took me to the appropriate page in the online encyclopedia at MotherNature.com. That page contained a link to another page that specifically discussed the use of zinc to treat cold symptoms, the precise information I needed.

Finally, Figure 1–4 shows that both individuals and organizations are linked through a computer-mediated environment. This makes interaction and feedback much easier. The online magazine Slate.com, for example, has a site labeled "Enter the Fray," where readers can post messages commenting on stories in the magazine. This environment allows people and organizations to be linked in unprecedented ways that permit totally new forms of interaction. The auction site e-bay joins buyers and sellers all over the world. The newsgroup humanities.classics brings together people who were probably never aware of one another and lets them talk about Descartes and Wagner. The Internet links producers and customers, and makes e-commerce possible (see Chapter 11). All in all, the new model, incomplete as it might be, suggests a new way of conceptualizing mass communication in the age of the Internet.

MASS COMMUNICATION MEDIA

Defining Mass Media

In the broadest sense of the word, a *medium* is the channel through which a message travels from the source to the receiver ("medium" is singular; "media" is plural). Thus in our discussion, we have pointed to sound and light waves as media of communication. When we talk about mass communication, we also need channels to carry the message. **Mass media** use these channels to carry the message. Our definition of a mass medium will include not only the mechanical devices that transmit and sometimes store the message (TV cameras, radio microphones, printing presses), but also the institutions that use these machines to transmit messages. When we talk about the mass media of television, radio, newspapers, magazines, sound recording, and film, we will be referring to the people, the policies, the organizations, and the technology that go into producing and distributing mass communication. A **media vehicle** is a single component of the mass media, such as a newspaper, radio station, TV network, or magazine.

In this book we will examine eight different mass media: radio, television, film, book publishing, sound recording, newspapers, magazines, and the Internet. Of course, these eight are not the only mass media that exist. For example, billboards, comic books, posters, direct mail, matchbooks, and buttons are some other kinds of mass media one could choose to examine. The eight types of media we have chosen, however, have the largest audiences, employ the most people, and have the greatest impact. They are also the ones with which most of us are most familiar.

The End of Mass Communication As We Know It?

The past two decades have seen a basic change in the mass communication process: It's become less mass-oriented and more selective. In the 1930s, for example, almost everybody tuned their radios to "Amos 'n' Andy." Today the top-rated network radio show gets about 2 or 3 percent of the audience. In the 1950s, virtually everybody watched Milton Berle on TV. The typical top-rated shows would attract about 45 percent of all TV households. Currently, top-rated shows get about 20 to 25 percent of the audience, thanks to competition from cable, broadcast networks such as Fox, the WB, Paxnet, UPN, VCRs, video games, and the Internet.

In the 1940s and 1950s, general-interest, mass circulation magazines, such as *Life, Look,* and *Collier's,* were popular. Today *Reader's Digest,* the most widely read general-interest magazine, is down from its all-time high of 18.4 million readers in 1977 to about 12.5 million in 1999. *TV Guide* lost about 5 million readers in the same period. In 1960, about 75 percent of the adult population read a newspaper. In 1999, that figure was down to about 55 percent.

What we are seeing is the fractionalization, or segmentation, of the mass audience. What are the forces behind this fundamental change? First, today's audiences are different. There has been an increase in one-parent families. In many households both the husband and wife bring home paychecks. Time has become a scarce commodity and much of it is devoted to commuting, working, and child raising. All this means less time devoted to the media, and when audience members do spend time with the media, they look for content geared to their special interests. Second, the emergence of new media, such as VCRs, cable TV, computers, and direct broadcast satellites, has given today's consumers more media to choose from. Consequently, the audience for any one media vehicle is divided into smaller and smaller segments.

Finally, manufacturers and service organizations have turned from mass to target marketing. This has led to an era where Americans now have more choices than ever before. Large movie theaters with a single screen have given way to 12- or 14-screen multiplexes. Instead of a handful of radio stations, most big cities now have a couple dozen. There are magazines for seemingly every demographic and special interest group. Back in the 1960s, most households could get just four TV channels. Now most get more than 60 and some get 100 or more.

Does all this mean that "mass communication" is no longer a meaningful term? Should this book be titled *The Dynamics of Segmented Communication?* Well, not quite yet. In the first place, the definition of mass communication given earlier still applies. Complex organizations still use machines to transmit public messages aimed at large, heterogeneous, and scattered audiences. Audiences are still large (even a flop TV show can reach 4 million households), scattered, and heterogeneous enough to justify using the term "mass communication."

Cable TV's great advantage is narrowcasting—through channels such as the Sci Fi Channel and the History Channel, that provide programs of interest to a small, homogeneous segment of the population. Can narrowcasting go too far? Below are the names of cable networks actually in operation or under development in 2000 along with the names of a couple of fictional ones. Can you pick out the bogus channels?

- Chop TV (for martial arts)
- The Museum Channel
- The Amphibian Channel
- The Outlet Mall Network
- The Wedding Channel
- The Church Channel
- The Professor Network
- The Puppy Channel
- Sewing and Needle Arts Network
- Soap TV (the opera kind, not the washing kind)

(Answer: All are legitimate except for amphibians and professors . . . but even they have potential.)

Second, we need to make distinctions regarding the terms mentioned above. The channels of mass communication are unchanged. There are, however, more and more mass media using these channels: about 13,000 radio stations today compared with half that number a couple of decades ago, more than 3,000 new magazines in the last decade, a record number of TV stations, and so on. Further, the messages sent by these mass media through the channels of mass communication have become more specialized. Magazines, newspapers, radio, TV, and websites are aiming their content at more defined audience niches, in part to meet the demands of advertisers and in part because it's more cost-efficient. Consequently, it's harder for any one media vehicle to reach a large number of audience members. Nonetheless, the potential is still there for the right message in the right medium to transcend the limits of specialized content and to attract a mass audience in the broadest sense of the term. This happened, for example, with *Roots,* "Who Wants to Be a Millionaire," *Titanic,* and the coverage of the opening hostilities of the Gulf War. More recently, it was estimated that 2.5 billion people watched the television coverage of the funeral of Princess Diana. Obviously, although the content of the media has become more specialized, the potential for reaching a mass audience still exists.

Mass Media Symbiosis

In biology, *symbiosis* is defined as the association of two organisms for mutual benefit. In mass media, the television and film industries demonstrate what we might call a form of symbiosis. The same companies produce works for both media; films that originally played in the theaters find their way to television in videocassettes, over cable, and over network and local stations. The sound recording and radio industries demonstrate another symbiotic relationship. Most radio stations depend on recordings to fill their airtime; most records need airplay to sell. MTV demonstrates a three-way symbiosis: Record companies use it as a promotional tool; MTV uses videos supplied by the record companies as a programming source; and radio stations use MTV as a sounding board for new releases. Some intermedia relationships have crossed traditional boundaries. Many local newspapers also operate a local cable TV channel. TV networks, movie companies, and publishers operate websites that promote their products. Newspapers use reporters and stories gathered for their print editions in their online versions.

The trend toward more mass media and more specialized content seems irreversible. Several consequences of this movement, however, bear scrutiny. To begin, the traditional media, whatever their shortcomings, did provide a national agenda for society and helped define a national consensus. They focused the attention of the nation and mobilized its resources. The fireside chats of Franklin Roosevelt, for example, were credited with helping the country survive the hardships of the depression. Could such a phenomenon take place in the 21st century? Douglas Cater is a media critic who was among the first to question whether media specialization was beneficial to society. In a 1973 *Wall Street Journal* article, Cater posed the fundamental question: "What happens when each minority group listens to its own prophets? When there are no more Walter Cronkites each evening to reassure us that despite its afflictions the nation still stands?"

Mass communication scholar Wilson Dizard described the traditional mass media as a kind of social "Elmer's glue" that bound people together (see the discussions of "Linkage" and "Transmission of Values" in the next chapter). Communication researcher Gladys Gantley in a 1991 *Washington Quarterly* article speculates that the growth in the number of specialized and personalized media might have political repercussions. Increased access to a greater range of information could serve as a democratizing force, but there might be a downside: "[If] [s]pread to millions of individuals throughout the world, each literally following his or her own agenda, such power could remove the glue of social cohesion . . . Power to the people could mean that nobody is in control."

Neil Postman, in his provocative book *Amusing Ourselves to Death,* suggests another troubling possibility. The proliferation of media and messages could result in a flood of trivialized content that distracts us from the key social issues of the day. We might, as his title suggests, amuse ourselves to death.

Although the following chapters discuss the various media individually, these media do not exist in a vacuum. In the future, we are likely to see more examples of the synergy that exists among all communication media.

Disintermediation

This rather ungraceful, tongue-twisting word refers to the process whereby access to a product or a service is given directly to the consumer, thus eliminating the intermediary, or "middleman," who might typically supply the product or service. The Internet and the World Wide Web have created a ubiquitous and easily accessible network where buyers and sellers make direct contact. The Internet has already provided several examples of **disintermediation.** Travelers bypass travel agents and book airline tickets directly online; traders bypass brokers and purchase stocks directly online; consumers bypass salespeople and buy insurance online. (Some businesses have more to fear from disintermediation than others. It's unlikely that consumers will bypass restaurants because of the Internet.)

Disintermediation is of obvious concern to mass media organizations. Those media that can easily be distributed over the Internet are the first to feel its effects. Take sound recording, for example: An artist can use the web to distribute a CD directly to the consumers via the net. The recording company, distributor, and retailer are no longer needed in the process. Or consider book publishing: An author can put a book directly on a website for readers to download, thereby bypassing publishing companies and bookstores altogether.

Other mass communication organizations, even though they may not have the immediate fears of the recording and publishing industries, will also have to face the implications of this phenomenon. For example, audience members can listen to radio on the web; local stations are no longer necessary. Before long, movie fans will be able to download current full-length films onto DVDs. Will motion picture theaters become obsolete? The chapters in Parts Two and Three of this book will have more to say about disintermediation and its impact on the various media.

■ MAIN POINTS

- The elements in the communication process are a source, encoding process, message, channel, decoding process, receiver, feedback, and noise.
- The three types of noise are semantic, environmental, and mechanical.
- The three main settings for communication are interpersonal, machine-assisted interpersonal, and mass communication.
- Each element in the communication process may vary according to setting.
- Mass communication refers to the process by which a complex organization, with the aid of one or more machines, produces public messages that are aimed at large, heterogeneous, and scattered audiences.

- Traditionally, a mass communicator was defined by formal organization, gatekeepers, expensive operating costs, profit motive, and competitiveness. The Internet has created exceptions to these features.
- New models have been developed to illustrate Internet mass communication.
- Communication content has become more specialized in the past 40 years, but the channels of mass communication still have the potential to reach vast audiences.
- Media have symbiotic relationships.
- The Internet makes possible disintermediation, eliminating the intermediary, or middleman. This phenomenon has implications for many media.

■ QUESTIONS FOR REVIEW

1. What are the eight elements in the communication process?
2. What are the three types of noise?
3. Compare and contrast interpersonal communication with machine-assisted interpersonal communication.

4. How has the Internet changed the characteristics of the sources of mass communication?
5. What is the difference between a "push" and a "pull" model of mass communication?

■ QUESTIONS FOR CRITICAL THINKING

1. What's the most embarrassing communication breakdown that's happened to you? Analyze why it happened. Semantic noise? Environmental noise? Mechanical noise?
2. Keep a media diary for a day. Tabulate how much of your time is spent in interpersonal, machine-assisted interpersonal, or mass communication. What conclusions can you draw?

3. What are some of the shortcomings of the communication models in Figures 1–3 and 1–4? Are there some elements that are missing?
4. Disintermediation is becoming more common as more people use the web. Can you find additional examples? Are there some mass media that won't be affected by this trend? Do you think this is a positive or negative develpment?

■ KEY TERMS

source (p. 4)
encoding (p. 4)
message (p. 5)
channels (p. 5)
decoding (p. 5)
receiver (p. 6)

feedback (p. 6)
noise (p. 7)
interpersonal communication (p. 8)
machine-assisted interpersonal communication (p. 9)

mass communication (p. 13)
gatekeepers (p. 18)
hypertext (p. 24)
mass media (p. 24)
media vehicle (p. 24)
disintermediation (p. 27)

◼ SUGGESTIONS FOR FURTHER READING

The books listed below are good sources to consult for further information about the concepts discussed in this chapter.

Baran, Stanley, and Dennis Davis. *Mass Communication Theory.* Belmont, CA: Wadsworth, 1995.

Barker, Larry, and Deborah Barker. *Communication.* Englewood Cliffs, NJ: Prentice Hall, 1993.

Berlo, David K. *The Process of Communication.* New York: Holt, Rinehart and Winston, 1960.

De Fleur, Melvin, and Sandra Ball-Rokeach. *Theories of Mass Communication.* New York: Longman, 1989.

Dennis, Everette. *Of Media and People.* Newbury Park, CA: Sage Publications, 1992.

Kaye, Barbara, and Norman Medoff. *The World Wide Web: A Mass Communication Perspective.* Mountain View, CA: Mayfield, 1999.

McQuail, Denis. *Mass Communication Theory: An Introduction.* Thousand Oaks, CA: Sage, 1994.

McQuail, Denis, and Sven Windahl. *Communication Models.* New York: Longman, 1993.

Perry, David. *Theory and Research in Mass Communication.* Manwah, NJ: Erlbaum, 1996.

◼ SURFING THE INTERNET

Listed below are sites that deal with interpersonal and mass communication.

http://excellent.com.utk.edu/jmce/
The home of *Journalism and Mass Communication Educator,* a periodical that examines instruction, curriculum, and leadership in mass communication education.

http://pertinent.com
A website that lists articles on various aspects of interpersonal communication, including business communication skills.

www.netgrab.com/fun/bulletin/
Examples of semantic and mechanical noise as seen in church bulletins.

http://students.washington.edu/ss2001/disintermediation2
Site that contains several examples of the disintermediation phenomenon.

CHAPTER 2

Perspectives on Mass Communication

There are several models that we could use to describe the relationships among media, society, and individuals. The "effects" model of examining mass communication, for example, emerged in the early to middle 20th century. The traditional effects perspective uses quantitative research to examine the impact that the media have on individuals and on society. Over the years, a substantial body of research using the effects paradigm (a **paradigm** is a model or a pattern that a person uses

Mourners gather outside John F. Kennedy Jr.'s home in New York City. Media coverage of his death brought the entire country together. *(AP/Wide World Photos)*

to analyze something) has accumulated. Chapter 18 discusses the methods used by effects research and reviews many studies that were done using this approach.

The effects paradigm is not the only one that has been used to examine media. This chapter introduces two other models that provide different ways of looking at media and society. The first of these, **the functional approach**, emphasizes the way that audiences use mass communication and the benefits people receive from media consumption. A second paradigm, which many have labeled the **critical/cultural approach,** examines underlying power relationships in media exposure and stresses the many meanings and interpretations that audience members find in media content.

A recent example highlights the differences among these three paradigms. On Friday, July 16, 1999, the small plane carrying John F. Kennedy Jr., his wife, and his sister-in-law vanished while on a flight from New York to Martha's Vineyard, Massachusetts. Almost immediately, the 24-hour news channels began nonstop coverage. The three major newsmagazines scrapped their planned covers and remade their issues to put Kennedy's face on the cover. Weekend newspapers devoted pages and pages to the story.

Eerily reminiscent of the reaction of the British to the death of Princess Diana, thousands of mourners placed bouquets of flowers outside Kennedy's residence in Manhattan. The public followed the developing story with great interest. Ratings for MSNBC, CNN, and Fox News continuous coverage of the crisis were up 300 to 500 percent.

The relentless media examination continued while the Coast Guard searched for and eventually found the downed plane and its occupants. The intense reporting did not let up until after the burial service for the victims. Let's use this tragic event to illustrate a few of the questions researchers representing the effects, functional and critical perspectives might have used.

A researcher who embraces the effects paradigm would be interested in such questions as how fast the news diffused across the United States; how many individuals first learned the news from TV, radio, print, or the Internet, and whether people shared the news with others. Another research question under the effects paradigm might be how exposure to the coverage affected people's attitudes toward the Kennedy family.

A researcher using the functional perspective would want to know why people watched the coverage and what gratifications they received. Did the coverage allow people to release their emotions about the event? Did the coverage link mourners from all parts of the nation? Moreover, the JFK Jr. tragedy took place in the Internet age. How did people use the Internet in this event? Chat rooms were flooded with comments after the news broke. On July 18, AOL logged one message posted every second concerning the search. A researcher guided by a functional perspective would be interested in analyzing these comments to see how individuals were using this new interactive medium.

A critical/cultural researcher would be interested in other elements in the process. For example, during John F. Kennedy Sr.'s presidency, the metaphor of Camelot, the mythical kingdom where justice and good prevailed, became part of the national culture. Did JFK Jr.'s death signal the end to this dream? Was he "The Last Child of Camelot," as one magazine described him? Is that why the outpouring of grief was so intense? Moreover, during his life, JFK Jr. was unpretentious and even self-deprecating. Why did the media elevate him to royalty status upon his death? *Time* called him "America's Prince," and "an icon of magic and grief." The *New Republic* labeled him "The People's Prince." *People* called him "The Little Prince." Finally, why do the tragedies of famous persons and the social elite take on such importance in American culture? Have the media created a culture of celebrity that has warped our perspective of what's important?

All in all, this one event could serve as the springboard for many disparate avenues of inquiry. This chapter will first examine functional analysis and then look at the critical/cultural approach.

 FUNCTIONAL ANALYSIS

In its simplest form, the functional approach holds that something is best understood by examining how it is used. In mass communication, this means examining the use that audiences make of their interactions with the media.

The functional approach has several advantages:

- It provides us with a perspective from which to examine mass communication.
- It generates concepts that are helpful in understanding media behavior.
- It makes us aware of the diversity of gratifications provided by the media.

By way of introduction, below are some actual responses given by college students to the following questions:

1. Why do you watch TV?
   - I like to watch when there's nothing else to do.
   - I like to vegetate sometimes.
   - I don't like eating alone.
   - It's easier to do than jog.
   - Television keeps me informed and entertained and it beats the hell out of studying.
   - It makes up for the newspaper I fail to read.
   - I watch TV to be entertained . . . also if the TV is on my girlfriend's mother thinks we're watching it.
2. Why do you go to movies?
   - Because movies take you to La-La Land, a fantasy place.
   - Movies are a good place to take a date.
   - To escape the everyday doldrums of life.
   - My boyfriend works at a movie theater and I get in for free.
   - I need an escape and movies are more socially positive than drugs.
   - I like to sit in the dark with sticky shoes.
   - I like the popcorn and the Jordan Almonds.
   - Movies are a fantastic way to be entertained while with a geek-me-out date.

Responses like these, varied though they are, have led to several generalizations about the functions that media have for a society and for its individual members. This section will focus on cataloging and describing those functions.

◼ The Role of Mass Communication

Maybe the best way to appreciate the role that mass communication plays in our society would be to imagine what it would be like if, all of a sudden, the whole system never existed. How would we find out what was on sale at the local supermarket? How would we know Britney Spears's current love interest? (Would there *be* a Britney Spears?) How could we find out what was happening in the Middle East? How could we avoid the traffic jams during rush hour? How would we spend our evenings? Obviously, the mass media are a pervasive part of our lives. Just how pervasive might become clear if we charted the various functions the media perform for us. Before we do this, however, we need to realize that different media have different primary uses. Not many people, for example, listen to records to find out the latest news or read the newspaper while driving their cars. Moreover, different groups of people use the same mass media content for different reasons. History professors, for example, might read articles in scholarly journals in order to keep up with their profession. Others who pursue history as a hobby might read the same journals in order to relax and be diverted from their normal routine.

One more qualification needs to be mentioned before we begin examining the functions and uses of mass communication. It is possible to conduct this analysis on at least two different levels. On the one hand, we could take the perspective of a sociologist and look through a wide-angle lens to consider the functions performed by the mass media for the entire society (this approach is sometimes called **macroanalysis**). This viewpoint focuses on the apparent intention of the mass communicator and emphasizes the manifest purpose inherent in the media content. On the other hand, we could look through a close-up lens at the individual receivers of the content, the audience, and ask them to report how they use mass media (this approach is called **microanalysis**). Sometimes the end results of these two methods are similar in that the consumer uses the content in the way that the source intended. Sometimes they are not similar, and the consumer uses the media in a way not anticipated by the mass communicator—a phenomenon noted by the effects, functional, and critical/cultural paradigms. Let's begin our analysis by using the wide-angle lens.

FUNCTIONS OF MASS COMMUNICATION FOR SOCIETY

For a society to exist, certain communication needs must be met. These needs existed long before Gutenberg bolted together his printing press and Morse started sending dots and dashes. Primitive tribes had sentinels who scanned the environment and reported dangers. Councils of elders interpreted facts and made decisions. Tribal meetings were used to transmit these decisions to the rest of the group. Storytellers and jesters entertained the group. As society became larger and more complex, these jobs grew too big to be handled by single individuals. Throughout the following discussion we will examine the consequences of performing these communication functions by means of mass communication as opposed to interpersonal communication. Furthermore, there may be instances where these consequences are undesirable from the point of view of the welfare of the society. These harmful or negative consequences are called **dysfunctions.** We will mention some of these as well. Lastly, these functions are not mutually exclusive. A given example might illustrate several different categories.

Surveillance

Surveillance refers to what we popularly call the news and information role of the media. The media have taken the place of sentinels and lookouts. The size of this surveillance apparatus is impressive; in the late 1990s, more than 90,000 people were employed in news-gathering jobs in radio, television, newspapers, news magazines, and wire services. The output is also substantial. The four major national television networks provide approximately 600 hours annually of regularly scheduled news programs. CNN provides a 24-hour news service to cable subscribers. Fox and MSNBC offer similar services. Many radio stations broadcast nothing but news. Newsmagazines reach nearly 10 million people. Approximately 1,500 daily newspapers and 7,500 weeklies also spread the news. In any given day, approximately 50 million to 60 million Americans are exposed to mass-communicated news. About 90 percent of the American public report that they receive most of their news from either the electronic media or newspapers.

The surveillance function can be divided further into two main types. Warning, or **beware, surveillance** occurs when the media inform us about threats from hurricanes, erupting volcanoes, depressed economic conditions, increasing inflation,

The headlines certainly got everybody's attention: "Giant Asteroid Heads for Earth," "Doomsday Asteroid Could Hit in 2028," "The End Is Near (Really It Could Be)." These headlines were about an asteroid dubbed XF-11, a mile-wide piece of rock floating in space that was discovered in 1998 by some amateur astronomers. Scientists at the International Astronomical Union examined the asteroid and did some very preliminary calculations that indicated the rock would pass extremely close to and maybe even strike Earth. The newspaper stories were based on these rough computations.

The next day, astronomers at NASA's Jet Propulsion Lab, using data not previously available, found that the asteroid would get no closer than 600,000 miles from Earth. The end of the world was averted.

As fate would have it, two movies were about to be released whose plots revolved around—guess what?—an asteroid about to strike Earth. Both *Deep Impact* and *Armageddon* appeared within two months of the scare. *Deep Impact* earned more than $210 million in admissions and rentals, while *Armageddon* topped the $300 million mark. Would they have done as well if XF-11 hadn't conveniently appeared? Did astronomers conspire to hype these two movies? Was it all a big coincidence? Draw your own conclusions.

or military attack. These warnings can be about immediate threats (a television station interrupts programming to broadcast a tornado warning), or they can be about long-term or chronic threats (a newspaper runs a series about air pollution or unemployment). There is, however, much information that is not particularly threatening to society that people might like to know about. **Instrumental surveillance** has to do with the transmission of information that is useful and helpful in everyday life. News about films playing at the local theaters, stock market prices, new products, fashion ideas, recipes, and teen fads are examples of instrumental surveillance.

Note also that not all examples of surveillance occur in what we traditionally label the news media. *People* magazine and *Reader's Digest* perform a surveillance function (most of it instrumental). Smaller, more specialized publications such as technical journals also perform the job of surveillance. In fact, the surveillance function can be found in content that is primarily meant to entertain. A soap opera might perform an instrumental surveillance function by portraying new hair styles and furniture arrangements.

What are some of the consequences of relying on the mass media to perform this surveillance function? In the first place, news travels much faster, especially since the advent of the electronic media. It took months for the news of the end of

This public-service campaign is an example of the warning function of the media. *(Tony Freeman/Photo Edit)*

DESIGNATED DRIVER
Don't leave the party without one.

GANNETT OUTDOOR

the War of 1812 to travel across the Atlantic. The famous Battle of New Orleans was actually fought after peace had been declared. It took weeks for news of Lincoln's assassination to spread to the rural Midwest. In contrast, when President Kennedy was assassinated, 90 percent of the U.S. population knew about it within one hour. And the beginning of the air war against Iraq was carried live by CNN. This speed sometimes leads to problems. Inaccuracies and distortions now travel just as fast as truthful statements. The live coverage of the Persian Gulf War, for example, was marked by inaccuracies that might have been corrected had more time been available for fact checking. One television network reported that Israel had been attacked by Iraqi Scud missiles that contained nerve gas, but no such attack had occurred.

During the coverage of the hotly contested 2000 presidential elections, the TV networks, in their haste to call a winner, first mistakenly reported that Vice President Al Gore was the winner of Florida's electoral votes. They later retracted that statement and prematurely reported that Governor George W. Bush had won Florida, a prediction that led Vice President Gore, temporarily, at least, to concede the election. Eventually, the networks decided that they didn't know who had won Florida. (See Chapter 18 for more on this story.)

The second consequence is a bit more subtle. In prehistoric times, if war broke out, it was fairly simple for people to find out about it: A stranger would appear and belt you with a club. The world of early men and women was small and easily surveyed. All of it was within the range of their eyesight, and seldom did it extend over the next hill. Today, thanks to the mass media, there aren't any more hills. Our world now extends well beyond our eyesight, and we can no longer observe all of it directly. The media relay news from environments beyond our immediate senses that we cannot easily verify.

Much of what we know about the world is machine-processed, hand-me-down information. News is prescreened for us by a complex arrangement of reporters and editors, and our conception of reality is based on this second-generation information, whose authenticity we do not usually question. For example, human beings have allegedly walked on the moon. Millions saw it—on TV. Not many saw it in person. Instead, we took the word of the TV networks that what we were seeing was fact, not fiction. However, some people feel that television staged the whole thing somewhere in Arizona as part of a massive, government-inspired publicity stunt. The same phenomenon occurred in 1997 with the Pathfinder landing on Mars. There were still some people who thought the pictures received from Mars were fakes. The point is this: In today's world, with its sophisticated system of mass communication, we are highly dependent on others for news. Consequently, we have to put a certain amount of trust in the media that do our surveillance. This trust, called **credibility,** is an important factor in determining which news medium people find the most believable. We will discuss the concept at length in Chapter 12.

The widespread use of the Internet for news does not change this basic idea. The stories posted on cnn.com or other websites devoted to news have been screened by several reporters and editors. Some websites that purport to present news, such as the Drudge Report, may not have a layer of editors, a circumstance that may affect the credibility of the information on that site. Whether the news is filtered or unfiltered, we still have to decide how much faith we invest in the media that provide it.

On the dysfunctional side, media surveillance can create unnecessary anxiety. Consider the tumult that surrounded the Y2K bug that was supposed to turn computers haywire at the beginning of the new millennium. The media carried many stories about what might happen: airplanes flying without radar, banks losing records of customers' deposits, power failures, and general disruption. Many so-called experts urged people to stockpile food to weather the chaos, and apparently some people followed their advice. Of course, the scare was bogus. The year 2000 began without any disruption in cyberspace. Let's look at just one other example of the media creating unneccessary anxiety. In August 2000, a group of tourists on an icebreaker discovered that there was no ice at the North Pole. Newspapers picked up this story and used it as evidence to support the theory of global warming. No ice at the Pole meant the Polar ice caps were melting and might lead to floods and general ecological disruption. Several scientists were quick to point out that the ice covering most of the Arctic Ocean has extensive cracks and huge holes in many places, even at the North Pole and particularly in summer. The open water at the Pole was not necessarily a sign of warming.

The fact that certain individuals or issues receive media attention means that they achieve a certain amount of prominence. Sociologists call this process **status conferral.** At the basis of this phenomenon is a rather circular belief that audiences seem to endorse. The audience evidently believes that if you *really* matter, you will be at the focus of mass media attention, and if you are the focus of media attention, then you *really* matter. Knowing this fact, many individuals and groups go to extreme measures to get media coverage for themselves and their causes so that this status-conferral effect will occur. Parades, demonstrations, publicity stunts, and outlandish behavior are commonly employed to capture airtime or column inches. In the early 1990s, the Ku Klux Klan staged a march in Washington, D.C. Only about 40 people participated in the march, but it still garnered the group extensive coverage on TV and in the print media.

Or take a more recent example. The 12 contestants on the TV program "Survivor" became media celebrities after the series was over. Susan Hawk, the truck driver, landed roles in TV sitcoms. Rudy Boesch, the former Navy SEAL, landed a role in the TV show "JAG" and appeared in an ad in the "Got Milk" campaign. Kelly Wiglesworth hosted an edition of the E! Network's "Talk Soup" and rode on a float in the Hollywood Christmas Parade. The only reason these people got all this status was because they had appeared on television.

Interpretation

Closely allied with the surveillance function is the interpretation function. The mass media do not supply just facts and data. They also provide information on the ultimate meaning and significance of those events. One form of interpretation is so obvious that many people overlook it. Not everything that happens in the world on any given day can be included in the newspaper or in a TV or radio newscast. Media organizations select those events that are to be given time or space and decide how much prominence they are to be given. Stories that ultimately make it into the paper, the newscast, or a media organization's website have been judged by the various gatekeepers involved to be more important than those that didn't make it.

Another example of this function can be found on the editorial pages of a newspaper. Interpretation, comment, and opinion are provided for the reader so that he or she gains an added perspective on the news stories carried on other pages. A

The March 6, 1999, issue of the *New York Times* contained a 4,000-word exposé claiming that China had advanced its nuclear weapons program by using secrets stolen from the Los Alamos National Laboratory in New Mexico. Specifically, the stolen information concerned the design of a W-88 nuclear warhead, the most advanced in the U.S. arsenal. The story went on to say that the FBI was investigating an unnamed Chinese-American scientist as a suspect in the case. Two days later, Wen Ho Lee, a nuclear scientist born in Taiwan, was fired from his research position in the laboratory.

Throughout the next several weeks, the *Times*, relying heavily on sources in Washington, D.C., published several stories that seemed to portray Lee as the villain. One story noted that Lee had once hired a Chinese citizen as his graduate assistant. The graduate student, the story reported, had disappeared. The obvious implication in the story was that the student might have taken nuclear secrets with him when he disappeared. Another story accused Lee of downloading to his personal computer top-secret files that put the nation's nuclear arsenal at risk. Other papers picked up on the *Times'* story and ran their own versions of the alleged spying incidents. Lee was eventually arrested on 59 criminal charges, 36 of which carried a life sentence. He was kept in solitary confinement and shackled whenever he left his cell.

As the story unfolded, however, other reporters found flaws in the *Times'* interpretation of Lee as a probable spy. A *Washington Post* reporter discovered that the reporters who broke the story for the *Times* had not even visited Los Alamos until five months after the story broke. The *Post* reporter also asked about the vanished graduate assistant. He was told the student had interned with Lee during the summer and was now at Penn State studying mechanical engineering. The student's name was even listed on Penn State's website. He had had no access to top-secret material. The reporters for the *Times* had apparently not asked anybody about the student's current whereabouts.

Another reporter talked to many of the scientists who worked with Lee. They were dubious that Lee even had access to the most sensitive nuclear files. Others noted that the *Times* relied heavily on leaks from a congressional committee headed by a conservative Republican with a political ax to grind, who was using the case to criticize alleged lax security measures by the Clinton administration. Chinese-American groups charged that Lee was the victim of racial profiling. Little by little, the case against Lee fell apart.

Eventually, the government dropped 58 of the 59 charges against Lee, who was released after pleading guilty to one count of mishandling secret information. The trial judge apologized to Lee for the harsh conditions of his incarceration. Subsequent media coverage focused on Lee as the innocent victim of a botched government investigation.

For its part, the *Times* published an article that examined its own reporting of this story and concluded that many of its interpretations may have been ill-founded and that its coverage fell short of its own standards. Why did the *Times* fall short in this case? It may be that the increased competition from other newspapers and magazines, 24-hour cable news networks, and Internet sites might have pressured the paper to look extra hard for possible high-profile stories. The potential competitive benefits from breaking a big spy story might have caused the paper to overlook some of its standards.

newspaper might endorse one candidate for public office over another, thereby indicating that, at least in the paper's opinion, the available information indicates that this individual is more qualified than the other.

Interpretation is not confined to editorials. Articles that analyze the causes of an event or that discuss the implications of government policy are also examples of the interpretation function. Why is the price of gasoline going up? What impact will a prolonged dry spell have on food prices? Radio and television also carry programs or segments of programs that fall under this heading. An editorial by Daniel Schorr or by the manager of the local TV or radio station is an example. TV documentaries are others. When the president broadcasts a major political address, network correspondents usually appear afterward to tell us what the president "really said." After the Supreme Court's pronouncement regarding the disputed Florida recount in the 2000 presidential election, various legal experts interpreted what the decision really meant.

Interpretation can take various forms. Editorial cartoons, which originated in 1754, may be the most popular form. Other examples are less obvious but no less important. Critics are employed by the various media to rate motion pictures, plays, books, and records. Restaurants, cars, architecture, and even religious services are reviewed by some newspapers and magazines. One entire magazine, *Consumer Reports,* is devoted to analysis and evaluation of a wide range of general products. Political "spin doctors" try to frame the way media cover news events in a way that is positive for their clients.

The interpretation function can also be found in media content that at first glance might appear to be purely entertainment. The comic strip "Dilbert" reflects a certain viewpoint about corporate America. "Martha Stewart Living" sends a message about what constitutes the "good life." Various interpretations of attitudes toward gay individuals are found in Dr. Laura Schlessinger's radio program and in the TV series "Will and Grace."

What are the consequences of the mass media's performing this function? First, the individual is exposed to a large number of different points of view, probably far more than he or she could come in contact with through personal channels. Because of this, a person (with some effort) can evaluate all sides of an issue before arriving at an opinion. Additionally, the media make available to the individual a wide range of expertise that he or she might not have access to through interpersonal communication. Should we change the funding structure of Social Security? Thanks to the media, a person can read or hear the views of various economists, political scientists, politicians, and government workers.

There are, however, certain dysfunctions that might occur. Since media content is public, any criticism or praise of an individual, group, or lifestyle is also public and might have positive or negative consequences for the medium involved. For example, in 1994 Amtrak pulled $2 million in advertising from NBC because it was offended by comic Jay Leno's jokes about Amtrak trains. Many advertisers refused to buy time on Dr. Laura's unsuccessful TV program because of her views on homosexuality.

Further, there is no guarantee that interpretations by media commentators and experts are accurate and valid. After the bombings in Oklahoma City and Centennial Park in Atlanta and the crash of TWA Flight 800, many in the media industry suggested these acts might be the work of foreign terrorists, an accusation that has yet to be substantiated.

Finally, there is also the danger that an individual may, in the long run, come to rely too heavily on the views carried in the media and lose his or her critical ability. Accepting without question the views of the *New York Times* or Rush Limbaugh may be easier than forming individual opinions, but it might lead to the dysfunctional situation in which the individual becomes passive and allows others to think for him or her.

Doris Kearns Goodwin is a frequent guest on talk shows, where she provides her interpretation of political events. *(Newsmakers/Liaison Agency)*

■ Linkage

The mass media are able to join different elements of society that are not directly connected. For example, mass advertising attempts to link the needs of buyers with the products of sellers. Legislators in Washington may try to keep in touch with constituents' feelings by reading their hometown papers. Voters, in turn, learn about the doings of their elected officials through newspapers, TV, radio, and websites. Telethons that attempt to raise money for the

As mentioned in the text, the online auction site eBay links sellers with buyers. One of the problems with that, of course, is that the seller doesn't know anything about potential buyers. Take the case of a Canadian firm that was commissioned to sell an antique bed on eBay. The firm had received several bids in the $11,000 to $12,000 range. Imagine the firm's surprise when a bid for the antique bed came in at $900,000. Not surprisingly, that was the winning bid.

When the firm called the winning bidder to discuss details of how to transfer the money, they were dismayed to find that the bid came from a 13-year-old boy who was apparently making bids just for fun. Over the course of a few weeks, the boy had placed more than $3.1 million worth of bids for various merchandise on eBay, including a $1.2 million offer for a medical office in Florida. The boy's parents were not amused. They terminated his Internet privileges.

treatment of certain diseases are another example of this **linkage** function. The needs of those suffering from the disease are matched with the desires of others who wish to see the problem eliminated.

Another type of linkage occurs when geographically separated groups that share a common interest are linked by the media. Publicity about the sickness known as Gulf War Syndrome linked those who claimed to be suffering from the disease, who formed a coalition that eventually prompted government hearings on the issue.

The best examples of linkage, however, are the various websites, newsgroups, and chat rooms on the Internet. The online auction site eBay, for example, links people who have some item to sell with people who are looking for an item to buy. A person in California looking to sell an Alex Rodriguez rookie baseball card might be linked with a buyer in Maine, a linkage that would have been much more difficult without the Internet. Match.com bills itself as the place where "You are just a few clicks away from meeting thousands of interesting, intelligent, and successful singles just like you!" WebMD offers subscribers various "communities" where they can share stories about their medical condition with others in the same situation.

This linkage function is present in other media as well. The magazine *Gambling Times* allows a person interested in games of chance to be linked to others with a similar interest. *The General,* a publication devoted to those who play board war games, contains a classified ad section where readers advertise for opponents. Some firms, with the help of the local phone company, are offering "party lines" or "gab lines." A person dials a number and is linked up with similarly minded folks. Most users of this service are looking for dates, and if two people hit it off, they can ask the operator to transfer them to a private line. One New York–based party line logged about 100,000 minutes in calls a day.

Of course, it is entirely possible that the media can create totally new social groups by linking members of society who have not previously recognized that others have similar interests. Some writers call this function the public-making ability of the mass media. A concrete example occurred in Virginia in 1996. Wal-Mart had proposed to the county board of supervisors that a new store be built near the site of George Washington's boyhood home. The board approved the request with little fanfare. The local newspaper, however, publicized the decision and ran a series of articles and cartoons against building the store near such a historic site. The series inspired citizens to unite against the proposal and protest the decision. Eventually, Wal-Mart agreed to move the store to a location about a mile away from the original location.

Anybody want to buy a Point Blank Armor Vest? You can probably find one for sale on eBay. Specialized websites, such as eBay, link sellers and buyers all over the world. *(The materials have been reproduced with the permission of eBay Inc. ©EBAY INC. ALL RIGHTS RESERVED)*

When the media perform in this role, one obvious consequence is that social groups can be mobilized quickly. For example, after *Pathfinder* landed on Mars in 1997, the National Space and Aeronautics Administration reported that its website was receiving millions of hits per day from people all over the world. Not surprisingly, coverage of the event created a new interest in Mars exploration and fueled the scientific debate over whether life ever existed there.

On the other hand, this linkage function may have harmful consequences. In December 1999, the World Trade Organization's meeting in Seattle was disrupted by violent street protests that injured many and did extensive property damage. The protesters included such disparate groups as the Teamsters' Union; the Ruckus Society from Berkeley, California; environmentalists; airline pilots; anarchists; and farmers. These groups were able to coalesce partly because they were linked by the Ruckus Society's website.

Transmission of Values

The transmission of values is a subtle but nonetheless important function of the mass media. It has also been called the **socialization** function. Socialization refers to the ways an individual comes to adopt the behavior and values of a group. The mass media present portrayals of our society, and by watching, listening, and reading, we learn how people are supposed to act and what values are important. To illustrate, let's consider the images of an important but familiar concept as seen in the media: motherhood. The next time you watch television or thumb through a magazine, pay close attention to the way mothers and children are presented. Mass media mommies are usually clean, loving, pretty, and cheerful. Ivory Snow laundry detergent typically adorns the packages of its products with a wholesome-looking mother and healthy child smiling out across grocery aisles. (Incidentally, the company was embarrassed a few years ago when one of their clean-scrubbed, all-American types went on to star in X-rated films.) The Clairol company sponsored an ad campaign that featured the "Clairol mother," an attractive and glamorous female who never let raising a child interfere with maintaining her hair. When they interact with their children, media mothers tend to be positive, warm, and caring. Consider these media mommies drawn from TV: Mrs. Cleaver (Beaver's mother), Mrs. Partridge, Mrs. Keaton ("Family Ties"), Marge Simpson, Mrs. Taylor ("Home Improvement"), Mrs. Barone ("Everybody Loves Raymond"), and Nikki Parker ("The Parkers"). All are understanding, reasonable, friendly, and devoted to their children.[1] Obviously these examples show that these media portrayals picture motherhood and child rearing as activities that have a positive value for society. Individuals who are exposed to these portrayals are likely to grow up and accept this value. Thus a social value is transmitted from one generation to another.

Sometimes the media consciously try to instill values and behavior in the audience. Many newspapers report whether accident victims were wearing seat belts at the time of the mishap. In 1989, TV writers voluntarily agreed to portray alcohol usage more responsibly in their programs and include references to designated drivers whenever possible. The next time you watch current TV shows, see if you can find anyone smoking a cigarette. The health concerns regarding smoking have prompted it to virtually disappear from prime-time TV.

There are probably countless other examples of values and behavior that are, in part at least, socialized through the media. At this point, however, let us examine some of the consequences of having the mass media serve as agents of socialization. At one level, value transmission via the mass media will help stabilize society. Common values and experiences are passed down to all members, thereby creating common bonds among them. On the other hand, values and cultural information are selected by large organizations that may encourage the status quo. For example, the "baby industry" in this country is a multimillion-dollar one. This industry advertises heavily in the media; it is not surprising, then, that motherhood is depicted in such an attractive light. To show mothers as harried, exhausted, overworked, and frazzled would not help maintain this profitable arrangement.

Mass media can also transmit values by enforcing social norms. In early 1993, two nominees for U.S. Attorney General were forced to withdraw from consideration when it was publicized that they did not comply with federal law when they employed domestic workers. In 1994, a newspaper photographer snapped a picture of two presidential aides boarding a presidential helicopter after playing a round of golf. The picture was carried by the wire services and prompted such an uproar that one of the aides in the photo was forced to resign and repay the $13,129 cost of the helicopter flight. Another example is found on college campuses. In an effort to combat binge drinking by college students, several campuses have launched information campaigns designed to show that excessive alcohol consumption is not as widespread or normal as some college students might think. If college students think that most of their peers drink only moderately or less, there is less pressure on them to drink to excess.

TV and Socialization   Of all the mass media, television probably has the greatest potential for socialization. By the time an individual is 18, he or she will have spent more time watching television than in any other single activity except sleep.

---

[1]OK, Peg Bundy of "Married . . . with Children" may be an exception.

A prime-time program that is popular with youngsters might draw an audience of 10 million 6- to 11-year-olds. Because of this wide exposure, several writers have warned of possible dysfunctions that might occur if television became the most important channel of socialization. For instance, since so many TV programs contain violence, it has been feared that youngsters who watch many violent programs might be socialized into accepting violence as a legitimate method of problem solving. In one survey among grade school youngsters, heavy TV viewers were more likely than light TV viewers to agree with this statement: "It's almost always all right to hit someone if you are mad at him or her." Or another possibility might be that the pervasiveness of television violence might encourage fearfulness about the "real world." One study, for example, found that children who were heavy TV viewers were more fearful of going out at night than were light TV viewers. We will discuss this topic at greater length in Chapter 18.

Surveys about television have indicated that this medium can also function as a source of knowledge about occupations. For example, during the 1970s, the two most common occupations held by leading female characters in prime-time TV were those of housewife and law enforcement officer. No other occupation came close to these two in frequency of portrayal. If she had no other sources of countervailing information, a girl growing up in this decade might have been socialized into believing she had two career choices when she grew up: to get married or to become a cop.

Finally, it has been argued that for many years the image of minority groups transmitted from one generation to the next by the mass media reflected the stereotypes held by those who were in power: white, Anglo-Saxon, Protestant males. As a result, Native Americans and black Americans endured many years during which Native Americans were seen as savages who murdered civilized whites, and blacks were depicted in menial and subordinate roles. These stereotypes were slow to change, partly because it took a long time for members of these minority groups to influence the workings of large media organizations.

■ Entertainment

Another obvious media function is that of entertainment. Two of the media examined in this book, motion pictures and sound recording, are devoted primarily to entertainment. Even though most of a newspaper focuses on the events of the day, comics, puzzles, horoscopes, games, advice, gossip, humor, and general entertainment features usually account for around 12 percent of the content. (If we considered sports news as entertainment, that would add another 14 percent to this figure.) Television is primarily devoted to entertainment, with about three-quarters of a typical broadcast day falling into this category. The entertainment content of radio varies widely according to station format. Some stations may program 100 percent news, while others may schedule almost none. In like manner, some magazines may have little entertainment content (*Forbes*), while others are almost entirely devoted to it (*National Lampoon*). Even those magazines that are concerned primarily with news—*Time* and *Newsweek,* for example—usually mix in some entertaining features with their usual reporting.

The scope of mass media entertainment is awesome. By late 2000, approximately 50 million people had paid money to see *Gladiator*. About 125 million people watched the last episode of "M*A*S*H." In a typical month, more than 5 million read (or at least look at) *Playboy*. Alanis Morissette's *Jagged Little Pill* album had sold more than 16 million copies by 1999. And the comic strip "Doonesbury"

Priorities in Order

For some perspective on the importance of the entertainment function, consider this: According to projections by a prestigious financial forecasting company, by 2003, Americans will spend more than $660 billion on entertainment. That's more than they'll spend on food.

is read by 18 million people. The importance of this entertainment function has grown as Americans have accumulated more leisure time. The work-week has decreased from about 72 hours at the turn of the 20th century to the current 40 hours.

Troubadours, storytellers, court jesters, and magicians fulfilled the entertainment function in the centuries before the media. What are the consequences of having this task now taken over by mass communication? Clearly, the media can make entertainment available to a large number of people at relatively little cost. On the other hand, entertainment that is carried by the mass media must appeal to a mass audience. The ultimate result of this state of affairs is that media content is designed to appeal to the lowest common denominator of taste. More programs that resemble "Survivor" and "Jerry Springer" will find their way to TV than will opera performances. Newsstands are filled with more imitators of *Playboy* than imitators of *Saturday Review*. We are more apt to see sequels such as *Star Trek VIII*, *Wes Craven's New Nightmare,* and *Lethal Weapon VII* than we are to see *Much Ado About Nothing II* and *More King Lear*. Rock stations outnumber classical stations 15 to 1.

One other consequence of the widespread use of media for entertainment is that it is now quite easy to sit back and let others entertain you. Instead of playing baseball, people might simply watch it on TV. Instead of learning to play the guitar, an adolescent might decide to listen to a tape of someone else playing the guitar. On more than one occasion, critics have charged that the mass media will turn Americans into a nation of watchers and listeners instead of doers.

 ## HOW PEOPLE USE THE MASS MEDIA

It is probably clear by now that statements made about the functions of mass communication in society could be paralleled by statements about how the media function at the level of the individual. Consequently, we will now focus on how the individual uses mass communication (in other words, we are moving from macro- to microanalysis). At the individual level, the functional approach is given the general name of the **uses-and-gratifications model.** In its simplest form, the uses-and-gratifications model posits that audience members have certain needs or drives that are satisfied by using both nonmedia and media sources. This discussion will be concerned more with media-related sources of satisfaction. The actual needs satisfied by the media are called media gratifications. Our knowledge of these uses and gratifications typically comes from surveys that ask people questions about how they use the media (much like the questions at the beginning of this chapter). Several researchers have classified the various uses and gratifications into a fourfold category system:

1. Cognition
2. Diversion
3. Social utility
4. Withdrawal

We will examine each in turn.

■ Cognition

Cognition means the act of coming to know something. When a person uses a mass medium to obtain information about something, then he or she is using the medium in a cognitive way. Clearly, the individual's cognitive use of a medium is directly parallel to the surveillance function at the macroanalytical level. At the individual level, however, researchers have noted that two different types of cognitive functions are performed. One has to do with using the media to keep up with information on current events, while the other has to do with using the media to learn about things in general or things that relate to a person's general curiosity. Several surveys have found that many people give the following reasons for using the media:

I want to keep up with what the government is doing.

I want to understand what is going on in the world.

I want to know what political leaders are doing.

These reasons constitute the current-events type of cognitive gratification. At the same time, many people also report the following reasons for using mass media:

I want to learn how to do things I've never done before.

I want to satisfy my curiosity.

The media make me want to learn more about things.

The media give me ideas.

These statements illustrate the second type of cognition—using the media to satisfy a desire for general knowledge.

One of the types of cognition is awareness of current events. Many people use the media to find out about breaking news, such as the continuing violence in the Middle East during 2000 to 2001. *(AP/Wide World Photos)*

◼ Diversion

Another basic need of human beings is for diversion. Diversion can take many forms. Some of these forms identified by researchers include (1) stimulation, or seeking relief from boredom or the routine activities of everyday life; (2) relaxation, or escape from the pressures and problems of day-to-day existence; and (3) emotional release of pent-up emotions and energy. Let's look at each of these gratifications in more detail.

Stimulation   Seeking emotional or intellectual stimulation seems to be an inherent motivation in a human being. Psychologists have labeled these activities "ludic behaviors"—play, recreation, and other forms of activity that seem to be performed to maintain a minimum level of intellectual activity. Many people report that they watch, read, or listen simply to pass the time. The media have taken advantage of this need to avoid boredom in many creative ways. Ted Turner has started an airport TV channel that beams news and commercials to passengers in airline terminals. Some airlines provide audio and video entertainment during long flights. Supermarkets have grocery carts with a video screen that displays the latest bargains. Some restaurants and coffeehouses have computers on their tables to allow customers to surf before they sup. There are now special magazines that are distributed only to doctors' waiting rooms. Advertisements are now found on walls and the backs of stall doors in rest rooms.

Relaxation   Too much stimulation, however, is undesirable. Psychological experiments have indicated that human beings are negatively affected by sensory overload, in which too much information and stimulation are present in the environment. When faced with sensory overload, people tend to seek relief. The media are one source of this relief. Watching "Leave It to Beaver" or reading *People* magazine represents a pleasant diversion from the frustrations of everyday life. The choice of material used for relaxation might not always be apparent from surface content. Some people relax by reading articles about Civil War history; others read about astronomy or electronics. Still others might relax by listening to serious classical music. The content is not the defining factor, since virtually any media material might be used for relaxation by some audience members.

Emotional Release   The last manifestation of the diversion function is the most complex. On the one hand, the use of the media for emotional release is fairly obvious. For instance, the horror movie has had a long history of popularity in America. Starting with *Dracula* and *Frankenstein* and continuing through *The Creature from the Black Lagoon, Them,* and *The Thing* right up to *Nightmare on Elm Street, Friday the 13th, Aliens,* and *Scream,* people have sat in dark theaters and screamed their lungs out. Tearjerkers have also drawn crowds. *Broken Blossoms, Since You Went Away, The Best Years of Our Lives, Terms of Endearment, Dying Young,* and *Titanic* have prompted thousands, perhaps millions, to cry their eyes out. Why do audiences cheer when Rocky goes the distance? Probably because people enjoy a certain amount of emotional release. People feel better after a good scream or a good cry.

Denzel Washington motivates a player in *Remember the Titans.* The movie provided theatergoers with an outlet for emotional release as they cheered for the heroes. *(Photofest)*

On the other hand, emotional release can take more subtle forms. One of the big attractions of soap operas, for example, seems to be that many people in the audiences are comforted by seeing that other people (even fictional people) have troubles greater than their own. Other people identify with media heroes and participate vicariously in their triumphs. Such a process evidently enables these people to vent some of the frustrations connected with their normal lives.

Emotional release was probably one of the first functions to be attributed to media content. Aristotle, in his *Poetics,* talked about the phenomenon of **catharsis** (a release of pent-up emotion or energy) occurring as a function of viewing tragic plays. In fact, the catharsis theory has surfaced many times since then, usually in connection with the portrayals of television violence. Chapter 18 contains a discussion of research that has dealt expressly with the catharsis notion.

Social Utility

Psychologists have also identified a set of social integrative needs, including our need to strengthen our contact with family, friends, and others in our society. The social integrative need seems to spring from an individual's need to affiliate with others. The media function that addresses this need is called **social utility,** and this usage can take several forms. First, have you ever talked with a friend about a TV program? Have you ever discussed a current movie or the latest record you've heard on the radio? If so, then you are using the media as **conversational currency.** The media provide a common ground for social conversations, and many people use things that they have read, seen, or heard as topics for discussion when talking with others. There is a certain social usefulness in having a large repository of things to talk about so that, no matter where you are, you can strike up a con-

Teens love to be terrorized—at least at the movies. Eighty percent of the audience for slice-and-dice films, such as the *Nightmare on Elm Street* series, is under the age of 21. In addition, the terror audience is almost always evenly split between males and females. This is not coincidental; slasher and splatter films are popular date movies. Apparently they serve an important function for their young audience. As one teenager, quoted in a recent issue of *Seventeen*, put it: "Sometimes you feel weird or self-conscious holding onto a guy's hand on the first date but this way you can just grab him." Said another teenage girl: "Guys like to take you to horror movies, hoping you'll be real afraid and need them to comfort you." Said a third: "You can get all rowdy with boys and jump into their lap."

Scientific studies seem to confirm that horror films are performing this social function for teens. In one experiment at the University of Indiana, female college students were paired with male confederates of the researchers. One male was instructed to remain silent while the couple watched a scene from a horror movie. A second male confederate acted wimpy, saying "Oh my God" at the gory scenes and generally acting afraid. The third male confederate acted macho, showing no signs of fear and shouting "All right!" during the gory scenes. Another condition in this experiment paired males with female confederates who acted the same way.

The results? Males enjoyed the horror film most when they were paired with the females who acted afraid. In contrast, females enjoyed the film most when paired with the macho males. The researchers concluded that horror movies encourage traditional gender-specific ways of behavior for both men and women, a conclusion supported by the preceding quotes from teen moviegoers.

versation and be fairly sure that the person you are talking to is familiar with the subject. ("What did you think of the Super Bowl?" "How did you like *Meet the Parents?*")

Social utility is apparent in other instances as well. Going to the movies is probably the most common dating behavior among adolescents. The motion picture theater represents a place where it is socially acceptable to sit next to your date in a dark room without parental supervision. In fact, many times the actual film is of secondary importance; the social event of going out has the most appeal.

Other people report that they use the media, particularly TV and radio, as a means to overcome loneliness. The TV set represents a voice in the house for people who might otherwise be alone. Radio keeps people company in their cars. In fact, some viewers might go so far as to develop feelings of kinship and friendship with media characters. This phenomenon is called a **parasocial relationship,** and there is some evidence that it actually occurs. For example, in one study done during the 1970s that examined parasocial relationships between the audience and TV newscasters, more than half the people surveyed agreed with the statement, "The newscasters are almost like friends you see every day."

TV sometimes reinforces the confusion. Many of you have probably seen the ad that starts, "I'm not a doctor but I play one on TV." The nondoctor then goes on to endorse a health-related product. Further, one local TV station tried to get closer to its audience by doing an entire newscast from the living room of one of its viewers.

◼ Withdrawal

At times, people use the mass media to create a barrier between themselves and other people or activities. For example, the media help people avoid certain chores that should be done. Children are quick to learn how to use the media in this fashion. This hypothetical exchange might be familiar:

"It's your turn to let the dog out."

"I can't. I want to finish watching this program. You do it."

In this case, attending to mass media content was defined as a socially appropriate behavior that should not be interrupted. In this manner, other tasks might be put off or avoided entirely.

People also use the media to create a buffer zone between themselves and other people. When you are riding a bus or sitting in a public place and don't want to be disturbed, you bury your head in a book, magazine, or newspaper. If you are on an airplane, you might insert a pair of stethoscopelike earphones in your ears and tune everybody out. Television can perform this same function at home by isolating adults from children ("Don't disturb Daddy. He's watching the game") or children from adults ("Don't bother me now; go into the other room and watch 'Sesame Street'").

Content and Context

In closing, we should emphasize that it is not only media content that determines audience usage, but also the social context within which the media exposure occurs. For example, soap operas, situation comedies, and movie magazines all contain material that audiences can use for escape purposes. People going to a movie, however, might value the opportunity to socialize more than they value any aspect of the film itself. Here the social context is the deciding factor.

It is also important to note that the functional approach makes several assumptions:

1. Audiences take an active role in their interaction with various media. That is, the needs of each individual provide motivation that channels that individual's media use.

2. The mass media compete with other sources of satisfaction. Relaxation, for example, can also be achieved by taking a nap or having a couple of drinks, and social utility needs can be satisfied by joining a club or playing touch football.

3. The uses-and-gratifications approach assumes that people are aware of their own needs and are able to verbalize them. This approach relies heavily on surveys based on the actual responses of audience members. Thus the research technique assumes that people's responses are valid indicators of their motives.

A great deal of additional research needs to be done in connection with the uses-and-gratifications approach. In particular, more work is needed in defining and categorizing media-related needs or drives and in relating those needs to media usage. Nonetheless, the current approach provides a valuable way to examine the complex interaction between the various media and their audiences.

CRITICAL/CULTURAL STUDIES

Both the functional approach and the traditional effects approach rely on empirical methods common to the social sciences. Researchers who use these approaches ask people questions and tabulate their results or enumerate characteristics of media content. In contrast, critical/cultural researchers use a more qualitative and humanities-oriented approach. This perspective takes a macroanalytic outlook and examines such concepts as ideology, culture, politics, and social structure as they relate to the role of media in society. Some background on this school of thought may be helpful.

History

Most scholars suggest that the beginnings of the critical/cultural model can be traced to the Frankfurt School during the 1930s and 1940s. The Frankfurt School was a group of intellectuals committed to the analytical ideas of Karl Marx. (Keep in mind that the following discusses Marxism as a philosophical system and an analytical tool. Marxism as a political and economic system has fallen on hard times of late.) In simplified terms, the core of this Marxist approach was that the best way to understand how a society worked was to examine who controlled the means of production that met the basic needs of the population for food and shelter. Marx noted that many Western countries had adopted a system of industrial capitalism where a system of mass production created wealth for the capitalists—the ones who owned the factories where the goods were produced. Mass production ensured that the basic needs of a society were met, but at a cost—tension between the haves (the wealthy) and the have-nots (the workers who worked in all those factories). In other words, the capitalist system exploited the working class and guaranteed their domination by the wealthy. Because capitalists were interested in creating more capital (or wealth), they had a vested interest in ensuring that the system stayed in place. Marx suggested that life would be better for all if some other, more equitable system of sharing wealth were in place.

The members of the Frankfurt School extended Marxist analysis into the cultural life of a society. They noted that, just as big firms controlled the production of economic goods, other big companies controlled the production of cultural goods. The radio industry, motion picture studios, newspaper and magazine publishers, and later the television business all adopted the capitalist model of production. According to the Frankfurt School, the culture industry exploited the masses just as capitalists did. They published and broadcast products based on standardized formulas that appealed to the mass audience and at the same time glorified and promoted the capitalist culture. For example, during the depression of the 1930s, Hollywood did not make films that advocated a different economic or political system. Instead, the studios churned out glitzy musicals and comedies that portrayed common people who get a break and make it big despite the bad economic times. The television sitcoms of the 1950s showed well-off families content with their lives in the suburbs: *Ozzie and Harriet* never agitated for a new economic system.

Much of the writing of members of the Frankfurt School was designed to show the exploitative character of mass culture and how the culture industry helped destroy individuality by promoting the social dominance of large corporations. The object of the critical theory espoused by these writers was resistance to this mass culture and exploitation. The media were so powerful and pervasive, however, that critical resistance to these forces was nearly impossible. The media continued to reinforce the status quo.

The viewpoint of the Frankfurt School was criticized for being pessimistic and gloomy and for underestimating the power of the audience. Nonetheless, this perspective caused many to analyze the impact of the media industries on the political and economic life of a society and to use interdisciplinary theories and methods in their investigations.

The next important stage in the development of the critical/cultural approach took place in Great Britain during the late 1950s and early 1960s. Scholars at the Centre for Contemporary Cultural Studies at Birmingham University noted that members of the British working class used the products of mass culture to define

their own identities through the way they dressed, the music they listened to, their hairstyles, and so forth. The audience did not seem to be manipulated by the media, as the Frankfurt School argued; instead, the relationship was more complicated. Audience members took the products of mass culture, redefined their meaning, and created new definitions of their self-image.

This emphasis on meaning was reinforced by studies of film and television. A theory developed by British film critics suggested that cinematic techniques (camera angle, editing, imagery) subtly but effectively impose the meanings preferred by the filmmaker on the audience.

This theory was later amended to acknowledge that, although films and TV shows could try to impose their preferred meanings on people, audience members were free to resist and come up with their own meanings of what they saw. For example, although the dominant theme in a documentary about efforts to control pollution might be how hard industry is trying to control the problem, some in the audience might see the program as nothing more than an empty marketing gesture by big companies.

Important to the cultural studies group were the values that were represented in the content. Again drawing from Marx, the group noted that the values of the ruling class became the dominant values that were depicted in mass media and other cultural products. Marx analyzed dominant values in economic terms. The cultural studies scholars extended the perspective to class, race, and, with the growth of feminist studies, gender. In Britain, and later in the United States, the dominant values that were represented were those of white, upper-class, Western males. The media worked to maintain those values by presenting versions of reality on TV and films that represented this situation as normal and natural, as the way things should be.

The audience, however, was not passive. The dominant values may have been encoded in complex and subtle ways (much critical/cultural research is aimed at describing and analyzing these subtle depictions), but viewers can supply their own meanings to the content (much critical/cultural research tries to catalog how various audience members interpret content in different ways). One of the classic studies examined how the audience made sense of a British TV program, "Nationwide." One group seemed to accept the dominant message of the program that British society was harmonious and egalitarian; another group "negotiated" their own, somewhat different interpretation; and a third group, young blacks who were not part of the mainstream, rejected it altogether.

The critical/cultural approach gained prominence in the United States during the 1970s and 1980s and was adopted by communication researchers and scholars doing feminist studies. Like Marxist analysis, feminist analysis saw inequalities in the way that wealth and power were distributed in society. Marx, however, argued that this inequality stemmed from industrial capitalism; feminist scholars suggested that it stemmed from male domination of women in society (sometimes referred to as patriarchy). Feminist critics examined how the media and other forms of culture strengthened the oppression of women. Advertising, for example, might suggest that the proper (or natural) place for a woman is in the home or that looking good is the preferred way for women to gain success.

Not all critical/cultural scholars, however, emphasize power relationships. James Carey, for example, contended that researchers should study how communication creates, maintains, or modifies a culture. He argued that it was valuable to look upon communication as a ritual—how it draws people together and how it represents a sharing of beliefs. Someone interested in the ritual role of mass communication, for instance, might examine the cultural meanings of males' gathering together to watch "Monday Night Football" and how this rite illustrates the social bonds that help maintain society. Other critical/cultural scholars have examined how cultural myths are embodied in mass communication. A myth is an expressive story that celebrates a society's common themes, heroes, and origins. Studying the way popular media programs utilize the collective myths of a culture might help us understand their success. "Star Trek," for example, has spawned a cult following, four TV series, and upwards of a half-dozen movie sequels. A mythic analysis of the TV show suggests that it draws upon myth deeply rooted in American history—the myth of the frontier where a wagon train heads hopefully into uncharted and potentially dangerous territory in search of better horizons. Note that the "Star Trek" prologue describes space as "the final frontier," the *Enterprise* takes the place of the wagon train, Klingons take the place of hostile Indians, and Kirk becomes the wagon master while Spock serves as scout.

As is probably obvious by now, the critical/cultural perspective is multidimensional and encompasses a wide variety of topics and analysis methods. It is difficult to summarize the important notions of such an eclectic approach, but the ones listed below have general relevance.

▪ Concepts

Like most other specialized ways of examining the audience, critical/cultural studies has developed its own specialized vocabulary. Some of the key terms are described below.

Cultural studies, naturally enough, broadens the study of mass communication to encompass the notion of **culture.** Culture is a complex concept that refers to the common values, beliefs, social practices, rules, and assumptions that bind a group of people together. Hence, it's possible to identify a street culture or an Asian-American culture or even a college student culture.

Culture is studied through the practices and texts of everyday life. A **text** is the object of analysis. Texts are broadly defined. They can be traditional media content such as TV programs, films, ads, or books, or they can be some things that do not fit into the traditional category, such as shopping malls, T-shirts, dolls, video games, and beaches.

Texts have **meaning,** the interpretations that audience members take away with them from the text. In fact, texts have many meanings; they are **polysemic.** Different members of the audience will make different interpretations of the same text. Some may interpret the way the source intended; others may provide their own unique meanings.

Ideology is contained in texts. Broadly defined, an ideology is a specific set of ideas or beliefs, particularly regarding social and political subjects. Mass communication messages and other objects of popular culture have ideology embedded in them. Sometimes the ideology is easy to see. Commercials, for example, illustrate the belief that consumption is good for you and for society. Other times the ideology is more subtle and harder to detect.

Hegemony has to do with power relationships and dominance. In the United States, for example, those who own the channels of mass communication possess cultural hegemony over the rest of us. Groups with political and economic power extend their influence over those groups who are powerless or at the margins of society. Hegemony, however, is not based on force. It depends on the dominated group's accepting its position as natural and normal and believing that the status quo is in its best interest. Media rules, regulations, and portrayals all help the dominant class present the status quo as customary and desirable. Hegemony creates the positions of the superior and the inferior and suggests that this division is unstable and continuously being negotiated through interpretations of meaning.

A couple of examples will illustrate how these concepts are used in the critical/cultural approach. One critical/cultural study used the long-running TV show "60 Minutes" as its text. The analysis found that predictable themes and formulas were found in the program. One common type of "60 Minutes" segment can be interpreted as the classic American detective story. Somebody, maybe a business that is ripping off consumers, is committing a crime. The "60 Minutes" reporters have to hunt down clues and gather information. They may sneak in a hidden camera to catch the wrongdoers in the act. The reporters become the heroes; the evildoers are the villains. The story is eventually resolved, and those who were committing the bad deeds are exposed or brought to justice.

This seems to be a meritorious service to the public. But upon closer inspection, it might be that this kind of "60 Minutes" story is reinforcing the hegemony of the dominant class. Note that these stories go after companies or businesses that have violated some basic values of American capitalism: "Thou shalt not cheat the customer"; "Thou shalt not promise more than thou canst deliver." The stories never question the basic ideology that capitalism is good for you. Instead, they imply that life would be fine if we could just expose all those companies that do not play by the rules of free enterprise and bring them back into the fold. Further, note how the program stands up for the little person. The reporters are our friends and champions. Everything is fine with the system, and CBS can continue to make money from selling ads in a top-rated program. It's easy for an audience member to come away with an interpretation that simply reinforces the economic and social hegemony of the powerful.

A second example concerns arcade video games as a text. These games are typically played by a relatively powerless segment of society—younger teenagers. Nonetheless, these players can find a meaning in the games that lets them resist, for a rather short time, forms of social control, allowing them to form their own cultural identity. The arcade games, for instance, reverse the traditional relationship between machine and machine operator. In industry, the two work together to produce some commodity. In the arcade, the player plays against the machine. The idea is to consume, not to produce.

Playing arcade games is regarded by some with a certain amount of disapproval; some games are violent and others have mature themes. There is also the view that game playing is just a waste of time, and this disapproval on the part of *non*players probably plays a role in the games' attraction to those who *do* play. In addition, the joy stick or steering wheel offers the player a direct means to control his or her environment, something that may not be possible in much of everyday life. These factors may account for the continuing popularity of this type of entertainment. Nonetheless, a closer look suggests that, although video games allow the player some freedom of cultural interpretation, the games still work to reinforce the dominant ideology—the social values contained in the games are the common ones in society. Arcade players get a chance to blow away monsters, aliens, drug runners, thugs, and other assorted bad guys; there is no opportunity to show disfavor with the prevailing social norms. And, of course, many of those quarters from the arcade go back to the video game companies, which maintain their economic hegemony and make more games that teens can play to make them feel as though they are resisting the dominant ideology while they are actually supporting it.

Throughout this book, we present a series of boxed inserts that illustrate the critical/cultural approach and demonstrate the range and diversity of critical/cultural topics. For example, in Chapter 5 you will find a critical/cultural analysis of *YM* magazine; in Chapter 6 an analysis focuses on Oprah's book club.

Before closing, we should point out that some friction exists between those who choose the traditional effects or functional approaches and those who adopt the critical/cultural approach. This discord seems unnecessary since these various paradigms ask different questions about media and society and use different tools to look for answers. In addition, each approach can learn from the others. No technique is somehow better than the rest. All are useful in the quest to understand the complicated relationships between mass communication and its audience.

■ MAIN POINTS

- Functional analysis holds that something is best understood by examining how it is used.

- At the macro level of analysis, mass media perform five functions for society: surveillance, interpretation, linkage, transmission of values, and diversion. Dysfunctions are harmful or negative consequences of these functions.

- At the micro level of analysis, the functional approach is called uses-and-gratifications analysis.

- The media perform the following functions for the individual: cognition, diversion, social utility, and withdrawal.

- The critical/cultural approach has its roots in Marxist philosophy, which emphasized class differences as a cause of conflict in a society.

- The critical/cultural approach suggests that media content helps perpetuate a system that keeps the dominant class in power. It also notes that people can find different meanings in the same message.

- The key concepts in the critical approach are text, meaning, hegemony, and ideology.

- Although they are different approaches, both functional analysis and critical/cultural studies can be valuable tools for the analysis of the mass communication process.

■ QUESTIONS FOR REVIEW

1. What is the difference between macroanalysis and microanalysis?

2. What is a dysfunction? What are some examples?

3. What is status conferral? How does it work?

4. What is meant by the uses-and-gratifications approach? What are its assumptions?

5. What are the key terms in the critical/cultural approach?

■ QUESTIONS FOR CRITICAL THINKING

1. Compare and contrast the functional approach and the critical/cultural approach. How does each view the audience? How does each view the media?

2. Compare your own reasons for watching TV and going to the movies with those that appear in the beginning of the chapter. Are there any similarities?

3. Can you find any more current examples of status conferral? Linkage? Media dysfunctions?

4. As mentioned in the text, one of the assumptions of the uses-and-gratifications approach is that people can verbalize their needs. Suppose this assumption is false. Is the uses-and-gratifications approach still useful?

5. Using the critical/cultural viewpoint, can you detect ways that the media preserve the current political and economic status quo?

■ KEY TERMS

paradigm (p. 30)
functional approach (p. 30)
critical/cultural approach (p. 31)
macroanalysis (p. 33)
microanalysis (p. 33)
dysfunctions (p. 33)
surveillance (p. 33)
beware surveillance (p. 33)

instrumental surveillance (p. 34)
credibility (p. 35)
status conferral (p. 36)
linkage (p. 38)
socialization (p. 40)
uses-and-gratifications model (p. 43)
catharsis (p. 46)
social utility (p. 46)

conversational currency (p. 46)
parasocial relationship (p. 47)
culture (p. 51)
text (p. 51)
meaning (p. 52)
polysemic (p. 52)
ideology (p. 52)
hegemony (p. 52)

■ SUGGESTIONS FOR FURTHER READING

The sources listed below are good places to go for additional information on this topic.

Andersen, Robin. *Consumer Culture and TV Programming.* Boulder, CO: Westview Press, 1995.

Avery, Robert, and David Eason. *Critical Perspectives on Media and Society.* New York: Guilford Press, 1991.

Bryant, Jennings, and Dolf Zillman, eds. *Media Effects: Advances in Theory and Research.* Hillsdale, NJ: Erlbaum, 1994.

Gauntlett, David. *Web. Studies: Rewiring Media Studies for the Digital Age.* London: Arnold, 2000.

Klapper, Joseph. *The Effects of Mass Communication.* New York: Free Press, 1960.

Lull, James. *Media, Communication, Culture: A Global Approach.* New York: Columbia University Press, 2000.

Marris, Paul, and Sue Thornham. *Media Studies: A Reader.* New York: New York University Press, 2000.

Perry, David. *Theory and Research in Mass Communication.* Mahwah, NJ: Erlbaum, 1996.

Smith, Joel. *Understanding the Media.* Cresskill, NJ: Hampton Press, 1995.

Stevenson, Nick. *Understanding Media Cultures.* London: Sage, 1995.

Wright, Charles R. *Mass Communication: A Sociological Perspective.* New York: Random House, 1986.

■ SURFING THE INTERNET

The following are useful sites that are related to the material in this chapter. In addition, scan some of the newsgroups on the net to see some of the special-interest topics that bring people together.

http://eserver.org/theory/
Page contains links to works using the critical/cultural approach in many disciplines.

www.aber.ac.uk/media/documents/short/usegrat.html
A site containing articles that discuss the uses-and-gratifications approach.

www.elm.mq.edu.au/ccs/ccsnews
The Critical and Cultural Studies Newsletter. A publication devoted to social and cultural analysis of media.

www.gu.edu.au/centre/cmp/newsletter.html
The online home of *Media & Culture Review.* This Australian-based publication contains articles relevant to critical and cultural studies.

www.shef.ac.uk/uni/academic/I-M/j/audpersp.htm
A discussion of the various approaches and models used to analyze the role of media in society.

CHAPTER 3

Historical and Cultural Context

The historical and cultural contexts of media are important because history tends to be cyclical. This fact has been apparent for centuries. Many ancient civilizations relied on storytellers to hand down the history and culture of their civilization so that they might learn from the past. The same is true for modern society. Knowing what happened many years ago might help us understand what is going on now. For example, when radio first started in the 1910s and 1920s, its future was uncertain. Many thought radio would compete with the telephone and telegraph as a means of sending messages from point to point, while others saw radio's future in aviation, providing radio beacons for aircraft.

The first organization to realize radio's importance was the military; the Navy led the way during World War I. After the war, as interest in the new medium increased, a totally new function emerged. Radio was used to broadcast information and entertainment to a mass audience. Many individuals and organizations scrambled to make use of this new means of communication: the telephone company, newspapers, businesses, and even universities. None had any clear idea how radio broadcasting would pay for itself. Eventually, the radio industry became a commercial medium, dominated by big business, that in less than 10 years reached an audience of 50 million. Radio changed America's news and entertainment habits and became a medium whose influence on popular culture is still being felt.

This modern-day storyteller keeps alive the oral culture of our ancestors and introduces another generation to the art of verbal communications. *(Michael Newman Photo Editor)*

Compare radio's development with that of the Internet, which was started by the Department of Defense to improve military communication. When first developed, the Internet was envisioned as a means of point-to-point

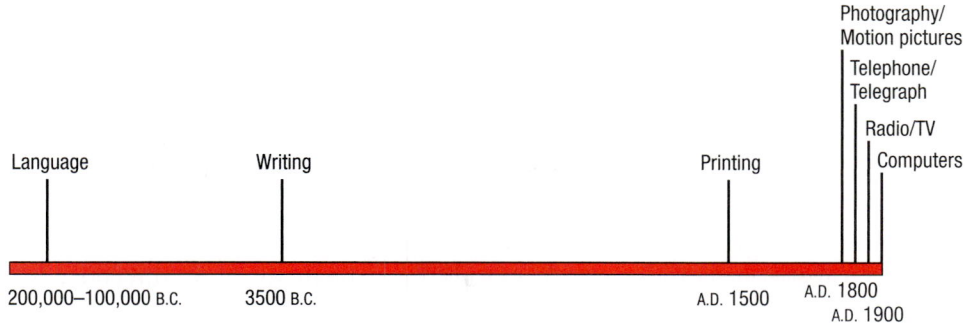

Figure 3–1

Media Time Line

Language | Writing | Printing | Photography/Motion pictures | Telephone/Telegraph | Radio/TV | Computers

200,000–100,000 B.C. | 3500 B.C. | A.D. 1500 | A.D. 1800 | A.D. 1900

communication. It gained popularity through the efforts of scientists and amateur computer enthusiasts. When the World Wide Web and newsgroups offered a place where anyone could post messages and reach a large potential audience, businesses, educational organizations, government agencies, and individuals all scrambled to stake out a site on the web. Everybody is currently trying to figure out how to make websites profitable. Will the web eventually become primarily a commercial medium dominated by big business? Will it change the way we get our news and entertainment? What sort of cultural impact will it have? History may help us answer these questions.

You have probably heard the old joke about the guy who was annoyed because he couldn't see the forest because of all the trees . . . or couldn't see the blizzard because of all the snow . . . or couldn't see the city because of all the tall buildings . . . (you probably get the idea by now). Well, sometimes it can be hard to see history because of all the names, places, dates, and events. Consequently, this chapter steps back and takes a broad view of media history, emphasizing major events and general trends. It also provides additional background information by examining communication in the days before mass communication developed.

Specifically, this chapter discusses seven milestones in the development of human communication: language, writing, printing, telegraph and telephone, photography and motion pictures, radio and television, and computers (see Figure 3–1). It is hoped that this overview of the historical and cultural context of mass communication will supplement and make more meaningful the specific histories of the various media presented in Parts Two and Three of this book.

 LANGUAGE

Obviously, our prehuman ancestors must have had some means of communication, probably nonverbal—maybe using gestures and body movements—and then eventually developed verbal communication using a spoken language. But why? Why didn't humans continue to depend on nonverbal communication and use their mouths just for eating and breathing? Such a scenario is certainly possible. Hearing- and speech-impaired people do this. What made spoken language superior? The truth is: We're not sure. Several theories have been advanced to explain the phenomenon. One theory notes that sign language is not very effective in the dark. If prehistoric humans were to be successful while hunting or moving about at night, they had to work out other means of communicating. Charles Darwin argued that language superseded gesture because language left both hands free to work with tools or handle weapons. Whatever the reason, early humans talked rather than gestured. When they started talking is another question that's hard to answer. Some scholars think the inception of verbal communication dates back hundreds of thousands of years; others suggest it developed around 40,000 B.C.

SOUNDBYTE

You Don't Say

Some of the theories that have emerged to explain how language developed:

- **The Bow-Wow Theory:** Humans imitated the sounds of animals. A cow, for example, might have been called a "moo-moo." (But how did inanimate objects, like rocks, get their names?)
- **The Pooh-Pooh Theory:** Words came from the sounds we make when we're experiencing various emotions; for example, when we're angry—a growl—or scared—a scream. This theory can't explain how words such as "head" or "water," with no emotional attachment, came to be.
- **The Grunt Theory:** Language grew out of the sounds humans make during physical exertion, such as "Aaaargh" or "Yow." This theory doesn't explain words that have no physical connections, such as "think."
- **The Play Theory:** First espoused by Charles Darwin, this theory posits that humans thought it was fun to make sounds while they went about their lives. Over time, some of these more or less random sounds got connected to certain objects or actions. This theory seems the most plausible of the bunch.

How exactly did language develop? Again, nobody knows for sure. There are some picturesque theories (see Soundbyte, "You Don't Say"), but none seems entirely adequate. What is fairly certain is that language was a tremendous factor in the advance of early civilization. For example, hunting became more efficient since directions could be given to coordinate the hunt (directions to a better place to camp could be reported to others in the tribe). Further, a more defined social power structure emerged, as the strong could issue commands to the weak. Instructions for making tools or utensils could be passed on to others. Language helped develop conceptual thinking and provided a means to manipulate ideas, transmit culture, and deal with abstractions. The birth of language marked a major development in the history of the human race.

Our ancestors developed an oral culture—one that depended upon language and the spoken word. Such a society (several examples still exist today) is tremendously dependent on memory. Much of the history, beliefs, and folklore of the culture is transmitted by individuals who memorize great amounts of information and recite it to those in the next generation who, in turn, pass it on to their offspring. This has several implications. Because there is a limit on what a person can remember, the growth of knowledge and information in such a society is slow. Further, there is the risk that an advance or breakthrough will not be remembered well enough to be transmitted. The Incas, for example, apparently made great strides in architecture that were lost because the oral tradition was too fragile to preserve them.

As humans developed further, so expanded the variety of food-gathering means: Farmers joined the hunters, reducing the need to roam over large territories seeking food. Instead, small agricultural villages developed. As more and more people settled in villages and towns, it became harder to rely on the oral tradition to fulfill their communication needs. Efficient farming needed a means to keep track of when to plant crops. It was also helpful to have records of who owned the domesticated animals that were part of the village. As the village's population grew, it was useful to monitor what belonged to each family. This need to keep more detailed, permanent, and accessible records was probably the impetus behind the next great communications revolution—writing.

 ## WRITING

Two problems had to be solved before a system of writing was invented. The first had to do with what symbols were to be used to represent spoken sounds or ideas and the second, with what surface the symbols should be written on.

The growth of international travel and global marketing has started a trend back toward pictographic communication, a method that cuts across languages. Airports all over the world, for example, have adopted a common pictograph system with symbols that denote baggage claim, rest rooms, ground transportation, and the like. Many products also use pictographs to convey information. Below are several pictographs. See if you can identify what they represent. (Answers are below.)

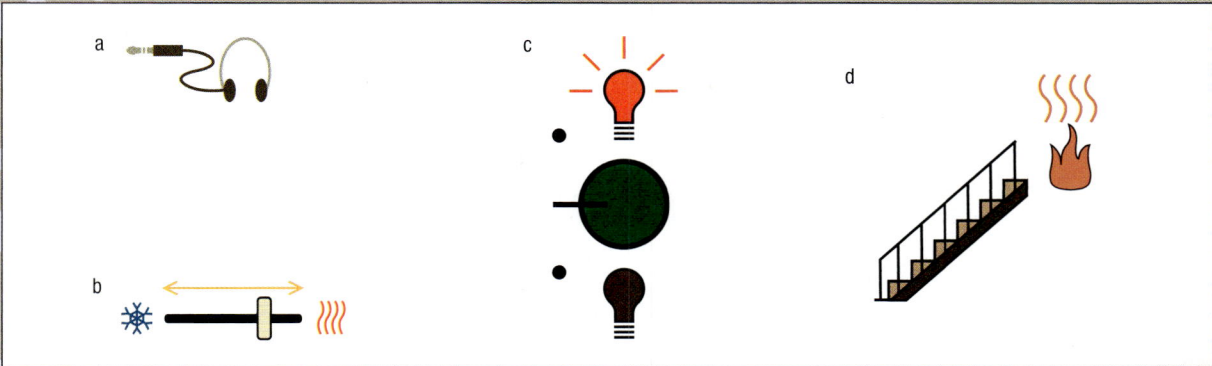

(a) headphone plug; (b) defroster in car; (c) power switch; (d) fire escape.

Sign Writing versus Phonetic Writing

The first problem was solved in two ways. One early symbol system might be called sign writing, in which each symbol was based on a picture that resembled the thing it stood for. Thus, a circle with wavy lines radiating from it might stand for the sun, while a series of wavy lines stacked on top of each other might stand for water. One early form of this style of writing developed in Sumeria (present-day Iraq) about 3500 B.C. A second, more familiar example, developed in Egypt a few hundred years later and came to be known as hieroglyphics. The most durable form of sign writing blossomed in China about 2000 to 1500 B.C. This method required learning thousands of different pictographs that represented various objects and actions.

The second type of writing system was based more on sound than signs. A group of letters, called an **alphabet,** was used to symbolize each of the sounds that make up a word. The Phoenicians are generally credited with having developed the alphabet that I am using to write this sentence. The Phoenicians were sea traders, and their invention gradually spread across the Mediterranean to Greece, where a standard alphabet of 24 letters was constructed. The epic poems of Homer were put into written form about 800 B.C. Later, the Romans modified the Greek alphabet into the 26 letters that are now standard in English. The alphabet was a more efficient way of writing than the pictographs used by the Egyptians and Chinese. For example, a computer keyboard with 47 keys can easily write any sentence in English complete with numbers and all punctuation marks. To do the same in the Chinese pictograph system would require about 9,000 keys. Eventually, even the pictographs used by the Egyptians evolved into an alphabet based on sounds.

Clay versus Paper

The problem of a writing surface was solved in various ways. The Sumerians used soft clay tablets and a wedge-shaped tool to record their pictographs. Clay was inexpensive and durable (many clay tablets still exist today). On the other hand, tablets were not very transportable, and it was difficult to make fine lines and delicate markings in clay. The Egyptians made papyrus from a plant that grew in the Nile region. Strips of papyrus were woven together, soaked, and pounded together into a flat surface that was polished with a rock until smooth. Hieroglyphics were painted or scratched on the papyrus with a brush or a pen. The Greeks wrote on parchment, made from treated animal hides. Parchment was more durable than papyrus but much more expensive to manufacture. Sheets of parchment or papyrus could be stitched together into long scrolls. It was the Chinese, however, who developed the writing surface that was to become the standard—paper. Mixtures of rags, tree bark, and other fibrous materials were soaked in tubs, pounded with mallets, pressed into sheets, and left to dry in the sun. The resulting paper had many advantages: It was lightweight, cheap, and easy to write on. Moreover, sheets of paper could be stacked and bound together, producing what we today would recognize as a book. The Chinese were making paper by about A.D. 100, but it took nearly another thousand years before paper became widely used in Europe.

Social Impact of Writing

The arrival of writing carried with it several consequences for early society. In the first place, it created a new division in society. Before writing, everybody had about the same degree of communication skills—they could speak and hear. But not everybody could read and write. Those who could had access to information not available to the rest of the population. And, as is usually the case, with greater access to information comes greater access to power. This power was concentrated in the rulers and the scribes who served the ruler. In Egypt, for example, only privileged children, who would later become priests or government scribes for the pharaohs, were taught to read and write.

Second, writing helped make possible the creation of empires. Writing made organization easier. Tax collection records could be kept more efficiently, as could the accounts of payments. An army could be established and paid regularly. Written orders to commanders simplified administration. Writing helped develop trade and increased a country's treasury. Although it's difficult to say what role writing played in its development, it is probably no coincidence that the first Egyptian dynasty under Menes (the ruler who united upper and lower Egypt and established a capital at Memphis) came into being about the same time as the Egyptians were developing their hieroglyphics. Additionally, writing helped establish and maintain both the Greek and the Roman empires. Note that this is not to say that writing caused empires to develop; other political, economic, and social conditions had to be present as well. But it is probably safe to say that writing made it *easier* for these empires to come about.

Early forms of picture writing such as this were developed in Sumeria and Egypt about 5,000 years ago. *(Robert Brenner/Photo Edit)*

Another, more subtle, effect had to do with the nature of knowledge itself. For the first time, it was possible to preserve and nourish a permanent body of knowledge. Before writing, the transmission of knowledge from one generation to the next was hampered by the limits of human memory, forgetfulness, and distortion. Knowledge that was written down, however, could be stored. The Greeks established the Great Library at Alexandria around 311 B.C., which eventually contained about a half-million scrolls. Scholars from all over the Greek world came to Alexandria to use the library and to further increase the store of knowledge.

Finally, writing made it possible to develop a consistent and enduring code of laws. Before the written word, legal decisions were made by local judges representing the particular village or community where they were located. There was no general, overarching, impersonal body of law on which decisions were based. With writing, law became tangible in the establishment of codes that transcended locale and individual circumstances. The first great legal document in history, the Code of Hammurabi, was written in Sumeria around 2000 B.C.

■ The Dark Ages

The Roman Empire came to an end around the sixth century and was followed by the feudal period in Europe. By this time, books were becoming more numerous but were far from common. Early books were copied by hand by scribes, a long and laborious process. As Christianity spread through Europe, bookmaking became centered in monasteries, where monks, writing on parchment in individual carrels, would carefully copy and illustrate the most important religious books of the period. Sometimes the original was garbled in the process since spelling varied widely from place to place and many authors used abbreviations known only to them. The resulting volumes were treated as works of art and were closely guarded; some were even chained to keep them from leaving the monastery. Another problem with many of the early books was that, once written, they disappeared forever in the monastery's library because there was no way for others to find them. Books were placed on the shelf in the order in which they were acquired by the library. There was no filing according to subject or author. Scholars had to depend on the librarian's memory to find anything. (Umberto Eco's 1980 novel, *The Name of the Rose*, provides a fascinating description of a medieval library.)

As trade increased throughout medieval Europe, the need for information grew. Merchants needed to keep track of financial information and to document the various currencies in circulation. The idea of a university probably originated in India and North Africa and eventually spread to Europe. The University of Paris was founded around 1150. Oxford began holding classes in the same century. As the feudal system gave way to strong, centralized monarchies, governments needed more information to help collect taxes and defend their borders. Lawyers needed to record the outcomes of legal cases. All this demand helped move the process of bookmaking away from the monastery and into lay society. Writing shops, or *scriptoria*, opened all across the continent. The copying business was helped by the widespread introduction of paper, which had finally made its way into Europe from China. Books copied on paper were cheaper than books on parchment, but they were still expensive. If you wanted a copy of a book in the early 14th century, for example, you would have to hire a scribe; negotiate a price; decide on the ink color, binding, and illustrations; and then wait, maybe as long as a year, for the book to be produced.

Demand for books still outran supply, however, and there weren't enough scribes to handle all the work. Consequently, the scribes were able to charge even higher fees, and books became even more a medium of the elite. Economic and social progress seemed to have hit a roadblock.

This problem was solved around 1450 with the invention of the printing press and movable type, the third of our communication milestones.

 ## PRINTING

The invention of printing is actually a story of many inventions. We've already mentioned the development of paper by the Chinese. China was also responsible for the development of block printing—character outlines were carved out of a block of wood, and the raised parts were inked and pressed against a piece of paper. The oldest surviving block-printed book was published in 868. The Chinese also perfected a system of movable type, first using clay and later, blocks of wood for individual characters. The Koreans were experimenting with movable metal type by the beginning of the 15th century.

The next major invention occurred in Germany, where Johann Gutenberg is generally credited with developing a printing press that used movable metal type. Gutenberg published his famous Bible around 1453, and his new printing method quickly spread across Europe. Only 30 years after Gutenberg's Bible appeared, there were printing presses in more than 110 towns in western Europe alone. The total increase in the number of books available in Europe is impossible to calculate, but it is probably safe to say that by 1500 there were hundreds of times more books available than in 1450. As books proliferated, their cost went down. Although still expensive, books were no longer the exclusive possession of the very rich. The printed book could now be afforded by those who were simply relatively prosperous.

Johann Gutenberg was a wine connoisseur as well as a metallurgist. His design for the printing press was borrowed from a similar device used in wine making. *(Brown Brothers)*

The consequences of the printing revolution are so far-reaching and extensive that it is impossible to discuss all of them. Most scholars seem to agree, however, on the most significant results.

■ Effects of the Gutenberg Revolution

First, the printing press helped the development of vernacular (everyday) languages across the European continent. Most of the pre–printing press, hand-lettered books had been written in Latin—the language of the Catholic Church and of higher education. Reading these works therefore required the knowledge of a second language, which restricted the type of people who might use them to the educated elite. Many early printers, however, recognized that a broader market for their books would be available if they were published in French, German or English. Many printers also felt closer ties to their home country than to the church, further encouraging the printing of books in native languages. This trend had other consequences. Bodies of information now became more accessible to more people, further encouraging the growth of literacy, and, in turn, prompting more books to be published. Finally, the use of the vernacular probably helped prepare the wave of nationalism that swept Europe in succeeding centuries.

The printing press played a role in the religious upheaval that swept Europe in the 16th century. Before the press, those clerics who disagreed with the doctrines and policies of the church had limited channels for expression. Handwritten copies of their views were few, had limited circulation, and could easily be censored or confiscated by authorities. The situation was forever changed after Gutenberg. Theologian and religious reformer Martin Luther's writings were translated from Latin into the vernacular, printed as pamphlets, and distributed all over Europe. It has been estimated that it took only a month for his famous Ninety-five Theses (the ones he nailed to the church door in Wittenberg, Germany) to be diffused across Europe. One of his later pamphlets sold 4,000 copies in a month. Despite efforts by the church to confiscate and burn his writings, the Reformation movement continued. In addition, the printing of the Bible in the vernacular meant that individuals now had direct access to the core of their religious belief system. The Bible could now be read directly and interpreted individually; there was no need for clerical intervention. This increased access to information further weakened the power of the Catholic Church and helped the spread of Protestantism.

Moreover, the arrival of printing speeded up the publication of scientific research. Although it would still be considered agonizingly slow today in an era of e-mail and the Internet, printing a book of scientific findings took far less time than it did when manuscripts were handwritten. Printing also ensured that identical texts would be read by scientists in different countries and helped them build on the work of others. Galileo and Newton came along in the 17th century, after advances in the 16th-century printing.

The printing press even helped exploration. The efforts of the Vikings are little known, due in part to the fact that they explored during a time when it was difficult to record and publicize their exploits. Columbus visited America after printing developed, and his deeds were widely known in Europe a year after his return. Printed accounts of the discoveries of early explorers found a ready audience among those eager to find wealth and/or bring religion to the New World. Many early developers published glowing (and sometimes overly optimistic) accounts of life in the new lands, hoping to promote investments and help business. The journeys of the early voyagers were helped by printed books that contained navigational and geographic information about the Americas.

Further, the printing press had a profound effect on the growth of scholarship and knowledge. Whereas access to handwritten textbooks was difficult, university students now had printed texts. (Think how hard it would be to take this course if everybody in the class had to use just one textbook.) As the number of books increased, so did the number of students who studied at a university. Literacy increased further. Interest in the classical works of Greece and Rome was revived as they appeared in printed books that were read by many. Books based on the scholarship of other countries appeared. The advances in mathematics made by the Indians, Muslims, and Arabs were disseminated. Without the printing press, the Renaissance of the 16th century might not have occurred.

Finally, the printing press led to the development of what we would today call news. As will be discussed in Chapter 4, early newspapers sprang up in Europe at the beginning of the 17th century. These early publications were primarily concerned with foreign news. It wasn't long, however, before these early papers focused on domestic news as well. This development did not sit well with some early monarchies, and government attempts to suppress or censor news content were not unusual. It took until the end of the 17th century to establish the notion of a press free of government control (more on this topic in Chapter Four). The early newspapers made government and political leaders more visible to the public and helped create a climate for political change in both Europe and America.

Technology and Cultural Change

Before leaving this topic, we should point out that it is easy to ascribe too much significance to the printing press. The above discussion makes it easy to assume that the printing press was the prime mover behind all these effects. Such a view is called **technological determinism**—the belief that technology drives historical change. A more moderate position suggests that technology functions with various social, economic, and cultural forces to help bring about change. Printing didn't cause the Reformation, but it probably helped it occur. And vernacular languages were growing in importance before Gutenberg, but his invention certainly helped them along. In any case, the birth of printing marks the beginning of what we have defined as mass communication, and it is certainly a momentous event in Western history.

The next centuries brought further refinements to printing. A metal press was developed by the late 1790s; steam power to drive the press was added shortly thereafter. Advances in printing technology helped usher in the penny press, a truly mass newspaper (see Chapter 4). A better grade of paper made from wood pulp came into use in the 1880s, about the same time as the Linotype machine, a device that could compose and justify a whole line of metal type. Photoengraving brought better visuals to the paper in the 1890s, as did the development of half-tone photography (see below) a few decades later. Hot metal type gave way to photocomposition and offset printing in the 1970s and 1980s, and the computer ushered in an age of relatively cheap desktop printing a few years later. Printing has changed a great deal over the years, but its consequences are still much with us.

The next two communication milestones occurred during what many have called the age of invention and discovery, the period roughly encompassing the 17th, 18th, and 19th centuries. The reasons behind the many achievements of this period are several. The great explorations of previous centuries had brought different cultures together, and scholars were able to share ideas and concepts. Further, there was a change in the way people generated knowledge itself. The traditional authority of the Catholic Church was eroding, and intellectuals looked less to revelation as a source of knowledge and more toward reason and observation. Philosophers such as Bacon, Descartes, and Locke argued for systematic research based on what the senses could perceive. In addition, scientific societies in Italy, France, and Great Britain helped advance the frontiers of knowledge. And, as we have already mentioned, the printing press helped distribute news of current discoveries to all, prompting others to new breakthroughs. Whatever the reasons, these three centuries saw such advances as Galileo's use of the telescope and the notion of a heliocentric solar system; the theory of blood circulating through the body; Newton's theory of gravitation; the roots of modern chemistry; electricity; and the discovery of microscopic bacteria. Inventions came along at a dizzying rate: the steam engine, the locomotive, the plow, the internal combustion engine, the automobile, the sewing machine, the dynamo, and a host of others. Not surprisingly, the field of communication also saw major developments, as the next two milestones demonstrate.

CONQUERING SPACE AND TIME: THE TELEGRAPH AND TELEPHONE

It's appropriate that we spend some time discussing the telegraph and telephone, two related technologies that presaged many of the features of today's media world. For instance, the telegraph harnessed electricity; it demonstrated the technology that would eventually be used in radio. It was also the first medium to use digital communication (dots and dashes). The telephone, with its interconnected network of wires and switchboards, introduced the same concept now at the core of the Internet: Everybody was linked to everybody else.

Development of the Telegraph

It's difficult for people raised in an age of cellular phones, CNN, fax machines, e-mail, and the Internet to appreciate the tremendous excitement that greeted the development of the telegraph. Before the appearance of the telegraph in the early 19th century, messages, with some minor exceptions, could travel only as fast as the fastest form of transportation. A messenger on horseback would clop along at around 15 to 20 miles an hour. A train carrying sacks of mail could travel about 30 miles in an hour. The fastest form of message transportation was the carrier pigeon, which could cover more than 35 miles an hour. Then along came the telegraph, which sent messages traveling over wires at the almost unbelievable speed of 186,000 miles per second, the speed of light itself. No wonder that when it first appeared, the telegraph was described as the great "annihilator of time and space." It was the first device that made possible instantaneous point-to-point communication at huge distances. It was also the forerunner of what we today might call, to use an overworked cliché, the information superhighway.

The technology necessary for the telegraph dates back to the discovery of electricity. Many early inventors realized that electricity could be used to send messages simply by varying the time the current was on and off. Experiments with early versions of the telegraph (*telegraph* comes from Greek words meaning "to

Wanted. Young, skinny, wiry fellows. Not over 18. Must be expert riders. Willing to risk death daily. Orphans preferred.

So went the ad in an 1860 California newspaper. Young men who responded found that they were applying to join the Pony Express, a short-lived but evocative mail system that captured the imagination of people all over the world and is a permanent part of the culture of the Old West.

In 1860, it took eight weeks to get information from the East Coast to California. With the Civil War approaching, it became imperative for the government to keep California in the Union by providing reliable, dependable, and rapid information from Washington and other locations in the East. The solution was the Pony Express, a rapid horse-and-rider mail system that stretched from Missouri to California, which began service in April 1860.

Approximately 165 stations were set up along the route. Riders rode at full gallop and changed horses about every 15 miles. After about 75 or 100 miles, a new rider took over. Riders had to weigh less than 120 pounds. They carried 25 pounds of equipment, including four mail pouches, a light rifle, a Colt revolver, and a Bible. It took about 10 days in good weather to get a letter from one end of the route to the other.

The Pony Express lasted only about 18 months. It was made instantly obsolete by the completion of a transcontinental telegraph system. Instead of taking days, information now traveled across the plains in a matter of minutes. Although it may have been faster, the telegraph never inspired the romance and folklore that grew up around the Pony Express.

write at a distance") were performed in the late 1700s. By the 1830s and 1840s workable telegraph systems had been developed in England and in the United States.

Samuel Morse was the principal force behind the creation of the telegraph in America. His device consisted of a sending key, a wire, and a receiver that made marks on a paper tape in concert with changes in the electrical current. Later versions let the operator read messages by listening to the clicks made by the receiver and did away with the paper tape. To simplify message transmission, Morse developed a code consisting of dots and dashes that is still in use today.

Morse demonstrated his device in the late 1830s and eventually received a grant from the government to continue his work. He constructed a line between Baltimore and Washington, D.C., and opened the nation's first telegraph service with the famous message, "What hath God wrought?"

Cultural Impact of the Telegraph

Public reaction to the new machine was a combination of awe and amazement. The telegraph wires that swayed between poles were called lightning lines. The early telegraph offices set out chairs so that spectators could watch as messages came in from distant cities. Some people refused to believe the new invention worked until they traveled to the source of the telegraphic message and verified it with the sender. Some were afraid that all that electricity flowing around above them posed a danger to their health, and they refused to walk under the wires.

Despite these fears, the telegraph grew quickly and the lightning lines quickly crisscrossed the nation. By 1850 almost every city on the expanding Western frontier could communicate with every other city. Maine could talk to Texas at the speed of light. By 1866 a cable was laid underneath the Atlantic Ocean, linking Europe and America. Four years later, the overland wires and undersea cable carried more than 30 million telegraphic messages (telegrams).

SOUNDBYTE

Skeptic

Some were skeptical about the benefits of the telegraph. Maine might be able to talk to Texas, but, as Henry David Thoreau pointed out, what if Maine and Texas have nothing important to talk about?

Alexander Graham Bell demonstrates a later version of his telephone for representatives of the business community. Bell and his colleagues eventually received 30 patents for telephone-related inventions. *(The Granger Collection)*

The telegraph was changing communication at about the same time another invention was changing transportation—the railroad. Interestingly, the telegraph wires generally followed the railroad tracks, and station masters were often the first telegraphers. The telegraph made it possible to keep track of train locations and coordinate the complex job of shipping goods to various parts of the country—particularly to the West. The telegraph helped the train bring settlers to the frontier and played a role in the country's westward expansion.

The conduct of war was changed by the telegraph. Troops could be mobilized quickly and moved, usually by railroad, in response to tactical and strategic developments. The significance of the telegraph for the military was demonstrated many times during the Civil War.

Morse's invention had an impact on commerce as well. It sped up communication between buyers and sellers, reported transactions, and organized deliveries. Instant communication brought about standard prices in the commodity markets. Before the telegraph, the price of corn varied with local market conditions and might be several dollars cheaper in Chicago than in St. Louis. After the telegraph connected all markets, local variations were evened out.

Further, as we will discuss in more detail in Chapter 4, the telegraph greatly enhanced the newspaper's ability to transmit news. Information from distant places had previously taken weeks to reach the newspaper office. With the telegraph and Atlantic cable, even news from Europe could make the next day's edition. Newspaper publishers were quick to realize the potential of this new device and used it heavily. Many incorporated the word "Telegraph" into their name. The telegraph also helped the formation of news agencies, or wire services as they were also called. The Associated Press made great use of the expanding telegraphic service to supply news to its customers. Finally, the telegraph changed the style of reporting. Since the early telegraph companies charged by the word, news stories became shorter. Rather than the wordy, reflective, and interpretive reports that characterized news reports in the early 19th century, the telegraph placed an emphasis on scoops, breaking news, and the bare facts.

■ Government and Media

The telegraph also set the precedent for the relationship between the government and large media companies. In many other countries, since the telegraph was used to deliver messages, it seemed an extension of the post office, and the government agency that assumed responsibility for the postal service also administered the telegraph. This model was not followed in the United States. Although some in the government endorsed a federal takeover of the telegraph system, the prevailing sentiment was in favor of private, commercial development. By the end of the 19th century, telegraphic communication was dominated by a large company, Western Union. As we shall see in later chapters, other mass media—motion pictures, radio, television—were also developed as private rather than government enterprises and were dominated by one or more large companies.

A Change in Perspective

Finally, another consequence of the telegraph was subtler and harder to describe. In some ways, the telegraph changed the way people thought about their country and the world. By erasing the constraints of space, the telegraph had the potential to function as an instant linkage device (see Chapter 2) that tied people together. Morse wrote how the telegraph would make a neighborhood of the whole country. A Philadelphia newspaper, shortly after the successful demonstration of the device, wrote that the telegraph destroyed the notion of "elsewhere" and made everywhere "here." The paper declared the telegraph "will make the whole land one being." An article in a magazine of the period was even more expansive. The telegraph "binds together by a vital cord all nations of the earth." It may not be too much of an overstatement to contend that the telegraph introduced the notion of a global village that was to be popularized a hundred years or so later by Marshall McLuhan. It created a sense of unity among Americans and encouraged them to think in national and international terms.

The telegraph was joined by a companion invention, the telephone. Like the Morse invention, the telephone also conquered time and space and had the added advantage of requiring no special skills, such as Morse code, for its use. It transmitted the human voice from point to point. There was some confusion over the precise role the telephone would play in society, but eventually the notion of linking phone users by wires and the development of the switchboard made it possible to interconnect one place with many others. This arrangement helped it become a fixture in businesses and homes across the nation. The telephone made private communication easier to achieve. It was now possible for people to converse away from the watchful eyes of parents, bosses, and other authority figures. Finally, like the telegraph industry, the telephone industry would also be dominated by a large corporation, AT&T, which would eventually gain control of Western Union.

In sum, the telegraph and the telephone enabled people to communicate vast distances in what we now call real time and had far-reaching impact in the political, economic, and social development of the United States and the rest of the world. We will discuss this impact in detail throughout the book. In many ways, it is still making itself felt today.

CAPTURING THE IMAGE: PHOTOGRAPHY AND MOTION PICTURES

The telegraph and the telephone drew upon advances in the science of electricity. The next communication advance we will examine could not have occurred without advances in the field of chemistry.

Early Technological Development

Two things are required to permanently store an image. First, there must be a way to focus an image on a surface. Second, the surface must be permanently altered as a result of exposure to the image. The first requirement was fulfilled in the 16th century with the discovery of the camera obscura, a dark chamber with a pinhole in one wall. The light rays that entered the chamber through the small hole projected an image on the opposite wall. The second requirement took longer to

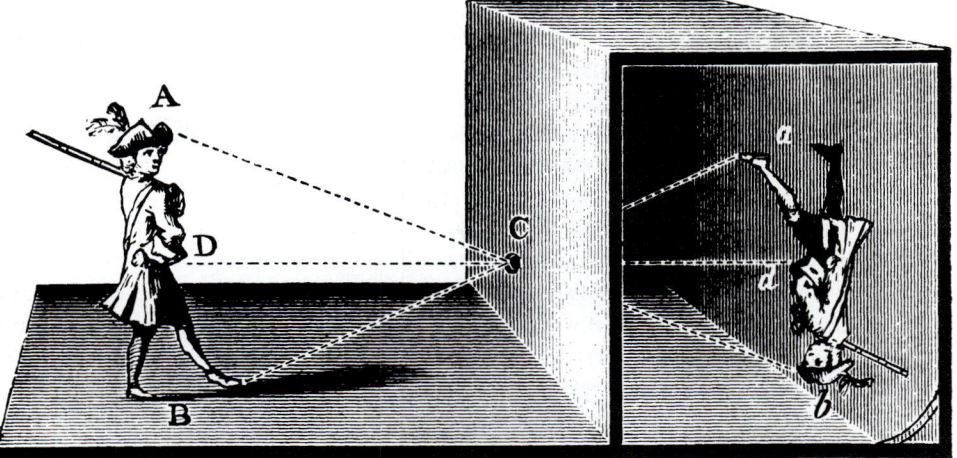

In the camera obscura, a small opening containing a lens produces an inverted and reversed image of an object. Many artists used the camera obscura to help them draw precise images of people, landscapes, and buildings. *(The Granger Collection)*

achieve. In the 1830s, two Frenchmen, Joseph Niepce and Louis Daguerre, experimented with various substances that changed upon exposure to light rays. Eventually, silver iodide provided the best results and Daguerre sold his discovery to the French government. An English scientist, William Fox Talbot, working at about the same time as Daguerre, refined the process by capturing his images on paper in the form of negatives, permitting copies to be made. Other advances quickly followed, including the use of flexible celluloid film. George Eastman's company introduced the Kodak box camera in the 1890s with the slogan, "You press a button. We do the rest." The Kodak was designed for the mass market. Amateur photographers simply loaded a roll of film in the camera, pressed the button, and sent the film off to Kodak to be developed, printed, and returned to the photographer.

There were several long-range consequences of these technological advances. Early photos (called Daguerreotypes) required long exposure times, making them particularly suitable for portraits, where the subject could remain still. These early portraits provided a way to preserve and humanize history. Our images of George Washington, for example, are from paintings that show him in an idealized manner, usually in noble poses where he appears distinguished and powerful. Our images of Abraham Lincoln, however, come from the many photographs that were taken of him during his term in office. The early photos, done around 1860, showed him in flattering poses. The later photos, taken after years of war, showed a man grown visibly older, with lines creasing his forehead, and tired eyes.

Mathew Brady's famous 1864 photo of a war-weary Abraham Lincoln. Part of this portrait was later used on the five-dollar bill. *(The Granger Collection)*

■ Mathew Brady

The Civil War was the first American war to be photographed. Before the camera, the public's view of war was

The U.S. government granted Mathew Brady authorization to take his camera equipment to the battlefields of the Civil War but was reluctant to promise him any firm financial support. The best the government could offer was a vague promise to buy his negatives at the end of the war. Further, his photos could not be reproduced in the periodicals of the time. (Woodcuts from his pictures appeared in *Harper's Weekly*, but although they brought him publicity, Brady apparently made little if any money from them). Despite these problems, Brady was willing to take a chance. Thinking that his war pictures would make a handsome profit from exhibitions and books, he paid his own expenses during the war years.

Brady did make a sizable amount of income from the thousands of photos he and his colleagues took, particularly from his New York exhibition, but not enough to pay off his costs. An expensive book of his photos published after the war failed miserably.

Brady was soon bankrupt. Congress finally voted to pay him $25,000 for his pictures, but this came too late to do him much good. By that time, he had forgotten where he had stored many of his photos. The glass photographic plates that eventually became government property were forbidden to be shown or published for commercial gain, a decision that kept people from seeing them. Government workers did not realize the significance of Brady's work. Hundreds of glass plates were broken through sheer carelessness. Eventually, the government thought the glass plates were more valuable than the photographic record they contained. Some plates were sold to greenhouses as replacement glass; the sun quickly faded their images and valuable history was lost. Other negatives were used to make face plates for World War I gas masks. Brady himself faded from the public eye. He died in a hospital charity ward in 1896.

probably shaped mostly by paintings and etchings that showed magnificent cavalry charges and brave soldiers vanquishing the enemy, not the horror and the carnage of combat. Mathew Brady persuaded the U.S. government to give him access to the battlefield. (Brady apparently thought the government would cover the costs of his venture, but his expectations were never met and many of his photos were lost. See Media Probe, "Mathew Brady and His War Photos.") Because early photography was not able to capture action scenes, Brady was limited to photographing scenes of the aftermath of a battle. These images, however, were powerful enough. In 1862, Brady's colleagues photographed the battleground at Antietam just two days after the battle and before all the dead had been buried. The resulting photographs were the first to show the actual casualties of war. When the photos went on view in a New York gallery, they caused a sensation. The carnage of battle was revealed to all. As Oliver Wendell Holmes remarked, "Let him who wishes to know what war is like look at this series of illustrations." A hundred years later, other communication advances would bring scenes of horror from the Vietnam War directly into American living rooms.

Photography had an impact on art. Now that a means had been developed to preserve realistic images, artists were free to experiment and develop different ways of portraying the world. Again, although it's hard to say how much of a role photography played in the movement, the impressionist, postimpressionist, and cubist schools of painting came to prominence at about this same time. At the other end of the spectrum, photography itself became a fine art, as virtuosos such as Alfred Steiglitz, Margaret Bourke-White, and Edward Steichen created masterpieces of graphic reproduction.

Photography's Influence on Mass Culture

You didn't have to be an artist, however, to take pictures. Everybody could and did. Advances in film and camera technology put cameras in the hands of the masses. Ordinary people took photos of significant people, objects, and events: marriages, new babies, new cars, pets, vacations, family portraits, family reunions, proms, and so on. Photo albums quickly became a part of each family's library. Photography enabled each generation to make a permanent record of its personal history.

Advances in the printing process, such as half-tone photography, made it possible for photographs to be published in magazines and newspapers. By the beginning of the 20th century, dozens of illustrated dailies and weeklies were published in the United States. This development created a new profession—**photojournalism**—and changed America's conception of news. Photojournalism reached new popularity in the 1920s when the pace of life increased, and many innovations cropped up that promised to save time for the consumer—lunch counters for fast meals, express trains, washing machines, vacuum cleaners, and so forth. When it came to news reporting, the biggest time-saver was the picture. Readers could look at photos more quickly than they could read the long text of a story. As a consequence, printed columns decreased and space devoted to pictures increased, helping popularize the tabloids and picture magazines such as *Life* (see Chapter 5).

Photojournalism had more subtle influences as well. For one, it changed the definition of news itself. Increasingly, news became that which could be shown. Accidents, natural disasters, demonstrations, and riots were natural photo opportunities. This visual bias in news reporting continues to be a topic of concern even today. Second, as photo historian Vicki Goldberg put it, photography created "a communal reservoir of images." Certain historic events were fixed forever in the minds of the public by their photos: the fiery crash of the Hindenberg, a suspected Viet Cong member executed on a Saigon street, the young girl screaming over the dead body of a student at Kent State, the rescue worker holding a critically injured baby after the Oklahoma City bombing. All these images have been permanently etched on the national consciousness.

▣ Pictures in Motion

The technology behind photography led to the development of another way to capture an image. The goal behind *this* new milestone, however, was to capture an image in motion. Chapter 9 details the early history of the motion picture medium and traces how it evolved from a series of toys into a giant entertainment industry. It is significant that this new medium evolved while three significant trends were occurring in the United States. The first was industrialization. The Industrial Revolution, which began in the early 19th century, continued into the 20th century. Production and manufacturing both increased significantly. Along with industrialization came urbanization, as people moved into the cities to be near the plants and factories where they could find jobs. In the United States, one-fourth of all Americans lived in an urban area by 1914. The third trend was immigration. About 25 million people immigrated to the United States between 1871 and 1914, and most of them wound up in cities where they went to work in manufacturing plants.

The culmination of these trends was the creation of an audience that was drawn to the new medium of motion pictures. The first movie houses sprang up in the cities. They were called nickelodeons, storefronts that had been turned into makeshift theaters, with uncomfortable benches or folding chairs for the audience, a tinkling piano, and poor ventilation. Nonetheless, the nickelodeons were big hits among the newly arrived immigrants. By 1910 there were more than 10,000 of

Some news photos, such as this one of a young man blocking the path of a line of tanks during the 1989 Tiananmen Square demonstrations, are forever etched in the national consciousness. *(AP/Wide World Photos)*

these nickelodeons around the country, and film exhibitors and filmmakers quickly realized that there was a market for filmed entertainment. The motion picture business had started. Film eventually moved to plusher theaters and tried to appeal to the middle class, but it left its mark on the immigrant population. Many learned the customs and culture of their new country from the nickelodeons.

Motion Pictures and American Culture

The long-range impact of the motion picture lay mainly in the areas of entertainment and culture. As the demand grew for feature-length films, only very large companies were able to come up with the money needed to pay production costs. As will be noted in Chapter 9, these large companies came to dominate the production, distribution, and exhibition of movies. Today's film industry is controlled by global conglomerates that still follow many of the patterns established in the 1920s.

Movies forever altered America's leisure time. Vaudeville soon died out. Going to the movies became an important social activity for the young. Saturday afternoons that once were spent going to parks and friends' houses were now spent inside a darkened theater.

The movies became a major cultural institution. Photography and the mass-appeal newspaper had made it easier for people to recognize and follow the fortunes of their favorite celebrities, but motion pictures raised this process to a new level. Hollywood produced cultural icons, the movie stars. The popularity of motion pictures was based on their appeal to all social classes. Unlike serious drama, opera, and ballet, which appealed to the elite, movies attracted the masses. The movies helped bring about the notion of a popular culture, a phenomenon whose benefits and liabilities are still being debated.

In 1915, American poet Vachel Lindsay published *The Art of the Moving Picture.* This volume signaled the beginnings of a new popular art form. Lindsay's book was the first of many serious attempts to develop a theory of film. Although a

Edwin S. Porter's *The Great Train Robbery* was the first American film to tell a story. This classic Western was actually shot in New Jersey. *(The Granger Collection)*

popular entertainment form that blended business and art, film soon became a topic worth serious study, a trend still with us today as evidenced by the many universities that teach film as part of their curricula.

In the early 1930s, the Payne Fund was set up to study the possible harmful effects of attending motion pictures. This was the first of many studies that tried to establish just what impact film and, later, broadcasting had on society (see Chapter 18 for more details). The Payne Fund studies were significant because they marked the first time the public had decided that a medium, in this case motion pictures, did something to society and was deserving of serious examination.

Finally, although film played its most prominent role as a medium of entertainment, it's important to note that it had influence on journalism as well. Started around 1910, newsreels appeared weekly or semiweekly and pictured the major events of the period. The big movie studios eventually controlled the production of newsreels. They standardized the content of the 10-minute reels so that audiences could expect to see something from Europe, some national news, sports, a feature or two, and perhaps a human-interest story. The newsreels were discontinued in the 1950s and 1960s as pictorial journalism moved to television. These early news films, however, influenced many of the conventions and expectations of broadcast news reporting.

NEWS AND ENTERTAINMENT AT HOME: RADIO AND TELEVISION BROADCASTING

Radio, the first medium that brought live entertainment into the home, would not have been possible without advances in physics. The discovery of electromagnetic waves caught the attention of many scientists, who looked for ways to use this new force to send messages. Advances in wire telephony in the United States made it possible to send voice and music over the air and prompted AT&T to fund a massive research program in the area. Radio development, however, was stymied by patent problems. Had it not been for World War I, radio's development might have taken far longer. The war had a couple of major consequences for radio's development. The U.S. Navy solved the legal problem by asserting control over all patents which made possible major advances in technology. Further, a large number of soldiers went into the Signal Corps, where they learned the fundamentals of the new medium. When they came back from the war, these men kept interest alive in radio, helping popularize many amateur radio clubs, and provided the basis for a ready-made audience for early broadcasting.

Broadcasting

The shift from using radio as a point-to-point communication device (like the telegraph) to a point-to-many broadcasting medium caught many by surprise. Thanks to the popularity of early radio stations, broadcasting became a national craze, and by the early 1920s the stage was set for the emergence of another mass communication milestone. Radio was the first mass medium that brought sports, music, talk, and news into the living room.

In addition to World War I, other historical circumstances influenced radio's development. It's easy to overlook today, but when radio first started out, there was no system in place that permitted it to support itself. Many radio stations went on the air simply for the novelty of it, with little thought as to how to fund their operations. Significantly, modern radio came about in the Roaring Twenties, when economic conditions were vigorous, consumer goods were easily available, stocks were soaring, and many people in the business world were accumulating fortunes. In the midst of this climate, it was easy for radio broadcasting to turn to commercials for its economic base. Accepting advertising brought quick profits and was in tune with the business-is-good philosophy of the times. Business was so good, in fact, that the federal government generally kept out of it. Radio, however, needed government intervention. Interference from too many radio stations broadcasting on too few frequencies was a serious problem. In 1927, Congress created a Federal Radio Commission (FRC), whose main authority was in regulating the technical side of the medium. Unlike the situation in some European countries, the FRC and its successor, the Federal Communications Commission, took a generally light-handed approach to regulation and favored the fortunes of commercial broadcasters.

It was also the era when newspaper chains and many other businesses were consolidating their operations. The development of radio networks fit nicely into this model, and it wasn't long before national programming was supplied by two, and later three, national radio networks. Further, tabloid newspapers were capturing readers and Hollywood films were booming. These trends were to have an impact on the future of radio programming. In concert with its evolution as an advertising medium, radio moved toward mass-appeal programs that provided an audience of consumers for those who bought commercial time on the new medium.

Ironically, the depression of the 1930s, which did some financial damage to radio, also helped its programming. Many performers from vaudeville, the recording industry, and the theater, rendered unemployed by the depression, took their talents to radio, particularly network radio. As a result, the level of professionalism and the caliber of entertainment improved, and the networks solidified their grasp on the industry. By 1937, almost every powerful radio station in the country was a network affiliate. News broadcasting came of age about this same time, and radio soon became a more important source of news than the newspaper.

Cultural Impact of Radio

In a look at the long-term impact of this medium, several elements stand out. First, and most obviously, radio helped popularize different kinds of music. One of the early radio stations with a powerful signal was WSM in Nashville, which carried broadcasts of "The Grand Old Opry," a program that probably introduced country music to many thousands. Broadcasts of black rhythm-and-blues music crossed the race barrier and gained listeners among whites. In more recent years, radio helped popularize rock and roll, reggae, and rap.

Radio made its own contributions to the popular culture. Although early programs recycled many vaudeville acts, genres original to the medium soon developed. One of these was the soap opera, whose familiar formula later successfully made the transition into television. In 1940, soaps accounted for more than 60 percent of all network daytime programming. Entertainment series aimed at children introduced youngsters to "Jack Armstrong—The All-American Boy" and "Captain Midnight." The significance of these programs may be less in their style or content and more in the fact that they signaled the radio broadcasters' attitude that children were a viable market and that it was acceptable to send advertising their way. Situation comedies, such as "Amos 'n' Andy," and action-adventure programs, such as "Gangbusters," were other formats that persisted into TV.

After a somewhat shaky start, radio news came of age in the 1930s and 1940s. Audiences tuned to the new medium for live coverage of the events leading up to the start of World War II. Listeners could hear live the voices of world leaders, such as Adolf Hitler and British prime minister Neville Chamberlain. Commentators would then provide what in a more modern era would be called instant analyses of what was said. Radio personalized the news: Unlike newspapers, where a byline might be the only thing that identified a reporter, radio news had commentators and reporters with names, voices, distinctive delivery styles, and personalities. A list of famous radio news personnel of the period would include H. V. Kaltenborn, Edward R. Murrow, and Lowell Thomas. These individuals became celebrities and introduced a new component into journalism—the reporter as star. This trend would also carry over into television as network anchors and reporters were able to command multimillion-dollar salaries in the same range as movie stars or sports heroes.

Finally, like the movies, radio changed the way Americans spent their free time. Radio was the prime source of entertainment and news. Families would faithfully gather around the radio set in the evenings to listen to the latest episode of their favorite programs. By the 1940s, average household radio listening time averaged more than four hours per day, most of it in the early evening hours. A new phrase grew up to describe this period of peak listening activity. It was called "prime time," another concept that passed over to TV.

Television

Television, as will be discussed in Chapter 10, also had its beginnings in the 1920s and 1930s and, like radio, a war intervened during its development. World War II halted the growth of TV as a mass medium. Early transmitting stations went off the air during the war, and TV receivers were no longer manufactured. The technology behind TV, however, received a substantial boost from the war effort, as new discoveries in the field of radar were translated into an improved TV system.

Also, like radio, television became popular during an age of relative prosperity. After a period of retooling, American industry was churning out consumer goods.

The self-denial of the war years gave way to a fulfillment of long-repressed desires, as Americans bought new cars, dishwashers, barbecue grills, and air conditioners. The TV set was the most sought-after appliance. Television swept the country during the 1950s. It took the telephone about 80 years to reach 85 percent of the country's homes. The automobile did it in 49 years. Television did it in 10. Approximately 10 million homes had TV in 1950. By 1959, that number had more than quadrupled. While new, labor-saving appliances increased leisure time, more often than not, that leisure time was spent watching TV. Household furniture had to be rearranged to accommodate the TV set in the living room.

Cultural Impact of TV

Television grew up surrounded by other dramatic social trends and events. Americans were moving into the suburbs, and thus commuting became a ritual. Women were beginning to enter the workforce in greater numbers. The 1960s saw the beginnings of the Civil Rights movement, the war in Vietnam, and the growth of the counterculture. Television brought these happenings into the nation's living rooms.

Today, television is in 99 percent of all households, and the set is on about seven hours every day. In an astoundingly short period, TV replaced radio as the country's most important entertainment and information medium and became a major cultural and social force. In fact, television probably hasn't been with us long enough for us to see all of its ultimate consequences. Some, however, are fairly obvious. Television has become a major consumer of time. Sleeping and working account for the most time in a person's day, but TV watching ranks third. TV has transformed politics. Political conventions are staged for TV; candidates hire TV consultants; millions are spent on TV commercials; candidates debate on TV; and so on. TV has exerted a standardizing influence on society. Clothing, hairstyles, language, and attitudes seen on TV pervade the country and, for that matter, the rest of the world. Television news became the most important and believable source of information. Like the motion picture, television created a whole new slate of stars and celebrities. It has been suggested that television has become an important source of socialization among children and that TV programs inspire antisocial and other undesirable behavior. (Chapter 18 reviews the evidence for these assertions.)

Although the telegraph was the first to be called the "great annihilator of time and space," it appears that television might be a better candidate for that title. Audiences have seen TV pictures live from Baghdad, Earth's orbit, the moon, and Mars (well, as live as they can be from a place so far away). In fact, today's TV viewer expects to see live reports of breaking stories, no matter where they are; no place seems far away anymore.

Photography was credited with creating a reservoir of communal experience. Television, however, has widened and deepened that reservoir. For example, televised images of President Kennedy's funeral, the *Apollo 11* moon landing, the *Challenger* explosion, the trial of O. J. Simpson, and election officials squinting at ballots during the Florida recount following the 2000 presidential election have all been indelibly impressed upon the national consciousness.

THE DIGITAL REVOLUTION

In his book *Being Digital*, Nicholas Negroponte, director of MIT's Media Laboratory, summed up the digital revolution as the difference between atoms and bits. Traditionally, the mass media delivered information in the form of atoms:

Books, newspapers, magazines, CDs, and videocassettes are material products that have weight and size and are physically distributed. Negroponte maintains that this is rapidly changing: "The slow human handling of most information in the form of [recorded music], books, magazines, newspapers and videocassettes is about to become the instantaneous transfer of electronic data that move at the speed of light." In short, atoms will give way to bits.

As an example, consider the difference between e-mail and traditional paper mail. In the traditional system, a letter must be placed in an envelope with a postage stamp and given to the U.S. Postal Service, where it is sorted, transported, and physically delivered a few days later to its recipient. E-mail needs no paper, no postage, and no delivery by the post office. It's a series of bits of information that travels electronically and is delivered in minutes rather than days. With e-mail, the same message can be copied a thousand times and sent to a thousand different people much more quickly and cheaply than with paper mail.

At the risk of oversimplifying a rather complicated topic, we can describe **digital technology** as a system that encodes information—sound, text, data, graphics, video—into a series of on-and-off pulses that are usually denoted as zeros and ones. Once digitized, the information can be duplicated easily and transported at extremely low costs.

As will be discussed in Chapter 11, the computer was the first device to use the digital system to process information. The innovation quickly spread to other media. Digital technology makes possible the special effects now common in motion pictures and television as well as digital audio, digital video, digital photography, and digital equivalents of newspapers, magazines, and books.

The development of the Internet meant that computers could send digital information to all parts of the globe. All of a sudden, a new distribution medium was available that permanently changed the media environment. In short, digital technology and the Internet triggered a revolution in the way information was stored and transmitted. As a result, the traditional mass communication media found themselves in uncharted waters and had to figure out how they were going to cope with this drastic development. Newspapers, for example, used to exist only on paper (atoms). Now they exist in both paper and digital form (bits). Big recording companies used to distribute music on tape or on disk (atoms). Napster and other music-sharing sites proved that individuals could download music files (bits) from other individuals on the Internet, totally bypassing the recording companies. The chapters in Parts Two and Three of this book discuss how the media are adapting to the digital age.

The digital revolution, of course, has had profound impact not only on the mass media but on other institutions as well. It has, for example, transformed business. Even companies that deal in atoms rather than bits have found that they have had to devise whole new marketing and distribution schemes to capitalize on the new digital age. It's not possible (yet) to have a tennis racket physically delivered over the Internet, but you can go online, search the various sporting goods sites for bargains, and order one that appeals to you. The Postal Service or a package delivery company, however, still has to deliver the racket (atoms) to you. The importance of this new form of buying and selling has added a new noun, "e-commerce," to the global vocabulary.

The potential social and cultural implications of the digital age are considerable. First, the notion of community may have to be rethought. In the past, people developed friendships based on local geography. The digital world of the Internet makes possible virtual communities based on shared needs and interests rather than locale. African Americans, for example, no matter where they live, can visit websites such as NetNoir, BlackVoices, and BlackPlanet, and make friends, discuss relevant issues, and connect to African-American culture and lifestyles.

Second, there is the question of social isolation. Despite its positive points, membership in virtual communities may negatively affect interpersonal contact. A recent survey by Stanford University found that about one out of every four persons who use the Internet regularly reported spending less time talking with family and friends. The Internet is a solitary, individual activity. Will it reduce further our participation in interpersonal relationships?

Third, consider what the digital age might mean for politics. A huge amount of political information—party platforms, candidates' positions, and texts of speeches—is available in digital form on the web. Ideally, this should result in a better-informed electorate. Moreover, fund-raising is going digital. During his unsuccessful campaign for the 2000 Republican presidential nomination, Senator John McCain raised $3.5 million online in the two weeks after the New Hampshire primary. The confusion and bitterness surrounding the results of the 2000 presidential election in Florida prompted many to call for a system of online voting. Indeed, the Internet raises the possibility of true direct democracy. Our current representative democracy was conceived in part as a solution to the practical problem that all the people couldn't be physically present in one place to debate and vote. The Internet now makes it possible for computer owners to debate and cast a ballot at home. Do we still need representatives? Should we institute "digital democracy"?

Finally, there is the problem of the "digital divide." Access to digital information is not equal. About 70 percent of middle-class homes have Internet access, compared with about 35 percent of lower-income homes. Viewed from a global perspective, the divide is much wider. As of 2000, only about 5 percent of the world's population was connected to the Internet, mostly in the developed countries. In the future, those who have access to information will have more access to power than those who don't. Will this digital divide translate into more serious social, economic, and political divisions?

In 1981, Tony Schwartz, a telecommunications expert, published *Media: The Second God.* One section of the book was called "Communication in the Year 2000" and described how the communications landscape would appear in 20 years. Looking at Schwartz's book today, one is impressed with the accuracy of his predictions regarding media that already existed in 1981. There is, however, no mention of the computer as a personal communication device. Nor is there mention of the Internet. This prompts some observers to suggest that it's much too early to forecast how this new technological revolution will turn out. It may turn into something that we, at the moment, can't even fathom.

CONCLUDING OBSERVATIONS

What lessons can be drawn from an examination of these seven milestones?

First, it is difficult to predict the ultimate use of a new medium. When the telegraph emerged, many thought that it would have a profound impact on the world order. Since the nations of the world were linked by the telegraph, it was predicted that misunderstandings would cease, prejudices would vanish, and peace would

All the communication milestones discussed in this chapter changed the way information was stored or transmitted. Starting with the printing press, they all expanded the scope of human communication by making it possible for people to share information with other people in other places or at other times. This achievement prompted a rather optimistic attitude toward the social benefits of the media. The text points out how the telegraph was viewed as a force for morality, understanding, and peace. Both radio and TV were touted as means of bringing education, high culture, and refinement to the masses. Cable TV was supposed to bring new forms of entertainment to minority groups and open the way for two-way TV that would aid the democratic process by making possible electronic polling. None of these things has yet come to pass. Nonetheless, the Internet, with its ability to connect everybody to everybody, is currently being touted as an information revolution that will affect society as deeply as the printing press. Whether this will happen is a matter for future debate, but for now it might be useful to ask if new communication technologies automatically carry with them social benefits. Have they been liberating or constrictive?

A number of social critics have pointed out that new communication media expand the potential for freedom of expression and have greatly enlarged the scope of human culture. The cost of sending messages over long distances has dramatically decreased. Thanks to the telegraph, telephone, and the Internet, people can do business, socialize, and argue with people all over the world. The new media have made information available to all. And, if information is power, the new media will empower more individuals. New means of communication make it easier for democracy to function. Film, radio, and TV have opened up new art forms and patterns of entertainment.

Others suggest a different interpretation. The new communication media have spurred the growth of large conglomerate owners whose main goal is profit, not cultural enrichment. Further, new communication media create an overload of information, some of it overpowering and pervasive, such as commercials, junk e-mail, and telemarketing. The information made available by the new technologies may be neither interesting nor useful nor profound, and it may interfere with people's attempts to identify the truly significant.

Moreover, although technological advances—such as the telegraph, telephone, and Internet—have expanded the scope of communication, is any of the communication worthwhile? Check out any chat room and you will probably find that much of the communication consists of greetings, good-byes, flirting, and "how-are-you's." Newsgroups exchange recipes, talk about sports, review cigar brands, and discuss other information that most could live without. How much real dialogue actually occurs? Is it possible to have a meaningful conversation with people whom you can't see and who may not even be who they say they are? The new media have done little to promote political participation. Voter turnout in the United States continues to decline, and political apathy continues to increase. Most people would probably stay at home and watch TV instead of going to a political forum. Further, many critics would argue that the new media have provided little that is new and fresh in the arts and entertainment. Expanded TV channels have brought us more of the same.

In sum, advances in communication media have the potential for both positive and negative consequences.

---

reign. Things did not quite go in that direction. Alexander Graham Bell suggested that the telephone be used as a means of communication between the various rooms in a house or that phones be sold only in pairs, linking only two specific points, such as a person's office and home. Others thought the phone would serve as a sort of wired radio. When radio first started, most thought it would be used as a substitute for telegraph or telephone communication. It took a while for the idea behind broadcasting to develop. Will our predictions about the ultimate future of the Internet be any more accurate?

Second, it appears that the emergence of a new communications advance changes *but does not make extinct* those advances that came before it. The telegraph and the telephone did not kill the printed word; nor did film, radio, TV, and the computer. Television did not make radio extinct, but it did cause a major change in the way the medium was used. Likewise, the computer and the Internet will probably not cause any of the traditional media to evaporate, but they will probably change the way we use these "old" media. (See Media Probe, "The Dead Media Society.")

The text suggests that the arrival of a new medium doesn't cause existing media to become extinct; the older media change their content and function and coexist with the newer competition. Well, this is true with regard to the general media that we have talked about. But, if "medium" is defined more specifically as anything that carries a message, then many media have become extinct. To catalog and to preserve the memory of these departed media is the goal of the Dead Media Project. The project has its own website at **http://griffin.multimedia.edu/~deadmedia/dedmedia.html.**

Some of the media that have given up the ghost include

- Carrier pigeons.
- Pony Express.
- Scopitone—a 1960s jukebox that played what we might call music videos.
- Super 8-mm home movie films.

- Viewmasters—those plastic gogglelike devices that you could look through and see slides of various places.
- Magic lantern—an early form of the slide projector.
- Stenograph—a typewriter for shorthand symbols.
- Heliograph—a device that sent messages by reflecting the sun's rays.
- Sonovision—a combination record player–laser that projected onto a wall abstract visual patterns that changed with each note.

The site lists dozens of others. It also has a category called "endangered species" (the typewriter) and another called "soon to be extinct" (VHS videotape, the personal check, floppy disks, and CDs). If you have any other nominees, you can post them at the site.

Figure 3–1 is a time line that displays when each of the seven milestones occurred. A quick examination of the figure makes clear that the pace of communication innovations has accelerated. It took humans dozens of centuries to get from language to writing. The jump from writing to printing took about 5,000 years. The telegraph and telephone cropped up only 300 years later, followed quickly by photography and motion pictures. Radio was invented only a few years after that, as was TV. The computer followed on the heels of television. In fact, a person born in 1900 and who lived 100 years (an accomplishment becoming increasingly more common) would have lived through three milestones: film, radio/TV, and computers. Each advance in communication increases our power to convey and record information, and each has played a role in prompting significant changes in our culture and society. It is becoming difficult to digest fully the impact of one communication medium before another comes on the scene.

What's the next great communications revolution that will burst upon us and change the way we live? Time will tell.

■ MAIN POINTS

- Seven milestones in the evolution of human communication are language, writing, printing, telegraphy and telephony, photography and motion pictures, radio and television, and computers.

- Language led to the development of an oral culture where information was passed on by word of mouth from one generation to another.

- The invention of an alphabet and a usable surface made writing possible. Writing created a social division in society. Those who could read and write had access to more information than those who could not.

- Writing helped create and maintain empires as well as make storehouses of information, such as libraries, possible.

- Printing made information available to a larger audience. It helped the development of vernacular languages, aided the Protestant Reformation, and helped the spread and accumulation of knowledge.

- The telegraph and telephone were the first media to use electricity to communicate. They marked the first time the message could be separated from the messenger. The telegraph helped the railroads move west and permitted the newspapers to publish more timely news. The telephone linked people together in the first example of a communication network.

- Photography provided a way to preserve history, had an impact on art, and brought better visuals to newspapers and magazines. Motion pictures helped socialize a generation of immigrants and became an important part of American culture.
- Radio and television broadcasting brought news and entertainment into the home, transformed leisure time, and pioneered a new, immediate kind of reporting. Television has an impact on free time, politics, socialization, culture, and many other areas as well.
- The digital revolution changed the way information was stored and transmitted, and made e-commerce possible.
- In general, it is difficult to predict the ultimate shape of a new medium. New media change but do not replace older media. The pace of media inventions has become quicker in recent years.

■ QUESTIONS FOR REVIEW

1. What is the difference between writing based on signs and writing based on an alphabet?
2. Why was the telegraph labeled "the great annihilator of time and space"?
3. What exactly is the "communal reservoir of images" created by photojournalism? Can you think of other examples of images that are forever fixed by photographs?
4. What digits are used in digital technology? Why could the telegraph be considered the first digital device?

■ QUESTIONS FOR CRITICAL THINKING

1. Printing was known in China for a long time before Gutenberg appeared. Why wasn't there a social revolution in China as there was in Europe when printing appeared?
2. Suppose Henry David Thoreau (see page 66) were alive today. What do you think he would say about the Internet?
3. Many people would argue that of all the communication media discussed in this chapter, television has had the greatest impact on society. Do you agree?
4. When the Internet was first developing, the term "information superhighway" appeared frequently in news stories about it. Now that the Internet has been around for a while, news stories rarely contain that term. Why not?

■ KEY TERMS

alphabet (p. 59)
technological determinism (p. 64)

photojournalism (p. 71)

digital technology (p. 77)

SUGGESTIONS FOR FURTHER READING

Crowley, David, and Paul Heyer. *Communication in History: Technology, Culture, Society.* White Plains, NY: Longman, 1995.

Czitrom, Daniel. *Media and the American Mind: From Morse to McLuhan.* Chapel Hill: University of North Carolina Press, 1982.

Dizard, Wilson. *Old Media, New Media.* White Plains, NY: Longman, 1997.

Eisenstein, Elizabeth. *The Printing Revolution in Early Modern Europe.* New York: Cambridge University Press, 1983.

Fang, Irving. *A History of Mass Communication: Six Information Revolutions.* Boston: Focal Press, 1997.

Goldberg, Vicki. *The Power of Photography.* New York: Abbeville Press, 1991.

Hogben, Lancelot. *From Cave Painting to Comic Strip.* New York: Chanticleer, 1949.

Lacy, Dan. *From Grunts to Gigabytes.* Urbana: University of Illinois Press, 1996.

Marvin, Carolyn. *When Old Technologies Were New.* New York: Oxford, 1988.

Negroponte, Nicholas. *Being Digital.* New York: Knopf, 1995.

Schramm, Wilbur. *The Story of Human Communication.* New York: Harper and Row, 1988.

Slevin, James. *The Internet and Society.* Malden, MA: Polity Press, 2000.

Stephens, Mitchell. *A History of News: From the Drum to the Satellite.* New York: Viking, 1988.

SURFING THE INTERNET

Here are some sites that provide information on media history. Some of the sites mentioned in Chapters 4 through 11 are also of relevance here.

http://jefferson.village.virginia.edu/albell/homepage.html
The home page of Alexander Graham Bell. The site reconstructs Bell's path to the invention of the telephone.

www.cln.org/themes/history_film.html
Links to many sites that contain information about film history.

www.gutenbergdigital.de
Gutenberg's Bible on the web.

www.jls.palo-alto.ca.us/virtualmuseum/ushistory/morse
Page devoted to Samuel Morse and telegraphy. Contains diagrams of early telegraphs and a Morse code alphabet.

www.mediahistory.com/index
This is the best all-around site for media history. Contains an extensive time line, other net links, book reviews, articles, archives, chat boards, and pages on the history of specific media.

www.uni.mainz.de/UniInfo/Stadt/Museen/gutenberg.html
Find out more about Gutenberg and his printing press at this site maintained by the University of Mainz. It helps to know a little German so that you can understand the text, but the graphics communicate well in any language.

PART 11

Print Media

CHAPTER 4 Newspapers

Sometimes comic books are pretty close to real life. In 1999, mild-mannered reporter Clark Kent (aka Superman), Lois Lane, Jimmy Olsen, and Perry White lost their jobs when Superman's archrival, Lex Luthor, bought the *Daily Planet* and shut it down. In its place, Luthor started a website: www.lex.com.

The *Planet* eventually reopened, but that's another story. What's important for this chapter is the question posed by this comic book story line: What will happen to traditional newspapers in the age of the Internet? At the start of the new millennium, the newspaper industry was still struggling with this question. Almost all newspapers had started websites, and many had expanded their sites into more than just online versions of the paper. The result was an industry whose economic fortunes looked good in the short term but whose long-term prospects were still cloudy. Some of the trends that signaled trouble in the future included a continuing decline in readership, increased competition from electronic media and Internet news providers, and increased costs of raw materials. Despite these disquieting trends, newspapers continued to be highly sought-after investments, profit margins were healthy, and advertising revenue continued to rise. As we have mentioned before, the emergence of a new mass medium seldom kills off the existing media. Instead, existing media change and adapt. The newspaper business is currently going through this period of transition. This chapter looks at the history, structure, features, economics, and future of this seemingly paradoxical industry as it moves into the digital age.

Is this the future of the newspaper? A foldable, updatable, eight-page prototype that uses electronic paper and electronic ink. *(Evan Kafka)*

HISTORY

Journalism in Early America

Before we get to the details, it might be helpful to identify some general features of newspapers in early America:

- There were few papers.
- Printers and postmasters did most of the early publishing.
- News was not as timely as it is today.
- The idea of a free press was not endorsed by colonial governments.

In 1690, Boston printer Benjamin Harris published the first American newspaper, *Publick Occurrences both Foreign and Domestick*. One of the items in the paper alleged an affair between the king of France and his son's wife. This news story infuriated the Puritan officials of the colony, and they shut down the paper after one issue. The notion of a free press had yet to surface in America; most colonists believed that a paper had to have royal consent to be published.

Fourteen years later, John Campbell, the local Boston postmaster, published the *Boston News Letter*. Published with royal permission, the paper was dull and lackluster, with many news stories simply reprinted from European papers. Campbell's paper had only about 300 subscribers and never made a profit.

A few years later, another Boston paper, the *New England Courant*, came on the scene. Published by James Franklin, Ben's older brother, the paper was published without government permission. Eventually, the elder Franklin's paper got him into trouble with the local authorities and he was thrown into prison. Ben took over and the paper prospered under his leadership. Ben eventually moved on to Philadelphia where he started the *Pennsylvania Gazette*, which boasted such innovations as more legible type, headlines, and a cleaner layout.

Ben Franklin retired from a successful publishing career at the age of 42. During his career, he had started several papers, published one of America's first magazines, run the first

Benjamin Franklin became the publisher of the *Pennsylvania Gazette* in 1729, when he was 24 years old. The paper became the most successful colonial newspaper, and Franklin became the best-known colonial journalist and publisher. *(Brown Brothers)*

editorial cartoon, proved that advertising copy could sell merchandise, and, perhaps most important, demonstrated that journalism could be an honorable profession.

The Beginnings of Revolution

Tensions between the colonies and the Crown were rising during Franklin's tenure as publisher, and this controversy sparked the development of the early press. One example of this tension was the trial of John Peter Zenger. Zenger published a paper openly critical of the British governor of New York. The governor threw Zenger into jail and charged him with criminal libel. Zenger's lawyer argued that no American jury should feel bound by laws formed in England, and Zenger was acquitted, striking a symbolic blow for press freedom.

Newspapers grew in numbers during the Revolutionary War, and most were partisan, siding with the colonies or with the Crown. This period marked the beginnings of the **political press,** which openly supported a particular party, faction, or cause.

In 1776, when the Continental Congress adopted the Declaration of Independence, the text of the document was published in the *Pennsylvania Evening Post* on July 6, 1776. The next year the Continental Congress authorized Mary Katherine Goddard, publisher of the *Maryland Journal,* to print the first official copies of the declaration with the names of the signers attached. Under Goddard's direction, the *Journal* became one of the leading colonial papers during the war. Goddard was one of about 30 women who printed or published colonial newspapers.

The Political Press: 1790–1833

The politicization of newspapers did not end with America's victory in the Revolutionary War. Instead, partisan leanings of the press were transferred into another arena—the debate over the powers of the federal government. The participants in this controversy included some of the best political thinkers of the time: Alexander Hamilton, James Madison, Thomas Jefferson, John Jay. Newspapers were quick to take sides in this debate, and their pages were filled with Federalist or anti-Federalist propaganda. Heated political debate gave way to name-calling and quarreling between these two groups, and the content of many newspapers became colored by volatile and inflammatory language.

At the vortex of this debate between Federalists and anti-Federalists was the Constitution of the United States. Although the original document made no mention of the right of a free press, the Bill of Rights did contain such a provision. The **First Amendment** held that "Congress shall make no law . . . abridging the freedom of speech, or of the press." Thus the idea of a free press, which had grown during the Revolutionary period, became part of the law of the new nation when Congress ratified this amendment in 1791.

Newspapers grew with the country in the first 20 years of the new century. The daily newspaper began in 1783 and grew slowly. By 1800, most large cities had at least one daily paper. By 1820, there were 24 dailies, 66 semi- or tri-weeklies, and 422 weeklies. These newspapers were read primarily by the upper socioeconomic classes; early readers had to be literate and possess money to spend on subscriptions (about $10 per year or six cents an issue—a large sum when you consider that during those years, five cents could buy a pint of whiskey). The content was typified by commercial and business news, political and congressional debates, speeches, acts of state legislatures, and official messages.

Politics was still the main focus of many of the nation's papers, and several sent correspondents to Washington to report political news. James Gordon Bennett, whom we shall meet again later, covered Washington for a New York paper. The first woman to achieve recognition as a political journalist was Anne Royall, who published two papers in Washington between 1831 and 1854. Royall was a crusader for free speech and state's rights, and campaigned against graft and corruption.

During this period, several newspapers arose in response to the needs and interests of minority groups. *Freedom's Journal,* the first of over 40 black newspapers published before 1860, was founded in the late 1820s by the Reverend Samuel Cornish and John Russwurm. Written and edited by blacks, the paper championed the cause of black people by dealing with the serious problems arising from slavery and by carrying news of foreign countries such as Haiti and Sierra Leone that appealed to its black audience.

At about the same time, in 1828, another minority group, the Cherokee Indian nation, published the *Cherokee Phoenix,* written in both Cherokee and English.

Two early examples of the black press: *Freedom's Journal* was started in 1827 by John Russwurm, the first black to graduate from a college in the United States, and by Samuel Cornish. Cornish later edited *The Colored American,* a paper that had subscribers from Maine to Michigan. *(Schomberg Center for research in Black Culture, The NYPL)*

When the Cherokees were evicted from their home in Georgia and resettled in Oklahoma, a new paper, the *Cherokee Advocate,* was started and continued to operate until 1906.

Birth of the Mass Newspaper

Several conditions had to exist before a mass press could come into existence:

1. A printing press had to be invented that would produce copies quickly and cheaply.
2. Enough people had to know how to read to support such a press.
3. A mass audience had to be present.

In 1830, the U.S. firm R. Hoe and Company built a steam-powered press that could produce 4,000 copies per hour. This and subsequent steam-powered presses that were even faster made it possible to print an extremely cheap newspaper that everybody could afford.

The second element that led to the growth of the mass newspaper was the increased level of literacy in the population. The first statewide public school system was set up during the 1830s. The increased emphasis on education led to a concomitant growth of literacy as many people in the middle and lower economic groups acquired reading skills.

The third element was more subtle and harder to explain. The mass press appeared during an era that historians call the age of Jacksonian democracy, an age in which ordinary people were first recognized as a political and economic force. Property requirements for voting had died out. Every state but one chose presidential electors by popular vote. In addition, this period was marked by the rise of an urban middle class. The trend toward democratization of business and politics fostered the creation of a mass audience responsive to a mass press.

The Penny Press

Benjamin Day was only 22 years old when he launched the mass-appeal *New York Sun* in 1833. Day's idea was to sell his daily paper for a penny (a significant price reduction from the six cents a copy for other big-city dailies). Moreover, the *Sun* contained local news, particularly those items that featured sex, violence, and human-interest stories. Conspicuously absent were stodgy political debates. Day's gamble paid off as the *Sun* attracted readers, and the **penny press** was launched.

Others imitated the *Sun's* success. The colorful James Gordon Bennett launched the *New York Herald* in 1835, which was an even more rapid success than the *Sun.* The *Herald* introduced a financial page, a sports page, and an aggressive editorial policy that emphasized reform.

Another important pioneer was Horace Greeley. His *New York Tribune* appeared in 1841 and ranked third behind the *Herald* and *Sun* in circulation. Greeley used his editorial pages for crusades and causes. He opposed capital punishment and gambling and favored trade unions and westward expansion.

Greeley also favored women's rights. In 1845, he hired Margaret Fuller as literary critic for the *Tribune.* In addition to her commentary on the fine arts, Fuller published articles dealing with the hard lot of prostitutes, women prisoners, and the insane. Greeley's decision to hire Fuller is typical of his publishing philosophy: Like Fuller, he never talked down to the mass audience and attracted his readers by appealing to their intellect more than to their emotions.

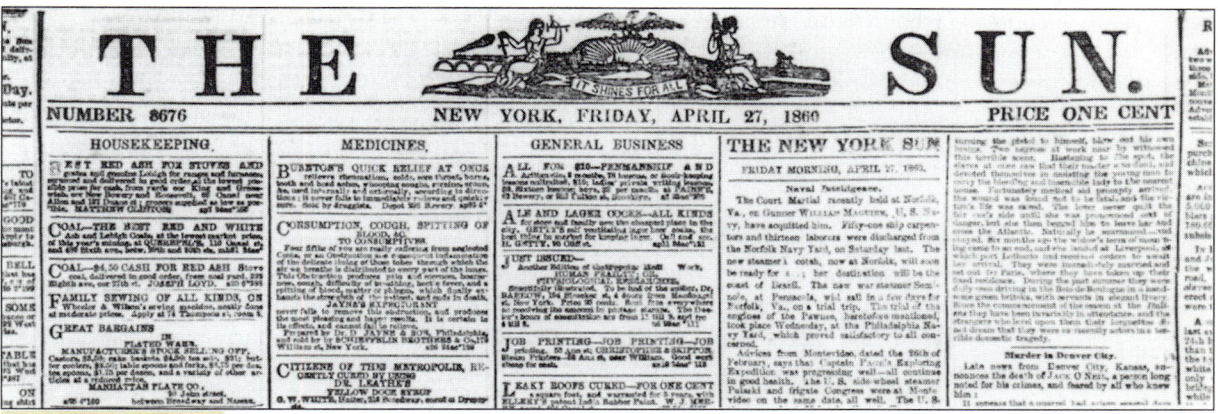

Front page of the *New York Sun:* Benjamin Day's reliance on advertising for revenue is illustrated by the several columns of classified ads appearing on the front page. *(Courtesy of the NY Historical Society, NYC)*

The last of the major newspapers of the penny-press era that we shall consider began in 1851 and, at this writing, is still publishing. The *New York Times,* edited by Henry Raymond, promised to be less sensational than the *Sun* or the *Herald* and less impassioned than Greeley's *Tribune.* The paper soon established a reputation for objective and reasoned journalism.

Finally, all these publishers had one thing in common. As soon as their penny papers were successful, they doubled the price.

Significance of the Penny Press   At this point, we should consider the major changes in journalism that were prompted by the success of the mass press during the period from 1833 to 1860. In short, we can identify four such changes. The penny press changed

1.   The basis of economic support for newspapers.
2.   The pattern of newspaper distribution.
3.   The definition of what constituted news.
4.   The techniques of news collection.

Before the penny press, most of a newspaper's economic support came from subscription revenue. The large circulation of the penny papers made advertisers realize that they could reach a large segment of potential buyers by purchasing space. Moreover, the readership of the popular papers cut across political party and social class lines, thereby assuring a potential advertiser a broadly based audience. As a result, advertisers were greatly attracted to this new medium, and the mass newspapers relied significantly more on advertising revenues than did their predecessors.

Older papers were distributed primarily through the mails; the penny press, although relying somewhat on subscriptions, also made use of street sales. Vendors would buy 100 copies for 67¢ and sell them for 1¢ each. Soon it became common to hear newsboys hawking papers at most corners in the larger cities. Since these papers had to compete with one another in the open marketplace of the street, editors went out of their way to find original and exclusive news that would give their paper an edge.

The penny press also redefined the concept of news. The penny press hired people to go out and look for news. Reporters were assigned to special beats: police, financial, sports, and religion, to name a few. Foreign correspondents were popular. Newspapers changed their emphasis from the affairs of the commercial elite to the social life of the rising middle classes.

This shift meant that news became more of a commodity, something that had value. And, like many commodities, fresh news was more valuable than stale news. Any scheme that would get the news into the paper faster was tried. Stories were sent by carrier pigeon, Pony Express, railroads, and steamships as the newspapers kept pace with the advances in transportation. The Mexican War of 1846 made fast news transmission especially desirable, and many newspapers first used the telegraph to carry news about this conflict. All in all, the penny papers increased the importance of speed in news collection.

■ Newspapers Become Big Business

A new reporting technique emerged during the Civil War as telegraphic dispatches from the war zones were transformed into headlines. Because telegraph lines sometimes failed, the opening paragraphs of the story contained the most important facts. If the line failed during a story, at least the most important part would get through. Thus, the "inverted pyramid" style of reporting was developed.

After the war, from about 1870 to 1900, the total U.S. population doubled and urban population tripled. Newspapers grew even faster than the population; the number of dailies quadrupled, and circulation showed a fivefold increase. As a result, newspapers became a big business and some big-city papers were making more than $1 million a year in profits by the mid-1890s. The thriving newspaper business also attracted several powerful and outspoken individuals who had a profound influence on American journalism. We will consider three: Pulitzer, Scripps, and Hearst.

Joseph Pulitzer came to the United States from Hungary and eventually settled in St. Louis. After a string of unsuccessful jobs, he found he had a talent for journalism and turned the *St. Louis Post-Dispatch* into a success. In 1883, he bought the *New York World.* In a little more than three years, Pulitzer increased the paper's circulation from 15,000 to 250,000.

What was Pulitzer's formula for success? Pulitzer stressed accuracy. He also introduced practices that appealed to advertisers: more advertising space and ads priced on the basis of circulation. Moreover, he aimed his paper at the large population of immigrants then living in New York by stressing simple writing and lots of illustrations. Pulitzer reintroduced the sensationalized news format of the penny press. The *World's* pages carried stories about crime, violence, and tragedy. Finally, Pulitzer endorsed the notion that a paper should promote the welfare of its readers, particularly the underprivileged. Although Pulitzer didn't originate the idea, he certainly put it into practice. The paper crusaded against unsanitary living conditions, corrupt politicians, and big business, all topics that gained Pulitzer many supporters among the working class.

Attempts to reach a working-class audience were not confined to the East. In the Midwest, E. W. Scripps started papers in Cleveland and Cincinnati, both growing industrial cities with large populations of factory workers. The Scripps papers featured concisely edited news, human-interest stories, editorial independence, and frequent crusades for the working class. Scripps pioneered the idea of a newspaper chain. By 1911, he owned 18 papers.

Perhaps the best-known of these three newspaper giants, thanks to the film *Citizen Kane,* was William Randolph Hearst. While Pulitzer was succeeding in New York and Scripps was acquiring papers in the Midwest, 24-year-old Hearst was given control of the *San Francisco Examiner,* thanks to the generosity of his wealthy father. Hearst went after readers by appealing to their emotions. Fires, murders, and stories about love and hate were given splashy coverage. Hearst banked heavily on sensationalism to raise his readership level. It worked. The *Examiner* shot to the number-one position.

■ Yellow Journalism

Hearst, like Pulitzer before him, then invaded the big league—New York City. In 1895, he bought the *New York Journal.* Soon, Pulitzer and Hearst were engaged in a fierce circulation battle as each paper attempted to outsensationalize the other. As one press critic put it, the duel between these two spread "death, dishonor and disaster" all over page one. Sex, murder, self-promotion, and human-interest stories filled the two papers. This type of reporting became known as **yellow journalism,** and whatever its faults, it sold newspapers.

The battle between Pulitzer and Hearst reached its climax with the Spanish-American War in 1898. In fact, many historians have argued that the newspapers were an important factor in shaping public opinion in favor of hostilities. When the battleship *Maine* was blown up in Havana harbor, the *Journal* offered a $50,000 reward for the arrest of the guilty parties. Circulation jumped over the 1 million mark. War was finally declared in April, and the *World* and the *Journal* pulled out

William Randolph Hearst, the successful publisher of the *San Francisco Examiner* and later the *New York Journal,* employed sensationalism (yellow journalism) to win the circulation wars of the late 1800s. He created a major publishing empire consisting of a chain of newspapers, a wire service, and four syndicates. *(Brown Brothers)*

all the stops. Hearst chartered a steamer and equipped it with printing presses. He also brought down his yacht and sailed with the U.S. fleet in the Battle of Santiago. The *Journal* put out 40 extras in a single day.

Although the period of yellow journalism was not the proudest moment in the history of the American newspaper, some positive features did emerge from it. In the first place, it brought enthusiasm, energy, and verve to the practice of journalism, along with aggressive reporting and investigative stories. Second, it brought wide exposure to prominent authors and led to some fine examples of contemporary writing. Stephen Crane, Frank Norris, Dorothy Dix, and Mark Twain all wrote for newspapers during this period (1880–1905). Further, yellow journalism helped popularize the use of layout and display devices—banner headlines, pictures, color printing—that would go on to characterize modern journalism.

■ The Early Twentieth Century

From 1900 to 1920, consolidation made itself felt in the newspaper business. Although circulation and profits went up, the number of daily newspapers decreased and the number of cities with competing newspapers dropped by 60 percent. What happened?

First, the cost of new technology—Linotype machines, high-speed presses— proved too expensive for many marginal papers. Second, advertisers showed a preference for the paper with the largest circulation in the market. Smaller-circulation papers saw their revenues shrink to the point where they could no longer compete. Third, consolidation had increased profits in the railroad, grocery, and hotel businesses, and newspaper publishers decided it could do the same for them. Consequently, newspaper chains—companies that owned several papers—grew quickly. By 1933, six chains—Hearst, Scripps-Howard, Patterson-McCormack, Block, Ridder, and Gannett—controlled 81 dailies with a combined circulation of more than 9 million, about one-fourth of all daily circulation.

Appearing with the consolidation trend and enjoying a short but lively reign was **jazz journalism.** At the end of World War I, the United States enjoyed a decade of prosperity: the Roaring Twenties. The radio, Hollywood, the airplane, Prohibition, and Al Capone all captured national attention. The papers that best exemplify jazz journalism all sprang up in New York between 1919 and 1924. All were characterized by two features: (1) They were **tabloids,** printed on a page that was about one-half the size of a normal newspaper page; and (2) they were all richly illustrated with photographs.

The *New York Daily News* debuted first. After a slow start, by 1924 the *News* had caught on. Its tabloid size was easy for people to handle while reading on buses and subways; it abounded with photos and cartoons; writing style was simple and short. The biggest content innovation of the *News* and the most noticeable was the lavish use of pictures. The entire front page was frequently given over to one or two pictures, and a two-page photo spread was included on the inside.

■ The Impact of the Great Depression

The depression had great social and economic impact on newspapers and magazines. During the 1930s, total daily newspaper circulation increased by about 2 million; the total population increased by 9 million. The total income of the newspaper industry, however, dropped about 20 percent in this decade. Marginally profitable papers were unable to stay in business, and approximately 66 dailies went under.

Although worsening economic conditions were one cause of the newspaper's decline, more important was the emergence of radio as a competitor for national advertising dollars. From 1935 to 1940, newspapers' share of national advertising revenues dropped from 45 to 39 percent, while radio's share jumped from 6 to more than 10 percent. By 1940, however, thanks to increased revenue from local advertisers, newspaper revenues were back up. Nevertheless, the economic picture was still not rosy, and the number of daily papers declined to 1,744 in 1945, an all-time low.

Postwar Newspapers

After World War II, economic forces continued to shape the American newspaper. Some trends of the postwar period were created by advances in print and electronic technology, but others had begun even before the war. For example, the postwar economy forced the newspaper industry to move even further in the direction of contraction and consolidation. Although newspaper circulation rose from approximately 48 million in 1945 to about 62 million in 1970, the number of dailies stayed about the same. There was actually a circulation loss in cities with populations of more than a million, and several big-city papers went out of business. Moreover, the number of cities with competing dailies dropped from 117 to 37 between 1945 and 1970. This meant that about 98 percent of American cities had no competing papers.

In 1945, 60 chains controlled about 42 percent of the total daily newspaper circulation. By 1970, there were approximately 157 chains that accounted for 60 percent of total circulation. Why had the number of chains continued to grow? One factor was the sharp rise in costs of paper and labor. Newspapers were becoming more expensive to print. The large chains were in a position to share expenses and to use their presses and labor more efficiently. Several papers could share the services of feature writers, columnists, photographers, and compositors, thus holding down costs.

The consolidation trend was also present across media, as several media conglomerates controlled newspapers, magazines, radio, and television stations. Black newspapers were also caught up in the trend toward concentration. In 1956, the *Chicago Defender* changed from a weekly to a daily, and its owner, John Sengstacke, started a group of nine black papers, including the Pittsburgh *Courier* and the Michigan *Chronicle*.

Another continuing trend was the competition among media for advertising dollars. The total amount of advertising revenue spent on all media nearly tripled between 1945 and 1970. Although the total spent on newspapers did not increase at quite this pace, the amount spent on television increased by more than a threefold factor. The rising television industry cut significantly into the print media's national advertising revenue.

Contemporary Developments

Investigative reporting received much attention in the 1970s because of the efforts of *Washington Post* reporters Bob Woodward and Carl Bernstein to expose the Watergate scandal, which eventually caused the resignation of President Richard Nixon.

The biggest development of the 1980s was the birth of *USA Today*. Following are some of the innovations sparked by this paper:

When Lyndon Johnson signed the Civil Rights Act of 1964, he invited leaders of the Civil Rights movement to join him in the Oval Office. Only one woman was among the group that witnessed the historic moment—Ethel L. Payne, an African-American journalist who had reported on civil rights for more than a decade.

Ethel L. Payne was the granddaughter of slaves. She originally wanted to become a lawyer but was denied admission to law school because of her race. In 1948, she went to Japan to work with African-American troops who were stationed there. Two years later Payne showed excerpts from her personal journal about the problems of black soldiers to a reporter for the *Chicago Defender* who was visiting Japan. Her stories became a series in the newspaper and launched Payne into a journalism career.

Based in Chicago, she won awards for her coverage of problems in the African-American community. She went to Washington in the mid-1950s to cover the beginnings of the Civil Rights movement. She wrote stories analyzing the historic *Brown v. Board of Education* Supreme Court decision. Payne made her presence felt at White House press conferences when she asked President Dwight Eisenhower pointed questions about the lack of progress on civil rights during his administration.

In 1956, Payne covered the arrest of Rosa Parks in Montgomery, Alabama, and the subsequent bus boycott. She reported the big stories of the Civil Rights movement, including the efforts to integrate the University of Alabama, the violence in Little Rock, Arkansas, the confrontation at Selma, Alabama, and the march on Washington in 1965. She was one of the first reporters to interview Dr. Martin Luther King, Jr.

In 1966, she traveled to Vietnam to cover African-American troops, who were involved in much of the fighting. She later accompanied Secretary of State Henry Kissinger on a six-nation tour of Africa. In 1978, at age 67, she ended her career with the *Chicago Defender* to write a syndicated column. Seven years later she became a leader in the effort to free South Africa leader Nelson Mandela.

Ethel Payne died in 1991. The *Washington Post* published a tribute to her on its editorial page. It praised her for being fair, straightforward, and independent, an assessment probably shared by her millions of readers.

- Splashy graphics and color.
- Short, easy-to-read stories.
- Lots of graphs, charts, and tables.
- Factoids (a *factoid* is a list of boiled-down facts—much like this list).

A somewhat controversial reporting philosophy surfaced in the mid-1990s. **Public journalism** (see Social Issues, "Public Journalism") embraces the view that newspapers should do more than just report the news; they should try to help communities solve problems and encourage participation in the political process. Some reporters think this philosophy exceeds the established tenets of journalism.

With the exception of the early 1990s, when a weak economy and a depressed advertising market caused several big-city papers to fold, the newspaper industry has enjoyed prosperity. By the late 1990s, layoffs, cost-cutting measures, and an increase in advertising revenue helped newspapers increase their profits.

The late 1990s also saw many newspapers start online editions. This trend continued into the new century as newspapers came to grips with the promises and pitfalls of the Internet.

NEWSPAPERS IN THE DIGITAL AGE

The newspaper industry is still experimenting to find the best way to incorporate an online presence with the traditional print editions. Fearful that online companies such as Yahoo! and Excite would use the web to steal away readers and advertising, many newspapers rushed to set up websites. The earliest newspaper sites were simply watered-down versions of the printed paper. They did little to promote the print version, nor did they generate enough revenue to pay for themselves. In short, for most papers, the website was simply a drain on finances and resources.

The debate over public, or civic, journalism is a debate over the basic philosophy of journalism. Consequently, feelings run high on both sides of the issue. Put simply, the fundamental principle behind public journalism is that journalists should put aside the traditional journalistic principle of detachment and become actively involved in public life. The basic rationale behind public journalism is as follows:

- Public and political life are in trouble. Basic problems cannot be solved. Journalism is also in trouble; the public thinks the press is arrogant and uncaring.
- The viability of public life and journalism are linked. If people withdraw from public life, they have no need for journalism.
- Public life cannot be improved using the traditional journalistic principle of detachment.
- Therefore, journalism must help citizens reengage in public life.

How is this philosophy put into action? A newspaper that practices public journalism helps encourage public discussion by providing a forum where citizens can explore the issues. It develops recommendations for change and prods both the audience and the government to action. Here are some specific examples:

- The Charlotte *Observer* published a series of articles that focused attention on a high-crime section of the city and helped improve the neighborhood.
- The Bremerton (Washington) *Sun* sponsored a series of town meetings and developed a plan to preserve open spaces.
- The *Wichita Eagle* sponsored a series of surveys and intensive interviews with members of the public to identify problems that the local government seemed unable to solve and subsequently listed groups working on those problems.

All the above seems pretty exemplary, so what could be a problem?

Those who oppose public journalism contend that it takes journalism into areas where it should not go. For example, Michael Gartner, a veteran newspaper publisher and former head of NBC News, called public journalism wrong morally, philosophically, and journalistically. "Newspapers are not to take sides," said Gartner, "even for Mom or apple pie. It ultimately will cost newspapers their credibility." He went on to argue that "newspapers should not be convening public meetings. They are supposed to tell the truth . . . and God knows that is hard enough to do by itself." Other opponents note that public journalism runs the risk of losing objectivity if the newspaper becomes involved with community leaders. As one put it, "When the editor and the real estate broker and the elected official form a team, whose ethics will prevail?" Finally, some critics have questioned the very assumptions that underlie public journalism. Veteran journalist Carl Sessions Stepp, for example, notes that public journalism assumes that government is broken and it is journalism's job to fix it. If that is the case, then the press and government become linked and objectivity might be lost.

Despite all the controversy, it seems clear that public journalism has had some positive effects. For one thing, it has prompted newspapers to view their readers not simply as consumers but as citizens who are capable of action. Second, it has prompted a reexamination of the role of journalism in society. In the long run, both of these consequences will help benefit journalism.

The pros and cons of public journalism are debated at length in Theodore Glaser (ed.), *The Idea of Public Journalism*, New York: Guilford, 1999.

Portals and Partners

That situation changed in the late 1990s, however, as papers gained knowledge and experience with their online ventures. For example, the fact that the 10 most popular websites are portals provided newspapers with incentives to get into the portal business. A **portal** is the first screen users see when they surf the net. These portals contained more than just news stories. There were searchable archives, links to other sites, chat rooms, e-mail services, online shopping, online polls, interactive restaurant and movie guides, a calendar of local events, and searchable classified ads. The more people who enter the web through a newspaper portal, the more revenue the paper earns from banner advertising.

Some newspapers that compete with one another on the newsstand are joining forces in cyberspace. The rivals *Fort Worth Star Telegram* and *Dallas Morning News* cooperated to launch the local portal dfw.com.

Online journalism has raised a host of ethical questions that reporters, editors, and publishers are struggling to answer. Here are just a few:

- *What's the proper separation of news and commerce at a website?* Traditionally, to preserve journalistic integrity, the editorial side of a newspaper was separated from the business side. Online, the boundaries are blurry. For example, a person who reads a book review at the *New York Times* online site can click a button and purchase the book from Barnes&Noble.com. The *Times* gets revenue from each such sale. Is this simply providing an additional service to the reader, or is it a conflict of interest? Can the *Times* be objective when reporting news about Barnes and Noble or its rival Amazon.com? What about an online paper that publishes movie reviews and offers a link where readers can purchase tickets to a local theater online and the paper gets a commission for each online ticket sale? Would the paper ever publish a bad review?

- *If an online paper has links to external sites, is it responsible for the content of those sites?* In a story pointing out the increasing danger of electronic eavesdropping and personal data snooping by private detectives, the *New York Times*

online provided links to the websites of the companies who engaged in such practices, seemingly exacerbating the problem. Another online *Times* story about convicted killer Charles Manson contained links to four websites maintained by less-than-credible organizations that proclaimed Manson's innocence. Again, is this simply another online reader service, or is the *Times* providing its audience with dubious and potentially misleading information?

Some online papers post disclaimers noting that they are not responsible for the content of linked sites, but is this enough to fulfill their ethical obligations to readers? Is it enough for the paper to simply wash its hands and not be responsible for any harm that might come from corrupted information?

- *What ethical obligations do online papers have when it comes to corrections?* A traditional newspaper usually has an explicit policy concerning when and where corrections will be published. Most online papers have no such policy. If they make an error, they will simply correct it when someone points it out, without acknowledging the mistake. Do they owe their readers more?

In that same connection, traditional competitors are teaming up to supply classified ads to national websites. The *New York Times* and *Newsday,* for example, supply automotive classified to cars.com. The *Washington Post* and the *Chicago Tribune,* along with about 80 other papers, contribute to CareerPath.com, a website that lists more than 300,000 job openings.

■ E-Commerce

Online newspapers have also embraced e-commerce. Newspaper websites charge for banner ads with links that will take a reader directly to a retailer. Some newspapers form a partnership with a retailer and get a small portion of each online sale. Newspapers have an advantage in e-commerce because most have a large fleet of delivery trucks that are idle for large periods of the day. These trucks can be used to deliver merchandise ordered online. The *Arizona Daily Star's* website offers a service that allows a customer to order something from the web and have it delivered within a couple of hours.

Newspapers are also realizing that local and regional e-commerce is an untapped market. The *Augusta Chronicle* uses its website to sell posters and other souvenirs from the Masters golf tournament and makes a profit selling home-grown pecans. The *Knoxville News-Sentinel* earns money by selling University of Tennessee memorabilia online.

Handheld Media

Many newspapers are looking beyond the conventional Internet site to other channels of distribution for the digital newspaper. One of the most promising channels involves handheld media, such as Internet-enabled cell phones and personal digital assistants (PDAs) such as the Palm handheld. About 3 million PDAs were sold in 1999, and the number will undoubtedly rise in the next few years. More than 70 million people in the United States have wireless telephone service, and many of those have web access. Not surprisingly, newspapers are already starting to tap into this market. The *Wall Street Journal* offers financial news to wireless customers. The *Sacramento Bee* sends local news reports to both PDAs and cell phones. The Knight-Ridder Company is a partner with AvantGo, a company that delivers content to wireless devices. Knight-Ridder supplies local and regional news, sports, and movie schedules, which AvantGo makes available to subscribers. The company reported that it was receiving about 7 million page views every month on the handheld devices. The advertising and marketing potential of this channel is enormous, because ads can reach people near the point of purchase. Reading sports scores on your handheld device? Press 1 and reserve tickets to a future game. Checking movie times? While you're at it, press 2 and reserve a table at a local restaurant for dinner after the movie.

Further, newspapers are closely watching developments in the book publishing industry, where flat-panel readers are being used to download and display books (see Chapter 6). One such reader, the Rocket eBook, lets readers access the online editions of the *New York Times* and *The Wall Street Journal*. In short, newspapers are preparing for the digital age by exploring all emerging media distribution platforms.

The Siphoning Dilemma

As digital papers add more content and become more attractive, timely, and accessible, they run the risk of siphoning off readers from their print counterparts. Online papers are free (with the notable exception of *The Wall Street Journal*), and many carry breaking news stories before the print editions. A 1999 survey found that more than 10 percent of online consumers canceled their newspaper subscriptions because they thought they could get the same information free online. This is the basic dilemma faced by the modern paper: How do you produce an online version that complements rather than cannibalizes the print version?

Of course, very few experts expect the print newspaper to vanish, but most think it will have to redefine itself, as it has done in the past. Radio news effectively killed off the "Extra" newspaper edition and became the first source for many breaking news stories. Television supplanted the newspaper as the main information source and cultural leader in America. The newspaper accommodated those changes and survived. The next few years will likely see the newspaper transform itself once again as it deals with the challenges and the unknowns of the Internet.

DEFINING FEATURES OF NEWSPAPERS

Both the online and the print renditions of the newspaper share some defining features. In the first place, the newspaper is made up of diverse content. Newspapers contain international, national, and local news. In addition, they feature editorials, letters to the editor, movie listings, horoscopes, comics, sports, film reviews, recipes, advice columns, classified ads, and a host of other material. Their range of content is extensive.

Second, newspapers are conveniently packaged. Both the print and online versions are organized according to content. There are sections devoted to general news, financial news, sports coverage, and entertainment. In addition, each story contains a headline that makes it easy for readers to decide if they want to peruse the rest of the story.

Third, newspapers are local. Reporters cover meetings of the local school board, the city council, and the zoning commission. They cover the local police station and tell about the newest store openings in the local mall. Sports sections cover the hometown Little League and high school teams. Local people with merchandise to sell use the classified ads. Newspapers are the only medium with the resources to report all the neighborhood activities in a community.

Fourth, more than any other medium, the newspaper serves as a historical record. One writer described newspaper journalism as "the first draft of history." The typical paper contains a record of daily events, some profound, some not so profound, that influence our lives. If a person wants to get a sense of what life was like in the 1940s, for example, he or she can flip through some old issues of the paper and see what events were on people's minds, what movies they were seeing, and what products were being advertised.

Fifth, as we have seen above, newspapers perform the watchdog role in our society. They monitor the workings of government and private industry for misdeeds and wrongdoings. They alert the public to possible threats and new trends.

Finally, newspapers are timely. News isn't useful if it's stale. Recognizing this fact, the largest-circulation newspapers in the United States publish daily and online editions that can break news any time of the day. Getting the news out fast has always been one of the characteristics of the newspaper business.

ORGANIZATION OF THE NEWSPAPER INDUSTRY

As is clear by now, there are two basic versions of a newspaper—print and electronic. Let's look at the traditional print version first.

The newspapers that are published in this country are many and varied. They range from *The Wall Street Journal,* a nationally oriented financial daily, to the *Journal of Commerce,* a small financial paper published in Portland, Oregon; from the *National Enquirer* to the *Daily Lobo,* the college newspaper of the University of New Mexico; from the million-plus-circulation *New York Times* to the 6,000-circulation Gallipolis *Daily Tribune* in Gallipolis, Ohio. Obviously, there are many ways to categorize an industry as diverse as this one. For our purposes, we will group papers by frequency of publication (dailies and weeklies), by market size (national, large, medium, small), and, finally, by their appeal to specialized interest groups.

Print Dailies

To be considered a daily, a newspaper has to appear at least five times a week. In 1999, there were 1,483 dailies, down 5 percent from 1996 (see Figure 4–1), and about 7,900 weeklies. Whether a daily or a weekly, the chief concern of a newspaper is its **circulation,** the number of copies delivered to newsstands or vending machines and the number delivered to subscribers. Weekday morning circulation

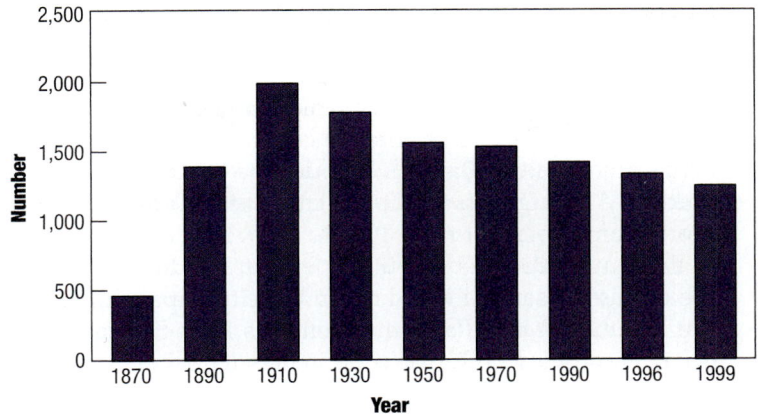

Figure 4–1

Number of Daily
Newspapers in United
States, 1870–1999

has increased and Sunday circulation has stayed about the same in the last 20 years. Evening circulation, however, has shown a major decrease. As a result, total daily newspaper circulation has declined to approximately 56 million, a figure that has dropped steadily from 1965 to 1999 (see Figure 4–2). At the same time, the population of the United States has been growing. Consequently, the ratio of newspapers per household has declined. To illustrate: In 1960, 111 newspapers were sold per 100 households; in 1999, about 58 newspapers were sold per 100 households. This circulation crunch has not hit all papers with equal force, and this becomes evident when we divide daily newspapers into market groups.

National Newspapers   Only a handful of papers fall into this category. These are publications whose content is geared not for one particular city or region but for the entire country. These papers typically use satellites to transmit images and information to regional printing plants where the papers are assembled and distributed. The newest addition to this category, with a circulation of about

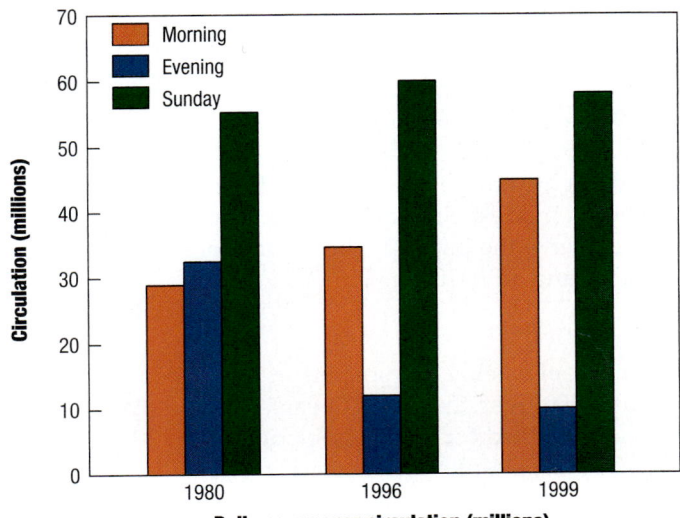

Figure 4–2

Daily-Newspaper
Circulation, 1980–1999

(Compiled by author)

1.7 million, is the Gannett publication *USA Today*, started in 1982. The paper's use of color and graphics and focus on such topics as sports and weather made a significant impact on other newspapers. Other papers with a national edition are the *New York Times, The Wall Street Journal,* and the *Christian Science Monitor.*

Large Metropolitan Dailies   The decline in circulation has hit these papers the hardest. Although the total population of the top 50 metropolitan areas increased more than 30 percent from 1960 to 1999, the circulation of newspapers published in those areas dropped about 45 percent. In addition, the last few years have seen the demise of several well-known big-city papers: the *Indianapolis Star and News,* the *Honolulu Star-Bulletin,* the Memphis *Press-Scimitar,* and the Dallas *Times-Herald,* to name a few. Why the drop in big-city circulation? There are several reasons, including migration from the central city to the suburbs, transient populations, rising costs of distribution, and increased competition from other media, most notably, television.

Suburban Dailies   Although suburban communities of between 100,000 and 500,000 residents are home to only 12 percent of total newspapers, they account for about 40 percent of all circulation. Suburban dailies, located in the areas surrounding the larger cities, are experiencing a period of growth. Circulation of these papers grew by about one-third from 1987 to 1999. One reason for this increase is the growth of suburban shopping centers, which have attracted many merchants formerly located in the central cities. To these merchants, suburban papers represent an efficient way of reaching potential customers. In addition, suburban residents are apparently less inclined to go to the city at night for dinner and entertainment, a factor that has cut down newsstand sales of city papers. Perhaps the best-known suburban paper is *Newsday,* aimed at the residents of Long Island. In 1999, *Newsday* had a circulation of about 575,000, thereby making it the eighth largest daily paper in the country.

In a quest to regain readers, large metro dailies have taken on the suburban press on the smaller papers' own turf. Big-city newspapers are putting out more **zoned editions,** sections geared to a particular suburban area. The *Philadelphia Inquirer,* for example, has eight "Neighbors" sections designed to compete with the 20 or so suburban papers that surround metro Philadelphia.

Small-Town Dailies   This category of newspapers has also made circulation gains. From 1979 to 1999, newspaper circulation in towns with 100,000 or fewer inhabitants grew by 19 percent. Recently, circulation among papers in this category has declined slightly, although dailies in towns with populations of less than 25,000 have shown modest circulation gains. Surveys have shown that readers of these papers perceive the papers to be sources of local information, for both neighborhood news and advertising.

Print Weeklies

The number of weekly newspapers in the United States has remained fairly stable at about 7,900 over the last 20 years. The circulation of weeklies, however, has more than doubled for this same period, from 29 million in 1970 to more than 74 million in 1999. Despite this increase in circulation, the rising costs of printing and distribution have made weekly publishers more cost-conscious.

The first weekly papers were published in small towns and in rural areas that did not have a population large enough to support a daily. Although many weeklies are still located in these communities, the past few decades have seen the emergence of weekly papers in local suburban neighborhoods. In the mid-1990s, it was estimated that more than one in three weekly papers was published in suburbia. Weeklies can offer advertisers more precise local exposure at prices that are more affordable. Daily papers are competing with the weeklies by introducing more zoned editions and special deals for local merchants. It's apparent that the future may bring even more competition.

Recapturing Readers

No matter what their size or frequency of publication, all print newspapers are faced with the task of maintaining their local readers while attracting new ones. Newspaper executives are aware that spending time with the daily paper is no longer the habit it once was. What are some of the things that newspapers are doing to attract readers?

- They are using more color. Readers generally like color, and papers are using it liberally throughout the newspaper. Even the gray and proper *New York Times* and the conservative *Wall Street Journal* have introduced color to their pages.
- They are changing their writing and editing style. Stories are shorter and accompanied by summary decks under the headline or have story-related information in sidebars on either side of the story. Some papers run highlighted synopses within long stories.
- They are changing the content of the paper. Many papers have become less dependent on lengthy stories dealing with local government. Appearing with more frequency are features dealing with lifestyles, fashions, and entertain-

Newsroom at a medium-sized paper: A substantial part of each reporter's and editor's day is spent at the computer.

CRITICAL / CULTURAL ISSUES

Rape in the Sports Pages

Contributed by Patricia Joyner Priest, Ph.D. As a media researcher and an advocate for rape survivors, I have a long-standing interest in how the media cover rape and how people learn about the topic. This is important because, among other things, knowledge—and myths—about rape and its aftermath influences (1) women's assessment of risk, (2) their decision to report the incident, (3) jurys' verdicts, and (4) rapists' beliefs that they can get away with the crime. Here's a quick example of the problem: Recently, when I did a search using the key word "rape," I was dismayed to find that eight of the first ten web pages listed were porn sites.

Barring some terrible firsthand knowledge, most of us learn about rape from newspaper reports that provide expansive coverage to stranger rapists who commit serial assaults. Acquaintance rape is rarely covered by the press, although women much more commonly are raped by people they know. The one place where reports of acquaintance rape occasionally surface is alongside news of grand slams and touchdowns: in the sports pages. Rapes are reported here because the prominence of people involved in news items is a key factor when editors determine newsworthiness.

There are several troubling aspects of the placement and character of these articles. First, if crime coverage is partly driven by a responsibility to inform people of possible risks, why place reports of rape in a section read less frequently by women? Most troubling is the framing of these stories: The reports cast the *woman* making the claim as the trouble-maker, because her allegations threaten the man's—and his team's—future. Sportswriters highlight the suspect's importance to the team with detailed statistics. The articles seem like the kind of handicapping information you might read at a horse race, not sobering indicators of what may be yet another instance of an urgent social problem.

These news stories are formulaic in other ways as well. Denials, often voiced by the man's parents, his defense attorney, and the player himself, are the most salient feature of the initial coverage. While it is *crucial* that the man have his day in court, balance is important, too, so that the sports section does not incessantly promote the insinuation that women who report rape are lying.

It is also common for the coach and teammates to praise the man's character, even though he may have had a history of serious violence. Another frequent theme suggests that the woman has ruined the man's career and life.

It is the woman's reputation, in fact, that is often ruined. Humanizing details about her are rarely provided except to mention negative information such as whether she had been drinking. Instead, she is often portrayed—most prominently by the defense attorney and the alleged assailant—as a prostitute, a "gold digger," a groupie, and a liar.

Statistics indicate the overwhelming odds faced by victims seeking justice. The authors of the book *Pros and Cons* write: "Of the 217 felony sexual assault complaints against college and professional athletes that were reported to police between 1986 and 1995, only 66 ever reached the trial stage. [Of these,] 85% were acquitted."

Women who think of rapists only as strangers who jump out from behind bushes are woefully uninformed about this basic, terrible fact: An acquaintance can get away with rape fairly easily, because the man can claim consent. It is that simple. And it's simpler still for sports heroes, accustomed throughout their lives to special treatment, even—or especially—when they step over the line.

The rare cases that make it to court are usually dropped for lack of evidence. Yet we warn women that resistance might make things worse. And, clearly, many of the suspects would be highly intimidating assailants, even if they do not brandish a weapon.

We rarely perceive these harmful cultural patterns of reporting about and responding to rape, but I've talked to people visiting the United States who are often puzzled by the victim-blaming stance of the public and the press. Perhaps it will help to consider this: What if a man went up to an athlete's hotel room—perhaps because the player said he had to get something or had to use the bathroom—and then the sports star raped *him*? Would we think the man was stupid, naive, or "asking for it"? See how gendered attitudes can shape our thinking, the criminal's behavior (if he knows he will probably get away with it), the response of the criminal justice system, and media coverage?

1. Think about coverage of rape you've seen (or look up some news stories about rapes). To what extent and in what ways do these stories reinforce the problems written about here?

2. If you were a reporter, what types of things do you think you'd want to include (or exclude) in rape stories?

3. What can we, as consumers and citizens, do to try to change this pattern of reporting about and responding to rape?

| Table 4.1 | Top 10 Newspapers by Circulation |

Although total newspaper circulation has declined slightly, there are some pronounced variations, as illustrated in the rankings below. Note particularly the changes in the volatile New York metro area (*New York Times, New York Daily News,* and *Newsday*).

Paper	1987 Circulation (millions)	1999 Circulation (millions)	Percent Change
1. The Wall Street Journal	1.961	1.752	−11
2. USA Today	1.324	1.671	+26
3. Los Angeles Times	1.113	1.078	−3
4. New York Times	1.022	1.086	+6
5. Washington Post	0.761	0.763	0
6. New York Daily News	1.285	0.701	−45
7. Chicago Tribune	0.765	0.657	−14
8. Newsday	0.641	0.575	−10
9. San Francisco Chronicle	0.568	0.457	−19
10. Detroit Free Press	0.649	0.361	−44

ment, and articles usually described as "news that you can use" (e.g., "How to Find the Perfect Babysitter," "Best Open-Late Restaurants," and "Managing Your Money").

Many of the above efforts are intended specifically to attract the audience segment that has been the hardest to recapture: teens and young adults. Surveys show that in the 1990s only one in three Americans under 35 regularly read a newspaper. Fifty percent of 18- to 24-year-olds don't read a newspaper at all. A recent study by the Times Mirror Center found that the current generation of people under 30 knows less, cares less, and reads the newspaper less than any other generation in the past 50 years.

■ Special-Service and Minority Newspapers

Special-service newspapers are those aimed at several well-defined audience segments. There are, for example, many newspapers published specifically for the African-American community. The African-American press in this country has a long history, dating back to 1827. Most early papers were started to oppose discrimination and to help gain equal rights and opportunities. The African-American press reached its circulation peak in the 1960s when approximately 275 papers had a circulation of about 4 million. Since that time, the African-American press has seen a significant decline in both numbers of papers and circulation.

In 1999, approximately 200 African-American papers were publishing in 35 states and the District of Columbia. Although some African-American papers were doing well, others were facing financial problems. In general, the problems faced by the African-American press stemmed from increasing competition from white-owned papers, decreasing circulation (which made it more difficult to attract advertisers), more expensive newsprint, and criticism from many in the African-American community that the papers were too conservative and out-of-date. In an attempt to recapture readership and advertisers, many African-American papers have

In the 1960s, after studying the civil disorder and racial violence that broke out in many American cities, the Kerner Commission concluded that part of the problem was the news media's failure to explore the causes of the violence. This failure, in turn, was due to a lack of minority reporters in the nation's newsrooms. Subsequently, most in the industry agreed that diversity in age, race, gender, and ethnicity on a newspaper's staff was helpful in providing more depth and perspective to news stories. In 1978, the American Society of Newspaper Editors set as its goal minority representation in the newsroom that equals that in the general population.

More than 20 years later, that goal has not been met. Minorities accounted for about 26 percent of the population in 2000 but make up only about 12 percent of newsroom employees. Hispanic/Latino journalists account for just 4 percent of this total, while Native Americans make up less than one-half of 1 percent. About 39 percent of U.S. papers have no minority employees at all.

Women in journalism have fared somewhat better, accounting for 37 percent of newspaper employees. The majority of these women work as reporters. About 22 percent are supervisors.

Why has minority employment stalled out in the past few years despite industry recruiting efforts? One reason may be that minorities are attracted to higher-paying professions. Another suggests that colleges and universities are not doing enough to attract minority students to journalism programs. In that connection, the Freedom Forum and the Knight Foundation announced in 2000 that they were setting aside $5.5 million for programs to encourage minorities to enter the journalism profession. Other reasons might be found in the results of a 1996 survey sponsored by the Associated Press Managing Editors (APME). The survey showed that the newsrooms in America were two different worlds. Minority and nonminority journalists had totally opposite attitudes about their experiences and expectations. For example, African-American journalists thought they were less likely than average to be promoted. Whites thought African Americans were more likely to be promoted. Minority members thought they spent more time in entry-level positions; nonminorities thought minorities spent less time in those types of jobs. Whites were far more likely than blacks to think their efforts were appreciated by management. Whites thought their papers did a good job in covering the minority community; minority journalists strongly disagreed.

These findings are troubling and suggest that the real benefits of diversity may be hard to realize. An increased number of minorities in the newsroom may be helpful, but changes in attitudes and perceptions have to take place before the more important advantages of diversity can be achieved.

---

changed their format and editorial focus and have begun to concentrate on local news. In the late 1990s it was estimated that the combined circulation of all African-American newspapers was about 2 million, down almost 50 percent from the 1960s. In an attempt to gain readers, many African-American newspapers were trying to appeal to upscale readers by emphasizing news about education, medicine, and economics. Many papers had added color and updated graphics.

Hispanics make up the fastest-growing minority group in America, and the Spanish-language press has grown along with them. According to the *National Hispanic Media Directory*, the number of Spanish-language publications has more than doubled, from 232 in 1970 to 515 in 1999. The most prominent daily Spanish-language paper is the New York City tabloid *el diario—La Prensa*, with a circulation of more than 70,000.

Many English-language papers, such as the *Miami Herald*, have introduced Spanish-language sections. Furthermore, English-language dailies in markets with a strong Hispanic population are attempting to expand their circulation by making deals with Spanish-language newspapers. In New York, for example, the *Times* teamed up with *el diario—La Prensa* in a joint promotion where a reader could buy both papers together for a reduced price. The *Los Angeles Times* and *La Opinión* have a deal where readers can subscribe to both papers at a discount.

There are many other ethnic newspaper publishers in the United States. Twelve cities have at least one Chinese-language newspaper, and eight cities have papers targeted toward Polish Americans.

The best-known member of the Spanish-language press is *el diario/La Prensa*, published in New York City. The paper has a circulation of more than 70,000. *(Courtesy el diario La Prensa)*

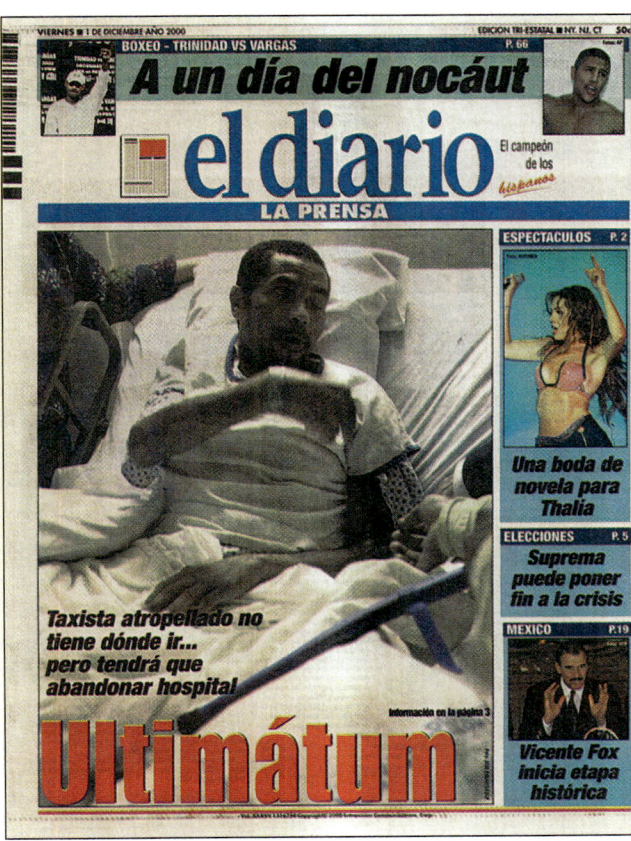

Another special type of newspaper is exemplified by the college press. Although numbers are hard to pin down, as of 1999 there were about 1,500 college papers published at four-year institutions, with a total circulation of more than 6 million. College newspapers are big business; consequently, more and more papers are hiring nonstudent professionals to manage their operation. Two of the largest college papers in terms of circulation are the University of Minnesota's *Minnesota Daily* and Michigan State University's *State News*, both with circulations of approximately 30,000. College newspapers get high readership scores. One survey noted that about 96 percent of students read at least part of their campus paper.

NEWSPAPERS ONLINE

Online papers do not differ from their print counterparts with regard to their primary function. Both gather, evaluate, and organize information. They differ significantly, however, in the way they distribute this news to their readers. Traditional newspapers use paper, ink, presses, trucks, and delivery workers; online papers are transmitted digitally to computers and handheld wireless media.

Online papers have certain advantages over traditional newspapers:

- Printed newspapers are limited by the **newshole**, the amount of news that can be printed in one edition. Online papers have no such limitations. The full text of lengthy speeches, transcripts of interviews, and extensive tables and graphs can be easily accommodated.

- Online papers can be updated continuously. There are no edition deadlines for online papers.

- Online papers are interactive. E-mail addresses, bulletin boards, and chat rooms allow readers to provide quick feedback to the paper. Many have searchable archives and links to other sites.

Many papers, such as the *Fort Worth Star-Telegram*, have turned their online editions into much more than electronic versions of the printed newspaper.

In 1994 about 20 daily papers had websites. In 2000, more than 1,100 are online. Of the top 150 papers, 148 offer their news online. The Newspaper Association of America's (NAA) website (www.naa.org) contains links to 1,153 online dailies, ranging from *USA Today,* with a print circulation of 1.7 million, to the *Americus* (Georgia) *Times-Recorder,* with a print circulation of 6,900. Online papers vary tremendously in their size and complexity. Large papers typically have extensive sites that offer more features and content than their print counterparts. Smaller papers may simply post a limited number of stories and classified ads. Weeklies and special-service papers have also branched out into the web. The NAA's site has links to more than 500 of these sites.

The relationship between the online and print versions of the newspaper varies from paper to paper. Many large papers have made the web version an autonomous operation, separate from the print side. Many other papers, however, have the web staff working under the direction of the newspaper's editors.

Online papers tend to have small staffs. A 2000 survey of newspaper editors disclosed that more than 80 percent have an editorial staff of five or fewer employees. Another survey found that only 40 percent of online editors thought their newspaper had a clear mission for the website and about 70 percent thought their website lacked needed technical resources.

Perhaps the biggest difference between online papers and traditional newspapers is one of newsroom atmosphere and attitude. Newspaper journalism has been around for more than 200 years and has established traditions and a particular culture. Online journalism has been around for less than 10 years, and its culture and traditions are still evolving. The staff at online papers tends to be younger and more casual. The atmosphere at many papers is more collaborative, friendlier, and a little irreverent. Traditional newsrooms have an established chain of command; online papers are more flexible. As a result, online papers sometime publish stories that might not make it into print. The *Baltimore Sun*'s web paper, for example, carried a three-part series by a 19-year-old journalist who reported what it was like to drink Jolt cola every day for three weeks.

NEWSPAPER OWNERSHIP

The two most significant facts about newspaper ownership are the following:

1. Concentration of ownership is increasing as large group owners acquire more papers.
2. There has been a decrease in the number of cities with competing papers.

Al Neuharth got into the newspaper business when he was 11 years old and delivered the *Minneapolis Tribune*. At 13, he had a part-time job in the composing room of a local weekly.

After serving in the military, he took a job as a reporter for a paper in South Dakota and later moved to the *Miami Herald*. Neuharth moved up rapidly through the ranks and eventually entered management. In 1960, he was appointed an assistant executive editor of the *Detroit Free Press*. His achievements there brought him to the attention of executives of the Gannett Company, who persuaded him to leave Detroit to manage two of Gannett's papers in New York. Neuharth's success there earned him a promotion to the position of chief of Gannett's operations in Florida. By 1970, Neuharth had become CEO of the company.

His emphasis was on the bottom line. During his tenure, Gannett's annual revenue increased from $200 million to $3.1 billion. Neuharth continued the strategies of his predecessors by acquiring small- and medium-market dailies that enjoyed a monopoly status in their markets and keeping costs down while raising ad rates. Stung by criticism that his papers emphasized profit at the expense of good journalism, Neuharth strengthened the editorial

Al Neuharth, the man responsible for making Gannett the nation's biggest newspaper. *(Cynthia Johnson/Gamma Liaison)*

operations of Gannett papers and by 1980, many had won awards for excellence in reporting.

Neuharth's biggest gamble came in the early 1980s when he decided to use a network of communication satellites and regional printing plants to produce *USA Today*, a national general-interest newspaper. The new paper was greeted with derision by critics, who dismissed it as a "McPaper" that served up flavorless "fast-food" journalism. *USA Today* was an immediate hit with readers, however, and quickly garnered more than a million readers. Advertisers took a little longer to get on board, but the paper eventually turned a profit.

Now most experts agree that after almost 20 years on the newsstands *USA Today* has had a significant impact on the industry. Most newspapers have incorporated color, a splashy page makeup, more charts and graphics, and shorter, more tightly written stories.

Neuharth retired in 1989 to become chair of the Freedom Foundation, an organization dedicated to furthering the cause of a free press in society. He also continues to write a syndicated newspaper column. The *Washington Journalism Review* named him the most influential person in print media for the decade of the 1980s.

The biggest newspaper group is the Gannett Company with 101 dailies and a combined circulation of about 6 million. Knight-Ridder Newspapers Inc. controls 34 dailies with about a 3.8 million circulation. Other newspaper chains that own dailies with a combined circulation of more than 2 million are Newhouse Newspapers, Tribune/Times Mirror Company, and the New York Times Company (see Table 4.2).

Table 4.2	Five Biggest Newspaper Groups, 2000	
Name	**Number of Papers Owned**	**Leading Papers**
Gannett Company Inc.	101	*USA Today, Nashville Tennessee*
Knight-Ridder Newspapers Inc.	34	*Philadelphia Inquirer, Miami Herald*
Newhouse Newspapers	23	*Cleveland Plain Dealer, Trenton Times*
New York Times Company	11	*Newsday, Los Angeles Times, Chicago Tribune*
Tribune/Times Mirror Company	21	*New York Times*

The Growth of Newspaper Group Owners

Concentration of ownership is not a new trend in the newspaper business. What is new, however, is the dominance of the industry by big group owners. The number of group owners has risen from about 8 in 1900 to approximately 130 in 2000. These 130 groups account for about 80 percent of newspaper circulation.

The newspaper market became more concentrated in 2000 thanks to the Tribune company's $6.5 billion deal for the Times Mirror Company and the Gannett Company's acquisition of 21 papers from Thomson Newspapers for $1.1 billion.

Big group owners are pursuing a strategy of regional consolidation. Gannett, for example, owns seven papers in New Jersey that account for almost 40 percent of the total newspaper circulation in that state. Newhouse owns eight papers located across central Michigan. Geographic consolidation saves money by allowing papers to share printing plants and editorial staff. It also increases advertising revenue by allowing one company to offer special deals to regional advertisers.

The Decline of Competition

Coupled with the growth of group ownership is the decline of newspaper competition within single markets. Back in 1923, more than 500 cities had two or more competing daily papers, including 100 that had three or more. By 2000, there were only a dozen cities that had independent competing newspapers. In another 13 cities competition was kept alive only through a **joint-operating agreement (JOA)**. A JOA is formed, under approval by the Justice Department, to maintain two newspapers in a city when otherwise one would go out of business. Functions of the two papers—circulation, advertising, and production—are combined to save money. Only the editorial staffs remain separate and competitive. JOAs exist between papers in Cincinnati, Tucson, and Birmingham, to name a few.

The Pros and Cons of Group Ownership

The pros and cons of group ownership and decreasing competition have been widely debated among newspaper executives and press critics. Critics maintain that fewer competing papers means a loss in the diversity of opinions available to the audience. They also claim that top management in group operations places profits above newspaper quality. A newspaper owned by a chain, say these critics, would likely avoid local controversy in its pages to avoid offending advertisers. It has also been charged that chain newspapers are usually under the direction of absentee owners, who may have little knowledge of or concern for local community interests.

On the other hand, those who favor newspaper groups argue that group owners can accomplish certain things that smaller owners cannot. For example, a large group owner could afford to have correspondents and news bureaus in the country's capital, Washington, D.C., and foreign cities—an arrangement too expensive for a small owner to maintain. The chains are also better able to afford the latest technical equipment. Last, chains have the resources to provide for more elaborate training and public-service programs than do individually owned papers. The validity of each of these arguments depends in great measure on the particular group owner involved. Many group-owned papers are doing excellent jobs. Others may not rate so highly.

PRODUCING THE NEWSPAPER

Departments and Staff

The departmental structure and staffing of a newspaper vary with its size. All papers, however, have certain common aspects. They have a publisher and are generally divided into three main departments. The publisher is in charge of the entire operation of the paper. He or she sets the paper's editorial policy and is responsible for the tone and overall personality of the newspaper. The three main departments at most newspapers are (1) business, (2) production, and (3) news-editorial. Figure 4–3 is a simplified departmental chart for a typical newspaper. The figure reflects the historical fact that news and opinion are kept separate. The editorial columns contain opinion, while the news columns contain objective reporting. The figure also assumes that the online version of the paper is an independent department.

The managing editor oversees the total day-by-day operation of the news department and coordinates the work of the newsroom. The wire editor scans the thousands of words transmitted by the major news services—Associated Press and United Press International—and selects those stories most relevant to the paper, edits them, and adds headlines. The city editor supervises the newspaper's local coverage. He or she assigns stories to local beat reporters or general-assignment reporters. Beat reporters have a specified area to cover: city hall, courts, police station, for example. General-assignment reporters handle a variety of stories, ranging from fires and accidents to the local flower show. The city editor also assigns photographers to go along with reporters on selected stories. The copyeditor usually works inside a special U-shaped desk (called the slot) in the newsroom and supervises the editing, headline writing, and changes in stories submitted by local reporters.

Figure 4–3

Departmental Chart for a Typical Newspaper

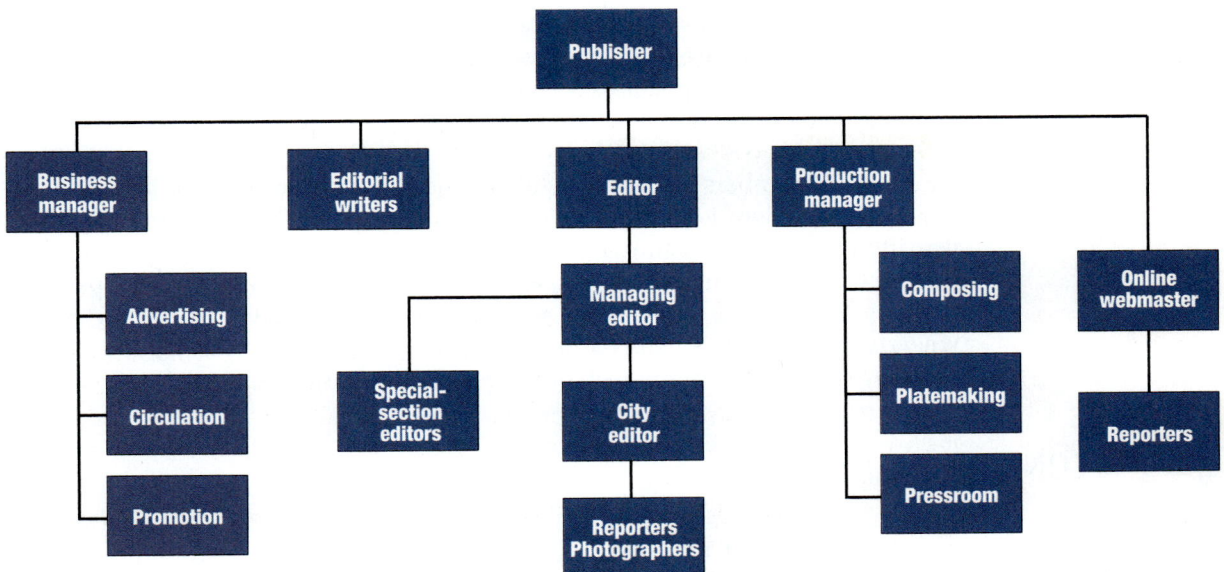

Who?

Beat reporters need to know the jargon of the area they cover lest embarrassing things happen. A case in point: A new reporter covering the legal circuit for a Virginia paper did not know that FNU (first name unknown) and LNU (last name unknown) were common abbreviations in Virginia law enforcement. Unaware of this jargon, the newcomer dutifully reported that a Mr. Fnu Lnu had been indicted by a grand jury.

Finally, there are specialized sections in the paper that generally have their own editor and staff. These may vary from paper to paper, but typically they include the sports, business, family, real estate, and entertainment departments.

■ Publishing the Newspaper

Getting out a newspaper is a 24-hour-a-day job. News happens at all hours, and many stories happen unexpectedly. Not only that, news is perishable; it becomes less valuable as it ages. Trying to cope with the never-ending flow of news and the constant pressure to keep it fresh requires organization and coordination among the paper's staff. This section will illustrate the coordination by sketching how a newspaper gets published.

There are two basic sources of news copy: local reporting and the wire services. Early in the day, the wire editor will scan the output from the wire machines and flag possible stories for the day's paper. At the same time, the city editor is checking his or her notes and daily calendar and making story assignments to various reporters. While all this is going on, the managing editor is gauging the available space, called the newshole, that can be devoted to news in that day's paper. This space will change according to the number of ads scheduled to appear on any one day. The more ads, the greater the number of pages that can be printed and the larger the newshole.

As the day progresses, reporters return from assignments and write and store their news stories at a personal computer. These stories are "called up" by copyeditors, who trim and make changes in the stories and code them for use in the paper. The newsworthy stories are then processed by the design desk. Decisions about page makeup and the amount of space to be devoted to a story are made as the deadline for publication appears. Other decisions are made about the ratio of wire copy to local and state news. Photographs and other artwork are selected for inclusion; headlines are written; space is cleared for late-breaking stories; updates are inserted in breaking stories. The stories are then sent to the composing room and finally to the press.

This routine does not necessarily apply to the online operation. The online editor and staff members discuss story ideas, and the editor assigns stories to the various staffers. There is no newshole limitation to worry about. Some content is rewritten from the print edition, while other content is original. The online staff, of course, works with more than just text and pictures. Sound and video clips could possibly be included with a story as could links to other sites. Stories are posted when finished; there is no need for a composing room or a press. Updates to stories may be posted continuously or at specific times of the day.

 ECONOMICS

Newspapers derive their income from two sources: advertising, which provides about 80 percent of the total, and circulation (revenue from subscriptions and single-copy sales), which accounts for the other 20 percent. Advertising revenue is closely related to circulation since papers with a large circulation are able to charge more for ads that will reach a larger audience.

The newspaper industry went through a period of cost cutting during the mid- to late 1990s. As a result, the industry was in good financial health at the start of the new century. The average pretax operating profit for newspapers was edging close to 20 percent in 2000, compared with about a 13 percent margin for all industries. Moreover, newspapers take in circulation and advertising revenues every day, making them good cash-flow businesses.

Online operations, however, continue to be a drain on profits for most papers. Not many online editions are in the black, and the sites of several major dailies are losing large sums of money. In 1999, for example, the *New York Times* online unit had an operating loss of $22 million. Only *The Wall Street Journal* has had success making money with its online edition. The *Journal* charges an annual access fee of $29 (for print subscribers) and $59 (for print nonsubscribers) for its online version. Other online newspapers have been unsuccessful in charging a fee for their content.

Ironically, one of the reasons that print newspapers were doing so well was the fact that Internet companies were spending large sums of money for newspaper advertising, a situation that changed in 2000 when the dot-com companies cut back on their spending.

A look at the longer term reveals several potential threats to continued economic good times. The percentage of people who regularly read newspapers has been dropping steadily for more than 25 years. Cable TV, radio, and direct mail are becoming aggressive competitors in the quest for local advertising dollars. Newsprint prices remain changeable. Finally, the newspaper is facing increased competition for classified ads, one of its major revenue streams. Web companies, such as monster.com, and portals, such as Yahoo! and Excite, have searchable classified ad categories that are much easier to use than the print classified section of the newspaper.

On the bright side, newspapers are still a fairly cost-effective way for local advertisers to reach local customers, and they continue to be the most important source of local news for their readers. Nonetheless, how long the current prosperity will last is anybody's guess.

■ Advertising Revenue

Advertising revenue comes from four separate sources:

1. Local retail advertising
2. Classified ads
3. National advertising
4. Prepaid inserts

Local retail advertising is purchased by stores and service establishments. Department stores, supermarkets, auto dealers, and discount scores are the businesses that buy large amounts of space. Classified advertising, which is bought by local businesses and individuals, is generally run in a special section in the back of the newspaper. Buyers and sellers purchase classified ads for a wide range of products and services. National advertising originates with manufacturers of products that need to reach a national market on a mass basis. The majority of these ads are for automobiles, food, airlines, and web-based companies. Prepaid inserts, or preprints, are advertising supplements put together by national, regional, and local businesses that are inserted into the copies of the paper. Companies such as Sears and Best Buy frequently use preprints. The paper charges the advertiser for the distribution of the preprints.

Local retail ads account for most advertising revenue, about 45 percent. Classified ads, however, are becoming more important, accounting for more than 40 percent of all advertising revenue, compared with about 35 percent in the early 1990s. Nonetheless, newspapers are worried that the classified category is not growing as fast as it might because of competition with online ad sites. National ads and preprints make up the remaining 15 percent.

Circulation Revenue

Circulation revenue includes all the receipts from selling the paper to the consumer. The newspaper, however, does not receive the total price paid by a reader for a copy of the paper because of the many distribution systems that are employed to get the newspaper to the consumer. The most common method is for the paper to sell copies to a distributor at wholesale prices, usually about 25 percent less than the retail price. Other methods include hiring full-time employees as carriers and billing subscribers in advance. These methods show promise, but they also increase the cost of distribution.

One closely studied factor important in determining circulation revenue is the effect of increased subscription and single-copy prices. In 1970, 89 percent of newspapers were priced at 10¢ a copy. In 2000, none cost less than 25¢. Most cost 50¢ or more. Sunday papers have shown similar increases. In 1970, the typical price was 25¢. By 2000, it was more than $1.50. The rising price of newspapers has probably had some negative impact on circulation revenue. Several papers have noted a decrease in subscriptions among older, fixed-income residents following a price increase.

General Expenses

The costs of running a newspaper can be viewed in several ways. One common method is to divide the costs by function:

1. News and editorial costs.
2. Expenses involved in selling local, national, and classified ads.
3. Mechanical costs, including typesetting and plate production.
4. Printing costs, such as newsprint (the paper), ink, and the cost of running the press.
5. Circulation and distribution costs.
6. General administrative costs, such as secretarial and clerical services and the cost of soliciting for subscriptions.

Some of these costs are variable. For example, the printing costs will increase as the number of printed copies increases. Distribution costs will also increase with circulation size. Other costs are fixed. The expense of sending a reporter to the airport to cover a visiting dignitary will be about the same for a paper with a circulation of 10,000 as for one with a circulation of 100,000. This means that the cost of running a newspaper will depend somewhat on the size of the paper. For a small paper (circulation about 25,000), general administrative costs would rank first, accounting for about one-third of all expenses. The cost of newsprint and ink would rank second, followed by mechanical costs. Total expenses for this size daily would run about \$3 million to \$5 million per year. In the case of a big-city daily (circulation 200,000), newsprint and ink costs rank first, followed by administrative expenses and mechanical costs. On the average, newsprint accounts for about 25 cents of every dollar spent by a paper.

FEEDBACK

The Audit Bureau of Circulations

The best-known feedback system for newspapers is that connected with the **Audit Bureau of Circulations (ABC).** During the early 1900s, with the growth of mass advertising, some publishers began inflating the number of readers in order to attract more revenue from advertisers. In an effort to check this deceptive practice, advertisers and publishers joined to form the ABC in 1914. The organization's purpose was to establish ground rules for counting circulation, to make sure that the rules were enforced, and to provide verified reports of circulation data. The ABC audits about three-fourths of all print media in the United States and Canada, about 2,600 publications.

The ABC functions in the following manner. Publishers keep detailed records of circulation data. Twice a year, publishers file a circulation statement with the ABC, which the ABC in turn disseminates to its clients. Once every year, the ABC audits publications to verify that the figures that have been reported are accurate. An ABC representative visits the publication and is free to examine records and files.

In an average year, the ABC's field staff of 90 travels approximately 300,000 miles and spends about 135,000 audit hours in verifying the facts on member publications' circulation. The cost of the ABC's services, about \$5 million per year, is financed through member dues and service fees.

Newspapers are turning to automation to save money. These robot paper movers work for the *Rocky Mountain News. (Courtesy FMC Corporation)*

The ABC has made its reports easier to understand by adding maps and bar charts that display five-year circulation trends. In addition, in 1993, the ABC approved guidelines for auditing electronic and online media.

Newspaper Audiences

As of 2000, approximately 56 million copies of morning and evening papers, either purchased at the newsstand or delivered to the doorstep, found their way into American homes every weekday. Daily newspaper circulation, in absolute terms, has decreased since 1970, as a glance at Table 4.3 shows. The population, however, has been increasing. To reflect this fact and to provide additional perspective, column four of the table presents the ratio of daily circulation to the total adult population of the United States (expressed in thousands). As can be seen, daily newspaper circulation is not keeping pace with the overall growth of the population.

The percentage of adults reading one or more papers every day has declined from about 80 percent in the early 1960s to about 57 percent in 2000. The most pronounced decline has occurred in the 18-to-29 and 30-to-44 age groups and among those who have not attended college. The overall drop in daily circulation has been most noticeable in urban areas. As Figure 4–4 shows, newspaper circulation in cities with more than a half-million residents has dropped about 24 percent from 1973 to 2000. Conversely, circulation in medium-size towns with populations from 50,000 to 500,000 has increased 46 percent. Circulation in smaller communities has decreased about 42 percent in the same period.

Why the overall decline? Some have attributed it to the increased mobility of Americans, the increase in single-person households, more expensive subscription and per-copy prices, a general decline in the level of reading ability among young people, and competition from other media.

Table 4.3	Daily and Weekly Newspaper Circulation			
Year	All Daily Papers	All Weekly Papers	Daily Circulation per 1,000 Adults	Weekly Circulation per 1,000 Adults
1930	39,589,000	—	455	
1940	41,132,000	—	415	
1950	53,829,000	—	487	
1960	58,882,000	21,328,000	475	172
1965	60,358,000	26,088,000	451	195
1970	62,108,000	29,423,000	428	203
1975	60,655,000	35,176,000	380	221
1980	62,201,840	40,970,000	360	245
1984	63,100,000	43,100,000	341	235
1990	62,327,962	56,181,047	329	298
1996	56,989,800	81,588,000*	312	432*
1999	55,979,332	74,457,621*	290	412*

Source: Compiled by author.

*1996 and 1999 weekly figures not comparable to prior years as a result of change in information collection procedures.

The traditional newspaper has always been an amalgamation of diverse content: local, national, and international news; sports scores; stock market reports; classified ads; editorials; weather; entertainment news; and so on. Over the years, the newspaper was the most convenient and cost-efficient form for packaging these items.

With the rise of the Internet, however, where publishing costs so little, niche websites can bleed off consumers who would have traditionally relied on the paper for information. The classifieds are the best example; they work much better on the net. They are searchable and not confined to a single geographic region. A job hunter can use a site such as monster.com to find job openings all across the country. People with odd items to sell find it cheaper and more effective to advertise on eBay rather than in the local paper. Some businesses have found it cheaper to set up their own

classified ad site, such as Realtor.com, rather than buy space in the newspaper. Since classified advertising is an important revenue stream for newspapers, it is not surprising that many papers have established partnerships with online classified websites.

Sports coverage is another example. Specialized sites such as ESPN.com or Sportsline.com offer more in-depth information and more up-to-the-minute scores. Current stock market quotes, analysis, and financial news are available on many websites. Entertainment news is available from numerous sites. The online news services offer breaking news all day long, not just at specific times in the morning, afternoon, or evening.

Will the print newspaper eventually come unglued, with all its parts being usurped by the web? Most experts think that scenario is unlikely. Most agree, however, that 10 years from now, the newspaper will be significantly different from today's model.

Print newspapers are losing some readers to online media. In 1995, about 4 percent of the U.S. population went online at least once a week to get their news. In 2000, the comparable figure was 25 percent. The key demographic group that reads most of its news online is young adults—the same group that reads print

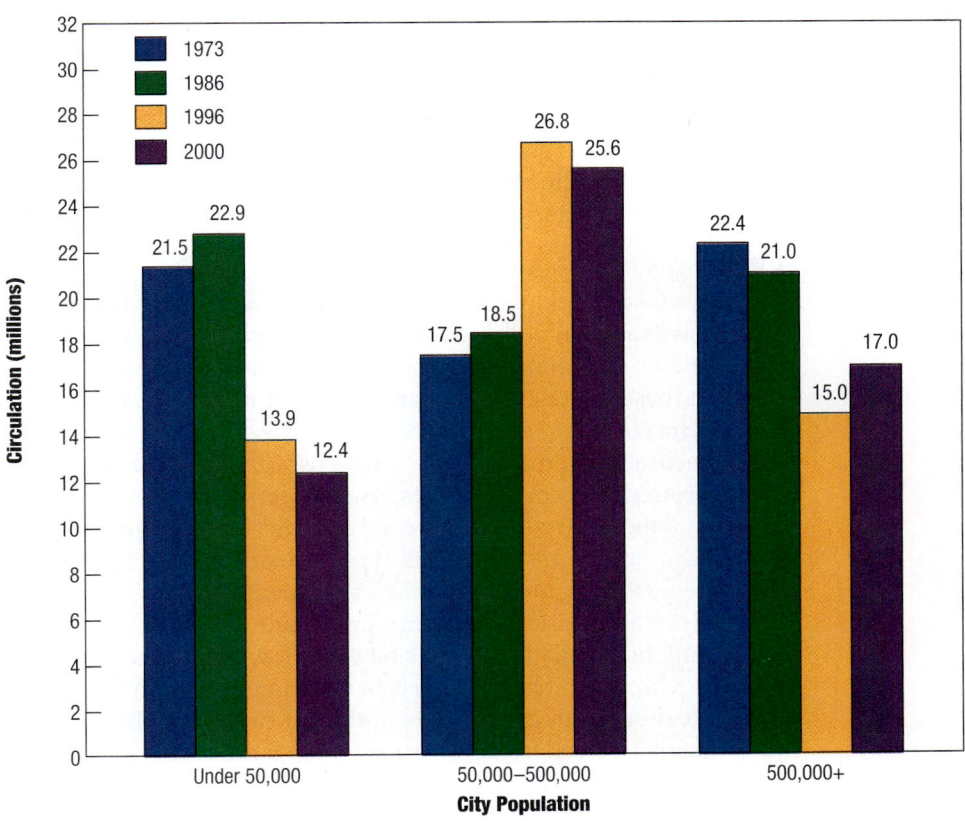

Figure 4–4

Fluctuations in Daily-Newspaper Circulation by Size of City, 1973–2000

papers the least. Some of these readers turn to online newspapers for their news; others go to portals, such as Excite and Yahoo!, or to other news sources, such as CNN.com, and skip newspapers entirely.

The number of people who visit the sites of online newspapers is impressive. On a typical weekday, *USA Today*'s website attracts more than 900,000 unique visitors. The *New York Times* online version is visited by about 300,000 people on an average weekday. Most experts agree that the number of people going online for news will increase steadily over the next few years.

THE NEWSPAPER INDUSTRY

The newspaper industry is a big employer. In 2000, newspaper employment exceeded 440,000 people. In fact, newspapers now rank among the leaders in the Labor Department's listing of the nation's manufacturing employees. Of these 440,000, about 70,000 are employed in the editorial side of the paper; an additional 50,000 work in promotion and advertising, and another 60,000 in the administrative area. The remainder work in the circulation and production departments. More women are entering careers in journalism. The 2000 workforce was about 48 percent female.

The economic prosperity of the past decade has helped improve the job market for those going into the journalism profession. More jobs were available, and average pay was increasing. Nonetheless, the newspaper industry has historically been one of the lowest-paying media industries. A 1999 survey by the *Columbia Journalism Review* found that entry-level reporters for print newspapers were making between $18,000 and $25,000, ranking them below their counterparts in broadcast and magazine journalism.

Online media have siphoned away many employees from print newspapers. One reason for this migration is financial. The same survey mentioned above found that average entry-level salaries for online reporters ranged from $30,000 to $35,000. Online media, however, cut back on personnel in 2000–2001 and many online reporters went back to the traditional print newspaper.

Entry-Level Positions

A person seeking an entry-level job as a reporter has the best chance of landing a job at a small daily paper or weekly. Starting out at a small paper will give a newcomer experience in several areas of newspaper work, since the division of labor at these papers is less clear. A reporter might also function as a photographer, edit wire copy, and write headlines. One possible way to break into the profession is to secure a summer job or an internship. Additionally, some people break into the profession as proofreaders, rewrite persons, or researchers.

Other entry-level jobs can be found in the business side of the paper. Students who are interested in this type of work should have a background in business, advertising, and economics, along with a knowledge of mass communication. Since advertising is such an important source of newspaper revenue, most newspapers will gladly accept a newcomer who wishes to work in the sales department.

Opportunities also exist in the circulation department for those interested in working with distributors and local carriers. Skills in organization and management are needed for these positions. Since controlling costs has become an important factor in operating a profitable paper, there are also beginning positions for accountants, cost analysts, and market researchers.

Of course, online newspapers represent a further opportunity. The kinds of jobs that are available are varied and are still being defined: Information has to be filed in the appropriate places, files must be updated, graphics need to be designed, e-mail must be answered, story leads suggested by subscribers need to be checked out, and so forth.

▨ Upward Mobility

A person who is selecting an entry-level position in newspapers should consider where the job might lead and how long it will take to get there. In the case of a reporter, upward mobility can come in one of two ways. A reporter can advance by becoming skilled in editing and move up to the position of copyeditor or perhaps state editor, regional editor, or wire editor. The ultimate goal for this person would be the city editor's or managing editor's slot. Other reporters might not wish to take on the additional administrative and desk work that goes with a managerial position. If that is the case, then career advancement consists of moving on to larger-circulation papers in big cities or to increased specialization in one field of reporting.

On the business side, the route for advancement in the advertising department usually leads from the classifieds to the national advertising division. This department works with manufacturers of nationally distributed products and services and plans display advertising for these companies. The national ad staff often works hand in hand with the newspaper's national sales representative. The national reps have offices in major cities where they solicit ads for local papers. Those who begin in the circulation department can eventually rise to the position of circulation manager. Ultimately, the top job that can be reached, short of publisher, is that of business manager, the person in charge of the entire business side of the paper.

■ MAIN POINTS

- Newspapers in colonial America were published with permission of the local government. A free press did not appear until after the Revolution.

- The mass newspaper arrived in the 1830s with the publication of Benjamin Day's *New York Sun*, the first of the penny-press papers.

- The era of yellow journalism popularized sensationalism, crusades, and human-interest reporting and introduced more attractive newspaper designs.

- Many newspapers were merged or folded during the early 1900s. Tabloid papers became popular. The trend toward consolidation would continue to the years following World War II.

- There are four types of daily papers: national newspapers, large metro dailies, suburban dailies, and small-town dailies. Other major types of papers include weeklies, special-service newspapers, and minority newspapers.

- More than 1,000 papers now have online versions.

- Newspaper ownership is characterized by large group owners and declining competition.

- Newspapers are currently enjoying financial prosperity but are worried about competition from online media.

- Newspaper audiences are measured by the Audit Bureau of Circulations. Newspaper readership has declined for the past several decades, with big-city dailies hardest hit by the decrease.

■ QUESTIONS FOR REVIEW

1. Trace the changes in the definition of *news* from the 1600s to 2000.

2. What are the defining characteristics of newspapers?

3. What are some of the advantages the traditional ink-and-paper newspaper has over the online version? What are some of the advantages the online version has over the print version?

4. What are the main revenue sources for newspapers?

■ QUESTIONS FOR CRITICAL THINKING

1. Why don't young people read a newspaper? What, if anything, could newspapers do to recapture this audience segment?

2. Has the growth of newspaper group owners helped or hurt the newspaper industry? Has it helped or hurt society?

3. What is your opinion of public journalism? Does it expand the role of the newspaper into areas that are controversial?

4. Will the online version eventually replace the print version of a newspaper? Why or why not?

■ KEY TERMS

political press (p. 86)
First Amendment (p. 86)
penny press (p. 88)
yellow journalism (p. 91)
jazz journalism (p. 92)

tabloids (p. 92)
public journalism (p. 94)
portal (p. 95)
circulation (p. 98)
zoned editions (p. 100)

newshole (p. 105)
joint-operating agreement (JOA) (p. 108)
Audit Bureau of Circulations (ABC) (p. 113)

■ SUGGESTIONS FOR FURTHER READING

The books listed below are good sources for additional information about the history and organization of the newspaper industry.

Emery, Michael, and Edwin Emery, with Nancy Roberts. *The Press and America.* 8th edition. Boston: Allyn and Bacon, 1996.

Folkerts, Jean, and Dwight Teeter. *Voices of a Nation.* 3rd edition. Boston: Allyn and Bacon, 1998.

Graham, Katharine. *Personal History.* New York: Vintage Books, 1998.

Hamilton, John, and George Krimsky. *Hold the Press: The Inside Story on Newspapers.* Baton Rouge, LA: Louisiana State University Press, 1997.

Keeble, Richard. *The Newspaper Handbook.* New York: Routledge, 1998.

Lauterer, Jock. *Community Journalism.* Ames, IA: Iowa State University Press, 1995.

Murray, Donald. *Writing to Deadline.* Portsmouth, NH: Heinemann, 2000.

Picard, Robert, and Jeffrey Brody. *The Newspaper Publishing Industry.* Needham Heights, MA: Allyn and Bacon, 1996.

■ SURFING THE INTERNET

The following are examples of some sites that deal with the newspaper industry. All listings were current as of late 2000.

www.cln.com/newsstand/current
Creative Loafing Online. A guide to the arts, culture, and entertainment. A good illustration of the non-traditional weekly press.

www.decaturdailydemocrat.com
A good example of a slick online paper published by a small-town daily.

www.naa.org
Site of the Newspaper Association of America, a major industry trade organization. Contains information on newspaper circulation, public policy, and diversity, as well as links to the organization's *presstime* magazine. A hot-link feature allows visitors to see a list of newspapers online in a chosen state.

www.theonion.com
It may look like an authentic online paper, but it's not.

www.usatoday.com
Colorful site of the national daily *USA Today*. Site will look familiar because it is modeled after the paper-and-ink version.

CHAPTER 5 Magazines

Every day, the Internet auction house eBay puts 1.8 million items up for sale, including old stuffed alligators, Barbie dolls, Furbies, and $200,000 Lamborghini automobiles. The site gets about 140 million hits every week.

Of more relevance to this chapter, however, is the 1999 launch of *eBay* magazine, a publication with a circulation of 400,000, which includes articles on collectibles, web navigation, and new technologies. It is interesting to note that eBay, a recent creation of the new digital world, has turned to one of the oldest traditional media, the magazine, to promote itself.

Indeed, *eBay* is a good example of how magazines are coping with the digital age. Of all the media discussed in Part Two, magazines have worked out the most symbiotic relationship with the Internet. Traditional magazines publish both print and online editions. Many magazines use their online versions to sell subscriptions to their print versions. Some magazine websites sell books, CDs, or other products manufactured by the magazine's parent company. And, as with eBay, the Internet has become a source of new magazines.

This chapter will examine the history, structure, and organization of the magazine industry, with particular emphasis on how magazines are handling their entry into the digital age.

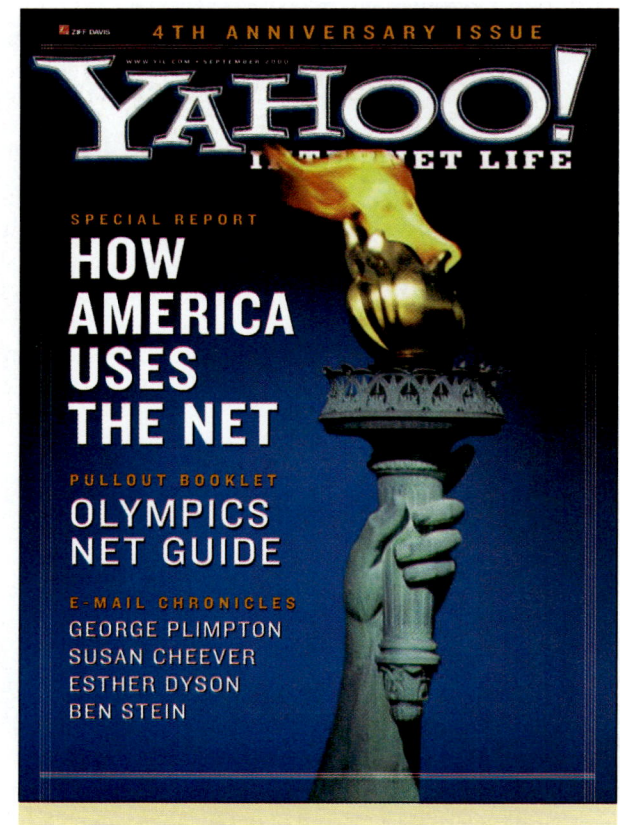

Old media/new media. *Yahoo! Internet Life* is a combination of one of the oldest mass media (the print magazine) and one of the newest (a website). *(Reprinted from Yahoo! Internet Life, September 2000, with permission. Copywright ©2001 Ziff Davis Media Inc. All Rights Reserved.)*

 **HISTORY**

The Colonial Period

In colonial times, *magazine* meant "warehouse" or "depository," a place where various types of provisions were stored under one roof. The first **magazines** printed in America were patterned after this model; they were to be storehouses of varied literary materials gathered from books, pamphlets, and newspapers, and bound together under one cover.

It was Ben Franklin who first announced plans to start a magazine in the colonies. Unfortunately for Ben, a competitor named Andrew Bradford got wind of his idea and beat Franklin to the punch. Bradford's *American Magazine* was published a few days before Franklin's *General Magazine* in 1741. The two publications carried political and economic articles aimed at an intelligent audience.

Both Franklin's and Bradford's magazines were ambitious ventures in that they were designed for readers in all 13 colonies and deliberately tried to influence public opinion; however, both quickly folded because of financial problems. The next significant attempt at magazine publishing occurred in Philadelphia when another Bradford (this one named William) started the *American Magazine and Monthly Chronicle* in 1757. This publication also contained the usual blend of political and economic articles mixed with a little humor; it was well edited and able to support itself for a year.

As America's political relations with England deteriorated, magazines, like newspapers, assumed a significant political role. Thomas Paine, who, in his rousing pamphlet *Common Sense,* argued for separation from England, became editor of the *Pennsylvania Magazine.* This publication strongly supported the Revolution and was a significant political force during the early days of the war. It became an early casualty of the conflict, however, and closed down in 1776.

All these early magazines were aimed at a specialized audience—one that was educated, literate, and primarily urban. Their overall impact was to encourage literary and artistic expression and to unify the colonies during America's struggle for independence from England.

After the Revolution

Magazines popular during the late 18th and early 19th centuries contained a mix of political and topical articles directed primarily at an educated elite. The birth of the modern news magazine can be traced back to this period. *Niles Weekly Register,* which reported current events of the time, was read throughout the country. The *North American Review,* started in 1815, was more parochial in its contents, focusing primarily on New England art and politics.

Politics was also reflected in other magazines of the period. One of the most influential was the *Port Folio,* edited by the colorful nonconformist Joseph Dennie. Dennie's intended audience was a select one; he wished to reach "Men of Affluence, Men of Liberality, and Men of Letters." Although the major thrust of the paper was political, Dennie interspersed travelogues, theater reviews, satirical essays, and even jokes.

Sara Josepha Buell Hale was responsible for having Thanksgiving declared an annual holiday and was the author of the popular nursery rhyme "Mary Had a Little Lamb." She was also one of the women who left a lasting impression on 19th-century American journalism.

Sara Josepha Buell married David Hale, a New Hampshire lawyer, who encouraged her to write articles and poems for the local magazines. By the time she was 38, she had published 17 poems, many magazine articles, two short stories, a literary review, and a novel.

Her literary accomplishments brought her to the attention of Louis Godey, publisher of *Godey's Lady's Book,* who offered her the position of editor. She brought to the magazine an intimate editor–reader relationship that proved so popular that the magazine had a circulation of 150,000 by 1860, a remarkable figure for the time.

Sara Hale not only edited *Godey's Lady's Book,* but also wrote about half of every issue. In addition, she found time to champion women's rights and was influential in persuading Matthew Vassar to start the college that still bears his name.

She spent 40 years editing the magazine and finally retired at age 89. Thanks to her efforts, *Godey's Lady's Book* is credited with being the best women's magazine of the period.

The Penny-Press Era

While the penny press was opening up new markets for newspapers (see Chapter 4), magazine publishers were also expanding their appeal and coverage. The *Knickerbocker, Graham's Magazine,* and the *Saturday Evening Post,* all established between 1820 and 1840, were written not so much for the intelligentsia as for the generally literate middle classes. By 1842, *Graham's,* under the direction of Edgar Allan Poe, had a circulation of 40,000. The growing social and economic importance of women was illustrated by the birth of *Godey's Lady's Book* in 1830 and *Peterson's* in 1842. These two magazines offered articles on fashion, morals, diets, and health, and printed elaborate, hand-colored engravings in their pages. *Godey's,* under the editorship of Sara Hale, was a pioneer for women's rights and was the first magazine to campaign for wider recognition of women writers. (See Media Probe, "Sara Josepha Buell Hale.")

In 1850, *Harper's Monthly* was started as a magazine that would present material that had already appeared in other sources (rather like the *Reader's Digest,* except that the articles were reprinted in full). *Harper's* also included elaborate woodcut illustrations along with its articles in double-sized issues. *Harper's Weekly* was instituted seven years later and was to become famous for its illustrations of the Civil War. In 1863, this magazine began publishing reproductions of Mathew Brady's war photographs.

The sensationalist and crusading approach of the penny press translated itself into at least two magazines. *Frank Leslie's Illustrated Newspaper* was a 16-page weekly that sold for a dime and concentrated on lurid illustrations of murders, morgues, and mayhem. The *New York Ledger,* started in 1855 by Robert Bonner, printed the best work of the period's popular writers and ran melodramatic serials in issue after issue.

The most famous crusade was probably that of *Harper's Weekly* against the corrupt political administration in New York in 1870. Under the control of William "Boss" Tweed, a group of unscrupulous politicians managed to bilk the city out of approximately $200 million. The editorial cartoons of Thomas Nast were credited with helping bring down this ring.

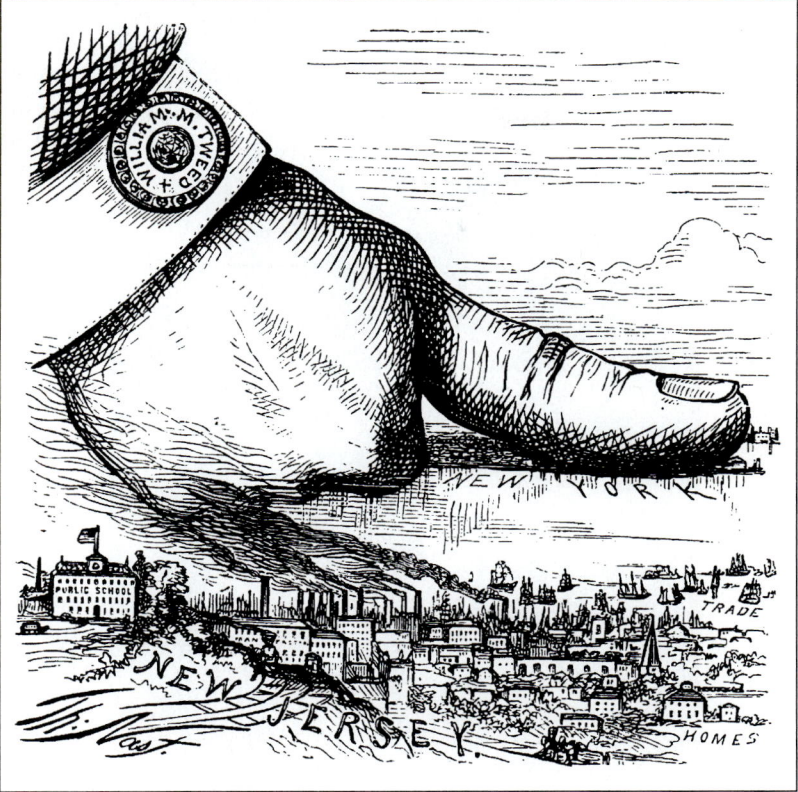

This political cartoon, titled "Under the Thumb," was created by Thomas Nast and appeared in *Harper's Weekly* during the summer of 1871. *(The Granger Collection)*

The Magazine Boom

In 1860, there were approximately 260 magazines published in the United States; by 1900, there were 1,800. Why the surge? The primary factors were more available money, better printing techniques that lowered prices, and especially the Postal Act of 1879, which gave magazines special mailing rates. It was possible to aim for a national market on a mass scale, and several magazines set out to do just that.

The most successful of the magazines seeking a mass market was the *Ladies' Home Journal,* founded by Cyrus Curtis in 1881. The first issue, eight pages long, contained an illustrated short story, an article on growing flowers, fashion notes, child care advice, needlework hints, and recipes. Curtis was the first to realize the potential for national advertising in the magazine industry.

The general crusading spirit of the press spilled over onto the pages of leading magazines of the late 1890s and early 1900s. Theodore Roosevelt dubbed the magazines that embraced this reform movement **muckrakers.** Corrupt practices in big business was the first topic to activate the muckrakers' zeal. *McClure's* ran an exposé of the Standard Oil Company by Ida M. Tarbell. Although it carried the innocuous title of "History of the Standard Oil Company," the article was filled with dynamite, for it revealed bribery, fraud, unfair business practices, and violence. Shocking stories on political corruption in big cities and another series on crooked practices in the railroad industry followed Tarbell's initial effort. Other magazines joined in. *Cosmopolitan* published "The Treason of the Senate" in 1906.

The beginning of life for *Life:* The magazine's first cover was shot by famous photographer Margaret Bourke-White. *(Courtesy LIFE Picture Service, Photograph by Margaret Bourke-White.)*

LIFE

NOVEMBER 23, 1936 **10** CENTS

It followed up with attacks on the International Harvester Company. By 1912, the trend toward crusades and exposés had spent itself. Many of the problems it uncovered had been remedied. Most important, the public had grown tired of it and magazines had to search for other ways to attract readers.

Between the Wars

The most striking characteristic of magazine development during the 20th century was a trend toward specialization. This movement was given impetus by the increasing importance of national advertising within the industry (in 1929 magazines received 42 cents out of every dollar spent on national advertising in the major media). A magazine had to not only please its readers, but also attract an audience that would be valuable to advertisers. So magazine publishers had to become experts in marketing procedures.

Shifting economic conditions and changing lifestyles in the decades following World War I also influenced magazine development. Three distinct types evolved in the years between World War I and World War II: (1) the digest, (2) the news magazine, and (3) the pictorial magazine.

The finest example of the digest genre, *Reader's Digest,* appeared in 1922. Although this magazine reprinted articles that had appeared elsewhere, it first condensed and edited the material so that it could be read by people in a hurry.

The idea of a news magazine was not new—examples could be found in the 19th century. *Time,* however, borrowed little from its predecessors. From its beginning in 1923, *Time* based its format on an original concept: the distillation and compartmentalization of news under various departments. Other innovations included the use of the narrative style to report news stories; group journalism produced by the pooling of the efforts of reporters, writers, and editors into anonymous articles; the institution of a large research department; and a brash, punchy, jargonish writing style. The magazine prospered slowly, but by 1930 it was turning a substantial profit. Two imitators, *Newsweek* and *U.S. News,* appeared in 1933.

In the mid-30s, two magazines, *Life* and *Look,* revived the tradition of the pictorial weekly originated by *Harper's* and *Leslie's. Life* was launched in 1936 and had almost a quarter of a million subscribers before it even had a name. *Life* featured public figures caught in unguarded moments, photo essays, occasional glamour

shots, and articles on the arts. In this format, *Life* would live for 36 years (it would reappear in the late 1970s in a totally different format). *Look* hit the newsstands in 1937, just two months behind *Life*. *Look* lacked the current-affairs emphasis of its forerunner and concentrated more on personalities and features. Over the years, it evolved into a family-oriented magazine. *Look* expired in 1972.

◼ The Postwar Period

Magazines of the postwar era reflected publishers' firm belief that the one way to become profitable was to specialize. Increased leisure time created a market for sports magazines such as *Field and Stream, Sports Afield, Golf Digest, Popular Boating,* and *Sports Illustrated.* Scientific advances also generated a resurgence of a popularized version of *Scientific American.*

The rapid expansion of urban communities and urban lifestyles gave rise to many specialized publications. Liberalized attitudes toward sex prompted such ventures as *Confidential* (1952) and the trendsetting *Playboy* (1953). During the 1960s, the rebirth of an interest in urban culture encouraged the rise of "city" magazines, of which *New York* is probably the best example. For the black press, the most significant development in the 1950s was the expansion of black magazines. John Johnson had started *Negro Digest* back in 1942 and used his profits to publish *Ebony,* whose format imitated that of *Life,* in 1945. In the early years of the 1950s, he added *Jet,* a weekly news magazine, and *Tan.* These were followed later by *Black World* and *Essence.*

◼ The Contemporary Magazine Industry

The 1980s and 1990s saw several notable trends in the magazine industry. Magazine publishing continued to become more concentrated as big publishing conglomerates owned more magazines. In 1999, the top five publishers accounted for about 33 percent of the revenue of the entire industry.

Circulation woes continued for general-interest magazines. *Reader's Digest* dropped 9 percent from 1998 to 1999, while *TV Guide* declined almost 12 percent. On the other hand, specialized publications, such as *Maxim* (men's interest), *Red Herring* (business technology), and *Cristina La Revista* (Spanish entertainment and lifestyle), showed large circulation gains for the same period.

Helen Gurley grew up in poverty in rural Arkansas. As a young woman, she worked as a secretary and later got a job writing copy at an advertising agency. After marrying movie producer David Brown in 1959, she published her account of her days as a "bachelorette" in *Sex and the Single Girl.* The book's message that single girls didn't have to marry to have sex was radical for its time and helped fuel the sexual revolution of the 1960s. Gloria Steinem called Brown a pioneer of early feminism.

In 1965 Brown took over the editorship of *Cosmopolitan.* At the time, *Cosmopolitan* was struggling and lacked focus. Brown decided to abandon *Cosmo*'s tradition as a serious current events magazine and reshaped it into a modern women's magazine. The new *Cosmo* had splashy graphics and provocative articles that were aimed at the same young women who had made *Sex and the Single Girl* a best-seller. She invented "That Cosmo Girl" to guide editorial policy, put sexy-

Helen Gurley Brown holds a copy of *Cosmopolitan,* the magazine she edited from 1965 to 1997. Under her leadership, *Cosmo* wrestled with the issue of how women should define themselves in the age of liberation. *(AP/Wide World Photos)*

looking women on the cover, and went so far as to include nude male centerfolds. The tag line on the *Cosmo* website sums up the *Cosmo* point of view: "Land that man, ace your job, and look your sexiest ever."

The new format was an immediate hit with its target audience. Circulation tripled to 2.5 million readers. In the 1990s, *Cosmo* was earning about $50 million a year. It was the largest-selling women's magazine in each of the 27 countries worldwide where it was published.

Many feminists criticized Brown for her emphasis on physical attractiveness and her apparent philosophy that women should focus their lives on attracting and pleasing men. Undaunted, Brown continued to edit the magazine her way for 32 years, until she stepped down from the editorship in 1996. At the turn of the century, at age 78, she was still serving as consulting editor for *Cosmo*'s 27 international editions.

It was also becoming harder for magazines to attract readers. Supermarkets and other retail outlets were becoming more selective about the number of magazines they would carry on their shelves. As a result, single-copy sales generally declined. Further, those sweepstakes promotions ("You may have already won $1 million!") that historically fueled subscription sales have come under legal pressure (see Ethical Issues, "Don't Hold Your Breath Waiting for the Prize Patrol") and are much less influential.

Salon.com was one of the first online magazines. *(This artical first appeared in Salon.com, at http://www.Salon.com. An online version remains in the Salon archives. Reprinted with permission.)*

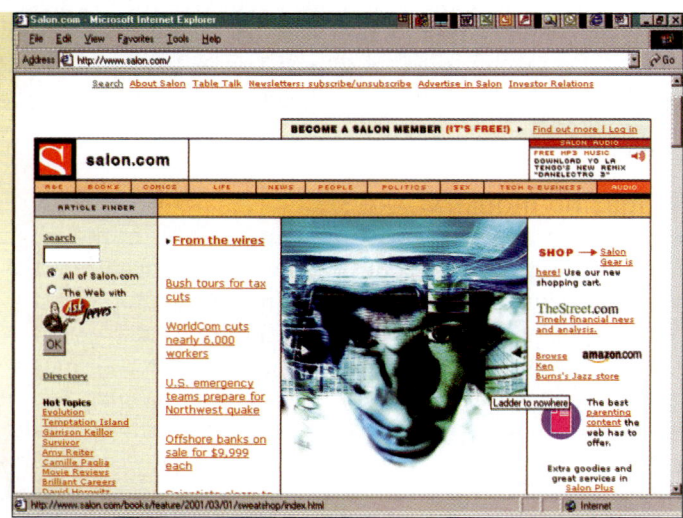

The biggest business development was the merger of the world's largest magazine publisher (Time Warner) with the world's largest Internet company, America OnLine (AOL). The new company offered many opportunities for cross-pollination between the print and digital media. All of Time Warner's magazines, for example, could sell subscriptions on AOL.

Several magazines, such as *Slate* and *Salon,* appeared in an online-only form. Many print magazine publishers viewed these new competitors with some apprehension because they feared that they would take away readers and advertising revenue. As it turned out, they needn't have worried. As a group, online-only magazines were generally money-losing propositions. A few narrowly targeted "e-zines" were successful (see Media Probe, "The Wonderful (and Sometimes Weird) World of E-zines"), but in general, as discussed in more detail below, the Internet turned out to be a friend rather than an enemy to traditional print magazines.

MAGAZINES IN THE DIGITAL AGE

When the Internet was first becoming popular, many publishers feared that it would spell the end for the printed magazine. It was thought that specialized web magazines available for free on the net would siphon readers and advertising from the traditional magazine. Online magazines were the "new" media that would inevitably replace the "old" glossy-paper magazine. Over the years, however, magazine publishers have come to the conclusion that the Internet is more of a complement to the traditional magazine that a competitor.

An *e-zine* is a magazine that exists only on the web. Small companies, organizations, or individuals with a common cause or common point of view start some e-zines. Other e-zines are started just for the fun of it. E-zines illustrate the tremendous diversity of web magazines. Go to *www.meer.net* to find a list of more than 4,000 e-zines. Some of the more intriguing are:

- *Eyewash:* The clearinghouse for Lee Marvin studies.
- *mutt:* Has nothing to do with dogs. It's a collection of fiction, poetry, and essays.
- *LatinoBaseball.com:* News and information about (surprise!) Latino baseball players.

- *My First Billion.com:* An optimistic journal about business administration.
- *FireGirl:* Everything you ever wanted to know about hot chiles.
- *Fascist Panties:* An e-zine that features political essays, rants, and poetry. (No, I don't know where they got that title.)
- *Lies People Tell:* The truth about the lies people tell. Which lies are the most common? (1) I've never felt better, (2) Sorry, I'm late; traffic was awful, (3) She (or he) is just a friend.

Symbiosis

At the start of the new century, almost all major print magazines had an online counterpart. One 1999 survey of consumer magazines found that only 7 percent did not have their own website. The same situation exists among business magazines. The trade organization American Business Press changed its name to American Business Media when it found that more than 90 percent of its members had websites. Most experts agree that it would be difficult to start a new print magazine without also starting a website. For example, *ESPN The Magazine* and *Cosmo-Girl!* debuted simultaneously in print and online.

The print version and the online version of magazines complement each other in various ways. Many magazines, such as *Newsweek,* refer readers to their websites for additional information and longer versions of stories. Visitors to magazine websites can subscribe online to the printed version. In addition, the website can be used to extend a magazine's brand and to attract new readers to the print version. Prevention.com features interactive tools, such as a calorie counter and a recipe search engine, as well as a section that lets visitors ask questions of experts. Many consumers are attracted first by the content on the website and then search out the magazine. In 1999, more than 45,000 subscriptions to *Prevention* were generated online.

Additional Revenue Streams

Many magazine publishers use their websites for e-commerce. Sometimes this takes the form of selling products produced by the parent company, such as books, DVDs, or CDs. Another arrangement is for a publisher to form a partnership with an online retailer and use the magazine's website to attract customers to the retailer. The magazine makes its money by taking a small percentage of the sales or by charging a flat fee to the retailer. *Modern Bride,* for example, has a partnership with Weddingnetwork.com.

Further, web-based companies, or "dot-coms," have become a significant source of advertising revenue. Web companies spent more than $900 million on magazine advertising in 1999, an increase of 348 percent from 1998. Put another way, dot-coms accounted for about 8 percent of all magazine advertising in 1999, compared with about 2 percent in 1998. Dot-coms, however, fell upon hard times in 2000–2001 and it's doubtful that their advertising purchases will be as significant in the future.

Reverse Launches

As mentioned at the beginning of the chapter, some online ventures have started their own print magazines. *Yahoo! Internet Life* has a circulation of about 1 million. A travel magazine spun off from Expedia.com was launched in 2000. Space.com launched *Space.com Illustrated* in the same year. One advantage for magazines that spring from existing websites is that they can use their online sites to promote their new product directly to the target audience.

Print to Portal

New technologies (see Media Probe, "Printed Page to Cyberspace in One Easy Step") will make it easier to make the jump from the printed magazine page to cyberspace. Scanning codes embedded in a print article or an advertisement will take readers directly to a website, making for a seamless transition between print and digital media.

In sum, unlike some other media industries (see Chapters 6 and 8), where there is genuine fear that the Internet will drastically change the customary way of distributing their products, the magazine industry has learned to work with the Internet to supplement its traditional print version and to expand and enrich the reading experience for consumers.

DEFINING FEATURES OF MAGAZINES

The first defining feature of magazines is that, of all the media discussed in this book, they attract the most specialized audiences. There are publications that are designed to reach specific demographic groups (*Modern Maturity, Maxim*); specific occupational groups (*Pointe,* the magazine for ballerinas, *Builder*); specific interest groups (*Cigar Aficionado, American History*); specific political groups (*National Review, Mother Jones*); specific geographic groups (*Southern Living, Arizona Highways*); and a host of other very specific groups (*Latin CEO*).

Second, magazines are the medium most in tune with social, demographic, economic, and cultural trends. As consumer and business needs and interests change, new magazines emerge and existing magazines fine-tune their content. The growing popularity of video games prompted the creation of several magazines with a focus on such games. The emergence of the home computer spawned several computing magazines. And the emergence of the Internet has been accompanied by the debut of several magazines devoted to the web.

Third, as we have seen, magazines can influence social trends. Magazines helped fuel the American Revolution. The muckrakers at the turn of the 20th century prompted social reform. In the 1950s, *Playboy* started the sexual revolution in the United States. In the 1970s, *Ms.* helped usher in the women's movement.

Finally, traditional magazines are packaged in a format that is portable and convenient, and that features high-quality print and exceptional graphics. Although online magazines will carve out a niche for themselves, the traditional print magazine will probably be around for a long time.

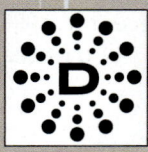

Almost every print ad these days carries the URL of the advertiser so that consumers can go to the website for more information. Unfortunately, that requires the reader to write down or remember the URL and then correctly type in a series of letters, dots, and slashes to get to the site.

A couple of new scanning technologies now make it possible for the reader to get to the appropriate website without typing in a single letter. One system, offered by a company called Digital Convergence, uses a tiny black bar that appears at the top or bottom of the printed page. The bar is actually a miniature Universal Product Code (UPC) that is linked to a web address. When a reader passes a handheld scanner connected to a computer over the bar code, the appropriate web page pops up on the computer screen. For example, a magazine ad for the Ford Motor Company's Taurus model would contain a bar code that would take the reader directly to the appropriate page at Ford's website.

The Digimarc Corporation presents an alternative technology. A tiny "D" symbol appears on the lower corner of the printed item. The symbol signals that the page contains a digital watermark that makes it "web ready." When the item is held up to a Digimarc MediaBridge enabled Webcam, the appropriate web page is displayed. This system made its debut in the August 2000 issue of *Wired* magazine.

There are, of course, some drawbacks to this approach. Consumers need to have handheld scanners, flat scanners, or Webcams for it to work. And they have to take the printed material to their computer for the system to work. Software is free and available on a variety of sites, including each of the company's own websites. The companies were also looking at ways to use the technology with personal digital assistants with wireless Internet access, thus making the technology more portable.

Whatever the final shape, the technology has tremendous potential. Website codes could be included on the business cards of salespeople, taking potential customers directly to the website. The codes could be placed on CDs or DVDs or even on cereal boxes, allowing almost any object to become an Internet gateway.

ORGANIZATION OF THE MAGAZINE INDUSTRY

One of the problems in discussing the magazine industry is deciding what exactly is a magazine. The dictionary defines *magazine* as a "periodical publication, usually with a paper cover, containing miscellaneous articles and often with illustrations or photographs." This definition is broad enough to include *TV Guide,* with a circulation of more than 11 million; *Water Scooter,* a magazine for boating enthusiasts; *Sky,* given away to airline passengers by Delta Airlines; *Successful Farmer,* the magazine of farm management; *Go,* distributed to Goodyear tire dealers; *The Journal of Social Psychology; Gloria Pitzer's National Homemakers Newsletter;* and the *Swine Flu Claim and Litigation Reporter.* There are around 11,000 to 12,000 magazines published in the United States. Both the number and the diversity of these publications are staggering. For example, *Standard Rate and Data Service (SRDS),* a monthly directory of advertising rates and other pertinent information about magazines, lists 83 automotive magazines, 41 horse-oriented publications, and four periodicals devoted to snowmobiling. There are more than 5,000 magazines sold regularly on newsstands, and the number of new consumer titles continues to go up: more than 894 in 1999. Obviously, classifying the magazine industry into coherent categories is a vexing problem. For our purposes, we will employ two organizational schemes. The first classifies magazines into five main content categories:

1. General consumer magazines.
2. Business publications.
3. Literary reviews and academic journals.
4. Newsletters.
5. Public relations magazines.

A glance at any newsstand will illustrate that consumer magazines fall into major general-interest categories such as sports, health, computers, business, and women's interests. *(M. Dwyer/Stock Boston)*

The second divides the magazine industry into the three traditional components of manufacturing: production, distribution, and retailing.

Content Categories

General Consumer Magazines A consumer magazine is one that can be acquired by anyone, through a subscription or a single-copy purchase or by obtaining a free copy. These magazines are generally shelved at the corner newsstand or local bookstore. (Other types of magazines are usually not available to the general public.) These publications are called consumer magazines because readers can buy the products and services that are advertised in their pages. One noticeable trend in the content of consumer magazines is, as we have mentioned, the movement away from broad, general appeal to the more specialized. *SRDS* lists approximately 50 content groupings of consumer magazines, ranging from "Antiques," with 25 publications, to "Women's," with 92 titles. Some of the better-known consumer magazines are *People, Time, Reader's Digest, TV Guide, Sports Illustrated,* and *Woman's Day* (see Table 5.1). Note that consumer magazines can exist in both print and online versions.

Business Publications Business magazines (also called trade publications) serve a particular business, industry, or profession. They are not sold on newsstands, and their readership is limited to those in the profession or business. The products

Table 5.1	Top 10 Consumer Magazines, 1999	
Title	**Circulation (in millions)**	**Percent Change from 1996**
Modern Maturity	20.5	0
Reader's Digest	12.5	−17
TV Guide	11.1	−15
National Geographic	8.5	−6
Better Homes and Gardens	7.6	0
Family Circle	5.0	−4
Good Housekeeping	4.5	−8
Ladies' Home Journal	4.5	0
Woman's Day	4.3	0
McCalls	4.2	0

Source: *Advertising Age,* March 13, 2000, p. 26.

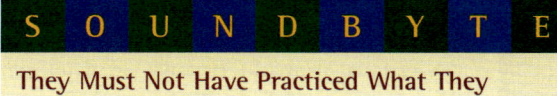

advertised in these publications are generally those that would be purchased by business organizations or professionals rather than by the general public. *Business Publications Rates and Data,* a companion publication to *SRDS,* lists approximately 4,000 titles of business magazines. Most of these magazines are published by independent publishing companies that are not connected with the fields they serve. For example, McGraw-Hill and Penton are two private publishing companies that publish business magazines in a wide variety of areas. Other business publications are put out by professional organizations, which publish the magazine as a service to their members. The degree of specialization of these magazines is seen in the medical field, which has approximately 375 publications serving various medical specializations. Some business publications are called vertical because they cover all aspects of one field. For example, *Pulp and Paper* reports on all segments of the paper mill industry. Other publications are called horizontal because they deal with a certain business function, no matter in what industry it exists. *Selling,* for example, would be targeted at salespeople in all industries. Leading business magazines include *Computerworld, Oil and Gas Journal,* and *Medical Economics.* Business publishers are also active in supplying databases and computer bulletin board systems to their clients. Like consumer magazines, business publications can exist in print and online.

Literary Reviews and Academic Journals   Hundreds of literary reviews and academic journals, generally with circulations under 10,000, are published by nonprofit organizations and funded by universities, foundations, or professional organizations. They may publish four or fewer issues per year, and a large number do not accept advertising. These publications cover the entire range of literary and academic interests, including such journals as *The Kenyon Review, Theater Design and Technology, European Urology, Journalism Quarterly, Poultry and Egg Marketing,* and *The Journal of Japanese Botany.* Some literary reviews and journals have online versions.

Newsletters   When some people hear the word "newsletter," they may think of a club, PTA, or church bulletin filled with helpful hints. Although these newsletters are important to their readers, they are not the kind we emphasize here. We are talking about newsletters typically four to eight pages long and usually composed by desktop publishing. They are sold by subscription, and in recent years they have become big business. In fact, there is even a *Newsletter on Newsletters,* published for those who edit newsletters. The coverage area of a newsletter may be broad or narrow. It might deal with one particular business or government agency, or it might report on a business function that crosses industry lines. The *Federal Budget Report,* for example, reports on just the president's budget and appropriations. On the other hand, the *Daily Labor Report* covers congressional actions that have an impact on many industries.

Newsletters are extremely specialized, with small circulations (typically under 10,000) but with high subscription prices. Typical fees are about $200 to $300 a year, but fees of $600 to $800 are not unheard of and some daily newsletters cost as much as $4,000 annually. Some influential newsletters are *Aerospace Daily, Oil Spill Intelligence Report,* and *Drug Enforcement Report.* In the mass communication area, the *Gallagher Report* and the *Media Monitor* cover events in the print and broadcast industries, and *Communication Booknotes* reviews new books about the mass media.

Public Relations Magazines   These are magazines published by a sponsoring company and intended specifically for one of its publics. An internal public relations (PR) magazine is aimed at employees, salespeople, and dealers. An external PR magazine would be directed to stockholders, potential customers, and technical service providers.

These publications typically carry little advertising, apart from promotional items for the sponsoring organization. *Marathon World* and *Target* are among the thousands of PR magazines that are published every year. These publications also have their own professional organization, the International Association of Business Communicators. Most PR magazines exist only in print, but some have online counterparts.

Function Categories

A second useful way of structuring the magazine industry is to divide it by function into the production, distribution, and retail segments.

The Production Function   The production phase of the industry, which consists of approximately 2,000 to 3,000 publishers, encompasses all the elements necessary to put out a magazine—copy, artwork, photos, titles, layout, printing, and binding. A subsequent section will describe in more detail how a magazine is produced.

The Distribution Function   The distribution phase of the industry handles the job of getting the magazine to the reader. It is not a simple job. In fact, the circulation department at a large magazine may be the most complex in the whole company. As with newspapers, circulation means the total number of copies of the magazine that are delivered through mail subscriptions or bought at the newsstand. There are two main types of circulation. **Paid circulation** means that the readers pay to receive the magazine, either through a subscription or by purchasing it at the newsstand. Paid circulation has two main advantages. First, periodicals that use paid circulation qualify for lower, second-class postal rates, and paid circulation provides a revenue source to the publisher in addition to advertising. On the negative side, paid-circulation magazines must undertake expensive promotional campaigns to increase subscriptions or to sell single copies. Paid-circulation magazines also have the added expense of collecting subscription payments and record keeping. Most consumer magazines use paid circulation.

The alternative to paid circulation is **controlled circulation.** Controlled-circulation magazines set specific qualifications for those who are to receive the magazine. Magazines that are provided to airline passengers or motel guests are examples. Two advantages of controlled circulation are that publications using it can reach all the personnel in a given field and that these publications avoid the costs of promoting subscriptions. On the negative side, controlled-circulation magazines gain no revenue from subscriptions and single-copy sales. Further, postage for these publications costs more. Controlled circulation has generally been used by business and public relations magazines.

No matter what method is chosen, the circulation of a magazine is an important number. The larger the circulation, the more the magazine can charge for its advertising space.

For a paid-circulation magazine, distributing copies to subscribers is a relatively simple affair. The complicated (and expensive) part of this process is getting subscribers. There are no fewer than 14 methods that are used by magazines to build subscription lists. They include employing cash-field agencies, which have salespeople make house-to-house calls to sell subscriptions directly to consumers; direct-mail agencies; direct-mail campaigns sponsored by the publisher; and, finally, what are called blow-in cards, those annoying little cards that fall out of a magazine as soon as you open it.

Single-copy distribution to newsstands and other retailers is a multistep process. The publisher deals with only one party, the national distributor. Four national distributors work with the nation's publishers. The national distributor handles anywhere from a dozen to 50 or more titles. At least once every month, representatives of the magazine sit down with the national distributor and determine the number of magazines to be distributed for an upcoming issue. The national distributor then delivers the magazines to wholesalers who sell magazines and paperback books within specified areas. In any given month, a wholesaler might receive 500 to 1,000 magazines to distribute to dealers.

The particulars of online magazine distribution, of course, are much different. Online magazines and newsletters can be distributed by e-mail, with "copies" going only to those who request them, or they can exist on a website, where they wait for readers. Whatever the arrangement, online magazines have no need for national distributors or wholesalers.

The Retail Function   The retailer is the last segment of the industry. The best available figures indicate that there are approximately 140,000 retail outlets in the United States. Of these, the supermarket accounted for 44 percent of all sales in 1998. Supermarket sales have become so important that publishers pay the stores a premium of about $20 per checkout rack to have their titles prominently displayed. When a dealer receives a magazine, he or she agrees to keep the magazine on the display racks for a predetermined length of time (usually a week or a month). At the end of this period, unsold copies are returned to the wholesaler for credit.

The tremendous diversity of the magazine industry is illustrated by this magazine display in a bookstore. Magazine publishers compete vigorously for prime space (front row, eye level) in such a display. (Mark Zemnick)

 MAGAZINE OWNERSHIP

Recent mergers and acquisitions have resulted in a magazine industry dominated by large corporations. Concentration of ownership, however, is not as pronounced as it is in some other media industries, such as newspapers or radio. Many of the conglomerates (e.g., Time Warner, Bertelsmann) had extensive holdings in other media (and have been mentioned in other chapters). Table 5.2 contains a ranking of the top 10 consumer magazine publishers by 1999 revenue and lists their well-known titles.

Table 5.2	Top Consumer Magazine Companies		
Company		**1999 Revenue (in billions)**	**Well-Known Titles**
1.	Time Warner	$3.79	*People, Time, Sports Illustrated*
2.	Condé Nast	1.49	*Vanity Fair, Vogue*
3.	Hearst	1.47	*Good Housekeeping, Cosmopolitan*
4.	Hachette Fillipi	1.13	*Elle, Woman's Day*
5.	Meredith	1.13	*Better Homes & Gardens, Ladies' Home Journal*
6.	Ziff-Davis	0.82	*PC Magazine, PC Computing*
7.	Gruner-Jahr (Bertelsmann)	0.75	*YM, McCalls*
8.	Primedia	0.74	*Seventeen, Modern Bride*
9.	Gemstar	0.65	*TV Guide*
10.	United News	0.61	*Internet Week, Computer Reseller*

Source: Compiled from *Folio,* July 1, 2000, p. 56.

Table 5.2 also illustrates that a significant foreign influence exists in magazine publishing. Three of the top 10 companies (Hachette, Gruner-Jahr, and United News) have foreign headquarters.

The business publication field is dominated by about two dozen publishers. The Disney Company has more than 40 publications, as does Reed Holdings; Penton has about 30.

PRODUCING THE MAGAZINE

Departments and Staff

A glance at the masthead (the page that lists the magazine's personnel) of a few magazines will show that, although there are many variations, a typical magazine is generally headed by a publisher who oversees four main departments: (1) circulation, (2) advertising, (3) production, and (4) editorial. Figure 5-1 shows a typical arrangement.

The publisher sets the general policy for the publication. He or she is responsible for budgeting, maintaining a healthy advertising position, keeping circulation high, and making sure the magazine has a consistent editorial direction. Strictly speaking, the publisher directs both the business and the editorial side of the publication, but most publishers tend to pay more attention to the financial operations and generally let the editor-in-chief make decisions concerning the content of the publication.

The Circulation Department   This department, under the supervision of the circulation director, is responsible for getting new readers and keeping current readers satisfied. Responsible to the circulation director are the heads of three divisions: (1) the subscription manager, who tries to increase the number of people on the magazine's subscription list; (2) the single-copy sales manager, who works with the national distributors, wholesalers, and retailers; and (3) the subscription-

Figure 5–1

Department Chart for a
Typical Magazine

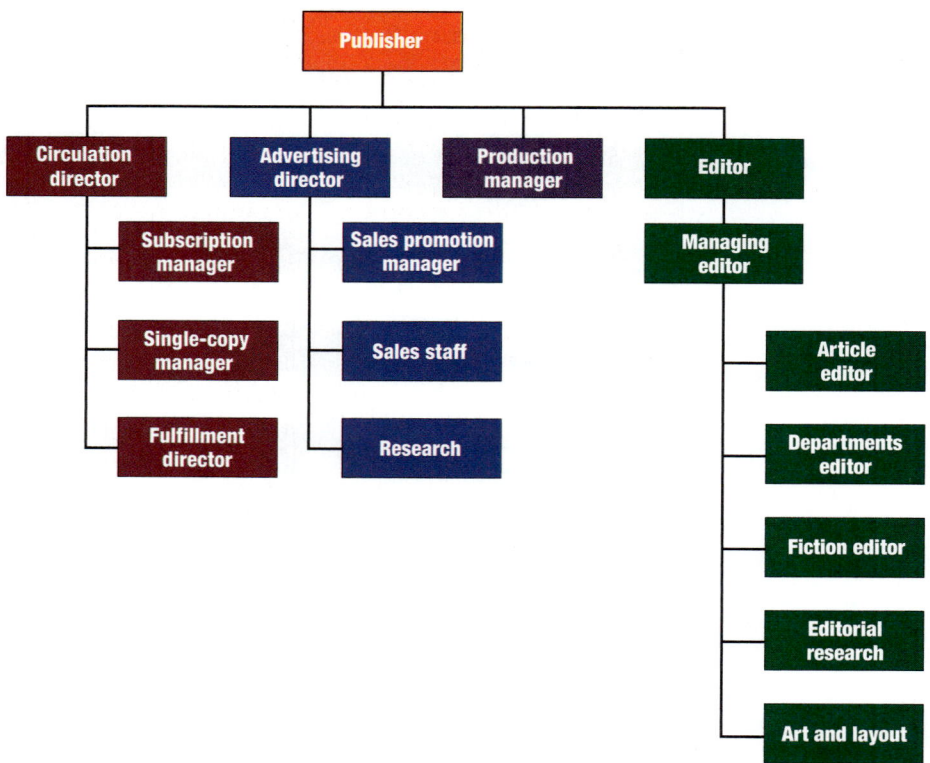

fulfillment director, whose division is in charge of making sure that the magazine gets to subscribers, by taking care of address changes, renewals, new subscribers, complaints, and so forth.

The Advertising and Sales Division   Under the supervision of an advertising director, the advertising and sales division is responsible for selling space in the magazine to potential advertisers. Also working in this department are the sales promotion manager, who is responsible for putting together new programs to enhance sales; the sales staff, which does the actual selling; and the research director, who studies the audience and compiles data of interest to advertisers.

The Production Department   The production department is concerned with actually printing and binding the publication. In charge of this department is the production manager, who buys paper, handles contracts with printers, orders new typesetting and computer equipment, and makes frequent visits to printing plants to make sure production is going smoothly.

The Editorial Department   The editorial department handles the nonadvertising content of the magazine. The person in charge may be called the executive editor, the editor-in-chief, or simply the editor. Much of the editor's time is spent in supervising the editorial staff, planning topics for upcoming issues, informing the advertising department about plans, and taking part in various public relations activities. The day-to-day operation of the magazine falls on the shoulders of the managing editor. Making sure all articles are completed on time, selecting artwork, writing titles, changing layouts, and shortening stories are all functions performed by the managing editor. Helping the managing editor with these tasks are several editors who handle articles, fiction, or other departments that appear regularly within the magazine. An art director designs the magazine, selects typefaces for headlines, and supervises the display of photos and other illustrations.

Some magazines might have an additional department to handle their online operations. Others incorporate the online function into the traditional departments listed above.

■ Publishing the Magazine

Everything moves in cycles. Early magazine publishers were printers as well as writers, but during the 19th century, the production function was divorced from the editorial function. Many magazines have now gone full circle: Computers allow writers and editors to set their words into type and make up pages, reuniting the production and editorial functions.

The first step in all magazine production is preliminary planning and generating ideas for upcoming issues. Once the overall ideas are set, the next step is to convert the ideas into concrete subjects for articles. At this point, preliminary decisions concerning article length, photos, and accompanying artwork are made. Next, the managing editor assigns certain articles to staff writers or freelancers.

The next step involves putting together a miniature **dummy,** a plan or blueprint of the pages for the upcoming issue that shows the contents in their proper order. This phase can now be done electronically, thanks to computer programs that allow editors to view 32 pages at a time.

At about this same time, schedules are drawn up to ensure that an article will get to the printer in time to be included in the forthcoming issue. A copy deadline is set—this is the day the writer must hand in the story to the editor. Time is set aside for editing, checking, and verifying all copy. A timetable is also set up for illustrations and artwork.

Most articles are now written and edited at the computer. Once they are in acceptable form, a computerized typesetter sets the copy in body and display-size type and the articles are sent to the press or posted on the magazine's website.

 ECONOMICS

There are four basic sources of magazine revenue: subscriptions, single-copy sales, advertising, and ancillary services such as e-commerce, custom publishing, and database assistance. This section will concentrate on the first three of these: subscriptions, single-copy sales, and advertising. At the beginning of this century, the magazine industry was taking in about $28 billion from these sources. Note, however, that this $28 billion is not an accurate estimate of the money that was actually received by magazine publishers. Some of this money went to distributors, wholesalers, and advertising agencies.

After some tough economic times in the early 1990s, the magazine industry was doing well at the beginning of the new millennium. Total magazine subscriptions were growing, and advertising revenue was increasing. Most of these increases were due to an increased number of magazine titles in the marketplace. However, there were some troubling trends as well. Single-copy sales continued to decline,

John Johnson is the founder of the company that publishes *Ebony* and *Jet*. (Johnson Publishing Company, Inc.)

off more than 15 percent from 1989 to 1999. Circulation figures for the most popular magazines (see Table 5.1) show that many have lost substantial numbers of readers in the past four years. Several notable magazines, including *Mirabella*, the reincarnation of *Life*, and *Women's Sports and Fitness*, ceased publication.

One problem for the industry was the change in the distribution process. Retail outlets wanted only those titles that were selling fast; they were not interested in cluttering their shelves with magazines that move slowly. The distributors responded by restricting the number of magazine titles they would handle and charging more for the slow-moving titles. This drove distribution costs up and made it difficult for new magazines to get shelf space.

Advertising is the number one revenue source for magazines, accounting for about 67 percent of the total. Subscription revenue makes up about 23 percent, while single-copy sales account for the remainder.

Of course, the relative importance of subscriptions, single-copy sales, and advertising varies tremendously from magazine to magazine. *Reader's Digest* gets about 54 percent of its revenue from subscriptions, 42 percent from advertising, and only 4 percent from newsstand sales. On the other hand, *Cosmo* gets 7 percent from subscriptions, about 68 percent from advertising, and 25 percent from single-copy sales, usually at supermarkets. *The New Yorker* displays another pattern: 72 percent of its revenue comes from advertising, 23 percent from subscribers, and 5 percent from single-copy sales. To gain some perspective on advertising fees, consider this: In 2000 it cost about $116,000 to run a full-page, black-and-white ad in *TV Guide*. The same ad in *National Geographic* would cost $33,000.

From the point of view of the consumer, one obvious fact is that magazines are getting more expensive. From 1986 to 2000, the average price readers have paid for a subscription has risen 25 percent, from $24 to $30. Cover prices have gone up even more sharply in the same time period, from $1.71 to $5.00, an increase of more than 100 percent. Magazines cost more because they are more expensive to produce. From 1970 to 2000, the cost of physically producing the magazine more than doubled. The typical expense dollar for a magazine breaks down as follows:

Advertising expenses	9¢
Circulation costs	31¢
Editorial costs	9¢
Manufacturing and distribution	40¢
Other costs	1¢
Administration	10¢

Two items included in the manufacturing and distribution category have increased at the fastest rate: paper and postage. The cost of coated paper, for example, rose about 20 percent from 1997 to 2000.

 FEEDBACK

The magazine industry, like the newspaper industry, depends upon the Audit Bureau of Circulations (ABC) for information about who is reading the publication. The ABC audits most consumer magazines and issues a "pink sheet"—so called because its report is printed on pink paper—every June and December. The ABC statement reports the magazine's average paid circulation and the magazine's **rate base.** The rate base is the number of buyers guaranteed by the magazine and is also the number that the magazine uses to compute its advertising rates. Other information in the report includes circulation for each issue in the past six months, state-by-state circulation data, and a report on five-year trends. The ABC also offers a service that tabulates the number of visitors to a magazine's website.

Another company, Business Publication Audit (BPA), specializes in business and trade magazines. It issues reports similar to those of the ABC, with additional information concerning the occupations of readers who receive controlled-circulation publications.

Although it is helpful to know the total circulation figure for a magazine, that number does not tell the whole story. Circulation measures the **primary audience,** those people who subscribe to the magazine or buy it at the newsstand. In addition, there is the **pass-along audience,** those people who pick up a copy at the doctor's office, at work, while traveling, and the like. **Mediamark Research Inc. (MRI)** provides data on the total audience for magazines. This company selects a large sample of the magazine-reading audience and conducts personal interviews with individuals to get an exposure score for each magazine. The reports issued by MRI are extremely detailed and encompass many volumes. They contain such specific information as what percentage of a particular magazine's readers make more than $50,000 per year and detailed product-use data, such as how many readers used a headache remedy in the past month. A small portion of an MRI report is reproduced in Figure 5–2.

Magazine Audiences

Although data on the audience for an individual magazine are readily available, information about the total audience for magazines is hard to come by, primarily because of the difficulty in defining what qualifies as a magazine. Nonetheless,

		ALL				**TIMES/LAST 7 DAYS**						
						HEAVY & MEDIUM 3 OR MORE				LIGHT LESS THAN 3			
	TOTAL U.S.	A	B %	C %	D	A	B %	C %	D	A	B %	C %	D
BASE: FEMALE HOMEMAKERS	*000	*000	DOWN	ACROSS	INDEX	*000	DOWN	ACROSS	INDEX	*000	DOWN	ACROSS	INDEX
ALL FEMALE HOMEMAKERS	85323	6628	100.0	7.8	100	4397	100.0	5.2	100	2231	100.0	2.6	100
MONEY	2719	*310	4.7	11.4	147	*214	4.9	7.9	153	*95	4.3	3.5	134
MOTOR TREND	499	*18	.3	3.6	46	*2	-	.4	8	*16	.7	3.2	123
MUSCLE & FITNESS	1109	*99	1.5	8.9	115	*86	2.0	7.8	150	*13	.6	1.2	45
NATIONAL ENQUIRER	11898	1134	17.1	9.5	123	770	17.5	6.5	126	*364	16.3	3.1	117
NATIONAL GEOGRAPHIC	12588	692	10.4	5.5	71	*416	9.5	3.3	64	*276	12.4	2.2	84
NATIONAL GEOGRAPHIC TRAVELER	889	*19	.3	2.1	28	*7	.2	.8	15	*13	.6	1.5	56
NATIONAL LAMPOON	*313	*21	.3	-	-	*21	.5	-	-	-	-	-	-
NATURAL HISTORY	662	*76	1.1	11.5	148	*6	.1	.9	18	*70	3.1	10.6	404
NEWSWEEK	8286	637	9.6	7.7	99	*447	10.2	5.4	105	*190	8.5	2.3	88
NEW WOMAN	3214	*206	3.1	6.4	83	*129	2.9	4.0	78	*77	3.5	2.4	92
NEW YORK MAGAZINE	728	*117	1.8	16.1	207	*87	2.0	12.0	232	*30	1.3	4.1	158
NEW YORK TIMES (DAILY)	1355	*67	1.0	4.9	64	*31	.7	2.3	44	*36	1.6	2.7	102
NEW YORK TIMES MAGAZINE	2087	*159	2.4	7.6	98	*116	2.6	5.6	108		1.9	2.1	79
THE NEW YORKER	1189	*81	1.2	6.8	88	*51	1.2	4.3	83	*43	1.3	2.5	96
OMNI	975	*102	1.5	10.5	135	*47	1.1	4.8	94	*30	2.5	5.6	216
1,001 HOME IDEAS	3610	*315	4.8	8.7	112	*290	6.6	8.0	156	*55	1.1	.7	26
ORGANIC GARDENING	1904	*35	.5	1.8	24	*28	.6	1.5	29	*25	.3	.3	12
OUTDOOR LIFE	1864	*121	1.8	6.5	84	*107	2.4	5.7	111	*6	.7	.8	31
										*15			

Figure 5–2

Excerpt from an MRI
Report

Source: Copyright © by
Mediamark Research Inc.

some figures are available. In the late 1990s, as reported to the Audit Bureau of
Circulations, total magazine circulation exceeded 360 million copies. Of these,
about 20 percent were bought at the newsstand, while the remaining 80 percent
were delivered as part of a subscription. If we examine circulation figures per
1,000 people, as we did with newspapers, we find that magazine circulation has
exceeded the growth in the adult population during the 1970s, 1980s, and 1990s.

It appears that almost everybody does some type of magazine reading. In an
average month, 94 percent of U.S. adults read at least one copy of a magazine.
Most read more. One study reported that adults read or look through an average
of 10 magazines a month. About 28 percent read a magazine on an average day,
and the typical adult spends about 25 minutes daily reading magazines. As far as
demographics are concerned, the typical magazine reader is more educated and
usually more affluent than the nonreader. Magazine readers also tend to be join-
ers. One survey found them far more likely to belong to religious, scientific, and
professional organizations than are nonreaders.

C A R E E R

O U T L O O K

THE MAGAZINE INDUSTRY

As best as anyone can tell, there are only about 140,000 people employed in the
magazine industry, thus making it a rather difficult industry to break into. Additionally, the headquarters of large magazine publishing companies tend to be
located on the East Coast, especially around New York City. For example, of the

CRITICAL/CULTURAL ISSUES

Lessons from *YM:* A Feminist Analysis

YM is one of the most popular magazines aimed at teenage girls, read by almost 8 million female teens. A typical *YM* issue contains articles on hair, fashion, cosmetics, dating tips, romance, sexual mores, and advice. A recent issue, for example, contained such articles as "Back to School Beauty and Fashion Blowout," "Guy Truths and Lies: What They Really Think about Fast Girls and Mushy Moments," and "Ten Little Love Lies Every Girl Should Tell."

What are the lessons that *YM* is teaching young females? This was the focus of a 1996 article in the *Journal of Communication Inquiry*. The authors, Margaret Duffy and J. Michael Gotcher, analyzed articles that appeared in *YM* between 1993 and 1995 and found several congruent themes that pictured a consistent view of gender relations: Getting the guy was the most important thing. The authors contend that *YM* portrays a world where the only power that's available to a young woman comes through seduction, beauty, and fashion, and that the magazine further convinces teens that this arrangement is natural and desirable.

Duffy and Gotcher point out that, in general, *YM*'s articles focus on romance, love, and sex—which are intimately linked to fashion, beauty, and cosmetics, and to information regarding stuff girls should know to get the guy. For instance, one prominent theme in *YM* suggests that a girl's power of attraction can be increased by getting the right information. The magazine typically runs articles such as "How Can I Get Guys to Notice Me?" "What Am I Supposed to Wear?" and "How Far Should I Go on a Date?" Answers and advice about these issues come from supermodels, celebrities, doctors, and psychologists. And, not surprisingly, a lot of the advice concerns products and services that young girls can purchase in hopes of becoming more attractive. The use of credible sources suggests that this information is an important and normal part of everyday life.

Another theme suggests that wearing the right clothes will provide young women the power they need to attract guys. Many photo layouts show young models in mildly suggestive costumes, and accompanying copy stresses the commanding strength that goes with looking good. Some illustrative titles: "Killer Clothes—They'll Knock Him Dead," "Flirty Dresses—They'll Have Him at Your Mercy," and "Totally Touchable Sweaters—Fuzzy Cover-Ups to Make Him Want to Cuddle You." These articles usually include brand names and prices for the clothing items shown. These displays suggest that buying high-priced clothing is the natural way for young women to become happy.

In sum, the authors note that *YM* portrays the pursuit of males as almost the only purpose in life. It is an unquestioned good thing to do. Nowhere in the magazine is it suggested that a young woman might find a rewarding life through personal achievements, education, friendship, public service, or other avenues. The world of *YM* provides young women with little information on occupational opportunities (other than modeling) and depicts a world where success is determined by how well a female meets the needs and expectations of males. Women are shown that they can gain power and happiness by purchasing the right dress or brand of cosmetics or by implementing some of the manipulative strategies mentioned in the magazine that are designed to get the guy. Duffy and Gotcher's article concludes by pointing out that *YM* provides an inadequate range of models for female teens to consult when attempting to find meaning in the world around them.

1. *YM* is aimed at female teens. To what extent are the themes contained in *YM* also present in magazines aimed at adult women (such as *Cosmo*, or *Ladies' Home Journal*)?

2. How might this emphasis on attractiveness, trendy fashions, and the pursuit of males affect the self-esteem of young women who may be overweight, or unable to affort the "right" clothes? What about the self-worth of young teens who are discovering they are lesbians?

3. What responsibilities might the editors of *YM* have in terms of presenting a more well-rounded, realistic picture of young womanhood?

top 10 magazine group publishers in terms of circulation, 8 are located in New York. The Los Angeles area is another region that contains a significant number of magazine publishers.

■ Entry-Level Positions

Most jobs in the magazine industry are found at small publications or at business and trade magazines. In the editorial department, the most common entry-level job is that of editorial assistant. Editorial assistants do a little bit of everything: proofreading, research, replying to authors' letters, coordinating production schedules, filing, indexing, cross-referencing, and answering readers' mail. In specialized publications, editorial assistants might be assigned duties somewhat far afield of actual editorial work. During her first days on the job, one editorial assistant at a fashion magazine spent her time carrying around clothing for one of the magazine's photographers.

Another beginning-level position at some magazines is that of researcher. A researcher spends his or her time pulling together assorted facts and data for staff writers or compiling folders and research notes for articles that are in the planning stage. This particular job requires a general education, skill at using the library, and familiarity with reference books and the Internet.

Many newcomers start out as readers. When articles or stories arrive at the magazine, they are assigned to a reader, who studies them, summarizes them for an editor, and may even make recommendations about what to publish. Some beginners become staff writers. The assignment editor gives the staff writers assignments such as preparing a calendar of upcoming events of interest to the readers or editing a section of helpful household hints.

Some beginners attempt to break into magazine work by freelance writing. Magazines give some of their assignments to freelance writers, who are paid per story. Other freelancers submit articles or stories on speculation, hoping that the magazine will be impressed enough with their work to buy it.

Newcomers in the circulation department are usually found in the subscription-fulfillment department, where they update subscription lists, send out renewal notices, and handle complaints. Other beginning-level positions in this department are subscription salesperson and assistant to the subscription director or to the single-copy sales manager. In the advertising department, entry-level positions are typically assistants to a staff member. Assistants to an advertising copywriter help prepare copy for leaflets and display cards, compile various reports, and assist in the preparation of direct-mail letters. Assistants to the sales promotion manager compile and verify statistical tables and charts, check promotional materials, handle routine correspondence, and suggest new promotional ideas.

The Internet has also had an impact on the magazine job market. Employees with web skills and HTML knowledge are generally at an advantage. Moreover, the Internet has opened new job opportunities: providing content for the online version of the magazine, selling ads in the digital version of the magazine, serving as a webmaster. Finally, the competition for skilled people between dot-com companies and traditional magazine publishers has given entry-level job applicants a bit of an edge. Many are able to command higher initial salaries and to negotiate terms whereby they can have flexible hours, work at home, or dress casually at the office. These perks, however, are a little harder to obtain now that many dot-coms have fallen on hard times.

■ Upward Mobility

Career advancement in the editorial department can follow two different routes. Editorial assistants move up the ladder to become assistant editors, usually assigned to a specific department of the magazine. The next step up is associate editor; the next position is senior editor. From there, the person may go on to be managing editor or perhaps even editor-in-chief. Another possible upward route finds the editorial assistant moving into the assistant copyeditor's slot. The assistant copyeditor then progresses to the rank of copyeditor. From this position it is possible, although not probable, that the person can become the managing editor.

In the circulation department, the next step up after an entry-level position is into the subscription director's or single-copy sales manager's slot. Advancement from this position consists of moving into the top management ranks by becoming circulation director. For many, the circulation director's job has led to a position as associate publisher or even publisher. In the advertising department, upward mobility consists of moving into the position the newcomer was formerly assisting, such as copywriter or sales promotion manager. Another route upward is to join the magazine's sales staff. Ultimately, the top position to aspire to in the advertising department is that of advertising director, a member of the magazine's top management team. The job of advertising director frequently serves as a springboard to the publisher's position.

The competition from the Internet has also had an impact on upward mobility. Many experienced employees have left magazines to pursue opportunities at Internet companies. As a result, there has been a talent drain in the industry and the pace of promotion has increased among those who stay. One publisher of a major consumer magazine estimated that, on the average, employees are working about 18 months in a particular job before being promoted.

■ MAIN POINTS

- The first American magazines appeared during the middle of the 18th century and were aimed at an educated, urban, and literate audience.

- The audiences for magazines increased during the penny-press era as mass-appeal publications became prominent.

- Better printing techniques and a healthy economy helped a magazine boom during the latter part of the 19th century.

- The muckrakers were magazines that published exposés and encouraged reform.

- Magazines began to specialize their content following World War I. News magazines, digests, and picture magazines became popular.

- The magazine industry has used the Internet to complement the print versions of their magazines.

- Magazines are specialized, current, influential, and convenient.

- The magazine industry is dominated by large publishing companies.

- The magazine industry can be divided into the production, distribution, and retail divisions.

- A typical magazine publishing company has several main departments, including circulation, advertising, production, and editorial.

- Magazines get revenues from subscriptions, single-copy sales, and advertising.

- MRI is a company that measures magazine readership.

■ QUESTIONS FOR REVIEW

1. What are the four defining features of contemporary magazines? Should any other features be added to this list?

2. Why did the general-interest magazines *Look* and *Life* go out of business?

3. How is the magazine industry learning to coexist with the Internet?

4. What are the major departments at a magazine?

■ QUESTIONS FOR CRITICAL THINKING

1. Are there dangers in having large corporations dominate the magazine publishing industry?

2. *Playboy, Cosmopolitan,* and *Ms.*—three magazines that influenced social trends—all came on the scene before 1980. Are there any more current magazines that have been influential in shaping American culture and society? If not, why not?

3. Is it possible for a magazine to become too specialized? How big does a specialized audience have to be to support a print magazine? A web-only magazine?

4. Muckraking by magazines never reappeared after its heyday in the early 20th century. Why not?

■ KEY TERMS

magazines (p. 121)
muckrackers (p. 123)
paid circulation (p. 133)
controlled circulation (p. 133)

dummy (p. 137)
rate base (p. 139)
primary audience (p. 139)

pass-along audience (p. 139)
Mediamark Research Inc. (MRI)
    (p. 139)

■ SUGGESTIONS FOR FURTHER READING

The following books contain additional information about the magazine industry.

Click, J. W., and Russell Baird. *Magazine Editing and Production.* Madison, WI: Brown and Benchmark, 1994.

Daley, Charles, Patrick Henry, and Ellen Ryde. *The Magazine Publishing Industry.* Boston: Allyn and Bacon, 1997.

Johnson, Sammye, and Patricia Prijatel. *The Magazine from Cover to Cover.* Chicago: NTC, 2000.

Mogel, Leonard. *The Magazine: Everything You Need to Know to Make It in the Magazine Business.* Portland, OR: Graphic Arts, 1998.

Tebbell, John. *The American Magazine: A Compact History.* New York: Hawthorne Books, 1969.

■ SURFING THE INTERNET

www.condenet.com
A site dedicated to good living. Links to Condé Nast's magazines, which feature food, drink, and travel.

www.ecola.com/news/magazine
Ecola's 24-hour newsstand. Contains links to hundreds of magazines and illustrates the vast diversity of the industry.

www.maddogproductions.com
A good example of an e-zine. Devoted to humor and commentary. Contains Plot-O-Matic, an online, instant movie script tool.

www.magazine.org
The site of the major trade association of the industry: Magazine Publishers of America. Contains statistics and latest news about magazines.

www.money.com/money/
Money magazine's site. Note the many interactive financial tools at the site and the way the site encourages visitors to subscribe to the print magazine.

CHAPTER 6 Book Publishing

Imagine the following. Classes have just begun for a new semester, and you haven't bought your textbooks yet. Rather than fight the crowds at the campus bookstore, you go to your computer and connect to an online bookseller. You search for the books you need. A few clicks and they're all in your shopping cart. You enter a credit card number and click again. Zap. The books are all downloaded to your lightweight, portable e-book reader. No crowds. No long checkout lines. No ink. No paper. No heavy books to lug around.

Sound fanciful? This scenario might not happen during your college career, but it (or some similar scenario) will almost certainly take place during your children's college experience. The book publishing industry will be profoundly affected by the shift to digital. But we're getting ahead of the story. Let's take a look at how book publishing has evolved over the years before we take a look at where it's going.

A portable e-book reader. A survey of college students done in 2000 found that 62 percent preferred digital texts over standard paper textbooks. *(Newsmakers/Liaison Agency)*

Many early medieval manuscripts, such as this hymn book, were "illuminated" with colorful drawings and graphics. *(Photo Edit)*

 HISTORY

Early books were inscribed by hand and lavishly decorated; many were valued as works of art. Until approximately the 12th century, most books in Europe were produced by monks in monasteries. As noted in Chapter 3, all this changed with the invention of movable type that worked with a printing press.

The invention of movable metal type suitable for printing is generally credited to Johann Gutenberg. Trained as a metalworker, Gutenberg developed a way to cast metal type and to encase it in a wooden mold that could then be attached to a printing press. In about 1455, Gutenberg printed his first book—the Bible. First put on sale at the Great Frankfurt Fair, the book cost the equivalent of three years of wages for the typical laborer of that time period.

Gutenberg's innovations spread quickly throughout Europe. The Protestant Reformation and the writings of Martin Luther spurred the printing of religious books. Printed books appeared in England in 1476. Although book publishing was not considered a socially important force, Henry VIII recognized its potential as a political force and required all printers to obtain government approval before setting up shop.

Colonial America

By the early 17th century, book publishers followed the early immigrants to North America. In 1640, the Puritans in Cambridge, Massachusetts, printed the *Bay Psalm Book*. About 90,000 other titles were to follow it as book publishing took hold in the American colonies. Early publishers functioned as printers and sometimes as authors. One of the early printer–publishers who went on to fame was Benjamin Franklin. His *Poor Richard's Almanack* sold about 10,000 copies a year. Most book content, however, was religious, such as *The Practice of Piety* and *Day of Doom*. Sentimental novels, many of them imported from England, also sold well. As the Revolutionary War approached, many book printers turned out political pamphlets. Thomas Paine's *Common Sense* sold 100,000 copies in just 10 weeks.

The Penny–Press Era

The change in printing technology and the growth of literacy mentioned in Chapter 4 also helped the book publishing industry. Many of the publishing companies still active today can trace their roots to the early 1800s. Many publishers specialized in professional and educational books, while others addressed their efforts to the general public. Book prices declined and authors such as James Fenimore Cooper and Henry Wadsworth Longfellow were popular, as were the works of English authors. Public education and the penny newspaper created a demand for reading materials. The number of public libraries tripled between 1825 and 1850. Book reading became a symbol of education and knowledge.

The novels of Charles Dickens and Walter Scott were best-sellers during this period, as were books by Herman Melville and Henry David Thoreau. Specialized books also appeared. In the late 1840s, textbooks were profitable, as were reference, medical, and engineering books. The most significant book of the period, however, was probably Harriet Beecher Stowe's *Uncle Tom's Cabin*, published in 1852. It sold 300,000 copies in its first year and was credited with converting many readers to an antislavery position.

The Paperback Boom

During the Civil War, soldiers turned to reading to fill the idle time between campaigns. This created a demand for cheap reading materials, and before long a series of paperbacks priced at 10¢ apiece flooded the market. These "dime novels" included the popular Frank Merriwell and Horatio Alger stories. By 1880, about one-third of all the books published in the country were paperbacks, and 15 firms were selling the softbound volumes at prices ranging from 5¢ to 15¢. Many of the best-selling paperbacks were pirated editions of best-sellers in England and other European countries. By the late 1880s, this problem was so bad that a new copyright law was adopted. The effect of this new law, combined with years of cutthroat competition and price cutting, spelled the end of this era of paperback popularity.

The Early Twentieth Century

The period from 1900 to 1945 saw the commercialization of publishing. Prior to this time, many publishing companies were family-owned and specialized in publishing one particular kind of book. Publishers were a closely knit group, and their dealings with one another resembled what might take place in a genteel private club. Several events altered this situation. First, a new breed of literary agents, concerned with negotiating the best bottom line for their authors, entered the scene. Forced to pay top dollar for the rights to books, the publishing business became more businesslike. Second, many publishing houses expanded into the mass market, publishing popular works of fiction. To compete effectively in the mass marketplace, these publishing houses introduced modern promotion and distribution techniques to the book industry. Third, a depression in the 1890s and a subsequent sluggish economy meant that the book industry was forced to depend more on banks for finance capital. The banks, of course, insisted that the book companies be run with the utmost efficiency, with an eye toward increasing profits. By World War II, all these factors combined to make the book industry more commercially oriented.

The content of popular books was highly variable during this time period. Outdoor adventures written by such authors as Jack London and Zane Grey were popular at the turn of the century. *Tarzan of the Apes* sold nearly a million copies on the eve of World War I. During the Roaring Twenties, light fiction, such as *The Sheik* and P. G. Wodehouse's *Jeeves* were best-sellers, but serious works sold equally well. H. G. Wells's *Outline of History* and Will Durant's *Story of Philosophy* reached the million mark in sales during this period. Detective fiction by Erle Stanley Gardner (Perry Mason was his hero) and Ellery Queen sold well during the depression. In 1936, two books broke the two million mark in sales, Dale Carnegie's *How to Win Friends and Influence People* and Margaret Mitchell's *Gone With the Wind.*

■ Postwar Books: Paperbacks and Consolidation

Shortly after the end of World War II, new paperbacks published by Bantam, Pocket Books, and New American Library appeared. These books were popular because of their 25¢ price and because new channels of distribution were used to market them. Wire racks filled with paperbacks appeared in train stations, newsstands, drugstores, and tobacco shops. A whole new audience was thus exposed to paperbacks. In 1950, the "quality" paperback appeared. These were serious nonfiction or literary classics that found their prime markets in education.

Moreover, expanded leisure time and more disposable income made book reading a popular means of recreation. All in all, the book publishing business looked like a good investment for the future. Consequently, large corporations began acquiring book companies. Between 1958 and 1970, there were 307 mergers or acquisitions of publishing companies. These mergers brought new financial and management resources to the book industry, which helped it stay profitable during the 1970s.

The content of popular books during this period was varied. The first big paperback best-seller following World War II was Dr. Benjamin Spock's *Baby and Child Care.* Other notable paperbacks followed. Mickey Spillane's Mike Hammer

Margaret Mitchell's *Gone With the Wind* was turned down by 25 publishers before Macmillan published it. The book still sells about 50,000 hardcover copies a year. *(Eric Sander/Gamma Liaison)*

was a hard-boiled private eye who appeared in six novels during the 1950s that sold 17 million copies. *Peyton Place*, a novel famous for its racy parts, sold 10 million in paperback. All in all, from 1946 to 1970, paperback sales were dominated by light fiction and an occasional how-to book.

The Contemporary Book Industry

The wave of consolidation that began in the 1970s continued until the end of the century. In 1998, media conglomerate Bertelsmann acquired Random House, and HarperCollins bought Morrow/Avon. As a result, book publishing was on its way to being dominated by a few big companies. The late 1990s also saw a major change in the way books were sold, thanks to the Internet. Amazon.com ushered in the world of e-commerce by first offering books for sale online direct to consumers. barnesandnoble.com followed suit with a similar service. In 1999, the two online booksellers sold more that a $1 billion worth of books.

The content of modern books is remarkably varied. Cookbooks and diet books are perennial favorites. In fiction, books by Stephen King, John Grisham, and Danielle Steele generally go to the top of the best-seller lists. In the late 1990s, J. K. Rowling's Harry Potter series (see Media Probe, "Harry Mania") was phenomenally popular with young readers. All in all, the varied content of modern books reflects the eclectic tastes of the modern reading audience.

As the new century began, however, the contemporary book industry faced many new challenges.

BOOKS IN THE DIGITAL AGE

The book industry has been using digital technology for more than two decades. Authors typed their manuscripts using word processing programs and submitted them to book publishers on floppy disks or by e-mail. Publishers edited and set type from these electronic texts. In the past, however, publishers then took the digital manuscripts and printed them on paper. The finished books were then bound together and shipped to bookstores and other sales outlets where consumers purchased them.

A book in digital form, however, doesn't have to be printed on paper to be distributed. Thanks to the Internet, the digital book, or **e-book**, can be distributed directly to consumers.

This new distribution channel and a glimpse of the possible future of book publishing was vividly demonstrated by Stephen King. While recuperating from a traffic accident injury, King wrote a 66-page novella entitled "Riding the Bullet" that was published exclusively online in early 2000. Some readers were able to download the work for free from the Amazon.com website; others paid $2.50 for it at other sites. By the time the smoke had cleared, about 500,000 copies of the novella had been distributed in just three days. (King was so impressed with the success of "Riding the Bullet" that he distributed another work on the Internet. His new venture was a serial offered to consumers at $1 per installment. Unfortunately for King, the new venture didn't succeed as many people downloaded the installments and didn't pay for them. Consequently, King stopped distributing the work.)

The biggest surprise in book publishing at the turn of the century was a series of books about an 11-year-old boy who learns that he has a talent for magic. A student at Hogwarts School, Harry Potter interacts with such fanciful characters as Professor Dumbledore, Ron Weasley, Hedwig the Owl, and Nearly Headless Nick.

Harry is the creation of the plenteous imagination of British author J. K. Rowling, but it's doubtful than even she could have imagined the success that the Harry Potter books have achieved. Rowling started outlining the Harry Potter saga while on a train between London and Manchester. She continued to develop the story while working in Portugal. Her luck turned bad, however, and a few years later, she was an unemployed single mother living on welfare. To stay warm, she and her young daughter would go to a cafe, where Rowling scribbled Harry Potter plot ideas. She finished her first manuscript in 1995. She was too poor to have it photocopied, so she typed another copy herself. A publisher paid her a $3,300 advance for the first Harry Potter book, *Harry Potter and the Philosopher's Stone.*

The most recent of Harry's adventures. *(HARRY POTTER, characters, names, and all related indicia are trademarks of Warner Bros. (2001))*

Then the magic struck. The book quickly sold 150,000 copies and went on to become a bestseller in the United States and Britain. Two more Harry Potter books followed, and they, too, went to the top of the lists. The fourth book in the series, *Harry Potter and the Goblet of Fire,* had a U.S. first printing of 3.8 million copies (a John Grisham potential best-seller usually has a first printing of about 2.5 million). Amazon.com got advance orders for almost 300,000 copies. Rowling will probably make an estimated $10 million on sales of the hardcover edition. Not surprisingly, a Harry Potter movie is in the works.

All in all, the Harry Potter series has made book readers of hundreds of thousands of TV-generation children who have never been fans of the printed page. That takes real magic.

■ Authors as Publishers and Retailers

E-books have the potential to change the structure of the book industry. An author could easily write a book, put it on a website, and offer it for sale, all without the aid of a traditional publisher or retailer. Some big publishers are fearful that a Tom Clancy or a Danielle Steele might use this method to publish a novel and leave the publisher totally out of the process—and the profits. In another variation of this arrangement, an author places a manuscript on a website run by a company that collects and distributes e-books. For example, a company called MightyWords accepts manuscripts from authors and puts them on its website, where they are called eMatter. You can buy a work of eMatter for just a few dollars, and the files are downloaded onto your computer. Promotion and marketing are left up to the author. Big booksellers, such as Barnes and Noble and Borders, are concerned that this new scheme will hurt their business as well.

Note that this is another example of the disintermediation process mentioned in Chapter 1. A content or service provider is connected directly to the consumer, bypassing the traditional distributor and retailer.

Back in 1971, Michael Hart was given a big chunk of free time on the mainframe computer at the University of Illinois. Not quite knowing what to do with it all, Hart began a most ambitious project, which has jumped from the Illinois computer to the web: creating a free library containing 10,000 volumes that made significant contributions to human culture and have made the world what it is today. All the books must be in the public domain.

The first document in this online library was the Declaration of Independence, followed by the Constitution, then the Bible, then Shakespeare's plays. Currently, about a thousand volunteers type or scan texts, adding about 50 a month. Hart eventually wants to input every book as soon as it falls into the public domain.

Hart has chosen a particularly appropriate name for this ambitious undertaking. He calls it Project Gutenberg. (You can check out what's available at www.gutenberg.net/list.html.)

New Devices

In years past, the conventional wisdom in the publishing industry was that only a few technologically advanced consumers would ever read books on a screen. (The conventional wisdom in the music industry was similar: Only a few geeks would ever download music from the Internet. Then came MP3 and Napster. See Chapter 8.) This conventional wisdom was somewhat justified because previous attempts at producing electronic devices for reading books have had limited success. But millions of people who now have personal digital assistants are used to reading e-mail and text on smaller screens. Moreover, several new devices have been designed to make reading e-books just as easy and convenient as reading the traditional paper-and-ink book. One is called SoftBook, a device a little larger than a PDA, with a touch-sensitive screen. Readers can even electronically dog-ear a page, display larger type, put in a digital bookmark, or mark up the screen.

Most experts expect this technology to improve even more in the coming years. In fact, at least two companies are working to develop ultrasharp, high-resolution video screens that are as flexible as paper. This electronic paper is expected to hit the market in about 5 to 10 years.

A big advantage of e-books is their convenience. A typical display device, such as SoftBooks, can hold the equivalent of 5 to 10 books at one time. No more struggling under the weight of a backpack filled with several heavy paper-and-ink books. Moreover, an e-book is searchable. Looking for a name or a particular passage in a novel or textbook? An e-book will let you jump to a particular page.

Printing on Demand

Another possibility made possible by digitalization is **printing on demand**. This is a less radical arrangement; traditional publishers and booksellers are still part of the mix, but books are printed and distributed differently.

Printing on demand works in a fashion similar to that of e-books. Publishers create a huge database of books in digital form. A customer goes to a bookstore, browses through a catalog, and selects a book. A machine in the bookstore then downloads the book and prints it while the customer waits. Folletts has installed printing-on-demand systems in selected college bookstores across the country. These systems can download and print a textbook in about 15 minutes.

The implications of printing on demand are impressive. Traditional book publishers look for books that will sell enough copies (usually a large number) to make a profit. They then print thousands of books, ship them to bookstores, and hope that most of them aren't returned as unsold copies. With printing on demand, however, publishers don't have to guess how many books they should print. They simply print one whenever somebody orders it. This eliminates all the expensive production and shipping costs and guarantees that no books will be returned unsold. Eliminating these costs and the guesswork involved in forecasting demand means that publishers can make money on a book that sells only a few hundred copies. This might open up the way for a multitude of special-interest books that would be too expensive to publish with the traditional method.

Moreover, a book title would never go out of print. It would be permanently stored somewhere on some hard drive or disk. Even the most esoteric or obscure titles could be easily accessed.

What Is a Book?

Finally, the digital age raises fundamental questions about what exactly constitutes a book. E-books could easily incorporate a sound track that plays while a person reads. Video clips that demonstrate how something works could be inserted into instruction books. Illustrations as lush as those done by monks during the Middle Ages are possible. The creative potential of e-books is still unexplored territory.

Does all this signal the death of the traditional paper-and-ink book? Probably not. People will still be drawn to the feel of books and the unique experience of reading paper pages bound between covers. Dick Brass, the executive in charge of Microsoft's e-book efforts, put it this way in a *Newsweek* article: "[Traditional] books will persist because they're beautiful and useful. They're like horses after the automobile—not gone but transformed into a recreational beast."

The rest of this chapter discusses the more concrete aspects of the book industry—its organization, ownership, production techniques, economics, and audiences. Keep in mind, however, that book publishing is in a state of transition as it quickly enters the digital age.

DEFINING FEATURES OF BOOKS

Books are the least "mass" of the mass media. It took about 40 years to sell 20 million copies of *Gone With the Wind*, but more than 50 million people watched the movie version in a single evening when it came to television. Even a flop TV show might have 10 million people in its audience, whereas a popular hardcover book might make the best-seller list with 125,000 copies sold. Even a mass-market paperback might sell only about 6 million copies.

Books, however, can have a cultural impact that far outweighs their modest audience size. *Uncle Tom's Cabin* is credited with changing a nation's attitude toward slavery. Dr. Spock and his *Baby and Child Care* altered the way parents brought up their children and became the target of critics who blamed him and his methods for the social unrest of the 1960s. *Silent Spring* changed the nation's attitudes toward the environment.

Finally, books are the oldest and most enduring of the mass media. Gutenberg printed a book back in the 15th century. Public libraries have been around for hundreds of years. Many individuals have extensive collections of books in their own home libraries. People throw away newspapers and magazines shortly after reading them, but most save their books.

ORGANIZATION OF THE BOOK INDUSTRY

The book publishing industry can be divided into three segments: publishers, distributors, and retailers.

Publishers

The publishing segment consists of the 2,000 or so establishments that transform manuscripts submitted by authors into books that are sought by readers. Every year these companies publish 50,000 to 55,000 new titles. Book publishing is a highly segmented industry. **Publishers** have developed a classification system for the industry based upon the market that is served. The following are the 12 major divisions suggested by the Association of American Publishers:

1. *Trade books* are aimed at the general consumer and sold primarily through bookstores. They can be hardbound or softbound and include works for juveniles and adults. Trade books include hardcover fiction, nonfiction, biography, cookbooks, art books, and several other types.

2. *Religious books* include Bibles, hymnals, prayer books, theology, and other literature of a devotional nature.

3. *Professional books* are aimed at doctors, lawyers, scientists, accountants, business managers, architects, engineers, and all others who need a personal reference library in their work.

4. *Book clubs* at first may sound more like a distribution channel than a division of the publishing segment, but some book clubs publish their own books and almost all prepare special editions for their members. Thus, it makes sense to include them here.

5. *Mail-order publications* consist of books created for the general public and marketed by direct mail. These are different from book clubs because the books are marketed by the publisher, and customers do not incur any membership obligations in an organization. The Time-Life Company, among others, has marketed books dealing with cooking, home repair, the Civil War, Western history, aviation, World War II, and other topics.

Books are portable and personal, and can be read whenever and wherever it's convenient. *(M. Granitsas/ The Image Works)*

CRITICAL/CULTURAL ISSUES

Labor versus Management in Journalism Textbooks

As mentioned in Chapter 2, the critical/cultural approach examines texts, broadly defined. In a paper presented at the 2000 convention of the Association for Education in Journalism and Mass Communication, Dr. Jon Bekken took a more literal approach and examined textbooks, in this case, journalism textbooks, to discover if these texts were instilling a professional ideology in their readers.

Dr. Bekken noted that studies of the coverage of business conflicts have generally found that the media cover these disputes from a perspective that does not favor labor or labor unions. For example, labor reporting focuses on the inconvenience strikes cause for consumers rather than on the issues that led to the strike. Wages rather than health and safety are portrayed as the central concern of labor. In addition, there is a trend toward ignoring labor news altogether. Fewer that a dozen newspapers employ even one full-time labor reporter.

Dr. Bekken wondered if these attitudes might have been fostered during a reporter's academic training. He was specifically interested in the way organized labor was portrayed in 29 media writing and reporting textbooks. After performing a critical/cultural analysis, he concluded that the texts marginalized labor, making it seem unimportant. For instance, he noted that some textbooks have exercises that ask students to write articles about layoffs or hiring freezes based on press releases or notes from interviews with corporate or government officials. The subtle lesson conveyed in these exercises is that the important perspectives do not include those of labor. Other texts simply make little or no mention of labor or labor unions despite the fact that many newspaper workers belong to the International Typographical Union and several newspapers have been plagued by labor–management troubles.

Most texts generally gloss over labor problems in the newspaper industry itself. Health risks such as carpal tunnel syndrome, working conditions, and inadequate pay are seldom mentioned. The idea that joining a union might help address some of these issues is not discussed.

Bekken chronicles other examples that show how labor is almost trivialized. One textbook devotes as many words to covering labor as it does to covering weddings. Another urges reporters to avoid an antibusiness attitude in their stories and to rely on corporate officials, financial analysts, and government regulators as sources for business news. When textbooks do discuss how to cover labor, their emphasis is on covering strikes, violence connected with strikes, or unfair labor practices. Some textbooks recommend that reporters cover how a strike will or will not disrupt the lives of consumers. Most say little about covering the issues that led to the strike.

What are some of the results of the way these texts depict labor? As Bekken says:

> Students carry blind spots towards labor inculcated in their academic training into newsrooms across the country. Editors and publishers have slashed the number of labor reporters . . . Reporters and editors typically do not look to the labor movement for news—rather they wait for strikes, or include labor in discussions of special interest groups said to dominate the political system.

Bekken ends his analysis by noting that in recent decades, textbook authors have tried to remove sexist language and pay more attention to cultural sensitivity. Moreover, newer editions of reporting texts have been expanded to cover topics such as reporting religious news and consumer news. Nonetheless, he points out, most journalism textbooks don't do a good job covering that large number of Americans who labor for a living. The fact that many of the students who read these books go on to ignore labor in their own reporting ought not surprise us.

1. What can textbook authors do to try to remove some of the promanagement bias Bekken discovered? How can teachers using these biased books help lessen the books' drawbacks? What can students do to try to raise awareness of these issues in class?

2. If you've taken or are taking a writing/reporting class, look at the text you're using. How and to what extent does it marginalize or trivialize labor?

3. To what extent—and why—does it matter whether such texts avoid discussing labor problems in the media industry or carry a promanagement bias?

6. *Mass-market paperbacks* are softbound volumes on all subjects that have their major sale in places other than bookstores. Typically, these are the books sold in wire racks in supermarkets, newsstands, drugstores, airports, chain stores, and so on.

7. *University presses* publish mostly scholarly titles or books that have cultural or artistic merit. University presses typically are run on a nonprofit basis, and most of their customers are libraries and scholars.

8. *Elementary and secondary textbooks* are hard- and softcover books, workbooks, manuals, and other printed materials, all intended for use in the classroom. Logically enough, schools are the primary market for these publishers. (This division is also referred to as "elhi" publishers—from *el*ementary and *hi*gh school.)

9. *College textbook* publishers produce texts and workbooks for the college market.

10. *Standardized tests* make up a relatively small segment of the industry. These publishers put together tests of ability, aptitude, interest, personality, and other traits. For example, the Educational Testing Service publishes the Scholastic Aptitude Test and the Graduate Record Exam.

11. *Subscription reference books* consist of encyclopedias, dictionaries, atlases, and the like. They are usually marketed in packages to schools, libraries, and individual consumers.

12. *Audiovisual and other media* supply tapes, films, slides, transparencies, games, and other educational material to schools and training companies.

Table 6.1 shows the relative importance of each of these segments to the industry. As can be seen, trade, professional, and textbook publishing are the major divisions, accounting for 74 percent of sales.

■ Distributors

The Internet has drastically changed the book distribution system. There are now two main channels by which books get to consumers. In the traditional method, the publisher usually ships copies of the book to a wholesaler or distributor who,

Table 6.1	Sales by Publishing Industry Division, 1999
Division	**Percentage of Sales**
Trade	27
Religious	5
Professional	20
Book clubs	5
Mail Order	2
Mass-market paperback	6
University press	2
Elhi text	14
College text	13
Standardized tests	1
Subscription reference	3
AV and other media	3

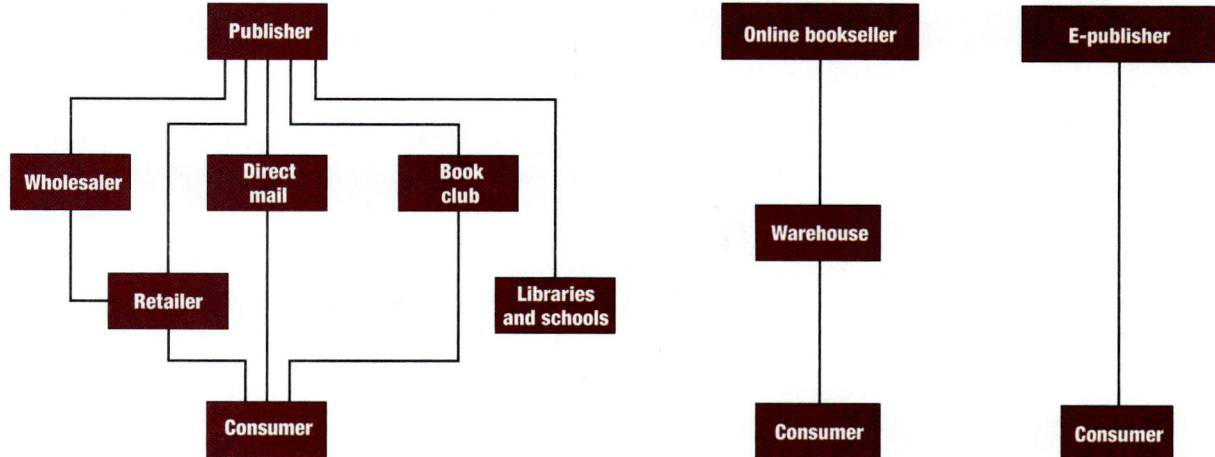

Figure 6–1

Channels of Book
Distribution

in turn, sends the books to a retail outlet where consumers can buy them. Online booksellers, such as Amazon.com and barnesandnoble.com use a different approach. The consumer orders a book from the website and the book is shipped from the seller's warehouse directly to the consumer, bypassing the distributor and retail outlet. E-books, of course, go directly from publisher to consumer, bypassing everything in between. Figure 6–1 illustrates these distribution arrangements.

Retailers

There are more than 20,000 traditional "brick and mortar" bookstores in the United States plus the big online booksellers mentioned above. Big chains, such as Barnes and Noble, Borders–Walden Books, Books-A-Million, and Crown Books dominate traditional bookselling. In 1999, these four firms took in about $7 billion in revenue, with Barnes and Noble in first place with about $2.8 billion in sales. Online retailers are not far behind. Amazon.com ranked third with $800 million, while Barnes and Noble's online operation ranked fifth.

Other retail channels include college bookstores and direct-to-consumer booksellers such as book clubs and mail-order sales.

OWNERSHIP IN THE BOOK INDUSTRY

The book industry is dominated by large conglomerates with interests in other media. The top five companies as of mid-2000 were the following:

1. *Pearson Publishing.* A global media company that is the world's largest educational publisher, with imprints such as Scott Foresman and Prentice Hall. It also owns the Penguin Group of consumer publishing firms (Penguin, Dutton, and Viking) as well as the *Financial Times* business newspaper. Its Pearson Television produces more than 150 programs worldwide, including the hugely popular "Baywatch." Publishing revenue was about $3.7 billion in 1999.

Jeff Bezos was always tinkering with things. When he was three, he took apart his bed. Eleven years later, he tried to make a hovercraft out of a vacuum cleaner. Sixteen years after that, he tinkered with the way books were sold and totally revolutionized a business by starting Amazon.com.

After growing up in Houston and Miami, Bezos enrolled at Princeton, where he studied computer science and engineering. After a couple of jobs in the financial marketplace, he wound up at a Wall Street investment company. One day in 1993, while doing financial research, he came across a startling statistic: The Internet was growing at a rate of 2,300 percent a year. Bezos recognized the tremendous selling potential of the net and decided to launch an online business. He reasoned that things that are big mail-order sellers should also do well online. Accordingly, he made a list of the top 20 mail-order products and determined that books would be the best item to sell. A virtual bookstore would have the space to list all the millions of books in print; no brick-and-mortar store could do that. Further, book wholesalers had already produced CD-ROMs that listed all available titles. Bezos realized that the existing book databases could easily be put online.

Bezos's family and friends invested $300,000 in his idea, and Bezos moved to Seattle, the home of many net-savvy programmers, who would be needed to get the business online. Seattle was also the home of one of the biggest book wholesalers in the country.

Working out of his garage, Bezos created a website that he tested among his friends. It seemed to work well, and Bezos decided to open the site to everybody. But what to call it? He originally wanted to call it Cadabra.com, as in "abracadabra," the magic incantation. When he tried this name out with his lawyer, the lawyer thought Bezos had said "Cadaver.com" and wanted to know why he would name his site after a dead body. Bezos went back to the drawing board and eventually settled on Amazon.com, after one of the world's longest and most powerful rivers.

The rest, as they say, is Internet history. The company grew quickly. In 1996, Amazon.com had 300 employees. In 2001, it had about 3,000. From a few thousand customers in its first year, it now has more than 20 million in about 150 countries. Sales in 2001 should exceed $3 billion. Its brand name is more recognizable than Burger King or Barbie. Amazon.com has also branched out from books and now sells CDs, toys, electronics, and gifts on its website.

Furthermore, Amazon.com is one of the companies that has defined the Internet economy, where growth seems more important than profits. As of 2000, the company had lost more than $1.5 billion dollars. Nonetheless, its stock was selling at $113 a share. Then reality set in. Like many other dot-coms, Amazon was hit hard by a stock slump in mid-2000 and its stock price dropped 76 percent. Despite this precipitous loss, investors value Amazon at $10 billion, more than Barnes and Noble, Kmart and J.C. Penney combined. Bezos has recently slashed costs and has projected that the company will turn profitable in the next couple of years.

No matter how profitable or unprofitable Amazon.com may become, one thing is certain: It has helped make pointing and clicking a significant part of Americans' shopping repertoire.

2. *Random House.* Part of the Bertelsmann media empire, which includes interests in 600 companies in 53 countries and is engaged in publishing, music, magazines, TV, and radio. Bertelsmann also owns 41 percent of barnesandnoble.com plus other Internet holdings. Random House had about $1 billion in revenue in 1999.

3. *HarperCollins.* Rupert Murdoch's worldwide communications company owns HarperCollins as well as 20th Century Fox, the Fox TV network, and various newspapers and magazines. HarperCollins had revenues of $764 million in 1999.

4. *Simon & Schuster.* This publishing house is part of the newly merged CBS/Viacom, a conglomerate that has TV networks, radio stations and a radio network, cable networks, theme parks, and a TV syndication company. Publishing revenue was $610 million in 1999.

5. *Time Warner Publishing.* Part of the AOL Time Warner company, the biggest media conglomerate in the world, with an online service, cable systems, magazines, and TV and radio, movie production, and other interests. The publishing group includes Warner Books, Time-Life Books, and Little, Brown and Company. In 1999 it had revenues of about $300 million.

PRODUCING THE BOOK

Departments and Staff

Figure 6–2 depicts the organizational arrangement at a typical publishing house. The titles may vary at other companies, but the functions will be basically the same. There are four major departments in the publishing company: (1) editorial, (2) production, (3) marketing, and (4) general administration or business.

The editorial department is in charge of dealing with authors. Essentially, it has a twofold task: selecting manuscripts and preparing them for publication. Some editors specialize in procurement and visit potential authors to solicit their work. Other editors read manuscripts, write reports on them, and recommend acceptance, rejection, or revision. Once an accepted manuscript is completed, copyeditors sift through it, checking grammar, punctuation, language, internal consistency, and accuracy.

As the name implies, the production department oversees the planning and design of the physical book. Type style, composition, paper, printing, and binding are the responsibilities of this division. The production manager and staff must keep track of many tasks, not the least of which is keeping the book on schedule.

The marketing department supervises sales, promotion, and publicity. The actual type of sales activity depends upon the kind of book being marketed. Publishers of elhi textbooks sell mainly to school systems; college text publishers sell to individuals or committees of professors. Mass-market paperbacks must be sold to retailers, who in turn must sell them to the general public. Advertising in trade magazines, listings in publishing catalogs, and posters are common promotional methods. For trade books, ads in literary magazines and reviews in respected publications can be influential. Publishers trying to promote mass-market books use other techniques.

For example, getting a book made into a movie, even a movie that's not particularly successful, will dramatically increase book sales. The paperback edition of *The Talented Mr. Ripley* sold thousands more copies once Matt Damon's picture was added to the cover. It also helps if an author can get on a TV talk show such as "Oprah" or "Larry King Live."

Figure 6–2

Organization of a
Publishing Company

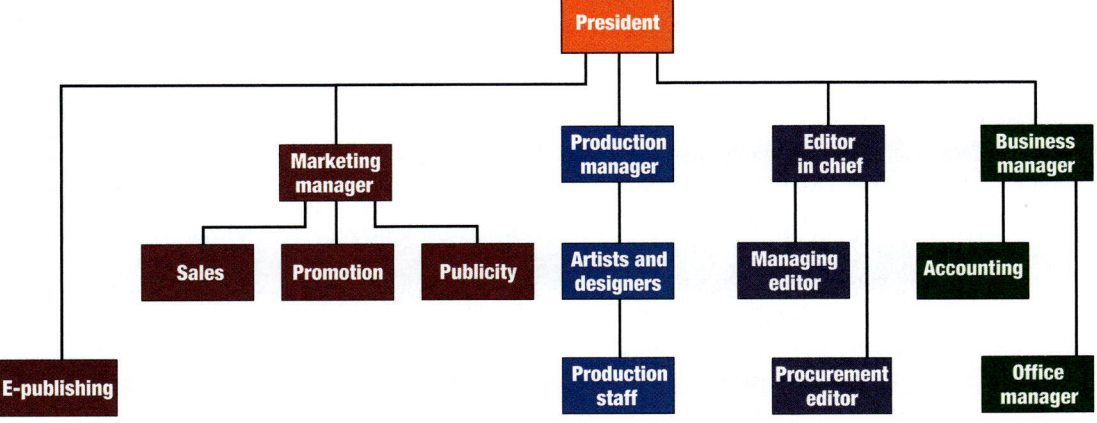

CRITICAL / CULTURAL ISSUES

Oprah Winfrey Sells Fictional Self-Help to Her Viewers

Contributed by Rita Van Zant   Oprah's Book Club has become the newest self-help narrative to be sold to women to influence their cultural perceptions of themselves. Oprah has created a frenzy in this country by promising her audience that their lives will be markedly improved if they will "Get with the Program" and read her fiction selections monthly. Because of her strong belief in the power of individual people to change their circumstances, Oprah feels that if she can get people to start reading books, they will become more self-aware. Using her book club, Oprah has offered her viewers, mainly women, the same "do-it-yourself" remedy for the mind, body, and soul that for years has been prevalent within the self-help industry.

The self-help world is big. During the last 40 years, the number of people who have joined self-help groups and purchased self-help books has grown exponentially. By the early 1990s, self-help discussion groups numbered well over 150,000. One in three adult Americans has purchased a self-help book. Of these, 75 to 85 percent are women. There is a reason for these statistics. The self-help marketing industry tends to toy with the emotions of women who feel inferior or victimized in some way, whether they are staying home caring for their children or seeking a career in the workforce. There is something wrong with them, women are told, but fortunately they can be "cured" by paying for some self-help therapy or buying self-help books. Many women have been exposed to this disease and have paid both financially and emotionally to "cure" it. The profound preoccupation with the self began with the "me" decade of the 1970s, which became the "me-first" decade in the 1980s and has become the "why me?" decade of the 1990s. By tapping into this phenomenon of bibliotherapy, Oprah Winfrey has become the most effective promoter of self-help for recovery on television today.

Oprah's Club reflects her New Age philosophy that women are responsible for their behavior and they can fix themselves if they want to intensely enough. In essence, what she says is that women are just not good enough as they are. They are told they must continue to strive for perfection, even though it is never attainable. The bar is always raised. This false paradigm is an important factor in the growth of the self-help market. For years, marketers have created an obsession with the self and made money from it. For example, women are told in various media that they are pathological because they shop too much; then they are told to buy books to learn how to stop shopping. The college-educated, middle-class women who are most likely to take advantage of this help are being told that the habits they have acquired are not normal. Oprah is shrewdly taking advantage of this unquenchable desire of women to become better people.

The Oprah Winfrey Show has become the major representative of a self-help panacea for women today. The anxieties that Oprah feeds her viewers do represent the real problems in our society—but in a twisted way. Many women are frustrated because they are working longer, harder hours both at home and at work with little to show for it except weariness. What Oprah doesn't discuss or even acknowledge is that women cannot solve this problem by themselves. The insistence by Oprah that self-help is the cure-all to the emotional and psychological concerns of her viewers obscures the real problem—that the inequality of the marketplace needs to be changed. Women need to be told they deserve their full share of the economic pie.

When Oprah advocates self-help as opposed to the changing of the hegemonic culture, she is helping the oppression continue. She sells products, not political solutions. Oprah continues to refine the "new woman"—but not necessarily to women's advantage. Thus women are really settling for a placebo. If Oprah would use her program to rally her viewers to vote as a block for women and family issues that would economically benefit them, their lives would change much more dramatically than by reading self-help books.

1. If you were Oprah's producer, how would you suggest she respond to criticisms such as this?

2. Van Zant argues strongly that self-help books are actually harmful to women. To what extent do you agree or disagree with her? Why?

3. Most readers of self-help books are women. What are some self-help books that might be created specifically for men, and what does this tell us about the social construction of gender in our society?

The publicity section spreads the news of the book to as many potential customers as possible. Getting the book reviewed by a reputable publication is a tremendous help. This is a challenging task, however. For example, a prestigious publication such as the *New York Times Book Review* might receive anywhere from 12,000 to 15,000 books a year, of which only 10 to 15 percent might be reviewed.

The business manager at a publishing company is responsible for several functions. One of the most important is accounting. This department oversees processing orders, controls credit, and provides balance sheets on the firm's overall operation. Further, it prepares budgets and makes long-range financial forecasts. The business department's responsibilities include dealing with internal personnel policies and supervising the general day-to-day operational needs of the company.

The newest department at most publishers deals with e-books. This department is in charge of building a diverse list of original material for electronic publication and coordinating the development and marketing of e-content. In addition, this department oversees the conversion of traditional print books into electronic form.

Publishing the Book

Editors get their books from three main sources: those submitted by agents, unsolicited books sent in by authors, and book ideas generated by the editor. Most trade manuscripts are submitted through literary agents. Agents are known quantities and will not generally submit manuscripts that they know are unacceptable to the editor. Unsolicited manuscripts are given an unflattering name in the business: "slush." As they come in, these manuscripts are put in the slush pile and eventually read, if the author is lucky, by an editorial assistant. Most of the time they are rejected with a form letter, but every once in a while an author gets lucky. *The Office Humor Book*, for example, went from the slush pile into five printings. Editors also generate ideas for books. If an editor has a good idea for a book, he or she will generally talk to one or more agents, who will suggest likely candidates for the assignment. This is another good reason why writers should have agents. In any case, the author typically submits a proposal consisting of a cover letter, a brief description of the planned book, a list of reasons why it should be published, an analysis of the potential market, an outline or a table of contents, and perhaps one or two sample chapters. The proposal usually goes to an acquisitions editor and is evaluated. If the publishing decision is favorable, then a contract is signed and the author begins work in earnest.

Editorial work starts as soon as the author submits chapters to the publisher. Editors look at the overall thrust of the book to make sure it makes sense and achieves its original intent. Moreover, the mechanics of the book are checked to make sure that the general level of writing is acceptable, that all footnotes are in order, that all necessary permissions to reproduce material from other sources have been obtained, and that all artwork is present. Eventually, both author and editors will produce a manuscript that is mutually satisfactory.

While all this editing is going on, other decisions are being made about scheduling, designing the interior look of the book, and designing the cover. When everything is in order, the book is printed, bound, and sent to the warehouse to await distribution or distributed online.

What ethical obligations to book publishers owe to their readers? Is it the responsibility of the publisher to make sure that all the facts in a book are correct?

In 1999, St. Martin's Press released a book which claimed that presidential candidate George W. Bush had been arrested in 1972 on a drug charge and that his father used his influence to have the charge expunged from the record. All the sources for this charge were anonymous. Bush denied the accusations and said they were fiction.

A few days after the book was published, facts began to surface that questioned the book's credibility. The author of the book was a convicted felon. His résumé stated that he had received a literary prize that apparently didn't exist. The book claimed that a Republican judge had expunged the record, but there were no Republican judges in office in 1972 in the jurisdiction where the alleged arrest had been made. Other inconsistencies also cropped up. Embarrassed, St. Martin's Press suspended publication of the book and had to trash 90,000 copies.

A postmortem analysis of the episode revealed that, despite the sensational nature of the charges against Bush, apparently no one at St. Martin's had done a very good job of checking out the claims in the book. It is true that most book contracts require an author to pledge that the facts contained in the book are true or are based on reasonable research. Nonetheless, when confronted with an accusation of this magnitude, perhaps a publisher has more than simply contractual arrangements to consider. There may be an ethical responsibility to the reader to assure that prudent care was taken to verify what was published. Otherwise, the publisher risks losing the trust of its readers.

Some critics have suggested that the current nature of the publishing business has exacerbated the problem. Pressures to cut costs are increasing, and publishers try to get books out faster to capitalize on their currency. At the time of the St. Martin's case, five other books about George W. Bush had been released or were in the works. In fact, St. Martin's moved up the publication date after the publisher learned of the explosive charges in the book, because the company was afraid it would be scooped by another publisher. All in all, this occurrence suggests that financial and competitive tensions ought not overshadow possible ethical considerations.

ECONOMICS

Despite economic ups and downs, changing lifestyles, and continued predictions that reading is a lost art, the book industry continues to prosper. Figure 6–3 displays book industry revenue over the past 33 years. Although 1999 was not a particularly good year for book publishers, more than $24 billion of books were sold, up 14 percent from 1997.

Why are books doing so well? First, the population is getting older; the fastest-growing age group is 35 to 49 years old—the age when people buy the most books. Second, people have disposable income to spend on books. Finally, federal and local governments continue to make education a funding priority. Per-pupil expenditures at the elementary and high school levels have increased and are expected to grow in the future, enhancing the market for texts, workbooks, and standardized tests.

At the consumer level, it's obvious that books have gotten more expensive. The average price of a hardcover book in 1999 was about $46, and the average price of a paperback was up to $6.00. In fact, many mass-market paperbacks were selling for $6.95, and some publishers were talking about breaking the $7 mark in the near future.

A publisher has two main sources of income: (1) the money that comes from book sales and (2) money from **subsidiary rights** (sales to book clubs, foreign rights, paperback rights, and reprint permissions). Of these two, the income from book sales is the most important. It should be noted, however, that the publisher does not get all the money from the sale of a book. The list price is discounted for wholesalers and booksellers. These discounts might amount to 40 percent for many books.

Figure 6–3

Book Publishing
Revenue, 1963–1999

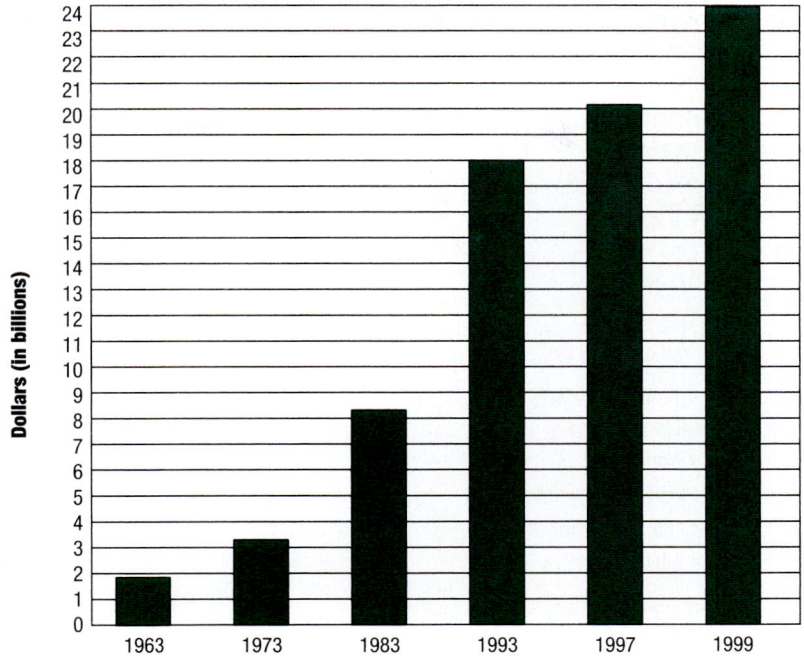

The costs a publisher incurs are many. First, there is the cost of manufacturing the book: printing, typesetting, and royalties paid to the author. These costs are variable and are tied to the number of books printed. For example, paper costs would be more substantial on a book with a press run of 20,000 than on one with a run of 2,000. There are also operating expenses, including editorial, production, marketing, and general administration expenses. Table 6.2 shows a hypothetical operating statement for an adult trade hardcover book published by a typical publishing company. It is assumed that the book has a list price of $20 (all numbers are rounded for convenience) and 10,000 copies were printed. After a year, 2,000 copies were unsold and were returned to the publisher for a credit. This means that 8,000 copies were sold. Allowing a 40 percent discount from the list price leaves the publisher with revenues of about $12 per book. Multiplying 8,000 times $12 gives us the gross sales amount: $96,000. From this are subtracted the costs of returns and allowances, leaving a balance of $77,000 in net sales revenue. Manufacturing costs and author royalties amounted to $45,400. This sum is subtracted from the net sales to find the gross margin on sales (the amount that net sales exceeded the cost of sales), in this case, $31,600. Table 6.2 also assumes that the publisher sold some subsidiary rights (to a book club or a paperback publisher) and received $6,900 in return. So far, the total income from the book is $38,500 ($31,600 + $6,900). Subtracting the total operating expense of $34,600 from $38,500 yields a net income of $3,900.

These figures, of course, would vary for other publishers and for other segments of the book industry. Profit margins typically varied from 2 to 20 percent during the period 1996 to 2000. Advances and acquisition rights are two of the big expenses in publishing. For example, Simon & Schuster paid Hillary Clinton an advance of $8 million for her memoirs.

Table 6.2	Profit-Loss Statement of Trade Hardcover with $20 List Price		
Press run	10,000 copies		
Returned	2,000 copies		
Gross sales	8,000 copies	@ $12	$96,000
Returns and allowances			(19,000)
Net sales			77,000
Cost of sales			
Manufacturing			27,700
Royalties			17,700
Total cost of sales			45,400
Operating expense			
Editorial			4,500
Production			1,600
Marketing and fulfillment			18,500
Administration			10,000
Total operating expense			34,600
Margin of net sales over cost of sales			31,600
Other income			6,900
Net income			3,900

The economics of printing on demand and e-books are much less complicated. There are no costs associated with printing, storing, shipping, or returns. One printing-on-demand company estimates that a publisher can produce a book for a just a few hundred dollars.

 FEEDBACK

The most important form of audience feedback in the book industry is the **best-seller lists** compiled by newspapers such as the *New York Times* and *USA Today* and the trade publication *Publisher's Weekly*. These organizations use slightly different methods to tabulate a rank ordering of the best-selling books, but all involve collecting data from a sample of the various channels of book distribution—chain bookstores, independent bookstores, newsstands, and price clubs—and then assigning various weights to the numbers to come up with the rankings. Making the best-seller list is important since many bookstores automatically order large numbers of all books that make the list. Consequently, appearing on the list can mean added sales for the book.

Amazon.com offers a unique feedback arrangement called purchase circles. These are highly specialized best-seller lists based on the zip codes of the customers who order books from the company. The lists are categorized by geography, by organizations, by companies, and by educational settings. For example, in mid-2000 the two top-ranking books on the Amazon.com purchase circle for the University of Georgia were *Autocad Conventions for Architects* and *The PDR Family Guide to Natural Medicine*.

Shortly after winning the 2000 Booker Prize for her novel *The Blind Assassin,* Margaret Atwood began a seven-month promotional tour that included stops in the United States, Canada, England, Sweden, and Germany. *(AP/Wide World Photos)*

Audiences

A book industry survey of readers revealed that two-thirds of all books are purchased by those over 40. Readers under 25 accounted for only 4 percent of all sales. Book reading was also positively related to income and education. Popular fiction was the most popular type of book read, accounting for more than half of all book sales, followed by cookbooks and books dealing with crafts.

C A R E E R
O U T L O O K

THE BOOK PUBLISHING INDUSTRY

Book publishing is a small industry; there are only 70,000 to 75,000 jobs nationwide in the entire business. Consequently, there is a lot of competition for many of the jobs, particularly those on the editorial side.

There are two general areas to pursue in book publishing: editorial and business. For someone interested in editorial work, the best training consists of courses in English and composition, with a strong emphasis on writing skills. Entry-level positions are competitive, and most newcomers typically join a publishing company as editorial assistants. There are numerous clerical tasks to be performed in publishing: answering authors' letters, reading manuscripts, writing reports about manuscripts, checking facts, proofreading, writing catalog copy, and so on. Editorial assistants do these and countless other tasks.

The next logical step up the career ladder is to become an assistant or associate editor. These individuals work with senior editors in several different areas: manuscript acquisition, copyediting, design and production, artwork, and so on. Eventually, this path leads to a position as an editor. After getting the necessary experience, editors are promoted to senior editors, managing editors, or executive editors, positions that carry a good deal of administrative responsibility.

On the business side there are several career paths open. Many people start as sales representatives and sell their company's books to the appropriate customers. Sales and marketing experience are so vital to the well-being of the industry that the path to top management usually begins in the sales department. At many companies, presidents and vice presidents are almost always former salespeople with extensive experience in marketing.

Understanding the Internet and having experience with web design and HTML are definite advantages for a newcomer as books move into the digital age. Many companies are offering substantial bonuses and perks to attract and keep such individuals on their staffs.

Finally, there are usually opportunities for newcomers in the advertising, promotion, and publicity areas of publishing. The usual career path is to find an entry-level position as an assistant to someone and gradually work up to the advertising, promotion, or publicity director for the company.

Before closing, we should mention that it is not always necessary to work for a publishing company to find employment in this area. Many people work as freelance editors, designers, proofreaders, indexers, artists, and photographers. These typically are people who have had some experience and have branched out on their own.

■ MAIN POINTS

- The book is the oldest form of mass communication. Early books were printed by hand until the invention of movable type and the printing press.
- In early America, publishers were also printers. Books became more popular during the 17th and 18th centuries.
- From 1900 to 1945, the book publishing industry became more commercialized. Continuing consolidation has resulted in a modern book industry that is dominated by a few large companies.

- The digital revolution may change the underlying structure of the book industry. Authors may self-publish their works on the web. New reading devices will make the e-book more convenient, and printing on demand will make narrow-interest books more accessible.
- The book industry consists of publishers, distributors, and retailers. The emergence of online booksellers has changed the way books are sold and distributed.
- Despite some ups and downs, book publishing has been profitable during the past few decades.

■ QUESTIONS FOR REVIEW

1. How has the content of popular books changed from the 17th to the 21st century?
2. What are the defining features of books?
3. What are the main revenue sources for book publishers?
4. What's the difference between a trade book and a mass-market paperback?

■ QUESTIONS FOR CRITICAL THINKING

1. With all the talk about declining literacy and complaints that nobody reads anymore, why do book sales keep increasing?
2. What implications for the industry will result from a shift to e-books?
3. What advantages or disadvantages are connected with a book industry dominated by a few big firms?
4. Have books become too expensive? What factors contribute to rising prices?

■ KEY TERMS

e-book (p. 150)

printing on demand (p. 152)

publishers (p. 154)

subsidiary rights (p. 162)

best-seller lists (p. 164)

■ SUGGESTIONS FOR FURTHER READING

The following books contain further information about concepts and topics discussed in this chapter.

Cardoza, Avery. *The Complete Guide to Successful Publishing.* New York: Cardoza Publishing, 1995.

Eisenhart, Douglas. *Publishing in the Information Age.* Westport, CT: Quorum Books, 1994.

Gallagher, Patricia. *For All the Write Reasons.* Worcester, PA: Young Sparrow Press, 1992.

Greco, Albert. *The Book Publishing Industry.* Boston: Allyn and Bacon, 1997.

Hamilton, John. *Casanova Was a Book Lover.* Baton Rouge: Louisiana State University Press, 2000.

Perkins, Wayne. *A Cheap and Easy Guide to Self-Publishing E-Books.* Downloadable electronic book, 2000.

Ross, Marilyn. *Marketing Your Books.* Buena Vista, CA: Communication Creativity, 1990.

Vanderbilt, Arthur. *The Making of a Best Seller.* Jefferson, NC: McFarland, 1999.

Also see *Publishers Weekly,* the leading trade magazine of the industry, and *Writer's Market.*

■ SURFING THE INTERNET

Remember, websites change all the time; some move, some evaporate, and some transform.

www.amazon.com

The online bookstore mentioned in the text. Try searching for a book, even an obscure one, in its database. You'll probably find it.

www.bookwire.com

Takes a look inside the book business. Includes news, features, and links to other related sites.

www.bisg.org.

Home of the Book Industry Study Group. Provides research information about the industry.

www.publishersweekly.com

The online version of *Publisher's Weekly,* the leading trade magazine. Includes job listings.

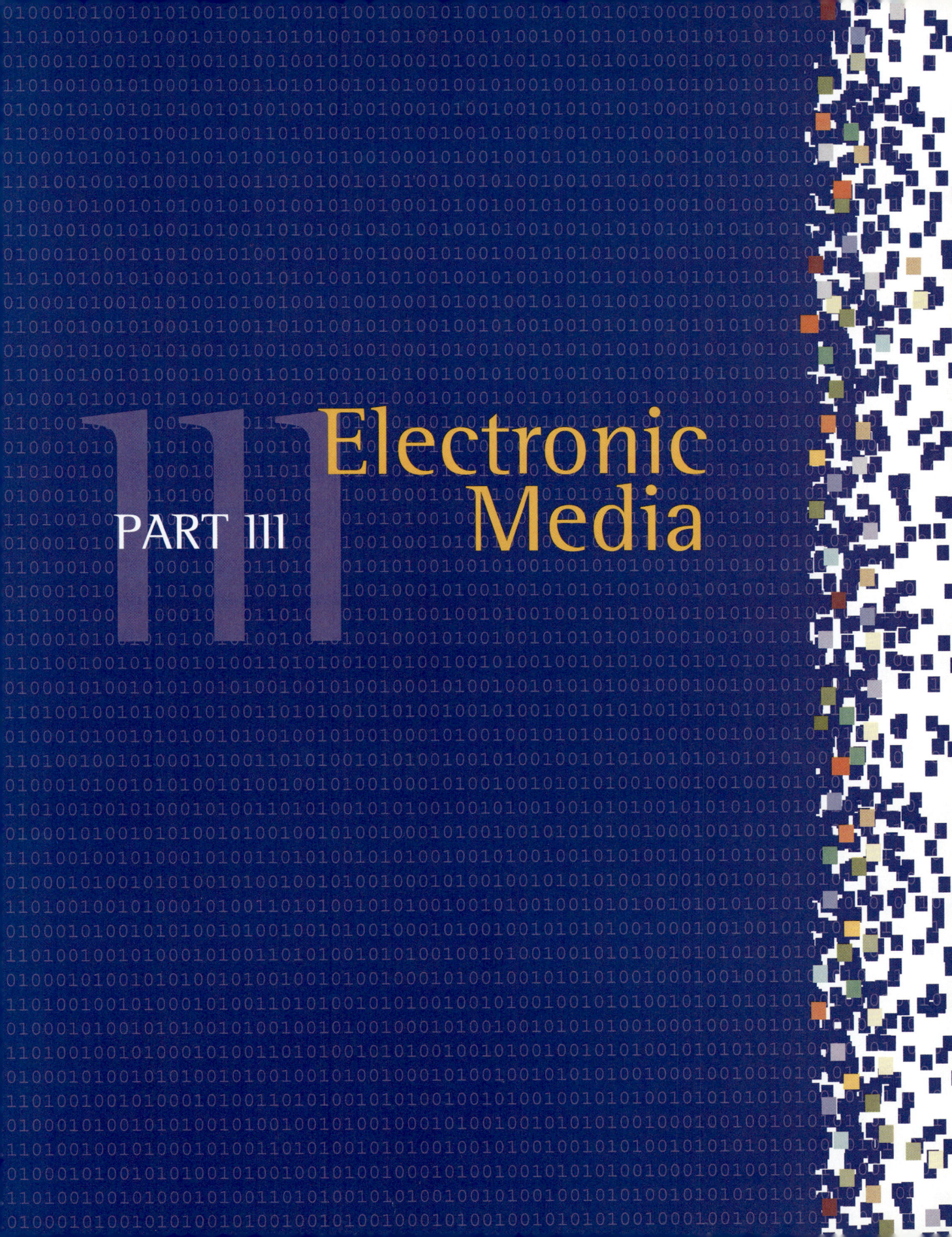

PART III

Electronic Media

CHAPTER 7

Radio

Heard at 8:36 A.M. during a commercial pod on a major-market AM radio station in the Southeast: commercials for (1) an insurance company, (2) an airline, (3) an online bill-paying service, (4) an office supply company, (5) a company that steam cleans driveways, and (6) a soft drink company, as well as a promotion for the station itself. Total time devoted to commercials during the pod: 6 minutes. Total commercial time for the 8–9 A.M. hour: 18 minutes.

The above example points out an interesting fact about radio circa 2000: It may be doing too well. Radio raked in more than $19.8 billion in ad revenue in 2000, an industry record. Radio industry revenues increased for 92 straight months from 1993 to 2000.

The result of all this success is more commercials per hour and less time for music and talk. In 2000, some AM stations reportedly were running more than 20 minutes of commercials per hour. How much will listeners tolerate before they turn to competitors created by the new technology of digital radio broadcasting?

Of all the media discussed in this book, radio is the one least affected by the digital revolution. In fact, radio stations still use the same basic analog technology that was used in the 1920s and 1930s. As the new century opened, however, there were signs that this situation is changing. But we're getting ahead of the story. Let's first take a look at how radio got to where it is today.

Radio listening is especially popular with young people. Teens average more than two hours per day. (©Corbis Images)

 HISTORY

In 1887, Heinrich Hertz, a German physicist, successfully sent and detected radio waves. Guglielmo Marconi used Hertz's efforts to build a wireless communication device that could send Morse code—dots and dashes—from a transmitter to a receiver. Marconi started a wireless telegraphy company that would play an important part in early radio's development.

Reginald Fessenden and Lee De Forest provided the breakthroughs that would make broadcasting—as opposed to sending dots and dashes—possible. Fessenden, with the help of the General Electric (GE) corporation, built a high-speed, continuous-wave generator that could broadcast the human voice and music. De Forest invented the vacuum tube, originally called the audion, which made it much easier to receive radio signals.

The development of early radio was hampered by legal battles over patent rights to various inventions. When World War I broke out, the U.S. Navy assumed responsibility for all relevant patents, and radio made great technical strides during the war.

Big Business

After the war, corporate America recognized the potential of radio. A new company, the Radio Corporation of America (RCA), was formed and acquired the assets of the U.S. division of the Marconi Company. Stock in RCA was held by some of the biggest companies of the period: AT&T, General Electric, and Westinghouse. Note that these companies thought RCA would be in the wireless telegraphy business. Despite the efforts of Fessenden and De Forest, it was hard to envision that broadcasting news and entertainment to the general public could make money.

Some individuals, however, were more prescient. David Sarnoff, an employee of the Marconi Company who later became head of RCA, suggested that one day this new invention would become a "radio music box." Sarnoff himself would be one of the central figures in the development of this new medium.

Mass Audience

Frank Conrad, an engineer for Westinghouse in Pittsburgh, tinkered with radio as a hobby. He built a radio transmitter in his garage and started broadcasting recorded music, reporting sports scores, and showcasing the musical abilities of his sons. In a short time, he had attracted an enthusiastic audience of radio fans. A local department store started selling radio sets so that more people could hear Conrad's programs. In turn, Westinghouse built a station so that Conrad's signal would be heard by more people. Westinghouse, meanwhile, would build the radio sets and receive "free" advertising because of its connection with the station. The station, KDKA, signed on in 1920 and is still on the air, making it the country's oldest station.

KDKA was a success. RCA, GE, and AT&T, along with many other companies and organizations, started radio stations. Radio listening became a national craze. By discovering that an audience existed for broadcast programs intended for the general public, radio found the role it would play for the foreseeable future.

A young boy listens to an early radio set. *(National Archives)*

Better Receivers

Early radio receivers were not user-friendly. They were powered by an assortment of large, bulky, and sometimes leaky batteries. Tuning required patience, a steady hand, and a knowledge of electronics.

By 1926, however, set manufacturers had improved their product. New radios ran on household current, could be tuned with just two knobs, had better antennas, and looked like a fashionable piece of furniture. Between 1925 and 1930, 17 million radio sets were sold and radio was becoming truly a mass medium.

Radio Goes Commercial

One of the curious things about early radio broadcasting was that very little of it was done by broadcasters. The early stations were owned by a polyglot of organizations. WLS in Chicago was owned by Sears, Roebuck (*World's Largest Store*); WGN by the Chicago Tribune (*World's Greatest Newspaper*); WSM in Nashville by the National Life Insurance Company (*We Shelter Millions*); and WHB in Kansas City by the Sweeney Automotive and Electrical School.

Early broadcasting wasn't expensive, and radio station owners figured they got their money's worth through the exposure they received through the station. Before long, however, operating expenses began to pile up and stations searched for a way to have their stations turn a profit.

Nobody knew quite how to do it. Some felt listeners should send in voluntary contributions; others wanted a tax on radio tubes. It was the phone company that finally came up with a workable plan. AT&T began selling time on WEAF, their flagship station in New York, to anybody who wanted to broadcast a message. The most logical customers for this new service were companies that had things to sell. Thus, in 1922, the Queensboro Realty Company paid $300 for five radio talks that extolled the benefits of living in the country, preferably on a lot bought from

Radio receivers in the 1930s no longer required a knowledge of electronics to operate. A family could simply sit back and listen. *(Stock Montage)*

the Queensboro Realty Company. Other companies quickly realized the advertising potential of this new media and bought time on WEAF and other stations. The problem of financing radio broadcasting was solved—broadcasting would be supported by advertising.

Networks

Linking radio stations into a **network** made good economic sense. Rather than having each individual station pay the costs of producing its own program, it was much cheaper for all stations to share the cost of a single program and broadcast the same show on all stations. Moreover, a linked network of stations could give advertisers the ability to reach a larger audience in a wider geographic area.

The first network was the National Broadcasting Company (NBC), a subsidiary of RCA, set up in 1926. NBC actually started two networks. One consisted of stations originally owned by RCA, and another was made up of stations acquired from AT&T when the phone company decided to get out of the broadcasting business. NBC got a competitor when the Columbia Broadcasting System (CBS) went on the air the next year. William S. Paley, whose career with CBS would last into the 1980s, headed the new network.

The two networks grew quickly. By 1937, NBC had 111 affiliated stations, while CBS had 105. Advertisers were spending more than $27 million annually on network radio. It was obvious that the network-affiliate arrangement would persist for some time to come.

Early radio commercials were polite and unobtrusive, almost as though the companies were embarrassed to invade the privacy of the home with their messages. Commercials were limited to merely mentioning the name of the product or the sponsor. Direct selling or quoting prices over the air was forbidden. There was even a good deal of discussion about the propriety of broadcasting commercials for a product so personal as toothpaste. These attitudes didn't last long.

At first, product names were incorporated into program names as indirect advertising became more accepted. Early listeners were treated to programs such as "The Eveready Battery Hour" and the "Balkite Hour." Other advertisers named performers after their products: the A&P Gypsies, the Clicquot Club Eskimos. From this it was only a short step to direct advertising over radio, and in 1928 Henry Field of KFNF in Shenandoah, Iowa, became one of radio's pioneer salesmen when he invited listeners to buy seeds, bacon, auto tires, fresh hams, prunes, paint, coffee, shoes, and pig meal from his general store.

By 1930, the 60-second spot announcement became the most widely accepted format. Radio commercials became more ambitious and elaborate. Dramatic situations were used to sell soap products. Wheaties, Pepsi-Cola, and Barbasol developed the singing commercial. But perhaps the form of advertising that will be best remembered from radio is that of the premium. All it took was a box top and maybe a dime and you could be the proud owner of a Little Orphan Annie Ovaltine Shake-Up Mug, a Tom Mix periscope ring, or a Lone Ranger Special Glow-in-the-Dark Belt. Most premiums were aimed at children, but the adults were not left out. The loyal listeners of "Clara, Lu, 'n' Em" could send in a box top from Super Suds Soap along with a dime and in return they would be sent a package of "Hollywood Flower Garden" seeds. In 10 days half a million seed packages were sold.

Revenues from advertising permitted the networks to hire big-name entertainers. Jack Benny, Ed Wynn, and George Burns and Gracie Allen were all well-known vaudeville entertainers who successfully made the transition to radio. The most successful program, however, was "Amos 'n' Andy," a comedy starring Charles Correll and Freeman Gosden, two white comedians working in blackface. Although considered racist today, the show was top-rated during the late 1920s and early 1930s and listening to it became a national habit.

Government Regulation

Early radio regulation did not anticipate the success of broadcasting. As more and more stations went on the air during the 1920s, interference became a tremendous problem and the government lacked the authority to do anything about it.

Congress finally acted to resolve this situation by passing the **Radio Act of 1927.** This act set up the Federal Radio Commission (FRC), a regulatory body that would issue licenses and try to clean up the chaos that existed. The commission defined the AM broadcast band, standardized channel designations, abolished portable stations, and moved to minimize interference. By 1929 the situation had improved, and the new radio medium was prevented from suffocating in its own growth.

Thus, by the end of the 1920s, the framework for modern radio broadcasting was in place. It would be a commercially supported mass medium dominated by networks and regulated by an agency of the federal government.

The Depression: 1930–1940

By most standards, radio was not hit as hard by the depression as were other industries. In fact, the amount of money spent on radio advertising tripled from 1930 to 1935. Profits may not have been as high as they might have been in better economic times, but the radio industry was able to weather the depression with relatively little hardship.

"This . . . is London." Edward R. Murrow's famous opening was familiar to millions of Americans who listened to his reports from the British capital during World War II. Murrow went on to a distinguished career in TV journalism. *(Culver)*

The most significant legal development for radio during the depression years was the formation of the **Federal Communications Commission (FCC).** President Roosevelt wanted to create a government agency that would consolidate the regulatory functions of the communications industry. In response to the president's demands, Congress passed the **Communications Act of 1934**, which consolidated responsibilities for broadcast and wire regulation under a new seven-member Federal Communications Commission. Aside from the expanded size of the commission and its increased duties, the fundamental philosophy underlying the original Radio Act of 1927 remained unchanged.

Birth of FM

In the mid-1930s, Edwin Howard Armstrong, a noted inventor, demonstrated frequency modulated radio, or FM, to his friend David Sarnoff, head of RCA. At the time, Sarnoff was more interested in promoting the development of television and, despite the technical advantages of FM, was not interested in backing Armstrong's creation. Armstrong tried to develop FM on his own. He set up his own transmitter for demonstrations and by 1940 had sold the rights to manufacture FM receiving sets to several companies. Sarnoff offered Armstrong $1 million for a license to his invention, but Armstrong, probably still angry over Sarnoff's earlier rejection, refused. FM's further development was interrupted by the start of World War II.

Radio Programs

Depression-era programs reflected a need for diversion and escape. Action–adventure series, such as "The Lone Ranger," were popular, as were daytime soap operas. Network radio news grew during the 1930s, and live coverage of special events, such as the abdication speech of Edward VIII of England, drew huge numbers of listeners. Broadcasts from Europe on the eve of World War II kept many listeners glued to their radio sets for the latest bulletins. During the war, Edward R. Murrow gained fame through his reports from war-torn London.

World War II

Radio did well during the war. The number of dollars spent on radio ads nearly doubled from 1940 to 1945. Helped by a newsprint shortage and an excess-profits tax that encouraged companies to advertise, radio broadcasting outpaced the newspapers as a national advertising vehicle in 1943.

The shape of modern broadcasting would be significantly altered by a court ruling that came in the middle of the war. In 1943, the Supreme Court ruled that NBC must divest itself of one of its two networks. NBC chose to sell the weaker network to Edward Noble, who had made his fortune selling Life Savers candy.

Noble renamed his network the American Broadcasting Company (ABC), and by the end of the war, ABC had 195 affiliates and was a full-fledged competitor for the older nets.

Innovation and Change: 1945–1954

The nine-year period following World War II was marked by great changes in both the radio and recording industries, changes that ultimately drove them closer together. The development of television delayed the growth of FM radio, altered the nature of network radio, and forced the radio industry to rely on records as the most important part of a new programming strategy.

FM   Despite the fact that FM sounded better than AM, was static-free, and could reproduce a wider range of sound frequencies, AM broadcasting had started first and FM had to struggle to catch up. FM had the misfortune of beginning its development at the same time as TV; in addition, because of technical considerations, both FM radio and TV are suited for about the same place in the electromagnetic spectrum. In 1945, the FCC decided to give the rapidly expanding TV service the space formerly occupied by FM. The commission moved FM "upstairs" to the 88- to 108-MHz band (where it is today), thus rendering obsolete about half a million FM radios.

TV   Of course, the biggest change in radio's fortunes came about because of the emergence of television. (We will have more to say about the development of TV in Chapter 10.) By 1948, it was apparent that TV would take over the mass entertainment function served by network radio. The emergence of TV meant changes in the content, economics, and functions of radio. Although many individuals believe that television cut into the revenues of the radio industry, no such thing happened. In fact, revenues rose steadily from 1948 to 1952 and, after a brief drop from 1953 to 1956, continued to rise. The part of the industry upon which TV did have a drastic effect was network radio. The percentage of local stations with network affiliations dropped from 97 percent in 1947 to only 50 percent by 1955. Network revenue dropped by 60 percent for approximately the same period. Faced with this loss, stations relied more heavily on revenue from ads for local businesses. In short, they redistributed the makeup of their revenue dollar. As TV became the new mass medium, local stations cut back on their budgets; relied more heavily on music, talk, and news; and began searching for a formula that would allow them to coexist with television.

Specialized Formats   By 1956 it was obvious that the networks would no longer be the potent programming source they had been in the past. In that year, radio networks were carrying only about 35 hours of sponsored evening programs each week. Finally, by 1960, all the once-popular evening programs and daytime serials had come to an end. Radio network service was limited primarily to news and short features, usually amounting to no more than two or three hours of time a day.

Local stations soon adapted to this change. Now that they no longer were tied to the networks for the bulk of their programming, the locals were free to develop their own personalities. Most did so by adopting a specialized format, a sound that had distinctive appeal to a certain segment of the audience. The most successful experiment occurred in the Midwest, where a station began monitoring the sales of records and sheet music and playing those tunes that were selling the most. Hence, the Top 40 format was born. Featuring a bright, continuous, and upbeat sound, the format was ruled by the **clock hour**, which specified every element of programming. The success of the Top 40 sound encouraged radio stations to experiment with other specialized formats. By 1964, at least a dozen different formats, ranging from country to classical, had sprung up.

Growth and Stabilization: 1955–1990

The number of radio stations continued to grow during these years, from 3,343 in 1955 to more than 7,000 in 1970. The Top 40 format was adopted by more and more stations and very quickly became the format of choice among young listeners—young listeners that, as it happened, had a good deal of money to spend on the records they heard played by their favorite disc jockey, or DJ. Since at this time the DJ had control of what songs were played on the air, he or she became the focus of promotional efforts by record companies to gain airplay for their new songs. All too soon this arrangement led to the growth of **payola** (see Media Probe, "Payola"), and a nasty scandal ensued.

The most significant development in radio during the 1970s and 1980s was the successful emergence of FM. As noted earlier, FM radio faced several hurdles in its development. By the early 1960s, however, conditions had improved enough for more individuals to consider buying FM stations. Licenses for AM stations were becoming harder to get. People who wished to invest in a broadcast station found it easier to procure an FM license. In 1965, the FCC had passed the **nonduplication rule**, which prevented an AM-FM combination from duplicating its AM content on its FM channel for more than 50 percent of the time. Faced with this ruling and the knowledge that specialized formats were becoming successful in radio, FM stations developed their own kind of sound (many stations adopted a rock format) that capitalized on FM's better technical qualities. Between 1960 and 1970, the number of FM stations tripled. In 1976, FM broadcasting went into the black as the industry as a whole reported earnings of $21.2 million.

Profits continued to increase for FM as it captured more and more of the listening audience. In 1990, FM accounted for about 70 percent of all audience listening time, with AM accounting for less than 30 percent. The only age group where AM garnered more listening time than FM was among people 50 or over. AM station executives began rethinking programming strategy in an attempt to stop the audience erosion. (See Figure 7–1).

A noncommercial radio network, **National Public Radio (NPR)**, went on the air in the early 1970s with an 80-station network. Over the next five years, its number of affiliates doubled, and by 1980 it was reaching a cumulative audience of more than 5 million people per week. Its most successful programs were its daily news programs "Morning Edition" and "All Things Considered."

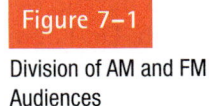

Figure 7–1

Division of AM and FM Audiences

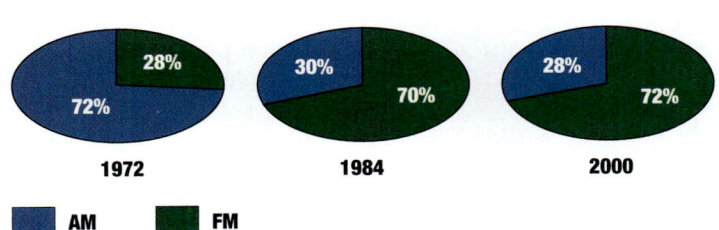

72% 28%   30% 70%   28% 72%

1972   1984   2000

■ AM   ■ FM

In the 1950s, the disc jockey (DJ) became an important figure in radio programming. In fact, many became stars in their own right. DJs sent out glossy pictures of themselves to their fans; they appeared at supermarket openings and record hops; they were the emcees at personal appearances by rock-and-roll groups. As the DJs became more influential, they also began to program their own shows. They picked the records that they would play during their airshifts.

Record promoters also realized the tremendous importance of airplay in the marketing of a hit. The more a record was played on the radio, the more it sold. Quite naturally, record promoters and DJs began to develop close ties. In the beginning, it was innocent enough. Promoters would make sure that DJs got the latest releases their companies were offering, and they also put in a good word or two about their companies' products. Competition got intense, however, and by 1959 about 250 new records were released every week. Some unscrupulous promoters resorted to more than words to advance their records. At first, they might send the DJs an elaborate Christmas gift. If that didn't work, some even "hired" the DJ as "creative consultant" and paid the disc jockey a fee every month. Others would cut the DJ in on the action and offer to pay a penny to the DJ for every record sold in the market. Eventually, most promoters stopped these charades and simply passed the DJ an envelope filled with money in return for airplay of their company's songs. In 1958 and 1959, record distributors reportedly spent over a quarter of a million dollars in the larger markets on payola.

The news of this illicit business practice did nothing to help the image of rock and roll or of broadcasting. Section 508 was added to the 1934 Communications Act to stop this practice, but it was not altogether successful. New payola scandals broke out in the industry in the early 1970s. At least one record company was accused of offering drugs to station personnel in return for increased airplay, and some concert promoters were accused of offering several monetary bribes. Payola resurfaced in 2000 when 80 program directors at Spanish-language stations were investigated for allegedly taking bribes from Fonovisa Records. Payola is a problem that doesn't seem to disappear.

The Volatile 1990s

The pivotal event for radio in the 1990s was the passage of the **Telecommunications Act of 1996.** The act was concerned primarily with encouraging competition in the new communication technologies, but the radio industry, through skillful lobbying, was able to include itself in the bill. Only a few sentences in the final version of the act concern radio, but those few sentences had an impact out of proportion to their length. A key provision completely erased the cap on the number of stations a company could own and increased to eight the number of stations a company could own in a single market.

Radio talk show star Don Imus (a.k.a. "The I-Man"). His syndicated program reaches about 15 million listeners every day. (Les Stone/Corbis Sygma)

The new law caused an avalanche of buying and selling of radio properties, and some stations were sold several times in a single year. In a typical year before the act, about $2 billion was spent on radio acquisitions and mergers. In 1996, the number hit $14.4 billion. That figure was eclipsed the next year when $15.3 billion was spent. New radio giants sprang up almost overnight. The radio industry became even more consolidated as a few large group owners dominated the industry.

On the programming front, talk became the hottest format on AM radio, thanks to the success of such performers as Rush Limbaugh, Dr. Laura Schlessinger, Tom Joyner, and Howard Stern. The trend toward format specialization continued on FM as stations realized that attracting as few as 2 to 3 percent of the audience was enough to keep them profitable.

CRITICAL/CULTURAL ISSUES

Radio and the Local Community

The philosophy that guided the development of radio in the United States was based on localism. Radio stations were licensed to serve the public interest of those who could hear their signals. Stations were expected to be integral parts of their local communities and responsive to the needs of local residents. The Federal Radio Commission set aside a number of AM channels that were dedicated to lower-power stations serving a particular town. Over the years, other regulations were enacted that favored localism. To encourage the development of roots in the community, owners were required to hold on to stations for three years before they could be sold. Stations had to survey their listeners and ascertain the needs of their community and provide programs to address those needs. Caps were placed on the number of stations one company could own to discourage large corporations from becoming out-of-town station owners with little or no ties to the community. In an effort to assure access for many voices, there were further caps on the number of stations that could be owned in one market.

As pointed out by Charles Fairchild in his article "Deterritorializing Radio: Deregulation and the Continued Triumph of the Corporatist Perspective in the USA," which appeared in a 1999 issue of *Media, Culture and Society*, this localist philosophy is not much with us today. His analysis of changes in the radio industry over the past two decades is a good example of a critical/cultural investigation that focuses on ideology and power relationships in society.

In essence, Fairchild argues that recent changes have removed the connection between a radio station and its local community. He suggests that there were two dominant ideologies in force that competed as definitions of the "public interest." One, the statist position, conceives of government as the protector of the public interest and an agency that assures that the broadest number of people benefit from the medium. The other, the corporatist view, holds that the market is the best determiner of the public interest. The most economically successful service is the service that succeeds best in the marketplace. In other words, the public interest is what interests the public.

Fairchild notes that the corporatist view has been the dominant model in recent radio operations. Thanks in part to an active industry lobby and the economic power wielded by large communications corporation, recent changes have almost erased the notion of local service.

Following are just a few of those changes: The three-year ownership rule has been dropped; the requirements for ascertaining the needs of the community have been minimized; and perhaps most importantly, the cap on the total number of stations that can be owned has been removed and the limit on the number of stations owned in a market has been raised to eight.

What were the effects of this change in ideology? The radio industry has become consolidated, with big corporations controlling hundreds of stations. Locally owned stations that had deep roots in the local community were gobbled up by big companies with headquarters in some faraway city and whose main interest was the bottom line. Consequently, local programming has been reduced in favor of standardized entertainment and news fed from some central location nowhere near the local community. Programming decisions are left to consultants and syndicators who have no local ties whatsoever. Hence, as Fairchild suggests, radio has become "deterritorialized," detached from a community connection.

Fairchild concludes that the corporatist ideology has triumphed: "local radio stations are the objects of unaccountable control from outside local communities and neither the government nor the public have any levers of power with which they can influence broadcasters to provide access to those voices which cannot gain any serious measure of volume elsewhere."

Read the Social Issues box on page 194 concerning efforts to increase diversity on the airwaves and see how the issues it raises fits in with Fairchild's analysis.

1. What effect might the Internet have on the amount of local news, information, and other services available in any given community? Might the Internet itself have any effect on the relevance or importance of the localism arguments?

2. If the government can deregulate radio, clearly radio could be re-regulated. What types of regulations would you like to see that would best serve the public interest, and where would you place the responsibility to ensure that citizens are indeed well-served by radio?

3. Who owns the radio stations in your hometown? Compare formats, amount of news, community activities—how do the locally owned stations compare with those that are corporate-owned? Had you noticed a difference before thinking about it now for this class? Does it matter?

Finally, as mentioned earlier, economic prosperity and an influx of advertising from dot-com companies boosted radio revenues to record levels. As the new century dawned, however, traditional analog radio was facing increased competition from some digital broadcasters.

RADIO IN THE DIGITAL AGE

Radio has moved slowly into the digital age. Thousands of radio stations have websites, and many now offer streaming audio. For the most part, however, these sites are used primarily to supplement the on-air station and its traditional analog signal.

IBOC

The technology for broadcasting a digital radio signal has been around for years, and several countries have systems already in operation. Digital radio has moved slowly in the United States because analog radio was doing well and broadcasters saw no need to disrupt a profitable situation. In addition, radio broadcasters wanted a digital system that was compatible with existing analog signals so that current radio sets could pick up the analog signal while new receivers picked up the digital signal. Broadcasters got their wish in the late 1990s when an **IBOC** (in-band, on-channel) system of digital broadcasting was developed.

Digital radio broadcasting has several advantages. First, it improves sound quality. An AM digital signal sounds as good as a traditional FM signal; digital FM signals sound as good as CDs. Further, digital signals are virtually static-free. On the other hand, it is still unclear if digital signals will produce the same coverage pattern as analog signals. Current plans call for some stations to start experimenting with IBOC digital radio in 2001.

Satellite Radio

Digital radio has paved the way for some potentially major competition to over-the-air radio. Two companies plan to start a "direct from satellite to car radio" digital service in 2001. These services will be commercial-free; subscribers will pay about $10 a month for up to 100 channels of music, sports, and talk programming. General Motors and Ford are major investors in this new venture.

Satellite radio faces some major challenges. The appropriate satellites have to be launched into the proper orbits. Further, people are not used to paying money for radio programming. These facts notwithstanding, the radio industry is somewhat concerned about the potential of satellite radio because it reaches consumers in their cars, a listening situation that analog radio currently monopolizes.

Internet-Only Stations

Another challenge to traditional analog radio comes from the 300 or so Internet-only broadcasters. While satellite radio services target listeners in cars, Internet-only stations are competing for the audiences that listen to radio at work. The web broadcasters offer dozens of specialized music genres (such as reggae and techno-rock) with limited commercials. Two of the most popular Internet services are Spinner.com (recently purchased by AOL Time Warner) and Broadcast.com (recently purchased by Yahoo!). In addition to the wider variety of music, Internet-only stations also offer chat rooms, e-commerce, and original content. Recent

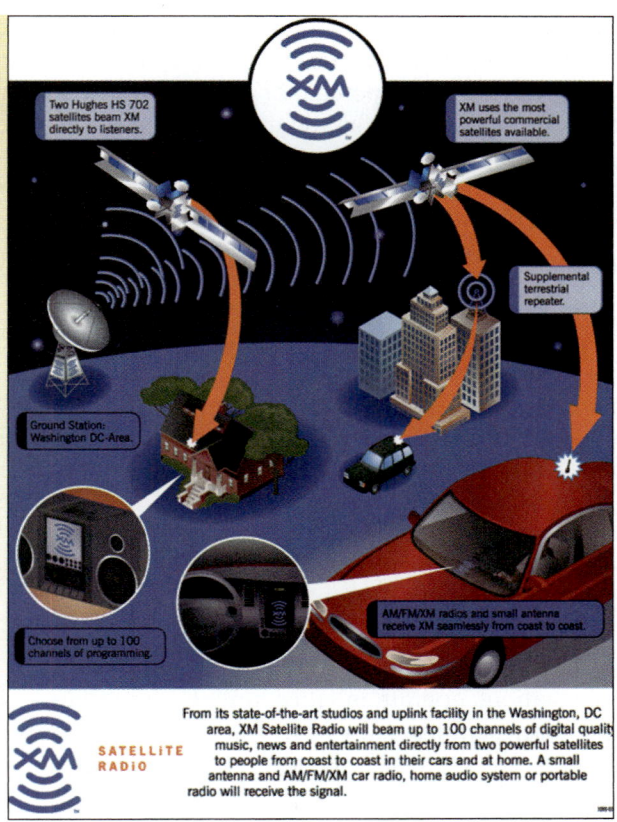

XM radio—digital radio sent directly to your car radio for a fee. *(Reprint permission granted by XM Satellite Radio Inc.)*

audience surveys disclosed that about 10 percent of respondents listened to a web radio in a month—a number that will probably grow in the future.

Satellite radio and Internet-only stations are interested in attracting audiences that are dissatisfied with traditional radio, and there are indications that quite a few may fit into that category. As the number of commercial minutes per hour has increased on radio stations, listening time has decreased. Since 1990, time devoted to commercials has doubled and the radio audience has shrunk 12 percent. What demographic group is most turned off by all the commercials on radio? Young people—the group most in demand by advertisers.

DEFINING FEATURES OF RADIO

Radio is portable. Some radio sets, like the Walkman, are small and personal. Others, like the boom box, are big and public. No matter their size, radio sets are easily transported and go everywhere—the beach, sporting events, jogging trails, the workplace. Car radios provide news and entertainment to commuters on their way to and from work. In fact, it's hard to find a place where radio can't go.

Radio is supplemental. Most radio listening occurs while we are doing something else—driving, working, studying, falling asleep, waking up, cleaning, and so on. Radio rarely is the prime focus of our attention; it provides an audio background for our activities.

Radio is universal. Virtually every household has at least one working radio. In fact, the average house has about six. Almost every car is equipped with a radio. In an average day, about 75 percent of Americans listen to radio.

Radio is selective. Much like the magazine industry (see Chapter 5), the radio industry has become a niche medium. Radio stations choose formats that attract a small, narrowly defined audience that is attractive to advertisers. As mentioned earlier, if a radio broadcaster can find a formula that attracts just 2 or 3 percent of the audience, odds are that the station will turn a profit.

ORGANIZATION OF THE RADIO INDUSTRY

There are more than a half-billion working radio sets in the United States. That works out to about two radios per person. There are about 12,000 radio stations in operation. Thanks in part to an FCC philosophy that encouraged competition, the number of stations grew from about 6,900 in 1970 to about 12,500 in 2000, an increase of 75 percent. To understand how this rapidly growing business is organized, we will examine it from several perspectives: programming, technology, and format.

Local Stations, Nets, and Syndicators

Local radio stations operate in cities, towns, and villages across the country. Big cities have many stations. New York City has 95; Los Angeles, 60. Smaller towns may have only one or two. Whitefish, Montana, for example (population 4,000), has two stations. Programming for these stations is provided by networks and by program syndication companies. Technically speaking, the distinction between a net and a syndication service is that all stations on a network carry the net program at the same time, while syndicated programming is carried at different times by the stations. In practice, however, much syndicated radio programming is satellite-delivered and carried simultaneously, and many network affiliates tape net programming and broadcast it later. To make it even more complicated, the traditional networks also offer syndicated programs. Consequently, the distinction between the two services may no longer be meaningful.

Networks were important programming sources during the earlier years of radio. After the emergence of TV, the importance of radio networks diminished and they provided only news and public-affairs programs to their affiliates.

Network radio staged a mild resurgence during the mid- to late 1990s. Listenership was not increasing, but advertising revenues were surging thanks to an influx of ad money from Internet companies. The leading radio networks at the turn of the century were ABC, Westwood One, and Premiere.

Many experts noted that the demand for syndicated shows was at an all-time high during the late 1990s. Rush Limbaugh continued to lead the syndication race. Radio counselor Dr. Laura Schlessinger was second. The drive-time shows of the controversial Howard Stern, along with those of Don Imus and Tom Joyner, are also popular.

Although Rush and Dr. Laura might receive the most attention, there are about 50 companies that provided syndicated programs of various length. For example, the American Comedy Network offers a library of 640 comedy bits on 13 CDs. The Motor Racing Network supplies coverage of 50 NASCAR races and NASCAR-related features to about 400 stations.

The WYNK humvee on a remote in Baton Rouge, Louisiana. Remotes are an important part of promotion for a local radio station. (*Photo courtesy of Carole Dominick*)

AM and FM Stations

Broadcast radio stations are either AM or FM. **AM** stands for amplitude modulation, and **FM** stands for frequency modulation. As we saw earlier in the chapter, since about 1975 the fortunes of FM radio have been increasing while those of AM stations are on the decline. In 2000, almost three-quarters of listenership went to the FM stations. Keep in mind, however, that some AM stations, particularly those in large markets, were doing quite well. In 2000, AMs were the top-rated stations in Chicago (WGN), San Francisco (KGO), Detroit (WJR), and Boston (WRKO).

All physical factors being equal, radio signals sent by AM travel farther, especially at night, than signals sent by FM. The AM dial on a typical radio set illustrates the precise frequencies in the electromagnetic spectrum where the AM station operates. AM stations are further classified by channels. There are three possible channels: clear, regional, and local. A clear channel is one with a single dominant station that is designed to provide service over a wide area. Typically, these dominant stations have a strong signal because they broadcast with 50,000 watts of power. For example, the 720 spot on the AM dial is a clear channel with WGN, Chicago, the dominant station, operating at 50,000 watts. The 770 position is also a clear channel with WABC, New York, dominant. A regional channel is one shared by many stations that serve fairly large areas. A local channel is designed to be shared by a large number of stations that broadcast only to their local communities.

FM signals do not travel as far as AM, but FM has the advantage of being able to produce better sound qualities than AM. FM radio is also less likely to be affected by outside interference such as thunderstorms. Similar to AM, FM stations are organized in classes. Class C FM stations are the most powerful, operating at 100,000 watts. Class B and Class A stations are less powerful. A glance at the FM dial of a radio reveals that FM stations operate in a different part of the electromagnetic spectrum than does AM. Figure 7–2 is a simplified diagram of the spectrum showing where AM, FM, and television signals are located. The AM versus FM distinction does not apply to digital radio signals.

Station Formats

Perhaps the most meaningful way we can organize radio stations is according to their **format**, a type of consistent programming designed to appeal to a certain segment of the audience. A format gives a station a distinctive personality and attracts a certain kind of audience that advertisers find desirable. In fact, the

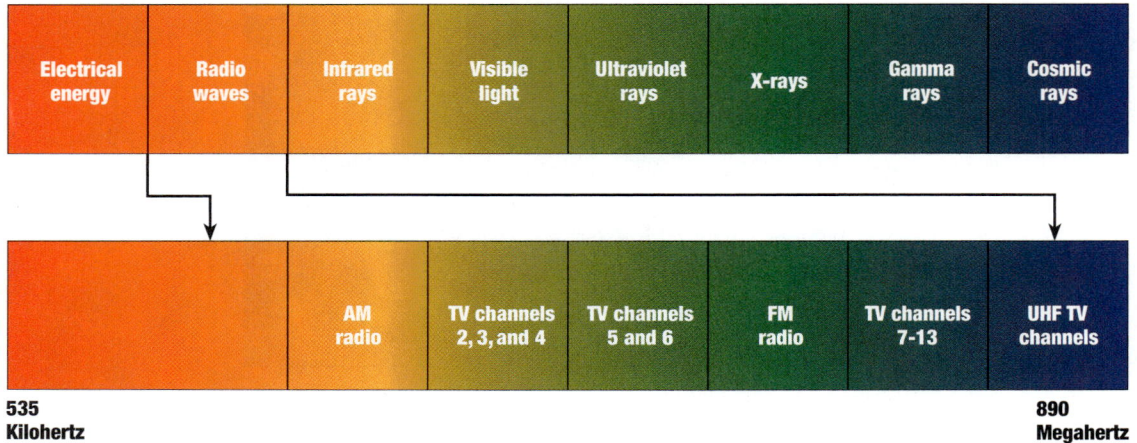

| Electrical energy | Radio waves | Infrared rays | Visible light | Ultraviolet rays | X-rays | Gamma rays | Cosmic rays |

| | | AM radio | TV channels 2, 3, and 4 | TV channels 5 and 6 | FM radio | TV channels 7-13 | UHF TV channels |

535
Kilohertz

890
Megahertz

Figure 7–2

Simplified Diagram of the Electromagnetic Spectrum

development of radio after 1960 is marked by the fine-tuning of existing formats and the creation of new ones that appeal to people in distinct demographic and lifestyle categories. Most modern stations can offer an amazingly precise description of the kind of listener they want their format to attract. An adult contemporary station, for example, might set its sights on men and women, aged 25 to 45, with college educations, making more than $40,000 a year, who read *Rolling Stone*, drive either a BMW or Volvo, and go to the mall at least twice a week. In our discussion we will cover three basic categories of radio formats: music, news/talk, and ethnic.

The Music Format   Music is the largest category and includes many subdivisions and variations. In 2000, the two most-listened-to music formats were adult contemporary (AC), with about 15 percent of all listening time, and country, with about 11 percent. AC is primarily an FM format, but a few AM stations carry it as well. It consists of a blend of suitable oldies and current soft-rock hits, usually about 20 percent current and 80 percent oldies. AC is splintering into four distinct subdivisions. One is soft AC, which emphasizes mostly subdued vocals from the past. A second type is oldies-based AC. These stations' playlists are dominated by softer hits from the 60s, 70s, and 80s. The third type, current AC, takes the opposite strategy. These stations play more contemporary hits and might feature several artists who would also appear on the Top 40 playlists. Finally, there are full-service ACs, which emphasize news, sports, weather, and DJs who are "personalities."

Top 40 features a small playlist of hit records in a fast rotation. The Top 40 format has shown a modest increase in listenership in recent years. This format does best with the 12- to 25-year-old age group.

Country stations, as the name suggests, play hit country-and-western singles and employ DJs who are down-home, friendly, and knowledgeable about country music. The country format has two main

Thanks to heavy radio airplay, Faith Hill had several hits on both the country and the adult contemporary charts. *(AP/Wide World Photos)*

divisions: (1) traditional country stations that play mainstream classic, twangy country music and (2) contemporary country stations that play more current artists who might use synthesizers and other modern sounds. A country station's audience still comprises mainly adults from 35 to 55.

The two fastest-growing formats of the past few years have been urban contemporary (UC) and modern rock. UC blends rap, dance, black, and Hispanic music and has strong appeal among city-dwelling 18- to 35-year-olds. The modern rock format blends Top 40 hits with artists who used to be featured only on alternative or college radio stations, such as Stone Temple Pilots, Foo Fighters, Pearl Jam, and Limp Bizkit.

Black and Ethnic Formats   These formats aim for special audiences that are defined primarily by race and nationality. There are about 175 stations that program for the black audience and about 260 stations that serve the Hispanic audience. Many of the black and Hispanic stations feature urban contemporary music and run news, features, and special programs of interest to their audiences. In addition, about 60 stations have formats aimed at other ethnic groups: Polish, German, Italian, French, Irish, and Greek.

Format Homogenization   Radio stations sound pretty much alike no matter where you are. Almost all the major music formats are represented in the large and medium markets, and it seems that every market has its morning "zoo crew"; an AC station that specializes in "the classic hits" of the 70s, 80s, 90s, and today; a modern rock station that calls itself "Power" or "Z" or "Q" something-or-other; an

Catherine Hughes, head of Radio One, the nation's largest radio group targeting black listeners, is the first African-American woman to head a publicly traded company. Her path to the top, however, was not an easy one.

Hughes started in radio by working in the sales department at Howard University's radio station. Eventually, she became the station's manager. She decided to start her own radio station in 1980 by buying WOL-AM in Washington, D.C. At the time, she was a single mother with limited financial resources. Bank after bank rejected her loan application. She finally found one bank willing to lend her part of the money she needed and got additional backing from a consortium of financiers who specialized in funding black business enterprises.

The station nearly failed. Hughes had her house and car repossessed and even sold some family heirlooms to pay the bills. She actually moved into the station, sleeping in a sleeping bag and cooking on a hot plate. She saved programming costs by doing her own talk show. Trying desperately to get advertising, she went door-to-door persuading small retailers to spend $10 for a minute of commercial time. Seven years later, the station finally turned a profit.

Hughes next decided that the time was right for expansion. She noted that African-American family income was growing along with its buying power. Taking advantage of relaxed federal ownership regulations, Hughes acquired another 11 stations over the next six years. She took her company public in 1999. Radio One's stock price nearly doubled in the first three months.

In 1999, Radio One generated more than $50 million in revenues. In early 2000, Radio One bought 21 radio stations in a $1.37 billion deal with Clear Channel, bringing its total number of stations to 47 and doubling Radio One's listenership. No more cooking on a hot plate for Catherine Hughes.

easy-listening station with a "warm" format that dedicates love songs at night; and maybe even an AM station that specializes in "golden oldies." Even the DJs sound pretty much the same.

There are several reasons behind this trend toward homogenization. First, many large-market stations are owned by groups, and what works for a group owner in one market is likely to work in another. Second, satellite-delivered music services are becoming more common. This means that stations all over the country are playing standardized music. Finally, radio has become so competitive that programming decisions are based on the recommendations of program consultants and audience research firms that compile playlists based on audience surveys and focus groups. There aren't many of these consultants and firms around, and the same records tend to score high from market to market. Consequently, the recommendations tend to be the same from radio station to radio station. Many stations prefer to adopt a "safe" format, one that has worked in similar markets, rather than risking a sizable amount of money on an untested format.

News/Talk Format   This format is becoming more and more popular on the AM band and accounts for 17 percent of all radio listening time. Some stations emphasize the news part of the news/talk format. National, regional, and local news reports are broadcast periodically throughout the day. Sports, traffic, weather, editorials, public-affairs programs, and an occasional feature round out the programming day. News stations appeal primarily to a male audience in the 25- to 54-year-old age category.

The talk format attracts listeners in about the same age group. Common types of programs that appear on stations using the talk format are call-in shows—usually hosted by an opinionated and maybe even abrasive host, interview shows, advice shows, and roundtable discussions. News, weather, traffic reports, and other feature material are blended in with these programs. Unlike the music formats, which do not demand their listeners' close attention, the talk format requires that its audience concentrate on the program in order to follow what is said.

Noncommercial Radio

Many of the early radio stations that went on the air during the 1920s were founded by educational institutions. As the commercial broadcasting system became firmly established, many educational stations were bought by commercial broadcasters, and the fortunes of noncommercial radio dwindled. In 1945, with the coming of FM broadcasting, the FCC set aside several frequencies for educational broadcasting. This action sparked a rebirth of interest in this kind of broadcasting, so that by 2000 there were about 1,900 noncommercial radio stations on the air.

Most noncommercial radio stations are owned by educational institutions or private foundations. Noncommercial radio gets its support from the institutions that own the stations. Ultimately, much of this support comes from tax revenue since taxes support most public educational institutions. Other sources of support are endowments (gifts), grants from foundations or the federal government, and listener donations.

Noncommercial stations are served by National Public Radio (NPR). National Public Radio, founded in 1970, provides program services to about 530 affiliates around the country. Member stations pay a fee based on audience reach and annual budget and receive in return about 50 hours of programming per week. Many of these shows are produced at NPR headquarters; others are produced at NPR stations and distributed by NPR. Probably the best-known NPR programs, as noted earlier, are the award-winning "All Things Considered" and "Morning Edition."

The public radio stations that help support NPR receive financial support from the Corporation for Public Broadcasting (CPB), a private, nonprofit organization funded by Congress. Member stations receive money from the CPB, and those that decide to affiliate with NPR pay some of this money to the network as a fee. NPR also receives grants directly from the CPB. Congress, however, has threatened to cut the CPB's budget, which, in turn, would lead to less money for stations and for NPR. Consequently, many public stations have resorted to underwriting, a practice in which the station accepts money from a person or an organization in return for an acknowledgment on the air. In some cases, these acknowledgments sound suspiciously like commercials. In contrast, NPR itself is committed to programming that is commercial-free and for the most part has resisted the pressure to air these minicommercials. In 1995, however, NPR relented a bit and allowed underwriters to broadcast brief slogans. At the same time, NPR is trying raise money in other ways. It has a telephone music ordering service and its own record label, NPR Classics. Public stations and NPR will probably struggle with their money problems for years to come.

The crew of NPR's "All Things Considered," a fixture of NPR programming for 30 years. *(Photo by Barbara Ries, Courtesy National Public Radio)*

The other noncommercial radio network, Public Radio International (PRI), was formerly known as American Public Radio. The

As the big companies in the radio industry get bigger and the smaller companies get swallowed up, a natural question is whether this consolidation is good for the listener and/or the few remaining stations that haven't been bought up.

Here are some arguments for "big":

- Bigness brings stability. Before consolidation, an economic downturn would spell the end for many small radio stations. As part of a larger chain, these stations would probably be able to withstand rough economic times.
- Large companies can benefit from economies of scale. Large group owners can use the same news bureaus for all stations; they can concentrate sales and advertising functions and streamline administrative costs.
- Advertisers benefit from consolidation. They can deal with only one organization and place ads to reach a market rather than dealing with several separate stations.

Here are some arguments against:

- Increased concentration means more control of information in the hands of fewer companies. Increased control over information could translate into political power.
- Consolidation costs jobs. When stations merge their respective news or sales departments, many people get laid off.
- Bigger might mean blander. In radio, the stations that have innovated programming ideas and formats have usually been smaller stations that have been losing money. They didn't have much to lose by trying something different. Stations that are part of large companies might play it safe because they might have more to lose.
- Consolidation might mean higher prices for advertisers. If one company controls all the top-rated stations in a market, the more economic leverage that company has over advertisers. (The Justice Department apparently agrees with this argument and has indicated it will look with disfavor on mergers that give one firm more than half of a market's ad revenues.)

Keep in mind that even with the recent wave of consolidation, the radio industry is still relatively less concentrated than the newspaper, sound recording, film, and TV industries.

Minneapolis, Minnesota, organization is a network that acquires and distributes programming from station-based, independent and international producers. Unlike NPR, PRI does not produce any of its programming but does finance program production at member stations. A noncommercial station can be an affiliate of both NPR and PRI.

OWNERSHIP IN THE RADIO INDUSTRY

As mentioned earlier, the Telecommunications Act of 1996 drastically changed the landscape of radio station ownership. The new rules prompted some huge deals, among them:

- A $23.5 billion merger between Clear Channel Communications and AMFM Incorporated, resulting in the largest radio company in history.
- A $4.9 billion merger between Westinghouse/CBS and Infinity Broadcasting, which created an 83-station group with multiple stations in top markets.
- Entercom's acquisition of the Sinclair Broadcast Group for $820 million.

Table 7.1 is a listing of the top five radio groups as of mid-2000. Keep in mind that this list will change as owners continue to make deals.

The pace of mergers and acquisitions had slowed by 2000. For one thing, there aren't that many large- and medium-market stations that aren't already controlled by large companies.

Table 7.1	Top Radio Groups, 2000 (ranked by number of listeners)	
	Company	**Number of Stations**
1.	Clear Channel	904
2.	Infinity	163
3.	ABC	43
4.	Entercom	85
5.	Cox Radio	58

Source: Compiled by author from industry reports.

 PRODUCING RADIO PROGRAMS

Departments and Staff

The departmental structure of a radio station varies according to its size. Obviously, a small station with five or six employees has a departmental setup different from that of a large station with a hundred-person staff. Figure 7–3 illustrates the arrangement at a typical medium-sized station.

The two top management positions are the general manager and the program director. The manager has the responsibility for planning and carrying out station policy, maintaining contact with the community, and monitoring program content, audience ratings, and sales information. The program director is responsible for the station's sound. He or she supervises the music or other program material that the station broadcasts and is also responsible for the hiring and firing of announcers and DJs.

Figure 7–3

Departments and Staff at a Medium-Sized Radio Station

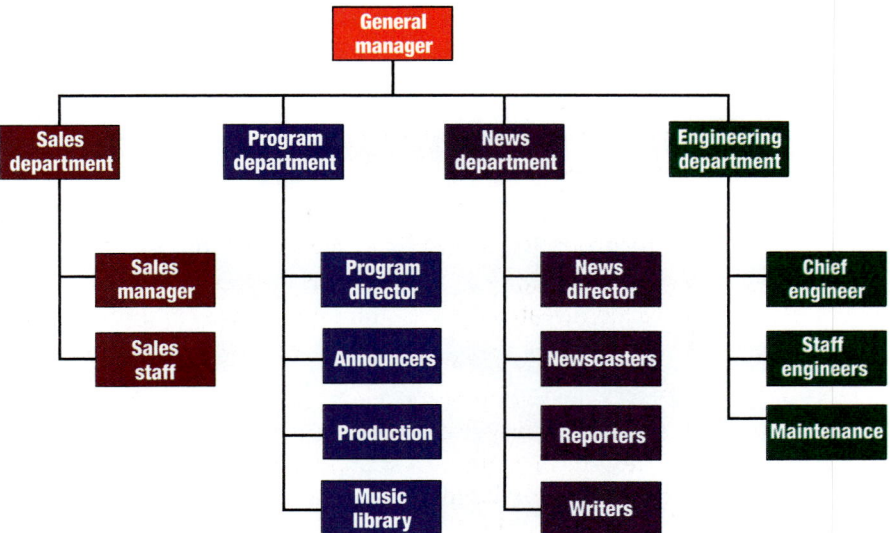

Most stations are divided into the four departments shown in Figure 7–3. The sales department consists of the sales manager and the station's sales force. The news department is responsible for compiling the station's local newscasts and rewriting the wire service reports of national and regional news. The engineering department, under the supervision of the chief engineer, is staffed with technicians responsible for keeping the station on the air and maintaining the equipment.

■ Putting Together a Program

This section will concentrate on how radio programs are produced for the music, talk, and news formats.

Music Format   When the staff of a local station puts together their program, the first step is generally to lay out a **format wheel** (also called a format clock), a pie chart of an hour divided into segments representing different program elements. Figure 7–4 is a simplified version of a wheel for a contemporary rock station.

Note that the music is structured to flow from one segment to another. Album cuts and hits from the past are spread around the wheel. Additional wheels would be constructed for the various parts of the broadcast day (i.e., one wheel for morning drive time, another for 10 A.M.–4 P.M., another for evening drive time, and another for 7 P.M.–midnight).

Talk Format   Most of the content of the talk format is produced by the local station. As is the case with the music format, the makeup of the audience is taken into account. During drive time, talk segments should be relatively short and liberally interspersed with news, weather, and traffic reports. The audience for the 10 A.M.–4 P.M. segment tends to be primarily female and, therefore, topics for discussion would reflect the interests of that group. The early evening audience is generally younger and contains more males.

Producing a talk show requires more equipment than does producing a simple DJ program. Speaker telephones and extra telephone lines are needed, as well as a delay system. This device gives the talk show moderator a 7- to 30-second delay period during which he or she can censor what is said by the caller. Another

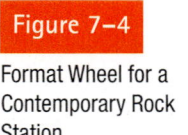

Figure 7–4

Format Wheel for a
Contemporary Rock
Station

important part of the talk show is the telephone screener. The screener ranks the waiting calls for importance, letting the most interesting callers go first, and filters out crank calls or calls from regulars who contact the station too frequently.

All-News Format   The all-news station also works with a programming wheel, similar to that of the music format. Instead of music, however, the news wheel shows the spacing between headlines, weather, news, sports, business reports, and commercials. It also illustrates the **cycle**, the amount of time that elapses before the program order is repeated.

The all-news format is the most difficult to produce. A large staff, consisting of anchorpersons, a managing editor, local reporters, editors, rewrite people, a traffic reporter, and stringers (freelance reporters who are paid per story), is needed. The list of necessary facilities is also long: radio wire services, sports wire, weather wire, mobile units, police and fire-frequency scanners, short-wave receiver, and perhaps even a helicopter.

ECONOMICS

Radio's recent financial performance has been impressive. From 1993 to 2000, the radio industry registered 92 consecutive months of revenue increases (the streak was still intact as this book went to press). Overall radio revenue was close to $20 billion in 2000, and radio's share of the total advertising market rose to a record 8 percent.

Part of this growth was due to the increasing consolidation in the industry as big radio companies offered advertisers greater reach and more efficiency for their ad dollars. Part was also due to the increase in radio advertising of the dot-com companies, which account for about 20 percent of current radio ad revenues. Most analysts think that despite competition from satellite services and web radio stations, as long as the economy is reasonably healthy, radio will continue to do well. The drive-time audience continues to grow, and average commuting times continue to increase. Radio programming is relatively cheap to produce (most music is supplied free from recording companies) and to distribute. Finally, radio supports target marketing. Radio permits advertisers to specialize by age, sex, ethnicity, and lifestyle.

Sources of Revenue

Radio stations earn their money by selling advertising time. The amount that a radio station charges for time is included in its rate card. A typical radio commercial costs several hundred dollars in large cities. The same commercial in a small town might cost only a few dollars.

The radio industry has three sources of income from the sale of commercial time. The first comes from the sale of spots on network programs to national advertisers trying to reach a broad market. The second is the sale of time on local stations to advertisers who wish to reach a specific region (e.g., the Northeast) or a specific type of market (e.g., rural areas). This is called national spot advertising. The third source is advertising purchased by local establishments that want their commercials to be heard only in the immediate community. In 1999, each of these sources represented the following amounts of each dollar of radio revenue:

Network	4¢
National spot	18¢
Local	78¢

As the numbers indicate, the overwhelming amount of revenue in radio came from local commercials.

General Expenses

Expenses in radio are divided into five areas: (1) technical, (2) programming, (3) selling, (4) general administration, and (5) news. Technical expenses include the payroll for the engineering staff and the cost of maintaining and replacing technical equipment. Program costs cover salaries paid to talent, cost of tape and CDs, and music fees paid to the music licensing organizations. Sales costs are made up of the salaries of the sales staff and all the other expenses that go with selling. General administrative expenses include the salaries of all management, secretarial, and clerical personnel; the depreciation of physical facilities; the cost of office supplies; and any interest that is due on loans to the station. News expenses consist of the costs involved in covering local and national stories.

As of 1999, general administration expenses ranked first, accounting for about 40 percent of all expenses. Programming came next, making up about 20 percent of the expense dollar, followed closely by costs associated with sales. News and technical expenses taken together accounted for about 15 percent.

 FEEDBACK

Ratings and Shares

In the radio industry, feedback is provided by ratings conducted by professional research organizations. The major company that measures the radio audience is **Arbitron.** Arbitron surveys radio listening in approximately 262 markets across the United States and reports its results to broadcasters and advertisers.

Within a given market, Arbitron chooses people at random from a listing of all telephone numbers in the market. Individuals who agree to participate in Arbitron's survey are sent a pocket-sized diary to record both in-home and out-of-home listening. Participants are instructed to fill in the diary on a day-to-day basis, noting the time spent listening to radio and identifying the station. Approximately 3,000 to 4,000 of these diaries are mailed in a given market, and Arbitron follows up with several reminder calls to persons in the sample. Nevertheless, only 45 to 50 percent of the diaries are returned in usable form. Figure 7–5 is an example of an Arbitron radio diary. Once all the diaries have been returned, Arbitron begins an analysis that typically takes three to four weeks. The end product of this process is a ratings book, which is sent to participating stations.

Measurements of radio and television audiences gathered by the diary method are usually expressed in terms of two related concepts: (1) ratings and (2) share of the audience. A **rating** is simply the ratio of listeners to a particular station to all people in the market. Suppose that in a market with 100,000 people, 20,000 listen to radio station KYYY from 9:00 A.M. to 9:15 A.M. The rating of KYYY would be 20,000/100,000, or 20 percent. A **share of the audience** is the ratio of listeners to a

Figure 7–5

Sample Arbitron Radio Diary

Source: Arbitron Ratings: Your Radio Ratings Diary. Copyright © Arbitron Ratings Company. Reprinted by permission.

THURSDAY

Time			Station			Place			
			Call letters or station name	*Check (✔) one*		*Check (✔) one*			
	Start	Stop	*Don't know? Use program name or dial setting.*	AM	FM	At Home	In a Car	At Work	Other Place
→ Early Morning (from 5 AM)									
→ Midday									
→ Late Afternoon									
→ Night (to 5 AM Friday)									

If you didn't hear a radio today, please check here. ☐

particular station to the total number of radio listeners in the market. For example, again suppose that 20,000 people are listening to KYYY from 9:00 A.M. to 9:15 A.M. and that in the total market 80,000 people are listening to the radio during the same period. KYYY's share of the audience would be 20,000/80,000, or 25 percent. Shares of the audience divide the listening audience among all stations in the market. When they are summed, shares should total 100 percent. Ratings books are important to stations because they are used to establish the rates stations will charge advertisers.

In an effort to improve the accuracy of radio ratings, Arbitron and Nielsen Media Research are testing a "peoplemeter" for radio. This new device is designed to be clipped to an individual's clothing. Radio stations encode a special inaudible, unique signal as part of their broadcasts. The peoplemeter "hears" this signal and records the station and the time spent listening. Such a device requires far less effort on the part of respondents.

Network radio is measured by RADAR (Radio All-Dimension Audience Research), a service of Statistical Research Inc.

Radio Audiences

There are about twice as many radio sets in this country as there are people. As of January 2000, there were more than 550 million radio receivers scattered around the United States, with car radios accounting for about one-third of this number. On a typical day at least three-fourths of all adults will listen to radio, and the average person will listen, or at least have the radio on, for about three hours.

In early 2000, the Federal Communications Commission (FCC), headed by William Kennard, approved a plan that would allow the licensing of a new breed of low-power FM stations. The stations would be dropped into the existing FM spectrum and would operate at less than 100 watts power (by comparison, a full-power FM station broadcasts at least 6,000 watts and many operate at 100,000). The new stations would have signals that would cover about a 4- to 6-mile radius.

Kennard and the plan's supporters saw these new stations as a means of increasing diversity in radio. Its proponents include such performers as the Indigo Girls and Jackson Browne, who argued that low-power stations would give outlets to local artists and musical groups who find it impossible to get airplay on big, commercially oriented stations. In addition, Kennard pointed out that the plan would provide opportunities for broadcasting by groups that have been shut out by the consolidation in radio— minorities, educational institutions, local governments, churches, community groups, and fans of music formats that appeal to a small niche audience.

Radio broadcasters, led by the National Association of Broadcasters (NAB), were strongly opposed to the plan. They argued that the new stations would almost certainly cause interference with existing FM stations and with each other. The NAB sponsored engineering studies that supported its claim.

In response, supporters of the plan charged that the NAB was simply trying to protect its own interests by limiting the amount of competition faced by current FM stations. Proponents dismissed the interference argument as bogus.

The NAB also argued that if these new stations were allowed to operate, they would sap audiences and advertising revenue from existing minority stations and perhaps force them out of business. Backers of the low-power stations rejected this argument as a scare tactic.

Although arguing against the proposal, the NAB went on the record as supporting the goal of diversity in radio but through different means. One proposal favored by the industry is to allow tax breaks to minorities who buy existing stations.

As the proposal was being debated in Congress, the broadcasting industry used some of its lobbying clout to impose restrictions on the plan that would drastically cut the number of low-power stations that could be built. Nonetheless, expect this issue to become more salient as concentration of ownership continues to increase in the radio industry.

Most people listen to radio in the early morning when they are getting ready for and driving to work and in the late afternoon when they are driving home. These two "day parts," consisting roughly from 6 A.M. to 10 A.M. and 4 P.M. to 7 P.M., are called drive time.

Perhaps the biggest change in the audience for radio over the past 15 years has been the steady increase in listeners for FM stations. In 1973, only 28 percent of the listening audience was tuned to FM stations. Today the figure is 72 percent, with the largest increase in FM audiences occurring among teenagers, probably because of the trend toward Top 40, album rock, and progressive rock apparent among FM stations.

Top 40 stations draw an audience composed primarily of 12- to 24-year-olds, with females outnumbering males by about three to two. Modern rock attracts 18- to 34-year-olds, in about equal proportions of men and women. Beautiful music, classical, and all-news formats generally attract an older crowd, with most of their audience coming from the 45-and-over age groups. Country music stations seem to have an across-the-board appeal to those over 25. As a person gets older, he or she tends to evolve out of the audience for one format and move on to another.

CAREER
OUTLOOK

THE RADIO INDUSTRY

About 150,000 people are employed at radio stations and radio networks. The average station employs about 14 full-time people. Competition is tight, but thousands of young people find jobs in radio every year. How does a newcomer gain experience? One good way is to volunteer to work at your college or university radio station. Try to do as many jobs as possible and learn as much as you can. Another possibility is to arrange for an internship at a local station.

Entry-Level Positions

The best place to break into radio is at a small-market station. Small stations hire people who are versatile. A DJ might have to work in sales. A salesperson might have to write commercial copy and produce radio ads. It would be virtually impossible to get this sort of experience at a large station.

Most employment counselors recommend that a beginner take any job that is offered at a station, even if the job is not exactly what you want to do. Once inside the organization, it is easier for you to move to your preferred area.

The two areas where most entry-level jobs occur are the programming and sales departments. Of these two, the programming area is the more competitive; many people who enter the radio field seem to want jobs as announcers or DJs. Nonetheless, it is possible to find a job if you are persistent and willing to work unusual hours. Volunteer your services for the midnight to 7 A.M. shift, or express a willingness to work weekends or holidays. Tell the program director you're willing to substitute any day time for a DJ who gets sick. Once you get your own air slot, you can prove yourself as a steady, competent professional and move to better things.

The best chance of landing a beginning job in radio can be found in the sales department. Radio stations, especially those in smaller markets, are usually in need of competent salespeople with a knowledge of and an interest in radio. If you are able to handle a sales job, it could be the start of a lucrative career in radio.

Upward Mobility

For talent, there are two distinct avenues of upward mobility. For DJs, it consists of moving up to larger markets and better time slots. The ultimate goal of most DJs is a drive-time air shift in one of the top 10 markets. In addition, many DJs progress within a station by moving up to chief announcer's spot and from there to program director. Radio news reporters also strive to move into the big markets, and those with an interest in administration move into the director's slot. An occasional program director or news director moves up to the general manager's job.

The sales department offers the best route for upward mobility. Competent salespeople are given bigger and more profitable accounts to service. Some will move up to the sales manager position. From sales manager, many will progress to general manager.

Remember that radio stations are not the only places of potential employment. Program syndicators hire announcers and those experienced in programming music formats. Companies that produce packaged feature programs need producers, writers, and directors. Radio wire services such as the Associated Press and United Press International need reporters and writers.

■ MAIN POINTS

- Radio started out as point-to-point communication, much like the telephone and telegraph. The notion of broadcasting didn't come about until the 1920s.

- The decade of the 1920s was an important one in radio. Big business took control of the industry, receivers improved, commercials were started, networks were formed, and the FRC was set up to regulate radio.

- The coming of TV forced local stations to adopt formats, such as Top 40 or country.

- FM became the dominant form of radio in the 1970s and 1980s. Sparked by a loosening of ownership rules, a wave of consolidation took place in the industry during the 1990s.

- Radio is moving slowly into the digital age. Satellite radio and Internet radio are two digital services that will compete with traditional radio.

- Radio programming is provided by local stations, networks, and syndication companies.

- Stations have refined their formats to reach an identifiable audience segment.

- The current economic picture of the radio business is positive. Most radio revenue comes from local advertising. Big companies now dominate large-market radio.

- National Public Radio is the best-known public broadcaster.

- Radio audiences are measured by the Arbitron Company using a diary method. The demographic characteristics of the radio listener vary greatly by station format.

■ QUESTIONS FOR REVIEW

1. What were the key developments during the 1920s that helped shape modern radio?

2. What impact did the Telecommunications Act of 1996 have on the radio industry?

3. What are the defining features of radio?

4. What is the function of a format wheel?

5. Why has radio prospered during the past few years?

■ QUESTIONS FOR CRITICAL THINKING

1. What might have happened if radio had developed during the 1930s—the depression years—instead of the Roaring Twenties?

2. What formats might radio stations have developed if rock and roll hadn't come along?

3. The radio industry is more consolidated than ever before. Consolidation may have helped radio's

bottom line, but is the listener better served? Why or why not?

4. Listen to the radio stations in your market. Are there audience segments in the market that are not being served?

■ KEY TERMS

network (p. 173)
Radio Act of 1927 (p. 174)
Federal Communications
    Commission (FCC) (p. 175)
Communications Act of 1934 (p. 175)
clock hour (p. 177)
payola (p. 177)

nonduplication rule (p. 177)
National Public Radio (p. 177)
Telecommunications Act of 1996
    (p. 178)
IBOC (p. 180)
AM (p. 183)
FM (p. 183)

format (p. 183)
format wheel (p. 190)
cycle (p. 191)
Arbitron (p. 192)
rating (p. 192)
share of the audience (p. 192)

■ SUGGESTIONS FOR FURTHER READING

The following books contain more information about the concepts and topics discussed in this chapter.

Adams, Michael. *Introduction to Radio.* Madison, WI: Brown and Benchmark, 1995.

Albarran, Alan, and Greg Pitts. *Radio Broadcasting Industry.* Boston: Allyn and Bacon, 2000.

Barnouw, Erik. *A Tower in Babel.* New York: Oxford, 1966.

———. *The Golden Web.* New York: Oxford, 1968.

———. *The Image Empire.* New York: Oxford, 1970.

Dominick, Joseph. *The Radio Standard.* New York: Gerson Lehrman, 1999.

Ditingo, Vincent. *The Remaking of Radio.* Newton, MA: Focal Press, 1995.

Hilmes, Michael. *Radio Voices: American Broadcasting, 1922–1952.* Minneapolis: University of Minnesota Press, 1997.

Sherman, Barry. *Telecommunications Management: Broadcasting/Cable and the New Technologies,* 2d ed. New York: McGraw-Hill, 1995.

Sterling, Christopher, and John Kiltross. *Stay Tuned.* Belmont, CA: Wadsworth, 1990.

■ SURFING THE INTERNET

Websites devoted to radio are about as changeable as the medium itself. With luck, these will still be functioning:

www.otr.com
A site devoted to radio's golden age. Listen to clips from kids' after-school serials, radio dramas, and classic comedy shows.

www.cbsradio.com
Home page of the CBS Radio Network.

www.kisw.com
KISW-FM is a Seattle rock station. Site includes local entertainment news, a ticket exchange, and "The Wall"—a place for listeners to exchange messages.

www.npr.org
The home of National Public Radio. In addition to the usual background information, the site has a link to current news and to the "Public Radio Ethics and Style Guidebook."

www.rab.com
Home page of the Radio Advertising Bureau. Filled with useful statistics and facts about radio.

www.spinner.com
"Where music lives online." Web-only radio site with 130 streaming music channels.

www.woodradio.com
Good example of a home page of a radio station. WOOD is a news/talk station in Grand Rapids, Michigan. Site allows visitors to jump to the show currently being broadcast.

CHAPTER 8

Sound Recording

For the recording industry, the future got here faster than expected.

Sometimes big ideas start in small places. Shawn Fanning was a 19-year-old freshman at Northeastern University in Boston who was interested in music, computers, and the Internet. In his dorm room one night, he developed Napster, a file-sharing program that made it ridiculously easy for users to download music for free over the Internet. Not surprisingly, Fanning's creation caused a major upheaval in the recording industry.

Napster is one example of how technology has influenced the development of sound recording. In the past, most innovations had to do with how sound recordings were permanently stored or with the fidelity of the recording. Napster, however, threatened to change the way recordings are packaged, marketed, and distributed. Not surprisingly, the music industry reacted by filing a lawsuit against Napster for copyright infringement. In February 2001, a Federal Court of Appeals ruled in favor of the industry and ordered Napster to remove copyrighted material from its system, a move that would effectively cripple the service. In the wake of this court decision, let's take a look at the history of sound recording to understand better where Napster fit in.

Napster: The sight that sent terror through many executives in the sound-recording business. The file-sharing program forced the industry to reexamine its distribution and marketing strategy.

 ## HISTORY

In America, Thomas Edison recited "Mary Had a Little Lamb" into a primitive recording machine consisting of a tinfoil-wrapped cylinder, needle, microphone, and crank. It's interesting to speculate what might have happened if Edison had sung the nursery rhyme rather than recited it. Perhaps the recording industry would have been more aware of the musical potential of this new medium and its

The phonograph is just one of Thomas Edison's inventions. His 1877 model was hand-cranked, and the sound waves were preserved as scratches in tinfoil. *(Brown Brothers)*

history might have been different. As it was, Edison and others thought his **phonograph**, the name he gave his 1877 invention, might best be suited to recording the spoken word. He eventually tried to sell it to the business community as an aid to dictation. At the time, the idea of using the phonograph to bring musical entertainment into the home was too wild to imagine.

Edison's phonograph faced new competition when Chinchester Bell and Charles Tainter patented a device called the **graphophone,** in which Edison's foil was replaced by a wax cylinder. In 1887, more competition emerged when Emile Berliner patented a system that used a disk instead of a cylinder. He called his new invention a **gramophone.**

By 1890, three machines that recorded and played back sound were on the market. At about this time, big business entered the picture as Jesse Lippincott, who had made a fortune in the glass-tumbler business, purchased the business rights to both the phonograph and graphophone, thus ending a bitter patent fight between the respective inventors. Lippincott had dreams of controlling the office-dictating market, but stenographers rebelled against the new device, and the talking-machine business fell upon hard times. Strangely enough, relief appeared quickly and financial solvency returned, a nickel at a time, thanks to a new idea: Using the phonograph to record music instead of voice.

One of Lippincott's local managers hit upon the idea of putting coin-operated phonographs in the many penny arcades and amusement centers that were springing up all over America. For a nickel, you could listen through a pair of stethoscope-like earphones to a cylinder whose two-minute musical recording had a technical quality that could only be described as awful. Still, these **nickelodeons** were immensely popular, and the demand for "entertainment" cylinders grew. Companies quickly scrambled for a share in the new recording production business.

Rivalry

The two decades spanning the turn of the 20th century were a time of intense business rivalry in the recording industry. While the two major companies, the Columbia Phonograph Company and Edison's North American Phonograph Company, fought one another, Berliner's United States Gramophone Company perfected the process of recording on flat disks. Ultimately, Columbia recognized the superiority of the disk and attempted to break into the market by selling the zonophone, its own version of the disk player. As for Berliner, along with machinist Eldridge Johnson, he formed the Victor Talking Machine Company, which had

The 100th anniversary of phonograph recording on a flat disk was reached in 1988. This technology was created by Emile Berliner, an immigrant from Germany, who worked as a stock clerk in a clothing store while investigating the intriguing world of sound amplification and recording. Berliner quickly noted that the cylinders used by Edison had too many disadvantages to be practical. He perfected a way to encode sound on a flat disk that could be easily duplicated by using a master mold, much like pressing waffles in a waffle iron.

His invention was slow to catch on in the United States because of competition from Edison, but it was a success in Europe. Eventually, Berliner introduced to the American market the phonautograph, which he renamed the gramophone. This eventually replaced the cylinder.

In one area, Berliner clearly saw the future. He predicted that prominent singers and performers would collect royalties from the sale of his disks. He was wrong on another count, however. He thought that musicians and artists who were unable to appear at a concert would simply send a record to be played on stage instead.

Berliner also developed the prototype of the modern microphone, and both his inventions—the disk and the microphone—came together when electronic recording was perfected during the 1920s. Even the modern CD owes him a debt. Like his original invention, the CD stores information in a spiral on a flat, rotating surface.

as its trademark the picture of a dog peering into the bell of a gramophone ("His Master's Voice"). Thanks to aggressive marketing, this new company was highly successful and in 1906 introduced the Victrola, the first disk player designed to look like a piece of furniture. By 1912, the supremacy of the disk over the cylinder was established.

On the eve of World War I, record players were commonplace throughout America. A dance craze in 1913 sent profits soaring, a trend that was to continue throughout the war. In 1914, 27 million records were manufactured; 107 million were produced in 1919 following the end of the war. The record industry had entered a boom period.

The boom continued when the years after the First World War ushered in the Jazz Age, a period named after the spirited, popular music of the Roaring Twenties. **Jazz**, which emerged from the roots of the black experience in America, was spontaneous, individualistic, and sensual. Because of its disdain for convention, jazz was widely denounced as degenerate during its early years (about 30 years later, another spontaneous and sensual musical innovation, rock and roll, would also be denounced).

The good times, however, didn't last. In the beginning, no one in the record industry regarded radio as a serious threat. Record company executives were sure that the static-filled, raucous noise emanating from a radio would never compete with the quality of their recordings. They were wrong.

The Impact of Radio on the Recording Industry

Radio gained popularity in the 1920s, and the recording industry felt the effects. By the end of 1924, the combined sales of players and records had dropped 50 percent from those of the previous year. In the midst of this economic trouble, the recording companies quietly introduced electronic recording, using technology borrowed from their bitter rival, radio. The sound quality of records improved tremendously. But despite this improvement, radio continued to be thought of as the medium for "live" music while records were dismissed as the medium of "canned" music.

In 1926, the record industry began to market radio-phonograph combinations, an obvious testament to the belief that the two media would coexist. This attitude was also prevalent at the corporate level. In 1927, rumors were flying that the Victor Company would soon merge with the Radio Corporation of America (RCA).

Frightened by this, Columbia, Victor's biggest rival, tried to get a head start by merging with the new (and financially troubled) radio network United Independent Broadcasters. All too soon, however, the record company became disillusioned and dissolved the deal. The much-discussed RCA and Victor merger came about in 1929, with the new company dominated by the radio operation.

The Great Depression

The Great Depression of the 1930s dealt a severe economic blow to sound recording. Thomas Edison's record manufacturing company went out of business in 1930. Record sales dropped from $46 million in 1930 to $5.5 million in 1933, and several smaller labels folded. The entire industry was reeling.

In the midst of all this gloom, the recording industry was saved once again by the nickel. Coin-operated record players, called jukeboxes (the origin of this term is obscure), began popping up in the thousands of bars and cocktail lounges that sprang up after the repeal of Prohibition in 1933. These jukeboxes were immensely popular and quickly spread to diners, drugstores, and restaurants. Starting in 1934, total record sales began to inch upward; by 1939, sales had increased by more than 500 percent.

World War II and After

The record industry did not do well during the war. First, the U.S. government declared shellac—a key ingredient of disks—vital to the national defense, and supplies available for records dropped drastically. Second, the American Federation of Musicians, fearful of losing jobs because of canned music, went on strike. The strike lasted from 1942 to 1944, and, as a result, record sales increased slowly

During the 1940s, the local record shop was the place to hang out with friends and listen to the latest releases. *(Nina Leer/Life Magazine © Time Warner Inc.)*

during the war years. However, it was also during the war that Capitol Records embarked on a novel approach to record promotion. The company mailed free records to radio stations, hoping for airplay. This marked formal recognition of a new industry attitude: Radio could help sell records. This new philosophy would revolutionize the recording industry.

The postwar years saw several important events that permanently altered the shape of the record industry. Using techniques and ideas that were developed in Germany during the war, the 3M Company introduced magnetic recording tape in 1947. The arrival of tape meant improved sound quality, easier editing, reduced cost, and multitrack recording.

The next year Columbia introduced the 33⅓ long-playing record (LP). The new disks could play for 25 minutes a side and were virtually unbreakable. Rather than adopt the Columbia system, RCA Victor introduced its own innovation, the 45-rpm extended-play record. The next few years were described as the "battle of the speeds," as the record-buying public was confronted by a choice among 33⅓, 45, and 78 records. From 1947 to 1949, record sales dropped 25 percent as the audience waited to see which speed would win. In 1950, RCA conceded and began issuing 33⅓ records. Columbia won only a partial victory, however. The 45 would become the preferred disk for single pop recordings, while the 33⅓ would dominate album sales. The 78 became obsolete. There were also changes in record players. High-fidelity sets came on the market in 1954, followed four years later by stereophonic record players. Record sales more than doubled during this period.

The mushrooming popularity of television during the 1950s had an impact on both radio and the recording industry. Television took away the big national stars from radio and forced local stations to experiment with new formats in an attempt to keep their audiences. One of the most popular radio formats that emerged was Top 40, a sound that relied on a set playlist based on record sales. The emergence of rock and roll (see next section) helped the new Top 40 format become popular with a young audience—a young audience that, as it happened, had a good deal of money to spend on the records they heard played by their favorite DJs.

The Coming of Rock and Roll

Rock had its roots in black rhythm and blues, commercial white popular music, country and western, and jazz. In July 1955, Bill Haley and the Comets moved into the number-one spot on the charts with "Rock Around the Clock." Less than a year later, another performer, who would enjoy a far more substantial career, came on the scene. "Heartbreak Hotel," recorded by a then relatively unknown Elvis Presley, would stay at the number-one position for seven straight weeks. A few months later a second Elvis hit, "Don't Be Cruel," would go to the number-one slot, followed by yet another number-one hit in 1956, a change of pace called "Love Me Tender." It was with Elvis that rock and roll first blossomed. Combining a country-and-western style with the beat and energy of black rhythm-and-blues music, Elvis's records sold millions. He appeared on Ed Sullivan's network TV show (from the waist up—Sullivan thought Elvis's pelvic gyrations too suggestive). Through Elvis, rock and roll gained wide recognition, if not respectability.

Presley's success inspired other performers from the country-and-western tradition. Jerry Lee Lewis combined Mississippi boogie-woogie with country music

Elvis Aron Presley sold more than 250 million records, starred in 33 movies, and forever changed American popular music. *(Gamma Liaison)*

to produce a unique and driving style. His "Whole Lotta Shakin' Going On" sold 6 million copies in 1957 to 1958. At about that time, Buddy Holly and the Crickets made the charts with "That'll Be the Day."

Several rock pioneers came from traditional black rhythm-and-blues music. Perhaps the most exciting (certainly the most energetic) was Richard Penniman, or, as he called himself, Little Richard. Except for a period of three months, Little Richard had a record in the Top 100 at all times from 1956 to 1957 (best known are "Long Tall Sally" and "Tutti Frutti"). About the same time, on the South Side of Chicago, Chuck Berry was singing blues in small nightclubs. Discovered by the owner of a Chicago-based record company, Berry was the first artist who paid more than passing attention to the lyrics of rock and roll. His style would later influence many musical groups, including the Beatles.

■ Rock Goes Commercial

By 1959, through a combination of bizarre events, all the pioneers of rock had disappeared. Elvis went into the Army. Buddy Holly was killed in a plane crash. Jerry Lee Lewis married a 13-year-old girl said to be his cousin and dropped from sight. Little Richard was in the seminary. And Chuck Berry ultimately entered federal prison. Thus the way was open for a whole new crop of stars. Economics dictated what this new crop would look and sound like.

Record companies realized that huge amounts of money could be made from the rock-and-roll phenomenon if it was promoted correctly. Unfortunately, rock and roll had an image problem. In 1959, the record industry was shaken by the payola scandals (see Chapter 7) that, arriving on top of years of bad publicity and criticism that blamed rock and roll for most of society's ills, threatened rock's profitability. Since rock and roll had too much moneymaking potential to be abandoned, the record companies decided to clean up rock's image.

As the 1960s opened, the new look in rock was characterized by middle-class, white, clean-cut, and more or less wholesome performers. Rock stars were young men and women you wouldn't hesitate to bring home and introduce to your parents. On the male side, Ricky Nelson, Bobby Vee, Bobby Vinton, Fabian, Paul

Anka, Frankie Avalon, and the Four Seasons were popular. Although there were fewer examples on the female side, those who had hits included Annette Funicello, Connie Francis, Brenda Lee, and Lesley Gore. All fit the new image of rock and roll. Consequently, the early 1960s saw few musical innovations. In 1963, however, the music changed again.

The British Invasion

Their name was inspired by Buddy Holly and the Crickets, but instead of the entomologically correct "Beetles," the group chose the spelling "Beatles" (which, it was later explained, incorporated the word "beat"). In early 1964, they took the United States by storm. Musically, the Beatles were everything that American rock and roll was not. They were innovative, especially in vocal harmony, and introduced the harmonica as a rock instrument. Ultimately, they would change the shape of the music business and American popular culture. The Beatles had seven number-one records in 1964; they held down the top position for 20 of the 52 weeks that year.

Their success paved the way for a veritable British invasion. Most British rock at this time resembled American rock: cheery, happy, commercial, and white. Not surprisingly, some of the first groups that followed the Beatles represented this school (Herman's Hermits, Freddie and the Dreamers, the Dave Clark Five, Peter and Gordon, to name a few). There was another style of British rock, however, far less cheery, as represented by the Rolling Stones and the Animals. This style was blues-based, rough-hewn, slightly aggressive, and certainly not bouncy and carefree.

American artists were not silent during this influx of British talent. Folk music, as performed by Bob Dylan and Joan Baez, was also popular. It was only a matter of time before folk merged with rock to produce folk rock. Soul music, as recorded on the Motown label, also made its mark during the 60s. The Supremes and the Four Tops had 11 number-one songs between them for this label from 1964 to 1967.

Transitions

The late 1960s was a time of cultural transition. Freedom, experimentation, and innovation were encouraged in almost all walks of life, and popular music was no exception. Sparked by the release of the Beatles' *Sgt. Pepper* album, a fractionaliza-

One of the strangest trends in the evolution of popular rock-and-roll music has been a small but persistent genre of records that can only be classified under the somewhat macabre title of "morbid rock." Although its roots probably go back further, it became especially notable in the 1960s. Among the first songs to become a hit was "Teen Angel," the tale of an unfortunate couple whose car stalled on the railroad tracks. Although the young man of the song is smart enough to run like crazy, the young woman goes back to the car to retrieve her sweetheart's high school ring. The train arrives at the same time. End of romance.

Another early example was J. Frank Wilson's "Last Kiss," a tragic tale of a guy and girl out on a date who plow into a disabled car. He survives. She doesn't. End of romance. "Tell Laura I Love Her" told the teary story of a young man who needs money to continue his romance with his lady friend and so resorts to stock car racing to provide extra income. He totals his car and himself. End of romance. "Patches" concerned the romance between a young woman from the wrong side of the tracks and a middle-class young man. Despondent, the young woman drowns herself in the river. At the end of the song, the young man is contemplating the same thing. Even wholesome Pat Boone got into the act with "Moody River," a song that also told the story of two people who throw themselves into the river and drown.

The trend was less noticeable in the early 70s, but a song entitled "Billy, Don't Be a Hero" enjoyed wide popularity. This effort was about a boy who goes off to war, against the wishes of his girlfriend, and gets killed. End of romance. (For those who are true fans of this genre, Rhino Records has collected 10 teen tragedy songs ranging from "Last Kiss" to the little-known but nonetheless moving "The Homecoming Queen's Got a Gun." Incidentally, the back cover of the LP doubles as a tissue dispenser.)

The trend resurfaced in 1999 when Pearl Jam's remake of "Last Kiss" went to number two on the charts. Apparently, morbid rock isn't dead yet.

tion of rock began to take place. Several trends of this period are notable. In 1968, Blood, Sweat and Tears successfully blended jazz, rock, and at times even classical, music. The Band introduced country rock. The Who recorded a rock opera, *Tommy*. In the midst of all this experimentation, commercial formula music was also healthy. The Monkees, a group put together by ads in the newspaper, sold millions of records. Proponents of bubble-gum rock, the Archies, kept "Sugar, Sugar" at the top of the charts for a month in 1969 (it replaced, oddly enough, a song by the Rolling Stones, "Honky Tonk Woman").

The 1960s was a decade of change in American music. Compare early 1960s recording star Annette Funicello (shown in her Mouseketeer costume) with late 1960s star Janis Joplin. *(The Everette Collection/Gamma Liaison)*

Berry Gordy began as an assembly-line worker in Detroit but ended up as the head of one of the largest black-owned businesses in America. Along the way he also introduced black performers to a wider audience and permanently shaped the evolution of American popular music.

In 1957, Gordy wrote a hit song for R&B artist Jackie Wilson. While Gordy and Wilson were in the studio working on other projects, a group called the Matadors auditioned for Wilson. Although Wilson was unimpressed with their songs, Gordy noticed the potential of their lead singer, a young man named Smokey Robinson.

In the next few years, Gordy continued to write and produce songs for a number of black artists. Unsatisfied with the way his songs were handled by the major record labels, Gordy decided to start his own. He took an $800 loan from his family and in 1959 opened what would later become Motown Records. The company released its first single in 1959 and had its first number-one hit two years later with the Marvelettes' "Please Mr. Postman."

Berry Gordy, Jr., and Motown star Diana Ross. *(Russ Einhorn/Gamma Liaison)*

In its early years, Motown appealed primarily to black audiences, but Gordy's strategy was to appeal to both whites and blacks. Motown's advertising slogan was "The Sound of Young America." During the middle 1960s, Gordy's company pioneered the Motown sound, which revolutionized the music industry. Artists such as Stevie Wonder, Marvin Gaye, Smokey Robinson, and Diana Ross and the Supremes became popular with both black and white record buyers. A few years later Gordy introduced the Jackson Five, featuring a young Michael Jackson as lead singer.

In 1988, Berry Gordy was inducted into the Rock and Roll Hall of Fame along with the Supremes, Bob Dylan, and the Beatles. That same year, Gordy sold Motown Records to MCA for more than $60 million. He continued, however, to head Motown's record publishing division and its film and television sections. The sound Gordy created will continue to influence the musical tastes of future generations.

Toward the end of the 60s and the beginning of the 70s, rock music became part of the counterculture; in many instances, it went out of its way to break with the establishment. Musically, many of the songs of this era were characterized by the **heavy metal** sound; amplifiers and electronic equipment began to dominate the stage. The artists also broke sharply with tradition. The pioneers in this style of rock were all vaguely threatening, a trifle unsavory, and definitely not the type you would bring home and introduce to the family. Consider Janis Joplin, Jimi Hendrix, Sly and the Family Stone, Alice Cooper, Rod Stewart, and David Bowie. They are a far cry from Frankie Avalon and Annette.

■ Industry Trends: 1970s–1990s

The recording industry enjoyed a boom period during the mid-1970s, resulting in large measure from the popularity of disco. A downturn during the early 1980s reversed itself during the second half of that decade thanks to Michael Jackson's *Thriller* album and a few popular movie soundtrack items. The 1990s saw the CD replace tape as the preferred playback medium. Record companies were happy about this since the profit margins on CDs were greater than for tape. As a result, recording industry revenues showed some fluctuation but generally increased during the 90s.

'N Sync performs live during NBC's "Today" program. 'N Sync was one of several "boy bands" to make it big at the turn of the new century. *(AP/Wide World Photos)*

MTV and music videos were surprisingly popular during the 1980s and helped launch many well-known performers, including Madonna and Bon Jovi. By the 1990s, however, MTV had lost much of its power as a promotional tool as the cable network changed its focus to more nonmusical programming.

With regard to content, the biggest trend was the growing popularity of rap music. Originally confined to radio stations with an urban format, rap moved more into the mainstream during the late 1990s. The end of the decade also saw the emergence of several boy bands, such as 'N Sync, the Backstreet Boys, and 98 Degrees, whose commercial sound helped them sell millions of CDs. Figure 8–1 depicts the evolution of rock music.

RECORDING IN THE DIGITAL AGE

The Impact of Napster

Explaining to an audience of college students how a file-sharing program such as Napster worked is like explaining the Super Bowl to a bunch of pro football players—both groups are already up to speed. For those who were not Napster users, here's a brief explanation of how it worked: People can download music from the Internet because of a technique called **MP3,** short for Motion Pictures Engineering Group Audio Layer 3, that takes digital audio (the kind that's encoded on CDs) and shrinks it into small packages that can be stored on a computer's hard drive, downloaded from the Internet, or sent via e-mail. A CD purchased at the local retail store can easily be converted to MP3 files.

Figure 8–1

The Rock-and-Roll Family Tree, Circa 2000, Greatly Simplified and Somewhat Subjective (If you disagree, draw new arrows and circles.)

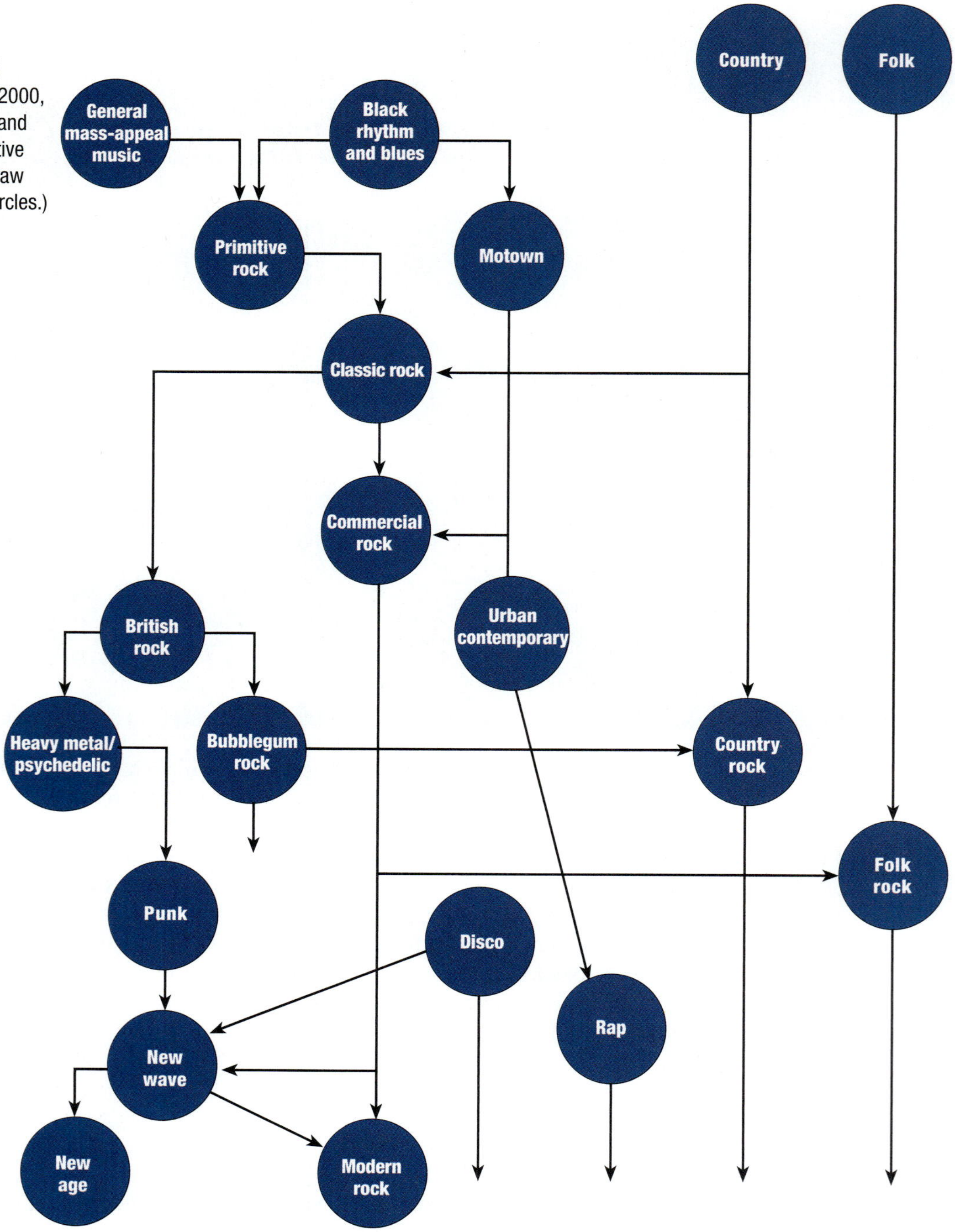

Once an individual downloaded the free Napster program, he or she sent a request to Napster to search for a song or an artist. The program then searched the hard drives of every online Napster user and displayed a list of all those users that had the song and even reported the size of the file and the source member's connection speed. The user double-clicked on one of the locations where the song was stored, and the music was copied onto the user's hard drive. Once copied, the

In December 1999, the Recording Industry Association of America (RIAA), representing the major record companies, filed suit against Napster alleging copyright infringement. In July 2000, a district court judge granted a preliminary injunction against the file-sharing service that would have shut it down. A court of appeals later overturned the injunction, giving Napster a stay of execution, as it were. That stay ended in 2001 when an appeals court found in favor of the record industry. The fight over Napster highlighted some significant issues in the struggle between legislation and innovation.

Napster was not the first media copying and sharing technology to find itself the topic of a lawsuit filed by a media industry. The motion picture and TV industry sued to stop the use of VCRs to record movies and TV programs. The case eventually went to the Supreme Court, which ruled that people could make personal copies for their personal use. (Ironically, the motion picture industry now makes most of its revenue from tape sales and rentals, a result of the popularity of the device they tried to stymie.) The RIAA also sued Diamond Multimedia, the maker of the Rio MP3 player, for copyright infringement, but the suit was unsuccessful. The RIAA was successful, however, when it sued MP3.com, an Internet site that offered free downloads of CD tracks.

The argument made by the RIAA was simple: Copyright law protects intellectual property and encourages creativity by making sure artists are compensated for their creative efforts. As the general counsel for the RIAA put it, "Napster is facilitating theft. This is a flagrant case of piracy." The RIAA cited surveys indicating that people who used Napster bought fewer CDs, thus harming the economic welfare of the industry. Napster cited surveys that showed the opposite: Napster users bought more CDs. The court apparently was more convinced by the RIAA argument.

Napster's defense was twofold. On the one hand, its lawyers argued that people who used Napster were engaging in a perfectly legal activity—making copies of songs for personal, noncommercial uses—an activity protected by federal law, just as making a taped copy of a CD to play in your car is perfectly legal. Napster's users were copying files for themselves and not selling them. The fact that millions of people were doing it was irrelevant as far as the law is concerned; just because large numbers of people were doing it doesn't make it illegal.

A more intriguing defense was one that goes to the heart of the purpose of copyright law. Copyright laws protect creativity by granting a monopoly. Monopolies, however, might harm the public's welfare. The government can impose restrictions on copyrights when they inhibit the spread of new technology. As one of Napster's legal defense team put it, "Copyrights are all about balance. The record labels don't see it that way. They view them as ironclad monopoly rights and [we think] they're not."

The Federal Court of Appeals decision was a clear victory for the record companies. The court found that Napster clearly knew that its members were infringing on copyright protection by trading copyrighted material and ordered Napster to remove all copyrighted material from its system. This decision might spell an end to Napster but it will not end the controversy over sharing copyrighted materials over the web. Other file sharing services similar to Napster have sprung up. Unlike Napster, however, these new services do not use a central server, which makes them almost impossible to shut down. It seems obvious that the final chapter in this saga has yet to be written.

music could be played over the computer's speakers or on an MP3 player, or "burned" on a recordable CD. Total cost to the user—nothing. The music was free.

Napster's quick rise in popularity was phenomenal. It took just a year for Napster to reach 20 million users. In contrast, it took AOL about 10 years (and lots of dollars in promotions and free disks) to reach 23 million subscribers. Downloading MP3 files became one of the most popular activities on the web. Many universities banned Napster because students were downloading so many Napster files, they were clogging up the university's computer system.

Napster raised many issues, some of them legal (see Social Issues, "Should Legislation Hamper Innovation?"), some of them ethical, some of them economic, and some that go to the core of the business model used by the recording industry almost since its inception. Traditionally, record companies made their money by controlling the production and distribution of music. They decided what acts to record and what songs would go on a tape or CD, produced physical copies of the music on tape or plastic compact disks, and then shipped those products to retail stores. The recording company, the artist, and the retailer received revenue from the sales of the physical product. When the music is liberated from the physical tape or CD and distributed digitally from one hard drive to another, as happened with Napster, there are no revenues for the recording company, the artist, or the retailer. Obviously, the recording industry was upset.

New Business Models

As we have seen, the first line of defense for the recording companies was the courtroom and they were successful in getting Napster to remove copyrighted material. Many experts, however, believe that this is a temporary victory and that many Napster clones will take its place and some of these clones might be located outside the United States where U.S. copyrighted law matters little. Once the genie is out of the bottle, it's hard to put it back in.

A more promising approach might be to rethink how music is marketed and sold, and some record companies are doing just that. Two big recording companies, Sony and Universal, have plans to sell music over the Internet. A post-lawsuit Napster figures in the plans of another big company. Bertelsmann has signed an agreement with Napster to use the service to distribute music by Bertelsmann's artists. Subscribers would pay a monthly fee for the right to download as many of the company's songs as they want.

Recording companies could also follow the radio model. Radio stations offer listeners "free" music and make money from selling ads; a site that offers downloadable music for free might do the same. Many advertisers would love to reach an audience of young people. The companies and their artists would receive income from the fees paid by advertisers who want to place ads on the site. Note, however, that although these plans create revenue streams for the record companies, they don't do much for the retail stores where tapes and CDs are currently sold.

More Diversity?

Once again, the availability of digital music on the Internet is an example of disintermediation (see Chapter 1). Recording artists can bypass the record companies and sell directly to the consumer. MP3.com, for example, operates a site where new artists can post their music for free. In late 2000, about 470,000 different songs were available for download. Of course, this increased diversity comes with a price. The really bad bands can post music just as easily as the really good ones. Garage bands have equal standing with Metallica. It will take substantial energy for consumers to find the good music.

Keep in mind that while all this is going on, some 19-year-old somewhere is probably working on a new piece of software that might shake everything up once again.

DEFINING FEATURES OF SOUND RECORDING

First, sound recording is a cultural force. Its products help characterize social groups and define movements and trends in American society. In that connection, recorded music has been at the center of a great deal of cultural and social controversy. Sound recording helped usher in the Jazz Age during the Roaring Twenties. This new style of music was condemned as corrupting the nation's morals. The same criticisms were heard during the 1950s when rock-and-roll music became the rallying point for a new youth culture. During the 1960s, recorded music joined the counterculture and big record companies (benefiting from the status quo) made great profits from selling albums that challenged the status quo. In the 1990s, rap music recordings introduced the hip-hop culture to the rest of America. All in all, the sound recording industry has played a major role in shaping modern culture.

Second, sound recording is an international enterprise. There are five giant companies that dominate the business, one in Japan, one in Germany, one in Britain, one in France, and one in the United States. Recording artists sell their music worldwide. Ricky Martin's eponymous album sold 14 million copies worldwide, 7 million in the United States. Celine Dion's greatest-hits album sold 5 million in the United States and 9 million internationally. Recording artists tour all around the globe.

Finally, the recording business is a unique blend of business and talent. Recording companies are continually searching for new artists and new sounds that will succeed in the marketplace. The singers and musicians may be the stars, but the recording companies are the star makers. Most hit recordings owe much of their success to the marketing and promotion efforts of their record labels.

ORGANIZATION OF THE RECORDING INDUSTRY

The recording industry consists of the various creative talent and business enterprises that originate, produce, and distribute records to consumers. Rock music accounts for more than 60 percent of the total sales of the record industry; country and rhythm and blues account for another 10 percent each; gospel, jazz, and classical account for the rest. Although this chapter concentrates on rock music, remember that the other music styles are also part of the industry. For our purposes, we will divide the business into four major segments: (1) talent, (2) production, (3) distribution, and (4) retail.

Recording artist Shania Twain. Her "Come on Over" album sold more than 14 million copies. *(Morrison Walffraat/Zuma/TimePix)*

■ Talent

The talent segment of the industry consists of all the singers, musicians, songwriters, arrangers, and lyricists who hope to make money by recording and selling their songs. The words "hope to make money" are important because far more performers are laboring in virtual obscurity in and around Detroit, Seattle, Nashville, New York, and Los Angeles than are cashing royalty checks from their recordings. Exactly how many people are "out there" hoping to make it big is impossible to pinpoint.

Performers start out as a beginning act. The initial motivation may be simply personal pleasure. Many begin performing during high school. For example, Bob Dylan (then known as Bob Zimmerman) started out with a high school band in Hibbing, Minnesota.

The novice musician or musical group, if it continues in the business, eventually graduates to being a traveling act, which plays anywhere and everywhere to gain experience, a little money, and maybe some recognition. Traveling acts play in bars and clubs where they are little more than human jukeboxes providing accompaniment or background music. REM played college clubs in Athens, Georgia, while getting its act together. Crossover star Shania Twain spent years singing in bars and lounges before being discovered. Matchbox 20 paid its dues by playing in various Florida hotels before its big break. Even Mariah Carey, who debuted on the charts when she was only 20, spent more than two years waiting tables and trying to sell songs before she was discovered.

If the act is talented and lucky, it may be noticed by an A&R (artist and repertoire) scout from a record company, an independent producer, agent, or manager. If things work out right, the act is signed to a contract by a recording company.

◾ Production

The recording company brings the act to a recording studio where a large number of songs are recorded. Audio engineers and elaborate sound-mixing facilities are used to get exactly the right sound. Eventually, a single or an album is put together. The company also supplies publicity, advertising, merchandising, and packaging expertise. Promotion, which in the recording industry consists primarily of getting the record played on influential radio stations and getting the music video on TV, is also the responsibility of the company. There are dozens of record companies, but five dominate the business: Sony, AOL Time Warner, Bertelsmann, Universal, and EMI.

◾ Distribution

There are five main outlets for tape and CD distribution: (1) direct retail, (2) rack jobbers, (3) one-stops, (4) direct consumer sales and (5) online sales. (See Figure 8–2.) Of these five outlets retail stores and rack jobbers are most important, accounting for more than 80 percent of all sales.

Direct retail refers to stores that specialize in the sale of CDs, tapes, and related products. Many retail stores are chain operations with several outlets in different parts of the country.

Rack jobbers service the tape and CD racks in variety or large department stores. Wal-Mart, Kmart, and Sears, for example, all have their tape and CD shelves serviced by rack jobbers. The rack jobber chooses the records that are sold in these locations, thus relieving department store management of the task of keeping up with the latest Britney Spears CD and such other tasks as reordering and returning unused merchandise.

One-stops purchase records from record companies and resell them to retail stores and jukebox operators. For example, a small, independently owned retail store might not qualify for credit from the record companies and so might purchase its records from a one-stop.

TV packagers and record clubs sell directly to the consumer. Many of you have probably seen TV ads for collections of music (*The Best of Heavy Metal, Connie Francis' Greatest Hits, Zamfir and the Pan Flute,* etc.). Packagers receive licenses from

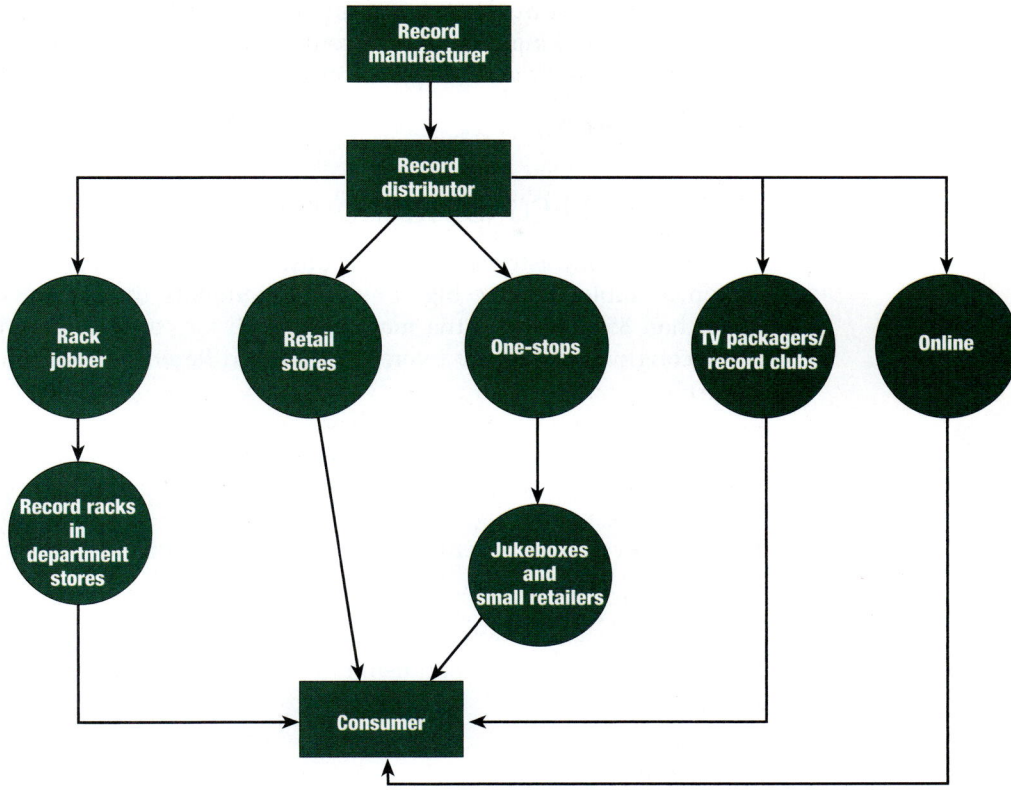

Figure 8–2

Record Distribution
Channels

record manufacturers and use TV advertising to market their products. Record clubs depend more on direct-mail advertising and usually offer an attractive introductory deal ("6 CDs for 99 cents") with the stipulation that consumers must buy a certain number of offerings in the next year or so.

Online distribution is simple: The consumer deals directly with an online retailer, and the product is delivered to his or her door.

▓ Retail

There are two major trends in the retail segment of the industry: consolidation and online selling. Big chains now dominate retail sales. The biggest, Musicland, which owns Sam Goody and Media Play, has about 1,300 locations. Transworld Music recently acquired Camelot Music and now has a total of approximately 900 outlets. Wherehouse Music bought out Blockbuster Music in the late 1990s and currently operates more than 600 stores.

Traditional brick-and-mortar retailers face increasing competition from Internet-only sales outlets, such as Amazon.com. They are also concerned that the big record labels will concentrate on selling online and will compete with the retail stores for customers. In response, traditional retailers are starting up their own online sales arrangements, becoming a click-and-brick hybrid operation that offers unique advantages to consumers. Wherehousemusic.com, for example, features hard-to-find used CDs that the pure online sellers don't stock. Other music retailers are expanding into related nonmusic merchandise.

Retailers are aware that programs such as Napster pose a threat to their operations and are looking for ways to compete. Plans call for at least two of the big retail chains to offer consumers the ability to burn their own custom CDs from a huge database of available music.

OWNERSHIP IN THE RECORDING INDUSTRY

The recording industry is one of the most concentrated of all media industries. As shown in Table 8.1, five big companies dominate the business, accounting for more than 85 percent of the market. In addition, these companies are multinational conglomerates, with interests in many different industries.

PRODUCING RECORDS

Departments and Staff

There are seven departments within the typical recording company:

1. Artists and repertoire (A&R)
2. Sales and distribution
3. Advertising and merchandising
4. Business
5. Promotion
6. Publicity
7. Artist development

Figure 8–3 shows a common arrangement.

The A&R department consists of talent scouts for the recording industry. The title "artist and repertoire" is a throwback to the 1950s, when the A&R department actually matched talent with potential songs. More recently, performers have

Table 8.1	Top Five Recording Companies, 2000		
Company and Location	**Major Labels**	**Top Stars**	**Other Interests**
Sony Records, Japan	Columbia, Epic	Pearl Jam, Celine Dion, Marc Anthony	Electronics, CD manufacturing, batteries
AOL Time Warner, United States	Elektra, Atlantic, Reprise	Faith Hill, Jewel, Goo Goo Dolls	Home video, Internet, books, TV, movies
Vivendi-Universal, France	MCA, Motown, Mercury, A&M	Hanson, LL Cool J, Vince Gill	Movies, Internet, theme parks, telecommunications
Bertelsmann, Germany	RCA, Geffen	Dixie Chicks, Whitney Houston, Elton John	Printing, book clubs, magazines, TV
EMI, Great Britain	EMI, Capitol	Garth Brooks, Pink Floyd, Radiohead	Consumer electronics, information technology

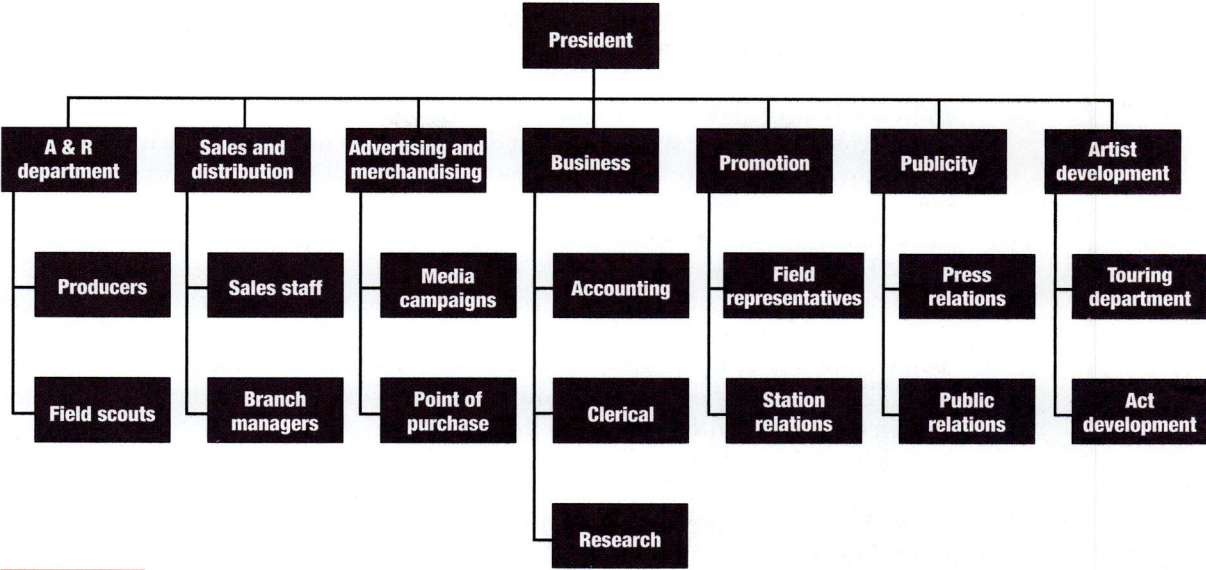

Departmental Chart for a Typical Recording Company

become more sophisticated in their approach to music and seldom accept advice from the A&R people. Performers now go to independent producers, who assist them in putting together a demonstration record. As a result, much of the creative work done by A&R people has been replaced by administrative functions: deciding how much it will cost to sign the act, whether the contract should be for a single or single plus album, what promotional strategies should be used, and so on. A major part of an A&R person's job is to listen to demonstration tapes sent in by hopefuls and to attend auditions. Major companies also send their A&R people out on the road, where they move from one club to another, enduring a succession of fourth-rate bands (in the slang of the business, such acts are called "garage bands") in the hope of discovering another Backstreet Boys or Britney Spears.

The sales and distribution department, as the name suggests, first sells the company's products and then makes sure that the tapes and CDs get to the stores where consumers can buy them. The actual selling of the tape and CD occurs about a month prior to the record's release. The distribution of the tape and CD is usually done through branch distributors.

The advertising and merchandising department aids sales by planning media ad campaigns and point-of-purchase displays in sales outlets. The advertising campaign goes hand in hand with the efforts of the promotion department (see below) to get airplay for the tape or CD. It includes television and print ads that remind consumers of the record that they have been hearing on the local radio stations. Point-of-purchase displays include posters, mobiles, neon signs, and life-size cutouts that are set up in the store to help trigger a sale.

The business department includes lawyers, accountants, market researchers, financial analysts, and secretarial and clerical staffs. It functions in the recording business in the same way that such a department would operate in any other business or industry.

In the recording business, promotion means getting the release played on radio stations. Since many contemporary stations restrict the music they play to a tightly controlled playlist, the job of the promotion department is a challenging one. Radio stations like to stick with tried-and-true hits; record company promotion people want to persuade the station to play their company's new releases. With about 5,000 singles and 2,500 albums released in the United States each year and only four or five slots open on a given radio station each week to devote to new releases, the job of the promotion department is made that much harder.

Another avenue of promotion is the music video. Once an important part of a company's promotional strategy, music videos became less significant in the late 1990s. The number of television outlets that featured videos decreased and some, like MTV, shifted their focus.

The publicity department attempts to get press coverage for new performers and new releases and has the responsibility of getting new acts and albums reviewed by such publications as *Rolling Stone* and *Billboard.* The publicity department also supplies the consumer and trade press with information and photos for feature stories and interviews with the label's stars.

The artist development department carries on a wide range of activities designed to further the career of a group or performer. Some of the duties supervised by this department are coordinating tour dates, making sure that the act has a well-produced concert show, and arranging for television appearances.

▨ Making a CD or Tape

For a performer or group to win a recording contract, they need to convince someone in a record company that they have a sound that will sell. The first step in the process is to produce a demonstration tape, called a **demo,** that can be sent to the appropriate persons. A demo is usually done in a studio with four-track mixing facilities and does not have to sound as good as the finished product released by the major studios. All the demo has to do is highlight the strengths of the group or performer and capture the attention of recording company executives.

The second step is to sell the demo. Sending an unsolicited tape to a recording company is probably the worst way to sell it. Although there are some exceptions, most of these tapes are never listened to. A better way is to hire a manager or agent to sell the demo for the act. If the agent is successful, step three entails going to the recording studio and making a master tape.

Resembling something you might see at NASA's mission control center, with banks of modern equipment, blinking lights, and digital readouts, the modern recording studio does multitrack recording. Professional studios have machines capable of recording up to 48 different tracks. This means that different instruments and vocals can be recorded on different sections of the same piece of tape. A piano might be recorded on one track, drums on another, bass on another, lead vocals on another, background vocals on yet another, and so on. So that one track does not leak onto another, the studio is set up with careful placement of microphones and wooden baffles—soundproof barriers that keep the sound of one instrument from spilling over into the mikes recording the other instruments. Once the session starts, the producer makes most of the creative decisions. The producer decides when the performers take a break, when the tune has to be played over because of a bad note, when the tape should be played back so that the group can hear itself and perhaps make changes in the arrangement, and so on.

The advent of multiple-track recording has revamped the music-making process. Currently, it isn't even necessary for band members to record together. The instrumentalists can come in one at a time and "lay down" their tracks, the lead singer or singers can add the vocals later, and everything can be put together at the mixing console.

After the recording session, the next step is the mix down, the technically exacting job of mixing down the multiple tracks onto a two-track stereo master. In the mix down, each track is equalized; echo, overdubbing, or other special effects are added and certain passages are scheduled for rerecording. If an album is being produced, each track has to be precisely placed on the stereo spectrum. A track can be placed in the left or right speaker or in the center, where it is heard as equal in both speakers. Mixing a 16- or 24-track tape down to 2 tracks can take several days. The job has been made somewhat easier in recent years thanks to computerized mixing boards. After the mix is completed, the master is reproduced on tape and disk for manufacture. At the same time, the promotion department is given a preview of the new release, and the advertising and publicity departments begin their efforts.

ECONOMICS

We will approach the topic of economics at two levels. First, we'll examine the economic structure of the industry as a whole. Next, we'll investigate the financial ups and downs of a typical musical group trying to make it in the recording business.

Economic Trends

The recording industry went through a few lean years during the mid-1990s when revenue growth stagnated. From 1997 to 1999, however, things picked up and recording industry revenue rose to $14.5 billion in 1999, an increase of nearly 20 percent from 1997. (See Figure 8–4.)

Part of that increase was due to an average price rise of $3 for a CD over the same period. This price increase attracted the attention of the Federal Trade Commission (FTC) and resulted in an antitrust investigation. The FTC charged that record companies were forcing some big chain stores to keep their prices above a specified level. In 2000, the industry and the FTC entered into an agreement whereby the record companies would stop that pricing practice.

Figure 8–4

Recording Industry Revenues, 1973–1999

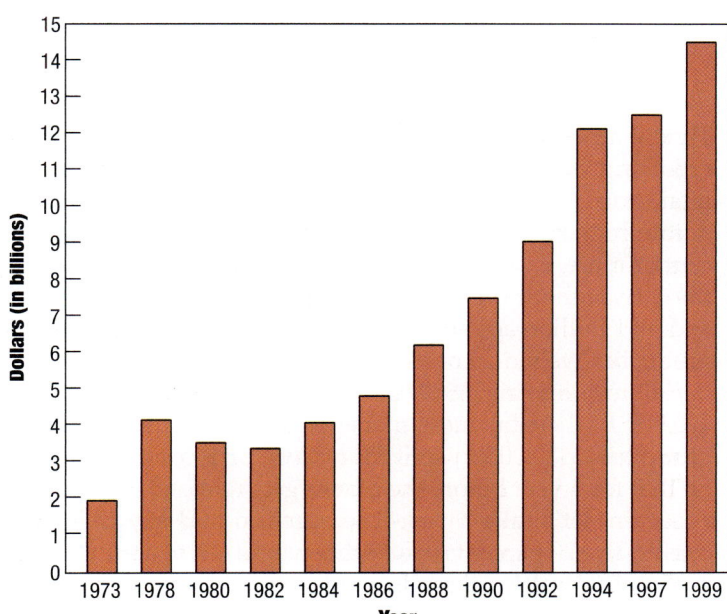

Table 8.2	Cost and Profits of a Typical CD	
Manufacturer's costs		
Recording expense		$0.65
Manufacturing expense		1.25
Packaging		1.30
Advertising and promotion		2.00
Artist's royalty		1.60
Freight		0.09
Payment to musicians' trust fund		0.65
Manufacturer's profit		2.94
Distributor's expenses and profit		1.50
Retailer's expenses and profit		5.00
TOTAL		**$16.98**

Table 8.2 breaks down the typical costs associated with a CD with a list price of $16.98. Keep in mind that the figures in the table are approximate and subject to change.

The CD has nearly replaced tape as the preferred medium for recorded music. In 1999, more than 83 percent of revenue came from the sales of full-length CDs, compared with about 8 percent from full-length cassettes. The remaining revenue came from sales of singles.

If Napster hurt recording industry revenues, it has yet to show up in overall sales data.

Rock Performers: The Bottom Line

Granted, most of the people who read this book won't go on to be rock stars. Nonetheless, the financial arrangements that surround the production of popular music can tell us a lot about the economics of the business. (The examples in this discussion come from Courtney Love's speech to the Digital Hollywood Online entertainment conference in May 2000.)

There are many stories about the fantastic sums of money earned by pop music stars. Well, some stars do make a lot of money. (R.E.M.'s most recent contract with Time Warner was for $80 million.) Others, however, are not quite as lucky. A new artist or group will receive a royalty rate of about 9 to 12 percent of the suggested retail price of a CD or cassette. A more established act might negotiate a rate that's a little higher, maybe 15 percent. Really successful performers might get 20 percent or more. Royalty rates on singles run about 6 to 9 percent. For simplicity, let's say a hypothetical group of four performers is getting a 20 percent royalty rate and a $1 million advance from their record company (totally unrealistic for a new group, but we'll do a best-case scenario). They spend half of the advance to record the album, leaving $500,000. They have to pay $100,000 to their manager and $25,000 to their business manager and their lawyer. After $170,000 in taxes, the group has $180,000 to split four ways, or $45,000 a person. The group has to live on that for a year before the album gets released.

Again, let's take a best-case scenario and say that the album sells 1 million copies. The 20 percent royalty rate works out to about $2 per album, or a total of $2 million in royalties. Sounds good so far.

Courtney Love has been an outspoken critic of the economics of the recording industry. *(AP/Wide World Photos)*

There are, however, expenses involved. The $1 million advance is recoupable by the record label. The record label spends $300,000 promoting the song; the costs are charged to the band. The band releases two singles and makes two music videos, costing a total of $1 million. A typical contract calls for half of that cost to be charged to the band. In addition, the band goes on tour, and since most tours lose money, the record label kicks in $200,000 in tour support, recoupable from royalties. After all the accounting is done, how much is left for the band? Nothing.

Of course, the band might make a little money from the sale of the singles and from TV appearances, overseas sales, and merchandising. Most artists, however, don't see much money until they've had a couple of back-to-back hits. And even that's no guarantee of riches. The group TLC, for example, declared bankruptcy after selling $175 million in CDs.

The truth is that relatively few acts are able to command large sums of money. The riches in the music industry are disproportionately divided, with a small number of artists at the top making most of the money. About 32,000 new recordings are released every year; only about 250 will sell more than 10,000 copies. Fewer than 30 sell a million copies.

 FEEDBACK

Billboard Charts

Feedback in the sound recording industry is characterized by stars, triangles, and bullets. These are common symbols used in *Billboard* magazine's charts of popular records. Stars stand for recordings that are movers; they are on their way up in the charts. Bullets go to singles that are 1 million sellers; triangles go to 2 million sellers. Every week disk jockeys, program directors, and record company executives scan the *Billboard* charts, the most important channel of feedback in the sound recording industry.

What determines the award of stars, triangles, and bullets? How is the *Billboard* chart put together? In general, the *Billboard* charts are based on two components: (1) exposure and (2) sales. For the Hot-100 Chart, for example, *Billboard* selects the top 50 markets in terms of total record sales in the United States (these markets are

A sophisticated mixing board such as this one handles as many as 48 separate sound tracks that contain recordings of instruments and vocals. Note the computer monitor. Computer programs remember previous mixing setups, making the process easier and faster. *(Mitch Leigh Studio, Walters/ Storyk Design Group, Photo by Robert Wolsch Designs)*

among the most populous), and within these markets the magazine subjectively chooses the most influential recording outlets. These can be retail record shops, record departments in department stores, and online stores. *Billboard* then examines sales data for the hottest-selling disks and tapes. About 185 outlets are surveyed weekly.

To measure exposure, *Billboard* surveys the playlist of leading radio stations. The survey includes approximately 240 stations that are weighted by audience reach (e.g., being the number-one record on a 50,000-watt station in New York City is worth more than being number one at a 5,000-watt station in a rural area). Note that another mass medium, radio, plays an important part in the feedback mechanism for sound recording. In addition, radio stations with a music format rely on the *Billboard* charts to determine what records they should play. Thus sound recording also functions as a feedback mechanism for radio. This reciprocity is another example of a symbiotic relationship between media (see Chapter 1).

When all the sales and exposure data have been collected, *Billboard* combines the two measures and winds up with a final index number for each album or single release. These rankings are then translated into the Hot-100 pop singles chart.

Other charts are prepared in basically the same way, but there are some differences according to format. The pop and country albums charts use electronically gathered sales data from 99 markets. The adult contemporary chart is based on airplay, as is the album rock chart. Figure 8–5 reproduces one of *Billboard*'s charts.

◼ Sound Recording Audiences

Information regarding the audience for sound recording (records, tapes, and CDs) is somewhat difficult to uncover, partially because the recording industry is supported by audience purchases and not by advertising. This means that recording companies concentrate on compiling overall sales figures and that detailed demo-

THE Billboard 200

THE TOP-SELLING ALBUMS COMPILED FROM A NATIONAL SAMPLE OF RETAIL STORE, MASS MERCHANT, AND INTERNET SALES REPORTS COLLECTED, COMPILED, AND PROVIDED BY SoundScan

FEBRUARY 3, 2001

THIS WEEK	LAST WEEK	2 WKS AGO	WKS ON CHART	ARTIST — IMPRINT & NUMBER/DISTRIBUTING LABEL (SUGGESTED LIST PRICE OR EQUIVALENT FOR CASSETTE/CD) — TITLE	PEAK POSITION
				◄ No. 1 ►	
1	1	1	10	THE BEATLES ▲³ APPLE 29325/CAPITOL (11.98/18.98) 1 8 weeks at No. 1	1
2	2	2	24	SHAGGY ▲² MCA 112096 (11.98/17.98) HOTSHOT	2
				◄ GREATEST GAINER ►	
3	11	41	4	SOUNDTRACK HOLLYWOOD 162288 (18.98 CD) SAVE THE LAST DANCE	3
4	3	3	10	VARIOUS ARTISTS ▲³ SONY/ZOMBA/UNIVERSAL/EMI 85206/CRG (12.98 EQ/18.98) NOW 5	2
5	4	6	69	CREED ▲⁸ WIND-UP 13053* (11.98/18.98) HUMAN CLAY	1
6	6	8	10	SADE ▲² EPIC 85185 (12.98 EQ/18.98) LOVERS ROCK	3
7	5	5	14	LIMP BIZKIT ▲⁵ FLIP 490759*/INTERSCOPE (12.98/18.98) CHOCOLATE STARFISH AND THE HOT DOG FLAVORED WATER	1
8	10	9	36	DIDO ● ARISTA 19025 (11.98/17.98) HS NO ANGEL	8
9	7	7	12	OUTKAST ▲² LAFACE 26072*/ARISTA (12.98/18.98) STANKONIA	2
10	9	10	13	LENNY KRAVITZ ▲² VIRGIN 50316 (12.98/18.98) GREATEST HITS	2
11	8	4	5	SNOOP DOGG NO LIMIT 23225*/PRIORITY (12.98/18.98) THA LAST MEAL	1
12	14	18	15	JA RULE ▲ MURDER INC/DEF JAM 542934*/IDJMG (12.98/18.98) RULE 3:36	1
13	12	11	30	NELLY ▲⁵ FO' REEL 157743/UNIVERSAL (12.98/18.98) COUNTRY GRAMMAR	1
14	17	21	14	LUDACRIS ● DISTURBING THA PEACE/DEF JAM SOUTH 548138*/IDJMG (12.98/18.98) BACK FOR THE FIRST TIME	4
15	13	13	11	R. KELLY ▲² JIVE 41705* (12.98/18.98) TP-2.COM	1
16	23	46	9	CRAZY TOWN ● COLUMBIA 63654/CRG (11.98 EQ/17.98) HS THE GIFT OF GAME	16
17	20	17	17	LIL BOW WOW ▲ SO SO DEF/COLUMBIA 69981*/CRG (11.98 EQ/17.98) BEWARE OF DOG	8
18	18	15	9	BACKSTREET BOYS ▲⁸ JIVE 41743 (12.98/18.98) BLACK & BLUE	1
19	19	16	12	U2 ▲² INTERSCOPE 524653 (12.98/18.98) ALL THAT YOU CAN'T LEAVE BEHIND	3
20	21	19	13	LINKIN PARK ▲ WARNER BROS. 47755 (11.98/17.98) [HYBRID THEORY]	16
21	15	14	9	TIM McGRAW ▲ CURB 77978 (12.98/18.98) GREATEST HITS	4
22	16	12	6	XZIBIT LOUD/COLUMBIA 1885*/CRG (12.98 EQ/18.98) RESTLESS	12
23	28	25	7	K-CI & JOJO ● MCA 112398 (12.98/18.98) X	21
24	22	20	9	ENYA ▲ REPRISE 47426/WARNER BROS. (12.98/18.98) A DAY WITHOUT RAIN	17
25	34	36	73	DIXIE CHICKS ▲¹⁰ MONUMENT 69678/SONY (NASHVILLE) (12.98 EQ/18.98) FLY	1
26	25	23	36	BRITNEY SPEARS ▲⁹ JIVE 41704 (11.98/18.98) OOPS!...I DID IT AGAIN	1
54	48	42	12	GODSMACK ▲ REPUBLIC 159688/UNIVERSAL (12.98/18.98) AWAKE	5
55	57	62	18	FUEL ● 550 MUSIC 69436/EPIC (12.98 EQ/17.98) SOMETHING LIKE HUMAN	17
56	54	45	13	SOUNDTRACK ▲ COLUMBIA 61064/CRG (12.98 EQ/18.98) CHARLIE'S ANGELS	7
57	53	49	7	MEMPHIS BLEEK ● ROC-A-FELLA/DEF JAM 542587*/IDJMG (11.98/17.98) THE UNDERSTANDING	16
58	52	39	10	THE OFFSPRING ▲ COLUMBIA 61419*/CRG (12.98 EQ/18.98) CONSPIRACY OF ONE	9
59	50	40	7	RAGE AGAINST THE MACHINE ▲ EPIC 85289* (12.98 EQ/18.98) RENEGADES	14
60	55	47	9	WU-TANG CLAN ▲ WU-TANG/LOUD/COLUMBIA 62193*/CRG (12.98 EQ/18.98) THE W	5
61	56	50	10	VARIOUS ARTISTS ARISTA/WARNER BROS./ELEKTRA/ATLANTIC 83412/AG (12.98/18.98) TOTALLY HITS 3	25
62	68	84	6	COLDPLAY NETTWERK 30162/CAPITOL (16.98 CD) HS PARACHUTES	62
63	62	65	9	DAVE HOLLISTER DEF SQUAD/DREAMWORKS 450276/INTERSCOPE (11.98/17.98) CHICAGO '85... THE MOVIE	49
64	58	54	7	FUNKMASTER FLEX ● LOUD 1961* (12.98/18.98) FUNKMASTER FLEX: 60 MINUTES OF FUNK, VOLUME IV: THE MIXTAPE	26
65	60	77	31	BILLY GILMAN ▲ EPIC (NASHVILLE) 62086/SONY (NASHVILLE) (11.98 EQ/17.98) ONE VOICE	22
66	63	66	52	KENNY CHESNEY ▲ BNA 67976/RLG (11.98/17.98) GREATEST HITS	1
67	65	58	74	CHRISTINA AGUILERA ▲⁷ RCA 67690 (11.98/18.98) CHRISTINA AGUILERA	1
68	75	67	8	MASTER P NO LIMIT 26008*/PRIORITY (11.98/17.98) GHETTO POSTAGE	26
69	64	61	32	BON JOVI ● ISLAND 542474/IDJMG (11.98/17.98) CRUSH	9
70	76	82	13	TAMIA ELEKTRA 62516/EEG (11.98/17.98) A NU DAY	46
71	71	76	19	THE CORRS ● 143/LAVA/ATLANTIC 83352/AG (11.98/17.98) IN BLUE	21
72	87	106	15	VARIOUS ARTISTS FLAWLESS/GEFFEN 490641*/INTERSCOPE (12.98/18.98) THE FAMILY VALUES TOUR 1999	32
73	73	79	35	LEE ANN WOMACK ▲ MCA NASHVILLE 170099 (11.98/17.98) I HOPE YOU DANCE	17
74	82	98	53	JAGGED EDGE ▲ SO SO DEF/COLUMBIA 69862/CRG (12.98 EQ/18.98) J.E. HEARTBREAK	8
				◄ HEATSEEKER IMPACT ►	
75	103	131	4	NELLY FURTADO DREAMWORKS 450217/INTERSCOPE (8.98/12.98) HS WHOA, NELLY!	75
76	72	69	39	DISTURBED ▲ GIANT 24738/WARNER BROS. (11.98/17.98) HS THE SICKNESS	29
77	78	71	39	MYA ● UNIVERSITY 490853/INTERSCOPE (12.98/18.98) FEAR OF FLYING	15
78	67	56	11	BLINK-182 ● MCA 112379 (12.98/18.98) THE MARK, TOM, AND TRAVIS SHOW (THE ENEMA STRIKES BACK!)	8
79	74	63	17	98 DEGREES ▲² UNIVERSAL 159354 (12.98/18.98) REVELATION	2

Figure 8–5

Excerpt from a *Billboard* Chart

graphic information about the audience is typically not sought after. True, some record companies have sponsored market research to find out more about their audiences, but the results of these studies are usually not made available to the general public. We do know that by the turn of the 21st century there were approximately 85 million stereos, with perhaps an equal number of tape playback units and 40 million CD players in use. It has been estimated that more than 90 percent of all the households in the country have some means of playing a record, tape, or CD. In 2000, this audience bought more than a billion tapes and disks.

In general, those people who have a sound system have paid about $500 to $800 for their equipment and have a typical collection of about 70 albums and approximately 30 singles. They listen to disks and tapes about an hour a day.

Record buying is related to age and sex. Older consumers are accounting for more record purchases. In the late 1990s, people over 30 accounted for about 55 percent of the total dollar value spent on prerecorded music, a 25 percent increase from 1988. At the same time, consumer spending by those age 19 and under declined from 32 percent to 21 percent. The percent of the dollar values of all purchases is currently split about evenly between males and females.

C A R E E R   O U T L O O K

THE RECORDING INDUSTRY

Of all the mass media, the recording industry employs the fewest employees. Not counting performers, there are only about 15,000 to 18,000 people in the entire industry.

SOUNDBYTE

Do You Hear What I Hear?

The words to many popular songs can be difficult to decipher. Some song lyrics, like those to "Louie, Louie," are so hard to hear that nobody understands what the song is about. Other songs have only a few lines that aren't clear. This doesn't stop people from providing their own translations. Sometimes these mishearings are rather different from what the songwriter intended. In the examples that follow, the real lyric is listed first, followed by the misheard lyric:

1. From Robert Palmer's "Addicted to Love":
    "Gonna have to face it, you're addicted to love" misheard as
    "Hyenas wear faces, you're addicted to love."
2. From Christina Aguilera's "Genie in a Bottle":
    "I'm a genie in a bottle, baby" misheard as
    "I drink martinis in a bottle, baby."
3. From the Backstreet Boys' "I'll Be the One":
    "I'll be the one to make all your sorrows undone" misheard as
    "I'll be the one to make all of your showers fun."
4. From the Beach Boys' "Help Me, Rhonda":
    "Well, since she put me down I've been out doin' in my head" misheard as
    "Well, since she put me down there's been owls pukin' in my bed."
5. From Elton John's "Tiny Dancer":
    "Hold me closer, tiny dancer" misheard as
    "Hold me closer, Tony Danza."
6. From the Beatles' "Lucy in the Sky with Diamonds":
    "The girl with kaleidoscope eyes" misheard as
    "The girl with colitis goes by."

A book ('Scuse Me While I Kiss This Guy) and several websites are devoted to listing these mishearings. Check out www.amiright.com.

■ Entry-Level Positions

Basically, there are at least three distinct career paths within the recording business: (1) engineering, (2) creative, and (3) business. We will examine each of these in turn.

Over the past two decades, the technical aspects of sound recording have become tremendously complex. Sometimes it takes two engineers to operate the giant control panel—one to run the tape machines and the other to do the actual recording. If the engineering side of the industry is of interest to you, it would be of some advantage to study at a college that has its own recording studio so that you can become familiar with the equipment. You could also take courses offered by the Recording Institute of America (RIA) in multitrack engineering and sound production. Alternatively, you might volunteer your services as an apprentice at a local recording studio and learn the skills by watching others.

If your interests lie more in the creative area and you wish to become a record producer, college courses in mass media, business administration, and music are relevant. Some colleges offer courses in the music industry, and a few even offer a bachelor's degree in the music business. You will also need some practical experience in directing a recording session. This can be done by working at a college that has a recording studio or, as previously suggested, by volunteering your services at a local commercial studio. Another possible route is to start out at a company in a low-level position, perhaps in the warehouse or mailroom, and work your way into the A&R department and try to gain experience as a demo producer.

If the business side of the profession appeals to you, a college background in business administration and mass media would be most helpful. Those interested in promotion and sales should start out by checking to see if there's a branch office of a major label or independent distributor located nearby. Your goal should be an entry-level position as a local promotion person or a sales representative in a particular market.

The same advice holds for someone interested in advertising and merchandising. A branch office might be able to start you off at a beginning position from which you can move up to the parent company. An alternative route would be to gain some experience at an advertising agency, preferably one that has a record label as an account, and then move to the recording company. Those seeking careers in publicity usually have a college background in journalism or public relations.

It is a little more difficult to provide advice on how to get started in the A&R department. Many A&R people come from the promotion department. Others start off as secretaries or clerks and work their way up within the division. A good ear and a knowledge of what will sell and how to sell it are essential for a career in this area.

■ Upward Mobility

There are several paths that lead toward advancement in the recording industry. Beginning audio engineers progress to staff engineers and ultimately to senior supervising engineer. Some engineers do cross over and become record producers, but this is rare. Once you've committed yourself to a technical career in the control room, you'll generally stay there.

People who start out as producers advance by becoming staff producers with major labels. The next step up would be the position of executive producer. The executive producer in the record business is analogous to the executive producer in motion pictures or TV. Another upward path is to start off with an established label and then go into independent production. Many independent producers go on to form their own labels.

Those who start off in one of the business departments at a recording company advance by moving up the corporate ladder. The most common route to top management has been through either the production or sales and distribution department.

Note that we have discussed only the most common careers in the recording industry. There are related careers such as agent or personal manager, as well as positions in the areas of concert promotion, music publishing, retailing, and marketing. Furthermore, although the recording business is hard to break into, the rewards come fast. Since most popular music is performed and purchased by young people, many top managers and producers are also young. Many people become top executives or producers in their late 20s and early 30s.

■ MAIN POINTS

- Thomas Edison pioneered the development of the phonograph, which was first used as a device to record voice and later, music. Emile Berliner perfected the modern technique of recording music in a spiral pattern on a disk. By the end of World War I, record players were found in most American homes.

- The coming of radio and the depression hurt the development of the recording industry, but the business was able to survive because of the popularity of jukeboxes.

- After World War II, the industry grew quickly because of the development of magnetic tape recording and the LP record, and, most of all, because radio stations began to play recorded music as part of their formats.

- Rock-and-roll music helped spur record sales and made young people an important part of the market for recorded music.

- The development of the CD meant increased sales. During the early 1980s, MTV emerged as an important factor in music promotion.

- File-sharing software such as Napster may transform the basic way the music industry conducts business.

- There are four segments in the recording industry: talent, production, distribution, and retail.

- Five big companies, three of them with foreign headquarters, dominate the record business.

- After some periods of slow growth in the mid-1990s, recording industry revenue has increased.

- *Billboard* magazine's charts are the most important form of audience feedback for the industry.

■ QUESTIONS FOR DISCUSSION

1. Trace the various media that have been used to record sound, from Edison's time to the present.

2. How do file-sharing programs such as Napster work? Why are they examples of disintermediation?

3. Trace the distribution arrangement in the sound recording business. How many of the distribution channels have you personally used?

4. If the chance of financial success is so small, why do so many people still try to make it in the recording industry?

■ QUESTIONS FOR CRITICAL THINKING

1. Why did it take the recording industry so long to figure out that radio airplay helped record sales? Will the same be true with Napster?

2. What are the implications of large corporate ownership in the record business? Are big companies less likely to promote new acts and risky musical styles?

3. What are the ethical implications of downloading and sharing music from services such as Napster? If you have ever downloaded music, did you feel guilty doing it? Why or why not?

4. What will be the future of the retail record store in the digital era? If you can download music direct to your computer, why go to a store? Do people go to record stores for purposes other than simply buying an album?

■ KEY TERMS

phonograph (p. 199)
graphophone (p. 199)
gramophone (p. 199)
nickelodeons (p. 199)

jazz (p. 200)
heavy metal (p. 206)
MP3 (p. 207)
rack jobbers (p. 212)

one-stops (p. 212)
demo (p. 216)
Billboard (p. 219)

■ SUGGESTIONS FOR FURTHER READING

Avalon, Moses. *Confessions of a Record Producer.* San Francisco: Miller-Freeman, 1998.

Fink, Michael. *Inside the Music Industry.* New York: Schirmer Books, 1996.

Haring, Bruce. *Off the Charts: Ruthless Days and Reckless Nights inside the Music Industry.* New York: Carol Publishing Group, 1996.

Hull, Geoffrey. *The Recording Industry.* Boston: Allyn and Bacon, 1998.

Krasilovsky, William, and Sydney Schemel. *This Business of Music.* New York: Billboard Publications, 1995.

Lathrop, Tad, and Jim Pettigrew. *The Business of Music Marketing and Promotion.* New York: Billboard Books, 1999.

Sanjek, Russell. *Pennies from Heaven: The American Popular Music Business in the Twentieth Century.* New York: Oxford University Press, 1996.

Sklar, Rick. *Rocking America.* New York: St. Martin's Press, 1984.

Szatmary, David. *Rockin' in Time: A Social History of Rock and Roll.* Englewood Cliffs, NJ: Prentice Hall, 1991.

Also, *Billboard* and *Rolling Stone* are two publications that provide extensive coverage of the recording industry.

Discography

A few albums that help illustrate some of the trends in popular music are the following:

The Beatles, *Sgt. Pepper's Lonely Hearts Club Band,* Capitol MAS 2653.

Eric Clapton, *Unplugged,* Duck/Reprise 45024.

Bob Dylan, *Bob Dylan's Greatest Hits,* Columbia KCS9463.

Michael Jackson, *Thriller,* Epic QE 38112.

The Notorious B.I.G., *Life After Death,* Bad Boy 73011.

Elvis Presley, *Elvis Presley,* RCA LSP 1254.

Little Richard, *Little Richard's Grooviest 17 Original Hits,* Specialty SPS 2113.

R.E.M., *Monster,* Warner Brothers, 45740.

The Rolling Stones, *Let It Bleed,* London NPS-4.

Bruce Springsteen, *Born in the USA,* Columbia QC 38653.

■ SURFING THE INTERNET

Websites for the recording industry are just as evanescent as the industry itself. The following were current as this book went to press.

www.billboard.com
Billboard magazine's online version. Contains the latest news about the industry plus recent charts.

www.bmgentertainment.com
Home of the Bertelsmann Music Group. Site lists all of BMG's top artists and has links to the company's various labels.

www.cdnow.com
A retail shopping site. Browse 18 different musical genres (with samples included for many new releases) or search for a particular CD.

www.musicpages.com
One of the most comprehensive sites on the web. Contains information about the industry, jobs, labels, music dealers, and distributors, 'zines, promotions, and music education.

www.riaa.org
Site of the Recording Industry Association of America. Contains industry data, latest news, and legal information.

CHAPTER 9 9 Motion Pictures

April 1896. A big crowd is standing in front of Koster and Bial's Music Hall waiting to get inside to see the first public exhibition of Thomas Edison's new invention, the Vitascope, a machine that projects moving pictures on a screen large enough for everybody in the theater to view at once.

After a vaudeville program, the movie starts. Forty-six frames of celluloid film whiz past the projector's lens every second. The audience is treated to scenes of dancers and of surf breaking, as well as a comic boxing match. The spectators love it; they cheer and cheer. The movies have arrived.

Let's flash forward (a common movie technique) 103 years.

June 1999. The big crowd standing outside the Cineplex Odeon on Route 4 in Paramus, New Jersey, is waiting to see another first: the digital version of *Stars Wars: The Phantom Menace*. There's no vaudeville this time, just some previews for upcoming films and some clips about visiting the concession stand. Finally, the movie starts.

But there are no celluloid film frames. Instead, the movie has been recorded as a series of zeros and ones and stored on 20 compact disks. A stream of digital information is sent to a complex device called a digital projector that uses a system of millions of tiny mirrors to project a sharp and detailed image onto the screen. The audience sees every freckle on Anakin's face and all the subtle shades of Queen Amidala's lipstick. Do they like it? As one 13-year-old puts it, it was "way cool." Digital movies have arrived.

The new digital technology promises to change not only the way movies are projected, but also how they are created, distributed, and marketed. It may also shake up the corporate power structure that has governed Hollywood movies since the Vitascope era.

This chapter examines the structure and history of the motion picture industry and investigates the potential impact of digital movies. We start by tracing the evolution of this medium, from Edison to Anakin.

Star Wars: The Phantom Menace was released in both analog and digital versions. *(Photofest)*

HISTORY OF THE MOTION PICTURE

Motion pictures and television are possible because of two quirks of the human perceptual system: the **phi phenomenon** and **persistence of vision**. The phi phenomenon refers to what happens when a person sees one light source go out while another one close to the original is illuminated. To our eyes, it looks like the light moves from one place to another. In persistence of vision, our eyes continue to see an image for a split second after the image has disappeared from view. First observed by the ancient Greeks, persistence of vision became more widely known in 1824 when Peter Roget (who also developed the *Thesaurus*) demonstrated that human beings retain an image of an object for about one-tenth of a second after the object is taken from view. Following Roget's pronouncements, a host of toys that depended on this principle sprang up in Europe. Bearing fanciful names (the Thaumatrope, the Praxinoscope), these devices made a series of hand-drawn pictures appear to move.

The Edison Lab

Before long, several people realized that a series of still photographs on celluloid film could be used instead of hand drawings. In 1878, a colorful Englishman later turned American, Edward Muybridge, attempted to settle a $25,000 bet over whether the four feet of a galloping horse ever simultaneously left the ground. He arranged a series of 24 cameras alongside a race track to photograph a running horse. Rapidly viewing the series of pictures produced an effect much like that of a motion picture. Muybridge's technique not only settled the bet (the feet did leave the ground simultaneously at certain instances) but also demonstrated, in a backward way, the idea behind motion picture photography. Instead of 24 cameras taking one picture each, what was needed was one camera that would take 24

An early version of the Praxinoscope. Later models would be able to project a moving image onto a large screen for many people to view at once. *(Corbis-Bettmann)*

pictures in rapid order. It was Thomas Edison and his assistant, William Dickson, who finally developed what might have been the first practical motion picture camera and viewing device. Edison was apparently trying to provide a visual counterpart to his recently invented phonograph (see Chapter 8). When his early efforts did not work out, he turned the project over to his assistant. Using flexible film, Dickson solved the vexing problem of how to move the film rapidly through the camera by perforating its edge with tiny holes and pulling it along by means of sprockets. In 1889, Dickson had perfected a machine called the **Kinetoscope** and even starred in a brief film demonstrating how it worked.

These early efforts in the Edison lab were not directed at projecting movies to large crowds. Still influenced by the success of his phonograph, Edison thought a similar device could make money by showing brief films to one person at a time for a penny a look. Edison built a special studio to produce films for this new invention, and by 1894, Kinetoscope parlors were springing up in major cities. The long-range commercial potential of this invention was lost on Edison. He reasoned that the real money would be made by selling his peep-show machine. If a large number of people were shown the film at the same time, fewer machines would be needed.

Developments in Europe proved Edison wrong as inventors there devised large-screen projection devices. Faced with competition, Edison perfected the Vitascope and unveiled it, as we have seen, in New York City in 1896.

Early movies were simple snippets of action—acrobats tumbling, horses running, jugglers juggling, and so on. Eventually, the novelty wore off and films became less of an attraction.

■ The Nickelodeons

Public interest was soon rekindled when early filmmakers discovered that movies could be used to tell a story. In France, Alice Guy Blache produced *The Cabbage Fairy*, a one-minute film about a fairy who produces children in a cabbage patch, and exhibited it at the Paris International Exhibition in 1886. Blache went on to found her own studio in America. Better known is the work of a fellow French filmmaker and magician, Georges Méliès. In 1902, Méliès produced a science fiction film that was the great-great-grandfather of *Star Wars* and *Star Trek*; it was called *A Trip to the Moon*. Méliès, however, did not fully explore the freedom in storytelling that film was capable of. His films were basically extravagant stage plays photographed by a stationary camera. It was an American, Edwin S. Porter, who in his *Great Train Robbery* (the ancestor of dozens of John Wayne westerns) first discovered the artistic potential of editing and camera placement. These new narrative films were extraordinarily popular with audiences and proved to be financially successful. Almost overnight, 50- to 90-seat theaters, called nickelettes or nickelodeons because of the five-cent admission price, sprang up in converted stores throughout the country.

Nickelodeons depended on audience turnover for their profits. Keeping the audience returning required that films be changed often—sometimes daily—to attract repeat customers. This policy created a tremendous demand for motion pictures, and new production companies were quickly formed. (In these early days, films were regarded as just another mass-produced product; hence, early film studios were called film factories.) New York and New Jersey served as the bases for these early film companies.

D. W. Griffith's *Birth of a Nation* was made to commemorate the 50th anniversary of the end of the Civil War. The film was based on a novel entitled *The Clansman*. In 1906, a stage play based on the novel had caused disturbances in Philadelphia when it opened, but Griffith chose to go ahead with his plans to turn the work into a movie.

The story paints the prewar South as a happy and idyllic place whose serenity is disrupted by the war. At the war's conclusion, Southern whites are shown being victimized by coarse renegade blacks, Northern carpetbaggers, and corrupt politicians. In response, whites form the Ku Klux Klan, which exacts vengeance on the blacks and restores the prewar utopia.

The NAACP objected to the film when it opened on the West Coast. About 40,000 blacks demonstrated in California. In response, the San Francisco city censor (several big cities had film censorship boards in this era) ordered a couple of the film's more controversial scenes cut out. A delegation called on the mayor of New York City to stop the premiere but was rebuffed. When the movie opened in Boston, several brawls occurred outside the theater. Unrest was averted in Chicago when the mayor agreed to seat a black on the city's film censorship board. Griffith, for his part, never understood black feelings toward the film. He responded to these actions by issuing a pamphlet about free speech.

Birth of a Nation is rarely screened today. Modern audiences find the racial depictions unacceptable. The film is remembered not so much for its content as for its technical achievements and because it served notice that motion pictures could exert a political and social force.

Zukor and Griffith

Adolph Zukor decided to copy European filmmakers, who were making longer, more expensive films aimed at a middle-class audience. He acquired the four-reel French film *Queen Elizabeth*, starring Sarah Bernhardt, the most famous actress of the period, and distributed it in the United States at the then-exhorbitant price of a dollar a ticket. His experiment was successful, proving that American audiences would pay more and sit still for longer films. Nevertheless, *Queen Elizabeth* remained essentially the filming of a stage play.

It was an American, D. W. Griffith, who eventually took full advantage of the film medium and established film as its own art form. Although controversial and racist in its depictions (see Media Probe, "Birth of a Controversy"), his brilliant Civil War drama, *Birth of a Nation*, was released in 1915 and became the most expensive American film produced to that date ($110,000). The three-hour movie, which was shot without a script, introduced history as a film topic. Griffith went on to top *Nation*'s figures with an even bigger epic, *Intolerance*, a piece composed of four scenarios dealing with life's injustices. The movie was completed in 1916 at a cost of about $2 million (the same film made in the 1990s would easily cost $80 million to $100 million).

In response to the controversy generated by *Birth of a Nation*, two African-American brothers, George and Noble Johnson, made films that presented a more realistic and accurate presentation of African Americans. The first of these, *The Realization of a Negro's Ambition*, demonstrated that there was an African-American audience that would support films that spoke to their community. The Johnsons' company, Lincoln Motion Pictures, stayed in operation until the early 1920s, when lack of capital and an inability to secure bookings at white theaters forced it out of business.

Birth of the MPPC

Events in moviemaking during the decade 1908–1918 had far-reaching effects on the future shape of the film industry. As the basic economic structure of the film industry developed, the center of filmmaking moved to the West Coast, and independent film producers, having survived attempts by the major studios to stamp them out, became an important force in the industry. The tremendous demand for new pictures brought enormous competition into the field. Small film companies cut corners by using bootlegged equipment (for which they paid no royalty fees) and started making films. Competition quickly reached the cutthroat level; lawsuits were filed with alarming frequency. In an effort to bring order to the business (and to cut down legal expenses), the leading manufacturers of films and film equipment banded together, pooled their patents, and formed the **Motion Picture Patents Company (MPPC)** to restrict moviemaking to the nine companies that made up the MPPC. Film exhibitors were brought into line by a two-dollar-per-week tax, which entitled the theaters to use projection equipment patented by the MPPC. Failure to pay this tax meant that the theater owners would no longer be supplied with MPPC-approved films. Eventually, to accommodate the growing industry, a new role, that of film distributor, was created. The film distributor served the function of a wholesaler, acquiring films from the manufacturers and renting them to exhibitors. This three-level structure—production, distribution, and exhibition—is still with us today. The MPPC was quick to take control of film distribution also.

To call the MPPC conservative would be an understatement. The organization refused to identify actors and actresses appearing in their films, for they were afraid that if performers were identified and became popular, they might demand more money. They didn't want to pay some actors more than others because they sold film by the foot, and film was priced the same per foot no matter who was in it. In addition, they were convinced that audiences would not sit through movies that ran longer than one reel in length (about 10 minutes). The MPPC also refused to use close-ups in their films, arguing that no one would pay to see half an actor.

Instead of squelching competition, the MPPC actually encouraged it. Annoyed by the repressive regulations, independent producers began offering films to exhibitors at cheaper rates than MPPC members. Full-length feature films, several reels in length, were imported from Europe. The MPPC declared war. "Outlaw" studios were raided and equipment smashed. Violence broke out on more than one occasion. In an effort to escape the harassment of the MPPC, independent producers fled New York and New Jersey. They were looking for a location with good weather, interesting geography, low business costs, and proximity to a national border so that the independents could avoid the MPPC's subpoenas. Several areas were tried. Florida proved to be too humid; Cuba was too inconvenient; Texas was too flat. Finally, they found the perfect environment—a rather sleepy suburb of Los Angeles called Hollywood. By 1913, this new home had so encouraged independent filmmaking that the MPPC could no longer contain its growth. By 1917, for all practical purposes, the patents organization had lost its power.

■ The Star System

The aura of glamour surrounding Hollywood and its stars might not have arisen if the MPPC had not been so stubborn. Whereas the patents company refused to publicize its performers, the independents quickly recognized that fan interest in film actors and actresses could be used to draw crowds away from the movies offered by the MPPC. Thus it was that Carl Laemmle, an independent producer, shrewdly publicized one of his actresses who possessed a poetic name—Florence Lawrence—until she became what we might call the first movie star. As Florence's fame grew, her pictures brought in more money, spurring other independents to create their own stars to maintain pace. The two artists who best exemplified the growth of the star system were Mary Pickford and Charlie Chaplin. In 1913, Chaplin was working in movies for $150 a week, a good salary in those days. Just four years later he was paid a million dollars for making eight pictures. Mary Pickford, nicknamed "America's Sweetheart," was paid $1,000 per week in 1913. By 1918, she was making $15,000 to $20,000 per week in addition to a cut of up to 50 percent of her films' profits.

In 1919, the star system reached its natural conclusion. Both Chaplin and Pickford joined with other actors and filmmakers to start their own production company—United Artists. The employees now owned the shop.

The star system had other, more subtle effects. Once stars became popular, the public demanded to see them in longer movies. However, feature-length films that ran one to two hours were more expensive to make. Furthermore, audiences couldn't be expected to sit for two hours on the wooden benches found in many of the nickelodeons. A need had been created for large, comfortable theaters that could accommodate thousands of patrons and, at the same time, justify higher admission costs. These new motion picture palaces were not long in coming. In 1914, the Strand opened in New York. With seats for more than 3,000 people, it occupied a whole city block and had space for an entire symphony orchestra. On

Charlie Chaplin, one of the first movie superstars created by the Hollywood star system, delighted film audiences throughout the world. This scene is from one of his earlier works, a 1916 short called *One A.M.* (*Photofest*)

the West Coast, Sid Grauman opened his Egyptian Theater (across from the Chinese Theater) in 1922 at a cost of almost a million dollars. His ushers were dressed in Cleopatra costumes. Clearly, the nickel was no longer the symbol of the movies.

Consolidation and Growth

The increased cost of filmmaking made it imperative for the producer to make sure that the company's movies were booked into enough big, new theaters to turn a profit. Under this economic pressure, the film industry moved in the direction of consolidation. Adolph Zukor, whose company would ultimately become Paramount Pictures, combined the production and distribution of films into one corporate structure. Paramount and its chief rival, Fox, began building their own theaters, and Marcus Loew, owner of a large chain of theaters, purchased his own studio (later to become MGM). Studio owners could exert control over independent exhibitors by another policy known as **block booking.** To receive two or three topflight films from a studio, the theater owner had to agree to show five or six other films of lower quality. Although this policy was not very advantageous to exhibitors, it assured the production companies of steady revenue for their films. Of course, all this was taking place while World War I was devastating Europe. When the war ended in 1918, the American film industry was the dominant force in the world, accounting for upwards of 80 percent of the worldwide market. By the beginning of the 1920s, the major production companies were comfortable and prosperous, and enjoyed as firm a lock on the film business as had the old MPPC, which they had replaced only a few years earlier.

The Roaring Twenties

The prosperity boom that followed the war exploded in Hollywood with more force than in other business sectors. Profits were up, and extravagance was the watchword as filmmakers endorsed the principle that the only way to make money was to spend money. Between 1914 and 1924, there was a 1,500 percent increase in the cost of a feature film. Salaries, sets, costumes, props, rights to bestsellers, all contributed to the mushrooming costs of films. Even the lawyer for United Artists was paid $100,000 a year. By 1927, the average film cost about $200,000, and many films easily topped that. *Ben Hur* (1925) was made for a reported $6 million.

Huge salaries created a boomtown atmosphere in Hollywood, and many people—some still quite young—were unprepared to deal with the temptations that came with sudden wealth. It wasn't long before newspapers were reporting stories about orgiastic parties, prostitution, studio call girls, bootleg whiskey, and drugs. Hollywood was dubbed "Sin City." Scandals were inevitable. In 1922, within a few short months, comedian Fatty Arbuckle was involved in a rape case, two female stars were implicated in the murder of a prominent director, and popular actor Wallace Reid died while trying to kick his drug addiction. Public reaction to these revelations was predictable: indignation and outrage. By the end of 1922, politicians in 36 states had introduced bills to set up censorship boards for films. The motion picture companies hired a well-respected former postmaster general, Will Hays, to head a new self-regulatory body for the industry. Called the Motion Picture Producers and Distributors Association, this organization was successful in heading off government control, and the basic standards it laid down would be in force for almost four decades.

Al Jolson in *The Jazz Singer.* This film convinced the public that talkies were possible, thus ushering in a new era in Hollywood. *(Photofest)*

The Coming of Sound

Since optical recording of sound on film had been feasible since 1918, why did Hollywood wait until the late 1920s to introduce sound films? Money.

Business was good during the 1920s, and the major studios did not want to get into costly experimentation with new techniques. Warner Brothers, however, was not as financially sound as the other studios. Since Warner did not own theaters in the big cities and could not exhibit all its pictures in the most lucrative markets, the company was willing to try anything to get its films into movie theaters. In 1927 Warner released *The Jazz Singer*, in which Al Jolson not only sang but spoke from the screen. Within two years the silent film, for all practical purposes, was dead.

The novelty of sound gave a boost to the film industry, despite the economic effects of the depression. In 1929, average weekly movie attendance was 80 million; by 1930 it had reached 90 million—a fact that led many to regard filmmaking as a depression-proof industry. They were quickly proved wrong as attendance dropped in 1931 and again in 1932. Innovations were needed to attract audiences. *Becky Sharp* was filmed in the new Technicolor process in 1935. Theaters also began the practice of showing **double features,** two feature films on the same bill. Animated cartoons were also emerging as a force to be reckoned with in the film industry. All this new activity called for Hollywood to produce even more films— almost 400 per year during the 1930s—to meet the demands of the market. This high production volume was a boon to major studios since they could churn out large numbers of films more economically. Moreover, the tremendous amount of money needed to convert to sound and the poor financial conditions created by the depression forced many small companies out of business and left eight major studios with a lock on the film industry.

The Studio Years

The 20 years from 1930 to 1950 were the studio years, with MGM, 20th Century Fox, RKO, Warner Brothers, Paramount, Universal, Columbia, and United Artists dominating the industry. These studios created hundreds of acres of back-lot movie sets, constructed elaborate sound stages, and built up showy stables of creative talent, carefully groomed for stardom. Audiences adored and emulated their favorite screen idols, who were presented as larger-than-life gods and goddesses inhabiting a glamorous fantasyland.

Individual studios left their imprint on the films of the period as a studio's products took on a distinct personality. For example, during this period, Warner Brothers became best known for its gangster films; 20th Century Fox for its historical and adventure films; and MGM for its lavish, star-studded musicals.

Busby Berkeley was the biggest influence on the movie musical during the studio years. His innovative dance numbers remain the purest blends of sight and sound ever to show up on film. As the 1930s wore on, films blending light comedy and romance, especially those by director Frank Capra, were popular.

The most significant period for motion picture achievement was the years 1939 to 1941. *Gone With the Wind*, which showcased the new Technicolor film process, was released in 1939. In that same year, two other classics, *The Wizard of Oz* and *Stagecoach* (starring John Wayne in his first major role), were released. Just two years later, Orson Welles directed and starred in *Citizen Kane*, which some critics consider the best American film ever made.

The financial backing and diverse holdings of the studio system helped the film industry survive the depression. Attendance and profits began climbing in 1934 and held steady throughout World War II. During the 1940s, going to a movie was just as much a part of American life as looking at television is today. In fact, the all-time peak for filmgoing was 1946, when average weekly attendance reached over 90 million. By 1948, however, all this was to change.

Orson Wells in a scene from the 1941 film *Citizen Kane*. Welles was 25 when he directed, produced, and starred in this film, considered by many critics the best American movie ever made. *(Photofest)*

Back in 1938, the Justice Department had filed suit against Paramount and the other major film companies, charging that the industry's vertical control of production, distribution, and exhibition constituted restraint of trade and monopolistic practices. The case had been set aside during the war, but by 1948, the courts had ordered the major studios to get rid of at least one of their holdings in these three areas. Most chose to divest themselves of their theater chains. The court also eliminated the block booking system and thus deprived the studios of guaranteed exhibition for all their films. As a result, the studios had to cut back on film production and reduce costs.

■ The Film Industry Reacts to TV

When television began building a sizable audience during the late 1940s, it cut into the motion picture industry's profits. The first reaction of the film industry was to fight back. Studios stubbornly refused to advertise their films on TV, and they would not release old films for showing on the newer medium. Many studios wrote clauses into the contracts of their major stars forbidding them to appear on TV. None of their efforts had an appreciable effect on television's growing popularity; more and more Americans bought TV sets, while film attendance slipped.

Hollywood looked for ways to recapture some of its audience from TV. By the early 1950s, the film industry thought it had found the answer—technical wizardry. The first technical gimmick was 3-D (three-dimensional film). The audience wore special polarized glasses to perceive the effect and were treated to the illusion of spears, trains, arrows, knives, birds, and Jane Russell jumping out at them from the film screen. Unfortunately, the glasses gave some people headaches, and the equipment was too expensive for most theater owners to install. Audiences quickly became bored with the novelty. It was soon apparent that 3-D was not the answer. The second technical gimmick concerned screen size. Cinerama, which involved the use of three projectors and curved screens, surrounded the audience with film. Less expensive techniques that enlarged screen size, such as Cinemascope, Panavision, and Vistavision, were ultimately adopted by the industry but did little to stem Hollywood's loss of money.

One of the problems with 3-D movies was the uncomfortable plastic glasses that audience members had to wear to appreciate the three-dimensional effects. *(Eyerman)*

The attitude of the movie companies toward TV during those early years was a clear example of shortsightedness. What the film companies failed to see was that they could have played a dominant role in TV's evolution. Because major networks were not eager to supply early television programs, film companies would have been logical sources for television shows. Somewhat belatedly, Hollywood recognized that it was in its best interest to cooperate with television. In the late 1950s, the studios began to release their pre-1948 films to TV and to supply programs to the networks. In 1960, post-1948 theatrical films were made available to the smaller TV screens.

By the 1950s, when it became clear that TV would be a formidable competitor, the film industry cast about for new ways to draw audiences back to the theaters. It tried big-budget, spectacle movies, such as *Cleopatra*, as well as films that addressed more adult subjects, such as adultery and homosexuality, that could not be shown on TV.

Realignments: Film in the 1960s and 1970s

In the film industry, the 1960s were marked by the waning power of the major studios and by a closer affiliation with their old competitor, television. The continued rise of the independent producer led to a concomitant loss of power by the studios. As major production houses cut back, they released many actors, writers, and directors who, naturally enough, formed small, independent production companies. Using the big studios for financing and distribution, these independents and the artists they employed frequently took small salaries in exchange for a percentage of the film's profits. By the mid-1960s, roughly 80 percent of all American films were independent productions.

Award Overload?

Hollywood is nothing if not self-congratulatory. You've probably heard of the Oscars, the Golden Globes, the MTV Movie Awards, and the Screen Actors Guild awards. But you probably never heard of the Crystal Awards, the Tiger Film Awards, or the Golden Frogs. All told, in 1999 the entertainment industry gave out 3,182 awards at 332 separate awards ceremonies. That's an average of more than 9 awards every day of the year. May I have the envelope, please?

The poor economic climate brought about other changes. Large studios, faced with ever-worsening financial conditions, were absorbed by larger conglomerates. In the early 1970s, both the MGM and 20th Century Fox studios were sold to make room for real estate developers.

The late 1960s also saw a change in the regulatory climate that surrounded films. The Supreme Court issued several decisions that loosened controls on content, and filmmakers were quick to take advantage of their new freedom. In 1968, the Motion Picture Association of America liberalized its attitudes toward self-regulation. Whereas the old production code attempted to regulate content, the new system attempted to regulate audiences by instituting a G-PG-R-X labeling system.

The relationship between film and television became even closer in the 1960s, as movies made expressly for TV appeared in the middle of the decade. In 1974, about 180 of these TV movies were shown on network television. In that same year, the major film companies distributed only 109 films to theaters.

Film history since the early 1970s has been marked by several trends: Revenue went up, as did the budgets of many feature films, and several motion pictures racked up astonishing gross receipts. Foremost among the trends was a reversal of the slump in box-office receipts that began in 1946 and finally bottomed out in 1971. With the exception of temporary declines in 1973 and 1976, the general trend has been upward. In 1977, total box-office gross was about $2.4 billion; by 1981, it had risen to nearly $3 billion, although some of this increase could be attributed to inflation.

With more cash flowing into the box office, more money became available for the budgets of feature films. In fact, films of the late 1970s and early 1980s were reminiscent of the extravaganzas of the 1920s. Perhaps the most interesting film phenomenon of the era was the rise of the super box-office blockbuster. From 1900 to 1970, only two films (*The Sound of Music* and *Gone With the Wind*) managed to surpass $50 million in film rentals; between 1970 and 1980, 17 films surpassed this mark (see Table 9.1 and Media Probe, "All-Time Top Moneymaking Films—Another Look").

The trend toward closer cooperation between the TV and film industries was reflected by the production of more movies aimed at a television audience. In 1978, Hollywood produced around 180 films expressly for the small screen; only two dozen more were made for release in motion picture theaters.

On another front, in 1985, the Motion Picture Association of America instituted a new rating category—PG-13. This category was designed for those films where parental guidance for children under 13 was recommended. Yet another new category, NC-17, replaced the X rating in 1990.

■ Contemporary Trends in Motion Pictures

The past 20 years have generally been favorable to the motion picture industry. Although theater attendance has increased only slightly, higher ticket prices have pushed box-office revenues to all-time highs. Video has eclipsed the box office as the main source of movie income. Revenues from the sale and rental of videocassettes and DVDs and from pay-per-view and premium cable have been greater than revenues from movie theater admissions.

| Table 9.1 | All-Time Top Moneymaking Films, as of 1999 |

The figures are based on film rentals, that is, the money received by film distributors from motion picture theaters. This figure is not the same as total box-office receipts, nor does it include videocassette rentals. The table includes rentals from the U.S. and Canadian markets only.

Rank	Title	Year	Rental (in millions)
1	*Titanic*	1997	$600
2	*Star Wars*	1977	461
3	*Star Wars Episode I: The Phantom Menace*	1999	431
4	*E.T.*	1982	400
5	*Jurassic Park*	1993	357
6	*Forrest Gump*	1994	330
7	*The Lion King*	1994	313
8	*Return of the Jedi*	1983	309
9	*Independence Day*	1996	306
10	*The Sixth Sense*	1999	293

Movies, in turn, have become more expensive as the blockbuster mentality that was prevalent during the 1920s reemerged. *Titanic* (1997) and *Dinosaurs* (2000) cost about $200 million to make. *Armageddon* (1998) and *Mission Impossible II* (2000) were not far behind. Hollywood continues to spend money freely because the rewards can be great. *Titanic*, for example, made more than $1 billion at the box office. Independent production companies, however, such as New Line and Miramax, have been successful in making smaller-budget films. Miramax's *Shakespeare in Love* (1998) was made for only $20 million but grossed more than $100 million at the box office.

The industry continues to be dominated by seven major companies: Sony, Universal, Disney, Fox, Warner Brothers, Paramount, and MGM. These companies typically control about 80 percent of the market.

The number of theater screens hit an all-time high in the 1990s. More and more theaters were multiplexes with 18 to 24 screens, featuring stadium seating and digital sound systems. The financial picture for movie theaters, however, was rather gloomy as the new century began.

The **digital videodisk (DVD)** was introduced in 1997 and by 2000 was supplanting videotape as the popular medium for the playback of rented movies. The DVD was significant in another way as well: It marked the beginning of the digital age for movies.

MOTION PICTURES IN THE DIGITAL AGE

The conversion from analog to digital will affect motion pictures at all levels. Some repercussions from this change have already been felt; it may take a few years before others are felt. Whatever the timetable, the motion picture industry is about to go through a period of significant transition.

Making Movies

Digital moviemaking is already a reality. The special effects in *Titanic*, *Dinosaur*, and *Chicken Run* were all done using digital technology. Digital editing is a reality, and it may not be long before digital cameras replace the traditional celluloid ones. In fact, George Lucas, the creative force behind the *Star Wars* series, has announced that he will shoot the next episode almost entirely in a digital format. At the other end of the moviemaking scale, independent filmmakers are experimenting with digital because of its cheaper costs.

Chicken Run contained more than 350 digital effects shots. *(Photofest)*

Digital Distribution

Under the current distribution system, hundreds of copies of a film are duplicated, put into big metal cans, and shipped to various theaters across the country. This is an expensive process. Each celluloid copy costs about $2,000 to make. A film that goes into wide release might need 200 to 250 copies. For example, it cost Columbia Pictures more than $4 million to make celluloid copies and ship *Girl, Interrupted* to theaters.

Digital movies can be distributed electronically. The local movie theater could receive digital movies over land lines or from a satellite at a tiny fraction of the cost of conventional distribution. There are other advantages as well. Each digital version can have multiple sound tracks. Thus a theater in a Hispanic neighborhood can switch from an English-language version to a Spanish one at the flick of a switch—a task that would be more difficult using reels of film.

The biggest problem with going digital is (you guessed it) cost. Each new digital projector costs about $100,000 to $200,000. Total tab for converting the industry to digital would be about $1.5 billion or so. Who would foot the bill? In the past, when new technologies, such as sound or Cinemascope, appeared, the motion picture exhibitors paid for them. There is no guarantee that the same pattern would be followed with digital. In the first place, the big savings in distribution costs made possible by a conversion to digital would benefit primarily the studios, not the theater owners. The costs aren't likely to be borne solely by those who don't get the big reward. Second, motion picture theater owners recently spent a bundle converting to stadium seating and surround-sound systems. Many do not have the cash available for digital. Will the big studios help pay for the costs? We'll have to wait and see.

The Netplex

Digital movies, of course, could be distributed on the Internet. In fact, there are several websites currently in operation that feature movies, usually short subjects, that audience members can watch on their computer screens. The iFilm Network, for instance, is an online community of independent and experimental filmmakers whose website contains more than 100 short films. Web distribution channels, such as iFilm, allow freelancers to reach a potential worldwide audience.

As the technology improves, it is likely that more full-length films will be available online. A preview of some of the possibilities of online movies occurred in August 2000, when a feature film premiered in a New York theater at the same time it was made available on iFilm's website.

Of course, it's not likely that many people would prefer to sit at their computer monitors for two to three hours to watch a movie, but the day is not far off when most Americans will have broadband, high-speed Internet access and the computer will merge with the TV set. When that happens, the Netplex becomes like a pay-per-view system in a hotel room: Viewers can watch what they want whenever they want it. Movies on demand, thanks to the net.

"Napsterization" of Movies?

The motion picture industry assumed that a file-sharing system like Napster would never be a problem because, unlike MP3 music files, DVD movie files are huge, several gigabytes, and would require a day or so to download. The files would be so huge that they would eat up most of the hard drive space on many computers. Transferring movies to a disk would be difficult since only a high-capacity DVD would have enough space; conventional CDs wouldn't be large enough to hold a movie. Burning a DVD would require special equipment and skills.

The film industry received a jolt in August 2000 when a new software program called DivX (not to be confused with a defunct DVD format) suddenly surfaced. The program compressed digital movie files so that they could be copied to a regular CD-R or stored on a hard drive. An individual with a high-speed modem could use the DivX software to download a movie in only an hour or so. As of late 2000, many Internet sites had full-length DivX movies available for downloading. Abruptly, the "Napsterization" of movies became a real possibility.

The movie industry is taking this possibility seriously. In 2000, the major movie studios filed suit and shut down Scour.com, an Internet site that let users copy movie files from other users' computers, à la Napster.

There are, of course, significant differences between movies and music that might prevent Napsterization from occurring. A DVD can be rented; music CDs cannot. A DVD rental costs only a few dollars; a music CD costs about $17. Will individuals go to all the trouble of downloading a movie that they could rent for only a couple of bucks more than the cost of a blank CD-R? Nonetheless, movie executives have nightmares about someone getting hold of an advance digital copy of the next *Star Wars* and putting it on a website where anybody can download it for free.

DEFINING FEATURES OF MOTION PICTURES

The most noticeable characteristic of motion pictures is their potential cost. Many big-budget Hollywood movies have production expenses that routinely top the $100 million mark. Tack on another $20 million or so for marketing and distribution and you're talking real money. No other media product—book, magazine, TV series, CD—costs as much as motion pictures. (There are, of course, independent filmmakers who put together films for a lot less and sometimes make big money—*The Blair Witch Project*, for example—but these tend to be rare events.)

Partly because commercial motion picture making is so expensive, the industry has become dominated by big conglomerates. As noted earlier, seven major companies control most of the market. These companies have the financial resources to risk $100 million or so on a few dozen films each year in hopes of finding a blockbuster. Making motion pictures tends to be only one of many media interests in which these conglomerates are involved. Some have holdings in TV and the Internet; others own publishing companies and recording companies.

Film has a strong aesthetic dimension. Of all the media discussed in this book, film is the one most often discussed as an art form. My university library lists 87 entries under the heading "motion picture aesthetics." This characteristic introduces a tension in the field because most big-studio films are produced to make a profit rather than to showcase their artistic merit. Many independent filmmakers, however, make films not because of the bottom line, but because they find their efforts artistically satisfying. Although this chapter discusses primarily mainstream Hollywood moviemaking, keep in mind that there are thousands of freelance filmmakers who work outside the established corporate structure and produce films of varying length on a myriad of topics.

Going to the movies continues to be a social experience. It is the only medium where audiences can still gather in large groups and be exposed to the same message. And, of course, moviegoing is still a popular dating activity. In some situations, the social dimension of moviegoing might be the most important.

ORGANIZATION OF THE FILM INDUSTRY

Although it may be true that film is an art form, the film industry is in business to make a profit. If an occasional moneymaking film also turns out to have artistic merit, so much the better, but the artistic merit is usually a by-product rather than the main focus. In our analysis of the film industry, we divide its structure into three levels: (1) production, (2) distribution, and (3) exhibition.

Production

Films are produced by a variety of organizations and individuals. For many years, the major studios controlled virtually all production, but independent producers have recently become prevalent. The major studios now finance and distribute many films made by independent companies. The influence of independent producers was demonstrated at the 1996 Oscars when four of the five nominated films were independently produced.

Probably the biggest change in production in the late 1990s has been the increased number of films that are released each year. Prompted in part by the additional revenues from home video and the theatrical box office, a total of 461 films were released in 1999, an increase of 12 percent since 1990. The major film production companies (Sony, Paramount, 20th Century Fox, MGM, Disney, Warner Brothers, Universal) will each produce 15 to 20 films a year. Table 9.2 shows the share of the domestic box office for each major studio in 1999.

Distribution

The distribution arm of the industry is responsible for supplying prints of films to the thousands of theaters located across the United States and around the globe. In recent years, distribution companies have also supplied films to TV networks and to makers of videocassettes and videodisks. Distribution companies maintain close contact with theater owners all over the world and also provide a

Table 9.2	Domestic Box-Office Shares, 2000	
Rank	**Company**	**Market Share (percent)**
1	Buena Vista (Disney)	15
2	Universal	15
3	Warner Brothers	11
4	Paramount	11
5	Fox	10
6	Sony	9
7	MGM	2
8	Others	28

transportation and delivery system that ensures that a film will arrive at a theater before its scheduled play date. In addition to booking the film at local movie houses, the distribution company is responsible for making the multiple prints of a film that are necessary when the film goes into general release. They also take care of advertising and promotion for the film. Most of the distribution of motion pictures is handled by the large studios listed above. These companies are firmly entrenched in both the production and distribution aspects of the business.

The nature of film distribution ensures that the large companies will control a large portion of the business. First, it's too expensive for an independent producer or a small distribution company to contact theaters and theater chains spread all over the globe. The big studios already have this communication network set up and can afford to maintain it. Second, the large studios can offer theater owners a steady stream of films that consistently feature big-name stars. A small company could not withstand that competition for long.

Distribution companies also serve as a source of financing for independent producers. These companies lend money to the film's producer to cover all or most of the estimated cost of the film. In this way, the major studios acquire an interest in films that they did not directly produce. This arrangement will be discussed further in the section of this chapter, which deals with film economics.

Exhibition

The exhibition side of the industry went on a building boom in the late 1990s, constructing new multiplexes with stadium seating and surround sound. The total screen count in the United States exceeded 37,000, an all-time high. As it turned out, the exhibitors overexpanded and opened too many new screens without shutting down older screens in unprofitable locations. Consequently, theater chains did not generate enough cash to cover the cost of all this expansion. In 2000, Carmike Cinemas, the third-largest exhibitor in the United States, filed for bankruptcy. Regal Cinemas and Loew's Cineplex, the nation's largest chain, were also in financial difficulty.

Multiplex theaters, featuring 12 or 18 screens clustered around a central concession stand, are still the rule. Most new theaters seat about 200 to 400 patrons. The massive movie palaces of the 1920s and 1930s have not reemerged, but there are noticeable changes inside the motion picture theater as exhibitors go after a

The trend in movie exhibition is big 18- and 24-screen multiplexes. Increased competition and declining profits forced some movie theaters to close during 2000 and 2001. *(Michele Burgess/ Stock Boston)*

slightly older market. Soundproofing to prevent spill from adjoining theaters is now common, and concession stands are putting real butter on popcorn, with a few even offering mineral water and cappuccino to their customers.

OWNERSHIP IN THE FILM INDUSTRY

Big conglomerates, many of them mentioned in earlier chapters, dominate the film industry. As of 2000, the top seven were as follows:

1. *The Walt Disney Company.* Headquartered in California, Disney has two movie enterprises: Touchstone, for mature-audience films, and Buena Vista, for general films. Disney has holdings in television, cable, and publishing in addition to its interests in theme parks, hotels, music, real estate, golf courses, and professional hockey (the Mighty Ducks). Disney also makes a tremendous amount of money licensing Disney characters for use by other companies.

2. *AOL/Time Warner.* Warner Brothers is the motion picture arm of this huge congolmerate, which has interests in the Internet, book and magazine publishing, recorded music, motion picture theaters, and cable TV, among others.

3. *Paramount (Viacom).* In 1994, Viacom acquired Paramount Pictures and the Blockbuster company. In addition to motion pictures, the company owns CBS, Infinity Broadcasting, video rental stores, cable networks, CD-ROMs, video games, theme parks, motion picture theaters, and publishing companies.

4. *Sony.* Sony Pictures Entertainment is the part of this Japan-based, worldwide conglomerate that manufactures video and audio devices. In addition to hardware, Sony has interests in music, video games, movie theaters, and television production.

5. *Vivendi–Universal.* Vivendi, based in Paris, announced plans to acquire Universal Studios in 2000. The new conglomerate would have interests in motion pictures, pay TV, music, theme parks, cable TV, and real estate.

6. *News Corporation.* Rupert Murdoch's Australian-based company owns 20th Century Fox. The company is also involved in satellite broadcasting and publishing, and owns a TV network and a cable news channel.

7. *MGM/UA.* This company was acquired by a French bank in 1992 and was subsequently purchased in 1996 by a consortium that included current management and an Australian TV network. In addition to the motion picture studio, the company has interests in home video and leisure-time products.

PRODUCING MOTION PICTURES

Departments

Film studios differ in the way they are structured. Figure 9–1 displays a conventional departmental chart, with three main departments. The distribution department handles sales and contracts for domestic and worldwide distribution. The production division is in charge of all those elements that actually go into the making of a film. The TV production division handles all the studio's work in the development and production of series and made-for-TV motion pictures.

Figure 9–1

Department Chart for a Typical Motion Picture Company

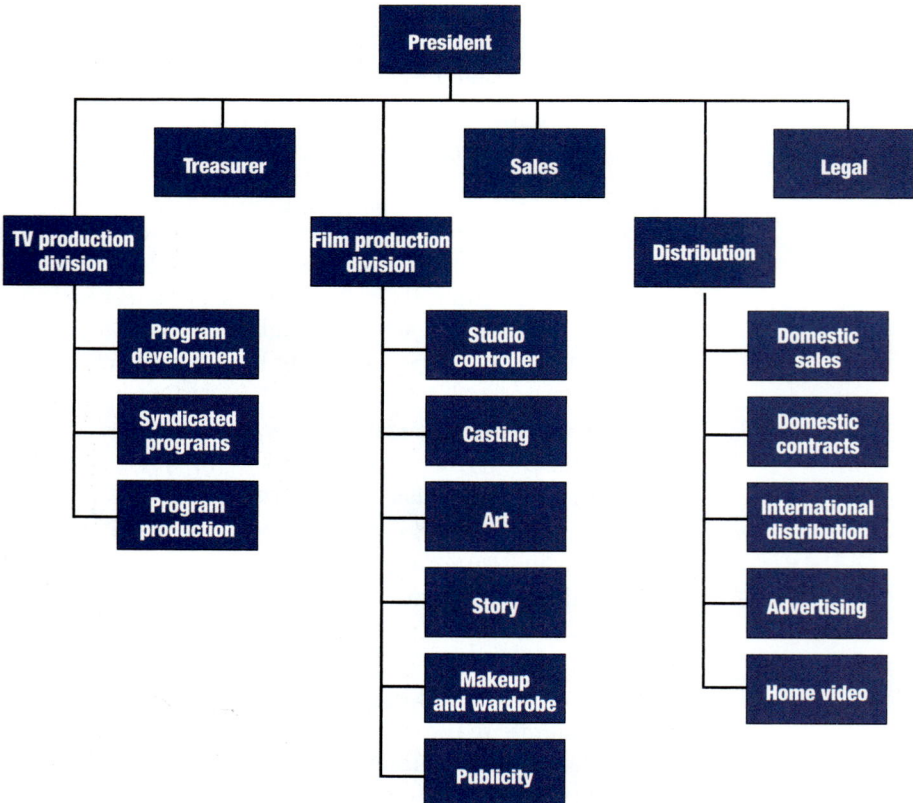

■ Preproduction

How does a film get to be a film? The three distinct phases in moviemaking are (1) preproduction, (2) production, and (3) postproduction. All films begin with an idea. The idea can be sketchy, such as a two-paragraph outline of the plot, or detailed, such as a novel or a Broadway play.

The next step of the preproduction process is writing the screenplay. In general, the route to a finished motion picture script consists of several steps:

1. Step one is called a treatment. This is a narrative statement of the plot and descriptions of the main characters and locations; it might even contain sample dialogue.
2. Step two is a first-draft script. This version contains all the dialogue and camera setups and a description of action sequences.
3. The third step is a revised script incorporating changes suggested by the producer, director, stars, and others.
4. Finally, step four is a script polish. This includes adding or subtracting scenes, revising dialogue, and making other minor changes.

While all this is going on, the producer tries to find actors and actresses (in the film industry, people who act in films are described by the generic term "talent," whether they have any or not) who will appear in the film. The contracts and deals that are worked out vary from astronomical to modest. One common arrangement is for the star to receive a flat fee. These fees have been rising in the past few years and are one of the reasons films cost so much to produce. For example, Sony Pictures paid Mel Gibson $25 million to star in *The Patriot*. Julia Roberts pocketed $20 million for *Erin Brockovich*. At the other end of the scale, the Screen Actors Guild has a contract that spells out the minimum salary that must be paid to talent in minor roles and walk-on parts.

Mel Gibson's fee was a big part of the $110 million budget for *The Patriot*. *(Photofest)*

Steven Spielberg started making movies at age 12 using his father's 8-mm camera. One of his earliest productions was a horror film starring his three younger sisters. He continued to make his own films during his college days and graduated with a degree in English (his grades were too low to get into film school). One of Spielberg's independently made films caught the attention of an

Steven Spielberg directing *Saving Private Ryan*. (Photofest)

movies, a strategy that movie studios still follow (consider *Twister, Independence Day,* and *The Patriot*). *Jaws* was also the first of the big movie blockbusters, raking in more than $250 million. Hollywood studios quickly adopted a "big budget equals big blockbuster" mentality.

Spielberg also hit upon a formula for making successful pictures that

executive at Universal Pictures, who hired the young Spielberg to direct episodes of TV series. The young director eventually wound up directing a made-for-TV movie, *Duel,* which won much critical acclaim.

On the basis of his success with *Duel,* Spielberg got approval to direct his first theatrical movie, *The Sugarland Express.* Although praised by critics, the movie did poorly at the box office. Nonetheless, the studio gave him the assignment of directing the movie version of a best-selling novel about a huge shark. The movie, *Jaws,* released in 1975, was a significant milestone in movie history. It marked the first of the big-budget summer action

resonated with U.S. moviegoers: Take tried-and-true, classic adventure themes and enhance them with cutting-edge special effects. The *Indiana Jones* trilogy, *Jurassic Park, E.T.,* and *Close Encounters of the Third Kind* are all examples of this formula. Spielberg also tackled more serious themes, as exemplified in *The Color Purple, Schindler's List, Amistad,* and *Saving Private Ryan.*

In a career that has spanned more than a quarter century, Spielberg has won two Oscars and numerous other movie awards. Among the top 25 all-time movie hits, 4 were directed by Steven Spielberg.

Meanwhile, the producer is also trying to secure financial backing for the picture. We will have much more to say about the monetary arrangements in film in the section on economics. For now, it is important to remember that the financial arrangements have to be worked out early in the preproduction process.

At the same time, the producer is busy lining up skilled personnel to work behind the camera. Of these people, the film's director is central. When all the elements have been put together, the director will determine what scenes get photographed from what angle and how they will be assembled in the final product. Working closely with the director is the cinematographer (the person responsible for the actual lighting and filming of the scenes) and the film editor (the person who will actually cut the film and assemble the scenes in the proper order). In addition, a movie crew contains dozens of other skilled people: set designers, makeup specialists, electricians, audio engineers, crane operators, painters, plumbers, carpenters, property masters, set dressers, caterers, first-aid people, and many others.

Shortly after the director has been signed for the project, he or she and the producer scout possible locations for shooting the film. Some sequences may be shot in the sound studio, while others may need the authenticity that only location shooting can provide. As soon as the locations have been chosen, the producer makes the necessary arrangements to secure these sites for filming. Sometimes this entails renting the studios of a major motion picture production company or obtaining permits to shoot in city streets or other places. The producer must also draw up plans to make sure that the filming equipment, talent, and technical crew are all at the same place at the same time.

■ Production

Once all these items have been attended to, the film moves into the actual production phase. Cast and crew assemble at the chosen location, and each scene is shot and reshot until the director is satisfied. The actors and crew then move to another location, and the process starts all over again. Overriding the entire production is the knowledge that all this is costing a great deal of money. Shooting even a moderate-budget film can cost $300,000 to $350,000 *per day.* Therefore, the director tries to plan everything so that each dollar is used efficiently.

The average shooting schedule for the typical film is about 70 days. Each day's shooting (and some days can be 16 hours long) results in an average of less than two minutes of usable film. Exhibitors prefer feature films that are about 100 minutes in length. This means the movie can be shown every two hours with a 20-minute break in between for people to visit the concession stand.

■ Postproduction

The postproduction phase begins after the filming has been completed. A film editor, working with the director, decides where close-ups should be placed, the angle from which the scene is shown, and how long each scene should last. The elaborate special effects that some films require are also added during postproduction. Once the scenes have been edited into an acceptable form, postproduction sound can be added. This might include narration, music, sound effects, and original dialogue that, for one reason or another, has to be redone. (About 10 to 15 percent of outside dialogue has to be rerecorded because of interfering noises.) Finally, the edited film, complete with final sound track and special effects, is sent to the laboratory where a release print of the film is made. In the case of some films, the final version is shown to special preview audiences. These audiences fill out preview cards that indicate their reactions to the film. If the reaction is overwhelmingly negative, the film may be returned to the editing room for more work. If the reaction is favorable, the film is made ready for distribution.

ECONOMICS

From 1970 to 2000, the box-office receipts of the movie industry showed steady growth. In 2000, total box office was $7.7 billion, up 2 percent from the previous year. Annual theater admissions have stabilized at about the 1.4 billion mark.

Movies are an expensive medium. In 2000, the average film cost $55 million to produce, up 500 percent since 1983, and another $20 million to $25 million to market and promote in the United States and overseas. Some films, like *Titanic,* cost much more. The rising costs of production and marketing have made it more difficult for many films to earn a profit for the studio. Having so many high-budget releases competing for the same audiences during the same season almost guarantees that many pictures will fail to break even.

Financial success is a function of U.S. and foreign box-office revenue, cassette sales, cable fees, broadcast TV rights, plus other things such as money from airline showings and pay-per-view, hotel, and satellite channels. The approximate contribution of each of these revenue streams for the typical Hollywood studio is as follows:

Domestic box office	22%
Foreign box office	20
Cassette sales and rentals (foreign and domestic)	28
Cable (foreign and domestic)	22
Broadcast TV (domestic)	4
Airlines, hotel, pay-per-view, and so on	4

The impact of the foreign box office can be striking. Some films do better overseas than they do in the United States. *The Matrix*, for example, took in $171 million in the United States and $285 million internationally. Other films don't have much foreign appeal: The comedy *Bowfinger* grossed $67 million in the United States but only $17 million overseas. Not surprisingly, studios carefully consider the potential for foreign income when deciding what movies to make.

Financing Films

Where do producers get the enormous sums of money necessary to make a film? Let's take a look at some common financing methods. If a producer has a good track record and the film looks promising, the distributor might lend the producer the entire amount needed to make the film. In return, the distributor gains distribution rights to the film. Moreover, if the distributor also has studio facilities, the producer might agree to rent those facilities from the distributor.

A second method is to arrange for a **pickup.** Under this arrangement, a distributor guarantees a producer that the distributor will pick up a finished picture at a later date for an agreed-upon price. For example, a distributor might agree to pay a producer $10 million 18 months in the future provided that the producer delivers a finished picture by that date. Although this money helps, it does not do the producer any immediate good. Armed with this agreement, however, the producer can arrange for a bank loan to secure the money needed immediately. If the bank is satisfied with the financial status of the distributor and feels that the producer can bring in the picture for $10 million or less, the bank grants the loan. But what happens if the bank feels that the producer won't be able to finish the film in 18 months or that the movie will go over budget? In this case, a third party, called a completion guarantor, is brought in to make sure that the loan will be repaid.

A third method is to finance the picture through outside investors, most frequently through a **limited partnership.** Under this arrangement, a number of investors put up a specific amount to pay for the film. Their personal liability is limited to the amount they invest; that is, they can't lose any more than what they put up, even if the picture goes over budget. The limited partners have no artistic control over the picture. They simply invest their money and hope to make a profit.

Ever wonder who gets a share of that $8 or so you plop down for a movie ticket? Here's a rough breakdown:

- The biggest share, about $3.20, goes to the theater where you see the movie.
- About $2.40 goes to the company that distributed the movie.
- About $1.43 goes to the company that produced the film.

- Another 80¢ goes to pay off the interest on the loan that the production company used to finance the film.
- The remaining 17¢ or so is divided among people who were promised a share of the movie's gross income as part of their employment contract. This usually includes big stars and big-name directors.

A fourth method is a **joint venture.** Under this arrangement, several companies involved in film production and distribution pool their resources and agree to finance one or more films. *Titanic* was financed using this arrangement.

The producer and distributor also agree on how to divide the distributor's gross receipts from the film (the money the distributor gets from the theater owners, TV networks, pay-TV operations, and videocassette and videodisk operations that show the film). Since the distributor takes the greatest risk in the venture, the distributor is the first to be paid from the receipts of the film. Distribution companies charge a distribution fee for their efforts. In addition, there are distribution expenses (cost of making multiple prints of the film, advertising, necessary taxes, insurance). Lastly, the actual production cost of the film must be repaid. If the distributor or a bank lent the producer $10 million to make the film, that loan has to be paid off (plus interest). Because of all these expenses, it is estimated that a film must earn two and one-half to three times its production cost before it starts to show a profit for the producers. Hollywood accounting tends to be complicated, however, and sometimes it's hard to determine when a film is profitable.

Dealing with the Exhibitor

The distributor is also involved in other financial dealings—this time with the exhibitors. An exhibition license sets the terms under which the showing of the film will occur. The license specifies the run of the film (the number of weeks the theater must agree to play the picture), holdover rights, the date the picture will be available for showing, and the clearance (the amount of time that must elapse before the film can be shown at a competing theater).

The license also contains the financial terms for the film's showing. There are several common arrangements. The simplest involves a specified percentage split of the money taken in at the box office. The exhibitor agrees to split the money with the distributor according to an agreed-upon formula, perhaps 50/50 the first week, 60/40 the second, 70/30 the third, and so on, with the exhibitor keeping more money the longer the run of the film. Another alternative is the **sliding scale.** Under this setup, as the box-office revenue increases, so does the amount of money that the exhibitor must pay the distributor. For example, if a week's revenue was more than $30,000, the exhibitor would pay the distributor 60 percent; if the revenue was between $25,000 and $29,999, the distributor would receive 50 percent; and so on. Another common approach is the 90/10 deal. Under this method, the movie theater owner first deducts the house allowance (called the "nut") from the box-office take. The house allowance includes all the operating expenses of the theater (heating, cooling, water, lights, salaries, maintenance, etc.), plus a sum that is pure profit for the theater (this sum is called "air"). From the revenues (if any) that remain, the distributor gets 90 percent and the house 10 percent.

Concession sales are a source of significant income for movie theater owners. According to industry figures, the average moviegoer spends about $3.50 on popcorn, soda, candy, and other concession munchies. Since slightly more than a billion tickets per year have been sold for the past decade or so, that translates to about $3.5 billion taken in at the concession stand. At some theaters, 90 percent of the profits come from concessions. (And no wonder—that $2.50 soft drink costs the theater owner less than 50¢.)

High ticket prices, coupled with large markups at the concession stand, mean that a trip to the movies can be an expensive proposition. For example, consider the costs for two at a theater in Atlanta: admission for two, $15.00; two small boxes of popcorn, $4.50; one package of Twizzlers and one box of Milk Duds, total $4.00; two large Cokes, $5.50. Total tab: $29.00.

Promoting the Film

A well-known film executive once said that a film is like a parachute: If it doesn't open, you're dead. The first week that a film is in release is crucial; in fact, since most films open on a weekend, the first three days are even more crucial. Films that open badly seldom do well.

Consequently, a good deal of promotion, marketing, and advertising is targeted to getting people into the theaters for that opening weekend. The most common strategy is to launch a media blitz that touts the film in the week or weeks before it opens. These campaigns do not come cheap. New Line Cinema spent more than $40 million promoting *Austin Powers II,* almost twice the industry average.

Movie studios are also relying on the Internet to aid promotion. Almost every big Hollywood movie has its own website. *The Perfect Storm*'s site, for example, featured scenes from the movie, discussion of how the special effects were done, a free poster offer, and show times at various theaters across the country. The biggest online promotional success of the late 1990s, however, was *The Blair Witch Project.* Before the film went into wide release, a website, www.blairwitch.com, was created. The company next screened the film on college campuses and spon-

Many websites that promote movies include photo galleries where fans can look through screen stills from the movie, like this one from *The Matrix. (Warner Bros.)*

sored a special about it on the Sci Fi Channel. Both these tactics led people to the website. By the time the film opened nationwide, the website had received more than 22 million hits, guaranteeing a good opening buzz. In addition, rather than open the movie on thousands of screens, the movie's producers opened the movie in only a few theaters and, of course, the movie quickly sold out. This encouraged even more people to check it out. Unlike most big Hollywood films, which can cost $20 million to $30 million to promote, *The Blair Witch Project* was marketed at a fraction of that cost—and was still widely successful, raking in more than $140 million. This lesson was not lost on traditional Hollywood executives, who began to explore alternative ways to promote their releases.

 FEEDBACK

Box Office

Feedback in the movie industry revolves around the box-office figures compiled and reported in the trade publication **Variety.** Each week, *Variety* reports the top-grossing films across the United States. An example of this listing is reproduced in Figure 9–2.

To compile these data, *Variety,* in cooperation with Entertainment Data Incorporated, surveys approximately 1,600 theaters located in about 20 major urban areas. The theaters in this sample usually account for about one-fourth the total box-office gross in the United States. Most of the column headings in *Variety*'s chart are self-explanatory. Each film's title is listed, followed by the distributor. Box-office gross for the listed week is then reported and ranked. The next four columns show the number of theaters showing the film for the past two weeks and the average revenue per screen. This is followed by the total earnings of the film to date in *Variety*'s sample cities. To estimate the film's total earnings in all

Figure 9–2

Excerpt from *Variety*'s Report on the 50 Top-Grossing Films

Source: Reprinted by permission from *Variety*.

VARIETY BOX OFFICE

TITLE/DISTRIBUTOR	Reported Box Office 1/19-1/25 (full week)	Reported Box Office 1/19-1/21 (weekend)	Percent Change in Box Office	Number of Engagements This Week	Last Week	Weeks Avg $ Per Engagement	No. Weeks Release	Domestic Box Office Cumulative	Foreign Box Office Cumulative	Worldwide Box Office Cumulative
Save the Last Dance (Par)	$18,674,203	$15,366,047	-40%	2539	2230	$7355	2	$49,546,387	—	$49,546,387
Cast Away (20th)	14,333,163	11,151,419	-37%	3061	3048	4683	5	185,152,150	44,237,173	229,389,323
Traffic (USA Films)	11,540,686	8,506,626	-29%	1571	1527	7346	5	49,726,154	—	49,726,154
Snatch (Sony/Screen Gems)	10,946,720	8,005,163	—	1444	—	7581	2	11,006,771	31,690,602	42,697,373
What Women Want (Par)	8,613,327	6,853,415	-36%	3025	3092	2847	6	164,002,564	12,669,322	176,671,886
Finding Forrester (Sony)	8,578,464	6,714,733	-34%	2002	2002	4285	6	31,064,844	—	31,064,844
Crouching Tiger ... (Sony Classics)	8,158,181	6,080,357	-27%	837	693	9747	7	39,365,351	31,371,755	70,737,106
Miss Congeniality (WB)	8,074,918	6,276,796	-34%	2603	2668	3102	5	89,120,147	—	89,120,147
Thirteen Days (New Line)	7,634,290	6,037,680	-41%	2034	2029	3753	5	21,268,905	11,000,000	32,268,905
The Pledge (WB)	7,437,045	5,765,347	—	1275	—	5833	1	7,437,045	—	7,437,045
Double Take (BV)	7,031,252	5,787,819	-46%	1631	1631	4311	2	20,102,085	—	20,102,085
The Emperor's New Groove (BV)	4,581,492	3,894,810	-46%	2016	2237	2273	6	76,735,637	3,525,181	80,260,818
The Gift (Paramount Classics)	4,464,812	3,461,903	—	805	—	5546	3	4,515,285	—	4,515,285
Chocolat (Miramax)	4,348,195	3,093,590	+70%	658	261	6608	6	14,068,964	—	14,068,964
The Family Man (U)	4,144,250	3,313,035	-46%	2277	2441	1820	5	70,362,020	21,710,579	92,072,599
Antitrust (MGM)	3,017,045	2,341,209	-52%	2433	2433	1240	2	9,361,583	—	9,361,583
O Brother, Where Art Thou? (BV)	2,365,121	1,633,678	-35%	419	431	5645	5	10,275,444	23,349,569	33,625,013
Vertical Limit (Sony)	1,616,970	1,256,307	-55%	1323	2042	1222	7	65,925,065	57,000,000	122,925,065
State and Main (Fine Line)	979,859	734,020	-52%	462	459	2121	5	5,403,836	—	5,403,836
Dracula 2000 (Miramax)	798,150	612,487	-64%	817	1604	977	5	32,397,653	—	32,397,653

markets, *Variety* suggests multiplying this column by 3 or by 4. (It varies, depending on the particular release pattern and the appeal of a film.) Note that this chart reports only a film's gross earnings; it does not show how much, if any, profit a film has made.

The economic feedback contained in *Variety* is extremely important in the movie industry. One or two blockbuster films can improve the financial position of an entire company. In addition, a film successful at the box office is apt to inspire one or more sequels and several imitators.

◼ Market Research

Audience research has become more influential in the movie business because of the tremendous cost of motion pictures. At most studios the first step is concept testing to find promising plotlines. The next step is an analysis of the script. If the script seems promising, the studio will make a rough cut of the finished film. The rough cut is then used by movie researchers in a series of test screenings. In addition, **focus group** sessions are held. A focus group is a small sample (usually about 10 to 15 people) of the target audience, which is asked detailed questions about what they liked or didn't like. With this information, the studio can add or drop a scene, modify the ending, change the musical score, or make other alterations. (The original ending of *The Perfect Storm* was changed when the studio found that test audiences didn't like a scene that focused on the doomed fishermen's final thoughts.) Once these changes are completed, the movie is released for a sneak preview. As mentioned earlier, audience members fill out preview cards that summarize their reactions to the film, its characters, and its stars. It is possible for the director to make limited changes in the film in response to this feedback, but it is usually too late to make wholesale changes.

◼ Motion Picture Audiences

Information on the motion picture audience is sketchy. Hollywood seems to put little faith in detailed audience study, preferring instead to concentrate on the bottom line, the amount of money a film brings in. In general terms, we know that after a slump during the early 1970s, movie attendance picked up. Average weekly attendance has been steady for about the past 20 years (see Figure 9–3). Attendance, however, is nowhere near the levels of the 1930s and 1940s, when film was in its heyday.

The movie audience is a young audience. One out of two moviegoers is under 30. Teenagers are a significant part of the movie audience. Although teens make up only 20 percent of the population, they make up nearly 30 percent of the film audience. The movie audience has changed in recent years. Older fans are now more likely to go out to a theater than they were five years ago.

Frequent moviegoers (those who see at least 12 films a year) account for 77 percent of all film admissions. These frequent fans are generally single, within the 16-to-20 age group (going to the movies continues to be a popular dating activity; only 6 percent of the audience goes to a movie alone), more educated, from middle-class families, and from urban areas.

The audience for movies is largest in July and August and smallest in May. The worst two weeks of the year for moviegoing are the first two weeks in December, when attendance drops 30 to 50 percent.

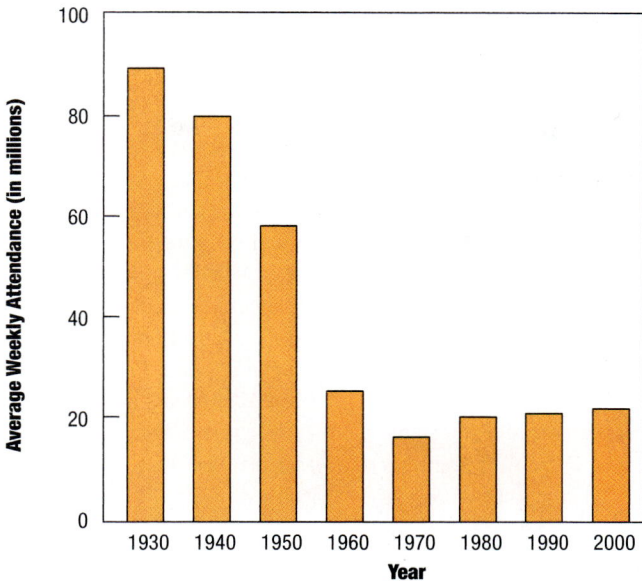

Figure 9–3

Average Weekly Film Attendance in the United States

Source: Motion Picture Association of America. Used by permission

What films have attracted the largest audiences? Some indirect information is available if we examine what the industry calls film rental fees, the money the theater pays to the distribution company to show the film. If we assume that films that earn large rental fees are attracting large audiences (a seemingly reasonable assumption), a list of the most popular films can be compiled. Table 9.1, page 237, contains such a list as of 1999. The large number of recent releases on the list reflects the current Hollywood philosophy, discussed earlier in the chapter, of aiming for a blockbuster.

CABLE AND HOME VIDEO: THE HOLLYWOOD CONNECTION

The cassette rental business boomed during the late 1980s and early 1990s but has recently showed signs of leveling off. Sales and rentals of cassettes brought in about $20 billion in revenue in 2000, with rentals accounting for about $8 billion of the total. About 6 million Americans rent a video on an average day, about twice as many as go to a movie. DVDs are becoming increasingly popular, and analysts predict that DVD movie sales will equal cassette sales in 2003.

The home video market, just like the theatrical box office, is driven by big hits. Movies that were popular on the big screen are almost always popular on the small screen. *Saving Private Ryan,* for example, took in more than $200 million at the box office and was rented more than 22 million times, generating an additional $63 million in rental fees. Some movies that were box-office duds do much better on videocassette.

Pay-per-view (PPV) television provides another revenue stream for movie companies. More than 30 million homes are equipped with PPV, and the number is growing steadily. In addition, the number of channels available on cable and satellite systems is increasing, and many of these new channels are devoted to PPV. Finally, Hollywood gets income from licensing its movies to premium cable channels, such as Home Box Office and Showtime, in addition to receiving money

The U.S. government spent $2.4 million in 1999 to screen antidrug messages before movie showings, hoping to get its message across to young people. These antidrug messages contrasted sharply with the messages about drug use that were in many of the movies they preceded.

Take *American Beauty*, for example, the Oscar winner for best picture of 1999. Its most sympathetic character is a marijuana-smoking drug dealer. The lead character in the film, played by Kevin Spacey, has his life take a turn for the better after he starts smoking pot. That film was R-rated, but drug references are now common in films aimed at a much younger audience. Take *Scary Movie*, where comic actor Marlin Wayans spends most of the film smoking marijuana. Then there's *Never Been Kissed*, which shows its main character becoming popular and hip after ingesting hashish brownies. In *Outside Providence*, the lead character wins the affection of the prettiest girl in school by supplying her with alcohol and pot. In *Go*, a character's overdose with the drug Ecstasy is played for laughs. These are just a few examples of how drug use is shown in Hollywood films. You can probably supply more.

Are filmmakers responsible for the potential harmful effects of these portrayals? Are these coy depictions really necessary, or is Hollywood simply trying to look cool and hip in an attempt to attract the young crowd?

If everybody agrees that we should discourage young people from experimenting with drugs, why should society tolerate motion pictures glorifying or at least trivializing drug use? Of course, parents still retain the primary responsibility for instilling proper behaviors and attitudes in their children, but as film critic Michael Medved recently put it, "Parents have no right to demand that Hollywood do their job of child rearing for them, but there's no reason that Tinseltown must make that job so much harder than it needs to be."

from selling the rights to movies to traditional over-the-air broadcasters. Given these numerous video aftermarkets, it's no surprise that TV generates more revenue for the movie industry than does the box office.

THE FILM INDUSTRY

Finding a job in the film industry is difficult but not impossible. Film is a young person's medium; as a result, motion picture companies are always looking for bright, young talent. Unfortunately, the industry is not large enough to accomodate all the newcomers who are seeking jobs, and competition is formidable.

A young person who has actual experience in films and filmmaking will probably enjoy more success in finding a job. How do you get this experience? In general, there are two ways: (1) taking college courses that deal with film and (2) making your own films. About 750 colleges and universities now offer courses in film, 227 offer bachelor's degrees, and many offer graduate degrees. The advantages of a university major in film are substantial. In the first place, it provides the student with an opportunity to practice with technical equipment: lights, meters, editing machines, cameras, and so forth. Second, students can take courses in film aesthetics and film history, and can learn by observing how others have made films. Third, students can take courses in other areas that relate to film, such as art, literature, history, music, and photography. Finally, during the course of his or her studies, the student may have the opportunity to make a film as a final classroom project. This finished film can be shown to potential employers as a sample of the student's capability.

The other approach to gaining experience is to become an independent filmmaker. This method is valuable because it allows a person to gain knowledge of every aspect of filmmaking. Of course, this approach requires that the individual have some money to invest in basic film equipment and the time necessary to devote to the film. A person looking to go this route should be prepared for some financial hardships while the film is being made. Sometimes people get lucky. The two creators of *The Blair Witch Project* were only a few years out of college when their film (made for only $30,000) took off.

Entry-Level Positions

Once a person has some experience, the next step is to find an entry-level job. This requires securing a job interview—not an easy task. The common technique of mailing a résumé to a potential employer seldom works in the film industry.

There are three ways to overcome this hurdle. The first is to know somebody. As is the case in most industries, if you have a friend or a friend of a friend in the industry, getting a job interview is less difficult.

The second way is to get yourself noticed. A newcomer accomplishes this by seeking out internships or training programs with production companies. The American Film Institute's *Guide to College Courses in Film and Television* lists such opportunities. Many times, help in finding out about and applying for internships can be secured from teachers or placement offices. Once you've gotten yourself into an organization, you will have better success in arranging an interview. Another way to get yourself noticed is to enter the many student film festivals. A newcomer who wins one or more awards at these festivals may find getting through the door into the film industry a little easier.

The third way is to be persistent. This is also the hardest way. Make a list of those companies where you wish to work and call on them personally. Since most film production companies are located in southern California and New York, this means that the job seeker might have to relocate. Once you've got your list together, start calling on the companies. Bring along a one-page summary of your education and special skills. If you have a completed film that is available for viewing, indicate it in your summary. Don't be discouraged if your first visit is fruitless. Keep checking back. As is the case with television, a newcomer should be prepared to take practically any job as a starter. Once inside the company, the path to more creative and challenging positions is easier to follow.

Upward Mobility

Select your first job with an eye toward future advancement. Some routes are best if your ultimate goal is producing and directing. Other avenues are better if top management is your ultimate goal. One early choice an aspiring filmmaker must make is the choice between editing and directing. Although there are some exceptions, most people who start in the editing room stay there, advancing ultimately to the post of supervising film editor. Those interested in producing and directing should begin as production assistants and progress to assistant directors, director, and perhaps producer. To reach high-level management, a person might consider breaking in with the distribution or sales division.

■ MAIN POINTS

- The motion picture developed in the late 19th century. After being a main attraction in nickelodeons, films moved into bigger theaters and movie stars quickly became the most important part of the new industry. Sound came to the movies in the mid-1920s.

- Big movie studios dominated the industry until the late 1940s, when a court decision weakened their power. Television captured much of the film audience in the 1950s. By the end of the 1960s, however, Hollywood had adapted to television and was an active producer of TV shows. A major trend in modern movies is the rise of big-budget movies.

- The transition to digital moviemaking may transform the film industry.

- The movie industry consists of the production, distribution, and exhibition components. Large conglomerates control the business. Producing a motion picture starts from the concept, proceeds to the production stage, and ends with the postproduction stage.

- Movie revenues have shown small but steady growth over the past 10 years. Videocassette sales and rentals and foreign box-office receipts are important sources of movie income.

- Movie audiences are getting older, but a significant part of the audience is still the 30-and-under age group.

- Motion picture studios are now using the Internet to promote their products.

■ QUESTIONS FOR REVIEW

1. What are the defining features of motion pictures?
2. What caused the rise and fall of the Motion Picture Patents Company?
3. How did the film industry react to TV?
4. What are the three main segments of the motion picture industry?
5. What are the various ways films are financed?

■ QUESTIONS FOR CRITICAL THINKING

1. Suppose the movie industry had never moved to Hollywood, staying instead on the East Coast. How might films be different?
2. What are the potential advantages and disadvantages of big corporations controlling motion picture production?
3. Do filmmakers have an obligation to be socially responsible for what they present on the screen? Why or why not?
4. Will the Internet help or hurt independent filmmakers? In what ways?
5. Someone once said that Hollywood producers don't make films; they make deals. Comment on the validity of this statement and its implications.

■ KEY TERMS

phi phenomenon (p. 227)
persistence of vision (p. 227)
Kinetoscope (p. 228)
Motion Picture Patents Company
   (MPPC) (p. 230)

block booking (p. 232)
double features (p. 233)
digital videodisk (DVD) (p. 238)
pickup (p. 248)
limited partnership (p. 248)

joint venture (p. 249)
sliding scale (p. 249)
Variety (p. 251)
focus group (p. 252)
pay-per-view (PPV) (p. 253)

■ SUGGESTIONS FOR FURTHER READING

The sources below contain further information about motion pictures.

Acker, Ally. *Reel Women.* New York: Continuum, 1991.

Asher, Steven, and Edward Pincus. *The Filmmaker's Handbook: A Comprehensive Guide for the Digital Age.* New York: Plume, 1999.

Cones, John. *The Feature Film Distribution Deal.* Carbondale: Southern Illinois University Press, 1997.

Gianetti, Louis. *Understanding Movies,* 7th ed. Englewood Cliffs, NJ: Prentice Hall, 1996.

Redding, Judith, and Victoria Brownworth. *Film Fatales: Independent Women Directors.* Seattle: Seal Press, 1997.

Smith, Scott. *The Film 100: A Ranking of the Most Influential People in the History of Movies.* Secaucus, NJ: Carol Publishers, 1998.

Stam, Robert. *Film Theory.* Malder, MA: Blackwell, 2000.

■ SURFING THE INTERNET

www.ifilm.com
An Internet cineplex. View short films of every description on your computer. Check out what avant-garde filmmakers are doing.

www.imdb.com
The Internet Movie Database. Everything you ever wanted to know about movies. Has information about stars, cast, plot, and box-office performance for just about every movie you can think of.

www.mgm.com
MGM Studio's website. View movie trailers for coming attractions, download movie music, see which MGM films are in theaters, and even check out MGM's corporate structure. Comes complete with the MGM lion's roar.

www.mpaa.org
The official website of the Motion Picture Association of America. Contains industry statistics and latest news releases. Has an extensive section that treats copyright issues.

www.mrcranky.com
Mr. Cranky reviews the movies. An offbeat review page featuring a reviewer who has high standards and a caustic style. Mr. Cranky rates movies by assigning a number of bombs. For example, four bombs means: "As good as a poke in the eye with a sharp stick."

www.variety.com
Website of the trade paper that is the bible of the entertainment industry. Includes latest industry news, global box-office charts, film reviews, and a section called a "slanguage dictionary," which translates *Variety's* showbiz language into English. For example, "to ankle" means to walk away from a job; a "sprocket opera" is a film festival.

CHAPTER 10

Television

It might be surprising to some to discover that one of the defining moments of modern television occurred on "The Drew Carey Show." The November 17, 1999, episode of the popular sitcom started off with Mimi Bobeck, Drew Carey's nemesis, looking into the camera and saying, "Hey, all you geeks out there. Both hands on the keyboard!" This rather peculiar line inaugurated one of the most enterprising examples of the convergence between television and the Internet: It was the first time a large-scale, streaming video webcast was used to enhance and expand the content of a prime-time, network television show.

Audience members for the segment, entitled "Drew-Cam," were encouraged to put their computers near their television sets. Those that visited the website for the show were treated to material not available to those watching TV. The storyline for the episode involved Carey's agreeing to have webcams installed in his apartment. Although there was some overlap with the tele-

Like "The Drew Carey Show," the quiz show "Who Wants to Be a Millionaire" also uses the Internet to enhance the viewing experience. *(Newsmakers/Liaison Agency)*

vised version, web viewers saw some scenes the TV audience didn't. In one segment, while Drew is at work, the webcams show his dog letting neighborhood mutts into his kitchen for a party. In another, Ed McMahon drops by with a $10 million check but leaves when he finds no one is at home. The experiment was a success. The website received a record 1.9 million clicks.

The "Drew Carey" experiment may have been the most visible example of TV and Internet convergence, but it is certainly not the only one. There is a web counterpart to "Who Wants to Be a Millionaire" in which web surfers play along with the show. ESPN.com synchronizes some of its content with ABC's "Monday Night Football" broadcast. The National Basketball Association (NBA) combines a special satellite-delivered NBA channel with complementary content from the NBA website.

The most important word in the above paragraphs is "convergence." Although people have been talking about the convergence of the computer and the TV set for about a decade, it seems likely, thanks to the growing availability of broadband Internet hookups, that convergence will shortly become a reality. When that happens, the whole digital video landscape will be redesigned . . . but we're getting ahead of the story.

This chapter will examine the rapidly changing world of TV. We will first examine the history and structure of the traditional TV industry, followed by a look at how the convergence scenario might play out. We will next look at cable TV and the newer video services: home video and direct satellite broadcasting.

 # HISTORY

Viewers who watched the webcast of "The Drew Carey Show" mentioned above saw a tiny image, a little blurry around the edges, that looked a little primitive. During the late 1920s, the earliest experimenters with television were also straining to see tiny, blurry images.

The two men who developed television in the United States could not have been more different. At the age of 16, Philo Farnsworth diagrammed his idea for a television system on the chalkboard in front of his somewhat amazed high school teacher. Farnsworth, an individualistic and lone-wolf inventor, worked at developing his new device, which he called an image dissector, and eventually patented it in 1930. In contrast, Vladimir Zworykin was an organization man, working first with Westinghouse and then with RCA. By 1928, he had perfected a primitive camera tube, the iconoscope.

Picture quality of the early television systems was poor, but technical developments during the 1930s improved performance. RCA, with Zworykin's help and with a patent arrangement that permitted it to use Farnsworth's invention, set out to develop TV's commercial potential. NBC, owned by RCA, gave the first public demonstration of television at the 1939 World's Fair.

The initial public response to TV was lukewarm. Sets were expensive and there weren't many programs for people to watch. Even early TV actors were somewhat skeptical about the future of the new medium. They had to wear green makeup to look normal for the TV camera and swallowed salt tablets because the intense heat of the lights necessary for TV made them perspire constantly.

World War II interrupted TV's development. When peace returned in 1945, new technology that had been perfected during the war greatly improved TV reception and the working conditions of the performers. New TV cameras required much less light. TV screens were bigger. There were more programs available, and stations were being linked into networks. All the signs pointed to big things for TV. In 1945, there were only eight TV stations and 8,000 homes with TV in the entire United States. Ten years later, there were nearly a hundred stations, and 35 million households, about 67 percent of the country, had TV.

TV's rapid success caught the industry and the FCC off guard. Unless technical standards were worked out, the TV spectrum was in danger of becoming overcrowded and riddled with interference just as happened with radio 30 years earlier. To guard against this possibility, the FCC imposed a freeze on all new applications for TV stations. The freeze, which went into effect in 1948, would last for four years, while the FCC gathered information from engineers and technical experts. When the freeze was lifted in 1952, the FCC had established that 12 VHF and 70 UHF channels (see page 271) were to be devoted to TV. In addition, the commission drew up a list that allocated television channels to the various communities in the United States and specified other rules to minimize interference. Also, thanks largely to the efforts of Frieda Hennock, the first woman to serve on the commission, TV channels were set aside for educational use.

The 1950s: Networks, Tape, UHF, and Color

The early television industry was modeled after radio. Local stations served their communities and, in turn, might be affiliated with networks. There were four TV networks during this time period: CBS, NBC, ABC, and DuMont, a smaller network that went out of business in 1956. Also much like the situation in early radio, the networks quickly became the primary programming sources for their affiliates. NBC and CBS were usually the most popular networks, with ABC trailing behind. Most early network programs were game shows, sports events, and interviews, with a few comedies and dramas interspersed throughout the schedule.

Most programs were broadcast live from New York or were filmed in California. Live programs, of course, couldn't be repeated and often had to be performed over again for the West Coast. In 1956, the Ampex Corporation developed videotape, a cheap and efficient way of storing TV programs. By the beginning of the 1960s, most of TV's live programming had switched to tape.

After the FCC-imposed freeze ended, TV stations and TV sets multiplied rapidly. The new UHF channels, however, were not doing well. Few sets equipped with UHF receivers were made during the 1950s. The UHF stations had smaller coverage areas than the VHF stations, and most advertising dollars went to VHF stations. As a result, UHF TV, much like FM radio, started off at a disadvantage.

Color television was introduced during the 1950s. Led by NBC (RCA, the parent company, was manufacturing color TV sets), the networks were broadcasting about two to three hours of color programming per day by 1960.

Mr. Television, Milton Berle, dressed in one of the outrageous outfits that became his trademark on the "Texaco Star Theater." *(AP/Wide World Photos)*

The Golden Age of Television

Many broadcast historians refer to the 1950s as the golden age of TV. Many shows aired during that decade became extremely popular. "Toast of the Town," hosted by

Robert Redford's 1994 movie, *Quiz Show*, was based on the events that surrounded the demise of the big-money quiz shows in the late 1950s. One of those shows, "The $64,000 Question," surprised everybody by becoming a runaway hit. On Tuesday nights when the program aired on CBS, the crime rate dropped drastically and movie attendance plummeted. At one point it was estimated that 85 percent of all the sets in use were tuned to the program.

On the assumption that a show that gives away $128,000 should be twice as successful as one that gives away $64,000, "The $64,000 Challenge" appeared soon after the premiere of "The $64,000 Question." Pretty soon both shows were at the top of the ratings. NBC countered with "Twenty-One," a show on which a contestant could win an unlimited amount of money. The ratings on "Twenty-One" were modest until an assistant professor at Columbia University, Charles Van Doren, became a contestant. Van Doren had charisma and audiences identified with him. Before long, Van Doren's winnings amounted to more than $100,000 and the show's ratings skyrocketed.

Troubled by the competition, "The $64,000 Question" quadrupled its stakes. A 10-year-old from the Bronx won $224,000 before stopping. A contestant on "The $64,000 Challenge" ran his winnings to $264,000, the most ever to be won during this time period.

While all this was going on, rumors were flying that some contestants were being coached and given correct quiz show answers. A grand jury was convened, but witness after witness denied everything. The American public seemed ready to believe that all was fine until a losing contestant on "Twenty-One" appeared with indisputable evidence. He produced three sealed, registered letters that he had mailed to himself before his appearances. The letters contained the questions that were to be asked on the show, the answers, and instructions as to how the contestant should act while answering. The lid was off. Other contestants testified that they were given answers. Charles Van Doren appeared before a congressional committee and revealed that he, too, was provided with the answers. Many of the earlier witnesses before the grand jury reappeared and changed their testimony. Twenty-three of them pled guilty to perjury.

The audience was stunned. The big-money quiz shows vanished almost overnight. Then, 40 years later, much to everybody's surprise, "Who Wants to Be a Millionaire" revived the genre. "Millionaire" and the other quiz shows that followed it were closely watched to make sure they did not run into any legal trouble.

Ed Sullivan, is still regarded as the best example of the variety series. "Texaco Star Theater," starring ex-vaudevillian Milton Berle, prompted many people to buy TV sets just to see what wacky stunts Berle would pull off on his next program.

Live prestige drama was also in prime time. Programs such as "Studio One" featured plays by Rod Serling, Gore Vidal, and Reginald Rose. Broadway stars such as Rex Harrison and Tallulah Bankhead performed in live TV drama. The growing popularity of videotape, however, put an end to these live productions.

By the end of the 1950s, a new genre, the adult Western, in which character and motivation overshadowed gunfights, dominated TV. By 1959, there were 26 Westerns in prime time, including "Gunsmoke," "The Life and Legend of Wyatt Earp," and "Wagon Train."

Coming of Age: Television in the 1960s

By the early 1960s, TV had lost its novelty and became just another part of everyday life. The number of TV stations continued to increase, and by the close of the decade, more than 95 percent of all American households owned at least one TV.

Television journalism came of age during the 1960s. NBC and CBS expanded their nightly newscasts from 15 to 30 minutes in 1963, and ABC followed suit shortly thereafter. In November of that year, TV journalism earned praise for its professionalism during its coverage of the assassination and funeral of President John F. Kennedy. The networks also covered the Civil Rights movement and the growing social unrest across the country. Perhaps the most exciting moment for television news came in 1969 with its live coverage of Neil Armstrong's historic walk on the moon.

Noncommercial broadcasting also evolved during the 1960s. About 69 educational stations were broadcasting by 1965. A report issued by the Carnegie Commission proposed that Congress establish a Corporation for Public Broadcasting. The commission's recommendations were incorporated into the **Public Broadcasting Act of 1967,** which set up the Public Broadcasting Service.

Another segment of the video industry was also experiencing growth during this time period—cable television. We will discuss the history of cable TV later in the chapter.

Television programs popular in the early 1960s included a number of rural comedies, such as "The Beverly Hillbillies" and "Green Acres." After the Kennedy assassination, however, fantasy and escapist programs dominated prime time. In 1964, for example, some of the shows that premiered included "Bewitched" (about a friendly witch), "My Favorite Martian" (about a friendly Martian), and "My Mother the Car" (self-explanatory).

■ The 1970s: Growing Public Concern

As the 1970s began, public concern over the impact of television programming was growing. A panel of scientists set up by the Surgeon General's office to investigate the impact of exposure to TV violence suggested that TV violence was related in a modest way to aggressive behavior in some young children. More on this topic in Chapter 18.

The early 1970s were also characterized by the growth of citizen group involvement in Federal Communication Commission (FCC) decisions. Groups such as Action for Children's Television and the Office of Communication of the United Church of Christ and coalitions of minority groups became influential in shaping broadcasting policy.

"The Beverly Hillbillies" was the most popular of the "bucolic" situation comedies. It was the number one show during the 1961–1962 TV season and spent nine years on the air. *(The Everett Collection)*

The three networks continued to dominate the industry during the early to mid-1970s. In an attempt to reduce the networks' power, the FCC issued the **Prime-Time Access Rule.** In effect, this rule took the 7:30 P.M. to 8:00 P.M. (EST) time slot away from the networks and gave it back to the local stations to program. The practical effect of this rule was to encourage the growth of television syndicated programming, which many stations used to fill the time.

By the end of the decade, the three networks were beginning

Live TV coverage of the first man landing on the moon in 1969 reached hundreds of millions of viewers. *(Ed Carlin/Index Stock)*

to feel the competition from the growing cable industry. Friction between the traditional over-the-air broadcasters and the cable companies would continue until the present.

The biggest trend in television programming during the early 1970s was the growth of law-and-order programs, for example, "The FBI," "Charlie's Angels," and "Mannix." By the middle of the decade, these shows were replaced by a number of adult situation comedies, shows that dealt with more mature themes. "All in the Family," "M*A*S*H," and "Sanford and Son" typified this trend. By the end of the decade, prime-time soap operas, such as "Dallas" and "Dynasty," topped the ratings.

■ The 1980s and 1990s: Increased Competition

The biggest trends in the TV industry in the 1980s and 1990s were the continuing erosion of the three big networks' audiences and the increased competition from new networks and cable channels. In the early 1970s the three networks routinely pulled down about 90 percent of the prime-time audience. By the late 1990s, their share had dropped to less than 60 percent. In addition, a fourth network, the Fox Broadcasting Company, owned by Rupert Murdoch's News Corporation, started broadcasting in 1987. In 1993, Fox further shook up the scene by convincing several large-market affiliates of CBS to switch to the Fox network and by snaring the rights to broadcast the National Football League's games. At about the same time, two other networks started up: the United Paramount Network (UPN) and the Warner Broadcasting Network (the WB). Both began with limited schedules but had plans to expand their offerings.

In August 1995, the world of network broadcasting was shaken by two megadeals: The Walt Disney

Company announced it was buying CapCities/ABC for $19 billion. The ink was barely dry on that deal when Westinghouse disclosed it was buying CBS for $5.4 billion.

Cable's Continued Growth

Cable reached more than 68 percent of the population by 2000. As cable systems increased their capacity, new cable programming services rushed to fill the new channels. By 2000, there were six national pay-per-view services, six premium services, including HBO and Showtime, and more than 75 cable networks, including the Sci Fi Channel, Animal Planet, and the Outdoor Channel. Many cable systems were providing more than 100 channels of television to their subscribers. Some new cable networks were having trouble because there was no room left on local systems to carry them. The growing popularity of cable channels further eroded the audiences of the traditional TV networks.

Advertising revenue also grew, topping the $11 billion mark in 1999 as some big advertisers, such as Procter & Gamble and Phillip Morris, moved significant parts of their ad budgets to cable. By the turn of the century, it was obvious that the cable industry was a full-fledged competitor of traditional broadcasting.

Zapping, Zipping, Grazing, and DBS

A development that had significant impact on both traditional TV and the cable industry was the spectacular growth of VCRs. Fewer than 5 percent of households had VCRs in 1982. By 2000, that figure became 90 percent. In fact, the VCR has been adopted faster than any other appliance except television. The effects of the VCR are many. First, the renting of movies on cassettes has become a multibillion-dollar business, with motion picture studios depending on cassettes for a large part of their revenue.

Second, the VCR encourages **time shifting**, playing back programs at times other than when they were aired. Although this has increased total audience by allowing people who might not otherwise view a program to do so, it has caused some new problems for advertisers. Some viewers have special machines that "zap" commercials: The VCR pauses while the commercial is aired and then starts up again when the program is on. Also, when viewers play back programs, many fast-forward, or "zip," their way through the ads.

Finally, the proliferation of the handheld remote-control device has also caused problems for advertisers and programmers. Remote units are in two-thirds of all households and have encouraged the tendency toward "grazing," rapidly scanning all the channels during a commercial or dull spot in a program in search of greener pastures.

After a slow start, direct broadcast by satellite (DBS) got a big boost in 1994 when two companies, DirecTV and United States Satellite Broadcasting (USSB), offered subscribers about 150 channels of programming beamed directly to their homes via a small (18-inch diameter) receiver. As of 2000, about 15 million households subscribed to a DBS service.

On the legal side, the biggest development was the Telecommunications Act of 1996, discussed in Chapter 15, which introduced program ratings and the V-chip, while encouraging competition between cable and phone companies, and easing ownership restrictions on TV stations. On the technology front, the most significant development was the move to digital TV, discussed in the next section.

Kweisi Mfume, president of the NAACP, speaking at his organization's national convention, criticized the four major TV networks for the lack of diversity in the new shows planned for the 1999–2000 season. He noted that none of the 26 series had a minority person in a leading or starring role. Mfume's criticism marked another chapter in the continuing controversy over the portrayals of minorities in prime time.

During the early years of TV, African-American performers were difficult to find. When they did appear, it was usually in a menial or subservient role. In 1965, however, a young Bill Cosby co-starred with Robert Culp in "I Spy" and paved the way for more substantial roles for African-American performers. By the 1970s, several shows that featured black casts appeared in prime time—most were situation comedies, such as "The Jeffersons." The number of African-American performers increased slowly but steadily during the 1980s. For most of the 1990s, the proportion of black characters seen in prime-time TV was about the same as the percentage of African Americans in the general population. This increase, however, was due in part to the emergence of UPN and WB, two networks that targeted several of their series to African-American viewers.

The apparent lack of diversity in the 1999–2000 season was especially troubling to Mfume. The NAACP also noted that minorities were hard to find behind the camera as well. Of all the writers who worked on TV sitcoms and dramas, only 6 percent were black. FCC data show that minorities own about 2.8 percent of all broadcast stations.

Mfume threatened a boycott of the networks and their sponsors unless something was done. The networks responded by adding some minority characters to the casts of existing shows. CBS aired *City of Angels*, a drama set in an inner-city hospital, that featured a predominantly black cast and creative team. The networks also planned to increase minority hiring and to appoint executives who will be in charge of their diversity efforts. These moves apparently satisfied Mfume, who called off plans for the boycott.

The 2000–2001 TV season did not spark similar protests. In addition to *City of Angels*, there were several new series with African Americans in major roles, including *Gideon's Crossing*, *Boston Public*, and *Welcome to New York*. The situation behind the camera and in minority ownership, however, was unchanged.

The situation for Hispanic Americans and Asians was bleak. These two ethnic groups make up less than 3 percent of all major characters in prime-time network TV.

Why should the networks present a diverse view of society? Many would argue that the networks have a social obligation to present an accurate view of society so that members of minority groups don't feel marginalized or disenfranchised from society. Other would suggest that TV should present role models for all groups. These benevolent reasons aside, it also makes economic sense for the networks to present a diverse menu of programs. The 2000 census will likely show that minorities may constitute more than 35 percent of the U.S. population, and their buying power is increasing each year. Presenting shows that appeal to these groups is simply good business.

Further, there are those critics who suggest that paying large amounts of attention to the way the broadcast networks portray minorities overlooks the gains minorities have made in cable. Black Entertainment Television draws a significant audience. Two Spanish-language networks, Galavision and Univision, are aimed at Hispanics. Lifetime presents *Any Day Now*, a series about the friendship between a black woman and a white woman, and Showtime runs *Resurrection Blvd.*, a series focusing on a Latino family's experiences in America.

Finally, consider the opinion of commentator Earl Ofari Hutchinson, who suggests that prime-time TV is not worth fighting for. He charges that the networks have oversaturated the airways with silly sitcoms and action shows designed to appeal to young, affluent whites. These types of programs, he argues, have no relevance for African Americans, who should focus their attention elsewhere. In a similar vein, Cynthia Tucker, the African-American editor of the editorial page of the *Atlanta Constitution*, suggests that the NAACP is misplacing its efforts by concentrating on network TV programs. Instead, she argues, the organization should encourage young African Americans to stop watching TV. "Let prime-time TV keep its bland cast of characters," states Tucker. "There are plenty of good books in which black youngsters can find themselves reflected."[1]

[1]Quoted in Richard Breyer, "Color TV," *Word and I*, March 2000, p. 84.

TV programming during the mid-1980s marked the return of warm, family-oriented comedies, such as "The Cosby Show" and "Family Ties." One reason for the popularity of these shows was economic. Family sitcoms did well in the syndication aftermarket (more on syndication later). The biggest programming trend of the early to mid-1990s was the growth of prime-time newsmagazines, such as "60 Minutes," "20/20," and "Dateline NBC." The 2000 season contained a record 10 hours of such programs. Once again, an economic factor helped this trend.

Newsmagazines are cheaper to produce than typical situation comedies and dramas. At the turn of the century, the astounding success of "Who Wants to Be a Millionaire" surprised many TV executives, as did the popularity of "reality" shows, such as "Survivor" and "Big Brother." Two HBO series, "The Sopranos" and "Sex and the City," also enjoyed popular and critical success.

TELEVISION IN THE DIGITAL AGE

The digital age for television began on April 3, 1997, when the Federal Communications Commission adopted rules that changed the way television is to be transmitted. The TV pictures on your set at the turn of the 21st century use the same basic technology that was developed during the 1930s—the analog method. A beam of electrons scans an image and creates an electrical signal; at the receiving end, the signal is converted back to an electron beam that bombards a fluorescent screen and creates an image. With **digital television (DTV),** the image is still scanned but the signal is a binary one, assigning bits of code to each pixel on a TV screen that define the color and the brightness of the pixel and recreate the original image.

Federal law mandates that all full-power TV stations must convert to digital transmission by 2003. Broadcasters are required to broadcast programs in both analog and digital formats from that year until all the older transmitters are shut down. Currently, most people receive digital TV on their old analog sets by means of a set-top converter box. The FCC hopes that the transition to digital will be complete by 2007, but even then, the old analog signals will still be broadcast in an area until more than 85 percent of viewers can receive the new signals. As of late 2000, about 125 television stations were already broadcasting a digital signal. Although the new digital standards apply only to traditional over-the-air broadcasters, cable companies and direct broadcast satellite (DBS) systems will support them as well.

Digital TV has many advantages. Digital pictures are clearer, and the sound quality is better. The new TV sets will have a different look. Instead of the current 3:4 aspect ratio, the digital TV will be more rectangular and look more like a movie screen. Moreover, digital television has more potential than the old analog system. A broadcaster can use most of the digital TV channel to broadcast high-definition television (HDTV). (Note that all HDTV is digital, but not all digital TV is HDTV.) The quality of HDTV pictures is on a par with 35-mm motion picture film. As of 2000, the major networks were presenting a few programs in HDTV. DirecTV, a DBS service, was also carrying some HDTV content, and HBO was transmitting some of its movies in the HDTV format. The Super Bowl and other major events are also carried in HDTV. The amount of available HDTV programming will increase in the future.

A broadcaster can also subdivide the digital channel and offer several lower-definition programs in the same space. For example, a local TV station might broadcast HDTV during prime time but at other times of the day switch to lower-definition signals and offer four different programs. When a viewer tunes in the channel, he or she will see a screen with four small windows. The viewer might be able to choose from the network feed of a soap opera, a local news channel, a weather forecast, or a syndicated show. Moreover, digital TV can send and receive e-mail, provide access to the Internet, and transmit data. Local stations might transmit program guides that a viewer can download and print.

There are some disadvantages as well. Digital sets are still expensive, about $2,000 to $3,000. HDTV sets cost about twice that amount. Consumers have yet to embrace HDTV, primarily because of the expense. This situation might change as costs decrease and more shows are televised in HDTV. Broadcasters also have some problems with HDTV. Firm technical standards have yet to be worked out, and switching over to HDTV equipment will be expensive. Accordingly, broadcasters have been in no hurry to implement the new system.

Digital TV will also speed the convergence between TV and the computer. Web TV lets subscribers access the Internet through their TV sets. A picture-in-picture feature permits simultaneous TV viewing and web browsing. The new digital technology makes TV interactive. If a viewer likes the tie that the local TV anchorperson is wearing, he or she can click on it and part of the TV screen turns into the website where the viewer can order the tie. Further, television transmitted on the Internet uses digital video. The next chapter contains more information about video applications on the computer.

One thing is for sure. Buying a TV set in the next couple of years will be more complicated. Should you wait for the new DTV sets to become cheaper? Spring for a big HDTV unit? Save money by purchasing a conventional set and a converter box? Hope you can use your PC to get Internet digital TV? Forget about TV and read a book?

DEFINING FEATURES OF TELEVISION

Like radio, TV is a universal medium. About 99 percent of the homes in the United States have at least one working TV set. In fact, most homes have more than one. Although not quite as portable as radios, miniature TV sets make it possible to take TV anywhere.

Television has become the dominant medium for news and entertainment for Americans. Surveys have consistently revealed that most people choose television as their main source of news. In addition, in the average American household, the TV set is on for about seven hours every day. Prime-time television series may draw an audience of 20 million households. In short, TV has become an important part of our society.

Further, TV, especially network television, is an expensive business. It costs the production company about $1.5 million to produce one episode of a typical one-hour prime-time series. Most series produce about 22 original episodes a year. A little math reveals that the total cost for one season of one prime-time hour for one network is about $33 million. Some more math discloses that the total tab for prime-time programming for the four major networks is more than $2 billion. Added to that is the cost of daytime programs and newscasts. TV advertising is also costly, averaging more than $100,000 for a 30-second spot in network prime time.

Finally, over the past several decades, the television industry has watched its audience fragment. Back in 1970, the major networks' share of the audience was about 90 percent. Today, the increase in cable networks, VCR usage, video games, and home video has cut that share nearly in half. The fragmenting audience is most apparent in the cable industry, where new cable channels are increasingly geared to a small, well-defined audience niche. And even those niche audiences are being divided up. There are two cable networks devoted to health programming, four specializing in women's programs, and five devoted to home and lifestyle topics.

ORGANIZATION OF THE BROADCAST TELEVISION INDUSTRY

The **commercial television** system consists of all those local stations whose income is derived from selling time on their facilities to advertisers. **Noncommercial television** consists of those stations whose income is derived from sources other than the sale of advertising time.

A local TV station is licensed by the Federal Communications Commission to provide TV service to a particular community. In the industry, these communities are customarily referred to as markets. There are 210 markets in the United States, ranging from the number-one market, New York City, with about 6.9 million homes, to number 210, Glendive, Montana, with about 5,000 homes. Some of these local TV stations enter into contractual agreements with TV networks. As of 2001, seven commercial networks in the United States supply programs to local stations: the American Broadcasting Company (ABC), the Columbia Broadcasting System (CBS), the National Broadcasting Company (NBC), the Fox Broadcasting Company (FBC), United Paramount Network (UPN), the Warner Broadcasting Network (The WB), and Paxnet. The Public Broadcasting Service (PBS) serves as a network for noncommercial stations. A local station that signs a contract with one of the networks is an affiliate. ABC, CBS, and NBC have about 200 affiliates scattered across the country; Fox has slightly fewer; and UPN, WB, and Paxnet have still fewer. Local stations that do not have network affiliation are independents.

Much like the film industry, the TV industry is divided into three segments: (1) production, (2) distribution, and (3) exhibition. The production element is responsible for providing the programming that is ultimately viewed by the TV audience. The distribution function is handled by the TV networks, cable, and syndication companies. The exhibition of television programs—the element in the system that most people are most familiar with—is the responsibility of local TV stations.

Production

Pretend for a moment that you are the manager of a local TV station in your hometown. Your station signs on at 6 A.M. and signs off at 2 A.M. That means your station must provide 20 hours of programming every day, or approximately 7,000 hours of programming each year. Where do you get all this programming? There are basically three sources:

1. Local production.
2. Syndicated programming.
3. For some stations, network programs.

Local production consists of those programs that are produced in the local station's own studio or on location with the use of the station's equipment. The most common local productions are the station's daily newscasts, typically broadcast at noon, in the early evening, and in the late evening. These newscasts attract large audiences, which in turn attract advertisers. As a result, the local news accounts for a major proportion of the ad revenue that is generated by a local station. Not surprisingly, local stations devote a major share of their production budgets to their news shows. Other locally produced programming might consist of local sporting events, early morning interview programs, and

S O U N D B Y T E

At Least the Floors Were Shiny

Sometimes mundane things can cause unforeseen hi-tech problems. At WLS-TV in Chicago, a cleaning person accidentally plugged in a floor buffer to the power outlet for the master control board. A short circuit caused sparks to fly, and the station's audio signal was knocked out for 20 minutes.

A local TV news program in Miami. News is the most common form of production at a local TV station and also produces the most revenue. *(The Image Works)*

public-affairs discussion shows. It would be difficult, however, for a local station to fill its entire schedule with locally produced programming. As a result, most stations turn to programming produced by other sources.

If the station is affiliated with a network (and most stations are), much of its programming problem is solved. Networks typically supply about 65 to 70 percent of the programming carried by their affiliates. Many of the programs supplied by the networks are produced by the networks themselves. News, sports, early-morning talk shows, and an increasing number of prime-time dramas and sitcoms are network productions. Independent production companies or the TV divisions of major motion picture studios supply other programs. Table 10.1 lists some programs and their production companies.

Many independent production companies sell their shows to syndication firms. Tribune Entertainment Company syndicates "Geraldo." King World Productions handles "Wheel of Fortune," "Jeopardy," "The Oprah Winfrey Show," and "Inside Edition." Programs that have already played on the networks (called off-net

Table 10.1	Example of Production Companies and Their Programs for the 2000–2001 Season
Production Company	**Programs**
Networks	
CBS	"Family Law," "Touched by an Angel"
NBC	"Will and Grace," "Providence"
ABC	"Monday Night Football," "20/20"
Independents	
Aaron Spelling Productions	"Charmed," "7th Heaven"
Steven Bochco Productions	"NYPD Blue," "City of Angels"
Studios USA	"Law & Order," "Deadline"
TV Divisions of Film Companies	
Warner Brothers	"The Drew Carey Show," "Friends"
20th Century Fox	"Dharma & Greg," "Dark Angel"
Paramount	"Nash Bridges," "Becker"

series) are also distributed by syndication companies. Twentieth Television, for example, syndicates "Dharma & Greg" and "The Practice," while Buena Vista Television handles "Sabrina" and "Home Improvement." These programs usually air during the late afternoon or early evening, not in prime time. In addition, packages of movies, made up from some of the 23,000 films that have been released for TV, can be leased from syndication companies.

■ Distribution

The three main elements in the distribution segment of television are the broadcast networks, cable networks, and the syndication companies. The network distributes programs to its affiliates by transmitting them by satellite. The station then transmits them to its viewers as they are received, or it videotapes them and presents them at a later time. The affiliation contract between a local station and the network is a complicated document. In simplified terms, the station agrees to carry the network's programs, and in return the network agrees to pay the station a certain amount of money for clearing its time so that the network programs can be seen. (Although it may seem contradictory that the network actually pays the station to carry the network's programming, remember that the network is using the local station's facilities to show the network's commercials.) The amount of money paid by the network varies by market size and is influenced by the competition. In general, each of the three older networks pays out about $150 million annually in affiliate compensation. The networks continue to examine their compensation arrangements, and it's likely that affiliates will be receiving less in the future. The network then sells time in its programs to advertisers seeking a national audience.

Cable networks beam their programs via microwaves to satellites where they are, in turn, downlinked to local cable systems. The local system then distributes the programming to its subscribers.

Inside a TV control room: The director is the man with glasses toward the upper part of the picture. It's his job to scan the monitors and choose the most appropriate shot. To his left in front of the large control panel, called the switcher, is the technical director, who actually pushes the buttons that put the cameras on the air.
(S. Gazin/The Image Works)

Syndication companies provide another kind of program distribution. These organizations lease taped or filmed programs to local television stations in each local market. Sometimes, as mentioned above, the syndication company also produces the program, but more often it distributes programs produced by other firms. Local stations that purchase a syndicated program receive exclusive rights to show that program in their market (a situation complicated by cable TV systems that bring in distant stations). Usually a station buys a package of programs—perhaps as many as 120 episodes or more—and the contract specifies how many times each program can be repeated.

Syndication companies try to sell their shows in as many TV markets as possible. The greater the coverage of the show, the more appealing it is to national advertisers. Top-rated syndicated shows, such as "Wheel of Fortune" and "Jeopardy," are seen in nearly all TV markets.

Syndication functions as an important aftermarket for prime-time TV shows. In fact, some prime-time series are produced at a deficit, sometimes $200,000 or more for each one-hour episode. Production companies gamble that they can make back this money in the syndication market. It's a risk, but if a show hits it big in syndication it might earn half a billion dollars or more. To be attractive in the syndication market, however, a prime-time show must have enough back episodes stockpiled so that stations can run episodes for a long time without repeats. Since 100 seems to be the magic number, series usually have a big party to commemorate the production of their hundredth episode. Since only 22 or 24 new shows are produced each season, it's obvious that those series that last four or five years are the best bets for syndication success.

■ Exhibition

At the start of 2001, there were approximately 1,300 commercial TV stations and 365 noncommercial stations in the United States. Some TV stations are licensed to broadcast in the very-high-frequency (**VHF**) band of the electromagnetic spectrum; these stations occupy channels 2 through 13 on the TV set. Other stations broadcast in the ultra-high-frequency (**UHF**) part of the spectrum; these stations are found on channels 14 through 69. As noted earlier, VHF stations have a signal that covers greater distances than UHF stations. Consequently, VHF stations tend to be more desirable to own and operate. These differences will not be as important after the move to digital TV.

As we suggested earlier, another important difference among stations concerns their affiliation with national networks. As of 2000, more than 80 percent of all commercial stations were affiliated with CBS, NBC, ABC, or Fox. The two new networks that started broadcasting in 1995, the United Paramount Network (UPN) and the Warner Broadcasting Network (The WB), started their services with significantly fewer stations than the 200 or so stations that are affiliated with each of the older nets. UPN now has 124 affiliates while The WB has about 180.

Those stations not affiliated with networks are called **independents.** For many years, independents were hampered because most were UHF stations and had less coverage area than VHFs. The emergence of cable, however, gave UHF independents more of a competitive advantage, since unlike the situation with over-the-air signals, both UHF and VHF stations have the same audience reach on the cable. Recently, most independent stations have signed on with either UPN, WB, or Paxnet. "Pure" independents are now hard to find.

■ TV Online

Promoting their products is the main function of the online sites of TV organizations. Each of the networks maintains at least one website. CBS, for example, previews its nightly program lineup, including the guests on David Letterman's show. NBC is more ambitious. In addition to its regular network site, it also offers NBCi, a page containing news and entertainment content that a person can customize and use as a home page for the web browser.

Local stations are well represented on the web. The website of WABC-TV in New York, for example, contains a weather report, traffic conditions, breaking news stories, and a guide to area cultural events and movies. Many local stations offer live video from their evening newscasts.

Major cable networks also are well represented on the web. Maybe the most well known is espn.go.com. CNN and the Discovery Channel also host popular websites, as does premium network HBO.

In addition, there are many sites devoted to specific series or stars. There are probably a hundred or more sites devoted to "Xena: Warrior Princess." Fans of the 1960s series "Gilligan's Island" have their choice of several dozen sites where they can find (for whatever reason) the lyrics to the theme song, a guide to all 98 episodes, and a full-color cast picture.

OWNERSHIP IN THE TELEVISION INDUSTRY

As of 2000, all the major networks were under the control of large conglomerates.

- NBC is owned by General Electric. In addition to its holdings in nonmedia areas, such as aerospace, aircraft engines, consumer products, and financial properties, GE has interests in TV stations; cable/satellite networks, including CNBC, MSNBC, and Court TV; as well as a video production company.
- ABC is owned by the Walt Disney Company, which also owns theme parks, a professional hockey team, a cruise line, retail stores, and media holdings that include daily newspapers, magazines, film production companies, radio networks, record companies, cable networks, and TV stations.
- Fox is controlled by Rupert Murdoch's News Corporation, which owns a major film and TV production company, more than 20 TV stations, cable networks, satellite networks, a record company, newspapers, magazines, and a book publishing company.
- CBS merged with Viacom in 1999. The new corporation has holdings in radio, TV, home video, publishing, theme parks, cable, and motion pictures.

The two newer networks, WB and UPN, are also part of large organizations. WB is owned by the giant AOL Time Warner conglomerate, while UPN is part of the Viacom organization.

At the station level, the Telecommunications Act of 1996 (see Chapter 15) allowed a person or organization to own as many TV stations as they wished, as long as the combined reach of the stations did not exceed 35 percent of the U.S. population. This change sparked a trend toward consolidation. By the start of 2001, big groups controlled most of the TV stations in the top 100 markets. Table 10.2 lists the top five group owners.

Table 10.2	Top Five Owners of TV Stations, 2000	
Company	Number of Stations	Percentage of Coverage
Viacom/CBS	35	40*
Fox	23	35
Paxson	60	34
Tribune	23	29
NBC	13	28

*May have to sell stations to meet 35 percent cap.

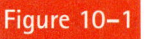 # PRODUCING TELEVISION PROGRAMS

Departments and Staff

There are many different staffing arrangements in television stations. Some big-city stations employ 300 to 400 people and may be divided into a dozen different departments. Small-town stations may have 20 to 30 employees and only a few departments. Figure 10–1 represents one possible staffing structure.

At the top of the chart is the general manager, the person ultimately responsible for all station activities. The sales department is responsible for selling time to local and national advertisers, scheduling ads, and sending bills to customers. Maintaining all the technical equipment is the responsibility of the engineering department. The production department puts together locally produced programming. At many stations the programming function is also handled by this department. Those involved in programming decide what programs should be broad-

Figure 10–1

Departmental Chart for a Medium-Sized Television Station

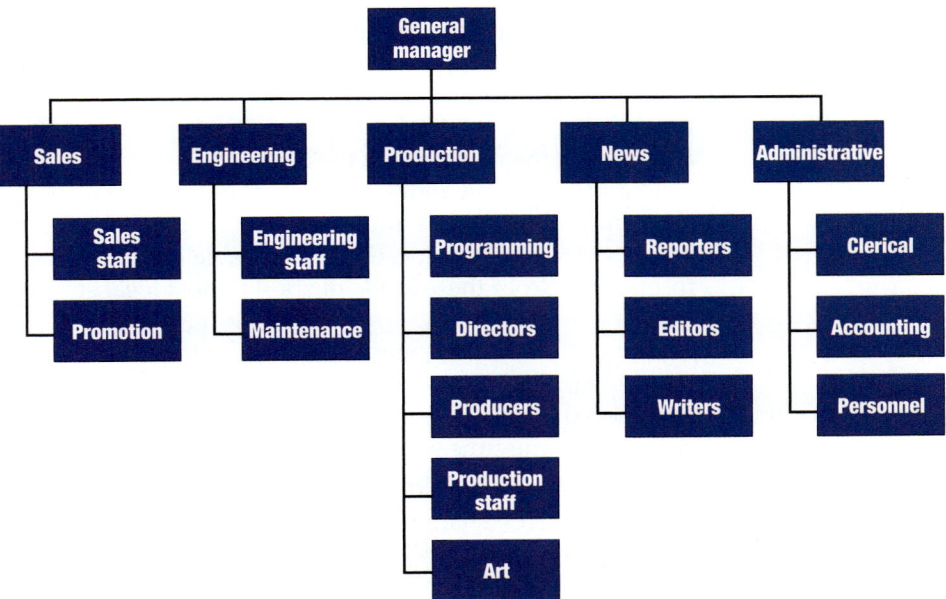

cast and at what times they should be presented. The news department includes the news director, anchorpeople, reporters, and writers responsible for the station's newscasts. The administrative department aids the station manager in running the station.

At the network level, the divisions are somewhat more complicated. Although the major networks differ in their setups, all seem to have departments that perform the following functions:

1. *Sales.* Handles sale of network commercials and works with advertising agencies.
2. *Entertainment.* Works with producers to develop new programs for the network.
3. *Owned and operated stations.* Administers those stations owned by the networks.
4. *Affiliate relations.* A very important job in the new century; supervises all contracts with stations affiliated with the network (and generally tries to keep the affiliates happy).
5. *News.* Responsible for all network news and public-affairs programs.
6. *Sports.* Responsible for all sports programming.
7. *Standards.* Checks all network programs to make sure they don't violate the law or the network's own guidelines for appropriate content.
8. *Operations.* Handles the technical aspects of actually sending programs to affiliates.

■ Getting TV Programs on the Air

At the local level, the biggest effort at a TV station goes into the newscast. Almost every station has a studio that contains a set for one or two anchorpeople, a weather forecaster, and a sportscaster. The station's news director assigns stories to reporters and camera crews, who travel to the scene of a story and videotape a report. Back at the station, the newscast producer and news director are planning what stories to air and allotting time to each. In the meantime, the camera crews and reporters return; the reporters write copy and editors prepare videotape segments. When the final script is finished (this may be only a few minutes before airtime), it is given to a director, who is responsible for pulling everything together and putting the newscast on the air.

In addition to the news, the local station might also produce one or two interview programs. Some stations produce a "magazine" program consisting of segments videotaped on location by portable equipment and later edited into final form. Aside from these kinds of shows, most local stations do little other production.

Because they are responsible for filling the hours when the biggest audience is watching (called prime time, 8–11 P.M., Eastern Standard Time), the networks must pay special attention to cultivating new shows. For the moment, let's concentrate on how a prime-time series is produced.

Everything starts with an idea. Network executives receive hundreds of ideas every year; some come from independent producers, some from TV departments of motion picture companies, some from network employees, and a good many from amateurs hoping for a break. From this mass of ideas, the networks select perhaps 50 to 75, usually submitted by established producers or companies, for further attention. After examining plot outlines and background sketches of the leading characters for these 50 to 75 potential series, the networks trim the list once again. For those ideas that survive, the networks request a sample script and a list of possible stories that could be turned into scripts. If the idea still looks promising, the network and producer enter into a contract for a **pilot,** the first episode of a series. In a typical year, perhaps 25 pilots are ordered by each net. If the pilot show gains a respectable audience, the network may order five or six episodes to be produced and may place the program on its fall schedule. From the hundreds of ideas that are sent to the network, only a few ever make it to prime time.

The process does not stop with the fall season. If a program does well in the ratings, the network will order enough episodes for the rest of the season. If the show does not do well, it will be canceled and another show will replace it. Meanwhile, network executives are sifting through the hundreds of program ideas for the next season, and the cycle begins once again.

ECONOMICS

The television industry has been profitable since 1950, and its total income has increased every year since 1971. In 2000, television advertising revenue amounted to $44.5 billion. The changing structure of the television industry, however, has had a significant economic impact on both local stations and the networks. More about this after we look at the traditional sources of television advertising revenue.

Commercial Time

Where did the $44.5 billion in revenue come from? It came from the sale of commercial time by networks, local stations, and cable systems to advertisers. A station, network, or cable system makes available a specified number of minutes per hour that will be offered for sale to advertisers. There are three different types of advertisers who buy time on TV:

1. National advertisers
2. National spot advertisers
3. Local advertisers

National advertisers are those that sell general-consumption items: soda pop, automobiles, deodorant, hair spray, and so on. These advertisers try to reach the biggest possible audience for their messages and usually purchase commercial time on broadcast network programs or cable networks.

In contrast, other advertisers have products that are used mainly in one region or locale. For example, a manufacturer of snowmobiles would gain little by having his or her ad seen in Miami or New Orleans. Likewise, a manufacturer of farm equipment would probably not find many customers in New York City. These companies turn to national spot buying. The snowmobile manufacturer would buy spots in several northern markets, such as Minneapolis, Minnesota; Fargo, North Dakota; and Butte, Montana. The farm equipment company would place ads in primarily rural markets.

Finally, there are many local businesses that buy advertising time from TV stations. They purchase time on one or more TV stations or cable systems located in a single market. The industrywide figures for 2000 showed the relative importance

Who's the biggest money winner on "Who Wants to Be a Millionaire"? It's not one of the contestants—it's ABC, the network that airs the show.

Let's do some arithmetic. Most estimates suggest that "Millionaire" costs ABC about $500,000 an episode to produce. In the 2000–2001 season, the show was on four times a week. That's a total of $2 million in production costs. Let's also suppose the show gives away a million dollars each time it's on. That's an additional $4 million. Total assumed cost per week: $6 million.

Let's assume that each one-hour episode of "Millionaire" sells about 15 minutes of commercial time at about $500,000 per minute. That totals $7.5 million per hourly episode. There are four shows a week, resulting in $30 million in revenue, or about a $24 million profit for every week the show airs. No wonder ABC is happy.

---

of these three types of advertising. Network spots (national advertising) accounted for 40 percent of the total amount of advertising dollars, while the remainder was divided about equally between national spot and local advertising.

Revenues depend upon the amount of money a station charges for its commercial time. The larger the audience, the more money a station can charge. The prices for 30- and 60-second commercials are listed on the station's rate card. The cost of an ad will vary tremendously from station to station. A 30-second ad might cost only $100 to $200 in a small market, while the same time would cost thousands in a major market. The same general pricing principles apply at the network level. Shows with high ratings have higher advertising charges than shows with low ratings. For example, in 2000, the average network 30-second spot in prime time cost about $180,000. On top-rated shows, spots were going for about $500,000; on lower-rated shows, the cost was about $85,000. To gain some perspective on how expensive it can get, consider that on the 2001 Super Bowl, a 30-second spot was going for more than $2 million.

A 30-second spot on "Everybody Loves Raymond" cost about $450,000 for the 2000–2001 TV season. *(Tony Esparza/CBS/Liaison Agency)*

■ Where Did the Money Go?

At the network level, one of the biggest expenses is programming. For example, a typical half-hour sitcom costs around $800,000 to $900,000 to produce. Hit shows, such as "Frasier," cost much more. An hour-long show, such as "ER," runs about $1.5 million to $1.75 million. ABC spends about $3 million for each "Monday Night Football" telecast.

At the local level, the costs are broken down differently, but the heavy

ETHICAL ISSUES Virtual Ads?

Television audiences watching the running of the 1998 Brickyard 400 saw logos for Pennzoil and Miller beer apparently emblazoned on the infield. Fans in the stands, however, saw only green grass. The same puzzling phenomenon occurred during the televising of the 2000 Indianapolis 500. Viewers saw ads for ABC Sports and Northern Light in the grass near the turns; those in person saw only grass.

What gives? The above are examples of virtual ads, computer-inserted brand images that are designed to look like part of the actual scenery. (This is the same technology that permitted CBS to insert a CBS logo in place of an NBC sign during its New Year's Eve coverage from Times Square. See Chapter 16.) Computer-generated ads have been around for three or four years, but because of increased commercial clutter and the rising costs of 30-second spots, they've recently become more popular. So far, they have been used mainly at sporting events such as races and baseball games (those advertising banners behind home plate are computer-generated in many baseball telecasts). Plans are on the drawing board that would also insert virtual ads between the goalposts during football games and on the mat during wrestling matches.

Further, advances in technology now allow advertisers to electronically insert products in episodes of TV series after they are produced and are in syndication. This makes it possible, for example, to insert a can of Coke in a scene from "Friends," or a box of Raisin Bran may magically appear in a syndicated rerun of "Seinfeld." A few weeks later the digital can of Coke could be replaced by a Pepsi can.

What are the ethical issues that spring from this practice? First, it represents a new level of commercial intrusion. With a tra-ditional TV ad, the viewer can leave the room or change the channel and not miss any program content. With virtual ads, there is no escape. If you want to watch the game, you must see the virtual ads. This seems to violate the principle of self-determination. Removing a person's free will is essentially treating that person as an object subject to manipulation.

Second, do advertisers and telecasters have the right to alter reality? Proponents of virtual ads point out that many broadcasts of football games now digitally insert a yellow line that indicates the first-down marker. They argue that viewers don't mind this modification to reality and many actually like it. In like manner, they note that viewers have made no concerted outcry against the practice of inserting virtual ads. On the other hand, there is the question of where the process will stop. Can TV networks digitally insert crowds of people to fill empty seats at a sporting event? How about digitally superimposing green grass over a snowy football field so that the viewer can more easily see the yard markers? Do the TV networks have an obligation to inform the viewer when such alterations take place?

The practice of inserting products into existing episodes of TV shows raises further questions. Virtual product placement takes away some creative control and freedom from actors and actresses. Digitally inserting a can of Coke into a actor's hand makes the actor an unwitting and perhaps unwilling endorser of Coke. A director who carefully frames a scene may not want the scene cluttered up with virtual products.

In sum, virtual ads can create some real problems.

---

cost of programming is evident there as well. Programming costs account for about 35 to 40 percent of the local station expense dollar, followed by administrative costs and expenses for news.

# PUBLIC BROADCASTING

A Short History

Public broadcasting in the United States has been in existence for more than 30 years. During its lifetime, its achievements have been considerable, but its evolution has been hampered by political infighting, a lack of a clear purpose, and, most of all, an insufficient amount of money.

Until 1967, noncommercial TV was known as educational television. In 1967, following the recommendations of the Carnegie Commission, Congress passed the Public Broadcasting Act, which authorized money for the construction of new facilities and established the Corporation for Public Broadcasting (CPB), to oversee noncommercial TV and distribute funds for programs. The government also created the Public Broadcasting Service (PBS), whose duties resemble those of commercial networks. Although this arrangement seemed to work well at first, internal disputes soon surfaced concerning which of these two organizations had final control over programming.

In addition, several cable channels began to offer programs that competed for public TV's audience. Many experts felt that much of the traditional programming on public TV would eventually move to cable or to videocassette. On top of this came further reductions in federal funds for public broadcasting.

Then things started to change. Somewhat surprisingly, cable turned out to be more of a friend than a foe to public TV. Since two-thirds of all public stations are in the UHF band, carriage by local cable systems increased their coverage area and helped public TV double its audience from 1980 to 1984. Public TV wound up as the primary cultural channel in the nation, with 90 million viewers every week.

In the mid-1980s, however, the Reagan administration cut funds for public broadcasting and proposed to freeze future funding at current levels. Congress restored some of the cuts, but in 1987 the system was struggling to get along on about the same amount of money it had in 1982. PBS funding became a major political issue again in the early 1990s. Faced with this financial uncertainty, public TV looked to other sources for funding: corporate underwriting, auctions, viewer donations, and sales of program guides. Some stations experimented with commercials.

Programming and Financing

In 1990, the Public Broadcasting Service presented an 11-hour documentary entitled "The Civil War," which became the highest-rated program in the history of PBS. Although it might be a bit of an exaggeration, much of the history of PBS programming can be described as a civil war between the local public stations and the centralized PBS organization. Each side has scored significant victories in this fray over the years, but most recently, the tide has turned in favor of the centralized authority. Let's quickly review how the system used to work and how it has changed.

Before 1990, PBS used a mechanism called the Station Program Cooperative (SPC) to determine which programs were carried by its member stations. The SPC system represented a decentralized decision-making process. Member stations were given a ballot that contained the descriptions of possible programs and voted for those they wished to broadcast. After several rounds, the initial list was pared down and stations voted again, but this time each station had to promise that it would help pay for the programs it voted for.

This system encouraged the broadcast of programs that already had some funding or series that could be acquired cheaply. Innovative or daring series that were expensive and had no prior funding commitments were seldom produced. The system also leaned heavily on a few big public TV stations that did the bulk of the production work. Finally, PBS had no cohesive national scheduling system.

In 1990, faced with declining funds and viewers, PBS suspended the SPC and moved toward more centralized programming. An executive vice president for national programming was appointed, with the power to develop and schedule new programs. By any measure, the first PBS season under the new centralized system was a success, exemplified by the fact that *The Civil War* series was watched by millions.

Successive seasons, however, were not as successful. For the entire decade of the 1990s, despite being one of the most established TV networks, PBS got an average prime-time rating of 2.0 (of all the TV homes in America, about 2 per-

Educational programs, such as this one on archeology, make up a significant part of the PBS schedule. *(The Everett Collection)*

cent watched PBS in prime time, about the same rating as UPN). In addition, PBS got into trouble with Congress when it was revealed that PBS stations, which are supposed to be politically neutral, were providing Republican and Democratic groups with their donor lists. Political parties might use these lists to solicit money.

In 2000, PBS named Pat Mitchell, a former programming executive at Turner Broadcasting, to be the new president of PBS. This marks the first time in the 30-year history of PBS that an experienced programmer has held the top position. Mitchell announced that she would make programming one of her top priorities.

PBS programs have earned numerous awards and substantial praise from critics. "Sesame Street" revolutionized children's TV by presenting educational content in an entertaining format. "Nova" and "Cosmos" introduced millions to the wonders of science. However, PBS programs have also come in for their share of criticism. Many critics have charged that PBS displays a liberal bias and have complained about the size of the salaries PBS paid to some of its performers.

Like commercial stations, public TV stations receive licenses from the FCC. As of 2000, there were 348 PBS stations operated by 173 licensees. About half of these licensees are community organizations, another one-third are colleges and universities, about 12 percent are state-operated networks, and the remainder belong to local educational or municipal authorities.

The audience for public TV is substantial. In 2000, more than half the homes in America watched public TV at least once a week. Viewing times, however, are far less than that for commercial TV. Average household daily viewing time for public TV is about 25 minutes, compared with more than four hours for commercial TV.

In addition to its broadcasting activities, PBS is also active in educational television. It is involved in the Adult Learning Service, which provides college-level courses to about 400,000 students. In addition, PBS operates a Teacher Resource Service, which provides instructional programs and educational materials for classroom use in grades K–12.

Unlike commercial TV, public television is funded from a number of sources. For 1999, about 43 percent of the budget of the Corporation for Public Broadcasting came from federal, state, and local governments; 25 percent from viewer contributions; about 15 percent from business; with the remainder accounted for by foundation grants, auctions, and other miscellaneous sources. For 1999, Congress appropriated about $300 million for CPB. This figure is less than the cost of a month of commercial programs on the four major networks.

CABLE TELEVISION

Cable television matured during the late 1990s and faced some of the problems that go along with growing up. The rapid expansion of earlier years slowed down, competition escalated from satellite broadcasters, legislation changed the media environment, and new cable channels found it difficult to find space on existing cable systems. Despite these difficulties, cable was holding its own. Before we discuss the current state of the cable industry, let's take a quick look at the past.

History

Cable TV began modestly in the 1950s as a device used to bring conventional television signals to areas that could not otherwise receive them. As cable grew, some systems imported signals from distant stations into markets that were already served by one or two local stations. The local stations, as you might imagine, were not pleased, since their audiences were being siphoned off by the imported signals. This situation caused some political maneuverings as stations affected by cable appealed to the FCC and to Congress for help. The FCC vacillated over the question of cable regulation before issuing, in 1965, a set of rules that retarded the growth of cable in large markets. In 1972, the FCC enacted a new set of less restrictive rules for cable. By 1980, in a move toward deregulation, the FCC dropped virtually all rules governing cable.

This deregulation move helped systems grow as cable companies scrambled to acquire exclusive franchises in communities across the nation (see Figure 10–2). Some companies made extravagant promises to win these contracts: 100 or more channels, local-access channels, community channels, shopping and banking at home, two-way services—and all at bargain prices. After the smoke cleared, the industry realized economic reality dictated that its performance would fall short of promises.

Cable quickly recovered from these setbacks and continued to grow. As of 1991, there were 7,500 cable systems serving about 55 million households. Keep in mind that this growth occurred despite the fact that cable companies generally avoided expensive urban installations. The growth rate slowed somewhat during the mid-1990s, but by 2000, there were about 68 million households that subscribed to cable.

Cable also scored several programming coups. ESPN signed a three-year deal with the National Football League to carry prime-time pro football games. CNN's coverage of the Gulf War, the O. J. Simpson trial, and the Clinton scandal demonstrated that it could be a formidable competitor to network news. Big-ticket network series bypassed the traditional syndication route and premiered first on cable.

On the economic side, cable advertising revenues exceeded $2 billion in 1990 and rose to about $7 billion by 2000. Although still small in comparison with the ad revenues generated by traditional television, the 2000 figure represents an increase of more than 40 percent over that of 1996.

R. E. "Ted" Turner inherited his family's outdoor advertising company in 1963, when he was 24. The Atlanta-based business was in poor economic shape, but the young Turner managed to turn it around. Six years later Turner learned that a financially troubled UHF television station was for sale. Disregarding the fact that the station's signal was so weak that he couldn't pick it up on his own home TV set, Turner bought the station, renamed it WTCG, and began to advertise it on his unused billboards around Atlanta. With a skillful programming mix of popular reruns and old movies, the station eventually became one of the few UHF stations in the country at the time to turn a profit. Turner, however, was not content with just turning the station around. He had much bigger plans for it.

One day in 1976 at a meeting of the station's managers, Turner placed a beat-up model of the RCA Satcom I satellite on the table and proclaimed that WTCG would soon be competing with CBS, NBC, and ABC. Turner had decided that he would use the new communication satellites to beam WTCG to cable systems all over the country, making it a national network. Not surprisingly, his managers were incredulous. Almost everybody dismissed Turner's idea as totally impractical.

There were lots of reasons why this bold move wouldn't work. Cable TV had not yet caught on; it was available in only 16 percent of the country, mostly in rural areas. Cable systems relied on terrestrial microwave signals; not many were equipped to receive satellite feeds. The FCC had a rule against leapfrogging that prohibited cable systems from importing signals from distant cities unless they also took the signals of stations closer to their market. Additionally, FCC regulations permitted cable systems to use only expensive 10-meter satellite dishes, which most systems could not afford. Undaunted, Turner pitched his idea to big cable operators. They were not impressed.

As fate would have it, however, two weeks later, the FCC dropped its leapfrogging rules and permitted stations to use smaller and cheaper satellite dishes. All of a sudden, Turner's idea didn't seem so far-fetched after all. In December, Turner renamed his station WTBS and started distributing it by satellite, thus creating the first superstation.

WTBS caught on slowly. When it first went on the satellite, the station was received by a grand total of four cable systems. Turner helped its fortunes by purchasing the Atlanta Braves baseball team and making their games available on WTBS. The new superstation continued to grow in popularity, eventually reaching 74 million homes. The success of WTBS inspired the creation of other cable networks and totally changed the cable TV industry. Turner proved that people would subscribe to cable not just to get good reception, but also to get programming.

Turner had other ideas. He had encouraged cable systems to carry WTBS by promising them that he would also provide them with additional cable networks. In 1980, he launched the first of those networks—CNN. Cable operators were lukewarm toward the new project. Most refused to provide money to cover start-up costs. Turner invested $21 million into the new venture, which was immediately derided by competitors for its bargain-basement approach to news. Critics labeled CNN the *Chicken Noodle Network*.

CNN started off losing money, but Turner kept the network alive with the profits from WTBS. Finally, CNN went into the black in 1985. Six years later, during the Gulf War, CNN scooped the other networks by having reporters on the scene in Baghdad when the war broke out. CNN's success spawned several 24-hour news service competitors, including MSNBC and Fox News Channel.

Several other Turner decisions have also paid off. In 1986, he paid more than a billion dollars for the MGM/United Artists film library. Turner used the films to help launch two other cable networks—Turner Network Television and Turner Classic Movies. Turner also bought the Hanna Barbera animation studio and started the Cartoon Network.

In 1996, Turner Broadcasting Systems merged with Time Warner and Turner became responsible for the new company's cable operations.

More recently, Turner has become interested in philanthropy. His United Nations' Foundation, funded by a $1 billion donation, grants about $100 million every year to organizations that are interested in population control and the environment. His Turner Foundation concentrates on improving the quality of life in the United States.

All in all, Ted Turner's decisions did much to build the landscape of the modern TV industry.

The most significant developments in the cable industry in the last two decades have been legal ones. In 1984, Congress deregulated the rates cable systems could charge consumers. Eight years later, in response to subscriber complaints, Congress reregulated the industry by passing the Cable Television Consumer Protection and Competition Act, which caused about a 17 percent reduction in rates and mandated that broadcasters could choose between *must carry* (the local cable system had to carry the station's signal) or *retransmission consent* (the local station had

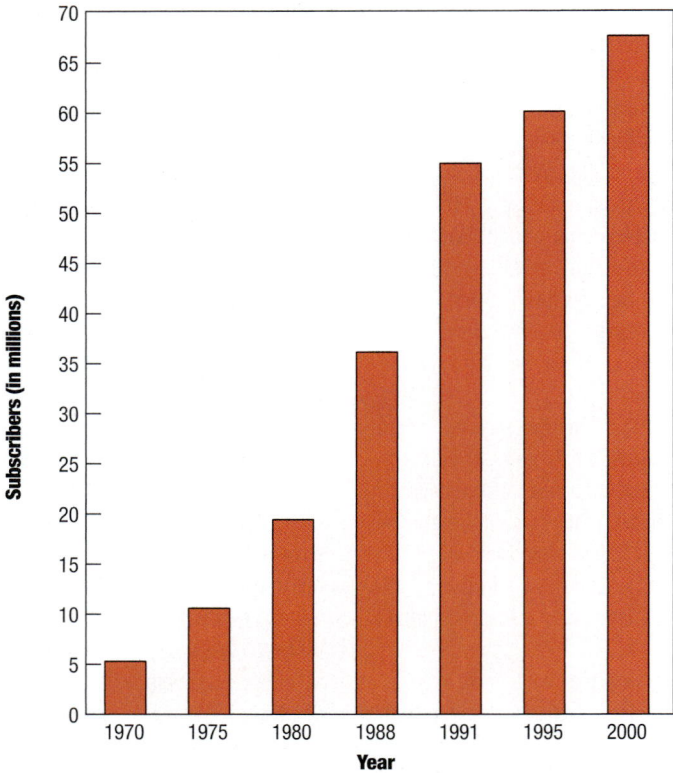

Figure 10–2

Growth within the U.S. Cable TV Industry

the right to negotiate compensation for carriage of their signal). Most broadcasters opted for consent and were compensated with promotional time on the system or were granted space for their own existing or planned cable networks.

The next major piece of legislation was the Telecommunications Act of 1996 (discussed in more detail in Chapter 15). The new law gave telephone companies the right to enter the cable business and gave cable companies the right to provide telephone services. In addition, both telephone and cable companies could own competing systems in the same community. Finally, the act allowed most cable companies to once again set their own rates. The ultimate consequences of this new legislation have yet to unfold. Some phone companies announced plans to start video services, while others acquired cable systems. A few cable systems were planning to start phone services. Both cable and phone companies have proceeded cautiously, but competition is growing. In the Atlanta area, for example, BellSouth (a regional phone company) offers phone service, cable TV programming, and Internet access to its customers.

Cable was also feeling problems resulting from its own growth. There were more cable networks around than available space on local systems. Some cable systems were making room for only those channels that would pay the system to carry their signals. Cable networks that lacked deep financial resources were having problems gaining access to local systems. In addition, like the broadcast networks, cable TV was becoming a victim of audience fragmentation.

Despite these difficulties, the long-range outlook seems positive. Cable continues to draw viewers away from the broadcast TV networks. In addition, thanks to their existing coaxial cable and optical fiber facilities, cable companies

Special-interest programs, such as Animal Planet's "The Crocodile Hunter," have fragmented the cable TV audience. *(AP/Wide World Photos)*

can offer subscribers high-speed Internet connections. Several cable companies have started online services, such as Time Warner's RoadRunner and AT&T's Excite@home, that offer community information. Finally, the websites of many cable networks are among the most popular on the web—CNN.com, espn.go. com, and the Discovery Channel Online.

■ Ownership

The ownership trend in the cable industry, as in other media, has been one of consolidation and of new players. Three big companies serve almost 60 percent of all cable subscribers: AT&T, AOL Time Warner, and Charter Communications. It is interesting to note that these three companies bought into the cable business for reasons other than the chance to provide TV service. AT&T bought out Tele-Communications Inc. for $50 billion in 1998, primarily to use the cable company's wires to provide local phone service. AOL acquired Time Warner, in part to get access to its cable lines to provide high-speed Internet access. Charter Communications is backed by Paul Allen, the co-founder of Microsoft, and is interested in using its cable lines to develop interactive services. These developments suggest that the convergence phenomenon is proceeding in cable television as well as in over-the-air broadcasting. The five largest cable systems are listed in Table 10.3.

■ Structure of Cable Systems

Cable systems are structured differently from those of conventional TV. There are three main components in a cable system (see Figure 10–3).

Table 10.3	Five Largest Cable System Operators, 2000
System	**Number of Subscribers (in millions)**
AT&T Broadband	16.4
AOL Time Warner	12.7
Charter Communications	6.1
Cox Communications	6.1
Comcast	5.7

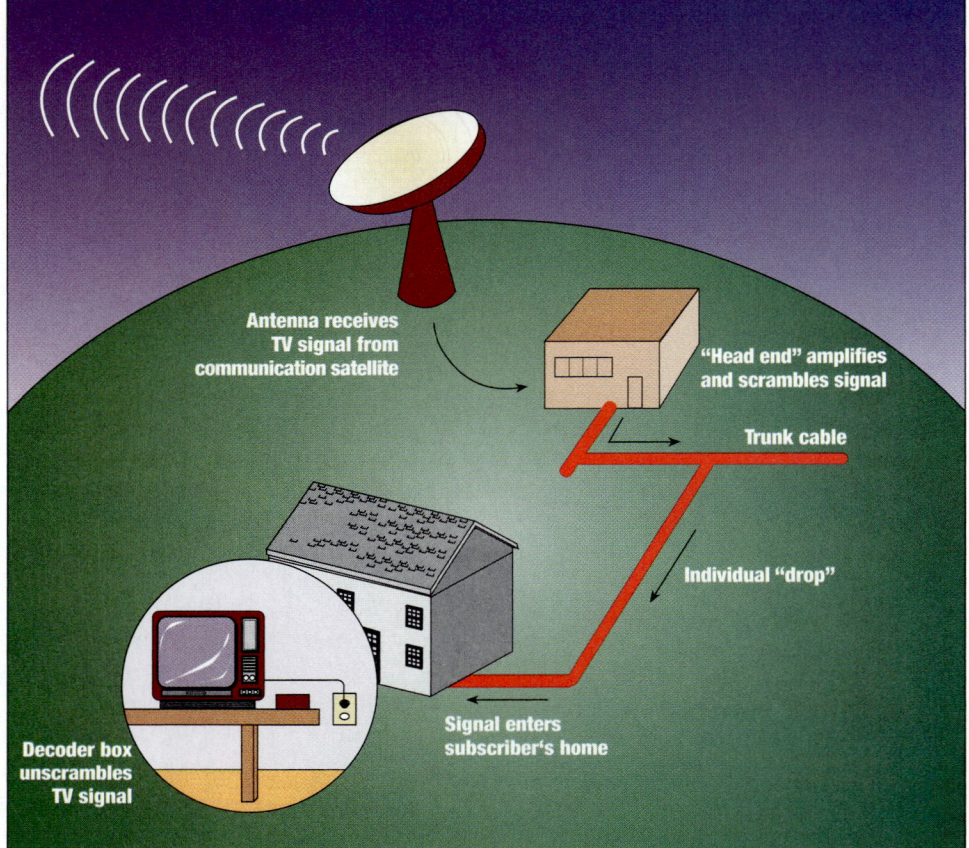

Antenna receives
TV signal from
communication satellite

"Head end" amplifies
and scrambles signal

Trunk cable

Individual "drop"

Signal enters
subscriber's home

Decoder box
unscrambles
TV signal

1. The head end
2. The distribution system
3. The house drop

The **head end** consists of the antenna and related equipment that receives signals from distant TV stations or other programming services and processes these signals so that they may be sent to subscribers' homes. Some cable systems also originate their own programming, ranging from local newscasts to weather dials, and their studios may also be located at the head end.

The **distribution system** consists of the actual cables that deliver the signals to subscribers. The cables can be buried or hung on telephone poles. In most systems, the main cable (called the trunk) has several feeder cables, which travel down side streets or to other outlying areas. Finally, there are special amplifiers installed along the distribution system, which boost the strength of the signal as it comes from the head end.

The **house drop** is that section of the cable that connects the feeder cable to the subscriber's TV set. Drops can be one-way (the signal travels in only one direction—from the head end to the house) or two-way (the signal can also be sent back to the head end by the subscriber). Fiber-optic cables make it possible to carry 500 or more channels.

The History Channel presents a biography of Thomas Edison. Special-interest channels have fragmented the cable TV audience. *(David Young-Wolff/PhotoEdit)*

■ Programming and Financing

We will examine these topics from two perspectives: (1) that of a local cable system operator and (2) that of a national cable network.

The sources of programming for a local system are as follows:

1. *Local origination.* This might range from a fixed camera scanning temperature dials to local news, high school football, and discussions. Other local origination programs include a government channel, which carries city council meetings or zoning board hearings. Some systems have set aside public-access channels available for anyone to use for a modest fee.

2. *Local broadcast television stations.* In addition to local channels, some cable systems carry signals from nearby cities.

3. *Superstations.* These are local stations whose signals are carried by many systems nationwide. There are six major superstations: WGN, Chicago; KTLA, Los Angeles; WPIX and WWOR, New York; KWGN, Denver; and WSBK, Boston. The original superstation, WTBS, Atlanta, changed its status in 1998 to that of a cable network.

4. *Special cable networks.* These are services distributed by satellite to cable systems. Most of these networks are advertiser supported. Examples include MTV, The Weather Channel, the USA Network, Black Entertainment Television, and the noncommercial C-SPAN (which covers Congress).

5. *Pay services.* These are commercial-free channels that typically provide theatrical movies and original programming: HBO, Showtime, The Movie Channel, and Cinemax, for example.

6. *Pay-per-view.* These are channels set aside for the showing of recently released theatrical films and special sports and entertainment events. Subscribers receive the programs for a specified price. Movies, for example, might be $4.95; special events, such as Wrestlemania, might be $20 to $30.

A local cable system has two basic sources of income: (1) subscription fees from consumers and (2) local advertising. Most systems charge a fee for local stations, superstations, and special cable networks. In addition, consumers might pay an additional fee to receive one or more pay channels. Cable is a capital-intensive industry: It takes a lot of money to start a system. The operating costs of a typical system are more reasonable. A good part of the basic cable monthly subscription fee goes to cover construction and maintenance costs.

Cable systems must also pay for their programming. In the case of pay services, the consumer fee is split between the cable system and the cable network. There has been a recent shift in the composition of cable system revenue. Pay-cable and pay-per-view receipts now account for more than half of cable operators' income. Local advertising on cable represents another source of income for operators. This sum is growing, but it still represents less than 20 percent of total income for local systems. In addition, cable systems that carry home shopping networks generally receive a percentage of the sales revenue generated in their market.

At the national level, cable networks draw upon three major sources for their programming: (1) original production, (2) movies, and (3) syndicated programs. The all-news channel, CNN, relies upon original production for virtually all its content. Most of ESPN's programming is also original, as is C-SPAN's. Movies make up most of the content on HBO and Showtime. Superstations program a mix of all three sources, while channels such as the USA Network and Lifetime depend heavily upon syndicated programs.

There are three main revenue sources for national cable services: advertising, carriage fees, and subscription fees. Pay-TV channels such as Showtime and HBO make their money from subscription fees paid by the consumer. Some cable networks, such as MTV and ESPN, will charge local operators a **carriage fee** (also called an affiliation fee) that ranges from about 5¢ to 30¢ per subscriber. Some channels, such as C-SPAN, support themselves entirely from this money. Other networks will sell advertising in addition to the carriage fee, while still others, such as TNN, support themselves entirely through ads. As mentioned earlier, advertising revenues for cable are growing, but cable still accounts for only a small percentage of the total TV ad dollars. Table 10.4 lists the top cable channels.

Table 10.4	Top Cable Services, 2000	
Top Pay Channels		
Channel	**Cable Subscribers (in millions)**	
1. HBO	19.2	
2. Encore	9.7	
3. Cinemax	8.9	
4. Showtime	8.1	
Top Basic Services		
Channel	**Subscribers (in millions)**	
1. WTBS	78.6	
2. ESPN	77.4	
3. CNN	77.3	
4. TNT	77.1	
5. USA	77.1	

■ Pay-per-view (PPV)

At the start of 2000, more than 30 million households were equipped with PPV, and the number is expected to grow. Experts estimate that future cable systems may have as many as 40 or 50 channels devoted to pay-per-view offerings. Sports and special events accounted for more than half of the approximately $600 million PPV revenue in 1999, with movies and adult services contributing the rest. As far as sports are concerned, boxing is the biggest revenue generator, accounting for more than half the receipts, with wrestling in second place. The biggest money-maker in PPV history was the Holyfield–Tyson fight in 1997, which grossed about $90 million. Experts suggest that PPV could easily generate $1 billion in revenue in just a few years.

HOME VIDEO

The home video industry came into existence because of the tremendous growth of VCR sales. By 2000, about 90 percent of homes in the United States were equipped with the device. Recently, the VCR has been joined by DVD (digital videodisk) players as the home video market evolves. DVD offers better pictures and sound than a videotape; can contain additional video material, such as outtakes and interviews with the director; and can have multiple-language soundtracks. DVD sales have skyrocketed; it is estimated that there are now more than 14 million in U.S. homes.

Both VCRs and DVD players are used to play back prerecorded cassettes and disks that can be purchased or rented from video stores such as Blockbuster. There are more than 30,000 prerecorded cassette and disk titles on the market, and many more are introduced each month. In addition, VCRs are also used to time-shift, to record TV shows for playback at a more convenient time. (Regular DVD players can't be used to time-shift because they can't record. Newer DVD players, however, will have this capability.) As of the turn of the 21st century, the shows that were time-shifted the most included soap operas and "Late Night with David Letterman."

Like most other businesses, home video can be divided into three segments: production, distribution, and retail. The production side of the industry consists of those companies that produce prerecorded cassettes and disks. Since much of the home video market consists of movies, many of the large motion picture studios also dominate the cassette/disk business.

These companies sell to distributors, who form the bridge between production and retail. Currently, some 90 distributors in the United States handle videocassettes. Major companies include Disney, Fox, Columbia, and Paramount. Moreover, the cassette/disk distribution business now resembles record distribution as a new breed of rack jobber is making it easy for many retail and department stores to get into the video renting business.

The retail side of the industry is the most volatile. It was estimated that in 2000, there were about 30,000 video rental/sales stores in the United States, in addition to the thousands of tape counters at grocery stores. The typical large retail store carries a library of about 3,000 to 5,000 different titles, representing a balance of current hits with other titles that have a longer shelf life. In contrast, other outlets stock only 200 to 500 titles, most of them current hits.

Imagine sitting in your favorite chair and being able to watch any movie ever made any time you want to watch it. That's the goal of video on demand, the couch potato's ultimate dream.

Here's how it works. The digital revolution makes it possible to store movies as computer files on a server. A searchable index contains the files of all the movies available. These files can be transmitted over regular cable TV lines. One server can deliver the same movie to about 20,000 different cable subscribers. Viewers need a special set-top box to be able to decode the movies. The boxes let consumers pause, stop, fast-forward, and rewind. You simply choose your movie, pay for it, and sit back and watch. No trips to the video store. No late fees.

How long before video on demand reaches your TV set? So far, the service is available on only a few cable systems. Experts, however, think the market is ready to bloom. Scientific Atlanta was recently hired to install the technology in 40 additional markets with 25 million viewers. Will it be expensive? The set-top boxes cost about $300, and individual movies would cost about $3 to $4 for each viewing.

There are still a few kinks to be worked out. Not every movie is yet available in digital form. Moreover, the Hollywood studios would have to change their release schedules to accommodate the new service. Currently, movies are released first to video rental stores, then to cable. For the new service to make a profit, it would have to have the movies at the same time as the video stores. Despite these problems, cable system operators are betting a lot of money that the system will succeed.

Large chains, with Blockbuster and Hollywood Video the most prominent, dominate the video rental business. Blockbuster alone accounts for 30 percent of all tape/disk rentals and sales.

Sales and rentals constitute big business. In 2000, consumers spent about $20 billion on cassettes and disks, with about half that sum going to rentals and the rest to tape/disk sales. The amount of revenue generated by DVD sales and rentals is still small in comparison with the total, but is increasing rapidly. The newest financial twist in the home video business is called **revenue sharing.** Before 1999, video stores bought copies of the tapes on their shelves at the whole-sale price and kept all the revenue. Under the revenue-sharing method, big chain stores such as Blockbuster agree to share the revenue from each tape rental in return for a drastically reduced wholesale price (maybe $10 per tape as opposed to $60 or $70). This arrangement lets the store buy three or four times as many copies of hit movies so that consumers can always find a copy on the store's shelves. The downside of this deal is that independent video stores who can't use their size as a bargaining chip will be unable to compete with the big chains, making the industry even more concentrated.

Finally, retailers are concerned about the growing competition posed by video on demand (see Media Probe, "Video on Demand") and direct broadcast satellites.

DIRECT BROADCAST SATELLITES

Subscribers to **direct broadcast satellite (DBS)** systems have access to dozens of movie channels as well as pay-per-view. As of 2000, there were about 15 million households equipped for DBS and market research suggested that these con-sumers were not only canceling their cable subscriptions but were also making fewer trips to the video store. It will take a few years, however, before the ultimate impact of DBS can be determined.

Satellite dishes come in two sizes. There's the 6-foot diameter dish that typi-cally sits in the backyard, and there's the newer 18-inch dish, about the same size as a large pizza, that hangs outside a window.

Web TV in action. A young viewer uses a wireless keyboard to browse the Internet on his TV set. *(AP/Wide World Photos)*

The 6-foot satellite dish collects faint microwave signals from an orbiting satellite and amplifies them about a million times. A cable carries these signals to a converter where they are changed so that they can be received over a normal TV set. Most 6-foot satellite dishes also have a remote-control device that permits the viewer to aim the dish at the appropriate orbiting satellite. A good backyard dish can pick up 75 to 100 channels.

The newer 18-inch dish uses digital technology to produce sharp pictures and CD-quality sound. When it was first introduced in 1994, the smaller dish retailed for about $700; by 2000, the dishes were selling for less than $200.

Subscriber growth was slow at first, partly because DBS systems were prohibited by law from carrying local television stations. In 1999, however, the Satellite Home Viewer Improvement Act granted satellite companies the right to retransmit the signals of some local broadcast stations. More subscribers were signing on in the wake of this development.

The two companies that dominate DBS are DirecTV and EchoStar. Both offer dozens of digital channels that carry movies, pay-per-view specials, sports packages, and the usual lineup of cable networks, such as MTV, ESPN, and CNN. DBS has more available channels than cable, and when computed on a cost-per-channel basis, DBS is cheaper than cable. On the other hand, DBS costs extra if a consumer wants to watch two different programs on two different sets. Finally, DBS signals tend to be affected by thunderstorms.

Like cable systems, DTV companies are preparing for the digital age by upgrading their set-top converter boxes to provide Internet access, e-commerce, and interactive TV to their subscribers. EchoStar, for example, has invested $50 million in iSKY Inc., a plan that offers two-way, high-speed Internet service and hundreds of TV channels.

 FEEDBACK

Measuring TV Viewing

This section will examine how the ratings for network TV shows are compiled and how ratings are gathered for local stations.

Network Ratings Nielsen Media Research, serving the United States and Canada, provides the networks with audience data through its Nielsen Television Index (NTI). To compile these ratings, Nielsen uses a device called a People Meter, introduced in the late 1980s. The People Meter consists of an apparatus about the size of a clock radio that sits on top of a TV set and a handheld device that resembles a TV remote-control unit. Demographic data are gathered from each household member and then each is assigned a number. While they are watching TV, each family member is supposed to periodically punch in his or her number on the handheld device to indicate viewing. People Meters can be used to tabulate all viewing—network, syndicated shows, and cable—and can even tabulate VCR playbacks. There are about 5,000 households in the Nielsen People Meter sample, and usable data are obtained from more than 90 percent of the meters. The sample is replaced every two years. The People Meter service is not cheap. Networks pay millions of dollars annually for the service.

Nielsen is also testing other systems. The most ambitious plan uses a passive meter and remote image recognition. Families agreeing to participate in this arrangement will be photographed and their facial features stored digitally in a black box atop the TV. At prearranged intervals, a tiny camera located in the black box takes a picture of a 120-degree arc in front of the TV and matches the faces of anyone watching the set with the faces stored in its memory.

Local-Market TV Ratings Nielsen surveys more than 200 markets in the United States at least four times a year, using a combination of the diary and electronic meter techniques. A computer selects phone numbers at random from all telephone directories in the area. The households selected into the sample are asked to keep a diary record of their television viewing.

Households that agree to participate receive one diary for every working TV in the household. The diary provides a space for entering the viewing of the head of the household as well as other family members or visitors. Participants are asked to record their viewing every quarter hour. In addition, the respondents are asked to record the sex and age of all those who are watching. At the back of the diary are questions concerning family size, the city where the household is located, and whether the family subscribes to cable. Diaries are kept for seven days and then returned to the ratings company. Nielsen reports that it is able to use approximately 50 to 55 percent of all the diaries they send out.

In about 50 markets, Nielsen has electronic meters that record any time a sample household's TV is turned on or off and what channel is viewed. The meters also record VCR usage. Data from this sample are compiled overnight and sent to subscribers early the next morning. These local meter data are augmented by information from the diary sample.

■ Television Ratings

Television viewing data for TV are reported essentially the same way as for radio. The following formula is used to calculate the **rating** for a TV program in a local market:

$$\text{Rating} = \frac{\text{Number of households watching a program}}{\text{Number of TV HH}}$$

where "TV HH" equals the number of households in a given market equipped with television.

Similarly, the **share of the audience** is found by using the following formula:

$$\text{Share of audience} = \frac{\text{Number of households watching a program}}{\text{Number of HUT}}$$

where "HUT" equals the number of households using (watching) television at a particular time.

Figure 10–4 reproduces a sample page from a local Nielsen ratings book. As can be seen, Nielsen reports shares, ratings, and an estimate of the number of people in the audience in various demographic categories for different areas in the market.

Four times every year (February, May, July, and November), Nielsen conducts a "sweep" period during which every local television market in the entire country is measured. Local stations rely on these ratings to set their advertising rates. Naturally enough, affiliated stations pressure the networks for special programming that will attract large audiences. All three networks generally go along with the affiliates' desires. As a result, blockbuster movies and specials are scheduled in competing time slots, leaving many viewers to wonder why all the good programs on TV always come at once.

Determining the Accuracy of Ratings Because the numbers in the rating books are the basis for spending vast amounts of money, it is important that they be as accurate and reliable as possible. During the early 1960s, in the wake of the quiz show and payola scandals, Congress took a close look at the broadcasting industry. In response to one congressional committee's criticism of audience-measurement techniques, advertising and broadcasting leaders founded the Electronic Media Ratings Council (EMRC). The task of the EMRC is basically threefold. It monitors, audits, and accredits broadcast measurement services. The council monitors performance of ratings companies by making sure that reported results meet the

Figure 10–4

Sample Page from a Nielsen TV Ratings Book

CHARLESTON, SC WK1 11/04-11/10 WK2 11/11-11/17 WK3 11/18-11/24 WK4 11/25-12/01

METRO HH		TUESDAY 7:30PM - 9:30PM		DMA HOUSEHOLD									DMA RATINGS																										
				RATINGS WEEKS				MULTI-WEEK AVG		SHARE TREND			PERSONS											WOMEN							MEN						TNS	CHILD	
RTG	SHR	STATION	PROGRAM	1	2	3	4	RTG	SHR	MAY '99	FEB '99	NOV '98	2+	18+	12-24	12-34	18-34	18-49	21-49	25-54	35+	35-64	50+	18+	12-24	18-34	18-49	25-49	25-54	WKG	18+	18-34	18-49	21-49	25-49	25-54	12-17	2-11	6-11
1	2			3	4	5	6	7	8	11	12	13	15	16	17	18	19	20	21	22	23	24	25	26	27	28	29	31	32	34	35	36	37	38	39	40	41	42	43
5			*R.S.E. THRESHOLDS 25+%*	*14*	*14*	*14*	*14*	*4*					*3*	*3*	*11*	*9*	*9*	*6*	*6*	*5*	*4*	*5*	*4*	*4*	*16*	*16*	*7*	*9*	*7*	*7*	*5*	*17*	*8*	*9*	*9*	*8*	*24*	*18*	*24*
1			*(1 S.E.) 4 WK AVG 50+%*	*4*	*4*	*4*	*4*	*1*					*1*	*1*	*3*	*2*	*2*	*1*	*2*	*1*	*1*	*1*	*1*	*1*	*4*	*4*	*2*	*2*	*2*	*2*	*1*	*5*	*2*	*2*	*3*	*2*	*7*	*5*	*7*
		7:30PM																																					
15	27	WCBD	JEOPARDY	9	12	18	19	15	26	24X	27	24	10	11	7	7	7	7	7	9	14	11	20	13	7	6	7	7	9	10	9	8	7	8	8	8	6	4	5
6	12	WCIV	HOLLYWD SQUARS	9	5	5	4	6	10	11X	13	14	4	4	6	6	4	4	4	4	3	3	2	4	3	5	5	5	5	4	3	4	4	4	4	4	9	2	2
9	16	WCSC	FRASIER	8	12	5	7	8	14	18	16	18	5	6	1	4	4	6	6	7	6	7	6	6	1	5	6	7	8	7	6	4	6	6	7	7	2	2	3
<<		WITV	FRONTRS-MEDCNE	<<	1	<<	<<	<<		2	2	2											1																
2	4	WMMP	STAR TREK VYGR	2	1	<<	3	2	3		1	1	1	1	1			1	1	1	1	2	1	1	1	1	1			1	1		1	1	1	2	1		
6	11	WTAT	MARTIN	8	6	7	3	6	11	13X	6	10	5	4	11	8	5	4	5	4	3	3	2	5	12	7	6	4	5	6	3	4	3	4	3	3	15	5	6
1	2	ABLN	DREW CAREY	1	1	1	<<	1	2	NR	NR	NR	1		2	2	1	1	1	1					3	1	1	1	1	1		1	1	1	1	1	4	1	1
56			HUT/PUT/TOTALS*	57	62	48	56	56		52	59	52	42	42	40	39	37	38	41	42	44	43	49	47	42	44	42	42	45	45	36	30	35	37	37	38	47	40	44
		8:00PM																																					
8	15	WCBD	JUST SHOOT-NBC	5	8	8	8	7	13	14	10	12	5	5	7	7	7	6	7	6	4	5	3	6	10	8	7	7	6	6	4	5	6	6	7	6	9	1	1
8	14	WCIV	AVG. ALL WKS	6	6	14	1	7	12	16	15	14	5	5	3	4	4	4	5	6	5	5	6	5	3	4	4	4	6	3	5	5	5	5	5	6	4	6	8
5	10		SPIN CITY-ABC	6	6		1	4	8				3	3	2	3	4	3	3	3	2	2	3	3	1	3	2	2	3	2	3	6	3	3	3	3	2	2	3
15	29		MILLNR-TU11/23			14		14	29				12	12		6	6	9	10	13	15	16	17	12			9				12		9	10					
13	25	WCSC	JAG-CBS	16	12	13	10	13	23	21X	24	22	8	10	4	4	4	7	7	9	13	12	16	10	5	4	7	7	7	8	10	3	7	8	9	10	5	2	1
2	3	WITV	AVG. ALL WKS	1	2	1	3	2	3	2	2	4	1	1	1			1	1	1	2	1	1	1	1		1	1	1	1	1		1	1	1	1	1		
2	3		S.C. REPORTS	1				1	2				1	1				1	1	1	1	1	1								2		1	1					
1	2		INTMTE STRANGR		2	1		1	2				1	1	1			1	1	1	1	1	1	1	1		1	1	1	1	1		1	1	1	1	2		
3	7		CHRSTMS-VIENNA				3	3	6				1	1		1		1	1	1	2	3	2	2			2				1		1	1					
<<		WMMP	AVG. ALL WKS	<<	<<	<<	1	<<		9	5	9			1																						1		1
<<			SHASTA MCN-UPN	<<	<<	<<		<<																															
1	3		WWF GRT HT-UPN				1	1	2				1			1																							
3	6	WTAT	AVG. ALL WKS	2	5	1	3	3	5	7	9	9	2	2	3	3	3	3	3	2	2	2	1	3	4	3	3	3	3	4	1	2	2	2	2	1	3	1	2

minimum standards of performance set up by the EMRC. Audits are performed on a continuing basis. If the ratings company passes the audit, it is accredited and is allowed to display the EMRC's seal of approval on its ratings reports.

Despite the EMRC's work, broadcast ratings are still subject to widespread criticism. One common complaint, voiced by many who evidently do not understand the statistical theory that underlies sampling, is directed at Nielsen's national survey. How can a sample of only 5,000 homes, these critics ask, accurately reflect the viewing of 100 million television households? In actuality, this sample size will generate tolerably accurate results within a specified margin of error. Other criticisms, however, deserve closer attention.

First, it is possible that the type of person who agrees to participate may have viewing habits different from those of the viewer who declines to participate. Second, in the case of the Nielsen reports (based on about 55 percent of the diaries sent out), it is possible that "returners" behave differently from "nonreturners." Third, people who know that their viewing is being measured may change their behavior. Fourth, ratings companies admit that they have a problem measuring the viewing of certain groups. For example, minorities—particularly blacks and Hispanics—may be underrepresented in the ratings companies' samples. Last, the stations that are being measured can distort the measurement process by engaging in contests and special promotions or by running unusual or sensational programs in an attempt to "hype" the ratings. The distinction between hype and legitimate programming, however, is somewhat fuzzy. Clearly, the ratings aren't perfect. Nonetheless, despite all their flaws, they present useful information at an affordable price to advertisers and to the television industry. As long as the United States has a commercial broadcasting system, some form of the ratings will always be around.

C R I T I C A L / C U L T U R A L   I S S U E S

Was Dan Quayle Right? Television, Politics, and American Values

During the 1992 presidential campaign, Vice President Dan Quayle criticized the TV sitcom "Murphy Brown" because the title character minimized the moral consequences of having a child out of wedlock. Quayle's criticism was based on the notion that long-term exposure to television programs and other media content shapes our sense of social reality and influences what our culture holds to be important or rightful. Many in the entertainment industry dismiss this reasoning. They argue that the media in general, and TV in particular, are not that powerful and portray far more conventional than aberrant behavior.

One problem in this controversy is its political connection. Not surprisingly, any assertion made by a politician is sometimes dismissed as merely an attempt to get votes. Further, the debate is sometimes shifted to tangential issues. Quayle, for example, was lampooned by many because he was criticizing a sitcom character. The American people, it was argued, were too smart to have their values shaped by a fictional character. Quayle was in an ideological and cultural dispute that was over his head.

The same debate occurred four years later. One of the key phrases of Bob Dole's unsuccessful presidential campaign was "family values." Dole admonished the entertainment industry for its emphasis on content that undermines America's standards and corrupts culture. He went on to charge that popular culture ridicules family values by bombarding society, particularly children, with

(Continued)

messages that glorify casual violence and casual sex. The entertainment industry, said Dole, hides behind the banner of free speech and artistic freedom and too often put profits ahead of decency.

Hollywood rejected Dole's charges. Many in the creative community pointed out that there were far more potent causes of the breakdown in American society than television. Dole's indictments of the industry were dismissed as conservative political rhetoric.

The debate about television and its influence on American values surfaced again in the 2000 election campaign, and this time, both sides seemed to agree about the power of the entertainment industry to shape values. Surprisingly, the most outspoken censure came from the Democratic side. Senator Joseph Lieberman, the Democratic nominee for vice president, had been an outspoken critic of gratuitous sex and violence on TV. Lieberman once accused entertainment executives of encouraging a "culture of carnage." The senator was one of the cosponsors of the bill that eventually mandated the installation of the V-chip in TV sets. Tipper Gore, wife of Vice President Al Gore, had campaigned against raunchy lyrics in rock songs. It sounded as though both Lieberman and Gore had decided that Dan Quayle had a point.

Did the entertainment industry feel threatened by these accusations? Did it attempt to rebut them and work against Gore and Lieberman's election? Just the opposite. The entertainment industry donated about $10 million to get them elected. Moreover, during the course of the campaign, Lieberman toned down some of his criticisms of the industry. Once again, the political context surrounding the question distracted attention from the core issues. Many in the industry wrote off Lieberman's contentions as just more political rhetoric.

Research, as discussed in Chapter 18, suggests that repeated exposure to the same media portrayals *can* have an impact (the cultivation effect) and that media are important in the socialization process. And, although television ranks below parents and peers and other forces when it comes to socialization, the media can still play an important role. Further, young people watch a lot of television and see many programs, popular and not so popular, that portray a wide range of values.

Before he became a media star, Ben Stein (*Ferris Beuller*, "Win Ben Stein's Money," and many commercials) wrote a book entitled *The View from Sunset Boulevard*, and subtitled "America as Brought to You by the People Who Make Television." Stein's thesis was that the programs on television don't reflect real life because they are put together by a small community of creative people who live in southern California with an idiosyncratic view of the world as shaped by their particular subculture. For example, in the TV world, business is often portrayed negatively and many crimes are committed by greedy businesspeople; small towns are shown as backward; poor people are portrayed as heroic or as innocent victims of society; alternative lifestyles are portrayed positively; and so on. Stein's book raises an interesting question about the portrayal of America's values in the media: Which Americans' values are to be shown? The values of people living in the Northeast, in Kansas, in Indiana, on Sunset Boulevard? Despite the glib charges of politicians and the predictable response of the industry, the issue of television's impact on cultural values is a complicated one that deserves serious consideration.

1. Why might the issue of TV and American values pop up in so many presidential elections?

2. To what extent should entertainment content be protected by the First Amendment?

3. This essay focuses on entertainment TV—to what extent should we also be concerned about the impact of TV news and newsmagazines? Why?

■ Questionnaires, Concept Testing, and Pilot Testing

In addition to ratings, the TV networks gather three special types of feedback from the audience to help them predict what television shows will be popular with viewers. The first kind of research consists of questionnaires that attempt to measure audience tastes, opinions, and beliefs. Perhaps as many as 100,000 people per year are questioned in person or over the phone as the networks try to identify what situations and topics might be acceptable for programs.

A second form is called **concept testing.** In concept testing, a one- or two-paragraph description of an idea for a new series is presented to a sample of viewers, who are asked for their reactions. Show ideas that do well in concept testing have an increased chance of getting on the air.

The third form is **pilot testing,** which consists of placing a group of viewers in a special test theater and showing them an entire program. The audience usually sits in chairs equipped with dials or buttons that are used to indicate the degree to which audience members like or dislike what is shown. For example, the audience might be told to press a green button when they see something on screen that they like and a red button when they see something they dislike.

The networks currently test pilots on cable TV systems since that is the closest thing to real TV viewing. In a cable test, several hundred cable subscribers in a certain community are telephoned and are asked to participate in the test. They watch the show on an unused channel of their cable system and then respond by telephone to a questionnaire that asks them about plot, character, relationship, and so on.

■ Television Audiences

The TV set has become firmly entrenched in the life of Americans. As of 2000, some 99 percent of all homes in the country had at least one working television set. About 75 percent had more than one. Cable television had more than 68 million subscribers in 2000, roughly 68 percent of all TV households.

The set in the average household is on for about seven hours a day, with each individual watching an average of more than three hours daily. The TV audience changes throughout the day, steadily growing from 7 A.M. until it reaches a peak from 8 to 11 P.M., Eastern Standard Time. After 11 P.M., the audience drops off dramatically. Figure 10–5 details this pattern of audience viewing.

Not surprisingly, the television audience is largest during the winter months and smallest during July and August, when people spend more time outdoors. The composition of the television audience changes during the day. Preschoolers

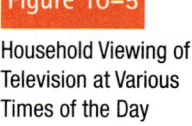

Figure 10–5

Household Viewing of Television at Various Times of the Day

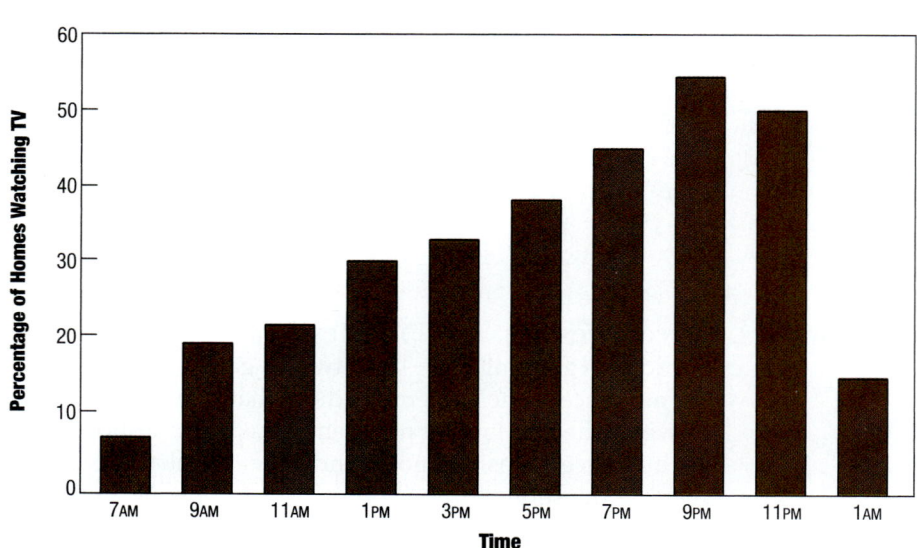

and females tend to predominate during the daytime hours from Monday to Friday. On Saturday mornings, most of the audience is under 13. Prime time is dominated by those in the 18- to 49-year-old age group.

Various demographic factors, such as age, sex, social class, and education, affect viewership. For example, teenagers watch the least. People in low-income homes generally watch more television than their middle-income counterparts. People with more education tend to watch less, and women watch more often than men. Cable subscribers are younger, have more children, and are more affluent than the average viewer. They also are dissatisfied with traditional television and want more program variety. Subscribers to the pay-cable channels have younger heads of households, are more affluent, and watch more TV than families in noncable homes.

THE TELEVISION INDUSTRY

Someone hunting for a job in TV quickly discovers that it's a relatively small industry. According to recent figures provided by the FCC, about 110,000 people are employed in commercial TV; 100,000 in CATV; 10,000 in noncommercial television; and about 16,000 at TV networks.

In any given year, probably 5,000 to 10,000 people are hired by the TV industry. Many of these people are replacing employees who have retired or gone on to other careers, while others are filling newly created positions. Also, in any given year, about 15,000 to 20,000 people are looking for TV jobs. Speaking conservatively, we can say that there are at least two people looking for each available position. In some areas of television, especially for the so-called glamour jobs (TV reporter, network page, on-camera host for an interview show, series writer), the competition will be much more intense.

■ Entry-Level Positions

Despite this competition, individuals who are skilled, intelligent, and persistent are likely to be successful in finding jobs. Here are some general hints on job hunting in TV:

1. *Think small.* As in radio, small-market TV stations offer more employment potential than larger-market stations. Moreover, at a small station, you have a chance to do more and learn more than you might at a larger station.

2. *Don't be afraid to start at the bottom.* Once you get in, it is easier to move upward into a position that might be more to your liking. Many successful people in TV started in the mailroom, secretarial pool, or shipping department.

3. *Be prepared to move.* Your first job will probably not be a lifetime commitment. Frequently, the road to advancement in TV consists of moving about and up—from a small station to a large station, from an independent station to a network affiliate, from the station to the network.

■ Upward Mobility

Those interested in producing TV shows might consider looking for jobs as camera operator, floor manager (the person who gives cues to the talent and makes sure everything in the studio goes smoothly during the telecast), or production assistant (a person who handles all the odd jobs that need to be done during a show). From there you might progress upward to become an assistant director or assistant producer or perhaps a writer. Eventually, you would hope to become a full-fledged director or producer.

If you are interested in being an on-camera news reporter, your best bet might be to find a general reporting job at a small station. If your interests lie behind the camera, you can start out as a news writer or news researcher or even a camera-person or tape editor. Most people interested in performing before the camera generally stay in that capacity. Upward mobility for general-assignment reporters consists of moving into the anchor position. For anchors, it consists of moving to bigger and more lucrative markets. For those behind the scenes, the first move up will probably be to the assistant news director slot and then on to the news director position.

Sales is the division that offers the most upward mobility. Most stations prefer people who have had some experience in selling (many move from radio sales to TV sales). Once a salesperson is established, however, the monetary rewards can be substantial. Salespeople advance their careers by moving to larger markets or by moving up to the sales manager position.

The highest level a person can reach at the local level is the general manager's position. In the past, most general managers have come from the sales department. This trend is likely to continue, but it is also probable that more people who started off in the news departments move into management, since news is becoming more of a moneymaker.

Other Opportunities

A television station is not the only place to look for employment. As cable provides more local programming and adds more channels, the industry will need more people in promotion, publicity, performance, marketing, and community relations. Allied with cable are the pay-TV services (HBO, Showtime, etc.). These organizations will also need skilled personnel.

Another emerging employment source is home video. The production of prerecorded cassettes and videodisks represents another area with opportunities. In addition, many large companies, such as IBM and Microsoft, use TV to produce employee training programs and to fill other internal communication needs. Although not as visible as some other parts of the industry, this is an important source of employment for a large number of people.

Finally, as the connection between television and the Internet becomes stronger, job opportunities for people with Internet skills will increase. Almost all TV stations, networks, cable systems, and cable networks need people to maintain their related websites. Producers of TV shows are looking for people who can design web content that promotes the program. In short, a knowledge of web page construction and production will be increasingly helpful for a career in TV.

■ MAIN POINTS

- Electronic television developed during the 1930s. After World War II, it quickly grew in popularity and replaced radio as the main information and entertainment medium.

- The three networks—NBC, CBS, and ABC—dominated early TV. Live drama, variety, and quiz and game shows were popular during the 1950s.

- Television matured in the 1960s and its content became more professional. The public television network began in 1967. Cable TV grew slowly during this decade.

- The 1970s saw TV programs criticized for excessive violence. The Prime-Time Access Rule helped companies that syndicated TV programs.

- In the 1980s and 1990s, the three traditional TV nets lost viewers to cable and to VCRs. The Fox network became a major competitor.

- The Telecommunications Act of 1996 had a significant impact on TV-station ownership and also introduced program content ratings. Rules for the eventual conversion to digital TV were announced in 1997.

- Changing from analog to digital signals will mean better pictures and sound. Consumers will have to buy a new TV set or a converter to receive the new signals. TV stations may use the digital signal to broadcast high-definition television or several lower-definition programs.

- TV is universal, dominant, and expensive. Its audience is currently fragmenting into smaller segments.

- The broadcast TV industry consists of program suppliers, distributors, and local stations.

- Big conglomerates own the major TV networks, and large group owners control most of the stations in large markets.

- Public broadcasting relies less on tax revenues and more on private sources of funding.

- Cable TV had reached maturity by the late 1990s and was facing problems associated with its rapid growth. The Telecommunications Act of 1996 permitted cable and phone companies to compete with one another.

- The costs and revenues connected with a cable system are different from those of a broadcast station.

- Home video is dominated by the major motion picture studios. Retailers are concerned about the eventual impact of direct broadcast satellite systems (DBS) on their business.

- DBS systems grew more slowly than expected, but their overall impact on the industry has yet to be determined.

- The Nielsen company compiles both network and local-station television ratings.

■ QUESTIONS FOR REVIEW

1. What are the defining features of the TV medium?
2. What are some of the advantages of being an affiliate of a major TV network?
3. Who owns the TV networks?
4. Trace the evolution of U.S. noncommercial TV programming.
5. What companies control the cable TV industry?
6. How has revenue sharing changed the home video industry?
7. Compare and contrast Nielsen's method of measuring network TV viewers with its technique for measuring local-market TV viewing.

■ QUESTIONS FOR CRITICAL THINKING

1. What does "convergence" mean? How will it change the TV industry? Will these changes be for the better?

2. What should be the goal of public television? Should the government support public broadcasting?

3. Large companies control both the broadcast and cable television industries. What are some of the good points and bad points of large corporate ownership?

4. The major broadcast networks have been losing viewers for the past two decades or so. Will they still be around 10 to 15 years from now? Why or why not?

5. In addition to the Nielsen People Meter, what are some ways that television viewing can be measured?

■ KEY TERMS

Public Broadcasting Act of 1967 (p. 262)
Prime-Time Access Rule (p. 262)
time shifting (p. 264)
digital television (DTV) (p. 266)
commercial television (p. 268)
noncommercial television (p. 268)
VHF (p. 271)

UHF (p. 271)
independents (p. 271)
pilot (p. 275)
head end (p. 284)
distribution system (p. 284)
house drop (p. 284)
carriage fee (p. 286)

revenue sharing (p. 288)
direct broadcast satellite (DBS) (p. 288)
rating (p. 290)
share of the audience (p. 291)
concept testing (p. 294)
pilot testing (p. 294)

■ SUGGESTIONS FOR FURTHER READING

The following books contain more information about the concepts and topics discussed in this chapter.

Barnouw, Erik. *Tube of Plenty.* New York: Oxford, 1990.

Brinkley, Joel. *Defining Vision: The Battle for the Future of Television.* New York: Harcourt Brace, 1997.

Dominick, Joseph, Barry Sherman, and Fritz Messere. *Broadcasting/Cable and Beyond,* 4th ed. New York: McGraw-Hill, 2000.

Newcomb, Horace. *Television: The Critical View.* New York: Oxford, 2000.

Seiter, Ellen. *Television and New Media Audiences.* New York: Clarendon Press, 1998.

Sterling, Christopher, and John Kittross. *Stay Tuned: A Concise History of American Broadcasting.* Belmont, CA: Wadsworth, 1990.

Van Tassel, Joan. *Digital Television: Advanced TV Systems.* Woburn, MA: Focal Press, 2000.

Walker, James, and Douglas Ferguson. *The Broadcast Television Industry.* Needham Heights, MA: Allyn and Bacon, 2000.

■ SURFING THE INTERNET

http://abc.go.com/primetime/drewcarey/drew_home.html
Drew Carey's home page. An offbeat, interactive site that offers several features that complement the TV show. Try taking the guided tour of Drew's wallet.

www.historychannel.com/
The History Channel's home page has more about history than it does about its cable network, but it's got good examples of interactivity and streaming video.

www.mtr.org/
Those interested in the history of television should visit the home page of the Museum of Television and Radio. Site contains a guided tour of the museum's New York and Los Angeles locations.

www.mtv.com
MTV online. Detailed site that contains links to just about everything on MTV.

www.netreach.net/~kaufman/
The "Kill Your Television" home page. If you don't like TV, this is the site for you. Includes a page that suggests things to do instead of watching TV.

www.nielsenmedia.com
Information about Nielsen Media Research, the firm that rates TV programs. Check out the Ratings 101 link for a basic description of how the TV audience is measured.

CHAPTER 11

The Internet and the World Wide Web

Halfway, Oregon, is a town of about 350 people situated in the eastern part of the state near the Idaho border. On January 19, 2000, the residents of the town voted to change its name to Half.com, the first "dot-com" city in the world. They were persuaded to make this change by the founders of Half.com, a new Internet company specializing in selling secondhand consumer products. As part of the deal, the Internet company provided a new municipal website and 20 computers for the local elementary school, gave residents stock options in the company, and opened a telephone customer service center in the town that would provide new jobs.

Well, things were going along pretty well for Half.com, Oregon, until June 2000, when Half.com (the company, not the town) was acquired by eBay, the online auction site. Apparently not wanting to be called Ebay, Oregon, the town's residents voted to return to their original name of Halfway.

What's in a name? Thanks to a promotion started by a new dot.com company, this Oregon town changed its name, temporarily at least, to Half.com. *(BBC Online)*

The continuing saga of Half.com (the town, not the company) is only one of the many consequences of the phenomenal growth of the Internet and the World Wide Web. "Dot-com" became a common expression in the language as hundreds of dot-com businesses rushed to the web, with varying degrees of success. To gain public visibility, many Internet business sites turned to promotional stunts (such as renaming a town) and expensive advertising. And, all the while, more and more people were using the web, until it has now become firmly embedded in the nation's communication repertoire. It's hard to imagine how we ever got along without e-mail, e-commerce, e-learning, e-dating, and eBay.

This chapter takes a look at how the computer became a mass communication medium, as well as at the development of the Internet, the coming of broadband, the new Internet economy, online audiences, feedback, and the legal and social implications of this new medium.

A BRIEF HISTORY OF THE COMPUTER

The earliest versions of the computer were basically adding machines, designed to take the drudgery out of repetitive arithmetical calculations. Back in the 17th century, French mathematician and philosopher Blaise Pascal (a modern computer language was named for him) created the *arithmatique,* a machine the size of a shoebox filled with interconnected 10-toothed wheels that could add numbers up to 1 million. A few decades later, the German mathematician Gottfried Wilhelm von Leibniz explored the subject of binary arithmetic, a system with just two possible values, 0 and 1. The binary system is the one used by modern computers.

During the 19th century, English inventor Charles Babbage, working with Augusta Ada Byron, the daughter of Lord Byron, the English poet, worked out plans for an "analytical engine," a steam-powered device about the size of a football field, that would quickly perform complicated mathematical operations. The existing technology, however, was not sufficient to build this machine and after 19 years of trying, Babbage and Byron gave up.

In America, Herman Hollerith developed a tabulating machine to help process data collected in the census of 1880. His machine used punched cards and electrical circuits to do calculations and worked so well that businesses all over the country clamored for it, prompting him to start his own company, International Business Machines (IBM).

In 1940, a Harvard University mathematician, Howard Aiken, made the next major breakthrough when he created a digital computer—one that worked with binary numbers, 0 and 1, or in Aiken's case, switch closed or switch open. Aiken's computer, the Mark I, was 50 feet long, 8 feet tall, and had 750,000 parts. When it was running, it sounded like thousands of knitting needles clicking together. A few years later, researchers at the University of Pennsylvania constructed the first

ENIAC, completed in the late 1940s, was the world's first all-electronic computer. The device took up most of the space in a good-sized room. ENIAC is a far cry from today's laptop computers. *(Courtesy Moore School Computer Museum)*

all-electronic computer, ENIAC. Although much faster than any previous mechanical computer, ENIAC's size was a drawback—it stood two stories tall, weighed 30 tons, and used about 18,000 vacuum tubes.

The invention of the transistor in the 1950s led to new electronic computers that were smaller, cheaper, and easier to maintain. Integrated circuits made it possible for many transistors to be embedded in a tiny silicon chip, which paved the way for the microprocessor. These advances opened up new markets for computer manufacturers. In the late 1970s, personal computers (PCs), using packaged software, appeared in new computer stores. Designed for home use, these computers were used primarily for word processing, financial management, and game playing.

A few years later, developments in hardware and software expanded the communication function of the computer. The **modem,** from *mod*ulate and *dem*odulate, enabled PCs to converse with one another and with larger computers located in other places over telephone lines. New communications software facilitated the development of local area networks (LANs), which linked several computers into a network. As miniaturization continued, laptop computers and wireless modems became more common.

The 1990s saw an explosion in computer communication. (One scholar coined the word "compucation" to describe this new process but it hasn't caught on.) Every day more than 500 million pieces of electronic mail (e-mail) are carried over the Internet. Companies specializing in providing online information and entertainment had 20 million subscribers. Every night thousands of individuals log on to computerized chat lines, check bulletin boards, visit websites, shop, read the news, play trivia and other games, engage in online conferences, and transfer information files. Perhaps the biggest reason for this surge in online communication has been the development of the Internet.

THE INTERNET

The Internet is a network of computer networks. You can think of it as a system that combines computers from all over the world into one big computer that you can operate from your own PC. Some computers are run by government agencies (like the National Aeronautics and Space Administration), some are run by universities, some by libraries, some by school systems, some by businesses, and so on. The connections between these networks can be ordinary phone lines, microwaves, optical fibers, or wires built specially for this purpose. A related example might be the phone system. When you call somebody in Cleveland, the call is routed through several different phone networks in different parts of the country. You really don't care what route it takes or what companies handle it as long as your call gets there. So, too, with the Internet. When you search for information, send mail, or chat online, several different networks may handle your messages. Just as there's no one phone company, there's also no one Internet company.

The Internet's seemingly chaotic structure arose from its somewhat fractured history. Maybe a little background will help.

From ARPANET to Internet

Back in the early 1970s, when the cold war was still raging, the U.S. Department of Defense was concerned about the vulnerability of its computer network to nuclear attack. The Pentagon did not want to lose all its computing and communication ability because of one well-placed atomic bomb. Consequently, defense computer experts decentralized the whole system by creating an interconnected web of computer networks. The net was designed so that every computer could talk to every other computer. Information was bundled in a packet, called an Internet Protocol packet, which contained the destination address of the target computer. The computers themselves then figured out how to send the packet. Thus, if one portion of the network happened to be disabled, the rest of the network could still function normally. The system that the Pentagon eventually developed was called ARPANET.

At about the same time, companies developed software that allowed computers to be linked to local area networks (LANs) that also contained the Internet Protocol programs. Not surprisingly, many of these LANs were also connected to ARPANET, causing the network to grow even more.

The users of this early network were primarily scientists and computer experts, and most observers thought it would continue to be of interest only to high-tech types. (The network was once uncharitably labeled a "Disneyland for geeks.") In the late 1980s, however, the National Science Foundation, whose own network was already connected to the net, created supercomputing centers at U.S. universities. Since they were so expensive, only five could be built. This meant that they had to be shared and interconnected. The ARPANET seemed like the obvious choice for interconnection, but there were too many problems involved. Instead, the National Science Foundation built its own system using the Internet Protocol and hooked together chains of regional networks that were eventually linked to a supercomputer. Thus the Internet was born.

Now that students, scientists, government workers, and others had access to supercomputers, the amount of information at their disposal increased tremendously. The Internet also served as a communications link that enabled scientists from all over the country to share data. Doctors, lawyers, journalists, authors, and business owners realized the potential of the net, and traffic increased.

The Internet was still used by only a small fraction of computer owners. Two developments, however, contributed to a meteoric rise in the Internet's popularity. The first was the development of the World Wide Web (WWW, or web) in 1990. Engineers working at a physics laboratory in Switzerland created an interconnected set of computers on the net that all used the same communications program. This communications program took advantage of **hypertext,** a navigational tool that linked one electronic document, either text or graphics, with another, thus creating a virtual web of pages. The web started off as an electronic information resource for scientists but was quickly discovered and utilized by the entire Internet community. Any organization or individual could create a page on the web as long as the person or organization used the communication rules developed in Switzerland. It wasn't long before conventional media companies, businesses, organizations, and individuals got involved with the web. By 1998, it was estimated that there were more than a million websites in operation.

The second development made it easier for consumers to find what they were looking for on the web. This happened in 1993 with the creation of user-friendly navigation tools that helped further spur the growth of the World Wide Web. The first of these **browsers,** called Mosaic, was able to retrieve data, determine what it was, and configure it for display. Mosaic created a graphical display for users that simplified navigating the Internet. In 1994, one of the developers of Mosaic formed a commercial company that was eventually named Netscape Communications, whose web browser is one of the most popular.

At the end of 2000, there were 150 million host computers connected to the net. The number of households in the United States with Internet access topped 100 million. Obviously, the net has grown to be a powerful mass communication medium. It is no longer just a playground for geeks.

STRUCTURE AND FEATURES OF THE INTERNET

As mentioned earlier, the Internet is a global network of computer networks. In more technical terms, this means that a group of two or more networks is electronically connected and able to communicate with one another. Together, they act as a single network. For this to work, however, the computers have to speak a common language. The common language, called a **protocol** by computer programmers, that was developed for the Internet is called the TCP/IP protocol. TCP/IP stands for Transmission Control Protocol/Internet Protocol. It is actually a set of protocols that govern how data travel from one machine to another over networks. IP is sort of like the address on an envelope. It tells a computer where to send a particular message. TCP breaks up the information into packets that can be transmitted efficiently and reassembles them at their destination.

Figure 11–1 presents a schematic view of the Internet and some of its major elements. At the bottom of the diagram is the audience, the people who provide content for and access content from the Internet. They gain access to the Internet in one of two ways:

Figure 11–1

Structure of the Internet

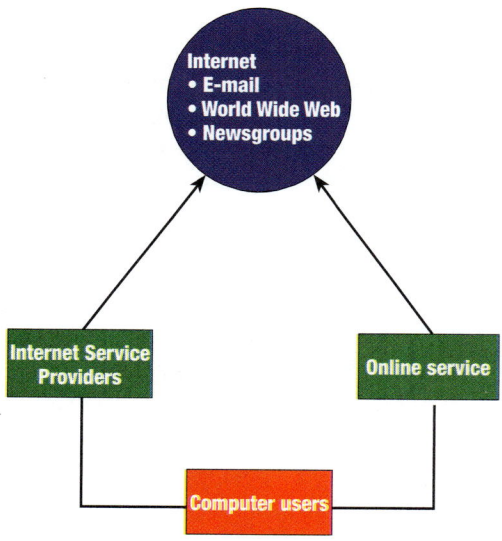

It's not surprising that the computer and the Internet have raised many new ethical questions. Computer experts at the Computer Ethics Institute, for example, have developed the Ten Commandments for Computer Ethics. The commandments are rather general and noncontroversial, such as "Thou shalt not use a computer to steal" and "Thou shalt not use a computer program for which you have not paid." There are other areas, however, where the issues are not so clear.

One such area involves anonymity. In the offline world, a person has to make an extra effort to remain anonymous. Hiding your true identity might require an unlisted phone number, a fake ID, and a disguise. On the Internet, however, anonymity is the default condition. User names generally are generic and say little about the true identity of the user. A person has to make an extra effort to establish his or her *real* identity.

Anonymity is not necessarily bad. For example, it disguises differences in race, sex, age, and physical appearance. To the extent that these items interfere with fairness, anonymity may serve as an equalizer. Further, people may be encouraged to reveal their true feelings if they know their identity will not be revealed. Battered spouses, for instance, might be better able to ask for help with their problem.

Conversely, anonymity creates problems. People are more apt to behave in undesirable ways when they act anonymously. They may send inflammatory or racist messages, post offensive material, and snoop into the affairs of others. It is also easy for a person to claim to be someone he or she is not or to become multiple persons with multiple identities. The best illustration of this is the case of a man who pretended to be a woman and participated in an online discussion group that dealt with women's issues. Is such behavior ethical? What if the man used his online female persona to arrange a date between his true self and a woman in the group?

Anonymity can undermine trust. In the offline world, people establish a history of dealing with certain other people and can decide whether a person is to be trusted. This is far more difficult in the online world where the same person might have multiple identities or the same identity might be used by more than one person. You have trouble developing a history because you're never sure with whom you are dealing.

Are there ethical principles (see Chapter 16) that can be applied to anonymity on the net? One possibility is situational ethics. There may be some situations where no one expects others to reveal their true identities. Adult-oriented chat rooms, for example, might call for a high level of anonymity (where everybody assumes that everybody else may not be who they purport to be). On the other hand, it would be unethical to participate in a discussion group about the consequences of child abuse by falsely claiming to be an abuse victim. As the popularity of the net continues to grow, much more attention will be paid to issues such as these.

1. Through an Internet Service Provider (ISP), a company that connects a subscriber to the net and usually charges a fee. Many companies, including some local phone companies, function as ISPs.
2. Through a commercial online service, such as America Online or MSN.

These services discussed in more detail below provide both a link to the Internet as well as some exclusive features of their own. Once connected to the net, an individual can make use of a variety of services and tools for communication and information exchange. Some of the more important applications are e-mail, newsgroups, and the World Wide Web.

■ E-Mail

Millions of people are connected to the Internet, and you can send mail to one of them or to a lot of them. **E-mail** works on the client/server arrangement. To send and read e-mail, users (clients) must access another computer (the server), where their mailbox resides. E-mail messages are not limited to text. Attachments, such as graphics or spreadsheets, can also be sent.

E-mail is usually fast, cheap, and reliable. It is the most widely used Internet resource. In 2000, more than 6 trillion e-mail messages moved through the net.

E-mail is helpful, but it also has some drawbacks. It's not as formal as a printed letter, so there may be some tasks for which it is inappropriate (like telling someone he or she has been fired). Secondly, e-mail is not as private as a letter in an envelope. Your e-mail message may travel through several computers where other people might have access to it.

Third, there is the ever-present threat of **spam.** Spam, the electronic equivalent of junk mail, includes unsolicited offers touting get-rich-quick schemes, miracle cures, and other merchandise that clogs up people's e-mail boxes and takes time to erase. Finally, e-mail itself can cause traffic jams, particularly in the business setting. The novelty of the system has encouraged people to use it for communication that normally would not take place or that would ordinarily be done face-to-face. In many offices, e-mail has caused cocooning as workers e-mail people in the next cubicle or at the next desk. Memos that used to go to a few people now get sent to everybody, and every decision—no matter how small—gets circulated via e-mail. As a result, the average worker at a *Fortune* 500 company sends and receives about 180 messages every day, creating communication congestion in a major way. Finally, many viruses are spread by e-mail.

Newsgroups

Newsgroups are collections of electronic bulletin boards, arranged according to topic, where people can read and post messages. Some newsgroups are devoted to current events, but the "news" in "newsgroups" refers to topical discussion groups, not news in the traditional sense. The information or "articles" that make up the news are written by people interested in the topic. Others can read the articles and comment on them. The newsgroups exist on a special network called Usenet, one component of the Internet.

Newsgroup categories are organized in a systematic hierarchy that moves from the general to the specific. For example, two general categories of newsgroups end in the suffixes "alt" and "sci." One subtopic in one of the alt categories is "algebra," and a subtopic under that entry is "help." Looking at the messages on this board reveals that they are about how to solve various equations. Under the sci category is a listing for "materials" and another subtopic for "ceramics." This bulletin board contained many articles about the tiles on the space shuttle.

There are more than 3,000 different newsgroups, with topics ranging from the highly intellectual to the downright weird. Each newsgroup is made up of messages about the topic. If one or more people reply to a message, those messages are grouped into a thread. For example, suppose you were browsing through the Elvis newsgroup. You might come upon one message asking about details of Elvis's performances in Las Vegas. Six people might have replied to that message, creating a thread seven messages long.

World Wide Web

As mentioned earlier, the **World Wide Web (WWW)** is a network of information sources incorporating hypertext that allows the user to link one piece of information to another. Note that the web is part of the Internet; the two terms are not synonymous. The web is nonlinear. This means that the user does not have to follow a hierarchical path from one piece of information to another. A user can jump from the middle of one document into the middle of another. In addition, the web incorporates text, graphics, sound, and motion.

Some terminology might be useful at this point. The structure of the web is based on the web server, a computer connected to the Internet that allows the transfer of hypertext pages. One server can hold thousands of hypertext pages. A

Cab-riding New Yorkers who get caught in traffic jams will no longer be cut off from Internet access. Thanks to a deal between Yahoo! and a taxi company, a fleet of 10 taxis will be equipped with Palm VII handheld computers and wireless Internet access. Riders can send e-mail, shop online, check flight times, and make stock trades as they travel to the airport or to their next business appointment or as they wait for traffic to clear. A similar test program in San Francisco was warmly received.

The new cabs will be easy to spot. All will be painted with the purple Yahoo! logo. (Don't worry about the driver being distracted; the computer can be operated only from the backseat.)

website is a complete set of hypertext pages linked to each other that contains information about a common topic. A **web page** is a hypertext page that is contained within a website. The home page of a website is the entry or doorway to the site that might contain links to other pages or to various sections of the site.

The protocols for navigating the web assign each web page a uniform resource locator (URL) and an Internet address. URLs are structured as follows:

protocol://server.subdomain.top-level domain/directory/filename

For example, the URL for the McGraw-Hill Publishing Company's Communication page (which has links to the latest updates of this book and other interesting stuff) is

http://www.mhhe.com/catalogs/hss/comm

This means that the page is in the hypertext transfer protocol, the server is linked to the www, the subdomain name is "mhhe," the top-level domain is "com," the directory name is catalogs, the file name is "hss," and the specific file is "comm." Not every URL will have a directory and a file name.

The tremendous variety of sites and the motives behind them make it difficult to describe websites in general terms. There are sites maintained by big media companies, such as the *New York Times* and the Walt Disney Company, that are used to promote their traditional media products and to build an audience for the online content as well. Other companies, such as Nissan and the Miller Brewing Company, use their websites to advertise their product lines. Government agencies, such as the IRS and the Department of Agriculture, have websites to serve their constituents and to promote good public relations; professional organizations, such as the Association for Education in Journalism and Mass Communication, use their sites to share information among their members. Groups with special interests, such as the American Diabetes Association, use their sites to disseminate information. Professors set up pages where they post syllabi, readings, and other resources for their classes. Some sites are on the web to make a profit; they sell advertising or charge a subscription fee. Some sites are simply search engines that let the user search other sites.

Many websites function as **portals.** A portal, as the name suggests, is an entryway, the first page a person looks at before zooming off into the web. The strategy behind a successful portal is to offer visitors useful information, such as news headlines, weather, stock information, chat rooms, and bargains, so that he or she doesn't go looking for these items at some other site. The longer a person stays at the portal, the greater the chance that he or she might see some of the advertising on the site. Some of the best-known portals are those provided by Yahoo!, Excite, MSNBC, and Netscape.

Jerry Yang was born in Taiwan in 1968. When he was 10, his family moved to the United States and settled in San Jose, California, soon to become ground zero for the burgeoning computer industry. Yang was a straight-A student and eventually enrolled at Stanford, where he earned a bachelor's and a master's degree in electrical engineering in just four years. Yang had the misfortune to graduate in 1990 during a recession when job prospects were bleak. Consequently, he decided to stay at Stanford and study for a Ph.D.

While in the program, he met David Filo, another doctoral student in electrical engineering. The two shared a crowded trailer while they worked on their doctoral dissertations. Like a lot of other doctoral students, Yang and Filo found other things to do instead of writing their dissertations. Yang, for example, became interested in the new Internet phenomenon called the World Wide Web. At the time, the web was growing quickly, but it was difficult for users to find exactly what they were looking for. Yang decided to compile an index of his favorite websites and classify them into categories. He developed software to let users locate and edit material stored on the web. He called his creation "Jerry's Guide to the World Wide Web." Filo added his own classification of websites to Yang's, and the index was renamed "Jerry and David's Guide to the World Wide Web." They put their guide on the Stanford computer system and were surprised to find that their classification was popular with thousands of other web surfers. In fact, the number of people using their database was so large that Stanford's computer system crashed. The administration told Yang and Filo to move their operation off campus.

Consequently, the two graduate students decided to turn their hobby into a full-time business, planning to make money by selling advertising space on their guide. After much discussion, they came up with a new name: Yahoo (short for Yet Another Hierarchical Officious Oracle). The next step was to find someone with money to invest in their creation. A venture capitalist with an investment firm visited their offices, where he found empty pizza boxes strewn around, golf clubs in the corner, and no chairs. Nonetheless, his company invested $2 million in Yahoo! (It was a wise decision. Today that investment is worth billions.)

Yahoo! became phenomenally successful. In 2000, the site boasted more than 60 million users. Yang and Filo wound up heading a $39 billion company. The *San Jose Mercury News* recently compared Yang's idea to the work of Carolus Linnaeus, the 18th-century botanist whose classification system organized the natural world.

Success has not changed Jerry Wang. He still prefers to wear jeans and sneakers, the same outfit he wore in graduate school. On his business card, he lists his title as "Chief Yahoo!"

Finally, some web pages are published by individuals (many of you reading this may already have your own web page). The motivations behind publishing a personal web page are many. Here, for example, is a section of a promotional blurb put out by BellSouth in an effort to encourage people to use BellSouth's personal web page service: "You can tell your life story, share information about your favorite hobby, post your résumé for prospective employers to see, tell the world about your small business, or you can just be plain silly . . . Imagine being part of an international community where your thoughts, ideas, and messages can be shared with the world." Sounds pretty neat, but the reality of the situation is that the web can be thought of as an incredibly huge magazine stand with more than a billion magazines on display. Some are glossy and have great graphics. Others are drab and grey. Some are displayed on eye level; others are way off in some dusty corner. Some have well-known logos, while others are totally obscure. The point is this: There are many websites out there and only a few of them are easy to find. Getting your message noticed is not easy. A web page might give you the opportunity to put your message about your small business into a new communication channel, but there is no guarantee that your message will ever be noticed by a receiver. You might want to share your thoughts with the world by putting them on the web, but the world might not pay any attention.

How big is the World Wide Web? The answer is hard to pin down because the web grows every day. As of 2001, the search engine Google estimated that there were about 1.4 billion unique pages on the web. Some evidence of the huge recent growth of the web is seen in the fact that the majority of those pages are less than a year old. Finally, although it's called the *World Wide* Web, it's primarily a web for industrialized nations. About 85 percent of the pages on the web are in English, Japanese, French, or German.

Online Information Services

Started back in the 1980s, online information services provide information and entertainment to their subscribers. As of 2001, there were three major companies:

1. *AOL Time Warner.* The biggest online service, AOL also owns CompuServe, giving it a total of about 23 million subscribers. One of the factors behind the recent merger of AOL and Time Warner was the fact that AOL could use Time Warner's cable lines for high-speed Internet access.

2. *Microsoft Network (MSN).* With more than 2 million subscribers, MSN runs a distant second to AOL. It features the most up-to-date and glitzy graphics. In 2000 Microsoft launched a new software package designed to make its service more user-friendly.

3. *Prodigy.* After restructuring itself in 1996, this company offers Prodigy Internet to consumers and Prodigy Biz to small businesses. It has slightly more than a million subscribers.

All these companies are concerned about the future. Much of the content that used to be exclusive has now migrated to the net, where people can access it directly. To keep their subscriber base growing, the online companies offer special features, such as easy web navigation, content filters, instant messages, games, personal web pages, chat rooms, and exclusive content such as special live online interviews with newsmakers and celebrities.

The Internet, with the many features we've just discussed—including e-mail, newsgroups, the web, and online information services—is not without problems, however. Since there was no master plan for the expansion of the Internet, it just grew. As a result, it's often difficult to navigate. Unless you know how to get to your destination, things may be hard to find. Some have described using the Internet as trying to find your way across a big city without a map. You'll see lots of interesting stuff but you may never get to where you set out to go. As noted, computer experts and software developers are hard at work trying to make the Internet more user-friendly.

Second, the Internet is not like a local phone company. If you think your bill is in error, the phone company has a number that connects you to a consumer service representative. If something goes wrong on the Internet—such as someone's stealing your password and running up a big bill—there's nobody you can complain to. Since the Internet is simply a collection of separate networks, there is no single person or organization in charge. An Internet Society, staffed by volunteers, does exist, but it has no regulatory power.

THE EVOLVING INTERNET

The net is changing so fast that predicting the future is risky. Nonetheless, here are several trends that most experts agree will significantly transform the net in the next few years.

■ Broadband

Most Americans still access the Internet through a dial-up phone connection and a 56k modem. Although this arrangement works OK for transmitting text, it is painfully slow when sending graphics and audio and is not very practical for video. The problem is that the phone line is too narrow to handle the tremendous amount of information needed for multimedia. It's like trying to drain a swimming pool full of water using a straw. As a result, the full audio and video potential of the net has yet to be realized.

The answer to this problem is called **broadband.** Broadband refers to any of the several Internet transmission channels that can carry information at 30 to 60 times the speed of a conventional dial-up modem. Let's return to the swimming pool example: With a broadband connection, it would be like draining a swimming pool with a pipe 5 feet in diameter. Broadband gives you much faster results.

This tremendous gain in speed makes it possible to send huge files in much less time. With broadband, you could send a whole encyclopedia across the world in just a few seconds. Even more noteworthy is that broadband's bigger pipes could make Internet television a reality and speed the convergence between the computer and the TV set. Broadband will make website builders into television programmers and vice versa.

Currently, there are four ways for a consumer to get broadband access:

1. *Integrated Services Digital Network (ISDN).* ISDN lines are dedicated connections that run from the user to a central office. An ISDN line is twice as fast as a 56k dial-up modem. Cost can range from $30 to $200 a month depending on hours of use. ISDNs will probably be eclipsed by the services discussed below.

2. *Satellite.* Satellite connections to the Internet transmit data about seven or eight times faster than a conventional modem. Subscribers, of course, must have a satellite dish. Cost is about $30 to $100 per month, depending on use.

3. *Cable Modem.* Download speeds with a cable modem, provided by companies that also carry cable TV, can be as fast as one megabyte per second. Subscribers with cable modems share bandwidth. If many users are online at the same time, speed is reduced. Also, if your cable TV service goes out, so does your modem. Cost is about $50-$75 per month.

4. *Digital Subscriber Line (DSL).* A DSL line piggybacks Internet service on a regular phone line. Speeds range from 640k per second to several megabytes per second depending upon the modem and the wiring used to connect the modem to the computer. DSL works only if you are three miles or less from a central telephone office (a central office is a building where the local switching equipment is housed), which makes it more practical for urban and suburban dwellers. Cost ranges from $45 to $150 per month.

One further advantage of the above access methods is that they are always connected to the net. There is no wait to establish a connection, nor do you hear those annoying beeps and hisses of a convention dial-up modem.

As of 2001, only 5 percent of American households had broadband access. This number is expected to grow to about 30 percent of all households by 2004. The cable modem was the most popular means of connection. Once they get broadband, consumers like it. A study done by the National Association of Broadcasters found that people with broadband access spend about 2½ hours online every day compared with 1 hour a day for those with dial-up access.

Streaming Video

The switch to broadband will make **streaming video** much more popular. When video files first showed up on the web, a user had to download the entire file onto his or her computer's hard drive and then play it back. Since even relatively small video files could be several megabits in size, it required the patience of a saint to download them. Streaming video, in effect, lets the user watch the beginning of a video file while the rest is still downloading. The first part of the video file is stored in a buffer and then played back while another portion is downloaded, making for a seamless stream of information.

Even with high-speed connections, the quality of streaming video is still a long way from that of regular TV. The picture is small and sometimes jerky, and it occasionally freezes because of congested traffic on the net. Nonetheless, most experts agree that future technological improvements will make streaming video competitive with TV. Even with today's standards, many companies are taking advantage of this new TV medium. Many corporations use streaming web video for sales presentations or to cover trade shows. MSNBC streamed live coverage of the hearings before the Florida Supreme Court during the contested 2000 presidential election. Zatso combines video from Reuters, local TV stations, and the Weather Channel that lets users compile their own personal newscasts by topic and location. PlayTV.com, for example, presents a 12-hour lineup of talk shows featuring local personalities. Pop.com, scheduled to launch in late 2001, will offer streaming video of the films of little-known directors. Finally, TooHotForFox.com, launched in 2000, streams the bloopers, animal attacks, and high-speed chases deemed too tasteless for the Fox TV network.

Interactive Web TV

Imagine the following: You're watching Chef Emeril on the Food Network whip up some fancy dessert when a message appears at the bottom of your TV screen: "If you want the recipe for this and other desserts, press the button marked I on your remote." A touch of the button and—BAM—a half-dozen recipes for scrumptious desserts appear on the bottom half of your screen.

Or suppose you're watching "Late Night" and David Letterman is about to do his "Top Ten" list. You want to make sure your friend in Cleveland is watching. You touch another button on your remote, the screen splits, and you're connected to the Internet. You send an instant message to your friend with a reminder to watch. Or maybe you're watching "Friends" and you see a great pair of sunglasses. Another touch of a button and you're taken to a screen that lists websites for some of the products seen in that episode. You can order the sunglasses online. These interactive scenarios are possible thanks to the convergence of the computer, the Internet, and the TV.

As of 2001, the two biggest providers of interactive TV were Microsoft's WebTV and the newly launched AOLTV. Subscribers to WebTV pay about $20 a month for a set-top box connected to their TV that lets them surf the web, chat with others, and send e-mail while watching TV. For an additional charge, subscribers can play interactive games (such as "Jeopardy") and have access to background information (such as how the scene was shot or character bios) about their favorite TV shows. About a million people subscribe to WebTV.

AOLTV, launched in late 2000, offers a similar service that includes TV listings, reminders for favorite shows, instant messages, online shopping, chat rooms, e-mail, and specialized web content. AOL is hopeful that its merger with Time Warner will help interest Time Warner's cable subscribers in the new service.

Some analysts suggest that interactive web TV will have a tough time generating subscribers. They point out that TV has been an essentially passive experience since its invention. Do viewers really want to do all these things while watching? Will the interactivity be just a distraction from TV programs? The next five years or so will hold the answer.

■ Microcasting

The word "broadcasting," as first used with early radio and then TV, meant sending a message to a large, heterogeneous group of people. When format radio and cable TV networks came into being, the word "narrowcasting" was coined. Narrowcasting meant targeting your message to appeal to a small, well-defined subsegment of the total audience. Top 40 radio stations, for example, narrowcast to 12- to 22-year-olds; ESPN narrowcasts primarily to male sports fans; C-SPAN, to aficionados of politics. Internet TV makes possible "microcasting," sending a message to just a few people.

For example, funeral parlors in the United States and Sweden have installed web TV cameras and microcast their services on the Internet so that mourners who cannot attend the service in person can at least watch streaming video of the ceremony. Several wedding chapels in Las Vegas and other cities offer web microcasts of marriage ceremonies. Several day care centers have web cameras that enable parents at work to periodically check in on their kids. Business meetings can be microcast to employees working at home.

The possibilities of microcasting are endless. A portable digital video camera and a wireless Internet connection would allow Dad to microcast Scott and Suzie's soccer games or band recitals to the grandparents. How about a web microcast of the prom to interested parents? How about streaming video of the local Little League games? Of traffic conditions around town? You can probably think of many other applications.

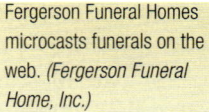

Fergerson Funeral Homes microcasts funerals on the web. *(Fergerson Funeral Home, Inc.)*

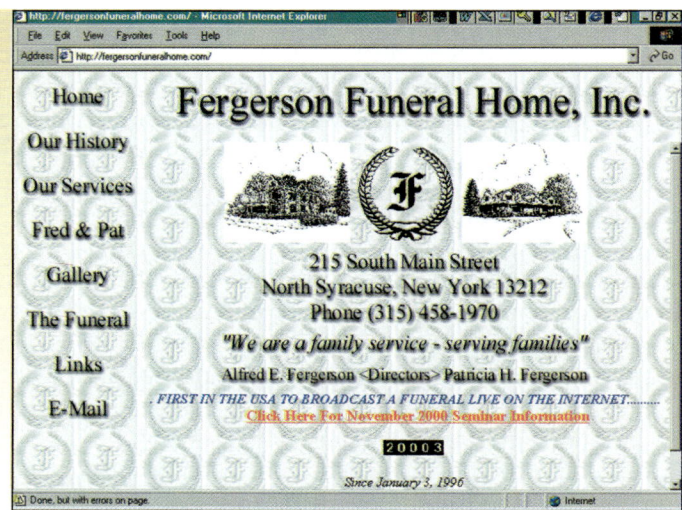

 ECONOMICS

This section will look at the general impact of the Internet on the national financial system, examine the economic impact of e-commerce, and then focus on the finances of individual websites.

The Internet and the National Economy

There is no doubt that the Internet has had an impact on the nation's financial condition. By reducing the cost of information and increasing its availability, the Internet allows companies to function more efficiently, thus increasing profits and productivity.

The period from 1998 to mid-2000 was the boom time for the Internet. In 1999, the Internet created more than 650,000 jobs, and net-related businesses collected more than half a trillion dollars in revenue. At the beginning of 2000, about 2.5 million workers were directly supported by the Internet economy. Dot-com companies became the darlings of Wall Street investors, and stock prices for these new companies rose astronomically, creating billions in new wealth. The advertising during Super Bowl 2000 was a sign of the times; it was dominated by dot-coms that happily paid $2 million for a 30-second spot. In fact, dot-com advertising created dramatic revenue increases in all commercially driven media.

By mid-2000, however, the boom was over. Poor planning, intense competition, and profligate spending pushed many dot-coms out of business and sent others to the brink of bankruptcy. Economic reality had apparently set in. Internet companies trimmed staff and drastically cut expenses, but Internet stocks plummeted. At the beginning of 2001, CNNfn estimated that the leading 280 Internet stocks had lost about $1.7 trillion dollars in value. Stock in Priceline.com, for example, (the one with William Shatner in some of its commercials) went from a high of about $100 a share in 1999 to about a $1 a share in 2001.

Despite this downturn, the long-range economic outlook for the net still seems positive. More traditional brick-and-mortar companies have incorporated the net into their business plans. Wal-Mart and Home Depot, for example, use the net as an additional revenue stream. Big corporations are turning to the net as a business tool (see below), using it to buy parts, handle customer relations, and allow workers to collaborate online. In short, the final economic impact of the net is yet to be determined, but most experts are optimistic.

E-commerce

"E-commerce" is the term used to describe selling goods, products, and services online. There are two kinds of e-commerce: the better-known type where companies sell directly to consumers and a less visible kind called B2B, or e-business, where companies sell to each other. Let's look at consumer e-commerce first.

The statistics concerning the rise of e-commerce are stunning. From being nonexistent in the early 1990s, e-commerce accounted for more than $20 billion in retail sales in 2000. The amount spent on e-commerce doubled from 1999 to 2000. The number of Internet users who actually bought an item online also doubled from 1997 to 1999. Despite the problems with inventory and delivery that occurred during the 1999 Christmas season and discouraged some consumers from shopping online, the dollar amounts devoted to e-commerce are expected to increase. The products that account for most of e-commerce are computer hardware, books, software, apparel and accessories, and music.

Progress can be compared to a seesaw. When one part goes up, another part comes down. Such is the case with online shopping. Without doubt, there are obvious advantages to ordering items over the Internet: no long lines, a bargain or two, no searching for parking places, home delivery, 24/7 convenience. There's a price, however, for all these advantages.

Let's start with the obvious. Going to a real brick-and-mortar store requires exercise. A consumer has to get dressed, travel to the store, walk around, pick things up, perhaps try them on, and transport the purchase back home. In contrast, sitting at a computer and clicking away on various items requires little exertion. In an age where lack of physical activity is a serious problem for many people, every little bit helps.

Second, for many people, shopping is a form of entertainment. Dressing up, walking around, seeing people, maybe running into a friend or acquaintance, and discovering new products are all forms of amusement that a computer screen has trouble duplicating.

Third, online shopping totally removes the human touch from the process. Shopping at a real as opposed to a virtual store means interacting with a variety of people, from clerks to store owners. Consider this a personal example: Recently, I was in the market for a certain piece of electronic equipment. I searched the web and found a few places where I could order the item, but I decided to check out a local electronics store. The store owner greeted me and struck up a conversation. It turned out he was from New York, where I lived for a while, and that we had several experiences in common. We also shared stories about moving to the South and our mutual interest in electronic gadgets. He had the item I wanted but recommended something else that ultimately worked much better. I paid for the component and left. Had I bought the item online, I would have saved about four dollars, but I would have missed a rather pleasant experience. Maybe a gratifying human interaction is worth more than saving a dollar or two.

Finally, another personal example: Not too long ago, I was standing in line at a department store waiting to pay for an item. The woman in front of me was paying with a credit card and was waiting for the transaction to be approved by a computer somewhere or other. She was drumming her fingers on the counter, and it was obvious that she was impatient with the process. After about a 35-second wait, the little machine on the counter spit out her receipt and as she was signing it, she remarked, "Doesn't take this long online." Has the Internet and online shopping made us so impatient that even a 35-second wait seems interminable? Why is speed so important these days? Maybe it's better for us just to slow down a bit.

Impressive as the consumer e-commerce market might be, it's small potatoes when compared with the B2B world. In 1999 the B2B online market in the United States was about $114 billion. By 2004, forecasters expect that this number will increase to $1.5 trillion. In that same year, experts predict that businesses worldwide will place orders totaling more than $3.2 trillion on the Internet.

The Internet allows businesses to deal directly with one another, making the process more efficient. Commerce One is a typical B2B site that matches buyers with sellers in industries ranging from auto parts to soft-drink bottling. Experts predict that B2B will save American businesses about $103 billion in 2003.

Now lets take a more specific look at the financial side of individual websites.

Website Economics

Once again, the tremendous variation in the kinds of people and organizations found on the Internet makes it hard to summarize its economic arrangements. Suffice it to say that the profit motive matters more to some than to others. A company that sells merchandise over the Internet is probably much more concerned with generating revenue than is a government agency or university that maintains a site as a service to its clients. Likewise, Uncle Max is probably not worried whether his personal web page ever generates a profit.

The rest of this section examines those online operations for which making money is an important consideration. There are three basic ways to make a profit over the Internet. The first is to create a site with content so compelling that people will pay to see it. One type of company that follows this model offers specialized

One way to make money with a website is to sell merchandise online as does ecost.com. *(eCOST.com)*

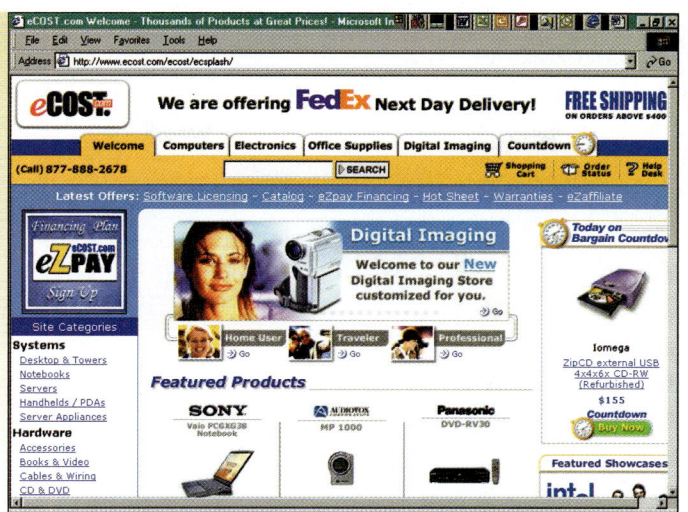

information that has value for a large number of consumers. *The Wall Street Journal,* for example, charges a subscription fee to access its online edition, which carries financial information. House of Blues Digital charges a fee for the netcast of a live concert. The other type of business that uses this system is sites that contain pornographic material.

Indeed, these sites are the most profitable on the web. At last count, there were thousands of them and some were raking in more than $3 million annually. Sex sells . . . even on the Internet.

The second way to profit from the net is to sell merchandise or services online. Amazon.com, for example, sells books and a wide range of other merchandise on the net. The Hotel Reservations Network offers travelers discounted hotel rooms online. It has been estimated that are thousands of virtual retailers online as of 2001. Are any making money? Some are, but plenty aren't. The Hotel Reservations Network finally turned a profit in 2000. EBay, the online auction house that takes a cut from sales conducted through its site, is also in the black. On the other hand, Amazon.com has yet to turn a profit. Online retailers Pets.com and Furniture.com both went out of business in 2000.

The third moneymaking method is for a website to sell advertising, usually consisting of banners that appear on the top and bottom of web pages. Clicking on the banners lets visitors order software, apply for a mortgage, or make online investments. Banner ads have recently fallen out of favor with advertisers after they discovered that very few people (less than 1 percent) actually click on them. Consequently, only the websites that draw large numbers of visitors (such as Yahoo! or Google) can use this method to generate a profit.

Of course, there are websites that use a combination of one or more of the above techniques. EBay, for example, charges for its services, sells advertising, and also markets its own customized T-shirts, toys, and coffee mugs.

 FEEDBACK

As with the other industries mentioned in Part Three, independent companies provide information about the Internet audience. Reliable data about audience size is important for advertisers who want to place banner ads on websites. The two companies that dominate the audience measurement field are Media Metrix and Nieslen/NetRatings. Both organizations use a panel of consumers to generate their data. Media Metrix samples about 40,000 people, using software that

Nielsen Media Research, the leader in the television ratings business, also measures Internet use. *(Net Ratings, Inc.)*

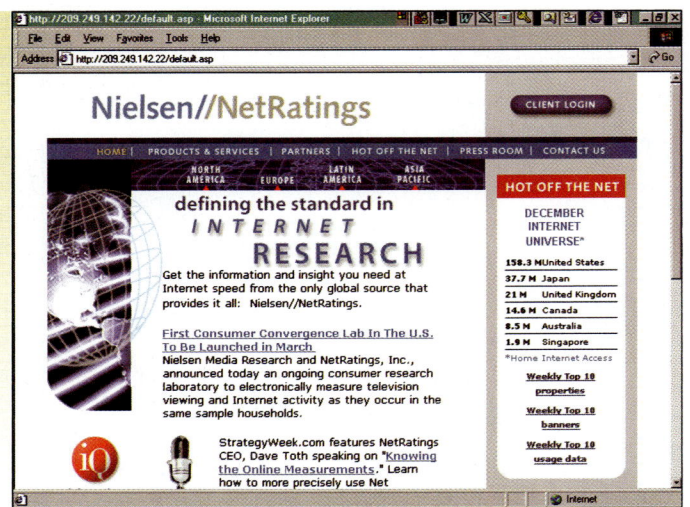

works with a computer's operating system to monitor Internet activity at home and at work. Nielsen uses a similar setup with a sample of about 65,000 people. Both services issue periodic reports that list the most popular websites. For example, in December 2000, Nielsen reported that American Online, Yahoo!, Microsoft, Excite, and Lycos were the top five sites.

Audiences

The Internet audience is changing rapidly. When the Internet first started, mostly young, affluent males were surfing the web. As of 2000, the audience was split nearly 50–50 between males and females, and the percentage of adults above the age of 50 had grown by 50 percent from 1998 to 2000. In short, the Internet audience is becoming more like the general population. More than 100 million people regularly use the Internet, with the typical user spending about 10 to 15 hours online per week. The main reasons for going online were to send e-mail or to find a specific piece of information.

SOUNDBYTE

Even Better than Cliffs Notes?

Don't have time to read all those novels for your English class? Never fear, the web is here. Check out rinkworks.com and its Book-A-Minute link for a really bare-bones summary of the plot. For example, with apologies to Charlotte Brontë, here is *Jane Eyre:*

People are mean to Jane Eyre.

Edward Rochester:	I have a dark secret. Will you stay with me no matter what?
Jane Eyre:	Yes.
Edward Rochester:	My secret is that I have a lunatic wife.
Jane Eyre:	Bye.

Jane Eyre leaves. Somebody dies. Jane Eyre returns.

Or how about Hemingway's *The Sun Also Rises?*

Stock Hemingway

Narrating Character:	It was in Europe after the war. We were depressed. We drank a lot. We were still depressed.

Now you can get started on all those book reports.

SOCIAL IMPLICATIONS

Now that you know the technical details of how the Internet is becoming a mass medium, let's discuss some of its social implications. In the first place, relying on the Internet diminishes the importance of the surveillance function of traditional mass media. When a news event occurs, interested parties immediately post messages on the Internet for others to read. This process represents a shift from traditional journalism, where the decisions flow from the top down. Editors decide what to cover and send reporters to collect the facts. Now the news starts at the bottom and is generated by people close to or with an interest in the news topic.

During the 1997 Pathfinder mission to Mars, for example, NASA's site contained the latest photographs from the planet and descriptions of the

First, some facts:

- Victoria's Secret 2000 Online Fashion Show cost corporate America about $120 million in lost worker-hours as many employees eschewed their usual spreadsheets and word processing documents to watch the online show.

- Playboy.com gets more hits during business hours than after work.

- About 60 percent of corporate managers think their employees spend too much time using e-mail and surfing the web for personal reasons during working hours.

Now that more and more workers have Internet access at their places of business, new problems are emerging about how much monitoring a company should do of its employees' online behavior. There are various software and hardware tools available that make it possible for an employer to monitor, down to the last keystroke, how a worker uses a computer: what websites were visited, what e-mails were sent, and so on. Some organizations think they have good reason to use these tools to monitor what employees are doing online.

Specifically, employers are concerned that workers are spending their time bidding on items on eBay, using e-mail to plan their high school reunion, and visiting sites such as britney.com instead of doing their jobs. In addition, companies worry that some employees may be using e-mail to send sexist or racist jokes to their colleagues, an activity that might trigger a lawsuit.

Workers argue that monitoring brings a "Big Brother" attitude into the office, creates an atmosphere of distrust between employer and employee, and invades a worker's privacy. Is it proper, they ask, for an employer to open a worker's locked desk and look through personal belongings? Similarly, it should not be appropriate for a boss to monitor e-mail or web surfing.

There are, of course, legal aspects to this issue, and so far, the courts have sided with employers. Court decisions have held that employees have no legal expectation of privacy when using company-owned computers and that employer monitoring of e-mail and online usage is legal. But what about the ethical dimensions of such scrutiny? Do employers have an ethical obligation to inform workers that their online activity may be monitored? When, if ever, is it ethical for an employer to disregard an employee's privacy?

Suppose a company has reason to believe that proprietary information and trade secrets are being leaked to competitors via e-mail. The company's responsibility to shareholders might take precedence over its regard for employee privacy. What about the situation where a company has no reason to believe that employees are improperly using their computers? Can it routinely sample employees' online activities to see who is being productive and who is wasting time? Is there enough justification for this intrusion?

Suppose a productive employee spends some time ordering personal items online or reading the latest movie reviews. Should this person be reprimanded for violating company computer policy? How much web surfing is too much? Then there is the question of who has access to the monitoring information. Is it ethical for a manager to tell others about what websites a person visits while at work?

Chapter 16 discusses an ethical principle known as utilitarianism. In brief, this principle suggests that the good consequences of a decision be weighed against the bad. This principle seems particularly appropriate for the current situation. There may be some positive outcomes from monitoring employee online behavior, but a company must decide if they are worth the distrust and suspicion that monitoring ultimately causes.

---

mission's progress. In addition, press releases, scientific reports, and personal observations were available on the net. During the long recount of the votes in Florida, many websites and postings on newsgroups contained personal observations from Florida voters concerning their experiences in the polling place. Thanks to the Internet, anybody with a computer can become a reporter, editor, and publisher. The implications of this for journalism are worth pondering.

Lack of Gatekeepers

As mentioned in Chapter 1, there are gatekeepers in the mass media. Computer networks—like the Internet—have no gatekeepers, and computer information services—such as America Online—have very few. This has several implications. For starters, the risk of overloading the system with unwanted, unrequested, trival, irrelevant, worthless, or inconsequential messages is increased tremendously. Suppose I think that this chapter is the most important chapter ever written in the history of the world, and I decide that everybody should have a chance to read it. I post it on every active bulletin board on the Internet so that millions of people can read it—whether they want to or not. Suppose everybody did that with stuff they thought important. The system would be clogged with traffic. There are no gatekeepers to keep unwanted material out of your system.

Gatekeepers also function as evaluators of information. Newspaper editors and television news directors consider the authenticity and credibility of potential news sources. If the system works properly, bogus news tips, unsubstantiated rumors, and false information are filtered out before they are published or broadcast. Information obtained on the Internet, however, comes without a guarantee. Some of it might be accurate; some of it you must use at your own risk. For example, the UFO-related newsgroups contain several accounts of UFO sightings and abductions by aliens. How credible these reports are is anybody's guess.

■ Information Overload

The Internet represents an information retrieval tool that is unparalleled—providing a person knows how to use and understand it. In the days before the net, students doing research would have to look things up in a text, reference book, or encyclopedia—sources that had some recognized authority. Today, students can post a request for information with the relevant newsgroup or use a search engine to look for the topic. The credibility of responses on a newsgroup, however, is open to debate when a web search indiscriminately displays a list of "sources," which may number in the thousands. Every source on the screen seems to have the same credibility, even though some may be from scientific documents and others from comic books.

For example, while doing research, I explored the web using a popular search engine looking for references to "virtual reality." My search turned up 17,033 matches, including some that were about virtual reality games, quite a few that were XXX-rated, a large number from multimedia companies that produce virtual reality software, some that described technical background, and one about the use of virtual reality techniques for law enforcement and explosive ordance training. (Of course, I might have narrowed my search using some advanced techniques, but the fact remains: There is so much on the web that it is sometimes more overwhelming than useful.) Further, other than making a reasoned guess from the titles, I had no clue as to which sources were more authoritative than the others. (Students doing a conventional search would also have to assess the credibility of their sources, but the profuseness of information and the sheer size of the net makes this extremely difficult to do.)

And, of course, having no gatekeepers means having no censorship. The Internet is like a huge city. There are some streets where the whole family feels comfortable and other streets where you probably wouldn't want to take your children.

■ Lack of Interpretation

Third, the Internet may diminish the interpretation function of the media. Usenet newsgroups and other computer bulletin boards, as we have seen, exist for an impressive array of topics. Want to know if a new movie is any good? You no longer have to rely on Roger Ebert or your local newspaper movie critic. Several newsgroups are devoted to current cinema, and you'll have no trouble sampling a wide range of opinion. Are the new TV shows on the networks any good? What did you think of the most recent episode of "The X-Files?" In addition to—or maybe instead of—your local TV critic, you can check into several newsgroups that evaluate and comment on new and existing shows. Which Mexican restaurant has the best burrito? No need to rely on restaurant critics. There's probably a newsgroup on the topic. Want to find out if the president's health care program is any good and don't have the time or inclination to watch "Meet the Press" or "Hardball"? Log on to the Internet and you will find no shortage of views.

Privacy Concerns

The Internet also raises a number of privacy concerns. Maintaining a person's privacy in the electronic age is not a new problem, but before the advent of the Internet, compiling a detailed dossier on someone required days or even weeks of searching through records scattered in dozens of places. Today, computerized databases let a person accomplish the same things with only a couple of clicks of a mouse. Examples illustrating this growing problem include the following:

- In Oregon, the state's entire Department of Motor Vehicles database was put into a website, making it possible for anybody to find out how many speeding tickets, parking violations, or drunk driving convictions a person might have. Residents complained so vehemently that the site was ultimately dropped.

- In 1997, the Social Security Administration started an online service that allowed Americans to access information about their accounts. It seemed like a good idea, but it was soon pointed out that an individual with just a few basic pieces of information about someone else—like place of birth, mother's maiden name, and social security number—could also pull up the account information. This meant that prying neighbors, private investigators, creditors, relatives, and ex-spouses, among others, could find out how much a person earned every year going back to 1951. The Social Security Administration quickly beefed up privacy safeguards for the site.

- Some states have put the names and addresses of sex offenders on websites. Although the motives behind this practice may be understandable, the potential for harm due to incorrect or outdated information is substantial. In North Carolina, a family was harassed because their address was listed online as the home of a known sex offender. The sex offender had actually moved away many months earlier, but the entry was never removed from the database. Many companies now charge as much as $150 to do online searches that will disclose someone's current address, social security number, bank account number, any criminal records, and a work history.

- Another growing concern is identity theft. A person can obtain someone's name, social security number, and date of birth from the Internet and can then apply for credit cards, get loans, and even commit crimes as someone else. Even more unsettling is the fact that the victim may not even know what has been done in his or her name. In California, a young man couldn't figure out why he was always turned down when he applied for retail jobs. He finally learned that someone had stolen his identity using the Internet and had been convicted of shoplifting. Whenever a potential employer ran a background check on the young man, the shoplifting conviction wrongly appeared on his record.

For the past few years, the government has wrestled with this privacy problem, and several bills have been introduced in state legislatures as well as the U.S. Congress that would restrict the availability of personal information. The issue is complicated because many are concerned that government regulation would be so rigid that legitimate searches for information would be difficult. Many prefer voluntary guidelines to laws.

■ Need for Regulation

The whole notion of how to regulate the Internet is a vexing problem (see Social Issues, "New Legal Models for New Media?"). Technology has once again outpaced legislation. The overall legal implications of the Internet are still nebulous. Copyright law is a good example: A 1997 conference organized by the United Nations World Intellectual Property Organization proposed new guidelines that covered digital forms of writing, music, and artwork, but the guidelines have yet to be ratified by the 160 nations that participated in the meeting. Even with these guidelines, questions remain. If copyright holders are given exclusive electronic rights, would there be a per-use charge for anybody who accesses the material? How would this fee be collected? Or suppose your website has a link to another site that contains copyrighted material used illegally? Are you liable for a copyright violation?

On another front, if someone posts a libelous message on a bulletin board, is the bulletin board operator liable? One recent case involving CompuServe ruled that the service was like a bookstore and cannot be sued for the comments of its users. The ruling, however, was based on the fact that CompuServe didn't interfere with the board's posting. Another service that monitored or edited content might not be in the same position.

What about pornographic content? In 1994 a couple operating a bulletin board in California were convicted of distributing pornography via computer when a postal inspector in Memphis, Tennessee, subscribed to the service using a false name and received sexually explicit pictures. This case raised the question of which local community standards should be used to judge whether the content was pornographic: California's, in which more liberal attitudes are evident, or those of the more conservative Tennessee?

Finally, will the computer encourage escapism? Some people are already spending lots of time (and money) engaging in computer chat, computer games, computer shopping, and maybe even computer sex ("compusex," as it's called). As more and more fun things come online, will we spend even more of our lives staring at computer screens? What happens when virtual reality becomes more appealing than "real" reality? Will large numbers of us abandon socially relevant pursuits for a romp in the media world? (Are you still reading this, or have you logged onto the Internet?)

C A R E E R

O U T L O O K

THE INTERNET AND THE WEB

The Internet and the web are so new that it is difficult to define career paths. Some careers that involve the Internet have been mentioned earlier—such as online journalism—and others, such as online advertising, will be discussed in subsequent chapters. The rest of this section examines general career opportunities for those interested in the online area. Keep in mind that the jobs listed below didn't exist 10 years ago. It is likely that many new jobs will be created in the next decade as well.

One interesting entry-level job might be called "web scout." Online companies—such as America Online—and web search companies—such as Yahoo! and

Contributed by Keisha L. Hoerrner, Ph.D. When the Supreme Court ruled in 1997 that parts of the Communications Decency Act were unconstitutional, legal scholars and Internet surfers hailed the decision as a victory. Why was everyone so excited that indecent material was deemed worthy of constitutional protection? Because the decision was about more than just the display of sexual pictures and such on the net. The case marked the first opportunity for the Court to determine how much constitutional protection the Internet as a medium deserved. And the Court stated unequivocally that the Internet deserves a great deal of protection under the First Amendment, not only in this case but in future ones.

To understand the significance of the decision, step back to early Supreme Court decisions dealing with radio and television. In 1934, the Supreme Court ruled that radio's "unique characteristic" of limited spectrum space made it distinct from print media such as newspapers and should, therefore, be treated differently under the First Amendment. In 1969, in a case called *Red Lion*, the Court reiterated the "spectrum scarcity" aspect of radio—which would also apply to over-the-air television—that warranted "medium-specific models" for determining constitutional protection. No longer would "freedom of speech and of the press" mean the same thing for all mass media. Those media falling within the "broadcast model" deserved less constitutional protection than those in the "print media model," according to the Court.

While Court watchers and media executives debated the Court's rationales for treating radio and television differently from newspapers, another problem was working its way through the judicial system. District and appellate court judges ruling on First Amendment cases involving cable television asked the obvious questions, "Where does cable fit? Which model do we use?"

The Supreme Court never really answered those questions. After 14 years of cable cases, the Court still has cable sitting somewhere in between the print model and the broadcast model but not fitting into either completely or comfortably. It's as though the Court has created a "cable model" without doing so explicitly.

The Court's indecision causes particular concerns for the cable industry but it points to a broader problem, a problem the Court faced in the Internet case and will face again each time a new medium is developed. Are two—or three—distinct models enough? Does every new medium deserve its own constitutional model? As media converge, how will the courts apply the different models? This gets even more complicated when you consider that in some areas of law, such as copyright and privacy, the medium in which the message was transmitted has no bearing on the outcome of the case. Yet in basic First Amendment cases where the Court is determining how much or little control the government is allowed to exact over the media, the medium seems to be the primary issue.

(Continued)

Excite—hire people who spend their days surfing the web, looking for sites that are unusual, interesting, or just unique. The scouts then organize these sites under various categories, such as art, science, and entertainment, and add them to a master listing that creates something like an index for the web. The parent company then uses this information to keep its listings current and handy.

Another typical entry-level job would be a web developer (also called a web designer or web publisher). Web developers are responsible for the actual creation of a website. They consult with the appropriate people about the content of the site and put together the content that will appear. Once the content has been assembled, the web developer converts the documents into hypertext and scans the text, graphics, and pictures into the server. Since many sites now incorporate multimedia, the developer might also include prerecorded or live audio and video. Developers also upgrade sites and make sure that the sites are easy to use.

The next step up from a web developer is a webmaster. This is a managerial position that involves working closely with web developers and members of the company that is supporting the site. Webmasters consult with staff members from departments such as engineering, customer support, and public relations. Webmasters are responsible for all aspects of a website. They design the overall look of a site and approve all materials that are published on the site. Webmasters make sure the site is performing as expected and is meeting the needs of users and the sponsoring organization.

(Concluded)

In its 1997 decision, the Court acknowledged that the Internet contained qualities resembling both print and broadcasting: "This dynamic, multifaceted category of communication includes not only traditional print and news services but also audio, video, and still images, as well as interactive, real time dialogue." Still, it found the Net to be less " 'invasive' [than] radio and television" and lacking a "scarcity" concern, two attributes of radio and television that the Court believes warrant less First Amendment protection.

Since the Internet doesn't fit into the broadcasting model, the Court was uncomfortable in allowing governmental interference into a growing, evolving medium. Justice John Paul Stevens, speaking for the whole Court, wrote, "The interest in encouraging freedom of expression in a democratic society outweighs any theoretical but unproven benefit of [governmental] censorship." Strong words of protection for the Internet. Why weren't they used for radio, television, or cable when they were growing and evolving industries? Will they be used for satellite television and other new technologies?

The Court's protection of the Internet can be viewed two ways. The Court could have simply found that the net resembles a newspaper more than it resembles either radio or television. Many web sites do look like the front page of a newspaper, and you do have to read words on the screen—as well as view pictures and advertisements on many sites.

On the other hand, the Court could be facing the recognition that medium-specific models are outdated and that new technologies will continue to blur the lines between media. Rather than forcing a new medium into a "print" or "broadcast" box, the justices may be ready to grant all media full constitutional protection. To quote Justice Thomas, "The text of the First Amendment makes no distinction between print, broadcast, and cable media, but we have done so." Should the justices collapse those distinctions and treat all media equally? Is it appropriate to grant the same or similar messages differing levels of First Amendment protection because of the medium in which it is transmitted?

The latest issue working itself through the judicial system is whether a software program that enables someone to decode DVD scrambling technology deserves First Amendment protection. A district judge in New York must decide whether computer language is "speech" worthy of constitutional protection. Whatever the judge's decision, it is sure to be appealed. So as this case works its way up the federal court system, the U.S. Supreme Court may be asked to render an ultimate decision. If computer code is speech, then is the computer industry a new mass medium? What level of First Amendment protection should it be granted?

While the Communications Decency Act case resolved some questions, it created more, and these questions about the constitutional protection of new media have long-range implications. If you were a Supreme Court justice, how would you rule?

As of this writing, there is no established curriculum that prepares students for online jobs. However, some colleges now offer courses in web page design or related topics. In addition to these, you should probably take courses in computer science, graphic design, journalism, public relations, and English . . . and be on the lookout for those jobs that haven't been invented yet.

■ MAIN POINTS

- The computer's ancestors were machines that performed mathematical calculations.
- By the 1970s, personal computers using packaged software went on the market.
- The Internet is a network of computer networks. It was started by the U.S. Department of Defense and in its early years was used primarily by scientists. The current Internet started in the 1980s thanks to the efforts of the National Science Foundation.
- The main features of the Internet are e-mail, newsgroups, and the World Wide Web.

- AOL Time Warner, Microsoft Network, and Prodigy are three companies that operate online information systems.
- The introduction of broadband Internet connections will encourage the growth of streaming video, interactive TV, and microcasting.
- The Internet has had a beneficial impact on the national economy, and e-commerce continues to grow.
- Some websites are profitable, but many have yet to make any money.

- Media Metrix and Nielsen/NetRatings provide Internet audience data for advertisers.
- The use of the Internet for communication has several implications. The surveillance function of the media has been altered by the Internet. The absence of gatekeepers makes it difficult to judge the credibility of items on the net.

- The Internet also lessens the interpretation function of the media. The Internet raises questions about privacy. How to regulate the Internet is still an open question.

■ QUESTIONS FOR REVIEW

1. How did the Internet come into being?
2. Distinguish between a website, a web page, and a portal.
3. What is broadband? How will it affect the Internet?

4. What's the difference between e-commerce and B2B net commerce?
5. What are some of the social implications of the Internet?

■ QUESTIONS FOR CRITICAL THINKING

1. Check out some of the newsgroups available on the net. Should there be some authority that controls what content is available?
2. Do a web search for your name. See how much personal information you can find out about yourself on the web. How easy was it for you to find the information? Could others have found it as well?
3. Rank the following media in terms of how credible each is as a news source: TV, newspapers,

Internet, radio. Why did you rank them the way you did?
4. How often do you click on banner advertising in various websites?
5. Some critics (Roger Ebert among them) have suggested that the era of free information on the Internet is about over and that ultimately, we will pay for most of the content we get over the net. Do you agree? Would you pay to access a search engine? Or a website such as CNN.com?

■ KEY TERMS

modem (p. 302)
hypertext (p. 303)
browsers (p. 304)
protocol (p. 304)
e-mail (p. 305)

spam (p. 306)
newsgroups (p. 306)
World Wide Web (WWW) (p. 306)
website (p. 307)

web page (p. 307)
portals (p. 307)
broadband (p. 310)
streaming video (p. 311)

■ SUGGESTIONS FOR FURTHER READING

Albarran, Alan, and David Goff. *Understanding the Web: The Social, Political and Economic Dimensions of the Internet.* Ames: Iowa State University Press, 2000.

Cozic, Charles. *The Future of the Internet.* San Diego, CA: Greenhaven Press, 1997.

Hafner, Katie, and Matthew Lyon. *Where Wizards Stay Up Late: The Origins of the Internet.* Carmichael, CA: Touchstone Books, 1998.

Lessard, Bill, and Steve Baldwin. *Net Slaves: True Tales of Working the Web.* New York: McGraw-Hill, 2000.

Porter, David. *Internet Culture.* New York: Routledge, 1997.

Slevin, James. *The Internet and Society.* Cambridge, UK: Polity Press, 2000.

■ SURFING THE INTERNET

http://marcussharpe.com/vidstream.htm
A good site to visit if you want to see examples of
streaming video. Check out the video of the host's
backyard and several hundred other video choices.

http://www.aoltv.com/about.html
Learn about AOLTV. Check out its features, and
decide if you think it will be successful.

http://www.excite.com
The address of one of the many popular web portals.

http://www.fcc.gov/broadband
The Federal Communications Commission site that
deals with the progress of broadband in the United
States. Some of the information is highly technical.

http://www.funeral-cast.com/
The site for the microcasting of funerals over the web.
(I included this site to prove that I didn't make it up.)

http://www.isoc.org/internet/history
Contains links to various sites that detail the growth
and history of the Internet.

PART IV

Specific Media Professions

CHAPTER 12 News Gathering and Reporting

The past 10 years or so have seen an explosion in the number of news media serving Americans. There are newsmagazines, local and national newspapers, three full-time all-news cable networks (CNN, MSNBC, and Fox), a weather channel, a couple of sports channels, three financial news channels, a channel that specializes in technical news, and a channel that concentrates on entertainment news. Some cities even have a 24-hour cable news channel that carries only local news. In addition, there are all the news sites on the Internet. Moreover.com aggregates news content from 1,500 online news sites. ENewswires.com provides updates every 15 minutes from more than 25 general news sites, 12 business news sites, 11 high-tech news sites, 6 sports sites, 4 weather sites, 9 health news sites, and numerous other newspaper, broadcast, and magazine sites. More news is available now than at any other time in human history.

Obviously, news is an important commodity for Americans. Before anything becomes news, however, it must be reported. A rise in gasoline prices, a city council meeting, an accident—all must be filtered through the eyes and ears of a journalist. A reporter must be aware of the qualities that characterize a news story, the types of news that exist, and the differences in the way the various media cover news. This chapter examines these topics and looks at the process of news gathering and reporting.

The set of the Ohio News Network, a 24-hour, statewide cable news channel. Local cable news channels have helped fuel the recent increase in the number of news media serving in the United States. *(AP/Wide World Photos)*

You may have noticed that in our discussion of the explosion of news media, no mention was made of radio. That's because for the past 15 years or so, the number of radio stations with newsrooms has decreased markedly as has the number of radio news reporters. In fact, many stations have gone "news-free" or have only the briefest news headlines.

The decline started in the mid-1980s. As part of a trend toward deregulation, the Federal Communications Commission relaxed guidelines that had previously encouraged stations to present news and public-affairs programming. Many stations with a Top 40 or progressive rock format were convinced that news segments were driving away listeners and were quick to reduce or eliminate their newscasts.

The trend was accelerated by the Telecommunications Act of 1996, which encouraged a wave of consolidation in the industry (see Chapter 7). In many markets, one company acquired six or seven stations, and it made economic sense to consolidate news operations. Thus, instead of six stations doing separate news reporting, there was one news staff serving all six.

In addition, many radio newsrooms were closed when management discovered it could provide news at no cost by outsourcing. Companies such as Metro Networks or Shadow Broadcast Services provide local news, weather, and traffic reports for stations in return for a couple of minutes of commercial time during the newscasts that they can sell to advertisers. The newscasts usually consist of headlines and are often rewritten from the local newspaper. A single announcer can do the news on many stations in the same market. Listeners may not even be aware that the newscaster may be located in some other city. In Washington, D.C., for example, 21 stations get their news from either Metro or Shadow. Only two stations have their own radio reporters.

Will television stations follow radio's example? Will station owners pursue greater cash flow at the expense of local reporting? Stay tuned.

DECIDING WHAT IS NEWS

From the millions of things that happen every day, print, broadcast, and online journalists decide which few things are worth reporting. Deciding what is newsworthy is not an exact science. News values are formed by tradition, technology, organizational policy, and, increasingly, economics. Nonetheless, most journalists agree that there are common elements that characterize newsworthy events. These include:

1. **Timeliness.**   Put glibly, news is new. Yesterday's news is old news. A consumer who picks up the evening paper or turns on the afternoon news expects to be told what happened earlier that same day. News is perishable, and stale news is not interesting.

2. **Proximity.**   News happens close by. Readers and viewers want to learn about their neighborhood, town, or country. A train derailment in France, for example, is less likely to be reported than a similar derailment in the local train yard. Proximity, however, means more than a simple measure of distance. Psychological proximity is also important. Subway riders in San Francisco might show interest in a story about rising vigilantism on the New York subways, even though the story is happening 3,000 miles away.

3. **Prominence.**   The more important a person, the more valuable he or she is as a news source. Thus, activities of the president, other heads of state, and sports and entertainment figures attract tremendous media attention. Even the infamous have news value. The past lives and recent exploits of many criminals are frequently given media coverage.

4. **Consequence.**   Events that affect a great many people have built-in news value. A tax increase, the decision to lay off thousands of workers, a drought, inflation, an economic downturn—all these events have consequence.

5. **Human interest.**   These are stories that arouse some emotion in the audience—stories that are ironic, bizarre, uplifting, or dramatic. Typically, these items concern ordinary people who find themselves in circumstances with which the audience can identify. Thus, when the winner of the state lottery gives half his winnings to the elderly man who sold him the ticket, the story becomes newsworthy.

In addition to these five traditional elements of news value, economics plays a large role. First, some stories cost more to cover than others. It is cheaper to send a reporter or a camera crew to the city council meeting than to assign a team of reporters to investigate city council corruption. Some news operations might not be willing to pay the price for such a story. Conversely, after spending a large sum of money pursuing a story, the news organization might run it, even if it had little traditional news value, simply to justify its cost to management.

By the same token, the cost of new technology is reflected in the types of stories that are covered. When TV stations went to electronic news gathering (ENG), stories that could be covered live became more important. In fact, many organizations, conscious of the scheduling of TV news programs, planned their meetings and/or demonstrations during the newscast to enhance their chances of receiving TV coverage. Further, after helicopters became an expensive investment at many large TV stations, traffic jams, fires, beautiful sunsets, and other stories that lent themselves to airborne journalism suddenly became newsworthy.

Newspapers are not immune to the pervasive influence of the bottom line. As more corporations and large newspaper chains dominate the business, more businesspeople than journalists are becoming newspaper executives. The topics of greatest interest to this new breed of manager are marketing surveys, budget plans, organizational goals, and strategic planning—not the news-gathering process. This new orientation usually shows up in the newspaper's pages. The paper's "look" improves—more color, better graphics, an appealing design—and there are more features—food sections, personal finance columns, entertainment guides, and reviews. The paper becomes a slickly packaged product. At the same time, however, the amount of space devoted to local news decreases, reporters are discouraged from going after expensive investigative stories, and aggressive pieces about the local business community tend to disappear. Many experienced editors fear that the new corporate breed of managers will change the traditional news values of American journalism (see Ethical Issues, "What You Don't Read or See").

The media cover the Florida recount. *(AP/Wide World Photos)*

Economics alters news values in other, more subtle, ways. Ben Bagdikian, in *The Media Monopoly,* noted that the rise of media conglomerates (large corporations that own newspapers, broadcasting stations, and other properties) poses a problem for journalism. Can a newspaper or TV sta-

In 2000, a poll conducted among journalists by the Pew Research Center turned up findings that suggest money plays a big role in what does or doesn't get reported. Poll results indicated that 3 in 10 reporters have avoided covering a newsworthy story because they were afraid it would drive away advertisers. The proportion was even greater among investigative reporters: One out of two confirmed that some stories were never reported because they conflicted with the news organization's economic interests.

Market pressures were also apparent in a more subtle way. About 80 percent of the reporters surveyed said that at least some of the time, they kill important news stories because they are too complex or too dull. Apparently, they are afraid that such stories would drive away readers and viewers and would hurt circulation or ratings.

Even stories that do make it into print or are broadcast are not immune from outside pressure. About a third of the reporters related that they had softened the tone of a news story because it might harm the financial interest of the news organization.

How does self-censorship operate in the newsroom? Some journalists get signals from their bosses to avoid some stories. At times, these signals are direct, such as a clear instruction to avoid the story. At other times, the cues are subtler, such as the boss's simply not responding, or responding with little interest, or responding with suggestions that the reporter cover something else.

What are the topics that are likely to attract these negative signals? Stories about politics, economics, consumer finances, and corporate dealings. Some journalists conceded that they don't even bring up some possible story topics with their supervisors because they know that the stories will not be approved.

These results may also relate to another survey finding. The journalists were more pessimistic than ever about their profession. In a 1999 survey, about half of the journalists said that the news business did a good or excellent job of informing the public. In the 2000 survey, that percentage dropped to about 36 percent. It seems possible that corporate focus on the bottom line may be making journalists more skeptical about their own performance.

The survey highlights a basic ethical dilemma for reporters and editors. Do they have an ethical duty to report the news that their professional training tells them is important and necessary in a democracy even though it won't win big ratings or increase readership among 18- to 24-year-olds? Should news be determined by its news value or by its entertainment value? Should big corporations judge news operations by the same standards they use to judge sitcoms and tabloid newspapers?

tion adequately cover the actions of its parent company? For example, could ABC news objectively report the activities if the Disney Company were involved in some alleged wrongdoing? Or could a Gannett-owned paper adequately cover events at *USA Today*, another Gannett property?

Economics plays a part in local markets as well. Newspapers make their money from circulation figures, and it has been charged that some publishers pander to public taste to inflate circulation figures. When media baron Rupert Murdoch took over the *New York Post*, he was chastised for placing great emphasis on sensationalism in an attempt to attract new readers. A similar situation exists in local TV news. The local newscast is an extremely profitable item for most TV stations, and competition is fierce. During special ratings weeks—called sweeps (see Chapter 10)—when viewing in every market is measured, a whole new set of news values comes into play at many TV stations. Suddenly, special programs on teenage prostitution, UFOs, pornography, the singles scene, and similar topics appear on the news. The quest for higher ratings (and revenues) at the expense of traditional news values is evident.

CATEGORIES OF NEWS AND REPORTING

Generally, news can be broken down into three broad categories: (1) hard news; (2) features, or soft news; and (3) investigative reports.

Hard News

Hard news stories make up the bulk of news reporting. They typically embody the first four of the five traditional news values discussed above. Hard news consists of basic facts: who, what, when, where, how. It is news of important public events, such as government actions, international happenings, social conditions, the economy, crime, environment, and science. Hard news has significance for large numbers of people. The front sections of a newspaper or magazine and the lead stories of a radio or TV newscast are usually filled with hard news.

Print Media   There is a standard technique used to report hard news. In the print media, it is the traditional inverted pyramid form. The main facts of the story are delivered in the first sentence (called the lead) in an unvarnished, no-nonsense style. Less important facts come next, with the least important and most expendable facts at the end. This structure aids the reporter (who uses it to compose facts quickly), the editor (who can lop off the last few paragraphs of a story to make it fit the page without doing wholesale damage to the sense of the story), and the reader (who can tell at a glance if he or she is interested in all, some, or none of the story). This format has been criticized for being predictable and old-fashioned. More literary writing styles have been suggested as alternatives, but the inverted pyramid has survived and will probably serve as the model for online reporting as well (see below).

Broadcast Media   In the broadcast media, with the added considerations of limited time, sound, and video, broadcast reporting follows a square format. The information level stays about the same throughout the story. There's usually no time for the less important facts that would come in the last paragraphs of a newspaper story. TV and radio news stories use either a "hard" or a "soft" lead. A hard lead contains the most important information, the basic facts of the story. For example, "The city council has rejected a plan to build the Fifth Street overpass." A soft lead is used to get the viewers' attention; it may not convey much information. For example, "That proposed Fifth Street overpass is in the news again." The lead is then supported by the body of the story, which introduces new information and amplifies the lead. The summation, the final few sentences in the report, can be used to personalize the main point ("This means that the price you pay for gasoline is likely to go up"), introduce another fact, or discuss future developments.

The writing style of broadcast news is completely different from that of print news: It is more informal, conversational, and simple. In addition, it's designed to complement sound bites (the sound of the newsmaker) or videotape segments.

Soft News

Soft news, or features, covers a wide territory. The one thing that all soft news has in common is that it interests the audience. Features typically rely on human interest for their news value. They appeal to people's curiosity, sympathy, skepticism, or amazement. They can be about places, people, animals, topics, events, or products. Some stories that would be classified as soft news are the birth of a kangaroo at the local zoo, a personality sketch of a local resident who has a small part in an upcoming movie, a cook who moonlights as a stand-up comedian, a teenager who mistakenly gets a tax refund check for $400,000 instead of $40, and so forth.

Features are entertaining and the audience likes them. Many television and print vehicles are based primarily on soft content ("Entertainment Tonight"; *E!*, the cable entertainment network; *People*; "Life Styles of the Rich and Famous"; *Us* magazine; the "Life" section of *USA Today*). Even prime-time news magazines such as "60 Minutes" and "20/20" have substantial amounts of soft news. Likewise, the fiercely competitive early morning network TV shows are turning more to soft news.

The techniques for reporting features are as varied as the features themselves. In the print media, features seldom follow the inverted pyramid pattern. The main point of the feature is often withheld to the end, much like the punch line to a joke. Some features are written in chronological order. Others start with a shocking statement, such as, "Your secrets just might kill you," and then go on with an explanation: "If you have a medical problem, you should wear a Medic-Alert bracelet." Still other features are structured in the question-and-answer format.

TV features are more common than radio features. In some large TV markets, one or more reporters cover nothing but features. Almost all stations have a feature file where story ideas are catalogued. If a local station does not have the resources to produce local features, it can look to syndication companies that provide general-interest features for a fee. Broadcast features also use a variety of formats. Humorous leads and delaying the main point until the end sometimes work well, a technique often used by Andy Rooney in his features for "60 Minutes." Other times a simple narrative structure, used in everyday storytelling, will be quite effective. The interview format is also popular, particularly when the feature is about a well-known personality.

Investigative Reports

Investigative reports unearth significant information about matters of public importance through the use of nonroutine information-gathering methods. Since the Watergate affair was uncovered by a pair of Washington newspaper reporters, investigative reporting has also been looked upon as primarily concerned with exposing corruption in high places. This connotation is somewhat unfortunate for at least two reasons. In the first place, it encouraged a few short-sighted reporters to look upon themselves as self-appointed guardians of the public good and to indiscriminately pursue all public officials, sometimes using questionable techniques in the hope of uncovering some indiscretion. Much of this investigative journalism turned out to be insignificant. In the second place, this emphasis on exposing political corruption distracted attention from the fact that investigative reporting can concentrate on other topics and perform a valuable public service.

Investigative reports require a good deal of time and money. Because of this heavy investment, they are generally longer than

The crew of "60 Minutes" gather around the show's trademark stopwatch *(Reuters/Larry Downing/ Archive Photos)*

the typical print or broadcast news item. Broadcast investigative reports are usually packaged in documentaries, or in a 10- to 15-minute segment of a newsmagazine program (such as "Dateline NBC" or "60 Minutes"). Print investigative pieces are usually run as a series of articles.

The mechanics of investigative reporting are similar in the print and broadcasting media. First, a reporter gets a tip or a lead on a story from one of his or her sources. The next phase consists of gathering facts and cultivating news sources. Eventually, a thick file of information on the topic is developed. These facts are then organized into a coherent piece that is easily digestible by the audience. Here the differences between print and broadcast reporting techniques become apparent. The print journalist can spend a good deal of time providing background and relating past events to the topic. Additionally, the print investigative reporter can draw heavily upon published documents and public records. In television and radio, the investigative reporter usually has less time to explore background issues. Documents and records are hard to portray on TV, so less emphasis is placed on them. Instead, the TV reporter must come up with interviews and other visual aspects that will illustrate the story. Moreover, the length of the TV report will sometimes dictate its form.

Some noteworthy examples of recent investigative reports include these from 1999: The *Washington Post* published two stories revealing widespread abuses in Washington, D.C.'s program to care for the mentally retarded. Radio station KCBS in San Francisco ran a four-part series on problems with the city's workers' compensation program. WAGA-TV in Atlanta won a Peabody Award for an investigative report revealing that U.S. customs agents were unfairly targeting minorities for unwarranted and invasive searches.

THE NEWS FLOW

As mentioned in Chapter 1, one of the characteristics of traditional mass communication is the presence of a large number of gatekeepers. This fact is seen in the gathering and reporting of news for conventional print and broadcast media. Reporting is a team effort, and quite a few members of the team serve as gatekeepers. Online reporting, in contrast, may have only one or a few gatekeepers. This section will first examine the news flow in the traditional print and broadcast media and then look at online media.

Print Media

Figure 12–1 illustrates the typical organization in a newspaper newsroom. There are two main sources of news: staff reports and the wire services. Other, less important sources include feature syndicates as well as handouts and releases from various sources.

Let's first examine how news is gathered by newspaper personnel. The city editor is the captain of the news-reporting team. He or she assigns stories to reporters and supervises their work. There are two types of reporters: Beat reporters cover some topics on a regular basis, such as the police beat or the city hall beat; general-assignment reporters cover whatever assignments come up. A typical day for the general-assignment reporter might consist of covering an auto accident, a speech by a visiting politician, and a rock concert. Stories from the reporters are passed along to the city editor, where they are approved and sent to the copy desk for fur-

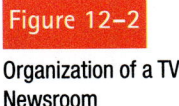

Figure 12–1

Organization of a
Newspaper Newsroom

ther editing. The managing editor and assistant managing editor are also part of
the news team. They are responsible for the overall daily preparation of the paper.
Let's review the news flow and the various gatekeepers in the process. The city
editor can decide not to cover a story in the first place or not to run a story even if
the event is covered. The reporter has a wide latitude of judgment over what he or
she chooses to include in the story. The copyeditor can change the story as needed,
and the managing editor has the power to emphasize or de-emphasize the story to
fit the day's needs.

Broadcast Media

The sources of news for the broadcast media are similar to those for the newspaper. Special wire services cater to television and radio stations, and local reporters
are assigned to cover nearby events. In addition, many broadcast newsrooms subscribe to syndicated news services or, if affiliated with a network, have access to
the net's news feeds.

The broadcast newsroom, as seen in Figure 12–2, is organized along different
lines from its print counterpart. At the local station, the news director is in charge
of the overall news operation. In large stations, most news directors spend their
time on administrative work—personnel, budgets, equipment, and so on. In

Figure 12–2

Organization of a TV
Newsroom

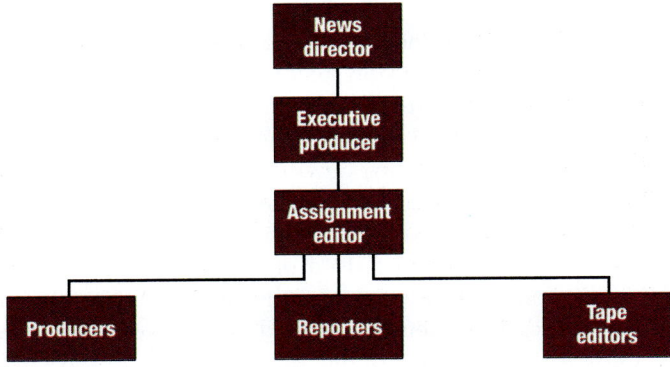

smaller stations, most news directors perform other functions (such as being the anchorperson) as well. Next in command is the executive producer. This person supervises all the producers in the newsroom. Typically, producers are assigned to the early-morning, noon, evening, and late-night newscasts. In addition to looking after the other producers, the executive producer might also produce the evening news, typically the station's most important program. Here are some of the things that a news producer does:

1. Decides which stories are covered, who covers them, and how they are covered.
2. Decides the order in which stories appear in the newscast.
3. Determines the amount of time each story is given.
4. Writes copy for some stories.
5. Integrates live reports into the newscasts.

The assignment editor, who assigns and monitors the activities of reporters, camera crews, and other people in the field, works closely with the news producer. Since speed is important in broadcast news, there is great pressure on the assignment editor to get the crews to the story in the shortest amount of time.

Then, of course, there are the "glamour" jobs—on-air reporters and anchors. Most reporters in broadcast news function as general-assignment reporters, although the large-market stations might have one or two regularly assigned to a beat, such as the entertainment scene. In many stations, anchors occasionally do field reports, but most of the time they perform their work in the studio, preparing for the upcoming newscast. In addition to the people seen on camera, there are quite a few workers whom no one ever sees or hears. Photographers accompany reporters to shoot the video. Tape editors trim the footage into segments that fit within the time allotted to the story. Big stations also have news writers and production assistants who pull slides and arrange other visuals needed during the newscast.

Obviously, the chain of gatekeepers in broadcast news is a long and complicated one. Starting with the assignment editor and ending with the anchor, usually more than a half-dozen people have some say-so over the final shape of the newscast. Sometimes, the way a story ends up might be drastically different from the way it started at the beginning of the gatekeeper chain. It is not unusual for a reporter to work all day on a story and then be told by a producer that the story will get only 40 seconds of airtime.

Online Media

The structure of an online news organization may take several shapes. In some operations, the online division may be a separate and independent entity; in others, the online segment may be integrated with the parent print or broadcast news organization. Figure 12–3 displays one possible arrangement.

The news flow in an online news department is similar to that in the traditional media. Top executives decide how the site will be structured and how many specialty areas (e.g., sports, financial, weather, entertainment) it will contain. Editors decide what content will be used on the website, which stories will have additional audio and video files, where the stories will be placed, and how often they will be updated. Staff members skilled in website design take care of the technical side. Online news departments that are affiliated with a broadcast or cable

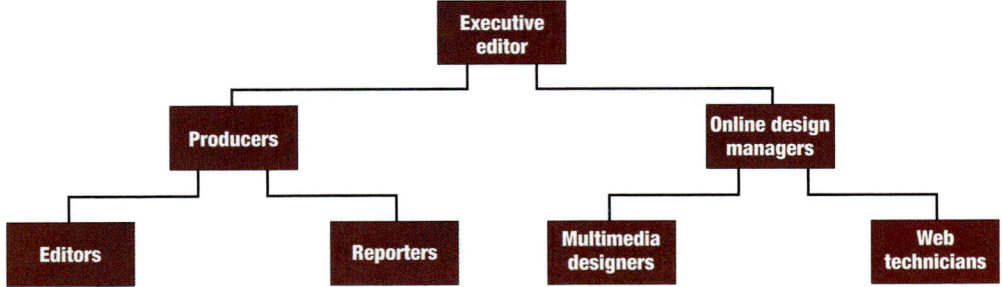

Figure 12–3

Organization of an Online Newsroom

network, such as CNN or MSNBC, will use the audio and video that appeared on the parent network, but may edit it differently. Other stories may be rewritten from wire copy or from copy that has appeared in print or on the air. Not all online news, however, is recycled. Most online news staffs also employ reporters who do original reporting for the website. During the 2000 election, CNN.com had dozens of reporters covering the various national and state races whose stories were posted on its site.

 TECHNOLOGY

Two technological developments that have had a tremendous impact on TV news are **electronic news gathering (ENG)** and **satellite news gathering (SNG).** The development of small, lightweight video cameras in the 1970s meant that pictures could get on the air much faster. Advances in satellite and microwave technology also made it possible to broadcast live from the scene of a major story. This new development brought both benefits and problems. ENG allowed TV news to take advantage of the immediacy of its live reports and added another dimension to its coverage. On the other hand, immediate coverage is unedited coverage, and this raises the probability that inaccuracies

A news reporter in action: Lightweight cameras and videotape recorders as well as electronic news-gathering (ENG) technology make it easy to broadcast from the scene of a news event. *(John Coletti/Stock Boston)*

might make it on the air. Also, live reports run the risk of violating the standards of ethics or good taste.

SNG uses a van or truck equipped with satellite links that enable reporters to send back pictures and audio from any location. More than 250 stations, most of them in large markets, now possess SNG capability. SNG enables local stations to cover national and international stories that used to be covered only by the networks. For example, many stations sent reporters to Sydney to cover the Olympics. Most local stations like the local angle and the additional prestige that go along with SNG coverage.

THE WIRE SERVICES

The next time you read your local newspaper, notice how many stories have the initials "AP" or "UPI" in the datelines. "AP" stands for Associated Press; "UPI," for United Press International. These two organizations are called wire services, and together they provide you with most of the news about what's going on outside your local community.

In simplified form, here's how the wire services work. A correspondent covers a local news event, such as a fire. He or she reports the event to the bureau chief of the local wire service. If the bureau chief thinks the story is newsworthy enough, the chief will send it on to the state bureau to go out on the state or regional wire. The state bureau chief then decides whether to send it on for inclusion on the national wire. All in all, the wire services are the eyes and ears for local papers and broadcasting stations that can't afford to have people stationed all over the country.

Local papers and broadcast stations rely on the wire services for national and international stories to which they would otherwise not have access. Shown here is the newsroom at UPI headquarters in New York City. *(Robert McElroy/Woodfin Camp & Associates)*

The AP has about 145 bureaus in the United States and about 95 foreign bureaus. Members of the association pay for this service according to their size and circulation. A large paper, such as the *New York Times*, will pay more than a small-town paper. United Press International also has dozens of domestic bureaus and a large number of foreign offices. As with the AP, member payment is based on the subscriber's size and audience.

In 2000, the AP had about 15,000 customers worldwide, including about 1,700 member newspapers. It also serves about 5,000 radio and TV stations, plus more than 500 cable systems. The AP offers a wide range of services to its clients, encompassing a weather wire, a sports wire, and a financial wire along with a broadcast wire used by TV and radio stations. In 1993, the AP introduced the AP NewsCenter, a fully automated TV newsroom, and began an international video news-gathering service.

In the past few years, UPI has been plagued by financial difficulties. The company was bailed out of bankruptcy in 1992 when it was bought by the Middle Eastern Broadcasting Company, which, in turn, sold it to News World Communications (the publisher of the *Washington Times*) in 2000. As a result of its economic troubles, UPI has reduced its domestic bureaus to six and now concentrates on providing news to Internet clients such as Excite.

AP and UPI are not without competition. Major newspapers, such as the *New York Times*, the *Los Angeles Times*, and the *Washington Post*, offer supplemental news stories generally not covered by other services. Some newspaper groups, such as Gannett, have their own wire services. There's competition overseas as well. The British-based Reuters agency has about 30 bureaus in North America. Agence-France-Press is another formidable worldwide service. Finally, there are specialized information services available on the Internet, such as Internet Wire and CNet.

MEDIA DIFFERENCES IN NEWS COVERAGE

It doesn't take a genius to see that broadcast journalism is different from print journalism and that both are different from web journalism. Over the years these differences have led many people to argue about which type of journalism is "best." Proponents of print journalism correctly point out that the script of a typical network evening newscast would fill up less than one page of a typical newspaper. They argue that the print media have the potential for in-depth reporting and lengthy analysis, elements that are usually missing from broadcast news because of time pressure. Moreover, some critics have taken to looking down on broadcast journalism, labeling it showbiz and commenting on its shallowness. The supporters of broadcast news answer that measuring a network newscast by comparing its word count with that of a newspaper is using the wrong yardstick. They suggest it is more appropriate to ask how many pages of a newspaper it would take to print the thousands of different visuals that regularly accompany a TV newscast. The emergence of 24-hour news channels and late-night newscasts, say these proponents, now makes it possible to cover news in depth. Print journalism is criticized for being slow, old-fashioned, and dull.

Critics of online journalism suggest that many web journalists are too quick to post stories and do not check their facts as thoroughly as do traditional journalists. They also note that many online news sites are slow to post corrections. Moreover, critics note that the line between reporting and commerce is blurry at many online sites. For example, online music and book reviews have links to places where readers can buy the material online, with part of the profits going to the online news site. Such an arrangement can cause pressure for good reviews. Finally, many people have a problem with how easy it is for someone to become an "online journalist." All that's needed is a website; no professional training or credentials are required.

And so the debate goes. Unfortunately, the argument covers up an essential fact: Print, online, and broadcast journalism have their own unique strengths and weaknesses. One should not be considered better than another. All play an important role in informing the public.

■ Words and Pictures

The inherent characteristics of all three media have an impact on what news gets covered and how it gets covered. In the first place, print and online journalism are organized in space; TV journalism, in time. Hence, the newspaper or online site can contain far more stories than the typical TV newscast and can provide more details about any one story. Given the time constraints of broadcasting (even including all-news channels), it is hard for television to provide more than a headline service and an in-brief look at a few stories. Even if a topic is treated in depth, the amount of information and detail included is typically much less than what is contained in its newspaper or online counterpart. Some observers have said that TV is better at transmitting experience or impressions, while the newspaper and online sites are better at providing facts and information. In any case, lengthy analysis and complicated interpretation tend to be better suited to the print or online media.

Second, print and online news has more permanence than broadcast news. A reader can go back and reread difficult and complicated parts as many times as necessary for understanding. Broadcast news does not have this luxury. TV newscasts are written to be understood with a single exposure. This means that complicated and complex stories are sometimes difficult to cover in the electronic media. Of course, television news has the advantage of the visual dimension. TV news directors ask if a story has action, visual appeal, something that can be seen. Faced with a choice between two events that are of equal importance, the television news organization will cover the one that has better pictures available. Obviously, the visual dimension is important and represents a powerful weapon in the arsenal of TV reporting. Some of the visuals carried by TV news are deeply ingrained in the national memory: the white Bronco on the Los Angeles freeway, the crowd scene where President Clinton embraces Monica Lewinsky, students fleeing Columbine High School. Nonetheless, it is easy for TV news to needlessly cater to the visual and run news items that have little news value other than their potential for dramatic pictures. There have been many examples of a small, relatively insignificant fire leading a local newscast simply because good pictures were available.

This is not to say that print and online reporters don't like a visual story. Quite the opposite. The advent of good color reproduction in newspapers and magazines and the ability of online sites to feature streaming video means that good visuals can accompany print and online stories. It is fair to say, however, that the print and online media are less likely to be influenced by the visual nature of a story.

■ Print, Online, and Broadcast Journalists

A second key difference has to do with the fact that in TV news, the appearance and personality of the reporter are an important part of the process. This situation is in direct contrast to print and online journalism, where the reporter stays relatively anonymous, with perhaps only a byline for identification. (Bob Woodward and Carl Bernstein, the newspaper reporters who broke the Watergate story, and Matt Drudge, the online reporter who broke the Lewinsky–Clinton scandal, are exceptions.) In TV, the person reading or reporting the news is part of the story. Repeated exposure of newscasters on the local and the network levels has turned many of them into celebrities in their own right. Some viewers evidently develop what amounts to a personal relationship or a sense of empathy with reporters and anchors. Many stories illustrate this peculiar audience–reporter relationship. When Dan Rather replaced Walter Cronkite at CBS, news executives tried all sorts of things to make him look appealing to the audience. Finally, one winter night in 1982, Rather wore a sweater under his jacket. Few people remember anything about what stories Rather reported that night, but almost everyone remembered his sweater. During her first years on the "Today" show, correspondent Jane Pauley received more comments about the way she wore her hair than about any of the stories she covered.

As personalities in TV news became more popular with the audience, they were able to command higher salaries. Annual salaries for the three network anchors range from $6 million to $7 million. Even at the local level, salaries between $250,000 and $750,000 are common in large markets.

News Consultants

Yet another difference between print, online, and broadcast journalism is the amount of control that outside news consultants have on the news itself. Market research consultants are employed by both newspaper and broadcasting organizations, but their activities are most noticeable at local TV stations. Consultants introduced the audience survey to local stations; they made recommendations to management based on what the public said they wanted to see in local news, not on what journalists thought should be in the newscasts—a fundamental shift in the traditional definition of news.

Recently, local TV newscasts have returned to a more traditional approach to covering the news. This doesn't mean that consultants have disappeared; they are still a strong force in local TV news. It's easy to see their influence, particularly if you travel across the country. The local TV news in Anchorage looks very much like the local TV news in Atlanta. Newscast formats, styles, and even the anchorpeople all seem quite familiar—a direct result of stations all over the country using the same consultants. (Compare this development with the format homogenization trend in radio. See Chapter 7.)

Similarities in the News Media

Before closing, we should mention that although there are significant differences between print, online, and broadcast journalism, there are many similarities as well. All journalists share the same basic values and journalistic principles. Honesty in news reporting is crucial for television, online, and newspaper reporters. Stories must be as truthful as humanly possible. The print or online journalist should not invent fictional characters or make up quotations and attribute them to newsmakers. Broadcast journalists should not stage news events or rearrange the questions and answers in a taped interview.

Another shared value is accuracy. Checking facts takes time, but it's something that a professional reporter must do with every story. A third common value is balance. Every story has two or more sides. All journalists must make sure that

Some TV images, such as this one, are replayed so many times that it's impossible to forget them. *(AP/Wide World Photos)*

they do not publicize or promote just one of them. Information should be offered on all sides of a story.

Print, online, and broadcast reporters share the value of objectivity. Objectivity means that the reporter tries to transmit the news untainted by conscious bias and without personal comment or coloration. Of course, complete and total objectivity is not possible because the process of reporting itself requires countless judgments, each influenced in some way by the reporter's value system. Nonetheless, journalists have traditionally respected the truth, refused to distort facts deliberately, and consciously detached themselves as much as possible from what they were reporting.

Finally, online, print, and broadcast reporters must maintain credibility with their audiences. The news media periodically undergo crises of confidence, when many people begin to doubt that journalists are telling them the complete and honest truth. Sometimes these crises appear when some journalistically unacceptable reporting is disclosed, as happened in 1998 when a reporter for the *Cincinnati Enquirer* used information in a story that he obtained by illegally tapping into the voice-mail system of the Chiquita Brands International food company. Other times credibility is called into question because of excesses in reporting, as occurred during the coverage of the Clinton–Lewinsky scandal. Whenever public opinion polls reveal that the news media have slipped another notch or two in credibility, journalists try to regain the lost confidence. After much soul-searching, the crisis usually passes. Credibility, however, is not something that should be examined only during journalistic crises. If a reader or a viewer loses trust or stops believing what is being reported, the fundamental contract between audience and reporter is undermined, and the news organization cannot survive. It matters little if the news organization is a newspaper, magazine, radio, online site, or TV station; credibility is paramount.

INTERMEDIA COMPARISONS

In June 2000, the Pew Charitable Trusts Research Center released a survey examining how Americans use the news media. The most significant finding of this survey was the fact that the Internet is quickly becoming a significant source of news. About 30 percent of Americans go online for news at least once a week, compared with 20 percent in 1998. At the same time, the number of people reporting that they watch network and local TV news has been declining. The survey also revealed that the number of people who regularly get their news from cable news channels or from the print media has been holding steady.

Although broadcast TV news viewership is declining, the Pew survey disclosed that TV is still the medium the audience believes the most. Print media (newspapers and magazines) ranked next in credibility. Online news sources

A news council is an independent body composed of journalists and private citizens that unofficially hears and adjudicates disputes over press conduct. People and organizations who feel that they have been wronged by news coverage but lack the time, energy, and money to pursue a libel case turn to news councils to help set the record straight. Those who bring complaints before a news council waive the right to file a lawsuit. Staff members look into complaints and the council holds hearings on those cases that raise significant issues. The council then votes on whether it thinks the complaint should be upheld. Councils have no legal power to enforce their decisions or to impose penalties. Their power stems from the publicity they bring to the case.

News councils are not a new idea. Wisconsin and Colorado had them; Minnesota and Hawaii still do. There was even a national news council that operated from 1973 to 1984 but was discontinued because of lack of money and lack of cooperation from influential media organizations. The idea of news councils resurfaced in 1997 when "60 Minutes" correspondent Mike Wallace suggested that the creation of a news council would help counter public skepticism and the negative feelings that members of the public have about the press. After the program was broadcast, residents from a number of states called the Minnesota News Council to ask how they could start their own news councils. In mid-2000, a news council started operation in the state of Washington and another was being planned in Oregon.

Most members of the news media do not share Wallace's enthusiasm for news councils. They make several arguments to support their view. The argument heard most often is that news councils are the first step toward government regulation. One of the reasons the *New York Times* refused to cooperate with the National News Council was its belief that the council would encourage an atmosphere of regulation in which government intervention might gain public support. Many journalists think that lawmakers would use the public complaints to justify more regula-

tion of the press. A second argument is that news councils would discourage hard-hitting stories. Journalists might be fearful of being unfairly targeted and forced to defend their decisions in controversial stories. If a council decision goes against a reporter, he or she might be afraid of doing any more such stories. Another argument contends that news councils substitute the judgments of people who don't know much about journalism for the judgments of professionals. How, ask the critics, can laypeople question the merits of a story when they don't know what went into producing it? In short, journalism should be left to the journalists. As one longtime journalist put it, "They have no damn business meddling in our business."

Supporters of the council idea first note that councils can prevent long and costly lawsuits. For example, they could give the principals in a defamation suit another forum in which to present the worthiness of their cases. Proponents also note that councils promote media fairness by making news outlets publicly accountable. Moreover, the councils give news media the chance to explain the reasons behind the choices they made and why they believed their decisions were proper. Such a discussion helps educate the public about some of the problems involved in the everyday practice of journalism and may help the public have a greater appreciation for the profession.

Supporters also contend that the press sees no problems in holding up other professions to public scrutiny but is unwilling to subject itself to the same treatment. They also note that there is wide public support for such an idea. Public opinion polls show that 85 percent of the general public likes the idea.

All things considered, the notion of a news council will be a hard sell to members of the news-gathering profession. Leading media outlets, such as the *New York Times*, still are adamantly opposed to the notion. Journalists have never been leading supporters of self-criticism. As Edward R. Murrow once said, when it comes to criticism, "The press is not thin-skinned. It is no-skinned."

---

varied widely in their credibility ratings. The major news sites (CNN.com, ABCNews.com, MSNBC.com) rated on a par with or slightly higher than their TV counterparts, while the credibility ratings of the news found on portals such as Yahoo! and Excite ranked below that of the print media. Online magazines, such as Slate.com and Salon.com, were rated lowest in credibility.

NEWS ONLINE

Let's take a look at some of the implications of the growing importance of online news. We'll first take the perspective of a member of the audience and then look at online news media from the perspective of the journalist and the news-gathering organization.

CNN.com is one of the leading sources for online news. The average visitor spends about 18 minutes on the site. *(CNN.com. Reprinted with permission.)*

For those who consume news, the Internet has meant an increase in the number of news sources available. General news sites appear to be visited most frequently (see Table 12.1). Also available are specialized sites that contain news about topics of narrow interest: automotive news, medical news, travel news, news with a conservative or a liberal slant, news about antiques, and so on. It's hard to think of an interest area that doesn't have at least one site devoted to it.

In addition, audience members can customize their news. The Internet portal Yahoo!, for example, offers visitors a number of different configurations that they can select. A person can pick specific categories of news to follow (entertainment, finance, sports), see the weather for chosen cities, monitor the prices of stocks in his or her portfolio, see local TV listings, and check the latest sports scores for favorite teams. Some sites even have programs that learn the kind of news that people like and refine the stories that appear within the personalized arrangement.

Finally, audience members can benefit because online news sites have memories. Most news sites have online archives that are searchable, providing the consumer the opportunity to look for more information about a topic. A person who was just diagnosed with high blood pressure might want to search archives of a medical news site to find related articles on the subject. Parents of a gifted child might look for past stories about special education programs.

Table 12.1	Top Five Online Sites for News, 2000

Site	Number of Unique Visitors per Month (in millions)
1. MSNBC (general news)	5.6
2. weather.com	5.5
3. ZDNet.com (technical news)	5.5
4. CNET.com (technical news)	5.4
5. CNN.com (general news)	2.8

Source: Data from *American Journalism Review,* September 2000, p. 27.

From a journalist's point of view, the Internet has provided a new set of tools for news reporting. As pointed out by Randy Reddick and Elliot King in their book *The Online Journ@list,* in the past, elite media organizations would send reporters to power centers and other locations where news happened to cover news events. Today, the reporter can sit at his or her desk and have instant access to documents, databases, government records, and expert sources. Journalists can now bring to their desks the information they previously went out to look for.

Many journalists now agree that the Internet is the most significant advance in reportorial tools since the telephone. Reporters covering a rash of wildfires that plagued the northwestern United States in 2000 were able to keep track of the fires by downloading the latest satellite pictures from the web. When a reporter found it difficult to arrange a face-to-face or telephone interview with the director of the media lab at MIT, she turned to e-mail as an alternative and was able to meet her deadline. Another journalist was preparing a report on euthanasia and was able to find a copy of a lengthy report on the subject on a law school website. When John F. Kennedy Jr. was killed in a plane crash, many reporters logged on to chat rooms to sample the reactions of young people to the tragedy.

The Internet can be a tremendous benefit, but journalists must learn new skills to be able to take full advantage of it. Today's reporters must know how to perform web searches, download files, construct e-mail attachments, set up listservs, navigate newsgroups, and analyze databases. These skills are sometimes lumped under the general name of **computer-assisted reporting (CAR).**

Writing news for an online service is somewhat different from writing news for a print or broadcast medium. Online reporters, for example, must be able to integrate hypertext links to related topics. An online story about a murder might contain links to a timeline of the crime, a transcript of a police press conference about the crime, and interviews with friends and neighbors of the victim. In addition, e-journalists have to be able to integrate sound and video clips that are relevant to the story. Online reporting is also interactive. Web-based news media can create bulletin boards where readers can offer opinions and even criticize the online news reports. The e-journalist must be ready to respond to readers' concerns. One skill that online journalists won't have to relearn is how to structure a story. The time-honored inverted pyramid style works fine on the web. Research has indicated that many readers don't like to scroll down through stories, so the most important information has to be included at the beginning. Somewhat ironically, what worked well 150 years ago still works well in cyberspace.

On a more general level, the growth of online news raises some fundamental issues for the profession, not the least of which is, Who exactly is a journalist? Before the Internet, it was relatively easy to identify journalists. They worked for formal organizations, such as the local paper, or a local TV station, or a national TV network, or a national magazine. As mentioned in Chapter 1, only companies with enough money to start and sustain a newspaper, magazine, or broadcast channel could reach a mass audience. The barriers to entry were formidable. Further, these organizations had chains of command. Journalists had editors; editors had managers. There were people who supervised the reporting process.

The Internet has changed all of that. Today, anybody with a computer and a connection to the Internet can set up a website and call herself or himself a journalist. No formal organization is needed; no editors or managers supervise what gets published. This development has both good and bad implications. On the one hand, the Internet makes it possible for a single journalist to become influential

Cyber journalist Matt Drudge demonstrated that big media organizations no longer have a monopoly on news. *(Amy Etra/TimePix)*

and make a difference. The Consortium, for example, is a site run by a single journalist that has published important stories about U.S. defense policies. Stories that might have been dismissed or downplayed by major news organizations can find a home on the web.

The expanded access provided by the Internet encourages lively debate between the public and members of the journalism profession. When Matt Drudge's website published reports based on questionable sources, the traditional news media were inspired to take a hard look at their own standards of credibility.

On the other hand, starting a web news site requires no formal journalistic education, no apprenticeship, and no exposure to the norms and ethics of the profession. Not surprisingly, many online news operations have been criticized for a lack of standards in their reporting. Will shoddy online journalism drive out the good?

Further, online journalists may have little investment in their site and thus take more liberties with the truth because they don't have much to lose. A traditional news operation has large sums of money invested in its reputation. If a newspaper, magazine, or broadcast news organization repeatedly makes misstatements of fact or distorts the truth, the resulting loss in credibility might cause the organization to lose large sums of money and maybe even go out of business, losing its entire investment. As a result, traditional news organizations normally pay close attention to what they report. A single person sitting at a computer has much less at risk from reporting untruths. In fact, he or she might even gain some notoriety if what is published is sensational enough.

Finally, will the news-consuming public be able to differentiate between legitimate journalism and the reporting of gossip and rumors that is found on some websites? If they cannot, the public might simply become cynical toward all news reporting and eventually tune everybody out.

NEWS GATHERING AND REPORTING

The career prospects for a young person interested in the news profession vary with the type of job desired. For those interested in newspaper journalism, the job market at the turn of the 21st century has never been stronger. *The Christian Science Monitor* reported recently that about 80 percent of small, local dailies and weeklies are desperate for staff. Part of the reason is that the supply of beginning journalists is dwindling. Fewer students are majoring in the subject, and there seems to be

A healthy skepticism is useful when dealing with some of the more sensational stories that find their way onto various "news" sites on the web. For example, it was reported that when asked her reaction to the death of King Hussein of Jordan, Mariah Carey replied that he was the greatest basketball player ever. Not true. This item appeared on a satirical website as a joke, but was treated as fact by many people, who e-mailed the story to friends. Similarly, another site apparently reported that designer Tommy Hilfiger had made racist comments on Oprah Winfrey's TV show. Again, not true. But some TV stations picked up the story and ran it before the truth was discovered.

Even more curious is the story of Mary Schmich, a writer for the *Chicago Tribune,* who wrote a column called "Use Sunscreen" as a spoof of a graduation speech. (The column eventually prompted a fairly successful song.) Somehow, an online news site apparently identified the piece as writer Kurt Vonnegut's speech to the graduating class at MIT. People liked it so much that Vonnegut was overwhelmed by requests to reprint it.

When it comes to the web, it pays to check things out.

little crossover into newspaper journalism from other professions. As a result, salaries for newspaper employees, although still relatively low when compared with those of other media professions, have been rising for the past few years.

Jobs in magazine journalism are harder to come by, primarily because there are so few of them. Most newsmagazines look for experienced people. Some even recommend that a prospective employee have a specialty in some area, such as law, finance, or science, along with journalism training.

Things are a bit tighter in broadcast journalism. Deregulation has meant that many radio stations have decided not to increase their news-reporting efforts. Consequently, the job market in radio journalism is sluggish. In television news, the glamour jobs of anchor and on-camera reporter continue to have far more applicants than there are available positions. There is some good news, however. The emergence of two-hour newscasts at large-market stations, the growth of all-news cable networks, and the increased prominence given to news at local stations have meant that there has been some expansion of the job market in news. Getting that first job, however, is still difficult, and the market is highly competitive. Most newcomers are content to start in a small market and work their way up. The outlook is a little brighter in the other positions. ENG camerapersons are in some demand, as are tape editors. The news producer position is another one where prospects for employment are favorable.

The prospects for online journalism were generally favorable as the new century began, but only time will tell if that situation continues. On the bright side, the new online news media have increased the number of jobs available for news reporters and editors. Furthermore, the online media were paying more than their print and broadcast counterparts. On the not-so-bright side, the financial viability of some news sites was in doubt. It is likely that the coming years will see some online news sites go out of business.

SOUNDBYTE

Cyber Anchor

This was probably inevitable. The Press Association of Britain has come up with a virtual anchorperson. Her name is Ana Nova. She has blue-green hair and matching eyes, wears bright red lipstick, and looks vaguely like Posh of the Spice Girls.

Click on ananova.com and Ana will read the latest news, sports, and entertainment headlines in the United Kingdom. For now, she appears a bit doll-like, with an otherworldly, computer-generated voice that sounds more American than British. Her facial expressions, however, are surprisingly lifelike and even include a faint smile.

One thing for sure: Ana works a lot cheaper than Diane Sawyer.

Ana Nova, the BBC's virtual anchor. (© Ananova Ltd. 2000, all rights reserved. Reproduced by kind permission of Ananova Ltd.)

■ MAIN POINTS

- The qualities that characterize news are timeliness, proximity, prominence, consequence, and human interest. Economics is also important.

- There are three main types of news stories: hard, soft, and investigative.

- Traditional print and broadcast news media have many gatekeepers. In contrast, online news media have only a few.

- The Associated Press and United Press International are two wire services that provide stories to print and broadcast journalists.

- Print, broadcast, and online journalism have their unique strengths and weaknesses.

- All forms of news media strive for credibility.

- Online news lets audience members select from more news sources and customize their news.

- Computer-assisted reporting using the Internet is a powerful news tool for reporters.

- Online news reporting raises fundamental issues about the journalism profession.

■ QUESTIONS FOR REVIEW

1. What are the characteristics that determine newsworthiness? Should others be added to the list?

2. What's the difference between hard and soft news? Is it possible to do a hard news report on a soft news topic, such as entertainment?

3. How does online news reporting differ from traditional print and broadcast reporting?

4. How is online news reporting similar to traditional print and broadcast reporting?

5. What is computer-assisted reporting?

■ QUESTIONS FOR CRITICAL THINKING

1. Should news be what the audience wants to know or what the audience needs to know? Who should decide?

2. Where do you get most of your news about what's going on in the world? Why?

3. What news medium is most believable? Print? TV? Online? Why?

4. Will the growth of online news help or hurt traditional news reporting?

■ KEY TERMS

timeliness (p. 327)
proximity (p. 327)
prominence (p. 327)
consequence (p. 327)
human interest (p. 328)

hard news (p. 330)
soft news (p. 330)
investigative reports (p. 331)
electronic news gathering (ENG) (p. 335)

satellite news gathering (SNG) (p. 335)
computer-assisted reporting (CAR) (p. 343)

■ SUGGESTIONS FOR FURTHER READING

The following books contain more information about the concepts and topics discussed in this chapter.

Applegate, Edd. *Print and Broadcast Journalism: A Critical Examination.* Westport, CT: Praeger, 1996.

Cloud, Stanley, and Lynne Olson. *Murrow's Boys.* Boston: Houghton Mifflin, 1996.

Cremer, Charles, Phillip Keirstead, and Richard Yoakam. *ENG: Television News.* New York: McGraw-Hill, 1996.

Cronkite, Walter. *A Reporter's Life.* New York: Random House, 1996.

Graham, Katharine. *Personal History.* New York: Knopf, 1997.

Gunther, Marc. *The House That Roone Built: The Inside Story of ABC News.* Boston: Little, Brown, 1994.

Herbert, John. *Journalism in the Digital Age.* Boston: Focal Press, 2000.

Reddick, Randy, and Elliot King. *The Online Journalist.* New York: Harcourt, 2001.

Stahl, Leslie. *Reporting Live.* New York: Simon and Schuster, 1999.

Tumber, Howard. *News: A Reader.* New York: Oxford, 1999.

■ SURFING THE INTERNET

There are hundreds of sites that have a connection to journalism. Only a few are listed here.

www.aim.org
Media watchdog group Accuracy in Media's site, which critiques the operation of the news media.

www.cnn.com
CNN Interactive's site. A good example of an online news service. Contains international and national spot news plus special sites for political, scientific, health, travel, financial, and entertainment news.

www.freedomforum.org
The Freedom Forum is an organization dedicated to exploring and improving journalism. This site has links to the First Amendment Center, Media Studies Center, and the Newseum.

www.mediachannel.org
Nonprofit site that offers criticism, interviews with journalists, and a discussion forum devoted to news reporting.

www.newslink.org
American Journalism Review's home page. In addition to the online version of the magazine, this site has links to other media sources as well as research tools.

www.trib.com
A good example of online journalism as practiced by a local paper—the Casper, Wyoming, *Star-Tribune.* Includes almost 50 links to other national and international news sources.

www.zatso.com
A personalized news service that lets a visitor construct his or her own TV newscast.

CHAPTER 13 Public Relations

In May 2000, the U.S. National Highway Safety Administration (NHSA) launched an investigation to examine if certain brands of Firestone tires had contributed to 21 fatal accidents. Most of the accidents involved Ford sport utility vehicles, where the tires had ripped apart at high speeds. What happened next presents an interesting example of how one company coped with a public relations (PR) nightmare.

Firestone made its first mistake when it failed to react quickly to the crisis. There was some evidence that the company knew about a possible problem months in advance of the investigation. Difficulties with the tires had cropped up earlier in Saudi Arabia and in some southern states, but the company refused to acknowledge a problem. In fact, after news of the NHSA investigation leaked out, the company blamed the mishaps on improper maintenance and underinflation. In doing so, Firestone committed another PR mistake: A company should not name blame the victims for its problems.

Ford CEO Jac Nasser meets the press during the Firestone recall. *(AP/Wide World Photo)*

Finally, under government and consumer pressure, Firestone announced a recall of 6.5 million suspect tires. The recall plan, however, caused further complications. Firestone is owned by a Japanese firm, but the company's response to the publicity generated by the recall featured U.S. executives as spokespersons. Another PR mistake: In the midst of a crisis, it's the CEO of the company who should step forward, not a subordinate. It would be weeks before CEO Masatoshi Ono, who preferred the Japanese model of keeping a low profile, spoke out. In contrast, the Ford Motor Company, also affected by the tire problems, spent $5 million on an ad campaign that featured its CEO assuring motorists that the automaker was responsive to their concerns.

Moreover, Firestone was not fully prepared to deal with the mechanics of the recall. The special phone numbers set up by the company were continually busy, and the company website was overloaded. A successful PR effort would have prepared for the increased consumer traffic.

Firestone also misread public response to its proposed recall scheme, which would be done in phases, with some consumers having to wait more than a year for replacements. Consumers were outraged, and the attorneys general of several states threatened lawsuits. An efficient PR enterprise would have alerted top management to possible hostile consumer reaction.

Firestone eventually weathered the crisis, but not before significant damage was done to its credibility and brand image. A better PR effort might not have prevented all the harm, but it certainly would have helped.

Firestone's PR problems may not be typical of those faced on a day-to-day basis by PR agencies and corporate PR departments, but they do illustrate the tremendous importance that favorable public relations has in corporate and consumer settings. In this chapter, we examine the role of public relations in contemporary society.

DEFINING PUBLIC RELATIONS

Before we try to explain what public relations is, it may be helpful to compare it with other facets of mass communication. There are, for example, similarities between advertising and public relations. Both are attempts at persuasion, and both involve using the mass media. Public relations, however, is a management function; advertising is a marketing function. Another difference is that advertising uses the mass media and machine-assisted communication settings; unlike PR, it does not involve interpersonal communications. A third difference is seen in the fact that advertising is normally sponsored. Public relations messages appear as features, news stories, or editorials, and the space or time involved is not paid for. In many instances, advertising, particularly corporate advertising, is used to help further the public relations program.

A concept that is sometimes confused with public relations is press agentry. Press agentry involves staging events or planning enterprises that attract media or public attention to a person, product, organization, or cause. Although press agents are useful in some PR campaigns, public relations encompasses a much broader area and involves more than just attracting attention.

Another concept that is sometimes confused with public relations is **publicity,** the placing of stories in the mass media. Publicity is a tool in the public relations process, but it is not equivalent to PR. For example, it is perfectly possible for a firm to have extensive publicity and bad public relations. Further, publicity is primarily one-way communication; public relations is two-way.

Having examined what public relations is *not,* we now turn to what it *is.* The term *public relations* has many interpretations and meanings. One PR veteran has compiled 500 different ones, ranging from the concise, "PR is doing good and getting credit for it," to the 100-word definition in the *Encyclopaedia Britannica.* Most of the leading textbooks on PR usually lead off with a chapter that attempts to define exactly what public relations is or isn't. Rather than catalog these many definitions, we find it more useful to define PR by examining what PR people do.

1. *Public relations involves working with public opinion.* On the one hand, PR professionals attempt to influence public opinion in a way that is positive to the organization. For example, in the Firestone episode, the company tried (although not always successfully) to reassure motorists that they were trying to fix the problem. In short, the public relations effort was designed to restore favorable public opinion. On the other hand, it is also the function of the PR department to gather information from the public and interpret that

information for top management as it relates to management decisions. This function was apparently absent in the incident; the hostile reaction of its customers surprised management.

2. *Public relations is concerned with communication.* Most people are interested in what an organization is doing to meet their concerns and interests. It is the function of the public relations professional to explain the organization's actions to various **publics** involved with the organization. Public relations communications is two-way communication. The PR professional also pays close attention to the thoughts and feelings of the organization's publics. Some experts refer to public relations as a two-way conduit between an organization and its publics.

   Note that the word "publics" in the preceding section is plural. This is because the organization typically deals with many different publics in its day-to-day operations. Several PR scholars divide these groups into internal and external publics. Internal publics include employees, managers, labor unions, and stockholders. External publics consist of consumers, the government, dealers, suppliers, members of the community, and the mass media. Public relations serves as the link for all these publics.

3. *Public relations is a management function.* It is designed to help a company set its goals and adapt to a changing environment. Public relations practitioners regularly counsel top management. Inherent in the specification of public relations is a planned activity. It is organized and directed toward specific goals and objectives.

Of course, public relations involves much more than just the three functions mentioned above. Perhaps it would be easier, for our purposes, to use the following definition approved by the World Assembly of Public Relations:

> *Public relations is the art and social science of analyzing trends, predicting their consequences, counseling organization leaders and implementing planned programs of action which serve both the organization's and the public's interest.*

A SHORT HISTORY OF PUBLIC RELATIONS

If the term is interpreted broadly enough, the practice of public relations can be traced back to ancient times. The military reports and commentaries prepared by Julius Caesar can be viewed as a triumph in personal and political public relations. During medieval times, both the church and the guilds practiced rudimentary forms of public relations.

It was not until the American Revolution that more recognizable public relations activities became evident. The early patriots were aware that public opinion would play an important role in the war with England and planned their activities accordingly. For example, they staged events, such as the Boston Tea Party, to gain public attention. They also used symbols, such as the Liberty Tree and the Minutemen, that were easily recognized and helped portray their cause in a positive light. Skillful writers such as Samuel Adams, Thomas Paine, Abigail Adams, and Benjamin Franklin used political propaganda to swing public opinion to their side. As a case in point, note that the altercation between an angry mob and British soldiers became known as the "Boston Massacre," an interpretation well suited to the rebel cause.

The Boston Tea Party was a PR move calculated to gain support for the Revolution. Such an event today would be done in daylight so that TV news crews would have an easier time covering it. *(Corbis-Bettmann)*

Later, the Industrial Revolution and the resulting growth of mass production and mass consumption led to the growth of big business. Giant monopolies were formed in the railroad, steel, and oil businesses. Many big corporations tended to disregard the interests of the consumer in their quest for more profits. In fact, many executives felt that the less the public knew about their practices and operations, the better. Around the turn of the century, however, public hostility was aroused against unscrupulous business practices. Led by the muckrakers (see Chapter 5), exposés of industrial corruption and ruthless business tactics filled the nation's magazines. Faced with these attacks, corporations hired communications experts, many of them former newspaper writers, to counteract the effect of these stories. These specialists tried to combat negative publicity by making sure the industry's side of the issue was also presented. These practitioners were the prototypes of what we might call press agents or publicists.

Public relations pioneer Ivy Lee *(Corbis-Bettmann)*

The debut of modern public relations techniques dates back to the first decade of the 1900s. Most historians agree that the first real public relations pioneer was a man named Ivy Lee. In 1903, Lee and George Parker opened a publicity office. A few years later, Lee became the press representative for the anthracite coal operators and the Pennsylvania Railroad. When confronted with a strike in the coal industry, Lee issued a "Declaration of Principles." This statement endorsed the concepts of openness and honesty in dealing with the public; it also marked the shift from 19th-century press agentry to 20th-century public relations. Lee went on to have a successful career

The National Credibility Index was started by PR professionals to measure how the American public perceives its leaders and public figures as believable sources of information. Fifty different sources of information were measured. As of 2000, these were the top five most credible sources:

1. Supreme Court justice
2. Teacher
3. National expert
4. Member of armed forces
5. Local business owner

These were the bottom five:

46. Head of a national interest group
47. Political party leader
48. Public relations specialist
49. Entertainer
50. Radio or TV talk show host

counseling people such as John D. Rockefeller, Jr. Among other achievements, Lee is credited with humanizing business and demonstrating that public relations is most effective when it affects employees, customers, and members of the community. Moreover, Lee would not carry out a public relations program unless it was endorsed and supported by top management.

The government got involved in public relations during World War I when President Woodrow Wilson set up the Creel committee (named for its chair, journalist George Creel). Creel enlisted the top figures in the public relations field to mount a campaign that persuaded newspapers and magazines to donate space for ads that urged Americans to save food and to buy war bonds. Creel advised Wilson on communication strategies and was instrumental in publicizing Wilson's war goal "to make the world safe for democracy." The work of the Creel committee was significant because it demonstrated the power of a well-planned and well-executed public relations campaign. In addition, it helped legitimize the field of public relations.

Following World War I, two more public relations pioneers, Carl Byoir and Edward L. Bernays, appeared on the scene. Bernays is credited with writing the first book on public relations, *Crystallizing Public Opinion,* published in 1923. In 1930, Byoir organized a public relations firm that was one of the world's largest.

The depression caused many Americans to look toward business with suspicion and distrust. In an attempt to regain public favor, many large corporations established their own public relations departments. The federal government, in its attempt to cope with the bad economic climate, also used good public relations practices to its advantage. Franklin Roosevelt introduced his New Deal reform program complete with promotional campaigns to win public acceptance. Roosevelt also recognized the tremendous potential of radio in shaping public opinion, and his fireside chats were memorable examples of personal public relations. The government intensified its public relations efforts during World War II with the creation of the Office of War Information.

During the second half of the 20th century, changes in American society created an atmosphere in which public relations grew tremendously in importance. What are some of the reasons behind the recent surge in this area?

1. Many corporations have recognized that they have a social responsibility to serve the public. Finding the means of fulfilling this responsibility is the task of the public relations department.

You've undoubtedly heard of Father's Day, Mother's Day, and maybe even Earth Day, but how about National Private Investigators' Day? Or Moon Day? Or Cheese Day? (An abridged list of these "national" days can be found at www.stayfreemagazine.org/13/holidays.html. I was surprised to find that my birthday is also National School Nurses Day.) Getting your own day (or week or month) is a big promotional plus, and there are PR firms out there who specialize in carving out spots on the calendar for their clients.

How can you get a day or week or month for your special interest? One way is to enlist a political PR firm that lobbies your case before Congress. If the effort is successful, Congress will pass a bill declaring a certain day to be whatever you want it to be. A second way is to hire a big PR firm to invent one. Such was the case when Hill and Knowlton came up with National Bladder Health Week to promote a new incontinence procedure, and when the Snack Food Association hired Porter Novelli to come up with National Snack Food Month (February). If you celebrated National Snack Food Month too heartily, don't despair. You can always look forward to National Diet Month (January). Of course, if you lack the money to hire professional PR companies, you can simply check the calendar and declare a day all by yourself. There's no copyright on the word "national" and nobody owns the calendar, so go for it. How about a National Introduction to Mass Communication Day?

2. A growing tide of consumerism has caused many corporations and government agencies to be more responsive and communicative to their customers or clients, a function served by the public relations department.

3. The growing complexity of modern corporations and government agencies has made it difficult for them to get their messages to the public without a department that is specifically assigned to that task.

4. Increasing population growth along with more specialization and job mobility have made it necessary for companies to have communication specialists whose task it is to interpret the needs of the audience for the organization.

All these trends have combined to make the past 50 years or so the "era of public relations." The profession has grown from about 19,000 members in 1950 to more than 300,000 people in 2000. Along with this growth has come increased professionalization among public relations practitioners. A professional organization, the Public Relations Society of America, was founded in 1947 and adopted a code of standards in 1954. Public relations education has also made great strides. Recent estimates suggest that about 400 colleges across the country offer courses in public relations. In 1967, the Public Relations Student Society of America was founded. It now has 220 chapters and 6,500 members.

The past decade has seen public relations become even more important. Spin doctors, specialists in political PR, became prominent figures in presidential elections and during the impeachment proceedings against President Bill Clinton. The emergence of dot-com firms and other high-tech industries changed the techniques of PR and sparked the growth of the industry. In 1999, the Bureau of Labor Statistics rated public relations as one of the three fastest-growing businesses in the United States (computers and health services were the other two).

ORGANIZATION OF THE PUBLIC RELATIONS INDUSTRY

Public relations activities are generally handled in two ways. Many organizations have their own public relations departments that work with the managers of all other departments. About 85 percent of the 1,500 largest U.S. companies have such departments. In many companies, these departments are part of top management, and the PR director is responsible to the president of the company. For example,

General Motors and AT&T both have about 200 people in their U.S. PR departments. Other organizations hire an external public relations counsel to give advice on press, government, and consumer relations. In business and industry, about one-third of the PR activity is handled by outside counseling firms. Many major corporations retain an outside agency in addition to their own internal public relations department.

Each of these arrangements has its particular advantages and disadvantages. An in-house department can be at work on short notice and has in-depth knowledge about the company; in addition, its operations tend to be less costly. On the other hand, it's hard for a corporate PR team to take an objective view of the company. Further, internal PR departments tend to have trouble coming up with fresh ideas unless new personnel are frequently added. An outside agency offers more services to its clients than does an internal department. Additionally, external counselors have the advantage of being objective observers, and many firms like the prestige associated with being a client of a respected PR firm. On the other side of the coin, outside agencies are expensive, it takes time for them to learn the inner workings of their client's operations, and their involvement may cause resentment and morale problems among the staff of the client's organization.

Internal or external, public relations professionals perform a wide range of services. These include counseling management, preparing annual reports, handling news releases and other forms of media coverage, supervising employee and other internal communications, managing promotions and special events, fund-raising, lobbying, handling community relations, and writing speeches.

Public relations is practiced in a variety of settings. Although the general principles are the same, the actual duties of the PR practitioner will vary according to the setting. Following are brief descriptions of the major areas in which public relations is practiced.

1.   *Business.* Public relations helps the marketing process by instilling in the consumer a positive attitude toward the company. Public relations also helps promote healthy employee–management relations and serves as a major liaison between the firm and government regulators. Last, all businesses have to be located somewhere, and the PR department makes sure the company is a good citizen in its community.

2.   *Government and politics.* Many government agencies hire public relations specialists to help them explain their activities to citizens and to assist the news media in their coverage of the different agencies. These same specialists also communicate the opinions of the public back to the agency. Government PR is big business; its total expenditures on public information rival the budgets of the four major TV networks. The Department of Defense, for instance, produces thousands of films and TV programs every year. The

This billboard is an example of a public-service PR campaign with a tie-in to a grocery chain. *(Bob Daemmrich/The Image Works)*

Are there certain clients that PR firms should not accept? For example, suppose you are asked to do PR work for the Ku Klux Klan? Or for a coalition that backs antienvironmental causes? Or for a militia group that advocates nonpayment of income taxes?

Existing ethical guidelines and standards in public relations don't offer much specific advice. One position argues that all clients deserve representation. This philosophy adopts the attorney model of PR and contends that PR professionals, like lawyers, have an obligation to represent clients even if they disagree with some of the clients' positions and causes. Like attorneys, PR practitioners should expect no retribution for such action because the client's beliefs are not attributed to the PR person.

The opposing viewpoint suggests that, no matter what the individual PR professional thinks, there are some organizations and causes that are not worthy of representation. This position maintains that the entire PR profession is harmed when firms take on undesirable clients. Consequently, an individual's duty to advance the reputation and standing of the profession takes precedence over individual choice. Advocates of this position also argue that the duty of a PR professional is to serve as the social conscience of an organization and promote social responsibility; by definition, then, a PR firm cannot represent an organization that is involved in socially undesirable activities.

This issue is not simply hypothetical; it surfaces from time to time in the public relations industry. In fact, Ivy Lee, one of the founders of modern public relations, was criticized because he represented the German Dye Trust during the 1930s when the trust was controlled by the Nazi government. More recently, Hill and Knowlton have come under fire for representing such clients as the Church of Scientology and an organization called Citizens for a Free Kuwait, whose main goal was to sway U.S. public opinion to the side of the Kuwaitis during the Gulf War. It was later disclosed that of the $12 million raised in support of this organization, about $200,000 came from private citizens and $11.8 million from the government of Kuwait.

Cases such as these illustrate the importance of establishing ethical boundaries for PR professionals.

Department of Agriculture sends out thousands of news releases annually. Political public relations is another growing field. A growing number of candidates for public office hire a PR expert to help them get their message across to voters.

3. *Education.* PR personnel work in both elementary and higher education. The most visible area of practice in elementary and high school concerns facilitating communication between educators and parents. Other tasks, however, are no less important. In many school systems, the PR person also handles relations with the school board, local and state legislative bodies, and the news media. Public relations at the college and university level, although less concerned with parental relations, has its own agenda of tasks. For example, fund-raising, legislative relations, community relations, and internal relations with faculty and students would be concerns of most college PR departments.

4. *Hospitals.* The rising cost of health care and greater public expectations from the medical profession have given increased visibility to the public relations departments in our nation's hospitals. Some of the publics that hospital PR staffs have to deal with are patients, patients' families, consumers, state insurance commissions, physicians, nurses, and other staff members. Despite the increasing importance of hospital public relations, many hospitals do not have a full-time PR staff. Consequently, this is one area that will see significant growth in the future.

5. *Nonprofit organizations.* The United Way, the Girl Scouts, the American Red Cross, and the Salvation Army are just a few of the organizations that need PR professionals. Probably the biggest PR goal in organizations such as these is fund-raising. Other objectives would include encouraging volunteer participation, informing contributors how their money is spent, and working with the individuals served by the organization.

6. *Professional associations.* Organizations such as the American Medical Association, the American Dairy Association, and the American Bar Association employ PR practitioners. In addition to providing news and information to the association's members, other duties of the PR staff would include recruiting new members, planning national conferences, influencing government decisions, and working with the news media.

7. *Entertainment and sports.* A significant number of PR experts work for established and would-be celebrities in the entertainment and sports worlds. A practitioner handling this type of client has two major responsibilities: Get the client favorable media coverage and protect the client from bad publicity. Additionally, many sports and entertainment events (e.g., the Super Bowl, a motion picture premiere) have PR campaigns associated with them.

S O U N D B Y T E

International PR Etiquette

International PR experts advise clients on the subtle intricacies of doing business abroad. Many tips involve minding your manners. For example:

- In some countries, crossing your legs and pointing your toe at someone is an insult.
- In many cultures, it is impolite to discuss business matters while dining.
- Be careful about bringing gifts. In Germany, red roses are for lovers only.
- Slurping your soup is frowned on in America, but it is accepted behavior in Japan.

8. *International PR.* Corporations with branches throughout the world, global news media such as CNN, an interrelated world economy, the shifting political scene in Europe—all these factors have combined to make this area one of the fastest-growing in public relations. International PR specialists might provide businesses operating in other countries with aid and information about local customs, language problems, cultural difficulties, and legal dilemmas.

9. *Investor relations.* This area (called IR for convenience) entails building a favorable image for a company and keeping shareholders happy. A public company needs to communicate information, both positive and negative, that might have an impact on its stock price to the financial community in general and shareholders in particular. To do this effectively, IR professionals must know the workings of the financial press as well as the various channels used to communicate with shareholders, such as annual reports, quarterly reports, and annual meetings. As more and more Americans invest in the stock and bond markets and as financial markets become more global, the importance of IR will surely increase.

10. *Politics.* The importance of public relations in political campaigns increases with every election. Building the right personal image, putting the proper spin on the interpretation of events, and responding to the charges of other candidates are all part of the job of a political PR specialist. There are many public relations firms who specialize in political campaigns.

11. *Crisis management.* Probably the ultimate test for the PR practitioner is dealing with a crisis. Such crises appear infrequently, but poor handling of the crisis can have long-term negative effects that might cripple a company and/or ruin the reputation of a PR firm. Tylenol faced such a crisis, for example, when several people were killed as a result of someone's tampering with its product. Pepsi-Cola faced a similar crisis when reports about hypodermic syringes in Pepsi cans began to surface. In both of these cases, the companies used their PR departments to cope successfully with their predicaments. In a crisis, the public seeks out more information and the

organization involved in the crisis is subjected to increased scrutiny by both the media and the public. Experts in crisis management PR generally counsel their clients to accomplish three goals: terminate the crisis, limit damage, and restore credibility.

From the above list, it appears that the profession requires PR specialists as well as generalists. In the next section, we will see how the PR function is typically organized and what jobs PR professionals perform.

DEPARTMENTS AND STAFF

This section discusses the structure of both internal public relations departments and external public relations agencies. The internal department setup will be discussed first. At the outset, remember that no two company departmental charts are alike, so the precise makeup of the PR departments will vary. Figure 13–1 displays a common organizational arrangement for a corporate PR department. Note that the PR director is directly responsible to the president (or the chief executive officer). Since PR affects every department, its supervision by the person who runs the entire organization makes sense. The figure also illustrates that the department is designed to handle communication with both internal and external publics. Corporate communications involves communicating with internal publics—workers, shareholders, unions—while community relations consists of dealing with external publics—community residents, customers, the government, and so forth. Press relations, of course, refers to dealing with the news media.

The organization of a public relations agency is more complex. Figure 13–2 shows one possible arrangement. As is apparent, the structure is somewhat similar to that of an advertising agency. Also, note that the range of services provided by the agency is more extensive than that of the internal corporate PR department.

THE PUBLIC RELATIONS PROGRAM

Pretend you're the public relations director for a leading auto company. The company is entering into an agreement with a foreign car manufacturer to produce a foreign model in the United States. Unfortunately, to increase efficiency and centralize its operations, the company will have to close one of its plants located in a

Figure 13–1

Organization of a Corporate Public Relations Department

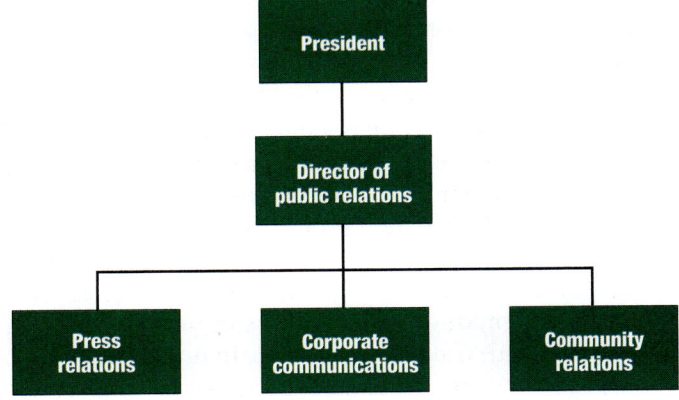

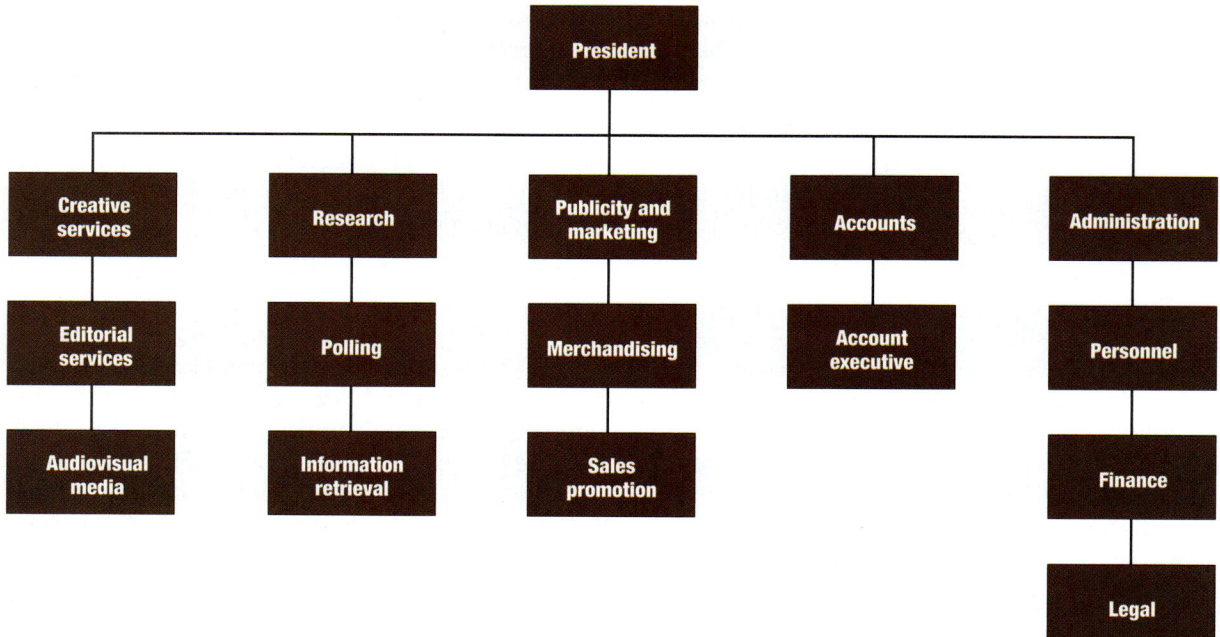

Figure 13–2

Organization of a Public
Relations Counseling
Agency

Midwestern city. About a thousand employees will have to be transferred or find
new jobs, and the community will face a significant economic blow. It will be
the job of the public relations department to communicate this decision to the
community.

   The thorny problem outlined above is a typical one for the public relations professional. Handling it requires a planned, organized, and efficient public relations
program. This section will trace the four main steps involved in developing a typical PR campaign:

1. Information gathering
2. Planning
3. Communication
4. Evaluation

■ Information Gathering

The information-gathering stage is an important one because what is learned from
it will influence the remaining stages. **Information gathering** can be achieved
through several means. Organizational records, trade journals, public records, and
reference books serve as valuable sources for existing data. Personal contacts, mail
to the company, advisory committees, and personnel reports represent other
sources of information. If more formal research methods are required, they might
be carried out by the PR department or by an outside agency that specializes in
public opinion polling or survey research. Let's return to our example. The PR
director at the auto company will need to gather a great deal of information. How
much will the company save by its reorganization? Exactly how many workers
will be transferred? Will the company help find new jobs for the workers who will
be unemployed? What will be the precise economic impact on the community?

Where does PR fit in the organization? Traditional thinking, as mentioned earlier in the chapter, treats PR as a management function. Another philosophy (which emerged during the mid-1990s), called integrated marketing communications, or IMC, argues that PR should really be part of the marketing function. This distinction involves more than just an organizational war for turf; it holds significant implications for the future of the field. If PR is subsumed within marketing, it loses much of its management component.

Those who advocate IMC point out that in addition to product and price, public and social issues also influence marketing. An integrated approach ensures that a company responds to all these concerns with a single voice. Additionally, proponents of IMC note that clients want their advertising, PR, and marketing activities coordinated and unified. Further, IMC saves a company money since a single IMC department can operate more efficiently than separate departments of advertising, marketing, and PR. Last, proponents argue that everything that a PR department does—

employee communication, crisis management, promotion—boils down to marketing functions.

Opponents of IMC argue that the credibility of PR efforts will be hurt if they are seen as simply another marketing tool. It is already difficult for PR practitioners to maintain feelings of honesty and believability on the part of the audience, and lumping the PR department with marketing will make the problem even worse. Another argument suggests that IMC hurts the diversity of opinion available to management. A separate PR department makes it more likely that different suggestions and alternative courses of action will be advanced. Finally, opponents argue that PR involves two-way communication that takes into account the needs of various publics, whereas IMC treats everybody as a customer and places top priority in sales.

One of the struggles for the industry in the years to come will be the development of a structure that recognizes the unique contributions of each of the departments that make up the modern organization.

What will become of the empty buildings that will be left behind? Will the employees believe what the company tells them? What do people expect from the company? Will the company's image be hurt in other areas of the United States?

Planning

Phase two is the planning stage. There are two general types of planning: **strategic** and **tactical.** Strategic plans involve long-range, general goals that the organization wishes to achieve. Top management usually formulates an organization's strategic plans. Tactical plans are more specific. They detail the tasks that must be accomplished by every department in the organization to achieve the strategic goals. Some plans that are drawn up might be used only once; others might serve as standing plans that set general organizational policy.

Planning is a vital part of the PR program. Some of the items involved in a PR campaign involve framing the objectives, considering the alternatives, assessing the risks and benefits involved in each alternative, deciding on a course of action, figuring up the budget, and securing the necessary approvals from within the organization. In recent years, many PR practitioners have endorsed a technique known as **management by objectives (MBO).** Simply put, MBO means that the organization sets observable and measurable goals for itself and allocates its resources to meet those objectives. For example, a corporation might set as a goal increasing sales by 25 percent over the next two years. When the time elapsed, it would be easy to see if the goal had been achieved. This approach is becoming more popular in PR because top management typically thinks in these terms, so it allows PR practitioners to speak the same language as chief executives. It also keeps the department on target in solving PR problems, and it provides concrete feedback about the efficiency of the PR process. In our hypothetical example, some possible objectives might be informing more than 50 percent of the community about the reasons for the move or making sure community and national attitudes about the company are not adversely affected.

■ Communication

Phase three is the communication phase. After gathering facts and making plans, the organization assumes the role of the source of communication. Several key decisions are made at this stage concerning the nature of the messages and the types of media to be used. Because mass communication media are usually important channels in a PR program, it is necessary for public relations practitioners to have a thorough knowledge of the various media and their strengths and weaknesses. Moreover, PR professionals should know the various production techniques for the print and broadcast media. Some common ways of publicizing a message through the mass media include press releases, video news releases, press kits, photographs, paid advertising, films, videotapes, press conferences, and interviews.

Public relations also makes use of other channels to get messages to its publics. These might include both the interpersonal and the machine-assisted settings. House publications, brochures, faxes, letters, bulletins, posters, websites, e-mail, billboards, and bulletin boards are possible communication channels used by a company to reach its own employees. On a more personal level, public meetings, speeches, demonstrations, staged events, open houses, and tours are other possibilities.

In the hypothetical example, our PR director would probably use a variety of messages and media. News conferences, ads, news releases, and public meetings are appropriate vehicles for explaining the company's position to its external public. Meanwhile, house publications, bulletin boards, speeches, and letters could be used to reach its internal public.

■ Evaluation

The last phase concerns **evaluation** of the PR program. How well did it work? The importance of evaluation in public relations is becoming greater because of the use of MBO techniques. If a measurable goal was proposed for the PR program, then an evaluation technique should be able to measure success in reaching that goal. Several different aspects might be measured. One easy method is simply to gauge the volume of coverage that the campaign generated. The number of press releases sent out, the number of letters mailed, speeches made, and so on, are simple to compute. In like manner, press clippings and mentions in TV and radio news can also be tabulated. It's important to remember, however, that volume does not equal results. A million press clippings mean nothing if they are not read by the audience. Measuring the impact of a campaign on the audience requires more sophisticated techniques of analysis. Some common techniques would include questionnaires distributed to random samples of the audience, telephone surveys, panels, reader-interest studies, and the use of experimental campaigns. It is likely that our hypothetical PR director would use many of these techniques.

Before closing, we should point out that the above discussion talks about these four steps as though they are distinct stages. In actuality, the PR program is a continuous process, and one phase blends into the next. The results learned in the evaluation stage, for example, are also part of the information-gathering phase of the next cycle of the PR program. In our continuing car company example, the PR department would use the results of surveys and focus groups to determine such things as whether the company's image has suffered, how much credibility the company has with consumers, and if there was any change in customer loyalty. These findings will help in terms of planning the goals of the next PR campaign.

Contributed by Dr. Vince Benigni   Ty Cobb, a member of Baseball's All-Century Team, retired in 1928 after a brilliant yet tumultuous 24-year career. The Ty Cobb Museum, located in his rural northeast Georgia hometown of Royston, opened its doors in 1998. Why so long to erect a "formal shrine"? The project didn't necessarily stall because of funding issues or even political wrangling. Instead, the project's decision makers had not addressed critical research and planning initiatives which spark a successful, multifaceted public relations campaign.

Cognizant of the need to objectively analyze the situation and canvass potential stakeholders, the museum committee consulted several University of Georgia researchers in fall 1997. Five students were then entrusted to develop a campaign for the client. Primary research, including benchmark surveys and in-depth interviews, concluded that the concepts of awareness and exposure were key developmental issues. Specifically, the public's knowledge of Cobb lagged far below respondents' "knowledge of baseball history." Statistics also revealed that a Cobb museum would be an appealing educational and entertainment venue to prospective patrons. *If you build it* (and successfully educate strategic publics through media gatekeepers and direct communication avenues) . . . *they will come.*

Setting measurable objectives, such as increasing the public's knowledge of Cobb commensurate to its historical knowledge, highlighted the campaign's planning stages, which also broached special events, a formal budget, and a long-range timetable. Communication initiatives targeted both media gatekeepers (press kits, pitch letters) and publics (web site, brochures).

However, the key to campaign success was not in distribution, but in the message. "The Other Side of Cobb" served as a boilerplate in external communications; Cobb is largely depicted by media and historians in unflattering terms, the result of assorted (and oft-embellished) transgressions. Instead of employing a defensive/denial posture, decision makers focused on *educating* the public—through written communications and in museum displays and videos—on Cobb's philanthropic legacy, which included donating funds for the local hospital and endowing a multimillion-dollar college scholarship fund.

The formal student presentation (to members of Ty Cobb Healthcare System, which administers the museum) was attended by print and broadcast media, and momentum for the project grew swiftly. In July of 1998, the newest Hall of Famer, Phil Niekro, headlined a list of luminaries at a grand opening honoring baseball's first Cooperstown inductee. Many members of the Cobb family were extremely touched by the special event, and their relationship to the museum has been paramount in terms of memorabilia acquisition and more importantly, issues of trust.

Recently, public relations efforts have shifted more to fundraising (silent auction, membership/donor plan) and community relations (a county Hall of Fame, sponsored trips to events). A multimedia kiosk is scheduled to debut in 2001, and a formal educational program with area schools is forthcoming. Events such as Ty Cobb's 100 Greatest Moments (featured in a prominent museum display), roundtable discussions, and book signings have proven gatekeeper- and patron-friendly, as have formal pitches to prominent regional and national media. Cobb Healthcare System has also aggressively publicized the museum and developed formal partnerships with key healthcare vendors to help fund major projects . . .

The museum's overarching mission is to foster education about Ty Cobb. Overcoming stereotypes—in this case, Cobb as "mean-spirited" and that museums can only prosper in highbrow, urban settings—is a continuous challenge. Like Cobb, the museum is a diamond in the rough. Sound public relations techniques will continue to smooth the legacy for both parties.

 ## ECONOMICS

Companies, nonprofit groups, and government agencies spend large sums of money on public relations. The total amount spent on corporate PR activities is hard to measure, but some information is available about the revenues of PR agencies. In 1999, the top 50 PR firms in the United States earned more than $2.8 billion in fee income, an all-time record. As was the case for other media, this increase was fueled mainly by an influx of money from dot-com firms.

The industry is dominated by giant PR firms owned by ad agencies. As of 2000, the biggest PR companies with ad agency parent companies were the Omnicom group (composed of Porter Novelli, Fleishman-Hilliard, Ketchum, and several other smaller companies); Young and Rubicam (Burson-Marseller, Cohn and Wolfe); and the WPP group (Hill and Knowlton, Olgivy PR). The largest independent PR companies were Edelman PR Worldwide and Ruder Finn. The PR business can also be volatile, especially for smaller agencies, whose fee income might vary by 40 to 80 percent from year to year.

PR agencies earn their money in a number of ways. Some perform a specific project for a fixed fee. An annual report, for instance, might cost $5,000. Some charge their clients a retainer every month, which might range from a few hundred to a few thousand dollars. Hill and Knowlton, for example, has a minimum monthly fee of $7,500. Other firms keep track of the time spent on various projects and charge clients an hourly rate. Still others bill for time plus special fees for extra services and materials.

PR ONLINE

The Internet has added another dimension to public relations. It provides more tools for the PR practitioner to use and opens up a new channel of communication with the public, but it also presents new and challenging problems.

The Internet has streamlined the way PR information is distributed to the media. E-mail and online services have replaced the paper-mail channel that was traditionally used for press releases. PR Newswire, for example, takes information from PR agencies and PR departments and makes this information available to newsrooms across the country. The online services provide everything necessary for the journalist to prepare a story: breaking news, background information about the company, bios, even audio and video clips.

PR practitioners who need to keep track of how various issues are being covered by the media can hire companies who scan the net for mentions of various topics. One such firm, eWatch, monitors 1,000 web-based newspapers, magazines,

The online home of PR Newswire. More than 35,000 journalists can access press releases through its web site. *(PR Newswire)*

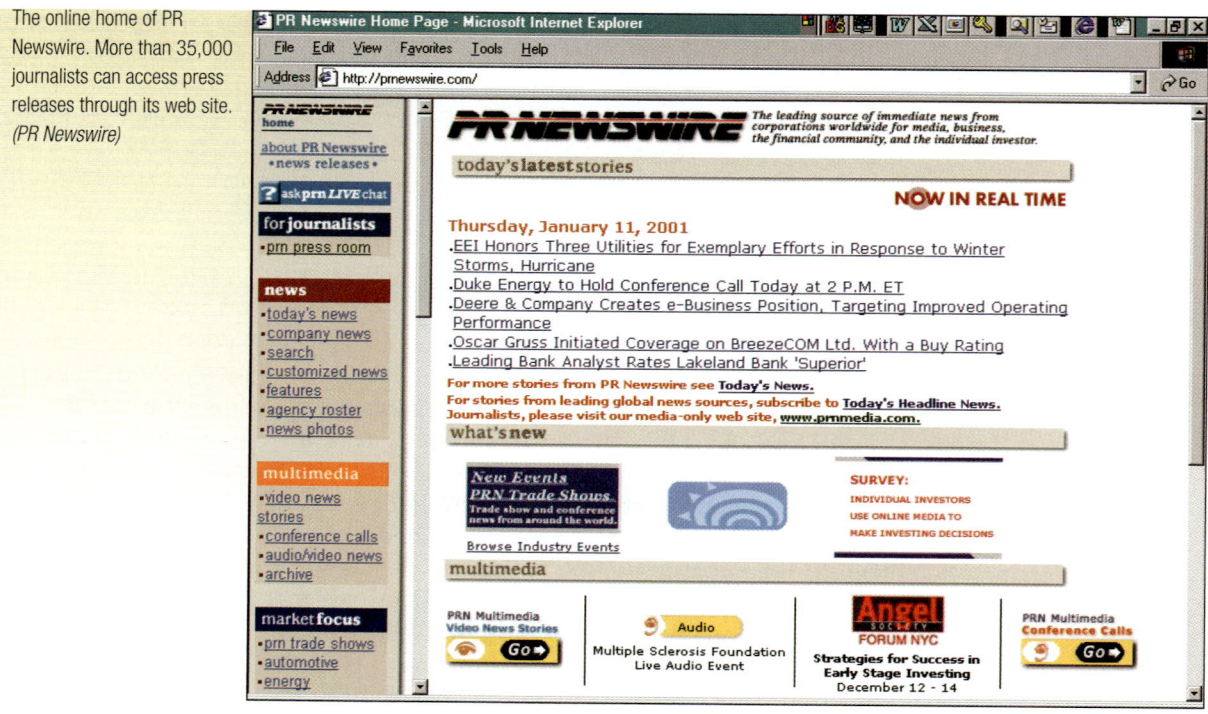

Here's another example of how the Internet makes PR more challenging. As you might have noticed, the fast-food restaurant that used to be called Kentucky Fried Chicken recently changed its name to KFC. In early 1999, an anonymous e-mail circulating on the net claimed that the name change was done because the product KFC was serving was some genetically manipulated organism that was so different from the real feathery bird that the company couldn't legally call it "chicken." The e-mail went on to claim that these mutant creatures had no beaks, feathers, or feet and that KFC had dramatically shrunk the bone structure to get more meat from them. The e-mail stated that the facts were from research done at the University of New Hampshire.

Luckily for KFC, the company was able to mount a PR campaign that effectively countered the rumor. KFC placed messages on its website denying the rumor. The University of New Hampshire issued a statement on its website saying no such research had been done on its campus. (The site was getting about 10,000 hits a day during the height of the rumor.) The national news media were sympathetic to KFC's plight and played the story as an example of how easy it is for unfounded rumors to spread on the net. Nonetheless, this episode illustrates how easy it is for one person with a modem to cause major headaches for a large corporation.

and news sites, such as CNN.com. Another firm, NetCurrents, monitors websites, newsgroups, and message boards for mentions about a specific company. If NetCurrents spots incorrect information about the company, it will automatically post a correction.

The Internet also furnishes numerous resources for PR professionals. Some photo archives are online and available for searching. Directories of editors and journalists are also accessible via the net. Other online services keep track of professional conferences and trade shows that might be of interest to PR professionals and e-mail them about registration deadlines. Market research can be done over the net using Internet surveys or focus groups.

Organizations have enlisted PR firms to turn their websites into new channels of communication. A corporate site might contain testimonials from satisfied buyers, new-product announcements, a consumer chat room, company history, news releases, and e-mail addresses. A website also allows PR professionals to respond quickly to events and crisis situations. Firestone's site, for example, contained detailed information about their voluntary recall as well as a message from the CEO outlining the company's response to the crisis.

The net has opened up channels of communications within companies as well. The Intranet, sort of an Internet within a company that contains information that is not available to the general public, has become a widely used tool for internal communication in many companies. Some Intranets contain an employee newsletter, travel guides, internal information libraries, company workplace policies, and training tutorials.

The Internet has also made the job of PR professionals more challenging. It's easy for unscrupulous individuals to post incorrect information on the web that may damage a company. In 2000, such a person sent a bogus e-mail press release to an online news service, where it was widely disseminated. The release incorrectly reported that the CEO of the Emulex Company, a high-tech firm, had resigned and that the company's profits would be less than expected. The false information caused the company's stock to temporarily lose about 60 percent of its value (about $2.5 billion) before the hoax was discovered. The stock eventually recovered, but some investors lost large sums of money. Monitoring the net for such incidents and responding quickly to them is a difficult task for the PR department at any organization.

The code of conduct of the Public Relations Society of America states in part: "We adhere to the highest standards of accuracy and truth in advancing the interests of those we represent and in communicating with the public." It goes on to state that a member shall "be honest and accurate in all communications." These statements seem fairly straightforward, but is there room for interpretation of what constitutes the "truth" and "accuracy"?

An example used by Thomas Schick in the winter, 1994/1995 issue of *Public Relations Quarterly* illustrates some of the issues associated with this question. Suppose you're the PR director for an historical park. The park recreates the home life, crafts, costumes, and general ambience of 19th-century life. The biggest attraction at the park is a restored antique train that visitors can ride around the park. Many people come to the park simply to ride the train. This year, however, the train is undergoing repairs and will not be operating.

The time has come for you to write a press release promoting the park for the upcoming season. What do you do?

(A)   Write the release stressing the benefits of visiting the park's other attractions and not mention the train repairs.

(B)   Write the release and include the fact that the train would not be operating.

Suppose you chose (A). There is nothing inaccurate in what you have prepared; you simply withheld some information. Is there an ethical difference between telling a lie and withholding a truth? How might you analyze this course of action? One method of ethical analysis suggests that a person weigh the good that would result from a decision against the bad. Let's try that method on this particular case.

You might argue that if you mentioned that the train would not be operating many people would stay away and would miss out on the educational benefits of all the other exhibits. You might also argue that mentioning the train's absence would decrease the number of visitors to the park and hurt the park's finances so much that it might be forced to close, therefore denying everybody the educational experience of visiting the park. Thus, there seems to be some good reasons for withholding the truth.

On the other hand, not mentioning the train's unavailability seems calculated to deceive the public. In the absence of other information, most reasonable people would expect the train to be operating. Some people would be inconvenienced if they make a long trip solely to ride the train and then leave when they find it's not operating. Others will suffer disappointment when they find the train is not operating. Many might not ever come back. This may cost the park in the long run.

Moreover, by issuing a press release the PR director has placed the message in the news media. The audience has a high expectation that information appearing in the news media is accurate and complete. By not telling the whole story, the PR director has also harmed the credibility of the news media and may have jeopardized future relationships with them. Editors may view any subsequent news releases with great skepticism and perhaps not run them.

In sum, it seems that the short-term gains realized by not telling the whole truth are outweighed by the long-term losses. In this case, telling the whole truth may be the best policy.

PUBLIC RELATIONS

Newcomers to the public relations field typically begin their work in the corporate area, with most people starting off in the public relations department of a medium-sized to large organization. A smaller number go directly into PR counseling firms. Others follow a different career path into the profession by first working at a newspaper or a broadcasting station and then moving into public relations. In any case, those in the PR industry recommend that prospective job seekers have excellent communications skills, particularly in writing, since many entry-level jobs entail writing and editing news releases, reports, employee publications, and speeches. Other qualifications that are desirable are a knowledge of public opinion research techniques, business practices, law, the social sciences, and computer-related skills.

New employees in the PR department are expected to perform a wide range of duties. More specifically, a newcomer would be expected to write news releases; update mailing lists; research materials for speeches; provide material for the organization's website; edit company publications; arrange special events; produce special reports, films, and tapes; and give public speeches.

The job market in public relations is expanding, thanks to the growth of dot-com companies. At the end of 2000, dot-com companies were creating more jobs faster than they could fill them. This growing job market has led to greater opportunities in both large and small PR firms. In addition to the high-tech sector, other areas where employment opportunities are increasing are biotechnology and health care.

Even with the improving job market, competition for entry-level positions will remain keen. One way that is helpful in gaining initial entry into the profession is to secure an internship with a public relations firm while still in college. A survey of recent graduates now working in public relations revealed that undergraduate internships turned into full-time jobs for about one-fifth of those surveyed. Internships may carry a modest salary, or they may involve no pay at all; some internships carry college credit, others do not. In any event, all internships can be valuable training experience.

As in other media-related work, the job applicant should not be too choosy about his or her first job. Most counselors recommend taking any job that is available, even if it lacks the glamour and the salary that the applicant was hoping for. Once you are inside the firm, it is much easier to move to those positions that are more attractive.

■ MAIN POINTS

- Public relations is difficult to define, but most practitioners agree that PR involves counseling management about communication strategies that can improve public opinion about an organization.

- Modern public relations began around the turn of the 20th century and has steadily increased in importance.

- PR is practiced in numerous settings, including business, government, and the nonprofit sector.

- A PR campaign consists of the following stages: information gathering, planning, communication, and evaluation.

- The Internet is an important part of PR. It is used to provide information to the public and to obtain background information for PR professionals.

■ QUESTIONS FOR REVIEW

1. Define *public relations.*
2. What are some of the major areas that make use of public relations?

3. What are the stages in a public relations campaign?
4. How has the Internet changed the practice of public relations?

■ QUESTIONS FOR CRITICAL THINKING

1. Can you think of any examples where you use PR in your personal life (like putting the best spin on a bad grade in a course)?
2. Why is the term *public relations* so hard to define? Is it important to have a definition that everybody agrees on?

3. What should Firestone have done differently in handling its recall crisis?
4. Many journalists look with disfavor on the field of public relations. What might account for this attitude?

■ KEY TERMS

publicity (p. 349)
publics (p. 350)
information gathering (p. 358)
strategic (planning) (p. 359)

tactical (planning) (p. 359)
management by objectives (MBO)
(p. 359)

evaluation (p. 360)

■ SUGGESTIONS FOR FURTHER READING

Cutlip, Scott. *Public Relations History*. Hillsdale, NJ: Erlbaum, 1995.

Cutlip, Scott, Allen Center, and Glen Broom. *Effective Public Relations*. Upper Saddle River, NJ: Prentice Hall, 2000.

Marlow, E. *Electronic Public Relations*. Belmont, CA: Wadsworth, 1996.

Matera, Fran. *Public Relations Campaigns and Techniques*. Boston: Allyn and Bacon, 2000.

Newsom, Doug, Judy VanSlyke Turk, and Dean Kruckeberg. *This Is PR: The Realities of Public Relations*. Belmont, CA: Wadsworth, 2000.

Wilcox, Dennis, Phillip Ault, and Warren Agee. *Public Relations: Strategies and Tactics*. New York: Longman, 1998.

■ SURFING THE INTERNET

Some of these sites are mentioned in the text. Others appear first on this list. Remember that the web is always changing. Some sites move, some change their focus, and others simply evaporate.

www.ewatch.com
The Internet monitoring service. Its promotional text says, "Safeguard stakeholder value, protect corporate reputation, monitor competition, identify trends, and pinpoint corporate activism." Includes sound bites from satisfied customers of companies such as Heinz and Mrs. Fields.

www.ketchum.com
The home page of Ketchum Public Relations Worldwide. Includes a description of the company, a list of the worldwide offices, a bulletin board where visitors can provide feedback, and links to some of the company's clients—including one to the Miller Genuine Draft Tap Room.

www.prcentral.com
Current news, issues, and controversies about PR. Also contains a directory of PR films.

www.prenewswire.com
A source of news about corporations for reporters and investors. Lists the day's top business stories and has links to specialized news about entertainment, autos, finance, and leisure activities.

www.prmuseum.com
A museum of public relations. Contains extensive information on the pioneers of PR.

www.prsa.org
The home page of the Public Relations Society of America. Includes general information about the society, a list of relevant publications, and a link to the PR student society. A recently added feature allows members to post their résumés in cyberspace.

CHAPTER 14 Advertising

Epidemic.com came up with a program that inserted banner ads into regular e-mail. Relatively unknown, the company decided to take a gamble and advertise during the 2000 Super Bowl to increase its name recognition. Epidemic.com joined 16 other dot-coms in shelling out nearly $2 million each for a 30-second spot. Epidemic.com's ad depicted people getting money for doing everyday things: A man was paid $1 by a bathroom attendant for using the rest room; a woman was paid $1 for sneezing in an elevator; another man was given money for sending e-mail—the company's selling angle. Although critics panned the ad, it did reach a potential audience of 125 million people and Epidemic.com reported increased traffic on its website the day after the game.

Unfortunately, the company had spent most of its marketing and promotion budget on that one Super Bowl spot. It couldn't sustain any momentum generated by its expensive spot. Five months after the game, Epidemic.com was out of business.

The saga of Epidemic.com illustrates several things about the advertising industry at the start of the new millennium. TV advertising, particularly during big events such as the Olympics, the Oscar award show, and the Super Bowl, has gotten more expensive. Dot-com companies have spent huge sums of money on advertising, raising the total amount spent on advertising to record levels. But the future of many dot-coms is in doubt, and this revenue stream may not be as lucrative as it was during 1999 and 2000.

This chapter will examine the advertising industry's history, structure, operations, and social concerns. In addition, it will take a closer look at how the Internet has affected advertising.

Advertising has gotten more expensive, and advertisers have found more imaginative ways to get their messages to the audience. Like the yellow first-down stripe, the FedEx logo in the middle of the field has been inserted into the picture electronically. During the 2001 Super Bowl, virtual ads like this one were placed in the international coverage but were not seen in the United States. *(AP/Wide World Photos)*

DEFINING ADVERTISING

Simply defined, advertising is any form of nonpersonal presentation and promotion of ideas, goods, and services usually paid for by an identified sponsor. Note three key terms in the above definition. Advertising is "nonpersonal"; it is directed toward a large group of anonymous people. Even direct-mail advertising, which may be addressed to a specific person, is prepared by a computer and signed by a machine. Second, advertising typically is "paid for." This fact differentiates advertising from publicity, which is not usually purchased. Sponsors such as Coke and Delta pay for the time and the space they use to get their message across. (Nonprofit organizations, such as the Red Cross or the United Way, advertise but do not pay for time or space. Broadcast stations, newspapers, and magazines run these ads free as a public service.) Third, for obvious reasons, the sponsor of the ad is "identified." In fact, in most instances, identifying the sponsor is the prime purpose behind the ad—otherwise, why advertise? Perhaps the only situation in which the identity of the advertiser may not be self-evident is political advertising. Because of this, broadcasters and publishers will not accept a political ad without a statement identifying those responsible for it.

Functions of Advertising

Advertising fulfills four basic functions in society. First, it serves a marketing function by helping companies that provide products or services sell their products. Personal selling, sales promotions, and advertising work together to help market the product. Second, advertising is educational. People learn about new products and services, or improvements in existing ones, through advertising. Third, advertising plays an economic role. The ability to advertise allows new competitors to enter the business arena. Competition, in turn, encourages product improvements and can lead to lower prices. Moreover, advertising reaches a mass audience, thus greatly reducing the cost of personal selling and distribution. Finally, advertising performs a definite social function. By vividly displaying the material and cultural opportunities available in a free-enterprise society, advertising helps increase productivity and raises the standard of living.

Types of Advertising

Advertising can be classified in several ways. One useful division is to distinguish the **target audience**—the specific segment of the population for whom the product or service has a definite appeal. Many target audiences can be defined; the most general are consumers and business. **Consumer advertising,** as the name suggests, is targeted at the people who buy goods and services for personal use. For example, Campbell's (known for its soups) uses consumer advertising to direct its ads to the adults and children most likely to buy soup at the grocery store. Most of the advertising that people are exposed to falls into this category. **Business-to-business advertising** is aimed at people who buy products for business use. Industrial, trade, and professional—as well as agricultural—advertising are all part of this category. Consumer advertising is the focus of most of this chapter, but we will also take a brief look at business-to-business advertising.

Geographic focus is another way to classify advertising. International advertising is used for products and services that are used all over the globe. Coca-Cola and McDonald's, for example, advertise in dozens of countries and in many

The most outspoken critics of advertising charge that it stimulates greed, envy, and avarice—three of the seven deadly sins—a claim that can be made by no other industry. Specifically, foes of advertising claim that it causes people to buy things that they otherwise would not. Flashy ads for new-model cars prompt people to trade in a perfectly good older model simply for the prestige and status of owning a new one. Even though the old VCR works fine, run out and buy the latest version with new bells and whistles. Still wearing last year's clothes? Shame on you. Go out and buy the latest fashions as seen in print and TV ads. In short, advertising *creates* needs and makes people buy things they don't *really* need or want.

In reply to this criticism, advertising practitioners point out that humans have a variety of needs; some are biological (the need for food) and basic (the need for a safe place to live). Others are more complicated (the need for self-esteem and self-actualization). Advertising, say its supporters, caters to a wide variety of needs, not just basic ones. There is nothing wrong in buying a new car every year if it helps a person's self-esteem. Buying the latest fashions can help a person's quest for self-actualization. Advertising is directed at many forms of need fulfillment, some of them subtle and personal. It's presumptuous of critics to tell consumers what they need or don't need. In this argument, advertising is pictured as catering to a variety of needs that are already present in consumers; it does little in creating new ones. As further support for this argument, advertisers point out that many heavily advertised products fail, and there is no evidence to suggest that advertising can compel people to purchase things they don't want.

A second line of criticism holds that advertising promotes materialistic values and lifestyles. Advertising persuades us to evaluate others not by who they are, but by what they possess. Material objects are portrayed as desirable goals. The people whom advertising presents as models to be emulated are not those who possess admirable personal qualities. Instead, we see people who drive fancy or powerful cars, wear expensive jewelry, write with the best pen, wear the trendiest clothes, or watch the biggest TV set. Advertising encourages people to spend and acquire, and makes consumption the most important activity in life. Critics go on to point out that this aspect of advertising is particularly disruptive among those with low incomes who do not have the means to attain the material goals portrayed in ads.

In response to this argument, supporters of advertising point out that advertising did not create the emphasis on materialism in American life. Writings about rampant materialism in American culture can be found from as early as 1830. Major holidays in the United States celebrate consumption and materialism. Christmas, for example, encourages gift giving; Thanksgiving, eating. Our basic economic system of capitalism stresses the production and consumption of economic goods. Advertising simply reflects the larger values of U.S. society and shouldn't be blamed for portraying them.

Finally, advertising is criticized for its intrusiveness. The typical American is the most advertised-to person in the world. U.S. companies spend more than $500 per person on advertising, more than companies in any other country. According to *Business Week*, you and I are exposed to about 3,000 commercial messages a day. In addition to the ubiquitous commercials on radio, on TV, and in print, advertising is now piped into supermarkets, airports, and doctors' offices; plastered on bathroom walls; splashed on the sides of race cars; snuck into the plots of feature films; displayed on blimps; and printed on the sides of hot dogs. Plans are even in the works to put ads in outer space. The avalanche of ads has made it difficult for advertisers to get consumers to notice their ads, let alone remember them. This causes additional pressure to find new channels and new attention-getting techniques and results in even more intrusiveness.

Even advertising's supporters agree that advertising is hard to avoid. But they go on to point out that this is a small price to pay for the social and economic benefits that it provides for society. Without advertising, television and radio would not be free and magazines and newspapers would cost at least twice as much. Advertising that appears on the sides of buses helps keep fares down. The uniforms worn by Little League teams were probably acquired for free in return for the advertiser's name on the back. Would you mind seeing ads for Coke in this textbook if it meant the price was $10 cheaper?

Obviously, these are complicated issues, made even more difficult because there is no simple way to sort out the effects of advertising from the effects of all the other factors in modern life. Nonetheless, because of its high visibility and its importance in determining the well-being of consumers, advertising will continue to be subjected to intense social scrutiny.

different languages. National advertising refers to advertising in many different regions of the same country. Delta, Wal-Mart, and Sprint, for example, run ads on TV networks and in national magazines to reach customers in many different markets across the United States. International advertisers, of course, also use national ads. Retail or local advertising is done within one specific market. The neighborhood restaurant or car dealership typically relies on local ads.

An example of a primary demand ad. The "got milk?" campaign was designed to promote milk drinking, not the purchase of a particular brand of milk. *(Serena and Venus Williams © 1999 National Fluid Milk Processor Promotion Board)*

Yet a third way to categorize advertising is by purpose. Some ads are for distinct products or services, such as frozen pizzas or muffler repairs, while others try to improve a company's image or influence public opinion on an issue, such as the ads run by oil companies describing their efforts to keep down fuel costs. Another distinction involves primary demand and selective demand ads. A **primary demand ad** has as its purpose the promotion of a particular product category rather than a specific brand. The campaign to encourage milk drinking that shows various celebrities with milk moustaches is an example of this type. **Selective demand type ads** are used by individual companies to sell their particular brand, such as a certain brand of milk. Finally, ads can be classified as direct action and indirect action. A **direct action ad** usually contains a toll-free number, coupon, e-mail address, or some similar device to allow the advertiser to see results quickly. In contrast, an **indirect action ad** works over the long run to build a company's image and increase consumer awareness.

Advertising is part of the overall marketing process. Broadly defined, **marketing** consists of the development, pricing, distribution, and promotion of ideas, goods, and services. Advertising is part of the general promotion process, along with personal selling, sales promotions, and public relations. It is an important element in marketing, but it is not the only element.

A BRIEF HISTORY OF ADVERTISING

Advertising's beginnings are impossible to pinpoint, but several examples date back thousands of years. Clay tablets traced to ancient Babylon have been found with messages that touted an ointment dealer and a shoemaker. The town crier was an important advertising medium throughout England and other countries in Europe during the medieval period.

In more recent times, the history of advertising is inextricably entwined with changing social conditions and advances in media technology. For instance, Gutenberg's invention of printing using movable type made possible several new advertising media: posters, handbills, and newspaper ads. In fact, the first printed advertisement in English, produced about 1480, was a handbill that announced a prayer book for sale. Its author, evidently wise in the ways of outdoor advertising, tacked his ad to church doors all over England. By the late 1600s, ads were common sights in London newspapers.

Advertising made its way to the American colonies along with the early settlers from England. Ben Franklin, a pioneer of early advertising, made his ads more attractive by using large headlines and considerable white space. From Franklin's time to the early 19th century, newspaper ads resembled what today are called classified ads.

The Industrial Revolution caused major changes in American society and in American advertising. Manufacturers, with the aid of newly invented machines, were able to mass-produce their products. Mass production, however, also required mass consumption and a mass market. Advertising was a tremendous aid in reaching this new mass audience.

The impact of increasing industrialization was most apparent in the period from the end of the Civil War (1865) to the beginning of the 20th century. In little more than three decades, the following occurred:

1. The railroad linked all parts of the country, making it possible for Eastern manufacturers to distribute their goods to the growing Western markets.

2. The population of the United States doubled between 1870 and 1900. More people meant larger markets for manufacturers.

An ad from the 1900s for Coca-Cola. Included at the bottom is a coupon for a free Coke. *(Culver Pictures)*

3. The invention of new communication media—the telephone, typewriter, high-speed printing press, phonograph, motion pictures, photography, rural mail delivery—made it easier for people to communicate with one another.

4. Economic production increased dramatically, and people had more disposable income to spend on new products.

This improved economic and communication climate helped advertising thrive. Magazines were distributed from coast to coast and

All the fuss started during the 2000 presidential campaign between George W. Bush and Al Gore. Hundreds of TV stations ran an ad paid for by the Republican National Committee that criticized Al Gore's prescription drug plan. The word "RATS" flashed on the screen for one-thirtieth of a second during the commercial. Democrats were outraged and accused the Republicans of using subliminal advertising, a tactic that violates Federal Communications Commission policy and could lead to a station's losing its license to broadcast. The argument revived the controversy over subliminal advertising and its alleged powers.

In psychology, a perceptual threshold is called a limen. Thus, anything that appears just below our perceptual threshold is called subliminal. Subliminal advertising consists of sending persuasive messages that we can't perceive but nonetheless have an impact on our subconscious.

The debate over subliminal advertising began back in the 1950s with an experiment in a movie theater. While the movie was playing, messages were flashed on the screen for about one–three-thousandth of a second, too fast for the conscious mind to perceive them. The messages said "Drink Coca-Cola" and "Eat Popcorn." The theater owners claimed that sales figures for Coke and popcorn increased significantly. When others tried to duplicate these results, however, they were unsuccessful. In fact, advertising professionals and researchers agree that there is no persuasive evidence that subliminal advertising works.

So what about the Bush ad? In the first place, it wasn't even subliminal advertising. People saw the word "RATS" flash on the screen; it was conscious perception. Was the quick glimpse of the word deliberately inserted into the ad? Probably not. The word appeared on-screen almost at the same time the camera zeroed in on the word "BUREAUCRATS," the last four letters of which are "RATS." Advertising experts suggest that a ghost image appeared on one or two frames of the film as the camera zoomed in, and the glitch wasn't noticed. It wasn't subliminal suggestion; it was just sloppy film editing.

---

made possible truly national advertising. The development of the halftone method for reproducing photographs meant that magazine advertisers could portray their products more vividly. By 1900, it was not unusual for the leading magazines of the period (*Harper's, Cosmopolitan, McClure's*) to run 75 to 100 pages of ads in a typical issue.

It is not surprising that the increased importance of advertising in the marketing process led to the birth of the **advertising agency,** an organization that specializes in providing advertising services to its clients. The roots of the modern-day agency can be traced to Volney B. Palmer of Philadelphia. In 1842, Palmer bought large amounts of space in various newspapers at a discount and then resold the space at higher rates to advertisers. The actual ad—the copy, layout, and artwork—was still prepared by the company wishing to advertise; in effect, Palmer was a space broker. That situation changed in the late 19th century when the advertising agency of N. W. Ayer & Son was founded. Ayer & Son offered to plan, create, and execute complete advertising campaigns for their customers. By 1900, the advertising agency became the focal point of creative planning, and advertising was firmly established as a profession.

The 1920s saw the beginning of radio as an advertising medium (see Chapter 7). Network broadcasting made radio an attractive vehicle for national advertisers; by 1930 about $27 million was spent on network advertising, and many of the most popular shows of the day were produced by advertising agencies. However, the stock market crash of 1929 had a disastrous effect on the U.S. economy, and total dollars spent on advertising dropped from $2.8 billion in 1929 to $1.7 billion in 1935. It would take a decade for the industry to recover. World War II meant that many civilian firms cut back on their advertising budgets. Others simply changed the content of their ads and, instead of selling their products, instructed consumers on how to make their products last until after the war.

World War II was followed by the cold war, when Americans were concerned about the rise of communism. Despite growth in mass consumption and economic prosperity, the prevailing mood of the country was one of fear and apprehension as many people were afraid that communists were secretly taking over the government and subverting the American way of life. This mood also had an impact on public opinion about advertising. After the Korean War (1950–1953), many stories surfaced about brainwashing and mind control of American prisoners. It wasn't long before advertising was indicted as a form of mind control that seduced people by subtle appeals to deep, subconscious urges. A best-seller called *The Hidden Persuaders* explained how advertisers used psychological research and motivational analysis to sell consumers things they really didn't need or want. It was during this time that the concept of subliminal advertising was introduced, which further deepened the suspicions about the advertising industry.

This paranoia gradually subsided during the 1960s, which were characterized by the growth of the creative side of advertising as art directors, copywriters, and TV directors had more input into the way advertising was presented. This trend weakened during the 1970s when a bad economic climate prompted a return to a more direct selling technique and a focus on efficient media planning.

The 1980s and 1990s saw the social and media environment for advertising change drastically. Cable television opened up dozens of new and specialized channels that siphoned advertising dollars away from the major TV networks. New video forms of marketing emerged, such as the infomercial and home shopping. Moreover, improved transportation and communication gave birth to the mega-ad agency with branches throughout the world. Political changes in Europe created new opportunities for global marketing. Changes in society also had an impact. Advertisers were facing a more culturally diverse marketplace that required more selective ads. Consumer attitudes toward products were changing, and new regulations promised to forever alter tobacco advertising. Liquor ads also drew criticism.

A new advertising and marketing medium, the Internet, arrived during the 1990s and saw remarkable growth. About $300,000 was spent on Internet ads in 1994; six years later, the total was nearly $6 billion. It seemed that nearly every company had a website, and print and television ads for dot-coms were everywhere. A favorable economic climate further fueled advertising spending. In sum, contemporary advertising seems healthy, but it must cope with social and technological change to adapt to the modern world.

ORGANIZATION OF THE CONSUMER ADVERTISING INDUSTRY

There are three main components of the advertising industry:

1. The advertisers
2. Advertising agencies
3. The media

Each of these will be discussed in turn.

Advertisers

Advertising is an important part of the overall marketing plan of almost every organization that provides a product or a service to the public. Advertisers can

CRITICAL / CULTURAL ISSUES

Cultural Meaning and Trade Characters

Tony the Tiger, Mr. Clean, the Maytag repairman, Ronald McDonald, the Jolly Green Giant, Betty Crocker, the Keebler Elves—these are examples of trade characters, fictional beings, both human and animated, created to help sell a product, service, or idea. Like slogans, trade characters are popular because they are an effective way of linking the product and its advertising so that consumers can easily remember the message. But trade characters do more than slogans; they give a product personality, style, and depth by creating an image with a clear cultural meaning with which the audience can identify.

An article by Barbara Phillips in a 1996 issue of the *Journal of Popular Culture* examines the role of trade characters in American culture. Phillips notes that mass-produced products have little cultural meaning. A Duracell battery is hard to distinguish from an Eveready battery, and neither is likely to arouse any emotional response. Trade characters, however, give meaning and significance to otherwise indistinguishable products by linking the product to an image that has a cultural meaning. One way that trade characters create this meaning is to rely on commonly accepted mythical symbols—images that possess cultural interpretations. Take the Jolly Green Giant, for example. The giant is a common mythical symbol whose size connotes strength, power, and authority. His green color is associated with freshness, while his hearty "ho-ho-ho" imparts warmth and humor. The giant's image on a can of peas makes the product less remote and more friendly.

The use of mythical symbols gives trade characters another advantage: They communicate messages without explicitly stating them. Mr. Clean, for example, immaculate in his all-white costume, symbolizes cleanliness and purity. His image suggests that using the product will have these results, but he never actually says these things. In contrast, an ad that proclaims "Our cleaner will leave

Created by the Leo Burnett Agency, the Jolly Green Giant has been ho-ho-ho-ing for more than 30 years. © *Tony Freeman/PhotoEdit*

your countertop spotless and pure" might be met with some degree of doubt. Since trade characters never directly state that a product has positive attributes, their "claims" are less likely to be rejected.

There are, of course, some drawbacks with trade characters. Cultural meanings shift over time, and advertisers must be careful to monitor changing attitudes in society. Perhaps the best example of this is Aunt Jemima. The Quaker Oats Company started using this trade character in 1889. Over the years, however, the image became an unacceptable stereotype. In 1968, during the Civil Rights movement, her image changed: She lost 100 pounds and became younger; her red bandana was replaced by a headband. In 1990, she was made over again into an image that was the black equivalent of Betty Crocker, an image the company hoped was more positive. Moreover, some trade characters may be entirely inappropriate. Joe Camel, for example, was the subject of much criticism because the cartoon character seemed designed to encourage children to smoke. Camel eventually phased him out.

In any case, trade characters have become an established part of American culture. Their ranks will undoubtedly increase in the future.

1. Why do marketers want us to have emotional connections to mass-produced products, and how might that affect our society? Those peas really *aren't* warm and friendly after all; why do we like it better when we think they are?

2. Besides the Aunt Jemima example (which in itself is worthy of further consideration), how else are expectations and stereotypes of race and gender reflected in trade characters?

3. If you can, look through some magazines from the 1950s, or even earlier. How do the trade characters you see there compare to the ones you see today, and what might that tell us about how (and whether) society has changed?

The boss as commercial spokesperson: Dave Thomas of Wendy's. *(Courtesy Wendy's International, Inc.)*

range from the small bicycle shop on the corner that spends $4 on an ad in the local weekly paper to huge international corporations such as Procter & Gamble, which spends more than $2.3 billion annually for ads.

At a basic level, we can distinguish two different types of advertisers: national and retail. **National advertisers** sell their product or service to customers all across the country. The emphasis in national advertising is on the product or service and not so much on the place where the product or service is sold. For example, the Coca-Cola Company is interested in selling soft drinks. It doesn't matter to the company if you buy their product at the local supermarket, at a small convenience store, or from a vending machine. **Retail advertisers** (also called local advertisers) are companies such as local restaurants, car dealerships, TV repair shops, and other merchants and service organizations that have customers in only one city or trading area. The retail advertiser wants to attract customers to a specific store or place of business. Some companies are both national and local advertisers. Sears and Kmart, for example, advertise all over the country, but their individual stores use local advertising to highlight their specific sales and promotions. Franchises, such as McDonald's and Burger King, keep up their national image by advertising on network TV, while their local outlets put ads in the paper to attract customers from the local community.

Naturally, the way organizations handle their advertising depends on their size. Some companies have their own advertising departments; a small retail store might have one person who is responsible for advertising and marketing and who may also have other job functions. Whether large or small, all advertisers must attend to several basic functions. These include planning the ads and deciding where they will appear, setting aside a certain amount of money for the advertising budget, coordinating the advertising with other departments in the organization, and, if necessary, supervising the work of an outside agency or company that produces the ad. In addition, some large advertisers have departments that can create and prepare all the advertising materials, purchase the space and airtime for the ads, and check to see if the ads were effective in achieving their goals.

■ Agencies

According to the American Association of Advertising Agencies, an **agency** is an independent business organization composed of creative people and business people who develop, prepare, and place advertising for sellers seeking to find customers for their goods and services. In the past, advertising agencies were located in a few big cities, such as New York, Chicago, and Los Angeles. That trend has changed, however, and many of the more memorable ad campaigns of recent years have been put together by agencies located far from Madison Avenue. When it comes to total income, however, the big-city agencies still dominate.

The last few years in the agency business have seen the spawning of super-agencies, or mega-agencies, resulting from the merger and consolidation of several large ad agencies. In addition, the business has been globalized, since these new mega-agencies have branches all over the world. The five mega-agencies listed in Table 14.1 dominated the industry at the close of 1999.

The global reach of advertising is apparent in the agency business as in many other media. Three of the megagroups in Table 14.1 are foreign-owned.

Agencies can be classified by the range of services they offer. In general terms, there are three main types: (1) full-service agencies, (2) media buying services, and (3) creative boutiques.

As the name implies, a **full-service agency** handles all phases of the advertising process for its clients; it plans, creates, produces, and places ads. In addition, it might also provide other marketing services, such as sales promotions, trade show exhibits, newsletters, and annual reports. In theory, at least, there is no need for the client to deal with any other company for help promoting its product.

A **media buying service** specializes in buying radio and television time and reselling it to advertisers and advertising agencies. The service sells time to the advertiser, orders the spots on the various stations, and monitors the stations to see if the ads actually run.

A **creative boutique** (the name was coined during the 1960s and has hung on to the present) is an organization that specializes in the actual creation of ads. In general, boutiques create imaginative and distinctive advertising themes and produce innovative and original ads. A company that uses a creative boutique would have to employ another agency to perform the planning, buying, and administrative functions connected with advertising.

Table 14.1	Top Five Advertising Agencies, 1999	
Company	**Headquarters**	**1999 Income (in billions)**
WPP Group/Young and Rubicam	London	$6.69
Omnicom Group	New York	5.74
Interpublic Group	New York	5.08
Havas Advertising	Levallois (France)	2.39
Publicis and Saatchi & Saatchi	Paris	2.17

It is not surprising that full-service agencies saw media buying services and boutiques as competitors. Consequently, the full-service agencies improved their own creative and media buying departments. It wasn't long before the services and boutiques began to feel the effects of the agencies' efforts. As it stands now, only a few services and a few boutiques still handle large national advertisers.

What does a full-service ad agency do for a client? To begin with, the agency studies the product or service and determines its marketable characteristics and how it relates to the competition. At the same time, the agency studies the potential market, possible distribution plans, and likely advertising media. The agency then makes a formal presentation to the client detailing its findings and its recommended advertising strategy. If the client agrees, the agency then launches the execution phase. This phase entails writing and producing the ads, buying space and time in various media, delivering the ads to the appropriate media, and verifying that all ads actually appear. Finally, the agency will work closely with the client's salespeople to make sure they get the greatest possible benefit from the ads.

Media

The last part of the advertising industry consists of the mass media. The media serve as the connection between a company and its customers. The media that are available for advertising include some obvious ones—radio, TV, newspapers, magazines, the Internet—and others that are not so obvious, such as direct mail, billboards, transit cards (bus and car cards), stadium scoreboard ads, and point-of-purchase ads. (Some other off-the-beaten-path advertising venues are discussed in Media Probe, "Is No Place Safe from Advertising?"). Chapters 4, 5, 7, 10, and 11 presented an overview of the mainstream mass media and discussed their dependence on various kinds of advertising. This section examines these media from the perspective of an advertiser.

Even the slickest and most imaginative advertising message will fail if it is delivered to the wrong people. To make sure that this catastrophe doesn't happen, advertisers employ highly skilled media planners to help them place and schedule their ads.

Advertising specialists evaluate media along four dimensions:

1. *Reach:* How many people can get the message?
2. *Frequency:* How often will the message be received?
3. *Selectivity:* Does the medium actually reach potential customers?
4. *Efficiency:* How much does it cost to reach a certain number of people? (This is usually expressed as cost per thousand people.)

Figure 14–1 summarizes how the various media rate on these dimensions.

In addition to the above considerations, advertisers have to take into account many other factors before deciding on which medium to use. An important part of any decision involves considering the creative limitations imposed by the physical properties of each medium. Television, for example, allows the advertiser to show the product in action. On the other hand, TV ads are short and cannot be used to present a great deal of technical information. A magazine ad can be in full color and can present a large amount of data, but it might not have the same impact as a TV ad. All in all, choosing which media to use in the final advertising mix is a difficult decision.

Ads seem to be creeping into every available space. Consider the following:

- Radio Shack bought advertising space on the side of a solar-powered rover due to be launched to the moon in 2003.
- Entire sides of buildings in New York City have been turned into huge billboards.
- Banner-toting airplanes now regularly fly over crowds at major sporting events.
- The Media Lab at MIT has invented wearable video. A leather jacket equipped with an ultrathin video screen in the back shows commercials as the wearer walks around.
- A company in San Francisco pays auto owners a monthly fee in return for painting advertising on the sides of their cars.

- A couple in Pennsylvania sold advertising space on their wedding invitations and thank-you notes to help pay for the ceremony.
- In New Mexico, a company paid to have its advertising slogan painted on the sides of cows that stood by the highway. (No, it wasn't "got milk?" It was a slogan for a dot-com firm.)
- A Mexican restaurant in San Francisco offered a free lunch for life to anybody who had the restaurant's logo (a kid in a sombrero) tattooed on a body part. Forty people accepted the offer and got tattooed. (If they all showed up every day for an $8 lunch for the next 10 years, it would cost the restaurant more than $1 million.)

ADVERTISING ONLINE

Online advertising began in 1994 when *HotWired*, the digital counterpart of the techno-hip *Wired* magazine, started a website with about a dozen sponsors who paid for advertising banners embedded throughout the site. Since that time, a whole new industry has grown up consisting of companies that sell ads, create ads, and measure how many people see ads. Most large companies now treat web advertising as part of their normal advertising media mix, along with radio, TV, print, and outdoor. In addition, the growth of the dot-com Internet companies has fueled the growth of web advertising. It's no surprise that companies on the net use the net to advertise. One recent survey disclosed that more than 70 percent of advertising on the web came from other Internet companies.

As mentioned in earlier chapters, the surge in advertising by Internet companies has helped increase revenue for the traditional media. Here are just a few examples: From 1998 to 1999, spending by online companies increased 900 percent for network TV advertising, 500 percent for outdoor media, 300 percent for cable TV ads, and 200 percent for magazine ads. Dot-com spending for advertising in business-to-business media increased as well.

Although on the increase, the amount of money generated by web advertising is still small when compared with the more traditional media. Estimates of Internet ad spending vary widely among industry analysts. Even with the most

Figure 14–1

Advertising Characteristics of Various Media

MEDIUM

CHARACTERISTICS	Newspapers	Magazines	Radio	TV	Outdoor	Direct Mail	Internet
Reach	High	Low	High	High	High	High	Medium
Frequency	High	Low	High	High	High	Medium	Medium
Selectivity	Low	High	High	Medium	Low	High	High
Efficiency	Medium	Medium	Low	High	High	High	Medium

optimistic assessment, the Internet accounted for about 2 percent of all advertising expenditures in 1999 (see Figure 14–3), or about $5 billion. To put this number in perspective, consider that General Motors by itself spent about $3 billion in advertising in traditional media that same year. Even so, everyone expects Internet advertising to become more important. Industry forecasting company Jupiter Communications projects that Internet ad revenue should be nearly $9 billion by 2002.

Moreover, companies are learning how to use Internet ads to their maximum potential. Some companies allow advertisers to buy space on a number of different sites, sort of like buying time on a radio or TV network. Doubleclick.com, for example, sells banner ad space on 490 websites and serves as a liaison between them and 3,100 advertising clients, such as General Motors Corporation and Visa International. Other companies, such as Digital City, have created cyber-based city websites in an attempt to gain a share of the multibillion-dollar classified ad market.

Not all is bright, however, for online advertising. Advertisers are beginning to have doubts about the efficacy of online banner ads. One study suggested that only about 0.5 percent of all people actually click on a banner ad and even fewer actually make a purchase. This percentage is even less than that of direct-mail campaigns (those ads that many people consider junk mail and toss away without opening). About 2 percent of direct-mail campaign recipients usually respond to the mailing. Advertisers are also discovering that acquiring customers through banner ads is much more expensive that using traditional media. As a result, many companies have cut their online budgets or are demanding cheaper prices for banner ads.

Finally, since so much of Internet advertising is done by dot-com companies themselves, an economic downturn among web companies will have a serious ripple effect on advertising. Such an event occurred in early 2000 when the financial failure of several high-profile dot-com companies meant that less money was spent on Internet ads.

Categories of Internet Advertising

There are several types of Internet advertising. **Banner ads** are the most common. These are the banners that appear on the top, bottom, or sides of a web page or are scattered throughout the content. Each banner displays a company logo or catchy phrase and some are even animated to attract attention. Visitors who click on these sites are provided with more information about the product and are given a chance to buy it online. Some advertisers pay websites according to the number of "click-throughs" they generate. As has been mentioned, very few banner ads ever get clicked.

An advertiser can purchase banner ads, or the advertiser can establish a **free-link exchange.** In this arrangement, one company offers banner ad space on its website to another company in exchange for space on the other company's site. An automotive repair service, for example, might set up a free-link exchange with a company that sells auto parts or with an online used-car site.

An example of an Internet banner ad.

Whenever you look at a page on the web, keep in mind that the page is also looking back at you. A cookie is an identifier program that many Internet sites install on your hard drive—without your knowing it. A cookie contains the name of the site you visited and what you did while you were there. Let's say you visit a site that contains entertainment news. The site asks your computer if it can store a cookie on your hard drive. Unless you have specifically told your Internet browser not to accept cookies, your computer will accept a cookie that says, in effect, "This is user 204140." While at the site, you click on a story about Jennifer Lopez, join a chat room discussion of the developments on "Survivor," and download a music clip from the latest album by Madonna. The site duly notes that you have these interests. The next time you visit the entertainment site, it finds the cookie on your computer and matches it to your interests. When the site comes up on your screen, there's an ad for the new Jennifer Lopez movie, a prime-time schedule for CBS, and a special offer on Madonna's new CD.

Cookies are not necessarily bad. They allow your browser to store passwords and user IDs so that you don't have to reidentify yourself every time you log onto a site that requires a registration. They also allow you to personalize your opening screen so that you see the information you are most interest in.

Fortunately, although most cookies can be traced to a computer, they can't be traced directly to you because they don't contain any information that will personally identify you. Thus, if you click on several sites that offer information on pets, you may receive more unsolicited e-mail about pet products, but you won't get any personal phone calls or personal mail about them. So you're protected against privacy invasion unless—and this is a big "unless"—you provided information about yourself by filling out an online form that appears on a web page that also has a banner ad. In this case, the banner ad, even if you don't click on it, might record the information on your form. Suddenly, you're not so anonymous anymore.

This issue was at the basis of a lawsuit that was filed against the DoubleClick company, the largest network of online banner ads, in 2000. It seemed that DoubleClick wanted to merge its online database of cookies, which might include some names and addresses, to a much larger database containing consumers' catalog shopping habits. That merged list might contain personal information as well as shopping habits, which would enable marketers to build a rather revealing personal portrait of your likes, dislikes, and shopping habits.

In response to the lawsuit, DoubleClick put its plans on hold pending some kind of government and industry agreement about what privacy standards should apply to the web. In the meantime, here's what you can do if you don't want cookies. You can set your Internet browser (Netscape or Microsoft Explorer) to not accept cookies, but this carries the risk that some websites may not work properly. You can also set your Internet browser to warn you before you accept a cookie; then you can decide if you want it or not. You might, however, get tired of all the warning messages. Or you can install a special program, such as CookiePal, that makes it easier to accept or reject cookies. If you decide to do nothing, remember that it's possible that all your site visits may be recorded and act accordingly.

In addition to banner ads, advertisers can sponsor chat rooms that are related to their product. A travel agency, for example, might sponsor a room that is devoted to travelers' cruise experiences.

Advertisers also use direct e-mail campaigns. These are similar to traditional direct-mail campaigns except that the advertising message is delivered to a targeted group of people via e-mail. Several commercial companies develop and maintain highly specific e-mail lists that advertisers can purchase. This form of advertising, although highly efficient, carries some risks because many consumers consider this content spam and react negatively.

Websites devoted to a product or company are another form of web advertising. Companies spend a great deal of time and energy creating the site most appropriate for their product. International diamond merchant De Beers, for example, created a "design your own engagement ring" site that allowed visitors to view various combinations of stone, setting, and sidestones online. After a visitor designed the preferred ring, she or he could e-mail the design to a friend (or fiancé).

Nike integrated its website with its offline advertising. TV ads put the viewer into immediate situations. Sample: "You're racing Marion Jones, fastest woman in the world. Look out for that glass door! What do you do?" The tagline then told the viewer, "Continued at whatever.nike.com." When the viewer got to the website, he or she could choose the ad's ending. Gap.com went for simplicity with an easy-to-navigate website. Products are displayed attractively in a way that recreates the in-store shopping experience. There are no high-tech, dazzling graphics or animations that take time to load and sometimes cause frustration among online shoppers.

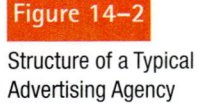 PRODUCING ADVERTISING

Departments and Staff

Figure 14–2 shows the departmental chart for a typical advertising agency. Remember also that many large companies have their own advertising departments, structured like agencies. There are four major departments:

1. Creative services
2. Account services
3. Marketing services
4. Administration

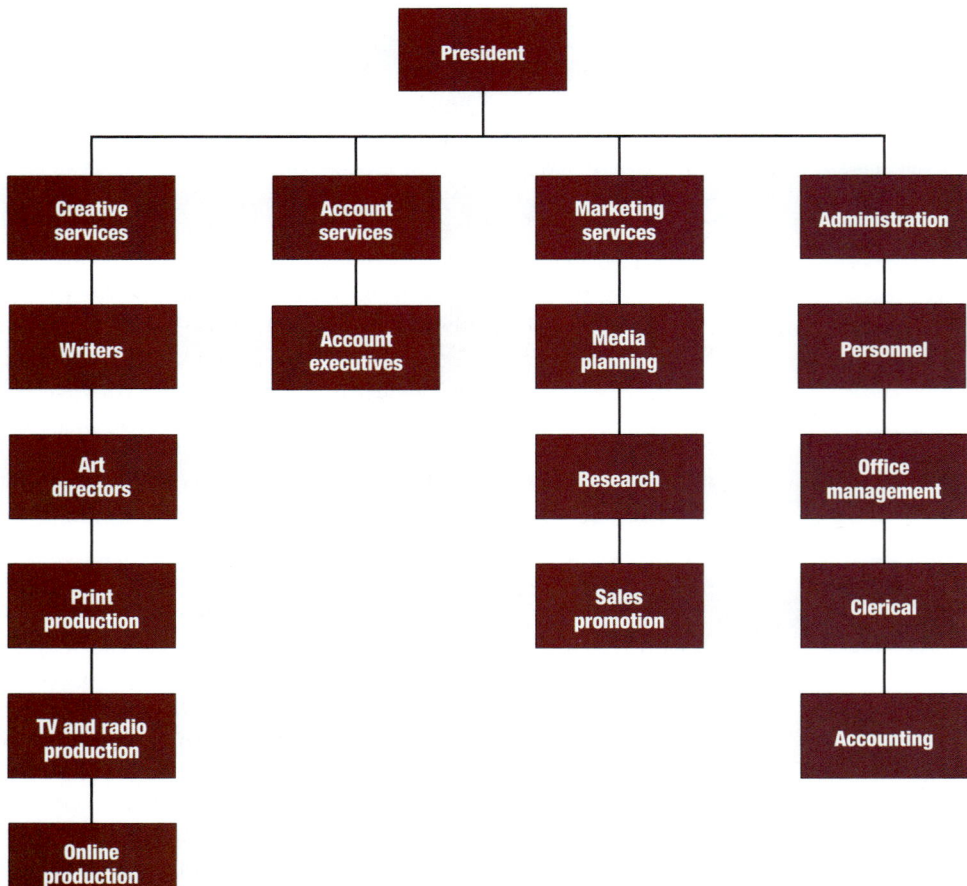

Figure 14–2

Structure of a Typical Advertising Agency

The creative department, as the name implies, actually produces the ad. The people in this department write the advertising **copy** (the headline and message of the ad), choose the illustrations, prepare artwork, and/or supervise the scripting and production of radio and TV commercials.

The account services department is responsible for the relationship between the agency and the client. Because the advertising agency is an organization outside the firm doing the advertising, it is necessary to appoint someone, usually called an account executive (AE), to promote communication and understanding between client and agency. The AE must represent the viewpoint of the agency to the client but at the same time keep abreast of the needs of the advertiser. Since the AE tends to be the person in the middle, his or her job is obviously an important one in the agency.

The marketing services department is responsible for advising the client as to what media to use for his or her messages. Typically, this department makes extensive use of the data collected by the Audit Bureau of Circulations, Arbitron, Nielsen, MediaMetrix, and the other audience research services mentioned in earlier chapters. This department is also in charge of any sales promotions that are done in connection with the advertising. These may include such things as coupons, premiums, and other aids to dealers.

Finally, like any other business, the advertising agency needs a department to take care of the day-to-day administration of the agency. This department is in charge of office management, clerical functions, accounting, personnel, and training of new employees.

> **S O U N D B Y T E**
>
> **Some Ads Aren't Meant to Be Taken Literally**
>
> In Pennsylvania, a shoe store named Shoestrings put up a big 14- by 48-foot billboard next to the highway with an ad that was meant to be a joke. Modeled after a newspaper coupon, the sign said, "Bring in this ad and you'll get a free pair of shoes." Three people took this offer literally. The three climbed up the billboard, took down the sign, and brought it to Shoestrings. The company agreed to give each a free pair of shoes if they returned the sign.

The Advertising Campaign

The best way to illustrate how ads get produced is to present a general discussion of an advertising campaign for a national product. A **campaign** consists of a large number of advertisements, all stressing the same major theme or appeal, that appear in a number of media over a specified time. Following is a discussion, greatly simplified, of these six phases of a typical campaign:

1. Choosing the marketing strategy.
2. Selecting the main appeal or theme.
3. Translating the theme into the various media.
4. Producing the ads.
5. Buying space and time.
6. Executing and evaluating the campaign.

In the first phase, a great deal of research is done to determine the target audience, the marketing objective, the appropriate price for the product or service, and the advertising budget. It is during this phase that the word **positioning** is often heard. Positioning has many interpretations, but in general it means fitting a product or service to one or more segments of the broad market in such a way as to set it apart from the competition without making any change in the product. For example, the Walt Disney company repositioned its theme parks as places where even adults without children would have a good time.

The Canandaigua Wine Company positioned Arbor Mist, a wine-plus-fruit drink, as a beer alternative for women. For years, the Red Lobster restaurant chain was perceived as a rather drab family restaurant. A new campaign launched in 2000 attempted to reposition the restaurant to appeal to upscale baby boomers with its "Escape to Red Lobster" campaign. One ad intercut shots of a group of young sunbathers baking themselves red with shots of plump lobster tails.

Sometimes positioning doesn't work. Minute Maid orange juice failed in its attempt to reposition its product from simply a breakfast drink to an all-purpose beverage. Despite an $18 million campaign that featured the message "Not Just for Breakfast Anymore," sales of orange juice remained flat as consumers failed to respond to the switch.

After the product or service has been positioned, an overall theme for the campaign is developed. Once again, considerable research is done to find the proper themes. Subway Restaurants introduced its "Gotta Have It Taste" campaign to appeal to young consumers who were more interested in taste than in the product's low-fat content. Research revealed that going to baseball games was not a popular choice as family entertainment. As a result, Major League Baseball launched a campaign with the theme "The First-Choice Destination for Family Entertainment" that showed parents and children bonding at the ballpark.

The next phase is translating the theme into print and broadcast ads. Advertisers try to achieve variety in their ads but with a consistency of approach that will help consumers remember and recognize their product. The recent "We Like to See You Smile" campaign for McDonald's is a case in point. Eight different TV commercials were created, but each centered on the "smile" slogan. The U.S. Army used its "Be All That You Can Be" theme for 11 years in print and broadcast ads and has only recently introduced variations.

The actual production of the ad is done in much the same way that other media content is produced. In the print media, the copy, the headline, subheads, any accompanying illustrations, and the layout are first prepared in rough form. The initial step is usually just a thumbnail sketch that can be used to experiment with different arrangements within the ad. The headline might be moved down, the copy moved from right to left, and so on. Next a **rough layout,** a drawing that is the actual size of the ad, is con-

The newest entry in McDonald's ad campaigns. The hamburger chain spent more than $250 million on prime-time TV ads during 2000. *(Courtesy DDB Chicago/"We love to see you smile," the campaign for McDonald's)*

structed. Usually, several layouts are prepared, and the best are used to produce the **comprehensive layout,** the one that will be used to produce the ad. Many agencies use outside art studios and printers to help them put together print ads and billboards.

Radio commercials are written and created in much the same way that early radio drama shows were produced. A script is prepared in which dialogue, sound effects, and music are combined to produce whatever effect is desired. The commercial is then either produced in the sound studio or recorded live on location. In either case, postproduction editing adds any desired special effects, and eventually, a master tape is prepared for duplication and distribution.

The beginning step in the preparation of a television commercial is a **storyboard,** a series of drawings depicting the key scenes of the planned ad. Storyboards are usually shown to the client before production begins. If the client has any objections or suggestions, they can be incorporated into the script before production. Once the storyboards are approved, the commercial is ready to go into production. Most TV commercials are shot on film (although some are now switching to videotape). Television commercials are the most expensive ads to produce. A 30-second commercial can easily cost $250,000. Special effects, particularly animation, can drive the costs even higher. In an effort to keep costs down, much of the time spent producing TV commercials consists of planning and rehearsing. As with the print media, many agencies hire outside production specialists to produce their commercials.

While the creative department is putting together the print and broadcast ads, the marketing department is buying time in those media judged to be appropriate for the campaign. If the product is seasonal (e.g., suntan lotion, snowmobiles), the ads are scheduled to reflect the calendar, appearing slightly before and during the time people begin buying such items. Other products and services might call for a program of steady advertising throughout the year.

The last phase of the campaign consists of the ads' actually appearing. Testing is done during and after this phase to see if consumers saw and remembered the ads. In addition, sales data are carefully monitored to determine if the campaign had the desired effect on sales.

Advertising Research

Advertising research takes place during all phases of the campaign and helps agencies and their clients make informed decisions about their strategy and tactics. **Formative research** is done before the campaign begins to help guide the creative effort. It can take several forms. One is audience definition—identifying the target market, such as "females 18 to 34" or "all adults." After this is accomplished, audience profiling is done to discover as much as possible about how the target market lives—what they think, what their attitudes are, how they decide to buy.

The next phase, **message research,** involves pretesting the messages that have been developed for the campaign. At its most basic level, pretesting determines if the audience can actually understand the ads. This type of testing guards against possible double meanings or overlooked sexual connotations that might have eluded the creative staff. In a second type of pretest, researchers show mock-ups of magazines that contain the prototype of the print ad and rough cuts of TV ads to test audiences. Consumers are tested to see whether they recall the main points of the ad and whether their attitude toward the product shows any change. Some

There's no doubt that advertisers have zeroed in on the child audience. The last few years have seen the growth of kid-specific media: Nickelodeon, websites, kid-oriented magazines, movie tie-ins, even hamburger wrappers. From 1993 to 1999, advertising in these media increased more than 50 percent, to $1.5 billion per year.

Part of the reason behind this increase is the fact that kids have become important factors in family buying decisions. First, they have more money to spend. The under-14 set gets allowances, earns money, and gets gifts to the tune of about $20 billion per year. In addition, kids probably influence another $200 billion worth of shopping decisions. Second, the increase in single-parent families and dual-career families means that kids are now making some of the purchasing decisions that were once left to Mom and Dad.

It is not surprising then to find that companies are intensifying their efforts to reach this market segment. And it's not just traditional toymakers, cereal companies, and fast-food restaurants that are in the mix. General Motors, for example, placed ads for its new minivan in *Sports Illustrated for Kids* and sent prototype vans to shopping malls where they showed previews of Disney's *Hercules* on a VCR inside the van. GM doesn't expect many six-year-olds to go out and buy a van, but the company knows through its research that kids can play an influential role in deciding which van to buy. In that connection, United Air Lines keeps its younger travelers happy by serving McDonald's Happy Meals.

Market research that examines children's psychology has been used to help sell goods. Researchers know that seven- and eight-year-olds like to collect things. This urge used to be satisfied by bottle caps, seashells, and baseball cards. More recently, the maker of Beanie Babies cashed in on this urge by creating a large number of different animals to collect, limiting production, and discontinuing models to create artificial scarcity.

The marketing even extends into the school. Companies donate money, equipment, and educational materials to schools in return for the opportunity to advertise their products. It all started with Channel One, a news program for students. In return for a donation of electronic equipment, schools agreed to show a newscast that contained commercials. Other companies did not take long to follow Channel One. Nike, for example, mailed out shoe-assembly kits to schools. Teachers were supposed to help kids make the sneakers while teaching a lesson on environmentally safe manufacturing (presumably by companies like Nike). McDonald's sponsored a seven-week curriculum on how to build a McDonald's restaurant and how to interview for a job there. Some school districts, hard up for cash, have sold advertising space on the side of school buses and in school hallways.

There are many who feel that all this selling to children isn't right. They argue that children are an unsophisticated audience and are vulnerable to the flashy, persuasive techniques of the advertising industry. Not many parents would allow a salesperson to come into the home and talk to their kids; why then should they allow TV to target their children? Additionally, they contend that advertising teaches values that are undesirable. Advertising focuses on the superficial and the material, and it glorifies consumption. Finally, critics contend that advertising creates conflicts between parents and children by encouraging kids to pester their parents for all the products they see advertised. Parents must continually say no and run the risk of possible strife. There is some evidence to support these positions (as discussed in Chapter 18). Even without this support, however, many people feel that advertising to kids is just plain wrong.

The advertisers reply that these critics don't give kids enough credit. They feel that kids are more sophisticated consumers than people realize and learn very quickly to see through the hype and manipulation that may be found in some ads. Additionally, the marketing community points out that kids are going to live in a world saturated by advertising. Coming into contact with it at an early age may help them learn how to deal with it when they become adults. Finally, they argue that kids get valuable information about new products and services from advertising, information that improves their lives.

The issue, of course, has legal as well as ethical overtones. To date, the government has weighed in on the side of kids. The Children's Television Act limits the amount of commercial minutes in TV shows that can be directed at children. The government and the tobacco industry worked out an agreement that prohibited the Camel cigarette company from using the cartoon character Joe Camel in its ads because the character appealed to children. There have been proposals to ban or limit beer, wine, and liquor advertising. Despite these efforts, it's clear that parents will be the ones to confront this issue head-on.

advertising campaigns go through pilot tests in actual markets. A split-cable transmission can show one version of an ad to one group of people and a second version to a similar group. The ads are compared to see which did a better job. A split-run of a magazine uses the same strategy.

Tracking studies examine how the ads perform during or after the actual campaign itself. Samples of consumers are studied to see if they recalled the ads, if their attitudes about the product changed, and if they actually bought the product or used the service advertised.

 ECONOMICS

This section will examine the economics of advertising on two levels. First, we will look at the total industry and trace expenditures in various media. Second, we will narrow our focus and examine how an agency makes money.

Advertising Volume in Various Media

About $215 billion was spent on advertising in the United States in 1999. Figure 14–3 shows how this money was divided among the various media. Since 1960, newspapers have seen a decrease in their relative share of advertising volumes—as have magazines. Television has shown a significant increase, while radio, outdoor advertising, and direct mail have shown modest growth. The Internet will probably account for more of the pie in the future.

Agency Compensation

How an advertising agency makes money is not well known outside the agency and media community. This section will discuss three common methods: (1) media commissions, (2) agency charges, and (3) fees.

Historically, the major mass media have allowed advertising agencies a 15 percent commission on the time and space they purchase. In simplified form, here's how the commission system works. Let's assume you have a new product and have enlisted the services of an agency to help you market it. You wish to run an ad in a particular magazine that will cost $1,000. Your agency places the order, prepares the ad, and sends it to the magazine. After the ad appears, the magazine sends the agency a bill for $1,000. The agency passes this bill on to you. You send $1,000 to the agency, which then deducts its 15 percent commission ($150 in this case) and sends the remainder ($850) to the magazine. If the total ad charges were $10,000, the agency would retain $1,500 in commission. Recently, however, the commission system has been declining in popularity. Many advertisers have struck pay-for-performance deals with ad agencies. Payments to ad agencies are based on sales or some other measure of performance. If sales go up, the ad

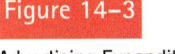

Figure 14–3

Advertising Expenditures in Various Media, 1999. (Dollar figures are in billions.)

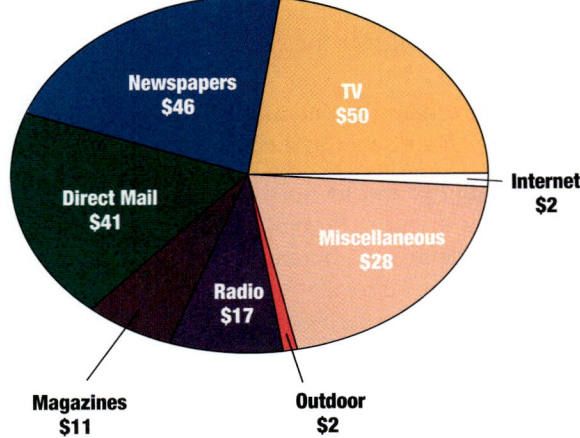

The medium of outdoor advertising has grown rapidly over the past decade. Modern billboards use striking new designs and graphics. *(Institute of Outdoor Advertising)*

agency gets more money. Other companies pay agencies a fixed fee, while still others use a combination of a flat fee plus performance-based incentives. A survey done in the late 1990s revealed that only 35 percent of advertisers were still using the traditional commission arrangement.

BUSINESS-TO-BUSINESS ADVERTISING

As its name suggests, business-to-business advertising is designed to sell products and services not to general consumers but to other businesses, typically via specialized trade publications, direct mail, professional journals, and display advertising at trade shows. Recently, however, some business-to-business ads have turned up in the mass media. There are four main categories of business-to-business advertising:

- *Trade.* Advertising goods and services to wholesalers and retailers who, in turn, resell these items to a more general audience.
- *Industrial.* Advertising those items that are used in the further production of goods and services, such as copy machines, forklifts, and drill presses.
- *Professional.* Advertising aimed at doctors, lawyers, architects, nurses, and others who might influence the buying process or use the product in their profession.
- *Agricultural.* Advertising aimed at farmers and possibly including products such as feed, fertilizer, seed, and chemicals.

Although its visibility might not be high, business-to-business advertising is big business, ringing up more than $150 billion in revenue in 2000. Some students ignore a career in business-to-business advertising because they feel it's not as glamorous as consumer advertising. There may be some truth to this: Selling a chemical solvent, bench-top fermenter, or blast furnace is not as flashy as designing a campaign for a sleek new sports car. In its own way, though, business advertising poses greater creative challenges. Coming up with a theme to sell the sports car is probably a lot easier than coming up with a winning idea for the chemical solvent.

An example of business-to-business advertising. This ad for Caterpillar industrial equipment contains far more technical information than would be found in a consumer ad. *(Courtesy Caterpillar)*

Consumer versus Business-to-Business Advertising

There are some obvious differences between advertising directed at consumers and business advertising. This section will list four.

First, the target audience in business advertising is much smaller. In some industries, the audience may number in the hundreds. Companies that manufacture storage tanks for petroleum products have determined that there are only 400 people in the United States authorized to purchase their product. In other areas, it may be in the thousands. This means, of course, that the media used to reach the target market must be selected carefully. In the nuclear reactor business, everyone in the market may read one or two publications.

Second, most of the products that are advertised tend to be technical, complicated, and high-priced. For the advertiser, this means that the ads will probably contain a great deal of technical information and will stress accuracy.

Third, the buyers will be professionals: purchasing agents whose only job is to acquire products and services for their company. Generally speaking, the decisions of the purchasing agent are based on reason and research. An error of a penny or two on a large purchase might cost the company thousands of dollars. Consequently, business advertising typically uses the rational approach. Additionally, it's important for the advertisers to know exactly who makes the buying decision, since most purchases in large business are generally made in consultation with others in the company.

Fourth, personal selling plays a greater role in the business arena and advertising is frequently used to support the sales staff in the field. As a result, ad budgets in the business sector may not be as high as their consumer counterparts.

Media

The media mix for business advertising is also different from consumer advertising. Since the target audience tends to be small, personalized media are best. Business publications tend to be the mainstay of campaigns. One study suggested that about 60 percent of industrial advertising dollars went to business and trade publications. Trade publications can be horizontal, dealing with a job function without regard to industry (such as *Purchasing Agent*), or vertical, covering all job types in an entire industry (such as *LP/Gas*).

Direct mail is also a valuable business advertising tool. Highly differentiated mailing lists can be prepared and ads sent to the most likely prospects. Research has shown that direct mail is perhaps more effective among businesspeople than among consumers. Whereas a large percentage of direct-mail material is thrown out unopened by the general public, about three-quarters of all businesspeople, according to a survey done in the early 1980s, read or at least scan their direct-mail ads.

Advertising in trade catalogs is particularly important to companies that sell through distributors rather than via their own sales staff. Since a catalog is a direct reflection of the company, extra care is taken to make sure it is up-to-date, accurate, and visually appealing.

Business-to-business advertising in the mass media used to be rare, but some large companies, such as Federal Express, IBM, and Xerox, have used it to great effect. Federal Express, for example, found that its business increased more than 40 percent after it started to advertise in consumer media. Purchasing time and space in the mass media must be done skillfully because of the expense and the chance of wasted coverage if the right decision makers are not in the audience. Specialized cable channels have made it possible for many business-to-business advertisers to use more general media with reduced chances of wasted coverage. CNN's "MoneyLine" and several shows on CNBC, for example, attract an audience that contains many business decision makers. General news magazines, such as *Time* and *Newsweek,* along with *Forbes, Business Week,* and *Fortune,* are rather obvious choices for this type of advertising.

It comes as no surprise that business-to-business advertising has embraced the Internet. Experts estimate that about $1 billion will be spent on this type of advertising in 2000. The majority of net advertisers are technology companies, but some other firms also have made use of the medium. Federal Express, for example, has spent considerable sums on net ads. This is one area of advertising that will see accelerated growth in the future.

■ Appeals

Close attention is paid to the copy in business-to-business advertising. A lot of consumer ads depend on impression and style to carry their messages. The copy tends to be brief and can cater to the emotions. Business copy tends to be longer, more detailed, and more factual. A premium is placed on accuracy and completeness. If the ad contains technical inaccuracies or exaggerations, the credibility of the product is compromised. Some of the most-used formats in business advertising are testimonials, case histories, new-product news, and demonstrations.

This is not to say, however, that all industrial ads should be stodgy and dull. In recent years, several ad agencies specializing in business ads have introduced warmth, humor, and creativity into their messages. The philosophy behind this movement is that businesspeople are also consumers and that they respond as consumers to business and trade ads. For example, Teddi, a California company that makes women's sportswear, placed special cover wraps on hundreds of copies of *Forbes* magazine that went to clothing retailers. The wraps featured Teddi clothes with headlines such as "As seen in Cosmo. Cosmopolis, Washington," or "As seen in Harpers. Harper's Ferry, West Virginia."

ADVERTISING

Although exact figures are hard to determine, there are more than 200,000 people working in the advertising business, with approximately 85,000 of those employed at advertising agencies. Job prospects appear bright for the future. The increasing amount of consumer goods being produced, along with more intense competition among existing companies, will create a sustained need for advertising specialists in the years ahead. Many experts think that opportunities will be the greatest in the advertising departments of large to medium-sized companies. No matter where a person intends to work, the following guidelines will be helpful in providing an overall view of the field.

Entry-Level Positions

A job applicant must make some basic decisions early in his or her professional training. Probably the first decision is whether to concentrate on the creative or the business side of the industry.

The creative side, as mentioned earlier, consists of the copywriters, art directors, graphic artists, photographers, and broadcast production specialists that put the ads together. Entry-level jobs include junior copywriter, creative trainee, junior art director, and production assistant. In most of these positions, a college degree in advertising or the visual arts is helpful, with a secondary concentration in marketing, English, sociology, or psychology also a benefit. Good web skills are also a plus.

Working on the business side of the industry refers to choosing a career as an account executive, a media planner, market researcher, or business manager. Proper preparation for this career includes extensive course work in both advertising and business, with particular emphasis on marketing. Common entry-level positions in these fields are assistant media buyer, research assistant, junior account executive, or account service trainee.

Agencies and advertising departments in private companies are not the only places to look for potential employment. A significant number of opportunities are available in companies that supply their goods and services to advertisers. Freelance artists, photographers, jingle writers, film and videotape producers, sound-recording specialists, and casting specialists are just some of the people needed by media suppliers. And, as has been pointed out in previous chapters, many people work for the various media in their advertising departments.

Upward Mobility

Opportunities for advancement in advertising are excellent. Outstanding performance is rewarded quickly, and many young people progress swiftly through the ranks. Beginning creative people typically become senior copywriters or senior art directors. Eventually, some may progress to become creative director, the person in charge of all creative services. On the business side, research assistants and assistant buyers can hope to become research directors and media directors. Account trainees, if they perform according to expectations, move up to account executives and later may become management supervisors. The climb to success can occur rapidly; many agencies are run by people who achieved top status before they reached age 40.

■ MAIN POINTS

- Advertising is any form of nonpersonal presentation and promotion of ideas, goods, and services paid for by an identified sponsor.

- Advertising can be classified by target audience, geographic focus, and purpose.

- Modern advertising began in the late 19th century and grew during the early 20th century as magazines and radio became mass advertising media.

- After World War II, advertising grew at a fast rate, particularly when TV came on the scene.

- The past two decades have seen the start of new channels for advertising, including cable TV and the Internet. Online advertising has grown in the past few years. It consists of banner ads, e-mail campaigns, and websites.

- The three main components of the advertising industry are advertisers, agencies, and the media.

- Advertising agencies put together large-scale campaigns for clients, consisting of a market strategy, theme, the ads themselves, media time/space, and evaluation.

- Although not as visible as consumer advertising, business-to-business advertising makes up a significant portion of the industry.

■ QUESTIONS FOR REVIEW

1. What are the three defining characteristics of advertising?

2. Briefly describe the three main components of the advertising industry.

3. Describe the main types of online advertising.

4. What is positioning? Why is it important to advertisers?

5. How does consumer advertising differ from business-to-business advertising?

■ QUESTIONS FOR CRITICAL THINKING

1. What would society be like without advertising?

2. Is it right to advertise to children? If you think it's appropriate to advertise to children, what special considerations, if any, should be applied to such ads?

3. Check the national media for ongoing advertising campaigns. What are some themes that are currently running?

4. How can you tell if an advertising campaign has been effective?

5. What will be the future of online advertising?

■ KEY TERMS

target audience (p. 369)
consumer advertising (p. 369)
business-to-business advertising (p. 369)
primary demand ad (p. 371)
selective demand ads (p. 371)
direct action ad (p. 371)
indirect action ad (p. 371)
marketing (p. 371)

advertising agency (p. 373)
national advertisers (p. 376)
retail advertisers (p. 376)
agency (p. 377)
full-service agency (p. 377)
media buying service (p. 377)
creative boutique (p. 377)
banner ads (p. 380)
free-link exchange (p. 380)

copy (p. 383)
campaign (p. 383)
positioning (p. 383)
rough layout (p. 384)
comprehensive layout (p. 385)
storyboard (p. 385)
formative research (p. 385)
message research (p. 385)
tracking studies (p. 386)

◼ SUGGESTIONS FOR FURTHER READING

Belch, George, and Michael Belch. *Advertising and Promotion: An Integrated Marketing Communications Perspective.* New York: McGraw-Hill, 2001.

Forbes, Thomas. *Advertising.* Gloucester, MA: Rockport, 2000.

Kilbourne, Jean. *Can't Buy My Love: How Advertising Changes the Way We Think and Feel.* New York: Simon and Schuster, 2000.

Russell, J. T., and Ron Lane. *Kleppner's Advertising Procedure.* Upper Saddle River, NJ: Prentice Hall, 1999.

Zeff, Robbin, and Brad Aronson. *Advertising on the Internet.* New York: Wiley, 1999.

◼ SURFING THE INTERNET

The sites below represent just a small sample of the hundreds and hundreds of sites that are relevant to this chapter. All were current as of late 2000. Keep in mind, however, that ad sites change rapidly.

www.aaaa.org
Home of the American Association of Advertising Agencies. Contains agency news, career information, and awards programs.

www.adage.com
Advertising Age is the leading trade publication for the industry. Its web page has current news, useful statistics, and critiques of website advertising.

www.chiatday.com
Chiat Day is an ad agency that handles Nissan and Apple. At first glance the site doesn't look like that of an ad agency, but don't let it fool you. A sampling of

the agency's current and past award-winning work is available.

www.clioawards.com
The Clios are advertising's counterparts to the Oscars. This site has a listing of winners and a searchable archive.

www.donnakaran.com
The fashion designer's website is a good example of consistency of execution. The tone and feel of this company's advertising is carried over to the website. Plus it's got some pretty neat clothes.

PART V

Regulation of the Mass Media

CHAPTER 15

Formal Controls
Laws, Rules, Regulations

For purposes of this chapter, formal controls over the media include laws, court decisions that refine those laws, and rules and regulations administered by government agencies. We will discuss six different areas where these formal controls are important: (1) the controversy over a free system of mass communication, (2) copyright, (3) restrictions on obscenity and pornography, (4) regulation of radio and television, (5) regulation of the Internet, and (6) regulation of advertising. Unfortunately, many students have the idea that the field of mass communication law and regulations is dull and boring. Nothing could be further from the truth. In what other textbook could you read about raunchy magazines, the CIA, mass murderers, women in men's locker rooms, juicy divorces, and a man who owned a submarine?

Over the years court decisions have had a major impact on the operations of the mass media.
(©Corbis Images)

THE PRESS, THE LAW, AND THE COURTS

A Free Press

As noted in Chapter 4, the idea of a free press did not catch on at first in America. The early colonial papers had problems if they were not "published by authority," that is, open to censorship by the Crown. Through the Stamp Act, the British government attempted to suppress hostile opinion by taxing printed matter. Recognizing these dangers to a free press, the framers of the Constitution added an amendment (the **First Amendment**) that stated in part that "Congress shall make no law . . . abridging the freedom of speech, or of the press." The precise meaning and interpretation of these words, however, have been open to some debate. Let's examine some key instances in which press and government have come into conflict.

Prior Restraint

When the government censors the press by restraining it from publishing or broadcasting material, that act is called **prior restraint.** Attempts at prior restraint have been relatively rare. Nonetheless, this area does illustrate that the provisions in the First Amendment are not absolute. The Supreme Court has ruled that under certain circumstances, prior restraint or censorship of the press is permitted, but the government faces a difficult task in proving that the restraint is justified. There are some obvious examples of legal censorship. During wartime, say, a newspaper could be prevented from publishing the sailing schedules of troop transports; a radio station could be prohibited from broadcasting the location and numbers of soldiers on the front lines. Other attempts at prior restraint have not been particularly successful; the Supreme Court has generally upheld the right of the press. There are two seminal cases in this area that are beneficial for us to examine. One is not widely known; the other made the front pages.

The Near Case   During the 1920s, the Minnesota legislature passed a law under which newspapers that were considered public nuisances could be curtailed by means of an **injunction** (an order from a court that requires somebody to do something or refrain from doing something). The motives behind this law may have been praiseworthy because it appears to have been designed to prevent abusive attacks on minority groups. Using this public nuisance law, a county attorney sought an injunction against the *Saturday Press* and the paper's manager, J. M. Near, on the grounds that the paper had printed malicious statements about city officials in connection with gangland activities allegedly controlled by minority groups. In 1931, the Supreme Court ruled that the Minnesota law was unconstitutional. Said the Court:

> The fact that for approximately 150 years there has been almost an entire absence of attempts to impose previous restraints upon publications relating to the malfeasance of public officers is significant of the deep-seated conviction that such restraints would violate constitutional rights.

It would be 40 years before this issue was raised again.

The Pentagon Papers   U.S. Attorney General John Mitchell was eager to see the Sunday, June 13, 1971, edition of the *New York Times*. Mitchell had attended the wedding of President Richard Nixon's daughter Tricia the day before, and he

wanted to see how the *Times* had covered it. On the left side of page 1, Mitchell saw a flattering picture of the president with his daughter on his arm. Next to the wedding picture, another story caught Mitchell's eyes: "Vietnam Archive: Pentagon Study Traces 3 Decades of Growing U.S. Involvement." As Mitchell read further, he realized that the *Times* article was sure to cause problems.

The basis for the story in the *Times* began three years earlier when Secretary of Defense Robert McNamara became disillusioned with the Vietnam War and ordered a massive study of its origins. This study, known eventually as the Pentagon Papers, was put together by 36 different people and ran for more than 7,000 pages. The final report was classified "Top Secret—Sensitive." During April 1971, one of those Pentagon staff members who compiled the report leaked a copy to a reporter for the *New York Times*. After much study and secrecy, the paper was ready to publish the story in nine installments. The U.S. Justice Department, under John Mitchell's direction, asked a U.S. district court judge to halt publication of the stories on the grounds that they would "cause irreparable injury to the defense interests of the United States." The order was granted, and for the first time in history, a U.S. paper was ordered by the courts to suppress a specific story. By then, however, other newspapers had obtained copies of some or all of the Pentagon documents and started publishing them. The Justice Department sought more restraining orders, but as soon as one paper was ordered to stop publishing, another newspaper in another part of the country would pick up the series. It was obvious that the Supreme Court would eventually have to intervene.

The Court did intervene and with uncharacteristic haste. On June 30, 1971, only 17 days after the story first appeared and only 4 days after hearing oral arguments on the case, the Court decided in favor of the newspapers' right to publish the information. Naturally, the staff at the *New York Times* was delighted. The paper called the decision a "ringing victory for freedom under law." Upon closer examination, however, the victory was not quite as ringing as it was made out to be. The Court did not state that prior restraint could never be invoked against the press. Instead, it pointed out that the government "carries a heavy burden of showing justification" for imposing restraint. The government, in the opinion of the Court, had not shown sufficient grounds for doing this. The government was free, if it wished, to bring other prior restraint cases to the courts to establish exactly how much justification it needed to stifle publication. In addition, each of the nine judges wrote a separate opinion that highlighted the ambiguities and complexities surrounding this topic.

More Recent Cases   After the release of the Pentagon Papers, the prior restraint problem cropped up several times in cases involving former CIA agents. In one instance the CIA was successful in having portions of a book deleted because they revealed classified information. When the Gulf War broke out in 1990, the Defense Department issued restrictive rules on how the press could cover military activities. Two news agencies challenged the constitutionality of the restrictions, but the war ended before the lawsuits could be heard.

In 1995, a judge ordered *Business Week* not to publish an article about a fraud case based on sealed court documents. The publication pulled the article but appealed the judge's decision. An appeals court later ruled that the original order barring publication was wrong. More recent examples of prior restraint include a 1999 ruling by a district court judge that the prohibition against prior restrain also included websites. The creator of a website devoted to news about the Ford Motor Company had posted documents obtained from anonymous Ford employees. The company obtained a ruling that prevented the website creator from posting the documents, but the order was overturned. Finally, prior restraint was considered justifiable in a South Carolina criminal court case. A judge had barred pretrial reporting on a secretly recorded conversation between a murder defendant and his lawyer that was obtained by the news media. The South Carolina Supreme Court ruled that the defendant's right to a fair trial outweighed the media's First Amendment rights, and the U.S. Supreme Court refused to overturn the decision. These cases illustrate that prior restraint is still a vital issue.

In sum, there is a strong constitutional case against prior restraint of the press, but gray areas exist where censorship might be legal. These areas will probably remain ambiguous until further court cases help define the limits of government authority in this area. It is likely, however, that the barriers against prior restraint will remain formidable.

PROTECTING NEWS SOURCES

Before we begin an examination of this topic, we should point out that the issues are fairly complicated. Conflicting interests are involved. Reporters argue that if they are forced to disclose confidential sources, those sources will dry up and the public's right to know will be adversely affected. Government arguments cite the need for the administration of justice and the rights of an individual to a fair trial.

A 1988 Supreme Court decision left little doubt that there was one area where authorities could exercise prior restraint—the high school newsroom. The case began in 1983 when a principal in Hazelwood, Missouri, deleted from the high school paper two articles, one on teenage pregnancy and one about divorce, on the grounds that they were inappropriate.

Three students, with the help of the American Civil Liberties Union, filed suit in district court, arguing that their First Amendment rights were being violated. The district court found in favor of the school system. The students appealed this decision and were delighted when the appeals court reversed the district court. Ultimately, however, the Supreme Court sided with the district court's decision in favor of the school system.

In its decision, the Court ruled that the paper was an integral part of the school's educational function: It was part of the regular journalism curriculum and was produced using school supplies and personnel. The staff was restricted to journalism students. As such, it was not a "public forum" and not entitled to First Amendment protection.

In the wake of the Hazelwood decision, many thought instances of censorship of the high school press would increase. Recent surveys of principals and publication advisors, however, found that they didn't much change in the amount of censorship they exercised. On the other hand, a 1994 study of student editors and advisors suggested a small increase in self-censorship following the Hazelwood verdict.

Perhaps a hypothetical example will help bring these issues into focus. Suppose you are a reporter for a campus newspaper. One of your sources calls you late one night and informs you that several students have started a drug ring that has monopolized the sale of illegal drugs on campus. To check the accuracy of this report, you call another one of your sources, one who in the past has given you reliable information on campus drug dealing. This second source confirms what your caller told you and adds more details. For obvious reasons, both of your sources ask not to be identified and you agree. On the basis of these reports and some additional research, you publish a lengthy article in the campus newspaper about the drug ring. A few days later you are summoned before a grand jury that is investigating criminal drug dealings. You are asked to reveal your sources. If you refuse, you will be charged with contempt and possibly fined or sent to jail. What do you do?

The Reporter's Privilege

Other reporters have found themselves in the same fix. One was Paul Branzburg. In 1969, Branzburg wrote a story for the *Louisville Courier-Journal* in which he described how two local residents were synthesizing hashish from marijuana. His article stated that he had promised not to reveal their identities. Shortly thereafter, Branzburg was subpoenaed (ordered to appear) by the county grand jury. He refused to answer questions about his sources, claiming, in part, that to do so would violate the First Amendment provision for freedom of the press. The case ultimately reached the Supreme Court, which ruled that the First Amendment did not protect reporters from the obligation to testify before grand juries to answer questions concerning a criminal investigation.

Initially, this ruling was viewed as a setback for reporters' rights. Upon closer examination, however, the Court did suggest some situations in which the reporter's claim to privilege would be valid. These included harassment of news reporters, instances in which grand juries do not operate in good faith, and situations in which there is only a remote connection between the investigation and the information sought. Additionally, the Court suggested that Congress and the states could further define the rights of a reporter to protect sources by enacting legislation (called **shield laws**) to that effect.

After the Branzburg decision, state courts were somewhat inconsistent in their rulings. On the one hand, several cases upheld the reporter's right to keep his or her sources secret. In Florida, Lucy Ware Morgan, a reporter for the *St. Petersburg Times,* refused to disclose her source for a story about a grand jury report on corruption in city government. She was promptly convicted of contempt of court and received a 90-day jail sentence. In 1976, however, the Florida Supreme Court overturned the conviction. Using the Branzburg decision as a guideline, the court concluded that the name of her source was not relevant to the investigation of a crime and that the contempt charge was designed to harass her.

Other decisions have narrowly defined the test of relevancy between the case at hand and the reporter's sources. In Virginia, a newspaper reporter refused to identify a source during testimony at a 1978 murder trial. The lawyer for the accused argued that the source's name was needed to question the credibility of a prosecution witness. The Virginia Supreme Court ruled in favor of the reporter and stated that a reporter's privilege must yield only when the defendant's need for the information is essential. To be essential, said the court, the information had to (1) relate directly to the defendant's guilt or innocence, (2) bear on the reduction of an offense, or (3) concern the mitigation of a sentence.

Just because these cases are taken from the 1970s, don't get the idea that reporters no longer go to jail or get fined. From 1999 to 2000, three reporters in California, a state with what many experts consider the strongest shield law in the country, got into legal trouble when they failed to reveal confidential information. One journalist went to jail for five days, while another was fined $1,000 a day for every day he refused to testify. Fortunately for the reporters, either the sanctions were overturned on appeal or the original requests were dropped.

As of 2000, 31 states and the District of Columbia have shield laws. Journalists generally recognize these laws as helpful, but most realize that they are not the powerful protectors of the press that many had hoped for. In addition, the laws themselves represent a bewildering collection of provisions, qualifications, and exceptions. Some states protect only confidential material; some protect the reporter from revealing the name of a source but do not protect the information obtained from sources. Other state laws confer less protection if the reporter is involved in a libel case. In some states, shield laws don't apply to reporters subpoenaed by a grand jury. Further, many courts are interpreting the shield laws on a case-by-case basis and ignoring or limiting the interpretation of judgments contained in the law.

Overall, since 1970 only about one in three shield law rulings have been against the press. The mid-1990s, however, saw an increase in the number of subpoenas that were upheld by the courts. On the positive side, many states that have no shield laws have recognized a reporter's privilege to resist a subpoena. It's obvious that reporters should consider their circumstances carefully before guaranteeing confidentiality.

■ Search and Seizure

Finally, there is the troublesome question of protecting notes and other records that might disclose sources. In this regard, the courts have offered little protection. Three particular cases have disturbed the news media. In the first case, in 1971, four police officers entered the offices of the *Stanford Daily,* the campus newspaper of Stanford University, and produced a search warrant authorizing them to search for photographs of a clash between demonstrators and police that the *Daily* had covered the day before. The newspaper brought suit against the authorities, charging that its First Amendment rights had been violated. In 1978, the Supreme Court ruled that the search was legal. (In 1980, however, Congress extended some protection to newsrooms by passing a bill that would require the government to secure a subpoena to obtain records held by reporters. The scope of a subpoena is somewhat more limited than that of a search warrant. In addition, a subpoena can be challenged.)

In the second case, the U.S. Court of Appeals in the District of Columbia decided another case that further eroded reporters' rights to protect sources. In 1974, the Reporters Committee for Freedom of the Press filed suit against the American Telephone and Telegraph Company (AT&T) because the company would not pledge to keep records of reporters' toll calls safe from government scrutiny. (An analysis of these calls might help locate a reporter's source of information.) The court of appeals ruled that it was legal for the government to examine such records without the reporter's knowledge or consent.

The third case involved *New York Times* reporter Myron Farber. During 1976, Farber had been reporting the investigation into mysterious deaths at a New Jersey hospital. The stories led to the indictment of a prominent physician on charges of poisoning five patients. Defense lawyers ultimately subpoenaed notes and documents pertaining to the case that were held by Farber and the *Times.* Both Farber and the paper refused to provide the documents, and both were convicted of contempt of court. Farber was sentenced to six months in jail and a $1,000 fine; the *Times* was slapped with a $100,000 fine and was ordered to pay $5,000 every day until it complied with the court's order. The *Times* ultimately turned over its files, but a judge ruled that the paper had "sanitized" them by removing some relevant material, so it reinstated the fine. Farber, meanwhile, had spent 27 days in jail. Eventually, Farber wound up spending 40 days in jail, and the *Times* paid $285,000 in fines. All penalties finally ended with the jury's verdict that the physician was innocent.

The privacy of computer-stored messages and e-mail received protection from the Electronic Communication Privacy Act, which requires the government to obtain a search warrant before examining online or stored messages that were intended to be private.

Judging from the above, perhaps the safest conclusion that we can draw is that a reporter's privilege in protecting sources and notes is unlikely to be absolute. Even those decisions that have favored journalists have been qualified. It also appears that further developments in this area will be put together on a piece-by-piece basis by lower courts unless the Supreme Court generates a precise decision or the legislature passes a comprehensive law. As for reporters, they must carefully consider these issues when they promise confidentiality to a news source.

COVERING THE COURTS

The criminal and civil trials of O. J. Simpson are the most striking examples of the conflicts of competing interests that repeatedly crop up when news media attempt to cover the courts. On the one hand, the Sixth Amendment guarantees a defendant the right to a trial before an impartial jury; on the other, the First Amendment guarantees freedom of the press. Trial judges are responsible for the administration of justice; reporters are responsible for informing the public about the workings of the legal system. Sometimes these responsibilities clash. In the Simpson

High-profile trials, such as the criminal trial of O. J. Simpson, highlight basic conflicts between the First and the Sixth Amendments. *(AP/Wide World Photos)*

criminal trial, cameras were allowed in the courtroom. In the civil trial, they were not allowed. The lawyers in both trials were extremely sensitive to pretrial publicity. Both judges considered gag orders that would have prohibited participants from talking to the press. The high-profile Simpson trials were the latest and most prominent example of the friction that sometimes develops in this area.

■ Publicity before and during a Trial

If a potential jury member has read, seen, or heard stories in the news media about a defendant that appear to indicate that person's guilt, it is possible that the defendant will not receive a fair trial. Although research has not produced definitive evidence linking pretrial publicity to prejudice, this concern has been at the heart of several court decisions that have castigated the news media for trying cases in the newspaper or on television instead of in the courtroom.

The 1960s saw a flurry of cases suggesting that the Supreme Court was taking a close look at pretrial publicity. In 1961, the Court for the first time reversed a criminal conviction entirely because pretrial publicity had made it impossible to select an impartial jury. The case concerned Leslie Irvin, a rather unsavory character who was arrested and charged with six murders. Newspapers carried police-issued press releases that said "Mad Dog" Irvin had confessed to all six killings. The local media seized upon this story with a vengeance, and many stories referred to Irvin as the "confessed slayer of six." Of the 430 potential jurors examined by attorneys, 90 percent had formed opinions about Irvin's guilt—opinions that ranged from suspicion to absolute certainty that he was guilty. Irvin was convicted—hardly a surprise—and sentenced to death. After six years of complicated legal maneuvers, made even more complicated because Irvin managed to escape from prison, the case went before the Supreme Court. The Court ruled that the pretrial publicity had ruined the defendant's chances for a fair trial and sent the case back to be retried. (Irvin, who had been recaptured, was again found guilty, but this time was sentenced to life imprisonment.)

Perhaps the most famous case of pretrial publicity concerned an Ohio physician. On July 4, 1954, the wife of Cleveland-area osteopath Dr. Sam Sheppard was found slain in the couple's home. Sheppard became a prime suspect, and the news media, especially the Cleveland newspapers, were impatient for his arrest. "Why Isn't Sam Sheppard in Jail?" and "Why Don't Police Quiz Top Suspect?" were headlines that appeared over page-one editorials. News reports carried the results of alleged scientific tests that cast doubt on Sheppard's version of the crime (these tests were never brought up at the trial). Articles stressed Sheppard's extramarital affairs as a possible motive for the crime. After his arrest, the news stories and editorials continued. There were enough of them with headlines such as "Dr. Sam Faces Quiz at Jail on Marilyn's Fear of Him" and "Blood Is Found in Garage" to fill five scrapbooks. Every juror but one admitted reading about the story in the newspapers. The sensationalized coverage continued during the trial itself, which produced a guilty verdict. Twelve years later the Supreme Court reversed Sheppard's conviction because of the extremely prejudicial publicity. This case assumed added importance because the Court listed six safeguards that judges might invoke to prevent undue influence from publicity. These safeguards included sequestering the jury (i.e., moving them into seclusion), moving the case to another county, and placing restrictions on statements made by lawyers, witnesses, or others who might divulge damaging information.

■ Gag Rules

Some judges have announced restrictive orders, or **gag rules**, that restrain the participants in a trial (attorneys, witnesses, defendants) from giving information to the media or that restrain media coverage of events that occur in court. For example, a superior court judge in a Washington murder trial ordered reporters to report only on events that occurred in front of a jury. Two reporters violated this rule by writing about events that took place in the courtroom while the jury was not present; they were subsequently charged with contempt. The Washington Supreme Court refused to review this ruling.

In other cases, the news media have won what might be called hollow victories. In New York in 1971, a judge closed a trial to both the public and the press. News organizations appealed, and the judge's ruling was ultimately declared incorrect. Although the press may have won a victory in principle, it lost one in fact—by the time the closure rule had been judged invalid, the trial had already been conducted behind closed doors. Two Louisiana reporters also won but lost when they violated a gag rule and reported testimony given in open court. They were found guilty of contempt and fined $300. A higher court ruled that the gag rule was unconstitutional, but the contempt fine was nonetheless upheld. The gag order, said the court, could not be ignored even though it might be invalid. Reporters must obey judicial orders until they are reversed, or reporters will suffer the consequences.

The whole question of gag rules reached the Supreme Court in 1976. A Nebraska judge had prohibited reporters from revealing certain information about a mass murder case. The Nebraska Press Association appealed the order to the Supreme Court. The Court ruled on the side of the press association and held that reporting of judicial proceedings in open court cannot be prohibited. Once again, upon first examination, this rule appeared to be a significant victory for the press. As time passed, however, it became apparent that the Nebraska decision had left the way open for court-ordered restrictions on what the trial participants could say to the press.

Recent developments indicate that gag orders on trial participants have become common. The Reporters Committee for Freedom of the Press found that one Texas judge had issued 219 gag orders in just two years. The committee also tracked 43 gag orders during early 2000 and found that only a few were imposed after a hearing. Most were issued routinely. Some gag rules were issued in cases decided solely by a judge, a situation in which there was no possibility that pretrial publicity could have an impact on a jury. One California judge issued a gag order that even prohibited discussion of the gag order itself.

The Nebraska decision mentioned above seemed to indicate that some legal proceedings, primarily those that take place before the actual trial begins, might be legitimately closed to the public. By the early 1980s, this was exactly what was happening. Although the press was left free to report what it chose, its news sources were muzzled by judicial order. During the late 1970s, judges began holding pretrial hearings in private to limit pretrial publicity. A 1979 Supreme Court decision held this practice to be constitutional. In 1980, the Court did go on record as stating that the press did, in fact, have a constitutional right to attend criminal trials. *Pretrial* events, however, such as those stated above, might still be closed. Because many criminal cases are settled out of court, these pretrial hearings are often the only public hearings held.

In the 1980s, the press gained wider access to court proceedings. In 1984, the Supreme Court ruled that the jury selection process should be open to the press except in extreme circumstances, and it established standards that judges must meet before they can close a pretrial hearing. A 1986 Supreme Court decision, however, gave the press a major victory in its efforts to secure access to pretrial proceedings. The Court held that preliminary trial proceedings must be open to the press unless the judge could demonstrate a "substantial probability that the defendant's right to a fair trial would be violated." Additionally, lower courts have held that the First Amendment right of access to trials also extends to documents used as evidence. Also in 1986, the Supreme Court ruled that the jury selection process, as well as the trial itself, must ordinarily be open to the public. The Court also provided a set of strict guidelines that would justify a private selection of a jury.

In summary, Supreme Court decisions do not give the press an absolute right of access to all court proceedings. Some parts of trials and pretrial hearings may still be closed if the judge can fulfill the court's guidelines regarding closure. Further, the recent Court decisions have not changed the legal status surrounding the privacy of grand jury hearings—they continue to have the right to secrecy. All in all, it might be safe to conclude that the press has been given a green light to report matters that occur in open court with little fear of reprisal. But gag orders on news sources and the closing of various legal proceedings threaten to be areas of tension between the press and the judiciary for some time to come.

Cameras and Microphones in the Courtroom

For many years, the legal profession looked with disfavor on the idea of cameras and microphones in the courtroom. There was a time when this attitude may have been entirely justified. The whole problem seems to have begun in 1935 when Bruno Hauptmann was put on trial for the kidnapping and murder of the son of national hero Charles Lindbergh. Remember that news photography and radio journalism were still young in 1935, and this fact may have contributed to some of the abuses that occurred during this trial (see Media Probe, "Canon 35 and the Hauptmann Trial"). After the trial, the American Bar Association adopted Canon 35 of its Canons of Professional Ethics. This provision stated that the taking of photographs in the courtroom and the broadcasting (later amended to include telecasting) of court proceedings should not be permitted. Although Canon 35 was not law, its language or some variation of it was adopted as law by every state except Colorado and Texas.

In 1965 the Supreme Court entered the picture when it ruled on the Billie Sol Estes case. Estes was on trial in Texas for allegedly swindling several farmers. The trial judge, over Estes's objections, had allowed the televising of the trial. Estes was found guilty, but he soon appealed that decision to the Supreme Court on the grounds that the presence of television had deprived him of a fair trial. The High Court agreed with Estes and argued for the prohibition of television cameras from

In 1935, nearly three years after the crime, Bruno Hauptmann was tried for the kidnapping and murder of the 19-month-old son of national hero Charles Lindbergh. The trial was held in the small town of Flemington, New Jersey. When it opened, more than 150 reporters were packed into a small area reserved for the press. During the trial, this number swelled to about 700 as members of the press corps prowled the corridors and surrounding rooms of the courthouse in an attempt to cover every aspect of the trial. Photography during the trial was forbidden, but photographers were allowed in the courthouse, and some were even allowed in the courtroom itself to take pictures when the trial was not in session.

As the trial progressed, the overcrowding got worse and it became obvious that the trial had turned into a media event. The ban against photography during court sessions was broken, but nothing was done about it. A newsreel motion picture camera was placed in the balcony of the courtroom, and despite a promise from the newsreel people that they would not take films during the trial, footage was taken of the testimony of Lindbergh, Hauptmann, and others. The film was shown in movie theaters throughout the country. Photographers, many of them freelancers, became more aggressive as the trial progressed and contributed to a general lack of courtroom decorum. The crush of reporters also aggravated the already severe overcrowding in the courtroom.

The crowds got so bad that the attorneys for both sides actually subpoenaed their friends in order to make sure that they got into the courtroom. One radio reporter, Gabriel Heatter, had no problem getting a seat. The judge's wife enjoyed his broadcasts so much that she prevailed on the judge to give Heatter a place in the front row. In an attempt to scoop the opposition, an Associated Press employee rigged a secret radio transmitter inside the courtroom.

Out of this confusion and carnival-like atmosphere came Canon 35, a rule adopted by the American Bar Association that limited courtroom reporting by photographers and radio and television reporters. Controversies that started in that overcrowded courtroom in Flemington are still debated today.

the courtroom. The decision said that broadcasting a trial would have a prejudicial impact on jurors, would distract witnesses, and would burden the trial judge with new responsibilities. But, the Court went on, there might come a day when broadcast technology would become portable and unobtrusive and television coverage so commonplace that trials might be broadcast. Thus the decision in the Estes case was not a blanket provision against the televising of trials.

Since 1965, the trend has been toward a general relaxation of the tension between the legal profession and the electronic press. In 1972, the American Bar Association adopted a new code of professional responsibility. Canon 3A(7) of this document superseded the old Canon 35. Canon 3A(7) still maintained the ban against taking photographs and broadcasting in the courtroom, but it did allow the judge the discretion to permit televising a trial to a pressroom or to another courtroom to accommodate an overflow crowd. In 1981, the Supreme Court ruled that broadcast coverage of a criminal trial is not inherently prejudicial, thereby clearing the way for the presence of radio and TV in the courtroom. The Court left it up to the states to devise their own systems for implementing such coverage.

As of 2000, several different systems have evolved in the various states. Some require the consent of all parties involved before electronic coverage is allowed; other states require the consent only of the prosecution and the defense. Forty-eight states allow some form of audiovisual coverage in courtrooms. Only Mississippi, South Dakota, and the District of Columbia forbid all recording and broadcasting of trials. Cameras are banned from federal trial courtrooms, and TV or radio coverage of proceedings before the Supreme Court is not allowed. The Supreme Court, however, did allow an audio recording of the Bush-Gore Florida recount hearings to be released shortly after the hearings concluded.

By the end of 1975, amendments to the Freedom of Information Act broadened the scope of information that was covered by the act. One area of information that became more accessible was FBI files. In the past 25 years, the FBI has handled more than 300,000 requests and released approximately 6 million pages of information.

In an effort to save time, money and paper, the FBI recently added an electronic reading room to its website (www.fbi.gov), which contains frequently requested documents. If you're really curious, you can find all sorts of interesting information about some of the topics that the FBI has been investigating over the years. For example, you can find:

- 248 pages on Beatle John Lennon, compiled after it was learned he donated money to a group that planned to disrupt the 1972 Republican convention.

- 600 pages on Elvis Presley. Elvis himself was not the target of an investigation, but the FBI kept copies of letters from people who commented on his performance, as well as newspaper clippings and documents suggesting that he was the target of extortion attempts.

- 80 pages on Marilyn Monroe discussing her alleged affairs and mysterious death.

- 1,600 pages on UFOs (but only one page on the alleged flying saucer crash near Roswell, New Mexico, in 1947).

Nowhere on the site is there mention of agents Scully and Mulder. Draw your own conclusions.

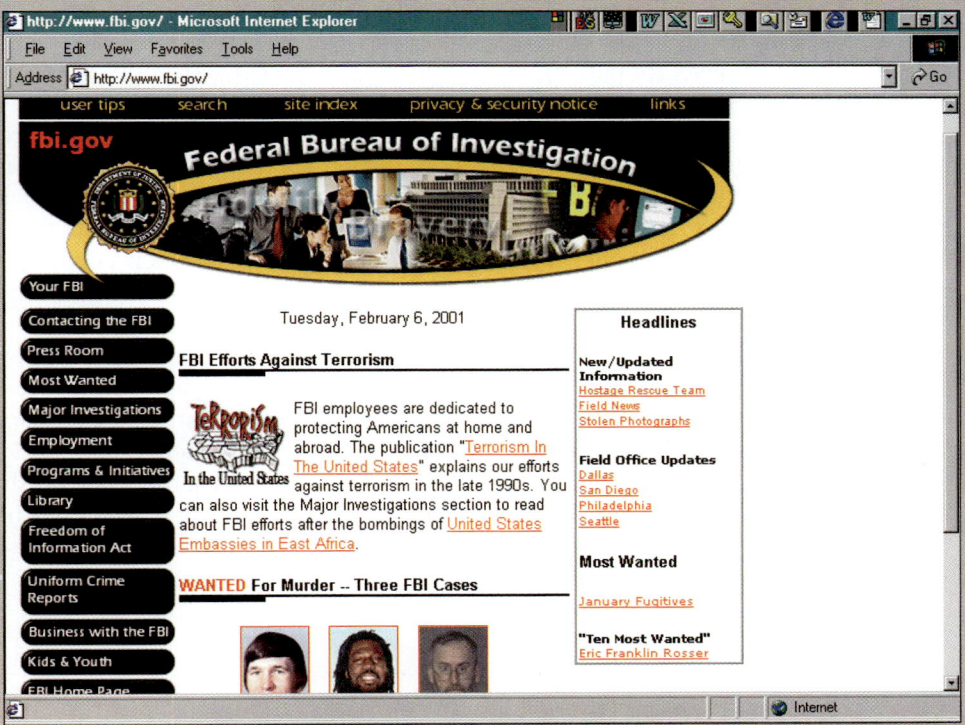

The files of the FBI's electronic reading room are organized into six categories: espionage, famous persons, gangster era, historical interest, unusual phenomenon and violent crime.

REPORTERS' ACCESS TO INFORMATION

Government Information

Reporting the doings of the government can be a frustrating task if the government insists that information about its activities be kept secret. After World War II, many members of the press complained that government secrecy was becoming a major problem. Reporters were being restricted from meetings, and access to many government documents was difficult to obtain. In the midst of continuing pressure from journalists and consumer groups, Congress passed the **Freedom of Information Act (FOIA)** in 1966. This law gave the public the right to discover what the federal government was up to—with certain exceptions. The law states that every federal executive-branch agency must publish instructions on what methods a member of the public should follow to get information. If information is improperly withheld, a court can force the agency to disclose what is sought. There are nine areas of exemptions covering material that does not have to be made public. Some of these exemptions are trade secrets, files of law enforcement investigations, and maps of oil wells.

In 1996, the Electronic Freedom of Information Act (EFOIA) was passed to make more information available on the Internet. Currently, many government agency websites contain a variety of information, ranging from statistics to press releases, that can be accessed via website visit rather than through an FOIA request. Nonetheless, many agencies have been slow to fully implement the requirements of the EFOIA.

Journalists are making increasing used of the FOIA despite some of the difficulties associated with it. The time lag between request and answer can be long, and journalists must have very specific information in mind when they request documents under this act. Nonetheless, the act has helped the development of many investigative projects. The authors of *Stolen Valor: How the Vietnam Generation Was Robbed of Its Heroes and History* used FOIA requests to obtain more than 1,500 military records and other documents in the preparation of their book.

A "Sunshine Act" ensures that regular meetings of approximately 50 federal government agencies will be open to the public. There are, however, 10 different situations that might permit the agency to meet behind closed doors, so the right of access to meetings is far from absolute. In addition, many states have their own versions of laws pertaining to information access and open meetings. The degree of compliance with these laws varies widely from state to state. A 1999 check of freedom of information laws in South Carolina, for example, found that in about one-third of the cases studied, public records were denied or not produced within the law's time limits. On the other hand, a survey in Kansas found compliance with the state's open records act in 84 percent of the cases.

■ Access to News Scenes

We have already mentioned this issue in our discussion of the right of the press to attend certain judicial proceedings. But what about the reporters' right of access to news settings outside the courtroom? The law here appears to be in the developmental stage. In the few decisions that have been handed down, the courts have given little support to the notion that the First Amendment guarantees a right of access. In separate rulings, the courts declared that journalists could be sued for invasion of privacy, for trespassing on private property, and for disobeying a police officer's legitimate command to clear the way at the scene of a serious automobile accident. Three of the most relevant Supreme Court opinions have focused on the question of access to prisons and prisoners. In these cases, the courts have ruled that reporters do not have the right to visit specific parts of a prison, to speak to specific prisoners, or to bring cameras inside. In general, the Court seems to be saying that the access rights of the press are not different from the access rights of the general public. When the public is not admitted, neither is the press.

Some rulings, however, have recognized a limited right of access. A Florida decision found that journalists who are customarily invited by police onto private property to view a news scene cannot be prosecuted for trespassing. The courts have also allowed access to news settings in order to halt discrimination among journalists. For example, in one case it was ruled that a female journalist could not be barred from entering a baseball team's locker room if male reporters had been admitted. In sum, the final words on this topic have yet to be written by the courts. A case as influential as the Branzburg or Estes decision has yet to be adjudicated in the area of press access. It is a good bet, however, that such a test will not be long in surfacing.

 DEFAMATION

The preceding discussions make it clear that in its news-gathering activities, the press often collides with the government. In addition, the right of free speech and the rights of a free press sometimes come into conflict with the right of an individual to protect his or her reputation. Protection for a person's reputation is found under the laws that deal with **defamation.**

To understand this somewhat complicated area, let's start with some general definitions:

Libel: Written defamation that tends to injure a person's reputation or good name or that diminishes the esteem, respect, or goodwill due a person.

Slander: Spoken defamation. (In many states, if a defamatory statement is broadcast, it is considered libel even though technically the words are not written. Libel is considered more harmful and usually carries more serious penalties than does slander.)

Libel per se: Some words are always libelous. Falsely written accusations, such as labeling a person a "thief" or a "swindler," automatically constitute libel.

Libel per quod: Words that seem perfectly innocent in themselves can become libelous under certain circumstances. Erroneously reporting that Mr. Smith was seen eating a steak dinner last night may seem harmless unless Mr. Smith happens to be the president of the Worldwide Vegetarian Society.

S O U N D B Y T E

Handle with Care

Below are listed red-flag words and expressions that are typical of those that may be libelous per se. Extreme care should be exercised in using these words in news reports:

bankrupt	corrupt	blockhead
intemperate	dishonest	rascal
unprofessional	amoral	scoundrel
communistic	disreputable	sneak
incompetent	illegitimate	deadhead
morally delinquent	hypocritical	fool
smooth and tricky	dishonorable	slacker
profiteering	cheating	skunk
sharp-dealing	unprincipled	poltroon
unethical	sneaky	ignoramus

(This list is also a handy reference guide for insults. Simply choose one word from the left list, one from the center, and one from the right, e.g., "You profiteering, amoral poltroon," or "You incompetent, corrupt deadhead"). Just make sure that you don't put it in writing and that no third party is listening. Otherwise, you may get hit with a defamation suit.)

For someone to win a libel suit brought against the media, that person must prove five things: (1) that he or she has actually been defamed and harmed by the statements; (2) that he or she has been identified (although not necessarily by name); (3) that the defamatory statements have been published; (4) that the media were at fault; and (5) in most instances, that what was published or broadcast was false.

Not every mistake that finds its way into publication is libelous. To report that James Arthur will lead the Fourth of July parade when in fact Arthur James will lead it is probably not libelous because it is improbable that leading a parade will cause harm to a person's reputation. (Courts have even ruled that it is not necessarily libelous to report incorrectly that a person died. Death, said the courts, is no disgrace.) Actual harm might be substantiated by showing that defamatory remarks led to physical discomfort (such as sleepless nights), or loss of income, or increased difficulty in performing a job.

Identification need not be by name. If a paper erroneously reports that the professor who teaches Psych 101 at 10 A.M. in Quadrangle Hall is taking bribes from his students, that would be sufficient.

Publication, for our purposes, pertains to a statement's appearance in a mass medium and is self-explanatory.

Fault is a little more complicated. To win a libel suit, some degree of fault or carelessness on the part of the media organization must be shown. As we shall see, the degree of fault that must be established depends on several things: (1) the person who's suing, (2) the subject matter of the suit, and (3) the particular state's laws that are being applied.

A 1986 Supreme Court decision held that private persons (as opposed to public figures) suing for libel must prove that the statements at issue are false, at least when the statements involve matters of public concern. For all practical purposes, however, proving that the media were at fault also involves proving the falsity of what was broadcast or published, so that virtually everyone who brings a libel suit must show the wrongfulness of what was published.

It should be emphasized that a mass medium is responsible for what it carries. It usually cannot hide behind the fact that it only repeated what someone else said. In most situations, a magazine could not defend itself against a libel suit by claiming that it simply quoted a hospital worker who said a colleague was stealing drugs. If, in fact, the hospital worker's colleague was not stealing drugs, the magazine would have to look to some other defense against libel.

Defenses against Libel Suits

What are some of the defenses that can be used? There are three. The first is truth. If what was reported is proved to be true, there is no libel. This defense, however, is rarely used since it is extremely difficult to prove the truth of a statement. In addition, since the Supreme Court's decision placed the burden of proving the falsity of a statement on the person bringing the libel suit, the defense of truth has become even less attractive.

A second defense is privilege. There are certain situations in which the courts have held that the public's right to know comes before a person's right to preserve a reputation. Judicial proceedings, arrest warrants, grand jury indictments, legislative proceedings, and public city council sessions are examples of situations that are generally acknowledged to be privileged. If a reporter gives a fair and accurate report of these events, no lawsuits can result, even if what is reported contains a libelous statement.

The third defense is fair comment and criticism. Any person who thrusts himself or herself into the public eye or is at the center of public attention is open to fair criticism. This means that public officials, professional sports figures, cartoonists, artists, columnists, playwrights, and all those who invite public attention are fair game for comment. This defense applies only to opinion and criticism, not to misrepresentations of fact. You can report that a certain director's new movie stank to high heaven without fear of a lawsuit, but you could not report falsely that the director embezzled funds from the company and expect protection under fair criticism. However, criticism can be quite severe and caustic and still be protected from lawsuit. In 1990, the Supreme Court ruled that expressions of opinion are not automatically exempt from charges of libel. Opinions that contain an assertion of fact that can be proved false might trigger a defamation suit.

In 1964, the Supreme Court, in the *New York Times* v. *Sullivan* case, significantly expanded the opportunity for comments on the actions of public officials and also changed the nature of the law governing defamation. The case involved the *Times* and an official of the Montgomery, Alabama, police department, L. B. Sullivan, and took place during the Civil Rights struggle of the early 1960s. A Civil Rights group published an ad in the *Times* concerning a protest in Montgomery that Sullivan claimed libeled him. Testimony in the case revealed that, indeed, several statements in the ad were false. An Alabama court awarded him $500,000, but the *Times* appealed the case to the Supreme Court.

The Court reversed the Alabama decision and enumerated three major principles that would affect future decisions concerning defamation:

1. Editorial advertising is protected by the First Amendment.

2. Even statements that are false might qualify for First Amendment protection if they concern the public conduct of public officials.

3. To win a libel suit, public officials must prove that false and defamatory statements were made with actual malice.

The Court also clarified what is meant by actual malice—publishing a statement with the knowledge that it is false or publishing a statement in "reckless disregard" of whether it is false or not. A few years later, the Court expanded this protection to include statements made about public figures as well as public officials. In 1971, it appeared that the Supreme Court would even require private individuals who become involved in events of public concern to prove actual malice before collecting for a libel suit. Three years later, the Court seemed to retreat a little from this position when it held that a lawyer involved in a civil lawsuit was not a public figure, that he was not involved in an event of public interest, and that he did not have to prove actual malice.

Even more protection was extended to the private citizen in 1976 in a case concerning the divorce of Mary Alice Firestone from her husband, tire heir Russell Firestone, Jr. The trial lasted 17 months and received large amounts of media coverage. Ms. Firestone even called several press conferences while the trial was taking place. When *Time* magazine erroneously reported that the divorce had been granted on the grounds of extreme cruelty and adultery, Ms. Firestone sued for libel. (Her husband had charged her with adultery, but adultery was not cited as grounds for the divorce.) *Time* argued that she was a public figure and contended that Ms. Firestone had to show not only that the magazine was inaccurate but also that it acted with malice. The Supreme Court ruled that she was not a public figure, despite all the attendant press coverage, and drew a distinction between legitimate public controversies and those controversies that merely interest the public. The latter, said the Court, are not protected, and actual malice need not be proved.

The Court affirmed this distinction in 1979 by noting that the fact that someone is involved in a "newsworthy" event doesn't make the person a public figure. When a U.S. senator presented a scientist with a satirical award used to denote wasteful spending of government funds, the scientist sued for defamation. The Court ruled that even though the scientist became the subject of media attention, his public prominence before receiving the satirical award did not merit labeling him a public figure. Therefore, he did not have to meet the actual malice standard.

Many people are confused by the meaning of the phrase "actual malice" as it applies to defamation. Some individuals mistakenly think that a person who is defamed has to prove evil motives, spite, or ill will on the part of the person or medium that allegedly committed the defamation. Not so. In the famous *New York Times* v. *Sullivan* case, the Supreme Court defined actual malice as (1) publishing something that is known to be false ("I know what I'm publishing is not true but I'm going to publish it anyway"); or (2) publishing something with reckless disregard for whether it's true or not ("I have good reason to doubt that what I'm publishing is true, but I'm going to publish it anyway").

A recent libel case involving CBS, Inc., and Walter Jacobson, a news anchor and commentator at WBBM-TV (the CBS affiliate) in Chicago, illustrates this definition. The Brown & Williamson Tobacco Corporation (maker of Viceroy cigarettes) claimed that Jacobson libeled their company when he charged during a TV commentary that Viceroy was using an ad campaign to persuade children to smoke. Viceroy, said Jacobson, was equating cigarette smoking with "wine, beer, shaving or wearing a bra . . . a declaration of independence and striving for self-identity . . . a basic symbol of the growing-up process." The commentary cited as evidence a Federal Trade Commission report that claimed the company had been advised by its advertising agency to launch such a campaign. Brown & Williamson, forced to prove actual malice on the part of Jacobson because of the company's position as a public figure, denied ever having launched such a campaign. In fact, company lawyers argued that Brown & Williamson was so outraged by its ad agency's advice that it fired the advertising firm. Further, Brown & Williamson argued that Jacobson knew this fact before he broadcast his commentary. In court, one of the officials for the tobacco company testified that a researcher for Jacobson had been told that the ad agency had been fired and that the campaign was not used. During the trial, Jacobson said that he had rejected a suggestion from this researcher that a disclaimer should be included in the commentary stating that Brown & Williamson had not used the campaign. Evidently, this fact was enough to convince the jury that Jacobson knew that what he was saying was false—thus establishing actual malice. The jury found in favor of the tobacco company and awarded Brown & Williamson more than $5 million in damages.

For their part, Jacobson and CBS still maintain that the commentary was an accurate summary of the Federal Trade Commission report and that Brown & Williamson had a strategy directed toward children, even if the company didn't fully implement it. In late 1985, CBS announced plans to appeal the decision. The appeal was decided in 1988 in favor of the tobacco company. CBS was ordered to pay $3.05 million in damages.

Private citizens, however, do have to show some degree of fault or negligence by the media. In many states, this means showing that the media did not exercise ordinary care in publishing a story. Establishing this will allow a private citizen to collect compensation for any actual damages that stem from the libel. The big bucks, however, come from punitive damages assessed against the media. These awards are designed to punish the media for their past transgressions and serve as a reminder not to misbehave again. To collect punitive damages, even private citizens must show actual malice.

The amount of money that juries award to the winners of libel cases can be substantial. Awards of a $1 million or more have become common. Singer Wayne Newton, for example, received a $20 million judgment against NBC. On the other hand, most libel cases are appealed and about 75 percent are either reversed or have the monetary awards substantially reduced. For example, the Wayne Newton verdict was eventually reversed.

The difficulty that public figures face in successfully bringing a libel suit against the media has prompted some news subjects to look for other remedies. In the past decade, several subjects of news stories sued the news media for the way they gathered the news rather than on the content of the story. Lawsuits concerning trespass and invasion of privacy by the media (see below) became more common.

For a private citizen to prevail in a defamation case, he or she must prove some degree of negligence on the part of the media. The standards for determining what constitutes negligence vary from state to state, and, like the actual malice standard, negligence is determined on a case-by-case basis. Nonetheless, some general statements can be made.

A common legal definition of negligence states that it is conduct that creates an unreasonable risk of harm. The standard of conduct that the possible negligence is measured against is whether a reasonable person under the same circumstances would behave in the same way. As far as the media are concerned, employees are to be judged against the appropriate practices and customs for their profession. Thus, in many cases, the issue of negligence boils down to whether the reporter or editor exercised reasonable care and followed the accepted practices of the profession in determining whether a story was true or false.

Some specific factors might also be taken into account. First: Was the story prepared under deadline? If sufficient time and opportunity were available, then reasonable care might require more checking of facts. Second: What was the interest being promoted by the story? Stories covering heated political debates have greater merit than gossip, but gossip can be extremely harmful. Hence, greater care should be exercised in the latter situation.

A concrete example might help illustrate negligence and show how it differs from actual malice. In a 1975 case in Massachusetts, a rookie reporter was covering a drug trial. The reporter was unaware that a table in the front of the courtroom was reserved for the press. Consequently, he sat in the back, where he had trouble hearing the testimony. One of the defendants was the 20-year-old son of a man named John Stone. John Stone ran the lunchrooms in a public school. When the prosecutor asked a marshal the question of who had the drugs, the reporter thought he heard the marshal say "Mr. Stone," and assumed he meant John Stone, the only "Mr. Stone" that the reporter knew. He wrote in his story that John Stone had possession of the drugs. When questioned by his editor, who knew John Stone personally and had a hard time believing that he could have possessed illegal drugs, the reporter said he had heard the name in court. In fact, the marshal was talking about Jeffrey Stone, the son of John Stone. John Stone, naturally enough, sued for libel.

The court found that the reporter was guilty of negligence because he didn't sit where he could properly hear and did not check with another source to confirm who the "Mr. Stone" was—two practices that were in keeping with the accepted procedures of journalism. By contrast, the reporter's conduct did not constitute actual malice since he was new in town and didn't have reason to doubt that the Stone mentioned in court was the only Stone he knew.

But what about the editor? The one who knew Mr. Stone personally and had trouble believing the story? The editor had reason to doubt the story but did not even make a phone call to check its accuracy. The court ruled that he had acted with reckless disregard for the truth of the report, which was enough to constitute actual malice.

Defamation and the Internet

The Internet has created new problems with regard to defamation. One basic question is whether defamation posted on the Internet is libel or slander. If you write a defamatory statement in a chat room, is that written or spoken defamation? Since defamation laws vary from state to state, there may be several different answers to this question.

Another problem involves who can be sued for defamation. Suppose you post a defamatory message on a CompuServe message board? Can someone sue both you and CompuServe? The courts have indicated that Internet service providers (ISPs), such as CompuServe and AOL, are generally not liable for the passive content they carry. If CompuServe did not actively moderate or edit the message board that contained the defamation, then it could not be sued. This position was codified by language in the Telecommunications Act of 1996. In a recent case that tested this provision, a public figure sought damages for libel from both Internet gossip columnist Matt Drudge and AOL, which provided Drudge's access to the Internet. The court ruled that AOL could not be sued because it had no control over the content of Drudge's site; the suit against Drudge, however, could proceed.

INVASION OF PRIVACY

The Right to Privacy

Closely related to libel is the right to privacy. In fact, a single publication will often prompt both types of suits. The big difference between the two is that while libel protects a person's reputation, the right of privacy protects a person's peace of mind and feelings. A second difference is that libel involves the publication of false information; invasion of privacy might be triggered by disclosing the truth.

There are four different ways that the mass media can invade someone's right to privacy. The first is intruding upon a person's solitude or seclusion. This generally occurs when reporters wrongfully use microphones, surveillance cameras, and other forms of eavesdropping to record someone's private activities. A TV news crew hiding in a van outside your room and secretly taping your activities while you were inside would probably constitute a situation of intrusion.

The use of tiny, hidden cameras and microphones by reporters in their quest for news has raised special problems in this area. In a 1999 decision, the California Supreme Court ruled that an ABC reporter committed an invasion of privacy when she went to work for a psychic hot line and secretly videotaped a conversation with a co-worker. Even though the conversation took place in an open office and was overheard by others, the court ruled that the co-worker had a reasonable expectation that a reporter would not secretly videotape his conversations. This decision suggests that reporters should give extra thought to the use of hidden recordings in their news-gathering activities.

The second occasion is the unauthorized release of private information. A newspaper's publishing private medical records that reveal that a person has a dread disease might be an example in this area. The courts allowed a suit claiming invasion of privacy to be filed when a newspaper published information about a person's sex-change operation without the person's consent.

A third method is publicizing people in a false light or creating a false impression of them. This invasion is most closely related to libel because falsity is also involved. Some TV stations get into trouble in this area through the practice of putting new narration over some stock tape footage, which sometimes creates a false impression. For example, a Chicago TV station was sued when it ran stock footage taken three years earlier of a doctor performing a gynecological exam with a story describing how another doctor allegedly used an AIDS-infected swab during a similar exam. The face of the doctor in the stock footage was readily identifiable and she sued the station, claiming the story made it appear that she performed the allegedly negligent procedure. (The station settled the suit out-of-court and paid the doctor an undisclosed amount of money.)

The last means of invading privacy is through appropriation of a person's name or likeness for commercial purposes. This commonly involves stars and celebrities who find their names or images used without their permission in some business or promotional activity. Model Christy Brinkley, for example, successfully filed suit to stop poster stores from selling her picture without her permission. The not-so-famous are also protected against appropriation. One man sued because he found that a camera company had used his picture without permission in their instruction manual.

The term "paparazzi" refers to freelance photographers who make a living taking pictures of celebrities and selling the photos to both tabloid and reputable newspapers. There is a lucrative market for these pictures, and some paparazzi have been paid hefty sums for them. Celebrities have a complicated relationship with the paparazzi. On the one hand, stars need publicity and the paparazzi provide needed exposure. On the other hand, sometimes the paparazzi may go too far in their quest for photos.

The alleged role of the paparazzi in the death of Princess Diana led to a reexamination of the conflict between the First Amendment and the privacy rights of individuals, especially celebrities. Three paparazzi bills were introduced in the U.S. Congress in mid-1998, shortly after Diana's death. These laws focused primarily on certain members of the paparazzi who were dubbed "stalkerazzi." The stalkerazzi are photographers who pursue and harass celebrities and who use telephoto lenses to invade their private moments.

Each of the bills created civil and criminal penalties for commercially motivated invasion of privacy through chases and through the use of "visual enhancement devices," such as telephoto lenses and satellite photographs, that could capture scenes that would be otherwise unavailable except through trespassing on private property. Thus, taking photographs of Madonna at the Grammy ceremonies would be fine, but shooting pictures of Madonna's wedding from a helicopter with a special lens might bring a lawsuit. Note that these laws would punish the behavior of the news gatherers even if what they reported was true.

Reporters and news organizations were against these laws for various reasons. One of their major concerns was that they gave celebrities a special privilege when it came to publicity. Movies stars and other public figures who build their careers by inviting public attention would be given the power to turn it off.

Reporters also argued that current state legislation dealing with invasion of privacy was adequate and that no new federal law was needed.

Those on the other side of the camera disagreed. Celebrities, including Michael J. Fox and Paul Reiser, presented horror stories of being stalked by photographers who pursued them in cars, staked out their houses, and yelled obscenities at them in the hope of provoking a violent response that would make a marketable photo. Others argued that stronger laws regarding privacy were needed, given the technological advances in lenses, cameras, microphones, and eavesdropping devices.

None of the proposed stalkerazzi bills made it into federal law. The state of California, however, home to many movie stars, enacted its own version of an anti-stalkerazzi bill in 1999. The California law made it possible for a person to sue someone who attempts to capture, through the use of an image-enhancing device, a visual or sound image of another person who is engaged in a personal or familial activity in a situation where the individual has a reasonable expectation of privacy. In addition, the only other way the image could have been obtained without the device would be by trespass. Thus, if you took a picture of Madonna sunbathing in her fenced-in backyard from a hilltop a mile away using a zoom lens, you might be sued. On the other hand, if there was no fence and you could see Madonna from the street, you could probably take a picture without fear of a lawsuit.

In the final analysis, prosecuting the stalkerazzi or paparazzi might be diverting attention from the real problem. Why do the tabloids pay money for pictures of people like Princess Diana, Tom Cruise, and George Clooney? Because people want to see them. The market exists because of people like you and me. If we were not so interested in celebrities and their lives, the paparazzi would go out of business.

Trespass

Trespass, defined as unauthorized entry onto someone else's territory, is a concept that is closely related to invasion of privacy. The close of the 20th century saw a significant increase in the number of trespass cases brought against the news media. These cases highlighted a fundamental question for news reporting: Do journalists have a special First Amendment privilege to break the law in pursuit of a legitimate news story that will advance the public interest? There have been several recent court decisions that suggest the answer to this question is no.

In one case, a Wisconsin court found that a TV photojournalist who had entered private property with permission of a police officer responding to a call was guilty of trespassing. Similarly, a 1999 circuit court ruling found that journalists who enter a private home with law enforcement officers but without consent of the homeowner could be sued for trespass. In another case, reporters who followed antinuclear demonstrators through a fence onto the property of a utility company were found guilty of trespassing. A related 1999 Supreme Court case found that law enforcement officers who permit the news media to accompany them across the threshold of a home when serving a search warrant were violating the Fourth Amendment's provisions against unreasonable searches.

Finally, consider the 1996 case of *Food Lion* v. *ABC.* Reporters for the newsmagazine "Prime Time Live" faked résumés to get jobs at a Food Lion supermarket and used hidden cameras to shoot video to document their story. After the program aired, Food Lion brought suit against the network not for defamation, but for fraud and trespass. Outside the courtroom, lawyers for Food Lion explained that they thought the story was libelous, but they thought they had a better chance of winning on the basis of the trespass and fraud charges. A jury found in favor of Food Lion and awarded the supermarket chain a whopping $5.5 million in damages. A district court judge reduced this amount to $350,000. Eventually, the circuit court of appeals dismissed most of the case, but it did uphold the trespass decision. The original jury awarded Food Lion only $1 in damages for the trespass, but now that the precedent has been set, it's possible that future lawsuits might seek far greater sums for trespass violations.

 COPYRIGHT

Copyright protects an author against unfair appropriation of his or her work. Although its roots go back to English common law, the basic copyright law of the United States was first enacted in 1909. In 1976, faced with copyright problems raised by the new communications technologies, Congress passed legislation covering literary, dramatic, and musical works, as well as motion pictures, television programs, and sound recordings. The law also states what is not covered. For example, an idea cannot be copyrighted, nor can a news event or a discovery or a procedure.

For works created on or after January 1, 1978, copyright protection lasts for the life of the author plus 70 years. Works published before that date are eligible for copyright protection for a total of 95 years. To obtain full copyright protection, it is necessary to send a special form, copies of the work, and a small fee to the Register of Copyrights. The owner of a copyrighted work can then reproduce, sell, display, or perform the property.

It is important to note that copyright protection extends only to copying the work in question. If a person independently creates a similar work, there is no copyright violation. As a result, one of the things that a person who brings a copyright suit must prove is that the other person had access to the work under consideration. Thus, if you contend that a hit Hollywood movie was actually based on a pirated script that you had submitted to the company, you must show that the people responsible for the movie had access to your work. (To guard against copyright suits, most production companies won't open the envelopes of what look like unsolicited scripts.) Note, however, that you don't have to prove that someone intentionally or even consciously copied your work.

In addition, the law provides that people can make fair use of copyrighted materials without violating the provisions of the Copyright Act. Fair use means that copies of the protected work can be made for such legitimate activities as teaching, research, news reporting, and criticism without penalty. The following factors are taken into consideration in determining fair use:

1. The purpose of the use (whether for profit or for nonprofit education).
2. The nature of the copyrighted work.
3. The amount reproduced in proportion to the copyrighted work as a whole.
4. The effect of the use on the potential market value of the copyrighted work.

Thus, a teacher who reproduces a passage from a long novel to illustrate writing style to an English class will probably not have to worry about copyright. On the other hand, if a commercial magazine reproduces verbatim a series of articles published in a not-for-profit magazine, it is likely that the copyright statute has been violated.

Recent cases involving copyright law have dealt with the new communication media. In what is popularly known as the "Betamax case," the Supreme Court ruled in 1984 that viewers who own videocassette recorders could copy programs off the air for later personal viewing without violating the Copyright Act. Such taping, ruled the court, was a fair use of the material. In 1991, a federal court ruled that commercial copying companies, such as Kinko's, had to get permission from the publishers before copying and selling copyrighted articles and book excerpts used for college courses.

The most recent issue concerning copyright law has to do with the Internet. One thing is clear: Copyright laws do apply to the online world. A 1995 presidential task force concluded that copying materials from the net is a form of reproduction that is protected by current copyright laws. What is unclear is what represents fair use of copyrighted digital material. This question was at the core of two 2000 court cases that involved digital music files.

The first case concerned MP3.com. One of the services available on the company's website was My.MP3.Com, which allowed users to listen to CDs that they already owned over their computers and portable MP3 players. The service worked like this: The company first copied large numbers of CDs onto its own computers. Users demonstrated ownership by simply inserting a CD into a computer's CD-ROM drive. Once the company verified that the person had possession of a CD, My.MP3.Com gave the user access to the music by going to its database of CDs and depositing an MP3 copy of the CD into the user's file.

The five major record companies sued MP3.com for copyright violations, claiming that the company copied CDs into its database without permission. The company reached out-of-court financial settlements with four of the five but was unable to settle with Universal Music, and the case went to trial. A federal judge ruled that MP3.com had indeed violated the Copyright Act and ordered the company to pay Universal up to $250 million in damages.

The other suit involved Napster and was previously discussed in Chapter 8. Here's a brief recap: Napster let users exchange music files directly with the computers of other users. Unlike MP3.com, Napster didn't have copies of the music stored on its computers. Instead it simply acted as a huge linkage device for its millions of users. Most of the music that was exchanged on Napster was probably copyrighted material that the recording industry claimed was being illegally copied. The record companies, however, could not realistically sue everybody who used Napster. They did, however, bring suit against Napster for contributory copyright infringement, arguing that the service made possible large-scale copyright violations.

The recording industry scored an early victory when a federal judge ordered Napster to stop carrying copyrighted material. This ruling was overturned by an appeals court, pending a hearing—a decision that kept Napster in operation for a while. Finally, in February 2001, the Ninth U.S. Circuit Court of Appeals ruled that Napster had to prevent users from gaining access to copyrighted material. The ruling further ordered Napster to police its system to prevent illegal file sharing. Napster officials conceded that the decision may force them to shut down the service. Other similar file-sharing systems sprang up to take Napster's place. It is likely that further legal battles are ahead.

OBSCENITY AND PORNOGRAPHY

Obscenity is not protected by the First Amendment; that much is clear. Unfortunately, nobody has yet come up with a definition of obscenity that satisfies everybody. Let's take a brief look at how the definition of this term has changed over the years. (If, when we are done, you are a little confused about this whole issue, don't feel bad. You are not alone.)

For many years, the test of whether something was obscene was the **Hicklin rule,** a standard that judged a book (or any other item) by whether isolated passages had a tendency to deprave or corrupt the mind of the most susceptible person. If one paragraph of a 500-page book tended to deprave or corrupt the mind of the most susceptible person (a 12-year-old child, a dirty old man, etc.), then the entire book was obscene. The standard was written in the 1860s and widely used for the next 80 years.

In a 1957 case, *Roth* v. *United States,* the Supreme Court tried its hand at writing a new definition. The new test for detecting obscenity would be the following: whether to the average person, applying contemporary standards, the dominant theme of the material taken as a whole appeals to prurient interests. (*Prurient* means "lewd" or "tending to incite lust.") The Roth test differed from the earlier rule in two significant ways. Not only did the entire work, rather than a single passage, have to be taken into consideration, but the material had to offend the average person, not simply anyone who saw it. Obviously, this standard was less restrictive than the Hicklin rule, but fuzzy spots remained. Should the community standards be local or national? How exactly would prurient interest be measured?

To gain an idea of the difficulties in this area, consider the following example of how someone tried to use the strict language of this test to beat an obscenity charge. In 1966, the case of Edward Mishkin came before the Supreme Court. Mishkin, who was appealing his sentence, operated a bookstore near Times Square in New York. The books he sold emphasized sadism and masochism. In his defense, Mishkin argued that his books were not obscene because under the literal interpretation of the Roth test, the books he sold would have to incite prurient interests in the average person. Since Mishkin's books appealed to a somewhat deviant crowd, the average person, he argued, would not find them lewd. In fact, the average person would be disgusted and sickened by them. Therefore, they were not obscene. Wrong, said the Court, and let his sentence stand.

The next few years produced more obscenity cases to plague the High Court. Other decisions added that the material had to be "patently offensive" and "utterly without redeeming social value" to be obscene. During the 1960s, the Supreme Court began considering the conduct of the seller or distributor in addition to the character of the material in question. For example, even if material was not considered hard-core pornography, it could be banned if sold to minors, thrust upon an unwilling audience, or advertised as erotic to titillate customers. A 1969 ruling introduced the concept of "variable obscenity" when it stated that certain magazines were obscene when sold to minors but not obscene when sold to adults.

By 1973, so many legal problems were cropping up under the Roth guidelines that something had to be done. Consequently, the Supreme Court attempted to close up loopholes in the case of *Miller* v. *California*. This decision did away with the "utterly without redeeming social value" test and stated that the "community standards" used in defining obscenity could be local standards, which, presumably, would be determined by local juries. The new test of obscenity would include these principles:

1. Whether the average person, applying contemporary community standards, would find that the work as a whole appeals to prurient interests.
2. Whether the work depicts or describes in a patently offensive way certain sexual conduct that is specifically spelled out by a state law.
3. Whether the whole work lacks serious literary, artistic, political, or scientific value.

Despite this new attempt, problems weren't long in coming. The language of the decision appeared to permit a certain amount of local discretion in determining what was obscene. The question of how far a local community can go in setting standards continues to be troublesome. The Supreme Court has since ruled that the motion picture *Carnal Knowledge* was not obscene, even though a state court said that it was. The Court has also said that *Screw* magazine and the *Illustrated Presidential Report of the Commission on Obscenity and Pornography* were obscene no matter what community's standards were invoked. The Court further clarified the third of the *Miller* guidelines in a 1987 case when it ruled that judges and juries must assess the literary, artistic, political, or scientific value of allegedly obscene material from the viewpoint of a "reasonable person" rather than applying community standards. These issues could be decided with the help of experts who testify about the value of a work. The first two guidelines, however, will still be decided with reference to contemporary community standards.

In 1982, the Court ruled that laws banning the distribution of pornographic materials involving children were not violations of the First Amendment. The Court ruled that a state's interest in safeguarding the physical and psychological well-being of children took precedence over any right of free expression. If it strikes you as somewhat bizarre that the members of the highest court of the United States have spent considerable time plowing through publications like *Screw* magazine and looking at such movies as *Deep Throat* to come to this decision, you are not alone.

Over the years, the Court has taken a somewhat more lenient view as to what constitutes obscenity. The Miller case suggests that the Court is encouraging the states to deal with the problem at the local level. Given the long history of controversy that surrounds this topic, however, it is unlikely that this predicament will end soon. In fact, the whole issue surfaced again in 1986 when the Justice Department released a report on pornography. The report, which had strong political overtones, called for more stringent laws concerning pornography. One such law, the Child Protection and Obscenity Enforcement Act, took effect in 1988.

More recent problems have concerned the Internet. Child pornography is illegal on the Internet just as it is in other media. The 1988 act noted above specifically mentions computers as one of the channels where this illegal material might be circulated. Sexual "stalking" over the net is also prohibited. In an effort to keep pornographic material from children, Congress passed the Communications Decency Act in 1996. Part of the act made it illegal to use a computer to create, solicit, or transmit any obscene, lewd, lascivious, filthy, or indecent communication. The Supreme Court eventually found the act to be unconstitutional and ruled that the Internet should be given the highest level of First Amendment protection, similar to that given to books and newspapers, rather than the more limited rights of broadcasting and cable, where regulation is more common. The Court noted that even though the government had a legitimate interest in trying to protect children from harmful content, this interest doesn't justify broad suppression of materials directed at adults.

A second attempt at protecting children from pornography also ran into legal difficulty. The Child Online Protection Act required commercial websites to require proof of age before delivering material that might be harmful to minors. In 2000, an appeals court upheld an injunction that blocked implementation of the act, ruling that the act raised serious First Amendment problems.

From a practical standpoint, legal restrictions concerning adult content on the Internet would be difficult to enforce. The net is worldwide and laws vary from one nation to the next. A more realistic solution might be the filtering programs, such as Net Nanny, that allow parents to block access to adult sites. In any case, along with its benefits, the Internet also brings new dangers.

 ## REGULATING BROADCASTING

The formal controls surrounding broadcasting represent a special case. Not only are broadcasters affected by the laws and rulings previously discussed, but they are also subject to additional controls because of broadcasting's unique position and character. When broadcasting was first developed in the early 20th century, it became clear that more people wanted to operate a broadcasting station than there were suitable frequencies available. As a result, the early broadcasters asked the U.S. Congress to step into the picture. Congress passed the Radio Act of 1927, which held that the airwaves belonged to the public and that broadcasters who wished to use this resource had to be licensed to serve in the public interest. A regulatory body, called the Federal Radio Commission (later known as the Federal Communications Commission), was set up to determine who should get a license and whether or not those who had a license should keep it. Because of this licensing provision, radio and television are subject to more regulations than are newspapers, magazines, films, and sound recording.

SOUNDBYTE

A 50 Percent Chance of Rain and a 20 Percent Chance of a Lawsuit?

Suppose you watch a weather forecast that says that the weather will be warm and sunny, and you then decide to spend the day at the beach. Suppose the weather forecast was wrong, and the day turns out to be cold and rainy, and your day is ruined. Can you sue the weather forecaster?

Apparently not, according to a recent decision by a Miami judge. Relatives of a Florida man who died in a storm sued the Weather Channel for contributing to his death. They claimed the man watched a Weather Channel forecast that predicted good weather, and he then decided to go out to sea. The man was taken by surprise by a storm and was lost at sea. The relatives claimed the Weather Channel knew about the storm but didn't include warnings about it in their weathercasts.

The judge ruled that forecasts were predictions of indeterminate reliability and that the Weather Channel was not liable if one of its predictions turned out to be wrong.

In addition to television and radio, the FCC also regulates telephone, telegraph, and personal communication devices. *(Paul Conklin/ PhotoEdit)*

◼ The Federal Communications Commission

The Federal Communications Commission (FCC) does not make law; it interprets the law. One of its big jobs is to interpret the meaning of the phrase "public interest." For example, the FCC may write rules and regulations to implement the Communications Act of 1934 if these rules serve the public interest. Moreover, the FCC awards and renews licenses if the award or renewal is in the public interest. Over the years, several significant FCC rulings have shed some light on this rather ambiguous concept. One of the first things the commission established was that it would examine programming and determine whether the public interest was being served. It was not enough for a station to adhere to the technical operating requirements of its license. It would also have to provide a "well-rounded" program structure. In its 1929 Great Lakes decision, the commission also put broadcasters on notice that the broadcasting of programs that tended to injure the public—fraudulent advertising, attacks on ethnic groups, attacks on religions—would not be in the public interest.

Localism is another important component of the public interest as it has been defined by the FCC. In a 1960 policy statement, the commission stated that programs featuring local talent and aimed at local self-expression were necessary elements in serving the public interest.

What can the FCC do to stations that do not operate in the public interest? It can take several official actions. At the mildest level, it can fine a station up to $250,000. The next level of severity is to renew a station's license only for a probationary period (usually a year). This action typically puts the station on notice that it has to improve its performance or face even more serious consequences. The most severe form of official action is the revoking or nonrenewal of a license. Revocation/ nonrenewal is more of a threat, however, than a reality. From 1934 to 1978, the FCC took away the licenses of 142 stations. This figure should be weighed against the thousands of renewals that the commission granted each of those years. In fact, it has been calculated that 99.8 percent of all licenses are renewed. Nonetheless, the threat of revocation is a potent one that is universally feared among broadcasters.

During the 1980s, as was the case in many industries, the prevailing philosophy that governed broadcasting was one of deregulation. The FCC and Congress had eliminated literally dozens of rules and regulations, including the controversial Fairness Doctrine (see the section devoted specifically to this doctrine). The rush to deregulation slowed during the 1990s as the FCC and Congress established new rules and regulations for broadcasting and cable.

Congress passed the Children's Television Act, which required that TV stations present programs designed to meet the educational and informational needs of young persons through the age of 16. The bill also created a $2 million endowment to fund children's educational programs. Additionally, the act limited the amount of commercial time during children's programming to 10 1/2 minutes per hour on weekends and 12 minutes per hour on weekdays, a limit that applies to both broadcasters and cable operators. Stations and systems that violate these standards could be subject to a fine. In response to a provision in the law that instructed the FCC to encourage children's programming, the commission mandated that stations devote three hours per week to informational and educational programs for children.

Indecent Content

When it comes to regulating indecent content, the FCC finds itself caught between the wishes of Congress and the rulings of the federal court system. A 1978 Supreme Court ruling gave the FCC the right to regulate indecency because the pervasive presence of broadcasting made it easily accessible to children. In the late 1980s, after many radio stations began to air raunchy content, Congress passed legislation that instructed the FCC to ban indecent programming 24 hours a day. A federal court declared that this ban was unconstitutional and ordered the FCC to establish a "safe harbor," a time when indecent material could be aired without much chance of reaching children. The FCC responded by banning indecent content between the hours of 6 A.M. and 8 P.M.. This did not satisfy Congress (there is some political benefit to be derived from being against indecency), which passed a law banning indecency before midnight. This law was ruled unconstitutional, and finally, a law that banned indecent content between 6 A.M. and 10 P.M. was approved. As should be clear by now, trying to protect children from indecency while protecting the First Amendment rights of adults is an exasperating task. Meanwhile, the FCC continues to be on guard against indecent programming. Radio stations carrying Howard Stern's talk show have been fined more than $2 million for airing indecent content.

The Equal Opportunities Rule

The **Equal Opportunities rule** is contained in Section 315 of the Communications Act and is thus federal law. Section 315 deals with the ability of bona fide candidates for public office to gain access to a broadcast medium during political campaigns. Stated in simple terms, this section says that if a station permits one candidate for a specific office to appear on the air, it must offer the same opportunity to all other candidates for that office. If a station gives a free minute to one candidate, all other legally qualified candidates for that office are also entitled to a free minute. If a station sells a candidate a minute for $100, it must make the same offer to all other candidates. Congress has made some exceptions to this law, the most notable of which are legitimate newscasts and on-the-scene coverage of authentic news events. This last exception provided the loophole by which the networks are able to broadcast presidential debates between the leading candidates; they are simply covering a news event that is under the sponsorship of another organization.

The Fairness Doctrine

The **Fairness Doctrine** no longer exists. The FCC repealed it in 1987. That doesn't mean, however, that it's dead and buried. There were several proposals in Congress to revive it, the most recent attempt in 1994.

When it was still in force, the Fairness Doctrine provided that broadcasters had to seek out and present contrasting viewpoints on controversial matters of public importance. On any issue, broadcasters had to make a good-faith effort to cover all the opposing viewpoints. This didn't have to take place in one program, but the broadcaster was expected to achieve balance over time. Note that the Fairness Doctrine never said that opposing views were entitled to equal time. It simply mandated that some reasonable amount of time be granted. In late 2000, the FCC announced it was reconsidering its 1987 decision to abandon the doctrine.

REGULATING CABLE TV

The regulatory philosophy of the FCC and Congress toward cable has shown wide variation over the years. In the 1950s, the FCC ruled that it had no jurisdiction over cable. This notion changed in the 1960s when the commission exerted control over the new medium and wrote a series of regulations governing its growth. By 1972, a comprehensive set of rules governing cable was on the FCC's books. The growth of cable during the 1970s led to successful lobbying efforts by the industry to ease many of these restrictions. In the 1980s, in line with the deregulatory philosophy of the Reagan administration, almost all the FCC rules concerning cable were dropped. Moreover, Congress passed the Cable Communications Policy Act in 1984, which gave cable operators great freedom in setting rates and deciding what channels they could carry on their systems. The law also allowed state and local governments the right to grant cable **franchises** (a franchise is an exclusive right to operate in a given territory).

In the years following the passage of this act, many consumers complained that their cable system raised rates and was insensitive to the needs of its customers. Consequently, in 1992, Congress enacted the Cable TV Act, which gave the FCC the authority to regulate the rates of most cable systems, required that cable systems carry the signals of any broadcast station with significant viewing in their market, and allowed commercial broadcast stations to waive their right to be carried in exchange for appropriate compensation from the cable system.

Two provisions in this law had important consequences. First, most consumers saw their monthly cable bills go down as the FCC instituted rate reductions of about 17 percent. As a result, a planned merger between cable giant TCI and Bell Atlantic fell through because the phone company thought the cable company was no longer as valuable as it once was. Second, the provision requiring cable systems to carry the signals of broadcast stations was challenged in federal court as a violation of the First Amendment rights of cable operators. In 1994 the Supreme Court ruled that cable operators deserved more First Amendment protection from government regulation than did broadcasters, but not as much as newspapers and magazines. Consequently, the Court declared that it was constitutional for Congress to pass laws to guarantee that the free flow of information not be restricted by a private company that controlled the means of transmission.

The issue of the constitutionality of the specific rules about which stations must be carried by cable systems was decided in 1997 when the Supreme Court ruled in favor of the "must carry" provision.

THE TELECOMMUNICATIONS ACT OF 1996

While all this was going on, Congress was wrestling with the regulatory problems caused by convergence and the information superhighway. The result of this struggle was the **Telecommunications Act of 1996,** the first major overhaul of communication laws in more than 60 years. The Telecommunications Act contained provisions that affected traditional broadcasters, cable companies, and telephone companies. The following are among the key provisions of the law:

- Removed limits on the number of radio stations that can be owned by one person or organization. Up to eight stations may be owned in a single market. (See Chapter 7.)
- Removed limits on the number of television stations that can be owned as long as stations don't reach more than 35 percent of nation's TV homes.
- Extended the term of broadcast licenses to eight years.
- Allowed telephone companies to enter the cable television business.
- Allowed cable TV companies to enter the telephone business.
- Deregulated the rates of many cable systems.
- Mandated that newly manufactured TV sets come with the ability to block unwanted programming based on an electronically encoded rating (popularly called the **V-Chip** [see below]).
- Mandated that the TV industry come up with a voluntary ratings system for violence, sex, and other indecent materials.

The section of the law that called for a ratings system for TV programs that could work with the V-Chip generated much controversy. One of the more interesting aspects of the act was the way in which it set up a mandatory voluntary ratings system. If the industry failed to come up with a system within a year, the FCC was directed to create an advisory board that would then do the job. Many in the industry suggested that the whole concept was unconstitutional, but the industry did not mount a legal challenge. Instead, leaders from the cable and broadcasting industry got together and eventually came up with a system that combined age-based ratings (much like the system used for rating motion pictures) with content warnings. (See Chapter 16 for more on the V-Chip.)

REGULATING ADVERTISING

Deceptive Advertising

"Rapid Shave outshaves them all!" At least that's what a 1959 commercial for that shaving cream claimed. To drive that point home, a demonstration was included in the ad. As an announcer extolled the benefits of the product, Rapid Shave was applied to a substance that looked like sandpaper. A razor then shaved the paper clean, whisking away every grain of sand. Unfortunately, the substance wasn't sandpaper. It was really sand applied to a sheet of plexiglass. The Federal Trade Commission (FTC) claimed that the commercial was deceptive. The FTC's investigations discovered that Rapid Shave could not shave actual sandpaper unless the sandpaper was first soaked with the stuff for about 80 minutes. The advertising agency that put together the commercial appealed the commission's ruling all the way to the Supreme Court. The Court sided with the FTC.

The problem of deceptive and potentially harmful advertising has been around a long time. The philosophy of *caveat emptor* (let the buyer beware) was dominant until the early 1900s. Exaggerated claims and outright deception characterized many early advertisements, especially those for patent medicines. Spurred on by the muckrakers (see Chapter 5), the government took steps to deal with the problem when it created the Federal Trade Commission in 1914. In the early years of its existence, the commission was concerned with encouraging competition through the regulation of questionable business practices, such as bribery, false advertising, and mislabeling of products; protecting the consumer was not the main focus. The consumer started to receive some protection in 1938 with the Wheeler-Lea Act, which gave the FTC the power to prevent deceptive advertising that harmed the public, whether or not the advertising had any bad effects on the competition.

Like the Federal Communications Commission, the Federal Trade Commission has several enforcement techniques available to it. First of all, it can issue trade regulations that suggest guidelines for the industry to follow. In 1965, for example, it ruled that auto ads must contain both the city and highway estimates of gas mileage. The FTC also uses **consent orders.** In a consent order, the advertiser agrees to halt a certain advertising practice, but at the same time, the advertiser does not admit any violation of the law; there is only an agreement not to continue. Somewhat stronger is a **cease-and-desist order.** This order follows a hearing by the commission that determines that a certain advertising practice does indeed violate the law. Violation of a consent order and failure to comply with a cease-and-desist order can result in fines being levied against the advertiser.

In the late 1960s and the 1970s, the FTC took a more active role in the regulation of advertising. The rising tide of interest in the rights of the consumer and the presence of consumer activist groups (such as Ralph Nader's Raiders) were probably behind this new direction. A flurry of activity took place. First, the FTC wanted documentation for claims. If Excedrin claimed to be more effective in relieving pain than Brand X, the advertiser was now required to have proof for that statement. The FTC also ordered "corrective advertising" in which some advertisers were required to clarify some of their past claims. Profile Bread, for example, had been advertised as a weight-reducing aid, with fewer calories per slice than normal bread. (This was literally true. Profile Bread had seven fewer calories per slice, but only because it was sliced more thinly.) The company agreed to run corrective ads with copy that included the following:

> *I'd like to clear up any misunderstanding you may have about Profile Bread. Does Profile have fewer calories than other bread? No, Profile has about the same per ounce as other breads. To be exact, Profile has seven fewer calories per slice. That's because it is sliced thinner. But eating Profile will not cause you to lose weight.*

(The corrective ads were so well received by the audience that the company wanted to present them more often than the ruling required.)

More recently, the FTC has been concerned about advertising inappropriately directed toward children. In 1997, the FTC issued an unfair advertising complaint against the R. J. Reynolds Tobacco Company. The FTC argued that ads featuring Joe Camel, the company's cartoon character, encouraged children to start smoking. In response, Reynolds announced it would no longer use the controversial camel in its ads.

In 2000, the FTC targeted the film industry for marketing R-rated movies to persons under 17. An FTC report found that marketing plans for 28 R-rated films included strategies for reaching children as young as 10. The report criticized Hollywood for routinely aiming their advertising at children for movies that their own rating system labels inappropriate. In response, eight movie studios announced plans to reform their promotional efforts.

Commercial Speech under the First Amendment

The 1970s marked a change in judicial thinking toward the amount of protection that advertising, or commercial speech, as it is called, receives under the First Amendment. Before the 1970s, advertising had little claim to free-speech

In the 1940s and 1950s, much cigarette advertising promoted the health benefits of smoking. This ad for Camels suggests that doctors endorse not only this brand of cigarette but smoking in general. *(PAR Archive)*

protection. In the 1940s, F. J. Chrestensen found this out the hard way. Chrestensen owned a former U.S. submarine. There is not much that a private individual can do with a submarine, aside from charging admission to view it. This was Chrestensen's idea, and he wanted to distribute handbills advertising the sub. No way, said the New York City police commissioner. The city's sanitation code did not allow the distribution of advertising matter in the streets. However, handbills of information or of public protest were allowed. Inspired, Chrestensen put his submarine advertising message on one side of the handbill, while the other side was printed with a protest against the City Dock Department. Sorry, said the city, the protest message could be handed out, but the advertising on the other side would have to go. Chrestensen appealed, and two years later the Supreme Court ruled against him and agreed with the city of New York that advertising merited no First Amendment protection.

Since that time, however, the Supreme Court has retreated from this view. In 1964, in the *New York Times* v. *Sullivan* case, it extended First Amendment protection to ads that dealt with important social matters. Seven years later, the Court further extended this protection when a Virginia newspaper ran an ad for an abortion clinic located in New York and thus violated a Virginia law against such advertising. The Supreme Court ruled that the ad contained material in the public interest and merited constitutional protection. More recent cases suggest that in many instances, commercial speech falls under the protection of the First Amendment.

In a 1980 ruling concerning advertising by an electric utility company, commonly called the Central Hudson Case, the Supreme Court enunciated a four-part test for determining the constitutional protection for commercial speech. First, commercial speech that involves an unlawful activity or advertising that is false or misleading is not protected. Second, the government must have a substantial interest in regulating the commercial speech. Part three asks if the state's regulation actually advances the government interest involved. Finally, the state's regulations may be only as broad as necessary to promote the state's interest.

A 1984 ruling illustrated the use of these principles: The Court upheld a prohibition against posting signs on city property. The Court first noted that, although the advertising was for a lawful activity and not misleading, the government has a substantial interest in reducing "visual blight" and that the ordinance directly advanced that interest and was not overly broad. Further, the Court affirmed that corporations also have the right of free speech and granted lawyers, doctors, and professionals the right to advertise their prices. Although all the questions surrounding this issue have not been answered, it seems safe to conclude that at least some commercial speech is entitled to First Amendment protection. Its status, however, is less than that given to political and other forms of noncommercial expression. In the future, it's likely that more and more advertising will fall into the category of protected speech.

Three other cases had repercussions for advertisers. In the first, a tobacco company was found partially liable for the death of a smoker from lung cancer, in part because early ads for cigarettes stressed their health benefits for smokers. Although it seems hard to believe, during the 1940s and 1950s many cigarettes were advertised as "just what the doctor ordered," even after information linking smoking to lung cancer and other diseases came to light. This case may have limited impact since it dealt primarily with pre-1966 claims, before health warnings appeared on packs. On the other hand, it raises the broader question of whether advertising contains an implied warranty for the product.

CONCLUDING STATEMENT

The term "half-life" is a useful concept in physics. It refers to the length of time in which one-half of the radioactive atoms present in a substance will decay. We might borrow this term and reshape its meaning so that it is relevant to this book. The half-life of a chapter in this text is the time it takes for half the information contained in the chapter to become obsolete. With that in mind, it is likely that the half-life of this chapter may be among the shortest of any in this book. Laws are constantly changing; new court decisions are frequently handed down and new rules and regulations are written all the time. All this activity means that what is written in this chapter will need frequent updating. In addition, it means that mass media professionals must continually refresh their understanding of the law. Of course, this also means that there will be a continuing stream of colorful characters, intriguing stories, and high drama as the courts and regulatory agencies further wrestle with the issues and problems involved in mass communication regulation.

■ MAIN POINTS

- There is a strong constitutional case against prior restraint of the press.

- Reporters have special privileges that protect them in some instances from having to reveal the names of their news sources. These privileges, however, are not absolute.

- Reporters can cover matters that occur in open court with little fear of reprisal. Some pretrial proceedings can still be closed to the press.

- All but two states now allow cameras in the courtroom on a permanent or experimental basis. Cameras and microphones are still barred from federal trial courts and from the Supreme Court.

- Defamation can be either libel or slander. To prevail in a defamation suit, a public figure must show that the published material was false and harmful and that the media acted with actual malice when it published the information. A private citizen must also show that the material was false and harmful and that the media involved acted with negligence.

- Invasion of privacy can occur when the media intrude upon a person's solitude, release private information, create a false impression, or wrongfully appropriate a person's name or likeness.

- Copyright law protects authors from unfair use of their work. There are instances, however, when portions of copyrighted material can be reproduced for legitimate purposes.

- The Napster online file-sharing system has raised serious questions about copyrights in a digital medium.

- Obscenity is not protected by the First Amendment. To be legally obscene, a work must appeal to prurient interests, depict or describe certain sexual conduct spelled out by state law, and lack serious literary, artistic, political, or scientific value.

- Special regulations and laws apply to broadcasting. The FCC is charged with administering the rules and regulations that deal with cable, TV, and radio. The Telecommunications Act of 1996 had a major impact on the electronic media.

- The Federal Trade Commission oversees advertising. Commercial speech has recently been given more First Amendment protection.

■ QUESTIONS FOR REVIEW

1. Whom do shield laws protect?

2. Whom do gag orders gag?

3. What is the Freedom of Information Act? How have reporters used it?

4. What's the difference between libel and slander?

5. What factors determine fair use?

6. Briefly explain the significance of the following court cases:
   a. The Betamax case
   b. The Pentagon Papers case
   c. *New York Times* v. *Sullivan*
   d. *Miller* v. *California*

■ QUESTIONS FOR CRITICAL THINKING

1. Why should reporters have special privileges when other professionals, such as architects, nurses, and accountants, have none?

2. Libel suits can be long and expensive for both sides. What are some other methods of conflict resolution that might cut down the time and the cost but still provide satisfaction for both sides?

3. Why are broadcasting and cable not entitled to the same amount of First Amendment protection as newspapers and magazines? Do you agree with this type of differentiation?

4. Keep up with the latest developments in the file-sharing controversy. Do you think these services aid in copyright infringement?

5. How can children be protected from exposure to adult-oriented content on the Internet?

■ KEY TERMS

First Amendment (p. 397)
prior restraint (p. 397)
injunction (p. 397)
shield laws (p. 400)
gag rules (p. 404)
Freedom of Information Act (FOIA)
   (p. 408)
defamation (p. 409)

libel (p. 409)
slander (p. 409)
libel per se (p. 409)
libel per quod (p. 409)
trespass (p. 415)
Hicklin rule (p. 418)
Equal Opportunities rule (p. 422)

Fairness Doctrine (p. 422)
franchise (p. 423)
Telecommunications Act of 1996
   (p. 423)
V-Chip (p. 424)
consent orders (p. 425)
cease-and-desist orders (p. 425)

■ SUGGESTIONS FOR FURTHER READING

The following books contain more information about the concepts and topics discussed in this chapter.

Creech, Kenneth. *Electronic Media Law and Regulation.* Boston: Focal Press, 2000.

Gillmore, Donald, et al. *Fundamentals of Mass Communication Law.* St. Paul, MN: West, 1996.

Hemmer, Joseph. *Communication Law: The Supreme Court and the First Amendment.* Lanham, MD: University Press of America, 2000.

Holsinger, Ralph, and Jon Paul Diltz. *Media Law.* New York: McGraw-Hill, 1997.

Middleton, Kent, Robert Trager, and Bill Chamberlin. *The Law of Public Communication.* New York: Longman, 2000.

Moore, Roy. *Mass Communication Law and Ethics.* Mahwah, NJ: Erlbaum, 1999.

■ SURFING THE INTERNET

There are many websites that deal with legal matters. The ones listed here seem most helpful for students.

www.aclu.org/library/foia.html
A primer on the Freedom of Information Act assembled by the American Civil Liberties Union.

www.commlaw.com/
The website of a law firm that specializes in communications and online services law. Contains updates about the latest communication law decisions.

www.fcc.gov/
The FCC's home page. Site contains an archive of recent speeches, a search engine, and consumer information along with more technical data.

www.freedomforum.org
Site contains a summary of recent First Amendment court decisions, relevant law articles, a First Amendment timeline, and a full text of relevant Supreme Court rulings.

www.rcfp.org
The Reporters Committee for Freedom of the Press maintains this site, which contains recent court decisions, legal news, and a link to their publication, *The News Media and the Law.*

CHAPTER 16 Ethics and Other Informal Controls

Laws and regulations are not the only controls on the mass media. Informal controls, stemming from within the media themselves or shaped by the workings of external forces such as pressure groups, consumers, and advertisers, are also important. The following hypothetical examples illustrate some situations in which these controls might spring up:

Like a winding road, the path to an ethical decision needs to be carefully navigated. *(©Corbis Images)*

1. You're the program director for the campus radio station. You get a call one morning from the promotion department of a major record company offering you a free trip to California, a tour of the record company's studios, a ticket to a concert featuring all the company's biggest stars, and an invitation to an exclusive party where you'll get to meet all the performers. The company representative explains that this is simply a courtesy to you so that you'll better appreciate the quality of her company's products. Do you accept?

2. You're a reporter for the local campus newspaper. The star of the football team, who also happens to be the president of the Campus Crusade for Morality, has been involved in a minor traffic accident, and you have been assigned to cover the story. When you get to the accident scene, you examine the football player's car and find a half-dozen pornographic magazines strewn across the backseat. You

have a deadline in 30 minutes; what details do you include in your story?

3. You're the editor of the campus newspaper. One of your reporters has just written a series of articles describing apparent health-code violations in a popular off-campus restaurant. This particular restaurant regularly buys full-page ads in your paper. After you run the first story in the series, the restaurant owner calls and threatens to cancel all her ads unless you stop printing the series. What do you do?

4. You're doing your first story for the campus paper. A local businessperson has promised to donate $5 million to your university so that it can buy new equipment for its mass communication and journalism programs. While putting together a background

story on this benefactor, you discover that he was convicted of armed robbery at age 18 and avoided prison only by volunteering for military duty during the closing months of World War II. In the more than 50 years that have passed since then, his record has been spotless. He refuses to talk about the incident, claims his wife and his closest friends do not know about it, and threatens to withdraw his donation if you print the story. Naturally, university officials are concerned and urge you not to mention this fact. Do you go ahead and include the incident as simply one element in your overall profile? Do you take the position that the arrest information is not pertinent and not use it? Do you wait until the university has the money and then print the story?

We could go on listing examples, but by now the point is probably clear. There are many situations in the everyday operation of the mass media where thorny questions about what to do or not to do have to be faced. Most of these situations do not involve laws or regulations, but instead deal with the tougher questions of what's right or what's proper. Informal controls over the media usually assert themselves in these circumstances. This chapter will discuss the following examples of informal controls: personal ethics; performance codes; internal controls, such as organizational policies, self-criticism, and professional self-regulation; and outside pressures.

PERSONAL ETHICS

Ethics are rules of conduct or principles of morality that point us toward the right or best way to act in a situation. Over the years, philosophers have developed a number of general ethical principles that serve as guidelines for evaluating our behavior. We will briefly summarize five principles that have particular relevance to those working in the mass media professions. Before we begin, however, we should emphasize that these principles do not contain magic answers to every ethical dilemma. In fact, different ethical principles often suggest different and conflicting courses of action. There is no perfect answer to every problem. Also, these ethical principles are based on Western thought. Other cultures may have developed totally different systems. Nonetheless, these principles can provide a framework for analyzing what is proper in examining choices and justifying our actions.

Ethical Principles

The Principle of the Golden Mean Moral virtue lies between two extremes. This philosophical position is typically associated with Aristotle, who, as a biologist, noted that too much food as well as too little food spoils health. Moderation was the key. Likewise, in ethical dilemmas, the proper way of behaving lies between doing too much and doing too little. For instance, in the restaurant example mentioned earlier, one extreme would be to cancel the story as requested by the restaurant owner. The other extreme would be to run the series as is. Perhaps a compromise between the two would be to run the series but also give the restaurant owner a chance to reply. Or perhaps the story might contain information about how the restaurant has improved conditions or other tempering remarks.

Examples of the **golden mean** are often found in media practices. For example, when news organizations cover civil disorders, they try to exercise moderation. They balance the necessity of informing the public with the need to preserve public safety by not inflaming the audience.

The London tabloids were just part of the sensational coverage of the crash that killed John F. Kennedy Jr. Sensationalism can raise serious ethical issues for journalists. *(AP/Wide World Photos)*

The Categorical Imperative   What is right for one is right for all. German philosopher Immanuel Kant is identified with this ethical guideline. To measure the correctness of our behavior, Kant suggests that we act according to rules that we would want to see universally applied. In Kant's formulation, categorical means unconditional—no extenuating circumstances, no exceptions. Right is right and should be done, no matter what the consequences. The individual's conscience plays a large part in Kant's thinking. The **categorical imperatives** are discovered by an examination of conscience; the conscience informs us what is right. If, after performing an act, we feel uneasy or guilty, we have probably violated our conscience. Applied to mass communication, a categorical imperative might be that all forms of deception in news gathering are wrong and must be avoided. No one wants deception to become a universal practice. Therefore, a reporter should not represent himself or herself as anything other than a reporter when gathering information for a story.

The Principle of Utility   **Utility** is defined as the greatest benefit for the greatest number. Modern utilitarian thinking originated with the 19th-century philosophers Jeremy Bentham and John Stuart Mill. The basic tenet in their formulations holds that we are to determine what is right or wrong by considering what will yield the best ratio of good to bad for the general society. Utilitarians ask how much good is promoted and how much evil is restrained by different courses of behavior. Utilitarianism provides a clear method for evaluating ethical choices: (1) calculate all the consequences, both good and bad, that would result from each of our options; then (2) choose the alternative that maximizes value or minimizes loss.

Looking at the mass communication area, we can easily see several examples of utilitarian philosophy. In 1971, the *New York Times* and other papers printed stolen government documents, the Pentagon Papers (see Chapter 15). Obviously, the newspapers involved thought that the good that would be achieved by printing these papers far outweighed the harm that would be done. (Note that the Kantian perspective would suggest a different course of action. Theft is bad. Newspapers do not want the government stealing their property, so they should not condone or promote the theft of government property.) Or take the case of a small Midwestern paper that chose to report the death of a local teenager who had gone East, turned to prostitution and drugs, and was murdered while plying her trade. The paper decided that the potential benefits of this story as a warning to other parents outweighed the grief it would cause the murder victim's family.

The Veil of Ignorance   Justice is blind. Philosopher John Rawls argued that justice emerges when everyone is treated without social differentiations. In one sense, the **veil of ignorance** is related to fairness. Everybody doing the same job equally well should receive equal pay. Everybody who got an 80 on the test should get the same grade. Rawls advocated that all parties concerned in a problem situation should be placed behind a barrier where roles and social differentiations are gone and each participant is treated as an equal member of society as a whole. Often Rawls's veil of ignorance suggests that we should structure our actions to protect the most vulnerable members of society. It is easy to see the relevance of this principle to the workings of the mass media. If we applied the veil of ignorance to the problem of hammering out the proper relationship between politicians and journalists, Rawls would argue that the blatant adversarial relationship so often found between the groups should disappear. Behind the veil, all newsmakers would be the same. Inherent cynicism and abrasiveness on the part of the press should disappear, as well as mistrust and suspicion on the part of the politicians. On a more specific level, consider the case of a financial reporter who frequently gets tips and inside information on deals and mergers that affect the price of stock and passes these tips on to personal friends who use this information for their own profit. The veil of ignorance suggests that the reporter must treat all audience members the same. Personal friends should not benefit from inside information.

Principle of Self-Determination   Do not treat people as means to an end. This principle, closely associated with the Judeo-Christian ethic and also discussed by Kant, might be summarized as "Love your neighbor as yourself." Human beings have unconditional value apart from any and all circumstances. Their basic right to **self-determination** should not be violated by using them as simply a means to accomplish a goal. A corollary to this principle is that no one should allow himself or herself to be treated as a means to someone else's ends. Suppose that sources inside a government investigation on political corruption leak the names of some people suspected of taking bribes to the press, which, in turn, publishes the allegations and the names of the suspects. The principle of self-determination suggests that the press is being used by those who leaked the story as a means to accomplish their goal. Perhaps those involved in the investigation wanted to turn public opinion against those named or simply to earn some favorable publicity for their efforts. In any case, the press should resist being used in these circumstances. The rights, values, and decisions of others must always be respected.

■ A Model for Individual Ethical Decisions

There are numerous instances where personal ethical decisions have to be made about what is or is not included in media content or what should or should not be done. These decisions have to be made every day by reporters, editors, station managers, and other media professionals. Too often, however, these decisions are made haphazardly and without proper analysis of the ethical dimensions involved. This section presents a model that media professionals can use to evaluate and examine their decisions. This model is adapted from the work of Ralph Potter.[1]

---

[1]Ralph Potter, "The Logic of Moral Argument," in *Toward a Discipline of Social Ethics*, P. Deats, ed. (Boston: Boston University Press, 1972).

The dean of the Harvard Divinity School resigned in 1999 after a computer technician discovered that he had stored numerous pornographic images on his Harvard-owned computer. This bizarre episode illustrates some of the novel ethical problems faced by individuals who deal with computers and the files they store.

In keeping with the model of ethical analysis discussed in this chapter, let's first establish some facts. The computer that contained the pornographic material was kept in the dean's personal residence. The dean looked at this material in the privacy of his own home. The dean had requested more storage space for his computer files. The technician came to the dean's residence and saw the pornography when he was transferring files to a new hard drive. The material was not child pornography nor was it illegal in any way, but it did violate Harvard policy against using a university computer to store obscene material.

What are the loyalties in this situation for the computer technician? Is the technician's primary obligation to respect the dean's privacy? Or is it to report the policy violation to the proper authorities? Did the technician have to look at the content of the files that were being transferred?

A few things are clear. If a technician finds evidence of illegal activity or conduct that is harmful to his or her employer, experts agree that the person has an ethical obligation to report it. But what about content that is not illegal, as in the Harvard case? Experts are divided on this question. Some suggest that the technician is obligated to respect the privacy of the client. Suppose a faculty member is checking out pornographic books from the university library. Should the librarian report the faculty member to the administration. Suppose a university moving crew transferring a faculty member's paper files from one filing cabinet to another uncovers a stash of pornography? Should they report it?

Others suggest that if a computer is used in violation of a company policy, then the technician has a responsibility to report it. In fact, the technician's loyalty to himself or herself may come into play. If the policy violation comes to light, the technician might be punished for covering up the infraction.

Note how the various ethical principles mentioned in the text come into play in this circumstance. If the technician endorsed a categorical imperative that favored privacy, the pornography would not be reported. If you don't want people disclosing what's on your hard drive, then you should not disclose what's on somebody else's. What about the principle of the golden mean? Was there a middle ground between silence and disclosing the existence of the pornographic material to Harvard officials? Could the technician have told the dean that he discovered the material and given the dean the chance to delete it?

The veil of ignorance also is relevant. The fact that the dean was head of the divinity school may have resulted in harsher judgment. Suppose the dean in question was the dean of the journalism school? Would the penalty have been as drastic? Finally, the principle of utility asks us to assess the benefits and the harm of our actions. What were the benefits in revealing that the dean had pornography on his computer? Policy is enforced. Harvard goes on the record as not condoning pornography. Technicians are protected against further exposure to potentially disturbing images. Perhaps the dean recognizes that he has a problem with pornography. What was the harm? A career is ruined. A human being undergoes profound embarrassment. The Harvard faculty loses an efficient dean. The right of privacy is eroded. Which action is better? It's a tough call.

In any case, the Harvard affair highlights the importance of establishing guidelines and ethical codes of behavior for technicians who deal with information stored on a personal computer.

DEFINITIONS → VALUES → PRINCIPLES → LOYALTIES → ACTION

In short, the model asks the individual to consider four aspects of the situation before taking action. First, define the situation. What are the pertinent facts involved? What are the possible actions? Second, what values are involved? Which values are more relevant to deciding a course of action? Third, what ethical principles apply? We have discussed five that might be involved. There may be others. Last, where do our loyalties lie? To whom do we owe a moral duty? It is possible that we might owe a duty to ourselves, clients, business organizations, the profession, or society in general. To whom is our obligation most important?

Let's examine how this model would work in a real-life situation. The October 10, 1999, edition of the *Los Angeles Times Sunday Magazine* was a 162-page special edition devoted to the Staples Center, a $400 million sports and entertainment facility in downtown L.A. that many hoped would revitalize the area. What readers did not know, however, was that the *Times* had agreed to split the advertising revenues generated by the special magazine edition with the Staples Center. A few days later, a local L.A. weekly paper broke the story, causing great distress and embarrassment to the *Times* and its employees. For reporters, this deal violated a long-standing ethical principle of the profession: Journalists don't enter into financial arrangements with the subjects they cover. How could such an ethical lapse have occurred at one of the most respected papers in the United States?

Establishing the Facts   First, let's establish some key facts. Top management at the *Times* was interested in the bottom line. The chief executive of the *Times* parent company was hired from General Mills, where he had a reputation for slashing jobs and cutting costs (his nickname at General Mills was the "Cereal Killer"). He had no prior newspaper experience. The paper's publisher, who conceived of the deal, also had no prior newspaper experience and had been on the job only a few months. Both had committed themselves to improving the paper's financial condition.

Moreover, the publisher never told the editor about the financial arrangement until shortly before the special edition was published. Nonetheless, the editor did have sufficient time to destroy copies of the magazine (a drastic and expensive course of action) or publish a disclaimer revealing the financial arrangement. The editor did neither. Several other executives knew about the deal in advance but apparently did nothing to stop it. Rank-and-file reporters and staff members were kept in the dark.

Clarifying Values   The values involved in this case are not hard to see. In business, there is great value placed upon making a profit. Profits are beneficial to shareholders and permit the business operation to go forward. Without profits, even the venerable *Times* would fold. Business also places value on entrepreneurship. Taking risks to gain a profit is at the heart of the free enterprise system, and searching for new revenue streams is encouraged.

On the other hand, journalists value credibility. Once credibility is lost, the whole structure of journalism is threatened. Striking deals with potential news subjects erodes credibility. If the audience thinks that advertisers can control news content, they will no longer believe what they read. Moreover, journalists value editorial independence. Decisions about what to cover and how to cover it should be based on the principles of newsworthiness rather than on profit/loss considerations. Journalism values place a wall between the business and editorial sides of a news-gathering organization.

Stating Principles   What principles are involved here? First, the principle of the golden mean needs to be considered. There may be some middle ground between the two extreme positions—publishing the magazine without any mention of the financial arrangement or destroying all copies of the publication before they were distributed. Perhaps the magazine could have been labeled an "advertorial," or perhaps full disclosure about the details of the deal could have been published as a foreword to the magazine. Another alternative would be to publish the magazine as a special commemorative document and distribute it at the Staples Center rather than through the paper. Several alternatives may have headed off the problem.

Second, there's the categorical imperative. Financial alliances between journalists and news subjects are wrong. Period. End of problem. Someone with this view would never have entertained such an arrangement.

Finally, let's consider the principle of utility. What is the possible good that might result from such an arrangement? We can probably think of several examples: greater profits, a business alliance with a highly visible local landmark, an increase in the stock price of the company, pleased advertisers. What about the downside? The negatives are also easy to list: eroded credibility, a hostile staff of reporters and editors, lowered morale, embarrassment in the profession, audience resentment, lack of faith in top management. Conducting such an analysis might have resulted in a different decision by the paper's executives.

Determining Loyalties   As for the loyalty dimension, there are conflicting obligations. The *Times* has an obligation to its parent company, its stockholders, and its employees to make a profit. Financially rewarding arrangements such as that with the Staples Center are one way to guarantee good economic health. There is also loyalty to the general public, who expects to be informed about openings of facilities such as the new arena. At the same time, however, the *Times* has an obligation to the profession to maintain accepted standards of journalism. In addition, news organization managers have an obligation to tell their employees about financial arrangements that may have an impact on editorial content. By the same token, newspaper employees have an obligation to tell management if organizational practices are violating established norms. In the Staples case, it seems obvious that the paper's top executives, with their lack of journalistic experience, were more committed to their business obligations than to their journalistic responsibilities.

What actions resulted from this incident? The *Times* publisher issued a public apology over the incident and vowed it would never happen again. The paper also published a front-page apology and a new statement of principles that addressed the relationship between journalists and advertisers. Finally, the paper ran a 14-page self-analytical section written by the paper's Pulitzer Prize–winning media reporter that was highly critical of the way the *Times* handled the whole affair. The last sentences of that report raised troubling questions: "[W]ill the [new] guidelines be followed diligently only until profit margins fall again and pressure for new revenue intensifies? Will the heightened sensitivity recede once the Staples Center controversy begins to fade?" It's likely that the growing corporate emphasis on the bottom line may well prompt more imbroglios like that involving the *Times* and the Staples Center.

◼ Another Example of the Ethics Model

A problem that directly concerns the college audience is the difficult and sensitive situation that surrounds the reporting of campus rape stories. Obviously, there are several conflicting values at issue in such situations. First, journalists support the free flow of information. On the other hand, the consequences of violating the rights of privacy of the accused and the accuser should not be taken lightly. This friction raises several questions: Does the rape victim have the right to determine if his or her name and the details of the incident should be made public? Does the accused have similar rights? And, a question that has been asked frequently in the late 1990s, do people who live in the residence hall or apartment building with or who attend classes with the accused person have a right to know about his presence?

Ethical principles can offer some guidance. The categorical imperative suggests that it is the job of journalists to disseminate information, not suppress it. No matter how stigmatizing or embarrassing to the persons involved, news should be published. The golden mean would recommend that some middle course be followed. For example, general information about the victim and the accused might be reported without identifying them by name. The utilitarian principle would suggest that the benefit of naming names and revealing details should be weighed against the potential harm to the individuals involved. One college newspaper adopted a policy of naming rape victims even without their consent because it might help ease the stigma of rape and help destroy the notion that rape victims were different from victims of other violent crimes. Although there may be no all-purpose formula to follow, a careful consideration of the values and ethical principles involved should help journalists, especially college journalists, balance the pressures that go with such a story.

Reporters and editors frequently face instances where they must weigh the public's right or need to know against possible repercussions on individual lives. Consider this illustration: A man suspected of a robbery has a perfect alibi because several witnesses testify that at the time of the crime, he was sharing a motel room with a woman who was not his wife. How much of this story needs to be reported? Is the apparent infidelity a necessary element? Or what of the reporter who gets crucial information "off the record"? Are there circumstances in which this confidence can be violated?

Most of the time, ethical decisions are made in good faith with a sincere desire to serve the public and reflect positively on the profession. Sometimes, however, ethical judgments may be adversely affected by other influences.

Acculturation

One of the factors that influences the judgment of some reporters is a phenomenon known as **acculturation.** Simply defined, acculturation in a media context means the tendency of reporters or other media professionals to accept the ideas, attitudes, and opinions of the group that they cover or with whom they have a great deal of contact. Many political reporters, for instance, come to share the views of the politicians they cover. So do many police-beat reporters. Publishers and station managers who spend a great deal of time with business leaders might come to adopt the point of view of industry. A 1977 study of reporters and legislators in Colorado revealed that political reporters and politicians held quite similar views. The study also revealed that many reporters identified with legislators, felt a sense of kinship with them, and actually considered themselves part of the legislative process. In the Potter model, these individuals have confused their loyalties. They see their duty to the group they are covering as more important than their duty to the profession of journalism.

Acculturation is not necessarily bad; it can cause concern, however, when it begins to affect judgment. Recently, a California newspaper learned that several off-duty police officers had terrorized a bar and had gotten into fistfights with some of its patrons. The disturbance was so serious that the chief of police recommended that three of the officers be dismissed. The paper, however, sat on the story for almost six weeks. It turned out that in the past, the police and the paper had developed an easy sense of cooperation. Police officers had been given the OK to look at the paper's files; in turn, the officers would give the paper mug shots if the paper needed a picture of a suspect. It is possible that this close and cooperative atmosphere led some journalists to identify with the police officers, which affected their news judgment in handling this particular story.

PERFORMANCE CODES

Many ethical decisions have to be made within minutes or hours, without the luxury of lengthy philosophical reflection. In this regard, media professionals are not very different from other professionals, such as doctors and lawyers. In these professions, codes of conduct or of ethics have been standardized to help individuals make decisions. If a doctor or a lawyer violates one of the tenets of these codes, he or she may be barred from practice by a decision of a panel of colleagues who oversee the profession. Here the similarity with the mass media ends. Media professionals, thoroughly committed to the notion of free speech, have no professional review boards that grant and revoke licenses. Media codes of performance and methods of self-regulation are less precise and less stringent than those of other organizations. But many of the ethical principles discussed above are incorporated into these codes.

The Print Media

During the colorful and turbulent age of jazz journalism (see Chapter 4), several journalists, apparently reacting against the excesses of some tabloids, founded the American Society of Newspaper Editors. This group voluntarily adopted the Canons of Journalism in 1923 without any public or governmental pressure. There were seven canons: responsibility, freedom of the press, independence, accuracy, impartiality, fair play, and decency. By and large, the canons are prescriptive (telling what ought to be done) rather than proscriptive (telling what ought to be avoided). Some of the canons are general and vague, with a great deal of room for individual interpretation. Under responsibility, for example, it is stated that "the use a newspaper makes of the share of public attention it gains serves to determine its sense of responsibility, which it shares with every member of its staff." This is a noble thought, but it is of little guidance when it comes to deciding if a newspaper should include the detail about the pornographic magazines in the football player's car. Other statements seem simplistic. Under accuracy, for example, one learns that "headlines should be fully warranted by the contents of the article they surmount." Before you get the wrong idea, it should be pointed out that these canons should not be dismissed as mere platitudes and empty rhetoric. They do represent the first concrete attempt by journalists to strive for professionalism in their field.

When the canons were first released, *Time* magazine held out grandiose hopes for the future of the profession: "The American Society of Newspaper Editors (ASNE) aims to be to journalism what the American Bar Association is to the legal fraternity." *Time* was overly optimistic. The legal fraternity, through its powerful bar associations, has the power to revoke a member's license to practice. Journalists have fiercely resisted any idea that resembles licensing as a restriction on their First Amendment rights. The ASNE has never proposed licensing or certifying journalists for this reason. In fact, the ASNE has never expelled a member in its history, even though it has had ample reason to do so. For example, just one year after the canons were adopted, Fred Bonfils of the *Denver Post* testified that he had accepted $250,000 to suppress stories about the Teapot Dome oil-lease scandal that was then plaguing the administration of President Warren G. Harding. (Ironically, Harding himself was a former newspaper editor.) Rather than expelling Bonfils, the ASNE decided to stress voluntary compliance with its canons.

The November 9, 1999, TV news reports in San Antonio were every parent's worst nightmare. Two TV stations were reporting that there had been a shooting at a local elementary school. Details were sketchy, but the stations were reporting that shots were fired, glass was shattered, and at least 14 people were injured. Frantic parents, the Columbine tragedy fresh in their minds, rushed to the school. In their haste, two parents were involved in traffic accidents. When the parents arrived at the school, however, they found there was no shooting. There was no broken glass, and nobody was hurt. Trying to be the first with a scoop, the TV stations got the story wrong.

The story behind this mistake illustrates some of the ethical problems caused by the modern news-reporting environment. What caused the blunder? Reporters in a TV newsroom routinely listen to reports on a police scanner. In this case, a garbled report apparently started the confusion. The school's custodian had the windows to his pickup truck shot out by another motorist in an apparent incident of road rage. The custodian waited until he got to the elementary school before he called police. The resulting communications between the police and emergency personnel were confused and garbled. As a result, they sounded eerily similar to communications that took place during other recent school shootings.

One station called sources at the emergency medical services center, who confirmed they had responded to reports of a shooting phoned in from a school. One station called the school, but the reporter was told that school officials were busy and couldn't come to the phone. That was enough. No reporters were sent to the scene, no helicopters were dispatched, and no further calls were made. The stations went with the story on the basis of what they had heard on the scanners and their phone calls. In the rush to be first with a potentially huge story, no station verified that a shooting had indeed taken place. It took about 20 minutes for the stations to realize their mistake and correct the story. By that time, however, many frenzied parents had already descended on the school.

The intense competition between local TV news stations and the pressure to be first can produce a situation where ethical values and loyalties can easily get mixed up. In this case, the TV journalists apparently put more value on being first with a story than on being accurate. Part of this problem can be explained by competition. No station wants to get beaten on a big story; it's professionally embarrassing and makes the station look clueless. Hence, the emphasis is on leading the way. The competition and pressure are likely to get worse in the age of the Internet and instant information.

On the other hand, paying close attention to the ethical principles discussed earlier in this chapter might have resulted in a different course of action by the TV stations. Consider the principle of utility. What harm could come from waiting to verify this story? If the story proved accurate, a station might get scooped and another station might gain, at least temporarily, a larger audience and an enhanced reputation. What good could come from waiting? If the story proved inaccurate, as was the case, dozens of parents would not have been needlessly panicked. Some would not have been involved in accidents. The station's dedication to accuracy and responsibility would be vividly illustrated. The good that comes from waiting seems to outweigh the harm.

The Society of Professional Journalists (SPJ) (formerly Sigma Delta Chi) adopted its code at about the same time as the ASNE. The code was designed to guide journalists working in all media. The SPJ code was unchanged for more than 45 years, but as journalistic ethics became more problematical, the code was revised in 1973, 1984, 1987, and again in 1996. The newly adopted SPJ code is organized around four main principles:

1. Seek the truth and report it. Journalists should be honest, fair, and courageous in reporting the news.
2. Minimize harm. Journalists should treat sources, subjects, and colleagues as human beings deserving of respect.
3. Act independently. Journalists should be free of obligation to any interest other than the public's right to know.
4. Be accountable. Journalists should be accountable to their audience and to each other.

In 1975, the Associated Press Managing Editors (APME) association adopted a code that also discussed responsibility, accuracy, integrity, and independence.

Revised in 1995, the APME code covers such issues as plagiarism and diversity. As with the ASNE's canons, adherence to the code is voluntary. Neither the SPJ nor the ASNE has developed procedures to enforce their codes.

In late 1999, the Gannett Company became the first newspaper chain to spell out ethical principles for its papers. Other newspaper chains have companywide guidelines covering general issues, but individual papers can set policy in their own newsrooms. The Gannett guidelines are the first to be newsroom-specific. The decision to establish guidelines stemmed from a growing public distrust of the media and a desire to reassure readers about the fairness and accuracy of newspaper content. The new guidelines forbid, among other things, lying to get a story, fabricating news, and publishing misleading alterations of photographs. The full text of the guidelines can be found at the company website (www.gan-nett.com).

Broadcasting

For many years, radio and television broadcasters followed the National Association of Broadcasters (NAB) Code of Good Practice. This code first appeared in 1929 and was revised periodically over the years. It was divided into two parts, one covering advertising and the other covering general program practices. In 1982, however, a court ruled that the code placed undue limitations on advertising, and the NAB suspended the advertising part of its code. The next year, to forestall more legal pressure, the NAB officially dissolved the code in its entirety.

Although the code is gone, its impact lingers on. In 1990 the NAB issued voluntary programming principles that addressed four key areas: children's TV, indecency, violence, and drug and substance abuse. The new guidelines were stated in a broad and general way. For example: "Glamorization of drug use and substance abuse should be avoided." "Violence . . . should only be portrayed in a responsible manner and should not be used exploitatively." To stay out of trouble with the Justice Department, the NAB declared that there would be no interpretation or enforcement of these provisions and that the standards were not designed to inhibit creativity.

Trying to resurrect a code for broadcasters is a favorite activity among politicians. In 1997, four U.S. senators introduced a bill that would exempt the broadcasting and cable industries from antitrust laws so that they could develop a new code. Other bills that urged broadcasters to develop a voluntary code of conduct were introduced in Congress in 1998 and 1999. More recently, Senators Joseph Lieberman and John McCain offered a bill to the 2000 Congress that would urge media companies to create a "uniform rating system" that would apply to video games, TV, movies, and music. As of this writing, none of these bills had been enacted into law.

In the broadcast journalism area, the Radio and Television News Directors Association has an 11-part code that covers everything from cameras in the courtroom to invasion of privacy.

The V-Chip and its companion ratings system represent an interesting interaction between formal and informal controls. The nuts and bolts of this arrangement are discussed in Chapter 15 as part of the Telecommunications Act of 1996. For purposes of this section, it is important to point out that the V-Chip represents an example of the government's pressuring the video industry to adopt "voluntary" guidelines that categorize programming. If the industry did not develop its own program ratings to work with the V-Chip, Congress left the door open for the FCC to do it for them. The threat of government action has been used before to prod broadcasters into reforms that they were reluctant to make on their own. In fact, scholars who have studied the FCC have even given this phenomenon a name: the "raised eyebrow" technique. The V-Chip legislation is a bit stronger than the raised eyebrow, but its end result is the same.

■ Motion Pictures

Codes of conduct in the motion picture industry emerged during the 1920s. Scandals were racking Hollywood at that time (see Chapter 9), and many states had passed or were considering censorship laws that would control the content of movies. In an attempt to save itself from being tarred and feathered, the industry invited Will Hays, a former postmaster general and elder of the Presbyterian church, to head a new organization that would clean up films. Hays became the president, chairman of the board, and chairman of the executive committee of a new organization, the Motion Picture Producers and Distributors of America (MPPDA). In 1930, the Motion Picture Production Code was adopted by the new group. The code was mainly proscriptive; it described what should be avoided in order for filmmakers to get their movies past existing censorship boards and listed what topics should be handled carefully so as not to rile existing pressure groups. The 1930 code is remarkable for its specificity; it rambles on for nearly 20 printed pages. The following are some excerpts:

> *The presentation of scenes, episodes, plots, etc. which are deliberately meant to excite [sex and passion] on the part of the audience is always wrong, is subversive to the interest of society, and is a peril to the human race.*
>
> *The more intimate parts of the human body are the male and female organs and the breasts of a woman.*
>
> *a.   They should never be uncovered.*
> *b.   They should not be covered with transparent or translucent material.*
> *c.   They should not be clearly and unmistakably outlined by garments. . . .*
>
> *There must be no display at any time of machine guns, sub-machine guns or other weapons generally classified as illegal weapons. . . .*
>
> *Obscene dances are those: which represent sexual actions, whether performed solo or with two or more; which are designed to excite an audience, arouse passion, or to cause physical excitement.*

A few years after the Production Code was drafted, a Roman Catholic organization, the Legion of Decency (see Media Probe, "The Legion of Decency"), pressured the industry to put teeth into its code enforcement. The MPPDA ruled that no company belonging to its organization would distribute or release any film unless it bore the Production Code Administration's seal of approval. In addition, a $25,000 fine could be levied against a firm that violated this rule. Because of the hammerlock that the major studios had over the movie industry at this time, it was virtually impossible for an independent producer to make or exhibit a film without the aid of a member company. As a result, the Production Code turned out to be more restrictive than many of the local censorship laws it was designed to avoid.

The Production Code was a meaningful force in the film industry for about 20 years. During the late 1940s, however, changes that would ultimately alter the basic structure of the motion picture industry also scuttled the code. In 1948, the Paramount case ended producer–distributor control of theaters, thus allowing independent producers to market a film without the Production Code seal. In

After World War I, during the roaringest part of the Roaring Twenties, the films that grossed the most money had titles like *Red Hot Romance, She Could Not Help It, Her Purchase Price,* and *Plaything of Broadway.* One movie ad of the period stated breathlessly: "brilliant men, beautiful jazz babies, champagne baths, midnight revels, petting parties in the purple dawn." It wasn't long before public opposition to such sensational movies began to form. The appointment of Will Hays, the creation of the Motion Picture Producers and Distributors of America, and the adoption of the Motion Picture Production Code were designed, in part, to forestall this public criticism.

Much of the code was suggested by a Roman Catholic layman, Martin Quigley, and a Roman Catholic priest, Father Daniel Lord. Despite the existence of the code, however, sensational films still appeared in significant numbers. This trend was disturbing to many segments in society, particularly the Catholic church. Keep in mind that at this time the United States was in the midst of a severe economic depression. Many individuals, including prominent Catholics, connected the country's economic poverty with the nation's moral bankruptcy as evidenced by the films of the period. Additionally, an Apostolic Delegate from Rome took the film industry to task in a blistering speech before the Catholic Charities Convention in New York.

In April of 1934, a committee composed of American bishops responded to the speech and to the general tenor of the period by announcing the organization of a nationwide Legion of Decency, whose members were to fight for better films. The legion threatened to boycott those theaters that exhibited objectionable films and sometimes made good on their threats. The Chicago chapter of the legion enrolled half a million members in a matter of days and was matched by equal enrollment in Brooklyn. Detroit Catholics affixed "We Demand Clean Movies" bumper stickers to their cars. Other religious groups joined the legion—Jewish clergy in New York, Lutherans in Missouri. Pope Pius XI praised the legion as an "excellent experiment" and called upon bishops all over the world to imitate it.

There were 20 million Catholics in the United States in 1934, and naturally, the film industry took this group seriously. The Production Code Administration was set up with the power to slap a $25,000 fine on films released without the administration's seal of approval. The Legion of Decency's boycotts hurt enough at the box office to force many theaters to book only films that the legion approved. In Albuquerque, New Mexico, 17 out of 21 theaters agreed not to book a film condemned by the legion. In Albany, New York, Catholics pledged to avoid for six months each theater that had screened the condemned film *Baby Doll.* Producers, frightened by this display of economic power, began meeting with legion members to make sure there were no lascivious elements in their films.

By the 1960s, however, the Legion of Decency was losing most of its clout. The restructuring of the film industry allowed independent producers to market their films without code approval. Many producers did just that and demonstrated that some films could make money even without the legion and Production Code approval. The increasingly permissive mood of the country encouraged an avalanche of more mature and controversial films. Moreover, the legion, renamed the National Catholic Office for Motion Pictures, painted itself into a corner when it condemned such artistically worthwhile films as Bergman's *The Silence* and Antonioni's *Blowup,* and endorsed such films as *Godzilla vs. the Thing* and *Goliath and the Sins of Babylon.* By the 1970s, this group had effectively lost all its power; it was essentially disbanded in 1980. Nonetheless, during its prime, the Legion of Decency was the single most effective private influence on the film industry.

---

addition, economic competition from television prompted films to treat more mature subjects. The industry responded during the 1950s by liberalizing the code; despite this easing of restrictions, more and more producers began to ignore them. Nonetheless, the code, outdated and unenforceable, persisted into the 1960s. A 1966 revision that tried to keep pace with changing social attitudes proved to be too little too late.

In 1968, the motion picture industry entered into a new phase of self-regulation when the Production Code seal of approval was dropped and a new motion picture rating system was established. Operated under the auspices of the Motion Picture Association of America (successor to the MPPDA), the National Association of Theater Owners, and the Independent Film Importers and Distributors of America, this new system, commonly referred to as the **MPAA rating system,** places films into one of five categories:

The Motion Picture Association of America's rating is a prominent part of this movie marquee. *(Michael Newman/PhotoEdit)*

G: Suitable for general audiences.

PG: Parental guidance suggested.

PG-13:   Some content may be objectionable for children under 13 (a new category added in 1984).

R: Restricted to persons over age 17 unless accompanied by parent or adult guardian.

NC-17:   No children under 17 admitted. (This category replaced the X rating in 1990. The MPAA made the change in response to several producers who argued that adult-themed, daring, but nonpornographic films should not be lumped into the same category as porno films.)

Unlike the old Production Code, which regulated film content, the new system leaves producers pretty much free to include whatever scenes they like as long as they realize that by so doing, they may restrict the size of their potential audience. One possible repercussion of this system may be the steady decline in the number of G-rated films released each year. Producers evidently feel that movies in this category will be perceived as children's films and will not be attractive to a more mature audience. During the first 11 years of the rating system's existence, the percentage of films in the G category dropped, while the percentage of films in the R category increased. X-rated or NC-17–rated films have never accounted for more than 10 percent of the total number of films submitted for review (of course, many low-budget, hard-core pornographic films are never submitted for classification). In 2000, about 12 percent of all movies released by the well-known studios and independent producers fell into the G and PG categories; 19 percent were rated PG-13, while 69 percent got R ratings.

In order for the MPAA rating system to work, producers, distributors, theater owners, and parents must all cooperate. There is no governmental involvement in the classification system; there are no fines involved. Moviemakers are not required to submit a film for rating. People evidently think that the system is a good idea. An industry survey done in 1988 disclosed that 67 percent of the adults surveyed considered the ratings "very useful" guides for children's attendance. How often parents actually pay attention to these classifications is still a bit unclear. One survey done in the 1970s found that only 35 percent of a sample of parents could name a movie that their teenage sons and daughters had recently seen and only 17 percent knew the film's rating.

The MPAA ratings system came under scrutiny once again in 2000 after it was revealed that movie companies were marketing R-rated films to children under 17. In response to this, the MPAA instituted new guidelines that included withholding all preview trailers for films rated R for violence from playing before any G-rated films. In addition, the organization urged movie theaters to enforce the age guidelines more conscientiously and actually check IDs of young people who attempt to see an R-rated movie without an adult. Despite these efforts, the Directors Guild of America called for a complete overhaul of the whole movie ratings system.

The Advertising Industry

In the advertising industry, several professional organizations have drafted codes of performance. The American Association of Advertising Agencies first adopted its Standards of Practice in 1924. This code, which covers contracts, credit extension, unfair tactics, and the creative side of advertising, contains provisions prohibiting misleading price claims, offensive statements, and the circulation of harmful rumors about a competitor. The Advertising Code of American Business, developed and distributed by the American Advertising Federation and the Association of Better Business Bureaus International, covers much the same ground. Memberships in these organizations and adherence to the codes are voluntary. In public relations, the Public Relations Society of America adopted its first code in 1954 and revised it during the 1980s. As with the other codes, enforcement is essentially voluntary and the society has no control over a practitioner who is not a member.

INTERNAL CONTROLS

Codes established by professional organizations and individual ethics are not the only informal controls on media behavior. Most media organizations have other internal controls that frequently come into play. Written statements of policy can be found in most newspaper, television, radio, and motion picture organizations. In advertising, a professional organization for self-regulation has existed since 1971.

Organizational Policy: Television Networks' Standards and Practices

For many years, each major network maintained a large department that was usually labeled "standards and practices" or something similar. Staff members in these departments would make literally thousands of decisions each season on the acceptability of dialogue, plotlines, and visual portrayals. During the late 1980s, however, network budget cuts took their toll, and most of these departments were scaled back dramatically. As criticism of television content increased during the 1990s, these departments were enlarged somewhat but still have far fewer people working in them than they did in the early 1980s. The departments at Fox, NBC, and ABC review everything their networks air, including commercials. At CBS, the standards department reviews children's programs, docudramas, ads, new shows, and about a dozen existing series. The efforts devoted to monitoring standards vary greatly among cable networks. MTV, for example, closely monitors all its programs; the Discovery Channel rarely has problems regarding taste. Pay channels, such as HBO, have more liberal standards.

The broadcast and cable networks are also relying more and more on the judgment of series producers to determine standards of acceptability. Producers, for their part, have a general notion about how far they can go without raising network displeasure. The networks will generally closely monitor the first few episodes of a series that may cause problems. After that, they will put more trust in the producers' standards.

It's probably obvious to any casual observer of broadcast television that network standards have become more liberal over the years. "NYPD Blue" shows partial nudity and routinely uses street language that would not have been acceptable 10 years ago. Characters on "The Practice" and "Ally McBeal" make direct references to oral sex. "Will and Grace" has a gay character as a star.

There are several reasons behind these changes. First, society has become more

"Will and Grace" is just one of a dozen new and returning TV shows in the 2000–2001 season that starred gay characters—an event that would have been unthinkable in the 1960s and 1970s. *(Bill Reitzel/NBC/Liason Agency)*

open-minded. Subjects that were once taboo, such as male impotence, are now discussed routinely in commercials. Second, the broadcast networks have to compete with the more permissive cable networks where shows such as "Sex and the City" have pushed the envelope of acceptability even further. Finally, the sex scandal involving President Bill Clinton and Monica Lewinsky put sexual topics on the evening newscasts and immediately erased a lot of taboos.

Despite this liberalization, the networks' standards and practices departments still exercise some caution. Same-sex kissing scenes are still, with some exceptions, generally frowned upon. Offensive stereotypes are not allowed. Networks traditionally have not aired ads for abortion clinics, contraceptives (some local stations have aired contraceptive ads), or massage parlors.

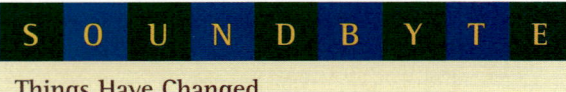

Things Have Changed

Below are selected results from a study done by the Parents Television Council that compared violence, sex, and profanity in four weeks of the 1989 TV season with four weeks of the 1999 TV season. As is obvious, standards are different now.

References to	1989	1999	Percent Increase per Hour of Programming
Oral sex	0	20	
Masturbation	2	17	700
Homosexuality	4	125	2,650
Genitalia	10	92	650
Kinky sex	13	60	357
Pornography	7	28	300

In addition to these network efforts, most local stations also have what is known as a **policy book.** This book typically spells out philosophy and standards of operation and identifies which practices are encouraged or discouraged. For example, most television and radio stations have a policy against newsroom personnel functioning as commercial spokespersons. Radio stations typically have a policy against airing "homemade" tapes and records. Other stations may have rules against playing songs that are drug-oriented or too suggestive. Commercials that make extravagant claims or ads for questionable products and services might also be prohibited under local station policy.

Organizational Policy: Newspapers and Magazines

Newspapers and magazines have policy statements that take two distinct forms. **Operating policies** cover the everyday problems and situations that crop up during the normal functioning of the paper or magazine. **Editorial policies** are guidelines that the newspaper or magazine follows to persuade the public on certain issues or to achieve specific goals.

Operating policies vary from one paper or magazine to another. In general, however, these policies cover such matters as accepting freebies, using deception to gather information, paying newsmakers for a story or exclusive interview (checkbook journalism), taking junkets, conducting electronic surveillance, using stolen documents, accepting advertising for X-rated films, and deciding whether to publish the names of rape victims. Also covered are outside employment of reporters and editors and conflicts of interest. Here, for example, are excerpts from *Rules and Guidelines* used by the *Milwaukee Journal:*

> *Free tickets or passes to sports events, movies, theatrical productions, circuses, ice shows, or other entertainment may not be accepted or solicited by staff members.*
> *A gift that exceeds token value should be returned promptly with an explanation that it is against our policy. If it is impractical to return it, the company will donate it to a charity.*
> *Participating in politics at any level is not allowed, either for pay or as a volunteer. Public relations and publicity work in fields outside the* Journal *should be avoided.*

Some newspapers and magazines are liberal; some are conservative. Some support Democratic candidates; others support Republicans. Some are in favor of nuclear energy; others against. These and other attitudes are generally expressed in the editorial pages of the newspaper. Editorial policy is generally clear at most publications. The *Chicago Tribune* has traditionally expressed a conservative point of view. The *New York Times* has a more liberal policy. The editorial policy of a paper will exert a certain amount of control over the material that is printed on its editorial pages. This, of course, the paper has a perfect right to do. There may be times, however, when the editorial policy of the paper spills over onto its news pages, and this might cause a problem with the paper's reputation for objectivity, responsibility, and integrity.

One problem that crops up periodically is called boosterism, a procommunity philosophy that sometimes causes not-so-good news to go unreported. In Flint, Michigan, when the local Fisher Body plant closed, TV networks and newspapers across the country announced the bad news that Flint was about to lose 3,600 jobs. The local Flint paper didn't mention the job loss until the 11th paragraph on an inside page. "Good news," however, got prominent play: A story about new shrubs being planted at the local Buick facility got front-page coverage.

Owners and publishers can exert editorial control over news policy in several ways. They can hire only those people who agree with their editorial views. (For example, the *New Orleans Times-Picayune* ran an ad in a trade magazine for a business reporter. One of the qualifications was a "probusiness philosophy.") They can also fire people who produce stories that the owner doesn't like, or they can issue orders to downplay some topics while paying large amounts of attention to others.

What is the significance of these examples for the news-consuming public? For one thing, we should point out that the above cases are probably exceptions to the norm rather than the norm itself. Nonetheless, they do illustrate the potential hazards of relying on only one source for news. The intelligent consumer of news and information should rely on several different media to get a more complete picture.

▪ Self-Criticism

Some informal control over media content and practices comes from within. Although the amount of internal media criticism has grown in the past few years, it is still small when compared with the amount of investigative reporting and critical analyses that newspapers, magazines, television, and radio conduct about other facets of society. Many newspapers and magazines have media critics and media reporters. The amount of meaningful critical writing done by these journalists, however, is highly variable. Some of the more well-known critics in the print media include Ken Auletta of *The New Yorker*, Mark Jurkowitz of the *Boston Globe*, and Howard Kurtz of the *Washington Post*.

Several journalism reviews regularly criticize media performance. The *Columbia Journalism Review* is the best known, but its circulation is only about 35,000. Others that are important include *Brill's Content*, the *American Journalism Review*, and the *Media Studies Journal*.

The Internet has opened up a new channel for media self-criticism. The Media Channel (www.mediachannel.org), for example, contains news, analysis of issues, and criticism about media across the globe. It even has a section called the "Whistleblower" where media professionals can single out companies with substandard performances. Journalist Jim Romenesko maintains a similar site at www.poynter.org. The impact of these and similar sites is yet to be determined.

Cable and broadcast television networks usually offer few programs with serious criticism of the media. Newspapers do a bit more in this area; *The Wall Street Journal* has occasionally run an in-depth study of the problems facing the newspaper industry. In film, the industry newspaper *Variety* has sometimes published an article critical of the film industry. *Billboard*, the trade publication of the sound-recording industry, has run analytical, if not critical, pieces on the recording industry.

Some newspapers and other media organizations have tried to incorporate an idea from Scandinavia into their operations to provide some internal criticism. An **ombudsperson** is employed by the company to handle complaints from audience members who feel they have gotten a raw deal. The ombudsperson also criticizes in general the performance of the organization's personnel. Although the number of ombudspersons in the United States remains small, interest in the position has grown in recent years primarily because news organizations are worried that they are losing credibility with their audiences. In 1999, the *Los Angeles Times,* the *Atlanta Journal-Constitution,* the *Miami Herald,* and National Public Radio all created such a position. There are about 40 ombudspersons in the United States, just about all at newspapers. The position is almost nonexistent in TV newsrooms. (One of the problems may be the difficult-to-pronounce title "ombudsperson." At one newspaper, letters were addressed to the "Omnibus person" or to "Dear Omnipotent.")

Professional Self-Regulation in Advertising

In 1971, the leading advertising professional organizations—the Council of Better Business Bureaus, the American Advertising Federation, the American Association of Advertising Industries, and the Association of National Advertisers—formed the National Advertising Review Council. Its objective is to sustain high standards of truth and accuracy in advertising. The council itself is composed of two divisions: the National Advertising Division (NAD) and the National Advertising Review Board (NARB). When a complaint about an ad is made by a consumer or competitor, the complaint goes first to the NAD, where it is evaluated. The NAD can dismiss the complaint as unfounded or trivial, or it can contact the advertiser for an explanation or further substantiation. If the NAD is satisfied that the ad in question is accurate, it will dismiss the complaint. If the NAD is not satisfied with the explanation, it can ask the advertiser to change the ad or discontinue the message.

If the advertiser disagrees, the case goes to the NARB, which functions as a court of appeals. Ultimately, if the case has not reached an acceptable solution, the NARB could call it to the attention of the Federal Trade Commission or other appropriate agencies. Sending a case to the FTC happens rarely. In 1993, the board turned over to the FTC the first fraudulent advertising case in the NARB's 22-year history. Most advertisers comply with NAD's wishes, but disagreements do occur. NAD found that a 1999 Visa card campaign that advertised the card as "the preferred lodging card" was misleading because its claim might be interpreted to mean that it was the card most preferred by the lodging industry, and the company had provided no evidence to back up that assertion. Visa appealed, but the NARB upheld the NAD decision and Visa voluntarily withdrew the ad.

Industry groups also exert control over advertising for their products. For example, the Distilled Spirits Council of the United States in 1996 ended a decades-old, self-imposed ban on advertising distilled liquor on television and radio. The major television networks declined to air any liquor ads, but many local stations accepted them. On the other side of the coin, the Miller Brewing Company and the Anheuser-Busch Company voluntarily agreed to remove their ads from MTV because they didn't want to appear to be encouraging underage drinking.

OUTSIDE INFLUENCES

The larger context that surrounds a media organization often contains factors that have an influence on media performance. This section discusses four: economics, pressure groups, press councils, and education.

It's no secret that many of the nation's public schools are short on money. This lack of funds is especially important today when expensive computers, Internet connections, and software are essential for a modern education. Wouldn't it be wonderful if schools could get these high-tech items for free? Well, they can—but it's not exactly free. A company called ZapMe! offers schools across the country a furnished computer lab, 15 Pentium II computers, built-in software, a high-speed Internet connection via a satellite dish, e-mail, and a printer free of charge to whoever wants the service.

What's the catch? As students use these computers to surf the net, they see advertisements in the lower left-hand corner of the screen. If they click on the ad, they see a full-screen version. Youngsters are a lucrative (elementary school–age kids spend more than $25 billion a year) but hard-to-reach market, and advertisers, such as Kodak, Frito-Lay, and Xerox, were quick to take advantage of the service. In addition, ZapMe! collects marketing information from the students. Students have to provide age, gender, and residence information when they register for the service. As a result, ZapMe! is able to tell which ads a 12-year-old boy from a high-income zip code clicks on. Since marketing to this age group is a big business, many companies are willing to pay large sums of money for such information.

As of late 2000, ZapMe! was providing its service to about 1.2 million teenagers in 1,200 schools with an additional 4,000 or so schools ready to sign up. The company projects that it will have an audience of 10 million teens by the end of 2001.

ZapMe! is the computer-age successor to Channel One, a service that provided free television sets and satellite dishes to schools in return for having students watch a specially prepared Channel One newscast complete with commercials. And, like Channel One, ZapMe! has triggered a wealth of controversy.

From an ethical perspective, the school systems that have signed up with ZapMe! have justified their decision from a strict utilitarian position. Some educators point out that without ZapMe! they would never have the kind of modern lab that the company provides. Granted, the service introduces commercialism into the classroom, but supporters point out that students will see ads whenever they use the Internet. In addition, students are smart enough to screen out the advertising and, after a while, most don't seem to notice it. The benefits of having such modern technology available for students who otherwise might not have access to it far outweighs any potential harm that comes from exposure to banner advertising. The students get much-needed computer and Internet experience from the service. As one teacher put it, "If the price for fifteen computers is a small strip of ad space, it's worth it."

Detractors, on the other hand, seem to be espousing the categorical imperative view. They presumably believe that advertising, no matter what the ancillary benefits, does not belong in the classroom. Consumer advocate Ralph Nader has charged that ZapMe! is a new "corporate predator" and is trying to take control away from parents over their children's experiences. "Parents, not corporations, should raise children," said Nader. Other critics endorse the notion of self-determination. They note that compulsory education laws force children to attend school. Making this captive audience watch ads violates their free will and treats them as objects that simply consume products rather than as students. In addition, they argue that taxpayer money is used to construct school buildings and pay staff. Using those taxpayer-funded classrooms as arenas for corporate advertising amounts to exploiting everybody who pays taxes as well as taking advantage of impressionable young people.

A deeper issue may be why schools are so poor to begin with. If adequate budgets were available, schools might not be so vulnerable to the pitches of companies such as Channel One and ZapMe!

Economic Pressures

Money is a potent influence on media gatekeepers. In commercial media, the loss of revenue can be an important consideration in controlling what gets filmed, published, or broadcast. Economic controls come in many shapes and forms. Pressure can be brought to bear by advertisers, by the medium's own business policy, by the general economic structure of the industry, and by consumer groups.

Pressure from Advertisers   The recording industry gets its revenue from the purchase of individual tapes and discs. Consequently, it earns virtually no money from advertisers and is generally immune from their pressures. The film industry makes most of its money from the sale of individual tickets. Advertisers have some limited influence through what's called "product placement"—an arrangement whereby an advertiser pays a movie studio to include the product in a film.

(*What Women Want*, for example, was filled with references to Nike.) Nonetheless, in relative terms, advertisers have only modest influence over motion picture content. In the print media, on the other hand, newspapers depend on advertising for about 75 percent of their income, while magazines derive 50 percent of their revenues from ads. Radio and television, of course, depend on ads for almost all their income. The actual amount of control that an advertiser has over media content and behavior is difficult to determine. It is probably fair to say, however, that most news stories and most television and radio programs are put together without much thought as to what advertisers will say about them.

Occasionally, however, you may find examples of pressure:

- *Esquire* killed a 1997 story about a gay college student because the Chrysler Corporation apparently expressed concern about placing advertising in that issue.
- Executives at the *Boston Herald* suspended a reporter who wrote columns critical of a merger between two big Boston banks. One of the banks was a big advertiser in the newspaper and held the mortgage on the newspaper's building. (Management eventually relented and reinstated the journalist.)

Finally, a 2000 poll conducted by the *Columbia Journalism Review* found that about one in three reporters said they avoided stories that would be detrimental to advertisers.

Business Policies   Economic pressure on media content is sometimes encouraged by the business practices of the media themselves. When the Supreme Court of Massachusetts ruled that a creditor could be sued for harassing those who owed money, the Boston newspapers declined to identify the retail store involved in the suit. The store in question was a big newspaper advertiser. In San Francisco, a newspaper killed a column that criticized the Nike Company. It so happened that Nike was the sponsor of the paper's "Bay to Breakers" race.

Trading news coverage for advertising space is a common problem. The *Architectural Digest* was criticized by the *Columbia Journalism Review* for its apparent policy of naming only advertisers in photo captions. In 2000, WCBS-TV in New York accepted more than $300,000 to run an ad on its website featuring a live webcast of laser eye surgery. Later that day, the station ran a story about the surgery, interviewing the patient and doctor who were involved. A station in Chattanooga, Tennessee, offered a local business positive news coverage in return for the purchase of $15,000 of advertising.

Then there is the problem of what a prominent editor called "revenue-related reading matter." This issue crops up when a new shopping center or movie theater or department store opens in town and receives heavy news coverage, maybe more than is justified by ordinary journalistic standards, in return for advertising revenue. In 1998, the Greensboro, North Carolina, newspaper devoted half its front page and 48 more column-inches to an inside page about holiday shopping to a recently opened Target store. The name "Target" appeared 17 times in the story, which included several color photographs of the new store. Not surprisingly, Target spends lots of money for newspaper advertising. That same year the Waco, Texas, newspaper devoted half its front page and two inside pages (including seven color photos) to the opening of a new supermarket. Supermarkets also spend heavily for newspaper advertising.

The aforementioned illustrations are not meant to criticize or impugn the reputation of any medium or profession. There are probably countless, less-publicized examples of situations where newspapers, magazines, television, and radio stations resisted advertising and economic pressure. What you should learn from this section is the nature of the close relationship that can sometimes exist between advertisers and media and the pressures that can result. Most of the time, this relationship will cause few problems. When professional judgment is compromised by the dollar sign, however, then perhaps the economic pressures are performing a dysfunction for the media.

■ Pressure Groups

Various segments of the audience can band together and try to exert control over the operation of mass media organizations. These groups sometimes use the threat of economic pressure (boycotts) or sometimes simply rely on the negative effects of bad publicity to achieve their goals. In radio and television, pressure groups (or citizens' groups, as they are often called) can resort to applying legal pressure during the license-renewal process. Because of broadcasting's unique legal position, it has been the focus of a great deal of pressure-group attention. In 1964, for example, a group of black citizens, working with the Office of Communication of the United Church of Christ, formed a pressure group and attempted to deny the license renewal of a TV station in Jackson, Mississippi, because of alleged discrimination on the part of station management. After a long and complicated legal battle, the citizens' group was successful in its efforts. This success probably encouraged the formation of other groups. John Banzhaf III headed an organization called ASH (Action for Smoking and Health), for example, which was instrumental in convincing Congress to ban cigarette advertising from radio and television. At about the same time, perhaps the most influential of all the pressure groups interested in broadcasting was formed: Action for Children's Television (ACT). From a modest start, this group was successful in achieving the following:

1. Persuading the networks to appoint a supervisor for children's programming.
2. Eliminating drug and vitamin ads from kids' shows.
3. Instituting a ban on the host's selling in children's programs (Captain Kangaroo cannot sell bicycles, for instance).
4. Reducing the amount of advertising during Saturday morning programs.
5. Helping a bill concerning children's TV pass Congress in 1990.

ACT disbanded in 1992. In its final press release, the organization said its major goal had been achieved with the passage of the 1990 Children's Television Act and that people who want better television for kids now "have Congress on their side."

In the mid-1970s, other self-interest groups whose primary interest was not broadcasting began to get involved in television programming. The American Medical Association and the National Parent Teachers Association both criticized TV violence. The National Organization for Women campaigned for more representative portrayals of women in the mass media. The American-Arab Anti-Discrimination Committee protested that Disney's *Aladdin* contained a song whose lyrics contained a slur against Arabs. More recently, Southern Baptists

American television operates in a system that encourages producers to provide content that satisfies the largest number of viewers. This is the notion behind cultural democracy. By watching a certain program on a certain channel at a certain time, we "vote" for that program. As a result, the content that gets the highest rating is the content that endures and is imitated. This approach assumes that the judgment of the TV audience is the best way to decide what content is of value.

This approach has intuitive appeal and seems consistent with the democratic ideals behind American society. It should come as no surprise that the cultural democracy concept is endorsed by many in the industry. But is it the best way to decide what programming gets aired? Do producers have an ethical duty to look beyond the numbers?

First, cultural democracy will inevitably lead to the lowest common denominator in programming. Shows that titillate and excite will draw bigger ratings than shows that make people contemplate. Perhaps programmers have a duty to society at large to present content of value that may not get the highest ratings.

Second, how can viewers register their dissatisfaction with current programming? Parents who think that certain programs are not desirable for their children can choose not to watch, but this action may not communicate their feelings to program producers. Dissatisfied viewers can write letters of protest and form watchdog groups (actions most viewers do not take); otherwise, cultural democracy allows little room for dissent.

Finally, cultural democracy makes it difficult for society to distinguish between content that is popular yet trivial and content that is important but lacks mass appeal. If value and worth are associated with popularity, then the unpopular will be perceived as valueless no matter what its intrinsic merit.

In today's ratings-driven television environment, it is easy to justify scheduling another clone of "Baywatch" or "Ricki Lake," because that's what the public wants. Popularity, however, may not equal significance.

called for a boycott against Disney products because the organization owned the company that produced "Ellen" (the program's title character was gay). Protests by gays and lesbians against the 2000 launch of Dr. Laura Schlessinger's TV show prompted many advertisers to back out from sponsoring the show and several stations to drop it altogether. Dr. Laura eventually apologized for some of her anti-gay remarks.

Pressure groups organized along political lines have also exerted control over media content and practices. One particularly vicious example occurred in the 1950s during the cold war period, when a massive communist scare ran throughout the country. A self-appointed group called Aware, Inc., tried to point out what it thought were communist influences in the broadcasting industry. Performers whose background was thought to be even the least bit questionable were blacklisted by the organization and were unable to find employment in the industry until they "rehabilitated" themselves by going through a rigid 12-step process. The blacklist went to the heart of the commercial broadcasting system. Its founders threatened to boycott the products of advertisers who sponsored shows with suspected communists. The investigation techniques of Aware, Inc., were slipshod and deficient. Many innocent persons were put on the blacklist and had their careers permanently damaged.

During the late 1990s, pressure groups were directing most of their attention to the TV program rating system ushered in by the Telecommunications Act of 1996. In fact, these groups, led by the Washington-based Center for Media Education (CME), were influential in getting the original age-based ratings system changed to include specific warnings against violent, sexual, and mature content. In addition, the CME sponsored campaigns to monitor local television stations to make sure they were in compliance with the FCC's rules and regulations regarding children's TV programming. In 1997, the CME released a report that criticized the websites of many alcohol and tobacco companies for encouraging underage smoking and drinking.

We can sum up by saying that there are both positive and negative aspects to the activities of these citizens' groups. On the one hand, they probably have made some media organizations more responsive to community needs and more sensitive to the problems of minorities and other disadvantaged groups. Citizen-group involvement with media organizations probably has also increased the feedback between audience and the media industry. On the other hand, these groups are self-appointed guardians of some special interest. They are not elected by anyone and may not be at all representative of the larger population. In addition, many of these groups have exerted unreasonable power, and some extremist groups, like Aware, may actually abuse their influence and do more harm than good.

Press Councils

Some of the general issues surrounding press councils, also called news councils, were discussed in Chapter 12. This section deals with more specific topics. The idea of a press council originated in Europe. A press council is an independent agency whose job is to monitor the performance of the media on a day-to-day basis. In Great Britain, for example, the council consists of people with media experience and some lay members. It examines complaints from the public about erroneous or deficient press coverage. The council has no enforcement powers; if it finds an example of poor performance, the council issues a report to that effect. Unfavorable publicity is the only sanction the council can bring to bear.

The idea of a press council has not been popular in the United States. As mentioned in Chapter 12, a National News Council existed in the United States from 1973 to 1984 but was hampered by lack of media cooperation. There are, however, a few local news councils in operation. The most active one is in Minnesota.

Education

Education also exerts informal control over the media. Ethics and professionalism are topics that are gaining more and more attention at colleges and universities. In fact, there has been a recent upsurge of interest in teaching ethics at many schools of journalism and mass communication. About 40 percent of the schools in the United States offer a special ethics course to their students. More than half of the approximately 40 books specifically devoted to mass media ethics have been published since 1980. Numerous workshops and conferences on how to teach ethics were held during the 1990s. Most of the experts in this area agreed that instead of teaching specific codes of ethics to students, a systematic way of thinking about ethics should be stressed, so that individuals can consider issues and arrive at decisions rationally.

Even this book can be thought of as a means of informal control. The hope is that after reading it, you will bring a more advanced level of critical thinking and a more sensitive and informed outlook to your media profession or to your role as media consumer.

■ MAIN POINTS

- There are several types of informal controls on the mass media, including ethics, performance codes, organizational policies, self-criticism, and outside pressures.

- The most important ethical principles that provide guidance in this area are the golden mean, the categorical imperative, the principle of utility, the veil of ignorance, and the principle of self-determination.

- All the media have performance codes that suggest principles to guide professional behavior.

- Many media organizations have standards departments that monitor the content that is published or broadcast.

- The National Advertising Review Council is the main organization that supervises self-regulation in advertising.

- Outside pressures from advertisers can sometimes influence media conduct.

- Special interest groups, such as Action for Children's Television, have been successful in modifying the content and practices of the TV industry.

- Although they exist in many foreign countries, only a few press councils operate in the United States.

■ QUESTIONS FOR REVIEW

1. What are the main ethical principles discussed at the beginning of the chapter?

2. Why was the NAB Code of Good Practice discontinued?

3. What is the difference between editorial policies and operating policies?

4. What is an ombudsperson? What does he or she do?

5. What are some ways advertisers can influence news content?

■ QUESTIONS FOR CRITICAL THINKING

1. How would you handle each of the examples mentioned in the introduction to the chapter?

2. What are some of the advantages and disadvantages of written codes of conduct?

3. Do special interest groups exert too much power over the media?

4. Do advertisers have too much power over the media?

5. Is it ever ethically correct to use deception to gather information for a news story? How would each of the ethical principles discussed in this chapter apply to this question?

■ KEY TERMS

golden mean (p. 431)
categorical imperative (p. 432)
utility (p. 432)
veil of ignorance (p. 433)

self-determination (p. 433)
acculturation (p. 437)
MPAA rating system (p. 442)
policy book (p. 446)

operating policies (p. 446)
editorial policies (p. 446)
ombudsperson (p. 447)

◼ SUGGESTIONS FOR FURTHER READING

The books listed below represent a good starting point if you want to find out more about informal controls on the media.

Bugeja, Michael. *Living Ethics: Developing Values in Mass Communication.* Boston: Allyn and Bacon, 1996.

Christians, Clifford, Kim Rotzoll, and Mark Fackler. *Media Ethics.* New York: Longman, 1998.

Day, Louis. *Ethics in Media Communications.* Belmont, CA: Wadsworth, 1999.

Fink, Conrad. *Media Ethics.* Boston: Allyn and Bacon, 1995.

Gordan, A. David, John Kittross, and Carol Reuss. *Controversies in Media Ethics.* White Plains, NY: Longman, 1999.

Kieran, Matthew. *Media Ethics.* Westport, CT: Praeger, 1999.

Limburg, Val. *Electronic Media Ethics.* Boston: Focal Press, 1994.

Sparks, Colin, and John Tulloch, eds. *Tabloid Tales: Global Debates over Media Standards.* Lanham, MD: Rowman and Littlefield, 2000.

◼ SURFING THE INTERNET

There aren't too many websites that deal with the topics discussed in this chapter, but the ones listed below are relevant.

http://jmme.byu.edu/
The home page of the *Journal of Mass Media Ethics.* Contains scholarly articles regarding issues of mass media and morality.

www.asne.org/ideas/codes/codes.htm
The American Society of Newspaper Editors has collected codes of ethics from about three dozen various media organizations.

www.cme.org
This colorful site is the home page of the Center for Media Education, one of the special interest groups mentioned in the text. Contains a detailed description of the group's efforts in the area of children's television.

www.mpaa.org/caramap
Information about the MPAA movie rating system is found in this site. Contains a database that lists the ratings of all recently released films.

www.poynter.org/classes/ethics.htm
The Poynter Institute's ethics page. Good for finding out the most current ethical issues.

www.spj.org/ethics/index.htm
The ethics page of the Society of Professional Journalists. Contains the latest ethics news and an "Ethics Hotline" that you can call for advice.

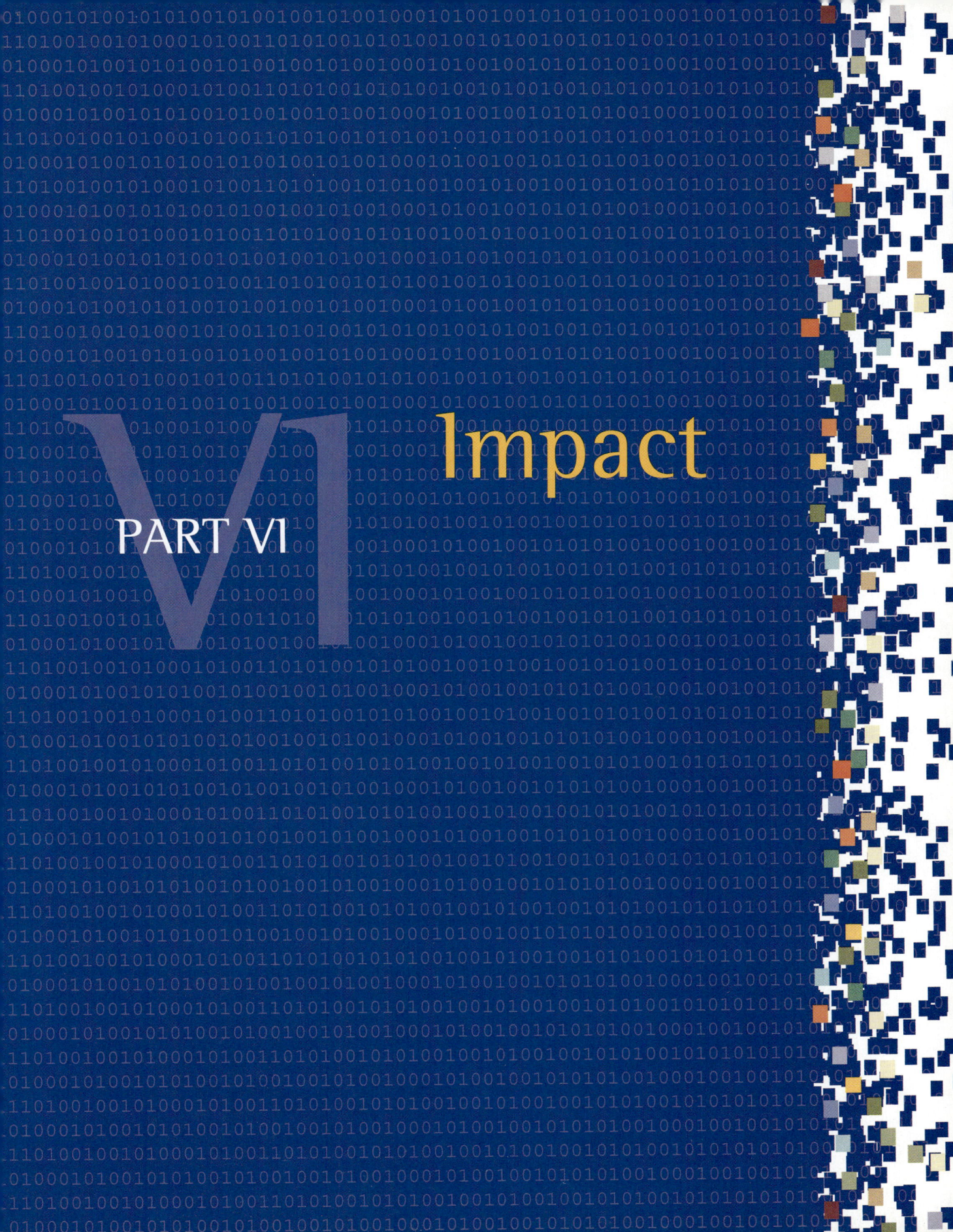

PART VI

V1 Impact

CHAPTER 17

The Global Village
International and Comparative Media Systems

About 35 years ago, media guru Marshall McLuhan predicted that mass communication would turn the world into a global village. With that in mind, consider the following.

What were some of the biggest hits on prime-time TV during 2000 to 2001? Well, there was "Who Wants to Be a Millionaire." The show was based on a British series of the same name. Then there was "Survivor." That program was based on a show that aired previously in Sweden. How about "Big Brother"? CBS paid $20 million for the rights to this show from the Dutch production company that produced the original program in the Netherlands. "Whose Line Is It Anyway?" was taken directly from a British

Iron Chef Masaharu Morimoto in action. The Japanese import became a cult favorite in the United States. *(Manny Milan/TimePix)*

show of the same name. Add to the list the Food Network's "Iron Chef," shot in Japan and dubbed into English, which became a cult favorite and one of the most-watched shows on the cable network.

Consider further the case of Sony Pictures, which recently hired Luc Besson to direct a movie based on the life of Joan of Arc. In other words, an American studio, owned by a Japanese conglomerate, hires a French director to shoot a picture in English about one of France's national heroes that will be shown in theaters around the world.

Viewers in St. Petersburg, Russia, get MTV. Viewers in the United States can watch the British Broadcasting Corporation's (BBC) cable network. Foreign newspapers and foreign

The recent wave of "reality" TV shows has its roots firmly in European television programming. As mentioned in the text, "Survivor," and "Big Brother" came from Europe, as did the successful series "The 1900 House" on PBS. What else is in the works? Below are a few other reality formats from Europe and other places that have been purchased or are under consideration by U.S. networks. By the time you read this, some of the shows may have already aired.

- "The Mole" (from Britain). Five men and five women are sent to an isolated location for a few weeks and try to work together to win prizes. One of them, however, is a mole, who tries to sabotage their efforts.
- "Treasure Island" (from New Zealand). Two teams follow clues leading to buried treasure at some isolated location.

- "Jailbreak" (from Britain). Contestants have several weeks to escape from a mock jail. There is a single big prize, and players have to decide whether they will go it alone and keep the whole prize or cooperate and have to share the prize with others.
- "Chains of Love" (from Holland). One woman is chained to four men and discards one a week until she decides on a winner.
- "Boot Camp" (from Britain). One hundred men and women endure a real-life boot camp run by real drill instructors. The one man and one woman left standing at the end receive a big prize.

magazines are available on the web. CNN, NBC, and the BBC, among others, operate 24-hour news channels that are carried on satellite and cable systems the world over. Radio listeners can tune in dozens of foreign shortwave and digital satellite radio stations. It's obvious that as a result of modern communications technology, national boundaries are becoming blurry. McLuhan's prophecy has come true; we're all neighbors in the global village.

INTERNATIONAL MEDIA SYSTEMS

The study of international mass media systems focuses on those media that cross national boundaries. Some media may be deliberately designed for other countries (as is the case with the Voice of Russia, the Voice of America, and the international edition of *Newsweek*); other media simply spill over from one country to its neighbors (as happens between the United States and Canada). Let's look first at those media designed for international consumption.

Global Print Media

Many newspapers provide foreign-language or international editions. The popular ones fall into two categories: general newspapers and financial newspapers. As far as U.S.- and British-based publications are concerned, the following were the leaders at the close of 2000:

- *The International Herald Tribune,* published by the *New York Times* and the *Washington Post* and headquartered in France, has a worldwide circulation of more than 200,000, most of it in Europe. The paper, which recently celebrated its 100th anniversary, is printed in 19 cities around the world, including New York, Singapore, and Tokyo.
- *USA Today International* is a newcomer to the scene, with a circulation of about 200,000, again mostly in Europe. The Gannett-owned paper is printed in London, Frankfurt, Milan, and Hong Kong. Most of its readers are U.S. citizens traveling abroad. *USA Today* recently became available in Russia.

- *WorldPaper,* published by the World Times Company in Boston, is distributed as a newspaper supplement primarily in Latin America, Asia, and the Middle East. It's printed in 25 different countries and boasts a circulation of more than 1 million.
- *The Financial Times of London,* as its name suggests, specializes in economic news and has a circulation of about 300,000.
- *The Economist,* also based in London, carries financial news and analysis. Easily available in the United States, the weekly is printed in Virginia, London, and Singapore. It reaches about 750,000 readers.
- *The Wall Street Journal*'s international editions reach about 1 million people, mainly in Europe, Asia, and South America.

Other papers that enjoy international status are the *New York Times, Le Monde* (France), *El País* (Spain), *The Times* (Great Britain), *The Statesman* (India), and *Al Abram* (Egypt).

The international flow of news is dominated by global news agencies. Reuters, Associated Press, Agence France-Presse, United Press International, and ITAR-TASS are the biggest, but in recent years, more specialized news organizations, such as the New York Times Syndicate and the Los Angeles Times Syndicate, have also become important.

As far as magazines are concerned, *Reader's Digest* publishes more than 40 international editions that are distributed to about 28 million readers in nearly 200 countries. Time Warner, in addition to the international edition of *Time,* which is distributed in about 190 countries, also publishes *Asiaweek* and a newsweekly in Chinese. The international edition of *Newsweek* reaches about a half-million readers. Hearst Magazines International oversees the distribution of eight major titles—including *Cosmopolitan, Good Housekeeping,* and *Redbook*—in more than 100 countries. *Cosmopolitan* alone is sold in 31 countries, including Japan, Poland, and Russia. The magazine's success in Russia has been phenomenal, achieving a circulation of 500,000 in just two years. *Elle* has 25 editions in 45 countries with about 15 million readers.

Smaller special-interest magazines are also growing internationally. A Spanish-language version of *Popular Mechanics* is sold throughout Latin America. *Men's Health* publishes a British edition as well as one for South America (where it's called *Hombre Saludable*). Many business magazines, including *Business Week* and *Fortune,* also have significant foreign readership.

Global Broadcasting

About 150 countries engage in some form of international broadcasting. Many of these services are government-run or at least government-supervised. Others, like WRMI, Miami, are private operations supported by the sale of commercial time.

In the past, international radio broadcasting was done exclusively in the short-wave part of the radio spectrum (see Chapter 7). Although it goes a long distance, shortwave radio is hard to pick up and prone to interference problems. In an attempt to improve technical quality, major international broadcasters have been striking partnerships with locally operated FM stations. The Voice of America, for instance, has a network of 400 local stations in Latin America that rebroadcast its signal. Further, many international radio services are available in digital form on the web.

Listed below are the leading global broadcasters as of 2001:

- The World Service of the British Broadcasting Corporation (BBC) has a worldwide reputation for accurate and impartial newscasts because, in theory at least, it is independent of government ownership. Along with its news, the BBC also carries an impressive lineup of music, drama, comedy, sports, and light features. The BBC pioneered the international radio call-in show in which prominent people, such as Prime Minister Tony Blair, answer calls from listeners around the globe. The BBC broadcasts 1,120 hours per week in 43 languages and has about 140 million worldwide listeners.

- Voice of America (VOA), now in its fifth decade of operation, broadcasts 870 weekly hours of news, editorials, and features in more than 50 languages to an audience of about 90 million people, about half of them in Russia and Eastern Europe. The United States also operates Radio Free Europe and Radio Liberty. With the end of the cold war, however, the long-term future of these two services is in doubt. The VOA is part of the International Broadcasting Bureau, which also includes Radio Martí, a special AM service beamed at Cuba; its TV counterpart, TV Martí; and the Worldnet TV service.

- Radio China International transmits about 1,400 hours of programming weekly in 40 foreign languages. Radio China International carried strident anti-American propaganda until the early 1970s, when improved relations led to a mellowing of its tone. Most of Radio China International's programming consists of news, analysis, commentary, and cultural information about China.

- Deutsche Welle (DW), "German Wave," broadcasts about 700 hours per week in 36 languages. DW's transmitters are located in Germany, Africa, and Asia. It has a large audience, particularly in Africa.

- Radio France International (RFI) broadcasts more than 300 hours a week to 45 million listeners, many on the African continent, in 20 languages. RFI programming consists of a blend of music, news, commentary, and locally produced features.

The biggest change in international broadcasting in recent years has been the proliferation of global news, sports, and music channels. The pioneer in this area was CNN, which now reaches thousands of hotel rooms and numerous cable systems in Europe, Africa, and Asia. CNN International (CNNI), started in 1990, reaches more than 150 million homes in about 200 countries. CNN International has been regionalized into four networks: CNNI for Europe/Africa and the Middle East, CNNI for Asia, CNNI for Latin American, and CNNI U.S. CNN International has also started broadcasting newscasts in several local languages as well as in English. CNBC offers 24-hour business news to 147 million households in 70 countries worldwide. In addition, BBC World, a full-time news channel, is available in Europe, Asia, Africa, and some U.S. locations.

Along with news channels, sports and music channels have audiences all over the world. MTV is available on every continent, reaching more than 200 million homes, and has versions in Japanese, Russian, Mandarin, Spanish, and several other languages. ESPN International (ESPNi) is the biggest global provider of sports programming. Launched in 1988, the service is seen in more than 140 countries and territories and reaches about 80 million households. ESPNi serves Canada, Asia, Latin America, the Pacific Rim, Africa, and the Middle East. The News Corporation also operates satellite services that beam news and sports programming to more than 175 million viewers in Europe and Asia.

On the set of CNN International. During its news broadcasts, CNN International links together anchorpersons from CNN bureaus all over the world. *(The CNN Inc.)*

■ TV and Film

A good deal of global electronic media traffic consists of films on videocassette that are shipped from one country to another and played back on home VCRs. It is not surprising that this market is dominated by Hollywood films. A major chunk of a film's revenue comes from the global home video market. Disney's *The Lion King,* for instance, made $300 million from foreign video sales, which is more than the film made at the U.S. box office.

The United States also dominates the international TV program market, but its influence is declining. There are still plenty of American shows that appear on foreign TV. "Oprah," for example, is seen in 135 countries, and "ER" and "Friends" are also popular worldwide. Nonetheless, the growth of local production companies and the influence of global conglomerates have made it more difficult for American series to be sold overseas. France's Canal Plus has become successful enough to produce series to fill up French prime time without buying American programs. In Latin America and Asia, Sony's and Time Warner's local operations are pouring money into native TV series. For the most part, locally produced shows dominate prime time in most countries. American shows appear in the late afternoon or early evening.

In many cases, the formats of popular U.S. series are licensed to overseas producers who transform them into local versions. There are dozens of foreign versions of "Jeopardy" and "Wheel of Fortune." Moreover, as we have seen at the beginning of this chapter, U.S. programmers have been paying close attention to programs popular in other countries and transplanting them to America.

American films still dominate the box offices of many foreign countries. At the turn of the 21st century, U.S. films accounted for more than half of all film revenues in France and Britain. Exporting films is big business. In 1999, film rentals from foreign countries amounted to $6.7 billion. Foreign box office now accounts for about half the revenue of an average film. Some films do better overseas than at home. *Mission Impossible II,* for example, made $215 million in the United States and $306 million overseas.

"Who Wants to Be a Millionaire" was the biggest international sensation at the start of the new century. Twenty-four countries broadcast their own versions of the program, and another 55 have bought the rights to it. It is interesting to note the cultural differences in the way contestants and audiences react to the program. In Britain, for example, contestants are cautious and rarely go for the million-dollar question. As of June 2000, no British contestant had won the big prize.

For audiences in India, the big draw, in addition to the money, is to appear with the host, Amitabh Bachcha, who has become an Indian heartthrob. In Holland and Germany, where there is a strong work ethic, the questions are much more difficult than in the U.S. version. Winners in these countries want to feel like they earned their money. Contestants in South Africa use up all their lifelines at the lower levels and have no help left for the big-money questions.

In Russia, the show is called "O Schastlivchik!" (O Lucky Man). The Russian economy is in such a bad state, however, that the show's producers have to push out a wheelbarrow full of rubles to convince the audience and the contestants that they actually have the money to give away. The Russian audience is jealous that the contestants have a chance to win big money while audience members can only watch. Consequently, when the contestant uses the "poll the audience" lifeline, audience members deliberately give the wrong answer.

The real challenge for the show may be Italy. A million lira amounts to only $521. Virtually everybody in Italy is already a millionaire.

Another aspect of international media is the problem of cross-border spillover. TV signals, of course, know no national boundaries, and the programs of one nation can be easily received in another country. The problem has caused some friction between the United States and Canada. Shows on ABC, NBC, and CBS are just as popular in Canada as they are in the United States and they take away audiences from Canadian channels. Fearful of a cultural invasion of U.S. values and aware of the potential loss of advertising revenue to U.S. stations, the Canadian government has instituted content regulations that specify the minimum amount of Canadian content that must be carried by Canadian stations. Not surprisingly, spillover is also a problem on the crowded European continent. More than a third of TV viewing time in Finland, Ireland, and Belgium is spent watching programs from another country's TV service. In Switzerland, 60 percent of viewing is "out-of-country."

WORLD MEDIA ONLINE

The Internet has come the closest to fulfilling McLuhan's global village concept. The World Wide Web provides access to worldwide media on a scale never before possible. Radio stations in other countries, for example, are available on the net. A scan of websites in early 2000 found stations in Japan, the Philippines, Hong Kong, Russia, Brazil, Great Britain, and many other countries broadcasting on the net. Live TV programs from other countries have yet to become common on the web, but the major international and domestic TV systems in many countries have websites that contain general information and programming highlights as well as live video.

At the turn of the 21st century, the hottest beer commercial in Canada had nothing to do with beer, but had a lot to do with national pride and American stereotypes. The ad for Molson Beer starts with a 20-something young man, called Joe Canadian, dressed in a flannel shirt, walking on stage. Speaking calmly at first, he starts dismissing Canadian stereotypes: "I'm not a lumberjack or a fur trader. And I don't live in an igloo or eat blubber or own a dogsled." At this point, he gets a bit more enthusiastic: "I have a prime minister, not a president. I speak English and French, not American. And I pronounce it 'about' not 'aboot.' " By this point, Joe Canadian is almost shouting: "And the beaver is a truly proud and noble animal. A toque is a hat. A Chesterfield is a couch. And it is pronounced 'zed' not 'zee.' " His voice rises to a fever pitch: "CANADA IS THE SECOND-LARGEST LANDMASS, THE FIRST NATION OF HOCKEY, AND THE BEST PART OF NORTH AMERICA. MY NAME IS JOE AND I AM CANADIAN."

The 60-second spot premiered in Canada during the Oscar telecast, right after the "Blame Canada" dance routine from the movie *South Park*. (The ad never ran in the United States.) It immediately struck a nationalistic nerve with Canadians. The actor in the commercial repeated his rant during intermissions at several hockey games. Wild cheering typically drowned out the last couple of lines. Thousands of people downloaded the soundtrack of the ad from the Internet. The commercial became a favorite topic on Canadian talk shows and prompted many newspaper editorials.

Not all Canadians, however, were thrilled by the ad. Many objected to its obvious anti-American tone, while others were upset that Molson was using nationalistic sentiments to promote its beer. Whatever the opinion, it was clear the ad revealed an unsuspected wealth of national pride among our neighbors to the north as well as their fear of being overwhelmed by U.S. culture. And, by the way, the ad sold a lot of beer.

News from Russia is easily available on the web. Kommersant Online is an influential business publication.

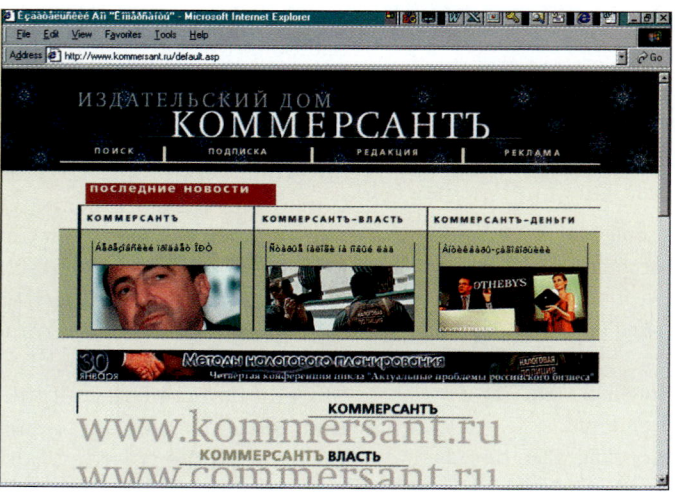

Individuals who want to read newspapers or magazines from other countries now have a wide selection at their disposal. In addition to the U.S. papers that have an international readership, such as the *New York Times* and *The Wall Street Journal*, papers from France (*Le Monde*), Germany (*Die Welt*), Great Britain (*London Times*), Japan (*Asahi Shimbun*), Australia (*Sydney Morning Herald*), and many other countries have online versions available. International magazines that have established websites include *Asia Week, Asia Online, New Woman* (Great Britain), *Beat* (Australia), *Der Spiegel* (Germany), *Playmen* (Italian equivalent of *Playboy*), *Tokyo Journal* (Japan), and *Art Bin* (Sweden).

Furthermore, e-mail has made it possible to send messages across the globe in seconds. Many newsgroups are devoted to news about international events and other cultures, and people all over the world have web pages that can be visited directly. The name *World Wide Web* is particularly appropriate for this global channel.

COMPARATIVE MEDIA SYSTEMS

Let's now turn our attention to media systems as they exist in individual nations. Before we start, we should note that the media system that exists in a country is directly related to the political system in that country. The political system determines the exact relationship between the media and the government. Over the years, several theories have developed concerning this relationship. In the sections that follow are examples of these theories in operation.

■ Theories of the Press

Since the 16th century, scholars and philosophers have attempted to describe the relationship between the government and the media and its implications with regard to freedom and control. Over the years, as political, economic, and social conditions have changed, various theories of the press have developed to articulate and explain this relationship. All theories, however, fall somewhere between two "isms" that reflect polar opposites in the amount of control the government exerts over the media—authoritarianism and libertarianism (see Figure 17–1). Current theories of the press represent modifications of these two fundamental principles. Let's look at each of them.

The **authoritarian theory** arose in 16th-century England about the same time as the introduction of the printing press in that country. Under the authoritarian system, the prevailing belief was that the ruling elite should guide the masses, whose intellectual ability was held in low esteem. Public dissent and criticism were considered harmful to both the government and the people and were not tolerated. Authoritarians used various devices to force compliance of the press, including licensing, censorship of material before publication, the granting of exclusive printing rights to favored elements of the press, and the swift, harsh punishment of government critics.

The **libertarian theory** is directly opposed to authoritarianism. Libertarians assume that human beings are rational and capable of making their own decisions and that governments exist to serve the individual. Libertarians believe that the common citizen has a right to hear all sides of an issue to distinguish truth from falsehood. Since any government restriction on the expression of ideas infringes upon the rights of the citizen, the government can best serve the people by not interfering with the media. In short, the press must be free from control.

Figure 17–1

Theories of
Media–Government
Relationships

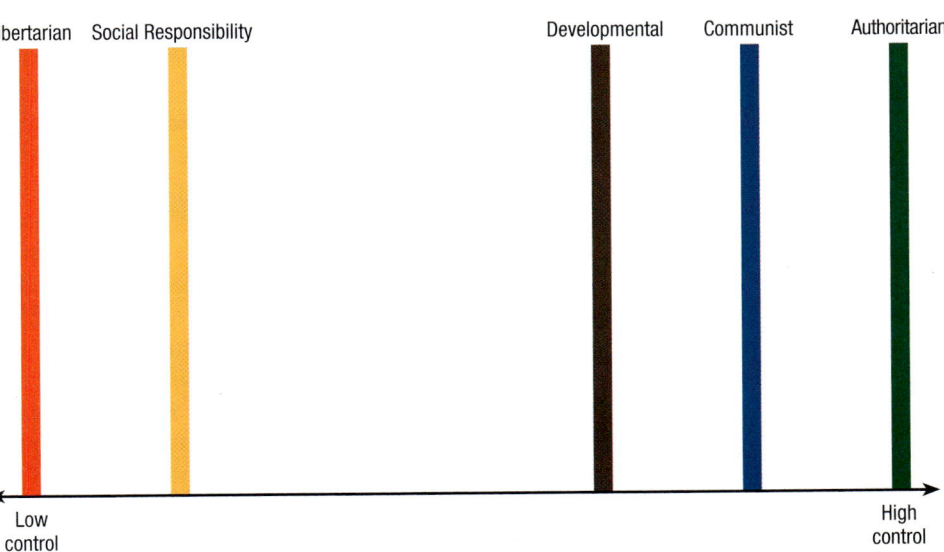

Libertarian   Social Responsibility   Developmental   Communist   Authoritarian

Low control   High control

"The Repeal, or the Funeral Procession, of Miss-Americ-Stamp." Colonial newspapers operated under an authoritarian philosophy as practiced by the British government. This English cartoon, published in 1766, satirized the repeal of the Stamp Act, an attempt to suppress hostile opinion by placing a tax on the pages of colonial newspapers. *(The Granger Collection)*

The libertarian theory fit well with the freewheeling political climate and rugged individualism of early America. By the mid-20th century, however, two world wars and a depression had changed world politics, media industries had become big business, and broadcasting had made it possible to reach millions of people instantaneously. As a result, new theories of the press emerged. In 1956, a book entitled *Four Theories of the Press* reexamined the libertarian and authoritarian philosophies and described two more modern approaches. The **social responsibility theory** (also referred to as the Western concept) incorporates part of the original libertarian approach but introduces some new elements as well. This approach holds that the press has a right to criticize government and other institutions, but it also has a responsibility to preserve democracy by properly informing the public and by responding to society's needs and interests. The press does not have the freedom to do as it pleases; it is obligated to respond to society's requirements. The government may involve itself in media operations by issuing regulations if the public interest is not being adequately served. The regulation of broadcasting by the Federal Communications Commission is a good example of this latter provision. The United States, Japan, Britain, and many other European countries are examples of countries that subscribe to this theory.

The other theory spelled out in *Four Theories of the Press* was the **communist theory.** This theory is a variant on the authoritarian scheme. The media are "owned" by the people as represented by the state. Their purpose is to support the Marxist system and to achieve the goals of the state as expressed through the Communist Party. Recent history has shown the communist approach to the press works best in a closed society where information is tightly controlled by the government. Once information is available from competing sources, people give little credibility to the official media.

This fact was illustrated by events in Russia and Eastern Europe at the end of the 1980s. The British Broadcasting Corporation (BBC), Voice of America, CNN, Radio Liberty, and Radio Free Europe unraveled the Communist Party's media monopoly. TV viewers in Eastern Europe saw Western TV shows beamed from West Germany or sent via satellite. Hollywood movies on videocassette were widely available. The people of Eastern Europe and Russia saw the shortcomings of their political and economic systems and clamored for change. As a result, the communist theory of the press has few proponents today. China, Cuba, Iraq, and North Korea are about the only places where it can be found, and even in those countries the official version of the theory often bears little resemblance to the actual practices of the media. In short, the communist theory has been rendered obsolete by events.

A more recent formulation is the **developmental theory,** which would fall more toward the authoritarian side of the spectrum. In this ideology, the government mobilizes the media to serve national goals in economic and social development. Information is considered a scarce natural resource and must be carefully managed by the government to achieve national goals. Some of the goals the media are expected to help achieve include political integration, literacy, economic self-sufficiency, and the eradication of disease. The notion of developmental journalism, discussed below, was one of the central issues in the debate about the New World Information Order. Until recently, many Third World countries espoused the developmental approach, but changing economic and political conditions have made it less prevalent. Many Third World countries, such as Brazil, Chile, and Pakistan, have replaced dictatorships with democracies, and democracies typically look with disfavor upon government control over the media. In addition, even in those countries where democracy has yet to appear, such as Kenya, the government has either privatized the formerly state-run media or allowed competition from independent channels. Consequently, the government has less control over the flow of information and is less able to promote the developmental approach. All in all, the growth of democracy and the growing popularity of free marketplace economics have resulted in more countries endorsing the social responsibility approach.

Control and Ownership of the Media

One helpful way of distinguishing among the various media systems throughout the world is to classify them along the dimensions of (1) ownership and (2) control. Finnish Professor Osmo Wiio has developed a useful analysis scheme, presented in Figure 17–2. As can be seen, ownership can range from private to public (public ownership usually means some form of government ownership), while control can range from centralized to decentralized. Note that this typology is an oversimplification. In many countries, there are mixed media systems in which part of the broadcasting system is owned by the government and part by private interests. In some countries, the print media could be placed in one cell of the matrix and the broadcasting system in another. Nonetheless, this model is helpful in displaying some of the major differences among systems.

In the upper-left cell are type A systems. These represent decentralized control and public ownership, a type best illustrated by the broadcasting systems in European countries such as France, Denmark, and Italy. Some of the broadcasting media are publicly owned, but no single political or special interest group can control their messages. In Great Britain, for example, the British Broadcasting

Figure 17–2

Typology of Media
Ownership and Control

Source: From "The Mass Media
Role in the Western World" by
Osmo A. Wiio in *Comparative
Mass Media Systems* by L. John
Martin and Anju Grover
Chaudhary. Copyright © 1983
by Longman Inc. Reprinted by
permission of Allyn and Bacon.

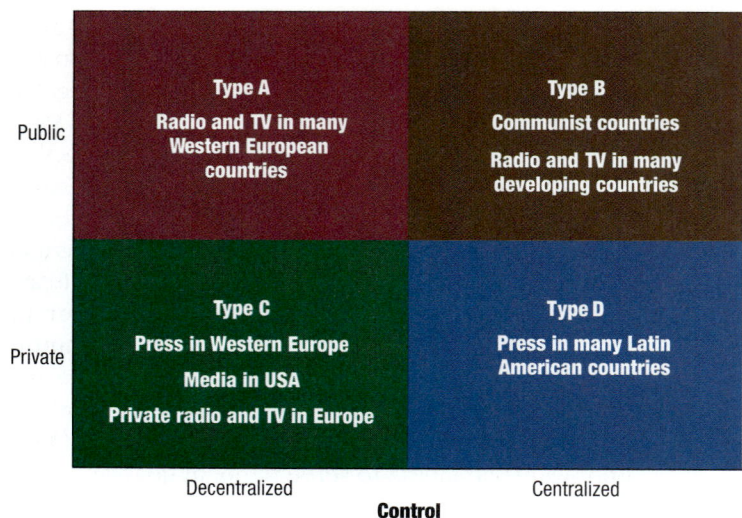

Corporation is a government-chartered, publicly owned corporation that is relatively immune to government censorship and interference. Private broadcasting
systems also operate in these countries.

In the upper-right cell are type B systems. This arrangement is typical of communist or socialist countries in which the media are publicly owned and controlled by the dominant political party. China would be an example.

In the lower-left cell is the decentralized-control, private-ownership model.
This is the system that currently operates in the United States and in many European countries. The media are owned by private companies and there is little, if
any, centralized control.

The lower-right cell is the centralized-control, privately owned system. In
many countries, particularly the developing countries of Africa and Latin America, the media are owned by private organizations but are firmly controlled by the
government.

Far fewer countries would fall into cell B of the matrix today than five years
ago. Only a handful of nations still exemplify the communist or socialist media
model. (Cuba, China, Iraq, and North Korea are examples.) In these countries the
ruling party exercises control, and freedom of the press belongs to the state, not to
the media. Communist countries feel that it is necessary to speak with one voice,
and antigovernment or antiparty criticism is forbidden.

Press control is exercised in several ways. First, the government controls the
source. Printing and broadcasting equipment are given only to approved organizations. In Cuba, for example, there is a newsprint shortage and only the government newspaper is supplied with it. Next, journalists are state-trained and state-
approved. Finally, news agencies are state owned and news sources state
controlled.

Those countries that have abandoned the communist philosophy have generally moved into cells A and C of the matrix. The state-run media organizations
have seen much of their control taken away, and private media outlets are permitted. Individual media outlets are given much more freedom to criticize the government.

The most significant trend in those countries that fall into cell A of the matrix has been a move toward pluralism in their broadcasting systems. State-owned monopolies in many countries, including France, Italy, Greece, Spain, and some of the Scandinavian countries, have given way to privately owned and commercially sponsored broadcasting systems. In addition, cable promises to bring even more video diversity to these countries.

Role of the Media in Various Countries

The role of a mass media system in a given country will differ according to its place in the above typology. For example, as mentioned above, in many developing countries where there is strong centralized control over the media, the principal role of mass communication is to help develop and build the nation. It is not surprising that many Third World countries are concerned primarily with economic and political development. This concern is translated into a rather focused definition of the role of mass media. In general, the media are expected to help further modernization or other national goals. In fact, a new term, "developmental journalism," has been coined to describe this philosophy. In short, **developmental journalism** means that the role of the media is to support national interests for economic and social development and to support objectives such as national unity, stability, and cultural integrity.

On the one hand, developmental journalism entails finding ways to make abstract stories about commodity pricing, agriculture, and educational goals understandable to readers and to highlight the developmental goals achieved by the nation. On the other hand, developmental journalism can also mean that the press refrains totally from any criticism of the government and will print only what the government deems helpful to is cause. The philosophy of many Asian, Latin American, and African developing nations falls somewhere between these two conceptions of developmental journalism.

The role of the media under the communist theory is straightforward: They are tools of propaganda, persuasion, and education. They function only secondarily as sources of information and entertainment. This philosophy dates all the way back to Lenin, who decreed that the communist press was to help further the revolution.

As we saw in Chapter 2, Western media inform and entertain, but their content is somewhat different from communist and Third World media. Most of the information carried by the media in the Western democracies is geared to the specific political and economic needs of the audience. An examination of the press in the United States and Canada, for example, would reveal a large amount of news about the local and national government, some of it unfavorable and critical. The role of government watchdog, based on the ideas presented in the social responsibility theory, is a function that would be unsettling to many of the countries in cells B and D of the matrix in Figure 17–2. Moreover, a great deal of content in the Western media is consumer-oriented, consisting of advertising, news, and entertainment. Further, there is, relatively speaking, little regulation of the content of the entertainment media. Aside from some regulations governing pornography and prohibitions against certain content on the broadcasting media, the government takes little interest in entertainment content.

It's the interpretation or editorial function where the biggest differences are found. The United States and other Western countries have a tradition of press freedom that recognizes the right of the media to present ideas to try to persuade the audience to some point of view. The philosophy of the **free marketplace of ideas** is endorsed by most countries in cells A and C of Figure 17–2. All relevant ideas concerning an issue are examined in the media, and a "self-righting" process occurs. Given the autonomous nature of the Western media, it would be difficult for the government to mobilize the media to support some national goal, as is typically done in developing and communist countries. There is a built-in tension and adversarial relationship between press and government that makes such efforts rare.

Economic Differences

In the United States, advertising plays a key role in media support (see Chapter 14). Newspapers, magazines, radio, and television all derive a significant amount of their total income from the sale of advertising time or space. Direct government subsidy or support of the media is minimal, limited to the funds given to public broadcasting. (Of course, the government also indirectly helps support the media by buying a lot of advertising.) In Western Europe, several countries provide indirect subsidies to the media, such as cheaper mailing privileges and tax concessions. Some Scandinavian countries have a system whereby newspapers controlled by various political parties are given direct financial assistance. Several different systems are used to support broadcasting. In the United Kingdom, for example, the British Broadcasting Corporation (BBC) is state-chartered and gets its operating funds from an annual license fee paid by the owners of TV sets. At the same time, the independent TV networks make their money from the sale of advertising time, in much the same way as do their U.S. counterparts. Many other Western countries follow this same model.

It is difficult to generalize about the means of economic support for media in the Third World. Where the print media are privately owned, money comes from circulation fees and advertising. Publishers are generally free to keep all profits, but in many countries, space must be provided free of charge for government announcements. Advertising and license fees are the two major sources of income for broadcasting.

In those few communist countries that still exist, most economic support for the media comes directly from the government. Since the media are state-owned, money for their operation is simply set aside from the government's budget. Because of this subsidy, the single-copy costs of newspapers and magazines tend to be cheap. Advertising used to be a minuscule source of income in communist countries, but recently, communist governments welcomed it as an important revenue stream.

EXAMPLES OF OTHER SYSTEMS

Let us now take a more detailed look at the mass media in three different countries. One is an industrialized nation, Japan. The second is Mexico, a developing nation, and the third is China, a communist country.

Japan

More than 127 million people live on this nation of islands. Japan's geography, culture, history, and economy have shaped its current media system. Education is highly valued in Japan, where the literacy rate is nearly 100 percent. This has helped the country develop a strong print media industry.

Newspapers in China are sometimes posted in public places for passersby to read. *(Stone/Dave Saunders)*

There are about 120 papers in Japan with a combined daily circulation of about 72 million, a total that exceeds that of U.S. dailies. Japan has 15 papers with daily circulations over the million mark, whereas the United States has 3. Japan's newspaper circulation of 576 copies per 1,000 people is the second highest in the world. There are five national newspapers, of which the *Yomiuri Shimbun*, *Asahi Shimbun*, and *Mainichi Shimbun* are the largest. (As you may have deduced by now, *shimbun* is the Japanese word for "newspaper.") The *Yomiuri Shimbun* (literally translated as the "Read-Sell Newspaper") has a combined morning and evening circulation of more than 14 million, making it the world's largest daily in terms of circulation. (By comparison, *USA Today* has a circulation of about 1.4 million.) Along with the national papers, Japan supports other regional and local dailies and about a dozen sports papers. Tokyo alone has 12 newspapers, 3 of them in English. By American standards, Japanese papers have circulations and penetrations that are unheard of. *Kyoto Shimbun,* in a city with a population of 1.5 million, has a circulation of 800,000. About 98 percent of the households in Japan subscribe to at least one newspaper.

Japan also has two newsmagazines and an influential business magazine. New leisure magazines are also making their appearance in Japan. The Japanese equivalent of *TV Guide* is also popular, as is *GQ Japan.* In addition, Asian editions of such familiar publications as *Time, Forbes, Newsweek*, and *Reader's Digest* are widely available.

Comic books in Japan sell more than a billion copies a year. These publications, while they bear a surface resemblance to American comics, are much more deeply rooted in the Japanese culture. Almost everyone reads them, from schoolchildren to business executives, and their content ranges from children's tales to science fiction and political intrigue. Comic books in Japan are available almost everywhere, from train stations to the local equivalent of the 7-Eleven.

Broadcasting in Japan started in the 1920s, and the Japanese government adopted the British model of a noncommercial system headed by a public corporation. Commercial broadcasting started after World War II, a result in part of the influence of the American forces who occupied the country. Japan's economy has helped it become one of the world's leaders in the development of electronic media, and Japan has one of the most technologically advanced broadcasting systems in the world.

The state-run noncommercial Japan Broadcasting Corporation (*Nippon Hoso Kyokai,* or NHK) is patterned after the BBC and has an annual budget of more than a billion dollars, all of which comes from a license fee imposed on all TV sets in Japan—$50 a year for a color TV and $30 for a black-and-white set. Competing with the three NHK channels are five commercial TV networks and two satellite channels. (The most viewed networks are commercial ones: Fuji Television, Nippon TV, and the Tokyo Broadcasting System, but NHK is not far behind.) TV and radio reach virtually 100 percent of the population as 11,000 transmitters blanket the country. Almost all the programs on Japanese TV are locally produced. American series don't do well in Japan. About 20 percent of all Japanese homes are equipped for cable. At present, however, cable is used to retransmit regular TV into areas that suffer poor TV reception. About 85 percent of all homes have VCRs, and the video software business is booming.

Because of its mountainous terrain, Japan pioneered the development of a direct broadcast satellite (DBS) system. NHK has spent about $2 billion in DBS research and now operates two satellite channels that beam entertainment, sports, movies, music, and specials direct from satellite to living room. NHK's system has about 4 million subscribers, but other privately operated satellite systems are struggling to stay in the black. Japan was one of the pioneers in HDTV. Unfortunately, NHK backed an analog system of HDTV, which has since been surpassed by the digital version (see Chapter 10). In early 1997, NHK finally announced that it too was backing a new digital system. NHK broadcast more than 300 hours of the 1996 Olympics in HDTV. Called Hi-Vision in Japan, the NHK system provides about 13 hours of HDTV signals daily over one of its satellite channels. Only a small percentage of the audience, however, owns an HDTV set, because of the high cost of this item.

Sony is heavily involved in movie production in Hollywood, and the movie scene in Japan is dominated by American releases, accounting for more than half of the Japanese box office. Movie attendance has been dropping the past few years, a result of increased competition from pay-TV and home video.

Japan has been a leader in developing new communications technology. This trend is evident in the fact that more than two-thirds of the population has cellular phones. About one in three homes has a computer, and Internet access stands at around 20 percent.

■ Mexico

The media situation in Mexico is typical of many developing countries. It demonstrates some of the many challenges faced by nations as they strive to form indigenous systems. The media system in Mexico has been influenced by economics, politics, and geography. A country with 97 million inhabitants and a literacy rate of 75 percent, Mexico has been saddled with massive foreign debt and high inflation. Sharp divisions exist between the rich and the poor. Many urban areas are characterized by relative prosperity, while some rural areas are mired in poverty. Literacy is higher in the cities than in the countryside. Moreover, various governments have taken different attitudes toward the media, vacillating between strict control and relative leniency. Finally, Mexico's media system always operates in the shadow of its neighbor to the north, the United States.

CRITICAL / CULTURAL ISSUES

Trivializing a Cause: Press Coverage of the Mothers of Plaza de Mayo

Contributed by Carolina Acosta-Alzuru News coverage of women's issues and women newsmakers is scant and inadequate. A recent study of news magazines showed that women accounted for only 13 percent of all news references. A similar study of network newscasts found that coverage of female leaders was minimal and that females were portrayed negatively more frequently than were males.

In general, analysis of the news coverage of women discloses certain common characteristics. Women and women's issues tend to be trivialized. Their opinions are treated as unimportant, and they are rarely used as news sources. Finally, women are often portrayed as victims with little power to change their fate.

The Mothers of Plaza de Mayo began marching in 1977 in defiance of a repressive Argentine military regime that had waged a "Dirty War" against anyone suspected of opposing the government's view. All of the Mothers of Plaza de Mayo had children who had "disappeared" as casualties of this Dirty War. More than 20 years later, these women still march in the Plaza de Mayo every Thursday at 3:30 P.M.

How have the media portrayed the Mothers of Plaza de Mayo? My study of the *New York Times'* coverage of this movement from 1977 to the 1990s revealed that the press treatment was superficial at best. The *Times* defined these women by their "motherhood" and not by their

"womanhood"; that is, the paper never noted that these women were the first Argentines to openly oppose the government. Their opinions were used in news coverage according to their standing in the Argentine public opinion. Their authority as sources was defined not by the merits of their cause but by their public approval.

The coverage contained little information about their confrontations with the government and their struggle to be heard. In fact, after 1985, the *Times* tended to trivialize the Mothers of Plaza de Mayo by mentioning them only in the travel section of the newspaper. They were portrayed as a tourist attraction, something from the past that seemed anachronistic in the present.

Finally, the women were often portrayed as powerless victims. In addition to being depicted as victims of the military regime, they were also represented as victims of their own children, who were described as "leftists," "terrorists," and "subversives."

These portrayals were consistent with the findings of prior research that highlighted the patriarchal ideology embedded in news stories that simplify women and disdain their activities as legitimate interlocutors of reality.

1. If you were an editor, how would you handle this story?

2. Can you think of any examples in other countries— including the United States—in which women's activities and concerns have been trivialized?

3. What can we, as citizens and consumers, do to let the media know whether we think their reporting and treatment of issues is appropriate? Can we make a difference?

Mexico has 309 daily newspapers, many of them topflight. The *Excelsior,* of Mexico City, with a daily circulation of 150,000, is the country's newspaper of record, comparable to the *New York Times.* Some provincial newspapers, such as *El Norte* in Monterrey, are also influential. The government publishes its own newspaper, *El Nacional,* which is modeled after *USA Today* and is distributed throughout the country. *El Nacional, El Norte,* and *Excelsior* all have online editions.

Total daily newspaper circulation in Mexico is about 10 million, or about 113 newspapers per 1,000 inhabitants. For comparison purposes, the comparable ratio in the United States is 230 per 1,000, while Japan's is 576 per 1,000.

Mexico publishes more than 200 periodicals. Media conglomerate Televisa is the world's largest publisher of Spanish-language magazines. Based in Mexico City, Televisa publishes 40 magazines in 20 countries, including 17 publications that are aimed at Hispanic Americans living in the United States. Televisa's best-known publication is the women's magazine *Vanidades.*

Freedom of the press has a checkered history in Mexico. The government and ruling party deflect criticism by having the government control the national supply of newsprint. If a newspaper or magazine prints something that offends the government, the publication may find its supply of paper cut off. The government has the power to withdraw broadcasting permits, and this fact has prompted television and radio stations to be careful about airing critical reports. In fact, many critics argue that the electronic media are merely conduits for government propaganda. Moreover, the government and the ruling party exert some press control by using the *mordida,* or bribe. Journalists in Mexico are underpaid (beginning salaries are about $600 a month) and are particularly susceptible to offers of money for favorable stories.

In the mid-1990s, the government appeared to be loosening its control. Mexico was receiving increased attention because of the North American Free Trade Agreement, and the government was under pressure to relax media controls. In addition, a short-lived armed revolt in a poor section of southern Mexico and an assassination of a presidential candidate increased demands for further democratic reforms, including a more independent press.

Press reform has been slow in coming. A few newspapers have become profitable enough without government support to achieve editorial independence. The 2000 election in Mexico brought an end to the rule of the PRI party, which had governed Mexico since the 1920s. Whether the new regime will encourage a more independent press remains to be seen.

Radio broadcasting developed in Mexico about the same time as it did in the United States. An official broadcast service signed on in 1923, and the model followed was heavily influenced by the U.S. system. In addition to state-run educational and cultural services, a system of private ownership of stations and commercial support was instituted. During the 1950s, the state sold most of its stations to private interests. Today, there are more than 800 commercial radio stations and only 50 noncommercial stations, along with a dozen commercial networks.

Television broadcasting was modeled directly on the U.S. system. It began as a commercially supported private enterprise, but a 1960 law dictated that TV had to

A typical scene from one of the steamy *telenovelas* popular in Mexico and other Spanish-speaking countries. *(Courtesy of Telemundo)*

perform certain social functions, such as fulfilling moral principles and preserving human dignity. Government became more involved in TV during the 1970s when an agreement with station owners set aside 12.5 percent of the broadcast day for government-produced programs. The government also acquired a Mexico City station as an outlet for its programs.

The private television and radio sector is dominated by Televisa, which controls about 70 of the 120 TV stations in the country. Televisa is the parent company of Univision, a U.S. Spanish TV network, and Televisa produces and exports *telenovelas,* the Spanish versions of U.S. soap operas, which are tremendously popular throughout

Latin America. For most of its existence, Televisa held a virtual monopoly on TV broadcasting, sometimes reaching 95 percent of all Mexican TV homes. In the past few years, however, it has faced competition from TV Azteca, which was government-owned until it was sold to a private firm in the mid-1990s. Broadcasting a program lineup that featured racy *telenovelas,* TV Azteca attracted about 15 percent of the audience in the late 1990s, and some big advertisers were abandoning Televisa in favor of the younger network.

Some U.S. TV programming is popular in Mexico, but the top-rated programs are generally Mexican productions. In 2000, for example, "Roseanne," "Dr. Quinn, Medicine Woman," and "Beverly Hills 90210" were aired on Mexican TV, but the top-rated programs were locally produced comedy–variety shows and *telenovelas.*

VCR penetration is about 60 percent, one of the higher figures in Latin America. About 15,000 different video releases are available in video rental stores. Like many developing countries, Mexico has a problem with pirated videos. One authority calculated that about 25 percent of all videos for rent in Mexico were pirated copies.

U.S. films do well in Mexico. All the top 10 films in Mexico City in 1996 were U.S. productions. An occasional Mexican film, such as *Like Water for Chocolate,* does well in the United States. The Mexican film industry was hurt by a nation-wide recession in the mid-1990s, and few films were produced. In the late 1990s, thanks to an improving economy, the industry was increasing its output. Televisa also plays a major role in Mexican film financing and production. The government-funded Mexican Film Institute helps the country's film industry by supporting new filmmakers and financing productions by first-time directors. There are about 1,500 movie screens in Mexico, many of them owned by Televisa.

In sum, the media scene in Mexico is changing. More competition is present and long-time giant Televisa is losing a little of its dominance. In addition, Mexico's proximity to the United States has had both positive and negative effects. Although a good deal of news and entertainment content flows from the United States to Mexico, there is now a significant flow in the other direction. The large

CRITICAL/CULTURAL ISSUES

Cultural Imperialism?

Cultural domination refers to the process in which national cultures are overwhelmed by the importing of news and entertainment from other countries—mainly from the United States and other industrialized nations. Residents of many countries are concerned that their national and local heritage will be replaced by one global culture dominated by U.S. values. They point out that American music, books, TV shows, and films are popular around the world. Many are fearful that audiences will become persuaded to adopt the values portrayed in this content—capitalism, materialism, consumption, and so forth. As a result, many countries, including Canada, Spain, and France, have placed quotas on the amount of foreign material that can be carried on their broadcasting systems.

The notion of cultural domination also spills over into the news area. For many years, the representatives of many developing nations have been arguing for a New World Information Order. They point out that the existing flow of news is one-way: from the industrialized West to the developing nations, sometimes referred to as the Third World. Under such a system, say the developing countries, news from the Third World is scant, and what news there is reflects unfavorably upon the developing nations. For example, what do you know about South

(Continued)

America? Most people will mention two things—revolutions and drugs—the two topics that dominate the news coverage. Most know little else about the whole continent. To remedy this imbalance, the developing countries advocated controls over the news and content that came across their borders. A resolution reflecting this philosophy was passed by the United Nations Educational, Scientific, and Cultural Organization (UNESCO) in the 1980s. The United States looked with disfavor on this proposal, and it was one of the factors that prompted the United States to withdraw from UNESCO back in the mid-1980s.

Is this charge of cultural imperialism a valid one? One claim of those who urged a New World Information Order had substance. News coverage of Third World Nations *was* unbalanced. In response, the Western media attempted to report more non-Western news and started programs to train journalists of former Third World countries. In addition, several other alternative news agencies have developed—including the Inter Press Third World News Agency, South North News Service, and the Pan African News Agency—that supplement and enlarge the coverage of the major Western news organizations.

Any consideration of this debate must also acknowledge that the whole controversy has economic implications. Those who champion the free flow of information across borders also champion their right to profit from the sale of their products across borders. Those who advocate controls in the name of avoiding cultural domination are also assuring themselves of less competition in the marketplace. If a country limits foreign television programs to 30 percent of its schedule, the other 70 percent must be produced locally. How much of the cultural imperialism debate is based on principle and how much on cash is hard to determine.

The cultural imperialism argument seems to assume that people in other countries are weak and simply absorb and accept cultural messages. One of the key things that the critical/cultural analysts point out is that the audience is anything but passive. It is likely that audiences in other cultures pin their own meanings and interpretations on media content. Those in other countries will reinterpret what they receive in light of their own culture and personal experiences.

The changing world political scene and the increasing trend toward market-driven economies and less oppressive governments have increased support for the Western model. The proponents of the New World Information Order received considerable backing from the Soviet Union and the communist countries of Eastern Europe. Now that these countries have changed governments, there is less support for the notion of increased media control. Consumers the world over seem to welcome the changes.

Those who campaign against cultural imperialism contend that American values are becoming dominant. This raises the question of exactly what American values are. The United States is currently experiencing a wave of multiculturalism, and the heritages of many ethnic and racial groups have influenced the cultural tastes and values of the entire country. In the music area, for example, reggae—which came from Jamaica—found a following among white Americans and went on to influence the development of African-American rap music. Is the global popularity of rap a manifestation of Jamaican, African-American, or white American values?

1. To what extent do you agree that American media products can influence the traditional values held in other societies?

2. If you were a political leader in another country, would you favor quotas on the amount of foreign material that could be broadcast? Why or why not? Does it depend on what country you're thinking about? Why of why not?

3. What foreign content have you seen in/on American media, and what have you learned about other cultures from that content?

Mexican-American population in the United States constitutes an enthusiastic audience for Mexico's media. In fact, although hard figures are difficult to find, it is likely that Mexico exports more media content to the United States than does any other nation. This trend is likely to continue.

China

The media in China have been expanding rapidly, particularly in the past 20 to 25 years. The past decade or so, with some exceptions, has seen a trend toward less government control and a more diverse media landscape. This trend is due in part to China's move toward a free-market economy and a greater dependence on advertising to support the media. Owners of many print and broadcast outlets are responsive to profit-and-loss considerations and act accordingly. As a result, the marketplace rather than the Communist Party is now the major influence on the content of Chinese media.

The country has about 2,000 newspapers, many started since 1980, with a combined circulation of more than 200 million. China has five national newspapers. The party-controlled *People's Daily* once dominated newspaper circulation, but since 1980, its circulation has dropped from 7 million to 2 million. Three other papers, *Xinmin Evening News, Yangcheng Evening News,* and the *Yangzi Evening News,* boast circulations of more than 1 million. One English-language paper, *China Daily,* is aimed at foreigners living in China and interested foreigners living in America and Europe. Xinhua, the Chinese state-run news service, has 80 overseas bureaus and transmits more than 50,000 words every day to Chinese media.

Chinese magazines, such as *Look* and *How,* are popular and attract significant sums of advertising revenue. In addition, Chinese editions of regional titles, such as *Elle China* and *Business Week China* are best-sellers.

Most Chinese live in rural areas, where the literacy rates are lower than in the cities. Consequently, many people rely on radio for news and entertainment. Radio is the number-one mass medium in the country, reaching about 95 percent of the population. The Central People's Broadcasting Station (CPBS), started in 1949, operates several networks that broadcast news, educational programs, and entertainment, including rock music. And, as we have mentioned, China manages an international service, Radio China International.

Television in China showed remarkable growth during the 1980s and the 1990s, with the number of TV sets exceeding 200 million. China Central Television (CCTV) operates seven national channels and one channel that is targeted at overseas viewers. Programming is a mix of news and entertainment, with some shows, such as "Baywatch" and "Funniest Home Videos," imported from the West. Television advertising is becoming big business. In the 20 years or so since the first commercial was shown on Chinese TV, advertising revenue has increased from zero to more than $10 billion. Like CPBS, CCTV is under the control of the State Ministry of Radio and Television. In addition to the CCTV networks, many large cities and regions have their own TV services. Moreover, cable and satellite systems reach about 40 million households.

Despite its more liberal attitude toward foreign programming, the Chinese government occasionally takes steps to limit what can be shown in the country. Regulations specify that no more than 15 percent of prime-time programming can come from foreign sources. The government does not allow foreign news programs to be shown on Chinese TV. In addition, the government can restrict certain content from being aired. In 1998, for example, the government banned Turner Network TV and the Cartoon Channel from Chinese TV for violating one of their programming rules. The government also banned the installation of satellite TV dishes that could be used to access foreign TV programs. The law, however, was rarely enforced, and a number of satellite networks obtained licenses from the state, enabling audience members to receive the networks legally.

The Internet is growing slowly as a mass medium in China, with about 10 million users. The state looks with suspicion on the net and has warned domestic users to register with local authorities. In a recent speech, a Chinese official called for China to take the "World" out of the World Wide Web and create a China web, presumably with content that is state-approved. Whether China will have success regulating this new medium is an open question.

In 1997, China took control of the former British colony of Hong Kong, a city-state with a population nearly 7 million. Hong Kong is both an economic and a media hub of Southeast Asia, with 20 daily newspapers, including two in English. *Time,* CNN, *Business Week,* and other Western media have offices there. It is also home to three television networks and a thriving film industry (Jackie Chan and John Woo are among its best-known principals).

Hong Kong has a tradition of free media, and the Chinese government has generally let the media function in their accustomed way—with one exception. In April 2000, a Chinese official ordered the Hong Kong media not to disseminate news that advocated the independence of Taiwan. In other areas, the Hong Kong media appear to have great freedom. They have carried stories critical of the government and have reported on the trials of Chinese dissidents. Nevertheless, some press analysts have noted that self-censorship may be occurring as Hong Kong journalists shy away from what they know are sensitive issues. When Deng Xiaoping died in 1997, the Hong Kong press barely mentioned his role in the Tiananmen Square violence. In the years to come, it will be interesting to see whether the Hong Kong media's tradition of freedom spills over to the Chinese media or if the controlled Chinese system exerts its influence over Hong Kong.

In sum, the media systems in these three countries illustrate the varying influences that economics, culture, geography, and politics have on the development of mass communication. Because of these and other factors, each nation will create a media system that is best suited to its needs.

■ MAIN POINTS

- Communications across international boundaries have increased in the past two decades.

- Newspapers designed for international consumption include the *International Herald Tribune, USA Today International,* and financial papers. Many magazines also have international editions.

- Global radio broadcasters include the Voice of America, the BBC, Radio China International, Deutsche Welle, and RFI.

- The leaders in global television are CNN, MTV, ESPN, BBC World, and CNBC.

- Comparative analysis of media systems allows us to view alternative ways of structuring the mass media.

- The four main theories of government–press relationships are the authoritarian, libertarian, social responsibility, and developmental.

- Media systems can be categorized by examining ownership patterns and degree of government control.

- The development of media systems in various countries is influenced by politics, culture, geography, history, and economics.

- The media systems in Japan, Mexico, and China illustrate how the factors mentioned above have operated in other countries.

■ QUESTIONS FOR REVIEW

1. Name the major international newspapers and broadcasting services.

2. Compare and contrast the four major theories of the press.

3. Distinguish between public and private ownership of mass media.

4. What is developmental journalism?

5. How has geography shaped the mass communication systems in Japan, Mexico, and China?

■ QUESTIONS FOR CRITICAL THINKING

1. Why has "Who Wants to Be a Millionaire" become such an international phenomenon? What factors influence the international success of a television series?

2. Strictly speaking, the term "global village" is an oxymoron. What are some ways today's international communication system is different from that in a traditional village? Is there another metaphor that is more appropriate?

3. Given the ubiquity of the Internet, is it possible for any nation today to use the authoritarian approach?

4. American media products are easily available in other countries. What media products from other countries are easily available here? Why is there such a difference?

5. As China moves more and more toward a free-market economy, what will happen to the country's media system?

■ KEY TERMS

authoritarian theory (p. 465)
libertarian theory (p. 465)
social responsibility theory (p. 466)

communist theory (p. 466)
developmental theory (p. 467)

developmental journalism (p. 469)
free marketplace of ideas (p. 470)

■ SUGGESTIONS FOR FURTHER READING

The following books contain more information about the concepts and topics discussed in this chapter.

Demers, David. *Global Media: Menace or Messiah?* Cresskill, NJ: Hampton Press, 1999.

Golding, Peter. *Beyond Cultural Imperialism: Globalization, Communication and the New International Order.* Thousand Oaks, CA: Sage, 1997.

Hachten, William. *The World News Prism.* Ames: Iowa State University Press, 1999.

Herman, Edward, and Robert Mc Chesney. *The Global Media.* London: Cassell, 1997.

Van Belle, Douglas. *Press Freedom and Global Politics.* Westport, CT: Praeger, 2000.

Volkmer, Ingrid. *News in the Global Sphere.* Luton, UK: University of Luton Press, 1999.

Wells, Alan. *World Broadcasting: A Comparative View.* Norwood, NJ: Ablex, 1996.

■ SURFING THE INTERNET

Many sites deal with international mass communication in general, and many others are the home pages of international media. Those listed below are a sampling of both.

www.aibcast.demon.co.uk/
The home page of the Association for International Broadcasting. Contains links to many international broadcasting stations.

www.bbc.co.uk/worldwide/television/html
BBC Worldwide Television handles the international operations of the BBC. This is part of the general BBC website.

www.cctv.com/english/
Home page of China Central Television. Includes a program schedule.

www.iht.com
Home of the *International Herald Tribune*, "The World's Daily Newspaper."

www.ipl.org/reading/news/
The Internet Public Library has links to online papers in every region of the globe.

www.tvradioworld.com
A directory of Internet radio and TV stations that includes the major international outlets.

CHAPTER 18

Social Effects of Mass Communication

"Duke Nukem" is a first-person shooter (FPS) computer game. Like "Doom" and other FPS games, "Duke Nukem" lets the player see through the character's eyes and control the character's actions, which in Duke's case usually consist of taking various weapons and blowing away an assortment of alien monsters who are invading Los Angeles. The realistic graphics show splattering blood and flying body parts.

In one particular scenario in the game, Duke enters the lobby of a movie theater, finds an automatic weapon, goes into the rest room and destroys some aliens who were lurking there, and finally goes into the theater itself to look for more aliens.

In 1999, a "Duke Nukem" fan in São Paulo, Brazil, went to a local cinema, entered the rest room, emerged with a weapon, walked into the theater, and sprayed the audience with at least 50 shots from an automatic handgun. Police said the shooter followed the game step-by-

Screen shot from "Duke Nukem," the computer game that puts players behind the gun.

step. While he was in the rest room, he fired one shot into the mirror. In the game, mirrors disintegrate when hit by bullets and sometimes reveal hidden weapons. The shooter even chose a shooting position in the movie theater that was exactly like the position in the computer game. Three people were killed on the spot and one died later. The assailant was overpowered when he stopped to reload.

This episode was not the first time that FPS computer games were linked to violence. At least one of the two teenagers involved in the Columbine High School tragedy was a big fan of "Doom."

These incidents sparked another round of controversy about the antisocial effects of media violence. The debate is not new. In 1993, a teenager was killed lying in the middle of a highway, apparently imitating a scene from the movie *The Program*. That same year, a young child was killed when a five-year-old, allegedly inspired by watching episodes of "Beavis and Butthead," set fire to the family house.

These events (and these are only recent ones; there are many more that span five decades) highlight the dramatic power that media sometime possess. Typically, of course, the effects are not that strong. Not everybody who plays an FPS game commits murder; not everybody who watched "Beavis and Butthead" burned down his or her house. Nonetheless, the media have the potential to influence what the audience knows, thinks, and does. Consequently, this chapter concentrates on the social effects of mass communication. The first part looks at the impact of media on people's attitudes, knowledge, and perceptions; the second part examines media influences on the way people behave. Before we discuss these effects, however, we need to examine how they have been investigated.

 INVESTIGATING MASS COMMUNICATION EFFECTS

There are many ways to investigate what is or is not an effect of mass communication. Some individuals claim that personal observation is the best way to establish proof. As we noted in Chapter 2, the critical/cultural analysts focus on the various meanings that audience members construct from specific texts. Others rely on

Beers and "Cheers"

Although this particular chapter spotlights the traditional effects-oriented model of mass communication research, the critical approach can also be a valuable tool in analyzing media impact. A good example of this method can be found in an article by Dr. Heather Hundley in a 1995 issue of the *Journal of Broadcasting and Electronic Media,* "The Naturalization of Beer on 'Cheers.'" Her analysis suggests that beer drinking on "Cheers" was portrayed as normal, acceptable behavior with little evidence of any harmful effects. In effect, it was shown as the natural, normal, and desirable thing to do.

To support her thesis, Dr. Hundley analyzed approximately 25 hours of "Cheers" episodes from its last season on the air. She identified three methods by which beer drinking was naturalized. First, jokes associated with beer drinking were common. For example, after taste-testing 22 different beers, Norm then went to "Cheers" to drink a few beers as his lunch. Even while suffering a hangover, Norm asks for a beer. Connecting humor to drinking distracts the audience from thinking about its potential negative effects and shows it as a harmless activity. A second method was camaraderie. People are brought together over beer, and beer drinking is connected to sociability and male bonding. For example, when Frasier first appeared on the program, he ordered Manhattans. He was not accepted as one of the boys until he switched to beer. The final method was detoxification. "Cheers" depicted characters who could seemingly drink beer all night and show no aftereffects. Norm, for example, consumed copious amounts of lager but never showed any evidence of drunkenness. Interestingly, the apparently harmless nature of beer drinking is contrasted with the harmful effects of drinking "hard" liquor. Norm's hangover, mentioned previously, came about as the result of consuming mixed drinks. In short, the show depicts the drinking of beer as being as harmless as drinking water.

In reality, of course, alcohol consumption is related to many social problems, and many problem drinkers start out at a young age by consuming beer. The nonrealistic depiction of beer drinking in "Cheers" seems to exacerbate this problem.

Who benefits from such a portrayal? The beer industry spends almost a billion dollars on advertising each year. TV networks get a significant chunk of that. As Dr. Hundley concludes, the "Cheers" message serves the economic and ideological interests of both beer producers and the television networks.

1. Some people respond to arguments such as this by saying "Lighten up!" It's only TV!" But is it "only TV?" How much do we learn from what we see, even when the producers are "only" trying to entertain us?

2. What else might Cheers have taught us? How did the show portray women . . . and people of color?

3. What responsibilities do producers have to let the audience know, for example, that heavy drinking (even of beer) isn't normal, desirable, or harmless?

The Hollywood tearjerker movie has had a long history. From D. W. Griffith's *Intolerance* through the story of Jack and Rose in *Titanic*, sad movies continue to draw crowds. Sad movies, however, draw predominantly female crowds. Tearjerkers are the one type of film that seems to elicit the strongest sex differences in viewer preferences. The common wisdom is that males stay away from these films in droves (or go reluctantly with a female significant other). In fact, the term "chick flick" (I apologize if readers find this term offensive) has been applied to many films of this genre.

Why do males and females differ in their enjoyment of tearjerkers? That was the research question examined in an article that appeared in the Spring 2000 issue of the *Journal of Broadcasting and Electronic Media*. This study serves as a good example of how the experimental method can be used to study media effects.

The researchers suspected that sex differences in the enjoyment of sad films would be greatest when the film featured feminine protagonists and relationship themes, such as the death of a loved one, the end of a romance, or strained family relationships. To investigate this assertion, the researchers conducted three studies. In the first study, they showed one group of males and females a sad scene from *Beaches* (about two women who are best friends and then one of them dies). Another group saw a neutral film segment (taken from *Our National Parks*). They found that females enjoyed the scene from *Beaches* more than males but that males didn't actually hate it; they also rated the scene from *Beaches* as more enjoyable than the neutral scene. Females just liked it more.

In the second study, they showed one group of males and females an entire movie, *Brian's Song*, a sad football story about a player who develops terminal cancer. Both main protagonists of the film were males. Another group saw a neutral film called *The Bear*, about a bear cub's first year of life. Results showed that females and males both enjoyed the sad film more than the neutral one, but unlike the results in the first study, females did not enjoy the sad film more than males. This suggests that the reason for the differences between males' and females' enjoyment of sad films may not be the fact that the film is sad but rather, that it contains female stars and relationship themes.

To check on this possibility, the research team conducted a third study, in which they asked subjects to pretend they were renting a video. Subjects were given various short descriptions of various videos and asked which they would like to watch. Some film descriptions depicted relational themes and some depicted nonrelational themes; some featured male stars and some featured female stars.

The results again showed that females were more likely to choose sad films and that females were more attracted to films with relationship themes. The sex of the main characters did not seem to matter in this experiment. Keep in mind, however, that subjects were reading only descriptions of films. Perhaps sex of characters might matter more if they had watched the actual film.

In short, this series of studies seemed to support the traditional notion that sad films are indeed "women's films" and that women especially prefer sad films about relationships. On the other hand, none of the studies suggested that males actively disliked this genre. They simply didn't enjoy it as much as females. Maybe the results of this study will make it easier for couples to understand why they disagree over what movies to see or videos to rent. Or maybe not.

Source: M. B. Oliver, J. B. Weaver, and S. Smith, "An Examination of Factors Related to Sex Differences in Enjoyment of Sad Films," *Journal of Broadcasting and Electronic Media* 44, no. 2 (Spring 2000): 282–300.

expert opinions and evaluations; still others point to common sense when they wish to support their views. All these methods are valuable, but this chapter will focus on the results of scientific studies of the media's impact on individuals. Keep in mind, however, that the scientific approach is only one of many ways to examine this topic.

When it comes to gathering information about media effects, scientists have typically used two main methods:

1. A **survey** is carried out in the real world. It usually consists of a large group of individuals who answer questions put to them via a questionnaire. Although the survey is usually not sufficient proof of cause and effect, it does help establish associations. A special kind of survey, a **panel study,** allows researchers to be more confident about attributing patterns of cause and effect in survey data. The panel study collects data from the same people at two or more different points in time. As a result, it is possible, for example, using sophisticated techniques that control the effects of other variables, to

see if viewing televised violence at an early age is related to aggressive behavior at a later date. Panel studies are expensive and take a long time to complete.

2. An **experiment** is performed in a laboratory and usually consists of the controlled manipulation of a single factor to determine its impact on another factor. A special kind of experiment, a **field experiment,** is conducted in a real-life setting. Experiments are useful because they help establish causality.

In the remainder of this chapter, we will focus on scientific findings about the effects of media on knowledge, attitudes, and behavior.

EFFECTS ON KNOWLEDGE AND ATTITUDES

The dividing line between attitudes and behaviors is fuzzy. In many instances, we can only infer that an attitude or perception exists by observing relevant behavior. Thus, many of the studies mentioned in this section involve the measurement of both behavior and attitudes.

We will examine five topics that have generated the most research interest:

1. The role of the media in socialization.
2. Cultivation analysis.
3. The impact of TV advertising on children.
4. Agenda setting.
5. Media exposure and cognitive skills.

Media and Socialization

In Chapter 2, we defined socialization as the ways in which an individual comes to adopt the behavior and values of a group. In this section, we will concentrate on the socialization of children. Socialization is a complex process extending over a number of years and involving various people and organizations, called **agencies of socialization,** who contribute in some degree to the socialization process. Figure 18–1 presents a simplified diagram of some of the more common agencies.

In many situations, the media's contribution to socialization will be slight. Parents might have greater influence ("Eat your spinach; it's good for you"). So might friends ("Don't be a tattletale"). So might direct experience ("I'd better not take my sister's stuff because the last time I did, she popped me one").

Figure 18–1

Agencies of Socialization

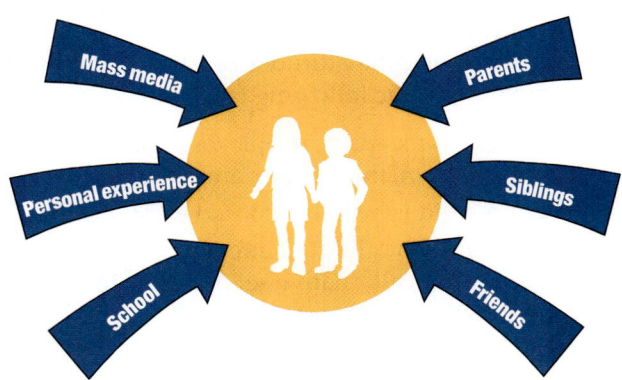

Could a media celebrity, such as Britney Spears, serve as an agency of socialization for young women? Could she influence their attitudes about what body type is desirable and what behaviors are appropriate for teens? *(AP/Wide World Photos)*

On the other hand, the media, especially television, may play an important role in socialization when it comes to certain topics. Let us now look at evidence pinpointing some of these areas.

■ The Media as a Primary Source of Information

Learning is an important part of the socialization process, and the media serve as important sources of information for a wide range of topics, especially politics and public affairs. For example, a survey of sixth- and seventh-graders found that 80 percent named a mass medium as the source of most information about the president and vice president, 60 percent named a mass medium as the primary source of information about Congress, and half named a mass medium as the chief information source about the Supreme Court.

Other research has shown that the media, primarily TV, serve as primary information sources for many age groups about a wide range of topics. Eight of ten Americans cited television as their primary source of information about the 1991 Persian Gulf War. Television was also named as the source of most information for local and congressional elections. This phenomenon is not limited to political and public-affairs information. There is reason to believe that media presentations, including those in entertainment programs, are important sources of information on topics such as occupations, crime, law enforcement, alcohol and drug usage, the environment, and minorities. One recent study of high school students, for example, found that about 2 in 10 students listed rock music as an important source of information about moral values and that 1 out of 4 specified it as an important source of information about interpersonal relationships.

■ Shaping Attitudes, Perceptions, and Beliefs

The mass media also play an important role in the transmission of attitudes, perceptions, and beliefs. Several writers have suggested that, under certain conditions, the media (especially TV) may become important socialization agencies in determining the attitudes of young people. Specifically, TV will be an influential force when the following factors are operative:

1. The same ideas, people, or behaviors recur consistently from program to program; that is, they are presented in a stereotyped manner.
2. A child is heavily exposed to TV content.
3. A child has limited interaction with parents and other socializing agents and lacks an alternative set of beliefs to serve as a standard against which to assess media portrayals.

All this means that under certain conditions, TV will be an influential force in shaping what children think about certain topics. Complicated though the task is, some researchers have identified some of the conditions, the topics, and the children to which the above theory applies. Moreover, they have specified some of the effects that may result when television does the socializing.

Creating Stereotypes   In the study of media socialization, it is helpful to identify consistent themes or stereotypes present in media content. For instance, consider how television programs typically portray law enforcement and crime. Programs about crime and law enforcement are a staple of prime-time television; between 20 and 35 percent of all program time consists of shows dealing with cops and robbers. However, the large percentage of law enforcement characters portrayed on TV does not accurately reflect the actual percentage employed in this capacity in real life. Furthermore—on television, at least—crime doesn't pay. One study found that some 90 percent of TV crimes were solved; real-life law enforcement agencies are not nearly as effective.

Television also overrepresents violent crimes, such as murder, rape, and armed robbery. One study found that violent crime accounted for about 60 percent of all TV crimes in one week of programming. To put this figure in perspective, consider that only 10 percent of crimes in the real world are violent. Last, television emphasizes certain aspects of the legal system (ask a young fan of any police show to name an arrested suspect's rights), while ignoring others (ask that same young fan what happens at an arraignment or what the functions of a grand jury are).

The war in the Persian Gulf focused attention on the way Arabs had been portrayed in the mass media. Content analyses of TV revealed that Arab men were typically portrayed via three main negative stereotypes: (1) terrorist, (2) oil sheik, and (3) Bedouin desert nomad. Arab women were rarely seen and when they appeared at all, were shown as belly dancers or members of a harem (harems were never common and none exist today). And how many Arab children have you seen on "Sesame Street"?

Although the mass media (particularly television) may influence the shaping of stereotypical images, the media also have the power to change such stereotypes. For example, in one study examining children's perceptions of sex roles, children were shown commercials specially made for Zing fruit drink. One set of commercials depicted women in conventional female occupations, such as model, file clerk, and telephone operator. A second set of commercials portrayed women in traditional male jobs, such as butcher, welder, and druggist. Girls who saw the women in male-dominated jobs were more likely to aspire to these occupations than were girls who saw women in the traditional roles.

In summary, there appears to be evidence that the TV world often presents images that are at odds with reality. In addition to the field of crime and law enforcement, stereotyping has also characterized sex-role portrayals, the depiction of occupations, methods of problem solving, portrayals of scientists, and the depiction of mental illness.

The Effects of Heavy Viewing   It seems probable that youngsters who are heavy TV viewers would display a pattern of beliefs and perceptions consistent with media portrayals. The earliest research in this area, completed in the 1930s, found that frequent viewing of crime and gangster movies could change attitudes on topics such as capital punishment and prison reform. More recently, other researchers have noted a connection between heavy viewing of violent TV programs and favorable attitudes toward the use of violence in real life. Further, children who were heavy viewers of cops-and-robbers TV programs were likely to

believe that police were more successful in apprehending criminals than were children who were not fans of these shows.

In other areas, several studies have linked high levels of television viewing with attitudes favoring traditional sex roles. In other words, children who were heavily exposed to television were more likely to feel, among other things, that men would make better doctors and that women would make better nurses or that raising children was a job for women rather than men.

Socialization by TV can also have positive effects. For example, a television program such as "Sesame Street" can help children develop skills and knowledge that will help them in school. "Sesame Street" is the most researched program ever to appear on TV. Findings have indicated that children who watched this program scored higher on tests measuring knowledge of numbers, letters, relationships, and vocabulary—concepts that the series was designed to teach. In addition, "Sesame Street" has been shown to affect general attitudes. Children who watched scenes in which white and minority children played together showed more tolerance in their racial attitudes than did children who had not viewed the scenes.

To be fair, we must again stress that this type of research *assumes,* but does not necessarily *prove,* that the mass media play a significant part in creating the attitudes held by these youngsters. Surveys can only highlight associations, not prove causality. Although some experimental evidence points to the media as the cause of certain attitudes, we cannot entirely rule out other interpretations. Nevertheless, it is likely that the link between media exposure and certain attitudes demonstrates reciprocal causation. What this means is best shown by an example. Watching violent TV shows might cause a youngster to hold favorable attitudes toward aggression. These favorable attitudes might then prompt him or her to watch more violent TV, which, in turn, might encourage more aggressive attitudes, and so on. The two factors might be said to be mutually causing one another.

The Absence of Alternative Information   Although research evidence is less consistent in this area than in others, it appears that, under some circumstances, television can affect young people's attitudes about matters for which the environment fails to provide firsthand experience or alternative sources of information. One survey that examined the potential impact of TV on dating behavior found that teenagers were more likely to turn to TV for guidance when they had limited real-life experience with dating.

A recent study noted that foreign students who depended mostly on television for their information about Americans had stereotyped beliefs about Americans. Chinese students who depended primarily on TV for most of their information and who had little interpersonal contact with Americans rated them as more pleasure-seeking and materialistic (two characteristics consistent with TV's portrayal of Americans) than did students who relied more on other sources.

Where media influence is indirect, it is difficult to pinpoint. This is particularly true when the media operate simultaneously with other agencies of socialization and when interpersonal channels outweigh media channels in forming attitudes and opinions. In the area of politics, for instance, the media probably supply youngsters with information and viewpoints that are subsequently commented on by parents and friends. Political beliefs and attitudes evolve out of this double context. In such cases, the socializing impact of parents and other interpersonal sources is more important than that of the media. One study dealing with attitudes toward police found that although children spent a great deal of time watching TV cop shows, friends and family were the important socializing agents. The point is this: The media play a significant role in socialization. Sometimes this role is easy to detect; sometimes it is indirect and harder to see; at still other times, it is apparently slight. Clearly, numerous factors are influential in determining how a child comes to perceive the world. The media (and television, in particular), however, have become important factors in the socialization process.

Cultivation Analysis

Directly related to socialization is an area of research called **cultivation analysis.** Developed by George Gerbner and his colleagues at the University of Pennsylvania, cultivation analysis suggests that heavy TV viewing "cultivates" perceptions of reality consistent with the view of the world presented in television programs. Cultivation analysis concentrates on the long-term effects of exposure—on both adults and children—rather than on the short-term impact on attitudes and opinions.

Methodology   The first stage in cultivation analysis is a careful study of television content to identify predominant themes and messages. Not surprisingly, television portrays a rather idiosyncratic world that is unlike reality along many dimensions. For example, television's world is usually populated by a preponderance of males: Two-thirds to three-quarters of all leading characters are men. Moreover, television overemphasizes the professions of—and, as previously mentioned, overrepresents the proportion of workers engaged in—law enforcement and the detection of crime. Last, the TV world is a violent one—around 60 to 80 percent of all programs contain at least one instance of violence.

Step two examines what, if anything, viewers absorb from heavy exposure to the world of television. Respondents are presented with questions concerning social reality and are asked to check one of two possible answers. One of these answers (the "TV answer") is in line with the way things are portrayed on television; the other (the "real-world answer") resembles actual life. For example:

What percentage of all males who have jobs work in law enforcement and crime detection?

Is it

_____ *1 percent or* _____ *10 percent?*

On television, about 12 percent of all male characters hold such jobs. Thus 10 percent would be the TV answer. In reality, about 1 percent are employed in law

The island nation of Fiji did not get television until 1995, when a local TV station began broadcasting shows such as "ER," "Seinfeld," and "Melrose Place." In the years that followed, there was an increase in bulimia and other eating disorders among young Fijian girls, disorders that were rare before the arrival of TV. In addition, there was a big jump in the number of females dissatisfied with their body image. A 1998 survey turned up the fact that three out of four female teens on the island reported feeling too big or too fat.

An anthropologist who has studied the Fijian culture since 1998 attributed these changes to the influence of television. The traditional Fijian female body type has been one that has been described as "robust" and "well muscled." The American TV shows, however, portrayed the ideal body type as thin and wispy. Fijian teen girls apparently believed that this body type was the one that was preferred in the modern world and tried to emulate it.

The Fiji case illustrates that TV shows contain more than just entertainment; they also embody the social values of the nation that produces them.

enforcement; thus 1 percent is the real-world answer. The responses of a large sample of heavy TV viewers are then compared with those of light TV viewers. If heavy viewers show a definite tendency to choose TV answers, we would have evidence that a cultivation effect is occurring.

Research Findings   Is there evidence to suggest such an effect? Most findings suggest that among some people, TV cultivates distorted perceptions of the real world. In one survey of approximately 450 New Jersey schoolchildren, 73 percent of heavy viewers compared with 62 percent of light viewers gave the TV answer to a question about the number of people involved in violence in a typical week. Youngsters who were heavy viewers were also more fearful about walking alone at night in a city. They overestimated how many people commit serious crimes, how often police find it necessary to use force, and how frequently police have to shoot at fleeing suspects.

In addition, results from a national survey of adult viewers indicate that cultivation is not limited to children. Heavy television viewers evidently felt that TV violence and crime presented an accurate depiction of reality, since they also were more fearful of walking alone at night and were more likely to have bought a dog recently or to have put locks on windows and doors than were light TV viewers. Although the differences in findings between heavy and light viewers were not large in the absolute sense, they were almost certainly not due to chance. Even more intriguing was the finding that heavy TV viewers were more likely to keep a gun to protect themselves than were light viewers.

Other cultivation research has focused specifically on college students. In one study, students' exposure to pornography was examined to see if stereotyped perceptions were being cultivated. Among males, those who were heavy users of pornography were more apt to report that they had less confidence in females doing certain jobs (e.g., mechanic, mayor). They also tended to agree more with stereotypes of sexuality ("Men have stronger sexual urges than women; women say 'no' to sex when they don't really mean it") than did light users. These relationships stood up even after rigorous statistical controls removed possible influences of other factors. Women showed no such effects from exposure. A 1993 study found that college students who had high exposure to televised portrayals of sexual behavior thought those behaviors happened more frequently in real life than did students with lower levels of exposure.

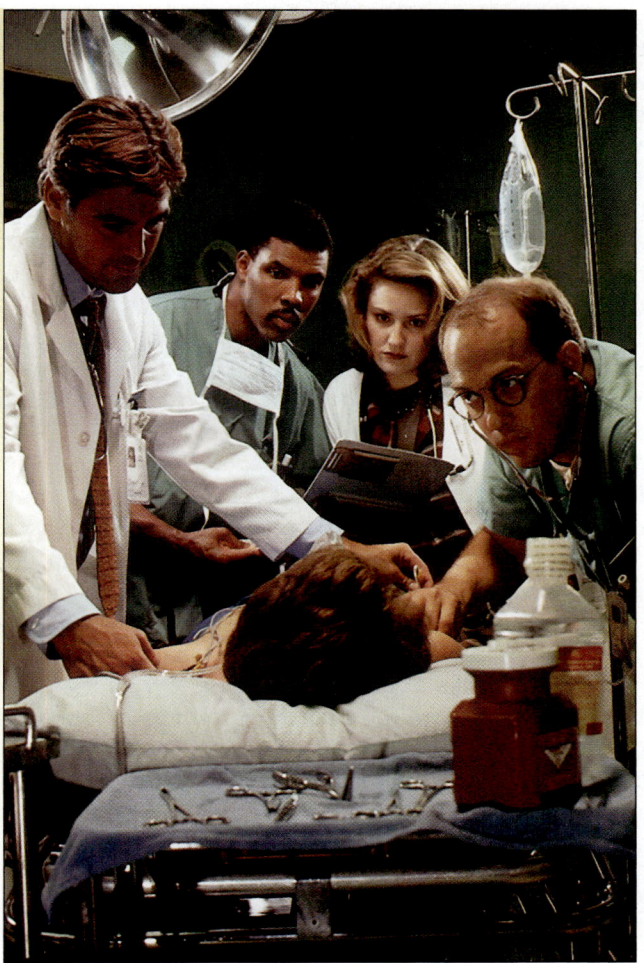

How many doctors in real life are like the doctors on NBC's "ER"? Cultivation analysis would suggest that for some heavy viewers, TV portrayals of doctors would influence perceptions of real-life MDs.

Although the results of cultivation-analysis studies are evocative and fascinating, conclusions are clouded by three problems. First, it is difficult to determine cause and effect. For example, does heavy TV viewing cause people to be fearful of walking alone at night, or does being fearful cause them to stay home and watch more TV?

The second problem concerns the fact that people differ in ways other than their TV viewing habits. Consequently, factors other than TV watching might affect the differences in perceptions and attitudes between heavy and light viewers. When certain factors that appear relevant to the cause-and-effect relationship (such as age, sex, and education) are statistically controlled, one factor at a time, the association between TV watching and perceptions is evident, but somewhat weakened. When two or more factors are controlled simultaneously (e.g., examining the relationship between TV viewing and anxiety, while simultaneously controlling for effects of both sex and age), some overall relationships disappear. We cannot conclude, however, that a relationship does not exist. In fact, recent research indicates certain subgroups will show a cultivation effect while others won't.

Gerbner and his associates, for example, have detected a phenomenon they have labeled **mainstreaming,** whereby differences apparently due to cultural and social factors tend to diminish among heavy-TV-viewing persons. They have also found evidence for what they call **resonance,** a situation in which the respondent's real-life experiences are congruent with those of the television world, thereby leading to a greater cultivation effect.

Third, technical decisions about the way TV viewing and attitudes are measured can have a significant impact on findings. For example, the precise wording of the questions has been shown to be important. In addition, some researchers argue that exposure to a particular kind of program (e.g., violent shows) gives a more accurate picture of cultivation than simply measuring overall TV viewing. Others note that deciding on the number of hours of viewing that differentiates high and low viewers has a bearing on the magnitude of cultivation.

Perhaps the most comprehensive summary of cultivation research is a 1997 review of more than 5,600 findings collected over two decades. The authors of this review concluded that there was evidence of a small but persistent cultivation effect that may have significance for the social, cultural, and political climate. As the authors concluded, "Certainly not all of the [cultivation] issues are resolved, but, taken as a whole, the data show that cultivation theory has amply demonstrated the nature, importance, and resilience of its findings."[1]

To sum up and perhaps oversimplify, we can say that, although not all mass communication scholars are totally convinced by the reasoning underlying cultivation analysis, a growing body of evidence suggests that the cultivation effect is indeed real for many people.

Children and Television Advertising

If you've ever watched Saturday morning television, you are probably familiar with Tony the Tiger, Captain Crunch, Count Chocula, Ronald McDonald, and Snap, Crackle, and Pop. This is not surprising because by the time you graduated from high school, you had already seen about 350,000 TV commercials. A typical child will see about 20,000 commercials every year, mostly for toys, cereals, candies, and fast-food restaurants. During the 1970s, the citizens' group Action for Children's Television brought this issue to the attention of the Federal Communications Commission (FCC) and the Federal Trade Commission (FTC). By the early part of the 1980s, most people had accepted the notion that children deserve special consideration from television advertisers, for the following reasons:

1. Children are a vulnerable audience and should not be exploited by TV advertising.
2. Children, especially younger children, might be deceived by TV techniques that make products appear more desirable than they really are.
3. The long-term effects of exposure to TV ads might have a negative effect on a child's socialization as a future consumer.

Using this threefold division, we will examine some of the many research studies that have investigated the effects of TV advertising on children.

Vulnerable Audience?   Adults can easily distinguish commercials from regular TV programs, but what about children? Research suggests that children from five to eight years of age can separate ads from the rest of the program, but they have little idea as to the purpose of the ads. Older children (from 9 to 12) are better able to identify ads and are aware that their purpose is to persuade people to buy things. Partly as a result of these findings, in 1974, the FCC concluded that some device was needed to clearly separate commercials from programs. Current programs aimed at children use such signals as "We will return after these messages" or "We now return to [name of show]." Experiments have shown that these program separators are not effective with kids under the age of five but are more effective with older children.

---

[1]This review was done by Michael Morgan and James Shanahan and appears on pages 1–46 of *Communication Yearbook,* edited by Brant Burleson and published by Sage.

The typical child sees up to 20,000 commercials in a year, many for popular games and toys. The impact of television advertising and its role in consumer socialization is a popular research topic. *(B. Glover/ Index Stock)*

Effects of Special Selling Techniques

When you were much younger, you may have had an experience like the following. On Saturday morning, while watching your favorite cartoon show, you saw an ad for a toy, perhaps a plastic model truck called "Toughie." In the ad, the truck, with headlights flashing and horn blowing, was shown dumping a load of sand in the middle of a miniature construction site, surrounded by miniature construction workers. The truck was then shown close up, practically dwarfing the young child in the background. Excited, you told your parents that Toughie was the one thing you wanted most for Christmas. When Christmas arrived and you were lucky enough to find Toughie under the tree, you were disillusioned to find that the actual truck was much smaller than it had appeared to be on TV. The headlights didn't flash and the horn didn't blow because batteries weren't included with the truck. There was no sand, no miniature construction site, no tiny construction workers. Somehow, it wasn't the same toy that you remembered.

It's obvious that toys and other products designed for children can be made to look more appealing through the use of special camera angles, lenses, advertising copy, sound effects, animation, and special lighting techniques. The ability of children to distinguish the illusion created by these techniques from the real object has been an area of continuing interest among policymakers and mass communication researchers. Recently, in response to tighter industry guidelines, commercials directed toward children have included disclaimers, messages such as "Some assembly required" or "Batteries not included" or "Accessories sold separately," which are read by an announcer and/or flashed on the screen. Some critics have argued that these disclaimers are not understood by children, and several research studies have examined this area.

The effects of these special selling techniques on children are hard to summarize. At least one study found that children who saw a commercial that purposely exaggerated the appeal of a building-block game were more disappointed with the game when compared with other children who saw an ad with a more realistic depiction. Other research has shown that the wording of product disclaimers is an important factor. Young children, for example, were far more likely to understand that a toy required some assembly when they heard a disclaimer that said "You have to put it together" than when they heard the standard "Some assembly required" disclaimer.

Consumer Socialization   Consumer socialization includes all those processes by which children learn behaviors and attitudes relevant to their future behavior as consumers. Research in this area is not clear-cut, but we can make some generalizations. First, as children get older, they tend to distrust commercials and even become cynical about them. One study revealed that the percentage of youngsters who believed commercials declined to only 7 percent by the fifth grade. Second, exposure to TV commercials is not related to consumer skills, such as price comparisons. Watching a lot of commercials on TV doesn't make a person an intelligent consumer.

Another area of investigation looks at the relationship between children's exposure to advertising and materialism—that is, a preoccupation with possessions and wealth. Several studies have turned up a link between heavy exposure to ads and endorsement of materialistic values. In one study, adolescents who favorably regarded TV ads also thought that money and physical possessions were necessary for happiness.

We have seen in this brief review that some criticisms voiced by public-interest groups such as Action for Children's Television appear to be supported by research. Some children, especially younger ones, have trouble understanding the basic intent of advertising. As a child matures, repeated exposure to commercials evidently results in disillusionment and cynicism about the merits of advertising. This whole topic raises questions of regulation. It is hoped that the construction of a public policy dealing with the general issue of advertising for children is a task that organizations such as the Federal Trade Commission and the Federal Communications Commission will accomplish in the near future.

Agenda Setting

One influence of mass media that has turned up in many studies of mass communication is called the **agenda-setting effect.** (An agenda is a list of things to be considered or acted upon.) When we say that the media have an impact on agenda setting, we mean that they have the ability to choose and emphasize certain topics, thereby causing the public to perceive these issues as important. To paraphrase Bernard Cohen in his book *The Press and Foreign Policy*, we can say that the media may not always be successful in telling people what to think, but they are usually successful in telling people what to think about.

Agenda-setting studies typically concern themselves with information media: newsmagazines, newspapers, television, and radio. Much of the research on agenda setting has been carried out during political campaigns. There are two reasons for this. First, messages generated by political campaigns are usually designed to set agendas (politicians call this tactic "emphasizing the issues"). Second, political campaigns have a clear-cut beginning and end, thus making the time period for study unambiguous.

To illustrate a typical agenda-setting study, one investigation of the 1968 presidential election asked a sample of voters to rank-order what they believed to be the key issues of the campaign. While this was going on, researchers examined newsmagazines, newspapers, and television newscasts, and a ranking of campaign issues was prepared according to the time and space the media devoted to each issue. When the media's ranking was compared with the voters' ranking, there was a strikingly high degree of correspondence. In other words, the voters perceived as important those issues that the media judged important, as evidenced by the amount of coverage they received. Similar studies of more recent elections have found similar results. Although such studies strongly suggest a relationship between personal agendas and media agendas, they do not address the question of causation, an issue that we have encountered before.

Some studies indicate that there are situations in which the direction of cause and effect is unclear—or will even depend on the medium under consideration. At least two studies report that newspapers exert a greater agenda-setting effect than does television. In fact, one survey found that during a political campaign, television appeared to alter its coverage to conform to voter interest, while newspapers appeared to shape the voters' agendas.

The type of topic being covered influences agenda setting. Coverage of a concrete issue (drug abuse, energy) has a more pronounced effect than coverage of an abstract issue (federal budget deficit, nuclear arms race). Moreover, a person's experience with a topic also influences the agenda-setting effect. Stories about inflation, a topic that most consumers experience directly, have little impact on the public's perception of the importance of this issue. On the other hand, coverage of foreign affairs, where most people lack direct experience, has been found to have a considerable agenda-setting effect.

Recent reviews published in scholarly journals noted two new directions of research interest. The first pertains to the notion of **framing,** the general way a news topic is treated by the media. This line of research posits that not only do the media tell us what to think about, they also tell us how to think about it by the way the story is framed. For example, suppose Congress is considering changes in the food stamp program. One way the media might frame this story is by concentrating on both the increased efficiency that might result from the changes and the savings to taxpayers. Alternatively, the media might choose to emphasize the hardships that might be experienced by people who will no longer qualify for the program. The particular choice of frames will affect the saliency of the story and our attitudes toward the revised program.

TV coverage of high-profile congressional hearings can help shape the public's agenda. *(A. Tannenbaum/ Corbis Sygma)*

A second direction concerns **agenda building.** Research on this topic examines how the media build their agenda of newsworthy items. Some factors that seem to have an impact include presidential press conferences, congressional hearings, and public relations efforts. One recent study, for example, found that a public relations effort by the Christian Coalition was influential in shaping the media agenda some

How willing are you to express your opinion on a controversial topic if you know that only a few other people share that opinion? That is the question at the center of "the spiral of silence," a concept originated by German political scientist Elisabeth Noelle-Neumann. In her conceptualization, audience members search the information environment for evidence that their personal opinion is or is not shared by others. Their search might involve reading the results of public opinion polls, watching news programs, reading articles in newspapers and magazines, monitoring Internet newsgroups, and so forth.

If, after scanning all the information sources, a person discovers that there is a good deal of support for his or her position, that person becomes more willing to express that viewpoint in public. On the other hand, if a person finds that his or her position is supported by a minority, then that person becomes less willing to express such an unpopular view in public. This reticence may be due to a fear of becoming isolated from the majority. Over time, the minority becomes even less vocal, and the "spiral of silence" results, leading to a situation where the minority viewpoint has little impact in matters of public policy.

Professor Noelle-Neumann acknowledges that there are circumstances in which those who hold a minority opinion might be more likely to voice it, particularly if they think that their opinion is becoming more widespread. Further, there are several demographic categories that tend to be more outspoken—for example, younger people and those with higher education.

The spiral of silence hypothesis is evocative and has intuitive appeal. The bulk of research studies that have examined it have supported its existence, some more strongly than others. Moreover, researchers have determined that the phenomenon may be more complicated than initially expressed. Factors such as the nature of the issue being considered, the intensity with which the opinion is held, and differences in the way an opinion may be expressed have been identified as important influences on the process. Despite these intricacies, the spiral of silence illustrates the dynamic nature of the media's role in the formation of public opinion.

three months later. Another recent study suggested that a journalist's own personal agenda (the issues that he or she considers important) might also have an impact on the media agenda.

Television and Cognitive Skills

Television has been charged with producing a generation of couch potatoes who simply vegetate in front of the tube, showing little sign of intellectual life. What does the research tell us? This section will briefly examine the connections between TV viewing, IQ, and school achievement.

At first glance, the relationship between TV viewing and IQ seems simple enough. Heavy-viewing children tend to have slightly lower IQs. On closer examination, however, age seems to be a complicating factor. A couple of surveys showed that in children up to the age of 10 or 11, heavy viewing was associated with a higher IQ. Older children showed the opposite pattern. After about age 12, the familiar negative relationship showed up. (It may be that the general level of TV programming is geared to the level of a bright 10- or 11-year-old. As these kids get older, they tend to outgrow their attraction to TV.) Note that these data do not establish that TV *causes* a lower IQ. It may be that youngsters with a low IQ are drawn to the undemanding world of TV for entertainment.

The relationship between TV viewing and school achievement became a hot news item because of the steep drop of SAT scores in the 1970s, 1980s, and 1990s. Some critics blamed much of this decline on TV viewing. Research findings suggest that there is a slight negative relationship between school grades and TV viewing. In one study that statistically controlled for IQ, heavy-TV-viewing students tended to score lower on tests of vocabulary and language achievement than did light-viewing students, but math achievement scores were not linked to amount of TV viewing. Another study noted that the type of TV content was important. Youngsters who watched a lot of news and educational programs did better than kids who watched lots of action–adventure shows.

Past studies of the relationship between reading achievement and TV viewing are hard to summarize. Most have found a slight relationship between entertainment viewing and reading skills, but this relationship was influenced by such factors as IQ, social class, age, and parental attitudes toward reading. A 1996 study done in the Netherlands, however, offers some fresh and somewhat disturbing insights into the relationship. A panel of 1,050 second- and fourth-graders were investigated over a three-year period to see if their TV viewing had an impact on their leisure-time book reading. The researchers used statistical techniques to control for the effects of gender, social class, and intelligence. The results were consistent with those of earlier studies. The more TV these students viewed, the less time they spent with books. The researchers also tested possible reasons for this relationship. Their data highlighted two causes. First, children have generally pleasant experiences with TV viewing that lead them to think that school will be equally amusing. Since this is seldom the case, they lose their enthusiasm for school-related activities such as reading. Second, the fast pace and rapidly changing images on TV decreased the students' ability to concentrate on reading.

In short, although TV has been linked to decreased intellectual performance, its effects are complicated and its impact is relatively light. On the other hand, the hours that youngsters invest in watching TV don't seem to pay off in better academic skills.

Although their effects vary in size and are hard to detect, the mass media, particularly TV, play a meaningful role in the way we think about and perceive the world. We next examine how the media influence the way we behave.

MEDIA EFFECTS ON BEHAVIOR: A SHORT HISTORY

It was early motion pictures that first inspired questions about the impact of the entertainment media on society. After all, children would sit for hours in a darkened theater, away from parental supervision, and watch films produced by the inhabitants of Sin City (more precisely, Hollywood). During the late 1920s and early 1930s, the gangster film became quite popular. It wasn't long before concerned parents and civic groups began to question the impact of these films on their children.

Consequently, in 1929 the first full-scale investigation into the effects of the entertainment film was begun. Experiments and surveys were carried out to address such questions as these: How do the mores of the movies compare with the mores of America? Do films directly or indirectly alter the conduct of children? Are films related to delinquency and crime? Although these studies did not conclusively prove that movies caused delinquency, their findings brought a tremendous amount of pressure to bear on the government and the industry to take action. As a result, the production code of the Motion Pictures Producers and Distributors of America, a powerful industry group, was strengthened to make sure that films did not portray gangsters in a favorable light.

Growing Public Concern

The potentially harmful effects of gangster and action–adventure radio programs were the subject of limited research attention during the 1930s. The area that aroused the most research interest, however, was the political impact of the mass

media, especially that of radio. Franklin Roosevelt used radio effectively during his first two terms in office. In Louisiana, Huey Long also used radio addresses to increase his political influence. Many people feared that a skilled political demagogue might use the new radio medium to shape popular opinion to his advantage. As a result, large-scale studies of the voting process were conducted during the 1940 presidential campaign to gauge the extent of media influence. After an interruption caused by World War II, the 1948 election was similarly studied by sociologists and political scientists. Somewhat surprisingly, these researchers found that the media had little direct effect on political decision making. Instead, personal influence was more important, and individuals called opinion leaders were thought to be important in transmitting political information.

The explosive growth of television in the early 1950s and 1960s refocused research attention on media impact on young people. This research went well beyond media effects on cognition that were discussed earlier. A British study, *Television and the Child*, published in 1958, discussed the results of interviews with several thousand youngsters. The researchers concluded that TV had an impact on children's values and perceptions of the world. An American study, *Television in the Lives of Our Children*, published in 1961, found that as children got older, heavy viewing was associated with lower IQ scores and unsatisfactory social relationships. The researchers found no evidence that TV caused violent or antisocial behavior in most normal children, but they did suggest that some children might be susceptible.

During the 1960s, there was considerable concern over the impact of the mass media, as evidenced by Senate subcommittee hearings in 1961 and 1964 on juvenile delinquency. The report of this subcommittee warned that violent television content might cause antisocial behavior among young people. The concern was reinforced by the assassinations and civil disorder of the mid-1960s, and in 1967 President Lyndon Johnson appointed the National Commission on the Causes and Prevention of Violence. The commission reiterated the need for more significant research in the area and concluded that a "constant diet of violent behavior on television had an adverse effect on human character and attitudes."

At about this same time, another national commission was preparing a report on a totally different topic. Because of less stringent laws governing pornographic and obscene materials, "adult-oriented" films, books, and magazines were becoming more prevalent. The National Commission on Obscenity and Pornography was established to examine the potentially negative effects of this material. When the commission released its report in 1970, it urged, among other things, that all laws prohibiting the distribution of pornographic materials be repealed.

TV Violence

In 1970, through the efforts of Senator John Pastore, the Office of the Surgeon General was given $1 million to sponsor a research program to determine the possible harmful effects of TV violence. The research was completed and a summary report was issued in 1972. The summary was greeted with controversy when many of the scientists who had contributed to the project complained that the report minimized the negative effects of TV violence. Subsequent hearings before a congressional committee clarified the main findings of the report and emphasized that exposure to television violence could increase the probability of antisocial behavior and that there was a causal link between the viewing of TV violence and real-life aggressive behavior. A 1982 follow-up study reinforced the findings of the original research.

Media violence was the center of attention throughout the 1990s. In the early part of the decade, the broadcast networks agreed to air advisories before programs that contained violence. As mentioned in previous chapters, the Telecommunications Act of 1996 contained the provisions for a program ratings system and a V-Chip to allow parents to block violent and other unwanted TV programs from their children. In 1999, in the wake of the violence at Columbine High School, several bills to regulate TV and movie violence were introduced into Congress but, as of this writing, none has become law.

We will now examine more closely some of the topics mentioned in this summary. We begin by considering the topic that has generated the most research attention: the effects of TV violence.

THE IMPACT OF TELEVISED VIOLENCE

Does television viewing prompt violent or other antisocial behaviors on the part of the viewer? As we have just seen, this question has been debated for the better part of three decades. It is a complicated issue, and the absolute answer has not yet been found. Nonetheless, enough evidence has been gathered so that we can begin to point to some preliminary conclusions. To arrive at these conclusions, we must examine research data from surveys and from experiments.

Survey Results

The following represent abbreviated and modified questionnaire items taken from surveys designed to analyze the viewing of TV violence and aggressive behavior.

About how often do you watch the following TV programs?

	Almost Always	Often	Sometimes	Never
The Sopranos	_____	_____	_____	_____
Malcolm in the Middle	_____	_____	_____	_____
NYPD Blue	_____	_____	_____	_____
Dharma & Greg	_____	_____	_____	_____
Cops	_____	_____	_____	_____
Walker, Texas Ranger	_____	_____	_____	_____

Next, what would you do if these things happened to you?

1.   Pretend somebody you know takes something from you and won't give it back. What would you do?

_____ Hit the other person and take my property back.

_____ Call the police.

_____ Ask the person to return it.

_____ Nothing.

2.   Pretend somebody is telling lies about you. What would you do?

_____ Hit the person and make the person stop.

_____ Ask the person to stop telling lies.

_____ Nothing.

As you can see, with measures like the above (assuming, of course, a questionnaire that was much longer), it would be possible to index a person's viewing of programs that generally contain violence. It would also be possible to measure that same person's tendency to report his or her willingness to use violence in everyday situations. If viewing violent TV does affect behavior, we would expect to find some relationship between reported heavy viewing of violence and an individual's own self-report of aggressive tendencies. If we do not find such a link, we might assume that exposure to media violence has no impact on subsequent aggressive tendencies. If, however, we do find a connection, we might conclude that media violence could actually cause aggression. We could not be sure, however, because survey data alone are not sufficient to establish a cause-and-effect relationship. We must also keep in mind that there are different ways of measuring exposure to TV violence and aggressive tendencies.

Viewed as a whole, surveys compiled over the years are difficult to sum up. Perhaps the most concise generalization is one that appears in a recent summary of television research findings. After carefully analyzing all survey results, the authors of this summary state: "We conclude that the evidence to date indicates that there is a significant correlation between the viewing of violent television programs and aggressive behavior in day-to-day life."

Nevertheless, as already mentioned, a relationship is not necessarily evidence of cause and effect. Remember, however, that the special survey technique known as a panel study gives us a little more confidence in making cause-and-effect statements based on survey data. However, since panel studies cost a lot and some-

What makes some children imitate the violent acts they see on TV? Scientists have been studying this question since the early 1950s. *(Stone/Edouard Berne)*

times take years to complete, not many exist. Further, the results from those that are available are not as clear as we might like them to be. One panel study was included in the 1972 Surgeon General's report on television and social behavior. Although its methods might have been stronger, it found evidence that viewing violent TV shows at an early age was a cause of aggression in later life.

Additional survey evidence appeared in 1982 with the publication of *Television and Aggression: A Panel Study.* This book reported the results of a three-year research project sponsored by the NBC television network. Data on aggression, TV viewing, and a large number of sociological variables were collected on six different occasions from children in two Midwestern cities. Eventually, about 1,200 boys in grades two through six participated in the main survey.

Lengthy and detailed analysis of the data suggested that there was no relationship between the viewing of TV violence and subsequent aggressive behavior. Later, other researchers were given the opportunity to reanalyze the NBC data. One reexamination did find some partial evidence of a causal relationship between TV violence and aggression, but its impact was tiny. In sum, if a causal relationship was present in the NBC data, it was extremely weak and hard to find.

In 1986, an international team of scientists reported the results of panel studies done in five countries: the United States, Finland, Australia, Israel, and Poland. The U.S. study and the Polish study found that early TV viewing was significantly related to later aggression. The Finnish study reached a similar conclusion for boys but not for girls. In Israel, viewing TV violence seemed to be a cause of subsequent aggression among boys and girls who lived in urban areas, but not for those who lived in the country. The panel study done in Australia was not able to find a causal relationship. Despite these differences, the five panels were consistent in at least two findings. First, the relationship between the viewing of violence and aggression tended to be somewhat weak. Second, there was a pattern of circularity in causation. Viewing violent TV caused some children to become more aggressive. Being aggressive, in turn, caused some children to watch more violent TV.

What are we to make of all these panel studies? On the whole, they seem to suggest that there is a mutual causal connection between watching TV violence and performing aggressive acts. This connection, however, is small and influenced by individual and cultural factors. At this point, we will turn to the results of laboratory studies to aid us further in forming a conclusion about what causes what.

Experimental Results

Imagine the following. It is a cold winter night. As part of the requirements of Psychology 100, a course in which you are enrolled, you are required to serve as a subject in three hours of research. Tonight is your night to fulfill part of your obligation. Thus, you find yourself trudging across campus to the Psychology Building. Upon arriving, you join several dozen other students in a large auditorium. Before long, an individual enters the room, introduces himself as Professor So-and-so, and tells you that you are about to begin your first experiment of the evening.

Professor So-and-so has a new IQ test that he is trying to develop and needs your cooperation. The test booklet is passed out, and you are told to begin. As soon as you start the test, you realize that it is unlike any IQ test you have ever seen before. There are questions about advanced calculus, early Greek architecture, and organic chemistry, which you have no idea how to answer. In a few minutes, Professor So-and-so starts making sarcastic comments: "You'll never finish college if this simple test takes you so long"; "It looks as if this group will certainly flunk out"; "High school students have finished this test by now." Finally, with an air of exasperation, the professor says, "There's no hope for you. Hand in the papers. Since most of you won't be in school after this semester's grades, let me say good-bye to you now." With that, the professor storms out of the room.

A few minutes go by, and then another individual enters the room and calls out two lists of names. Each group is assigned to another room down the hall. When you report to your assigned room, you find another professor already there. She tells you that this is the second experiment you will participate in tonight. It is a study to see how much people remember from films. You are going to be shown a brief excerpt from a film, and then you will be asked questions about it. The lights go out, and all of a sudden you are watching an eight-minute fight scene from a Kirk Douglas film called *The Champion*. In the movie, Douglas, playing a boxer, gets the stuffing beaten out of him as he competes for the championship. (Unknown to you, that other group of students is also seeing a film. At the same time you're watching Douglas get battered, they're viewing a totally different scene from *Canal Boats in Venice*.) When the film ends, you are asked several memory questions about its content.

You are then directed to yet another room. Once in this cubicle, you are told that the third and last experiment is to begin. You are seated in front of a rather strange-looking machine with a dial that can be moved from a setting of 1 to 11. You also notice a button and a light connected to something behind the machine. The researcher explains that you are to be part of an experiment designed to investigate memory. In another room, but wired up to this same machine, is a student who is learning a word-association test. Every time this other student makes a mistake, you are to punish him by giving him a shock. The dial on your panel determines the intensity of the shock; when you press the button, it will be administered. You can choose any level you like; you can hold the button down as long as you like. The experimenter then gives you a level-2 shock to show you what it feels like. You jump and wonder why you didn't take botany instead of psych. Your thoughts are interrupted, however, when the little light on the panel flashes on. The other student has made a mistake. It's your job to administer punishment. Your hand reaches for the dial . . .

■ The Catharsis versus Stimulation Debate

The above is an abstracted, simplified, and condensed version of the prototype experimental design used in several key studies to investigate the impact of media violence. The idea behind this experiment is to test two rival theories about the effects of watching violence. The first theory is thousands of years old; it is called the **catharsis theory** and can be traced back to Aristotle. This theory holds that viewing scenes of aggression can actually purge the viewer's own aggressive feelings. Thus, a person who sees a violent television program or movie might end up less likely to commit violence. The other theory, called the **stimulation theory,** argues just the opposite. It suggests that seeing scenes of violence will actually stimulate an individual to behave more violently afterward.

As you may realize, in the above hypothetical experiment, everybody was first insulted and presumably angered (this part of the experiment gave you some hostility to be purged); one group saw a violent film while the other saw a nonviolent film. Both groups were then given a turn at the punishment machine. If catharsis is right, then the group that saw *The Champion* should give less intense shocks; if stimulation is correct, then *The Champion* group should give more intense shocks.

The catharsis versus stimulation debate was one of the earliest to surface in the study of mass media's effects. One early study seemed to point to catharsis, but a series of studies carried out by psychologist Leonard Berkowitz and his colleagues at the University of Wisconsin found strong support for the stimulation hypothesis. Since that time, the bulk of the evidence seems consistent: Watching media violence tends to stimulate aggressive behavior on the part of the viewer. There is little evidence for catharsis.

Bandura's Experiment

The catharsis versus stimulation question was only one of several topics that sparked early experimental work in the investigation of the effects of the media. Another controversy arose over the possibility that TV and movies were serving as a school for violence. Would children imitate violent behavior they had just observed in films or TV programs? A series of experiments conducted by psychologist Albert Bandura and his colleagues during the 1960s indicated that, in fact, films and TV might teach aggressive behaviors.

Preschool children were shown films in which a model reacted violently to a large rubber doll (called a Bobo doll). When children were placed in a play situation similar to the one they had just observed, they mimicked the behaviors they had seen, performing far more aggressively toward the unfortunate Bobo doll than did children who had not seen the film. It was further determined that children would behave more aggressively if they were rewarded for doing so or if they saw the model in the film rewarded. Of course, as you are probably aware, there is a big difference between hitting an inanimate doll and hitting a human

A series of still photographs of the famous study by Bandura, Ross, and Ross (1961). In this experiment, children watched adults act aggressively toward a Bobo doll. When allowed to play in the same room, these children imitated the behavior of the adult models. *(Albert Bandura)*

being. To account for this, more recent studies have substituted a human being dressed as a clown for the faithful Bobo doll. Although more children were willing to hit the rubber doll, a large number also physically assaulted the human clown. This reaction did not occur among children who had not seen the violent film.

◾ Complicating Factors

Of course, many complicating factors might influence the results of such experiments. To begin with, many of these studies used specially made films and videotapes. In laboratory situations, the experimental "program" may not duplicate the impact of real-life TV or films. In those films and tapes produced especially for laboratory use, the violence is concentrated in a short period; there is usually a clear connection between the violence and its motivations and consequences. Films and TV shows are not this direct, and violence is usually embedded in a larger story line. Punishment for violence may not occur until the end of the program. Motives may be mixed or unclear.

Further, it is likely that a person's age, sex, social class, and prior level of aggression influence the ultimate effect of viewing televised violence. Boys, for example, tend to be more affected by TV violence than girls. Children who come from homes where there are no explicit guidelines condemning violence also seem to be strongly affected. It also appears that a similarity between the circumstances surrounding televised violence and the situation in which a person finds himself or herself immediately after viewing is an important factor. The more alike the two settings, the more aggressively the person is likely to behave.

Finally, the reactions of other people directly influence aggression. If children were watching an aggressive film in the company of an adult who made positive comments about the media violence, they acted more aggressively than children who viewed with a silent adult. Conversely, children who heard the on-screen aggression condemned committed fewer aggressive acts. It has also been shown that children who view violence in pairs act more aggressively than children who are alone.

◾ Field Experiments

In field experiments, people are studied in their typical environment, where they probably react more naturally than they do in the lab. Field experiments are therefore subject to the contaminating influences of outside events.

At least two field experiments done in the early 1970s revealed no link between TV and aggression. On the other hand, five field experiments have yielded data consistent with the survey and lab data. Their main conclusion is that people who watched a steady diet of violent programs tended to exhibit more antisocial or aggressive behavior.

One of the more elaborate field experiments involved identifying a Canadian town that did not receive a TV signal until 1974. Two similar towns were selected for comparison—one could get only Canadian TV, while the other could get Canadian and U.S. channels. The research team gathered data from all three towns in 1974 and again two years later. Children in the town that recently received access to U.S. TV showed an increase in their rate of aggressive acts that was more than three times higher than that of children living in the other two towns. Taken as a whole, the results from the field experiments tend to support the notion that viewing TV violence fosters aggressive behavior.

What Can We Conclude?

Let us now try to summarize the results of these surveys and experiments. Although no single survey or experiment can provide a conclusive answer, and although every study has certain shortcomings, there appears to be a thread of consistency running throughout these studies. Surveys and panel studies have shown a relationship between the viewing of violent programs and aggressive behavior. Lab and field experiments also have shown that watching violence increases the possibility of behaving aggressively. Taken as a whole, these results encourage a tentative acceptance of the proposition that watching violence on television increases aggressiveness on the part of at least some viewers.

However, viewing TV violence is only one of many factors that might prompt a person to behave aggressively and, in relative terms, its influence is not particularly strong. But is a weak relationship an inconsequential relationship? Much of the recent debate about TV violence has centered on this question. In statistical terms, researchers gauge the strength of any relationship by the amount of variability in one measure that is accounted for by the other. For example, height and weight are two factors that are related. If I know how tall you are, I can make a better guess about your weight than if I didn't know your height. I may not get your weight exactly right, but at least I'll be closer to the correct figure. Consequently, height "explains" some of the variability associated with weight. If two factors are perfectly related, one explains 100 percent of the variability of the other. If two factors are not related, (for example, weight and IQ), one would explain 0 percent of the variability of the other. Exposure to TV violence typically explains from about 2 percent to 9 percent of the variability of aggression. In other words, about 91 percent to 98 percent of the variability in aggression is due to something else. Given these figures, can we conclude that the impact of TV violence is really that important?

The answer to that question is more political and philosophical than scientific, but research does provide some benchmarks for comparison. In psychology, the relationship between undergoing psychotherapy and being "cured" of your mental ailment is only slightly stronger than that between TV violence and aggression. Psychotherapy explains about 10 percent of the variability in cure rates. In relative terms, however, this means that psychotherapy increases the success rate from 34 percent to 66 percent of patients, hardly an outcome to be labeled inconsequential. Moreover, the effect size for TV violence's impact on antisocial behavior is only slightly less than that of the effect size between viewing "Sesame Street" and readiness for school. "Sesame Street," of course, was regarded as a great success. Furthermore, the Food and Drug Administration has released for general use several drugs whose therapeutic effect was about as great or even less than the size of the effect between TV violence and aggression. Thus, although the effect might be small, it is not necessarily trivial.

ENCOURAGING PROSOCIAL BEHAVIOR

Most early research into the effects of mass communication dealt with the negative or antisocial effects of the media. Toward the end of the 1960s, however, sparked perhaps by the success of public television's "Sesame Street," researchers realized that positive behaviors could be promoted by television programs. (These behaviors are generally referred to by the umbrella term **prosocial behavior** and can include actions such as sharing, cooperating, developing self-control, and helping.)

Developing Self-Control

Laboratory experiments have shown that films and TV programs can affect a young child's self-control. These studies typically use a brief television program to depict a particular aspect of self-control. This program is shown to one group of children, while other groups see a different program or perhaps no program at all. For example, in a study designed to examine children's resistance to temptation, five-year-olds were brought into a room containing several attractive toys and a dictionary. The boys were told they could not play with the toys but could look at the dictionary (not exactly a five-year-old's idea of fun). These boys were then divided into three groups. One group saw no film; a second group saw a film in which a boy played with these toys and was even joined by his mother (this was called the "model-rewarded" condition). In yet a third condition, youngsters saw a film in which a boy played with the toys but was scolded for doing so when his mother entered the room (this was the "model-punished" condition). Each boy was then left alone in the room, and hidden observers measured how much time each spent playing with the forbidden toys and how long it took to disobey. As you might expect, those boys who saw the model-punished film resisted temptation for the longest period of time and spent the least time playing with the toys.

Cooperation, Sharing, and Helping

Experiments that have investigated sharing behavior usually use the same basic approach as described above in the self-control experiments. In this instance, however, children watch a film depicting a model playing a game and receiving a prize for winning (usually money). A film model then donates part of his or her winnings to charity. The child then wins at the same game and is also given the option to donate some money to charity. In general, the many experiments in this area indicate that observing a generous model prompts young people to behave more generously. Other experiments have shown that children are willing to imitate cooperative behavior that they have seen portrayed in a television program.

The lovable Blue from "Blue's Clues," a program with obvious prosocial messages. *(Ted Thai/TimePix)*

Survey Data

There is little survey research analyzing prosocial behavior. Some data exist, however. Research on the CBS series "Fat Albert and the Cosby Kids" revealed that about 90 percent of approximately 700 children who veiwed the show were able to express at least one prosocial theme from episodes of the series. Other research indicated that children who watched "Sesame Street" were able to identify accurately the cooperation messages contained in that program. Thus it appears that the prosocial messages are at least perceived. Do these messages influence the day-to-day behavior? One large-scale survey found little relationship between viewing prosocial programs and performing

"Sesame Street" is probably the most successful educational television program ever produced. After its debut in 1969, the show was showered with praise from critics, parents, teachers, and children. Initial projects indicated that the program was accomplishing its educational goals. However, "Sesame Street" did not succeed without generating some criticism.

Seven years after its inception, "Sesame Street" had established itself as an international favorite. The program was viewed regularly in more than 40 countries around the world, and Big Bird, Cookie Monster, and Oscar had become household words. Children in Latin America watched "Plaza Sesamo"; in Germany, "Sesamstrasse"; and in Holland, "Sesamstraat."

With international prominence came international problems. The Spanish-language version, "Plaza Sesamo," was faced with the difficult task of producing a program that would adequately reflect the diverse subcultures of 22 million Latin-American preschoolers. For example, the program ignored the language variations in favor of a standardized approach. Further, although Latin America has many varietes of folk music, the first series of "Plaza Sesamo" contained only one Latin-American selection per program; other selections consisted of American rock. Soon critics of the program charged that "Plaza Sesamo" was submerging local culture and substituting a standardized American-influenced culture in its place.

Despite good intentions, "Sesame Street" ran into political problems. A joint Palestinian–Israeli version of the show debuted in 1998 but quickly ran into trouble. Both the Israelis and the Palestinians criticized the show for perpetuating stereotypes. Production on the series was subsequently halted. A proposed South African version of the show had to use 11 official languages to satisfy political concerns.

Another criticism that emerged closer to home complained that "Sesame Street" was teaching too well. One of the program's original goals was to aid the intellectual growth of disadvantaged children, and the show was clearly meeting this goal. However, advantaged children were also watching "Sesame Street" and learning from it, sometimes at a faster pace than their disadvantaged counterparts. As a result, "Sesame Street" had done little to narrow the gap between the two groups and, in fact, might even have widened it. Other educators criticized the program's fast-paced format, which contrasted dramatically with the slower-paced classroom environment. Such a frenetic format, these educators claimed, might contribute to hyperactivity and other behavioral problems.

More recent criticisms have to do with the increasing trend toward commercializing the "Sesame Street" characters. Dolls and other figures based on the characters have always been popular (consider "Tickle Me Elmo"), but the latest trend has seen the program form partnerships with well-known companies. In 2000 the Keebler Company introduced a Cookie Monster line of cookies (they're chocolate chips with a C on one side and the Cookie Monster's likeness on the other). They will be joined by Elmo Tickles and Bert and Ernie Cookie Pals. In addition, Kmart has introduced "Sesame Street" clothing. One of its TV commercials ends with the line, "This is brought to you by the letter K—for Kmart." Or should that be K for Keebler? Is "Sesame Street" teaching kids that learning and consuming go hand in hand?

prosocial acts in school, when all other variables were statistically controlled. A recent study done among children in the Netherlands also found no relationship between TV viewing and prosocial behavior.

Judging from these studies, we can say that the relationship between viewing and prosocial behavior is much weaker than that between viewing and aggressive behavior. Closer examination indicates why this should be the case. Violent behaviors as portrayed on TV and in films are blatant, easy to see, and physical; prosocial behaviors are subtle, sometimes complicated, and largely verbal. Because children learn better from simple, direct, and active presentations, aggressive behaviors may be more easily learned from media content. Further, since most children are taught early in life that they should be friendly, helpful, and cooperative, media content may only reinforce what children already know. On the other hand, aggressive behavior is usually punished at home and at school, and frequent viewing of it on TV might serve to overcome children's inhibitions against performing this discouraged behavior. It appears that much more research evidence is necessary before the total impact of the media on prosocial behavior is known.

OTHER BEHAVIOR EFFECTS

Political Behavior

Trying to summarize the many studies that have been conducted about the influences of the media on politics would require far more space than we have available. Consequently, we will restrict our discussion to the more central findings. At the core of our current discussion will be an examination of the individual's most important political behavior, the ultimate payoff in any political campaign—namely, voting behavior.

Studies of Voter Turnout   Voter turnout in presidential elections generally increased from 1924 to 1960 (if we exclude the war years). From that time, however, the trend has been reversed, and fewer people have voted in presidential elections. Have the media had an impact in this area? The data are not conclusive, and many people have different viewpoints. At least one political scientist has argued that part of the increased voter turnout from 1930 to 1940 was due to the impact of radio. As this new medium reached those who were less educated, less politically involved, and beyond the reach of printed media, it apparently stimulated greater interest in politics and increased the tendency to vote. The parallel emergence of TV did not have such an impact, although many argued that the visual dimension of TV would make the political process more vivid and so further increase participation. But turnout has decreased, starting with the 1964 election (the first election in which the first "TV generation" would be eligible to vote). A current explanation for this drop holds the unique characteristics of TV news as partly responsible. TV news, it is argued, presents the news in such a way that it is hard to avoid messages about the opposition. Seeing an opponent making a good case for his or her position rarely converts a voter, but it might make that voter less sure of his or her own views and more confused. As a result, these voters might simply tune out and become less interested in politics and voting.

Data from presidential elections from 1960 to 1976 indicate that the frequency of reading a newspaper was strongly related to voter turnout, but radio and television exposure was not. These data suggest that the recent decline in newspaper reading among those of voting age might be part of the cause of the low turnout, rather than the alleged confusion that might result from viewing TV news. Obviously, the relationship between media exposure and voter turnout is complicated.

Recent political campaigns have centered attention on negative political advertising. Although there is no standard definition of this term, most political experts interpret it as a personal attack on the opposing candidate or an attack on

Presidential debates, such as those between George W. Bush and Al Gore in the 2000 campaign, have become a common sight. The average audience for this series of debates was the smallest ever, a result of competition from the baseball playoffs and new programming on the Fox network. *(Reuters NewMedia Inc./Corbis)*

what the opposing candidate stands for. There was much speculation that negative advertising would turn off voters, make them distrustful of politics, and make them less inclined to participate in the political process. Both survey and laboratory research suggested that most of these fears were unfounded. When compared with those who did not view negative ads, voters who were exposed to negative ads were just as likely to vote, were just as involved, and showed little difference in the amount of trust they placed in the political system. There was a tendency, however, for negative advertising to be related to more polarized attitudes, but this polarization didn't seem to have much impact on political behavior.

More recent surveys indicate that those candidates who use a lot of negative advertising tend to receive a lower proportion of the vote. This does not necessarily mean that negative ads are ineffective; it may be that candidates who are behind in preelection polls turn to negative advertising since they have little to lose. (For a summary of the rather voluminous literature on negative advertising, read Chapter 5 in *Television: What's On, Who's Watching, and What it Means,* by George Comstock and Erica Scharrer.)

Effects of the Mass Media on Voter Choice A person's decision to vote for a particular candidate is affected by not only the mass media but also many other factors, both social and psychological. Still, some tentative generalizations can be made. First of all, it would appear that conversion (changing your vote from Republican to Democrat, for example) is unlikely to result from media exposure, because it is difficult for the media to persuade someone whose mind is already made up to change, and because most people (roughly two-thirds) have already made up their minds before the campaign begins. Far more common are two effects that have a direct bearing on voter choice: **reinforcement** and **crystallization.** Reinforcement means the strengthening or support of existing attitudes and opinions. Crystallization means the sharpening and elaboration of vaguely held attitudes or predispositions. If a person approaches a campaign undecided or neutral, then crystallization is likely to occur. If the person has already made up his or her mind, then reinforcement will probably take place.

In recent national elections, there has been an increase in ticket splitting (supporting one party's candidate for president and another's for governor, for example). This phenomenon may be due to crystallization, which in turn results from exposure to mass media. The flow of information during the campaign evidently crystallizes a voter's vague intention, and, in many instances, these new choices do not square with party loyalty. On the other hand, when partisan voters are exposed to the media, reinforcement is likely.

These findings do not necessarily mean that the media are not influential. A key factor in winning any election is to keep the party faithful loyal (reinforcement) and to persuade enough of the undecideds to vote for your side (crystallization). Thus, even though widespread conversion is not usually seen, the media are still influential. Even more important, the media may have significant indirect influence on the electorate. By serving as important sources of political news, by structuring "political reality," and by creating an image of candidates and issues, the media may have a potent effect on a person's attitudes about the political system. Furthermore, our discussion has been mainly concerned with the effects of the media in national elections. Local elections present a somewhat different picture. Most research evidence indicates that the media, especially local newspapers, might be highly influential in affecting voter choice in a city, county, or district election.

The election night TV coverage of the 2000 presidential race will be remembered as the night the networks blew it—twice. Network projections of the winning candidate in a given state are a familiar part of election night coverage. These projections are based on exit polls and allow the networks to "call" a given state shortly after or even before the polls in a state have closed. The networks compete with one another to be the first to make these various calls. These calls are accurate the vast majority of the time, but not always, as the situation in Florida on election night 2000 proved.

Network policy is to hold off calling a state until the vast majority of the polls in the state are closed. The networks (ABC, CBS, NBC, Fox, and CNN) predicted that Vice President Al Gore had won Florida at 7:50 P.M., Eastern Time, when 95 percent of the state's polling places had closed. Since Florida extends across two time zones, however, polls were still open in the western panhandle of the state. As the evening wore on, and the actual votes began to be counted, it became evident that the initial call might be wrong. All the networks then shifted the state into the "too close to call" category. Shortly after 2 A.M., the networks reversed their earlier decision and declared that George W. Bush had won the state. An hour or so later, the networks were embarrassed to report that they had been wrong again and once more put the state into the "too close to call" category.

What went wrong? All the networks have different rules about when to call a state, but they all use the same exit poll data, supplied by the Voter News Service (VNS). VNS was set up in 1990 as a cost-cutting measure. Before VNS, each network did its own exit polling. It turned out that the VNS data were flawed, and each network used the same flawed data to make its call. Had each network done its own polling, as they did before 1990, it is unlikely that all of them would have made the same mistakes. In addition, the race to be first to call a key state prompted the networks to make predictions early, before the actual vote totals revealed the flaws in the exit polls.

The networks, of course, were mortified by their mistakes. NBC anchor Tom Brokaw said that the networks didn't have egg on their faces, they had "omelets all over their suits."

Did the bad calls have any real impact on the election? Remember that research has generally shown that early calls don't have much impact on the final totals. It would seem unlikely that the early call had much of an effect in Florida. In the first place, it was made only 10 minutes before the remaining polls were to close. Therefore, a person had to (1) be standing in line to vote or almost at a polling place, (2) hear about the early call, (3) believe it, and then (4) decide to go home and not vote for all the other statewide races on the ballot or vote anyway and just leave the presidential race blank. It would seem that the number of people who did all the above would be small. Still, in a race decided by a few hundred votes, even a small number might make a difference.

In addition, some claimed that people on the West Coast who heard the early incorrect call for Gore in the key state of Florida might have assumed that Gore was going to be the eventual winner and decided to not go to the polls in the first place. It was also argued that the incorrect call for Bush fostered a perception that he had been elected president, a situation that made the Gore recount battle more difficult to win.

In any case, after the dust had settled, bills were introduced in Congress to set a uniform poll-closing time for all the states so that early calls could never be made. This idea has come up before but has never been enacted into law. Perhaps the Florida fiasco might improve its chances.

The Debates   A basic knowledge of the effects of mass media on politics would not be complete without an examination of presidential debates. The 1960 debate, which pitted John F. Kennedy against Richard Nixon, was the first presidential debate in the electronic era. Because of this, it was also the most researched debate, inspiring 31 different studies. One of the more interesting research projects compared the opinions of people who had watched the first debate on television with those who had listened on radio. Among those who listened to radio, Nixon was more often perceived as the "winner" of the debate. Among those who watched on TV, Kennedy was seen as the winner. Subsequent analysis suggested Kennedy had a better and more appealing TV appearance than did Nixon. This outcome emphasized the importance of a successful TV image for a candidate seeking the presidency.

Other findings from these studies of the 1960 debate demonstrated that reinforcement seemed to be the main effect, since many had already made up their minds prior to the debate. There was also evidence of crystallization in that independent voters became more favorable to one or the other candidate throughout the course of the debates. Significantly, more independents shifted to Kennedy. All in all, the number of voters actually influenced appeared rather small. The 1960 election, however, was decided by a tenth of a percentage point. Thus, even a relatively small effect in terms of numbers might have an enormous social impact.

The two debates between Ronald Reagan and Walter Mondale in the 1984 campaign were studied extensively. Surveys showed that Mondale "won" the first debate, with even Reagan supporters conceding that he performed better than their candidate. The polls showed that Reagan scored a narrow victory in the second debate. In any event, the debates had apparently little effect in determining the final outcome. Reagan had a lopsided lead all through the campaign, which was translated into a landslide victory on election day. If anything, the 1984 debates again demonstrated the reinforcement effect. After the debates, about 85 percent of the moderate Mondale supporters and 75 percent of the moderate Reagan supporters made their final decision to vote for their candidate. The 1988 debates between George Bush and Michael Dukakis showed the same pattern.

The 1996 debates between Bill Clinton and Bob Dole also seemed to have little impact on voter choice. Clinton went into the debates with a big lead that did not diminish after the debates were over. In short, as noted in Friedenberg's book cited in the Suggestions for Further Reading at the end of the chapter: The principal effect of presidential debates is to reinforce rather than shift voter attitudes. TV debates crystallize opinion far more often than they convert.

Television and the Political Behavior of Politicians On a general level, it is clear that the emergence of television has affected the political behavior of politicians and political campaigns. A comparison of pre-TV practices with those occurring after TV's adoption reveals the following:

1. Nominating conventions are now planned with television in mind. They are designed not so much to select a candidate as to make a favorable impression on public opinion.
2. Television has increased the cost of campaigning.
3. Television has become the medium around which most campaigns are organized.
4. Campaign staffs now typically include one or more television consultants whose job it is to advise the candidate on his or her television image.

Bill Clinton's 1992 presidential campaign was significant because it was the first to use the newer communications media—the Internet, e-mail, satellite news conferences—and nontraditional media—talk radio, TV interview shows, MTV—to get its message across. By 2000, however, the novelty of this approach had worn off and presidential candidates relied more on traditional communications media to reach voters. Perhaps the most notable thing about the 1996 and 2000 elections was the emergence of the World Wide Web as a channel of political communication. Many candidates for federal and state offices established their own websites, where they presented their messages directly to voters.

Effects of Obscenity and Pornography

Research into the effects of obscene and pornographic material is not as advanced as is research in the other areas we have examined. The most concerted effort in this area was conducted by the Commission on Obscenity and Pornography, which sponsored a three-year study of the impact of such material. Although the commission was unable to issue a unanimous statement, its major research findings are of interest. The commission found that the most frequent users of pornography were middle-class and middle-aged males. It found no evidence that viewing pornography was related to antisocial or deviant behavior and attitudes. Further, the commission even stated that pornographic material served a positive function in some healthy sexual relationships. The majority of this commission went so far as to make the politically unpopular recommendation that all laws prohibiting the sale of this material to adults should be repealed. The Nixon administration repudiated the recommendations of this body in 1970, and since that time, the report has been largely ignored.

During the next decade, however, pornography became more abundant and more extreme. In addition, the results of new research cast doubt on the conclusions of the earlier commission. A new National Commission on Pornography was appointed in 1984 and released its report in 1986. Surrounded by political considerations, the new commission concluded that pornography, particularly violent pornography, was harmful and that its distribution should be curtailed. More recent studies have found that sexual arousal might be linked to subsequent aggressive behavior if other outlets for release are not available. Other research has indicated that the responses of males and females to this content are becoming more alike.

In addition, several studies done in the mid-1980s found a disturbing link between exposure to pornography and feelings of callousness toward women. In one experiment, college students were divided into three groups. One group saw 36 erotic films over a six-week period. A second saw 18 erotic and 18 nonerotic films over the same period, while a control group saw 36 nonerotic films. After the viewing period was over, all groups were questioned concerning their attitudes toward pornography, rape, and women in general. The group that received the heaviest dose of pornography was less likely to think that pornography was offensive, had less compassion for women as rape victims, and was less supportive of women's rights than were the other groups.

The most recent debate in this area is over the relative effects of violent versus nonviolent pornography. Several studies have noted a link between exposure to films that were both violent and pornographic and feelings of sexual callousness toward women. But is it the violence or the pornography that is the cause? At least one study has found the same result after viewing nonviolent pornography, but others have failed to replicate this finding.

In 1995, a comprehensive review of 30 experiments in this area produced some interesting conclusions. The authors found that exposure to erotic materials that contained only nudity was actually related to diminished subsequent aggressive behavior. There was also a relatively small connection between exposure to nonviolent pornography and aggression and a somewhat stronger link between violent pornography and the subsequent performance of aggressive behavior. In short, viewing pornography, whether violent or nonviolent, tended to increase aggressive behavior, at least as measured in the laboratory.

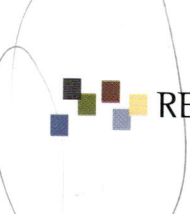

RESEARCH ABOUT THE SOCIAL EFFECTS OF THE INTERNET

Obviously, research concerning the effects of spending time on the Internet is still in a formative stage. Nonetheless, we can already identify three major trends in net studies:

1. The impact of Internet use on other media.
2. The relationship between Internet use and social involvement.
3. Internet addiction.

The Internet seems to have had the most impact on television usage. This is not surprising since much Internet use takes place during the evening—the same time that most TV viewing generally takes place. Magazine and newspaper reading, radio listening, and moviegoing seem not to have been significantly affected.

As mentioned in Chapter 12, the Internet is becoming more important as a source of news. At the same time, there has been a decline in the number of people who rely on broadcast TV and newspapers as their main sources of news. At the moment, however, online news sources are no threat to replace traditional TV and print journalism.

Research results concerning the Internet and social involvement have been contradictory. A 1998 survey of online users revealed that as people used the Internet more, they spent less time speaking with their family, experienced more loneliness and depression, and reported fewer friendships. In short, heavy net users seemed to be more socially isolated than those who were light users. A second survey done by researchers at Stanford University contained similar findings. (If the link is still active, you can read this report for yourself at www.stanford.edu/group/siqss.) Respondents to this survey who were regular Internet users reported spending less time with friends and family, going to fewer social events, and spending less time on the phone talking to friends and family.

Another survey released in 2000 by the Pew Internet and American Life Project found the opposite. This study reported that net use was an important factor in sustaining and strengthening social and family ties. About a third of the respondents to this survey noted that they had used e-mail or the web to resume communication with a family member or a friend they hadn't contacted in the past. (As of late 2000, this report was available online at www.pewinternet.org.) In short, it's a little too early to make a generalization about this topic. Perhaps subsequent studies can clear up the inconsistency.

Research has demonstrated that some individuals spend a great deal of time on the Internet. This has led to the suggestion by some social scientists that people can be addicted to the Internet in the same way they might be addicted to drugs, gambling, or alcohol. Psychologists have identified three characteristics of an addiction: increased tolerance, loss of control, and withdrawal. People who find themselves spending more and more time online, who can't control their Internet use, and who neglect family, friends, and other social obligations to spend time online would seem to fit these criteria. One recent study in the *Journal of Affective Disorders* examined the habits of 20 individuals who reported spending more than 30 nonworking hours online per week for three years. The individuals reported that they skipped sleep, ignored family responsibilities, and came late to work so that they could spend more time on the web. Many also suffered from marital problems, flunked out of school, or lost a job. There is even a website for those who think they may be addicted: http://www.computeraddiction.com.

Even though **Internet addiction** may be poorly researched and vaguely defined, with millions more people going online every year, it has the potential to be a significant social problem.

COMMUNICATION IN THE FUTURE: SOCIAL IMPACT

Let's close this chapter (and this book) with an examination of some of the relevant questions about the impact of the new communications technology on society. Advances in media technology usually have an upside and a downside. The telephone, for example, made communication at a distance much more convenient. It also meant that we could be interrupted, awakened, or bothered at any hour of the day or night. Radio and television brought immediate access to information and entertainment but also encouraged the growth of couch potatoes. What might the future bring?

Privacy

Cellular phones have greatly expanded the communications potential of the telephone. The new phones can go anywhere: to the supermarket, in the car, to a restaurant, wherever. Although we're still not quite to the point of the personal communicators worn by Spock and Kirk, the telephone is moving in that direction. On the downside, keep in mind that cellular phones are simply miniature radio stations and anybody with the right equipment, such as a scanner, can pick up all your conversations.

Computers are now common in the workplace. Word-processing programs have improved efficiency, and database programs have made it possible to analyze and manipulate large amounts of data. Computers, however, have opened up other threats to privacy. Some systems allow supervisors to monitor every keystroke of their employees to observe productivity. E-mail, no matter how personal, can be read by anyone with access to the system. Consumers who subscribe to computerized data services run the risk of having their personal files examined by unauthorized persons.

In the past, spying on our personal habits was made difficult simply because information was scattered about in different places. Now computers store huge amounts of information about us in one centralized place, the computer's memory, that is easily accessed from anywhere over phone lines. We willingly provide a lot of this information when we apply for a credit card, buy a car or a house, take out insurance, file a lawsuit, claim unemployment benefits, and so on. What many consumers don't know is that a lot of this information is sold to other organizations for other purposes. This is one of the reasons why many of us are hit with barrages of junk mail from organizations we've never heard of.

Computer scanning systems used at the checkout counters of supermarkets and drug and discount stores now record your every purchase. Such information is invaluable to marketers. The makers of Mylanta could offer discounts to people who regularly buy Tums to get them to switch to their product. Bumblebee Tuna could send free samples to Chicken of the Sea buyers. Although this is great for marketing purposes, it is troubling for consumers. If you're like the rest of us, there are some purchases you make that you might like to keep private. Do you want everybody to know what kind of birth control method you use?

Fragmentation and Isolation

The mass media are increasingly serving the needs of more specialized audiences. Magazines, radio stations, and cable TV networks, with their highly targeted niche audiences, are the best examples of this trend, but the other media are mov-

Will the home computer increase isolation as more people interact online and not in person? *(Mark Richards/PhotoEdit)*

ing in this direction. The media are increasingly directing individuals toward more selective content exposure. If this trend continues, it might result in a generation of consumers fragmented into smaller and smaller interest groups with little in common with the rest of society. If people are overspecialized in their interests, they may run the risk of being ignorant about the rest of the world.

This phenomenon has been labeled the cocoon effect by sociologists. From their perspective, it refers to the process, already evident in the 1990s, whereby people surround themselves with only the political and social information that they find comforting, appealing, or acceptable. It's as though people retreat into their informational cocoon to escape some of the uncertainty of modern life and to help reduce the multitude of choices that have to be made in today's society. It seems possible that this cocooning could generalize into cultural and recreational use of knowledge as well.

Moreover, as telecommuting becomes more popular, more and more people will stay at home. The computer will let people work, bank, shop, and be entertained at home. Services such as webvan.com and kozmo.com deliver books, groceries, flowers, movies, meals, medicines, diapers, and deodorants direct to a consumer's door. With worries over personal safety mounting daily, will people decide to just stay at home?

Overload in the Information Society

As is fairly evident, the United States and a good portion of the rest of the world have entered the information age. News, data, and entertainment have become the most important products of society as we move into the postindustrial age. This transition means that the individual is faced with a plethora of choices for knowledge and recreation: thousands of magazines, 500-channel cable TV systems, dozens of radio stations, thousands of books, print and electronic newspapers, movies on videocassette, pay-per-view TV, direct broadcast satellites, websites, and so forth. The world's knowledge base is doubling every eight years. A study done in Japan found that the production of information is growing at a rate that is four times faster than the consumption of information. Some observers have said we are creating an "infoglut." How can an individual manage this flood of information without drowning in it?

It's likely that those who succeed in the future will be the ones who can maximize the efficiency of their information-seeking behavior. Since there is a finite amount of time in a day, it makes sense to examine the media menu available to us and to select only those items that will fulfill our most important needs. It's not too early for you to start this process. Analyze your own patterns of media consumption. How well do they stack up against your long-term needs and requirements?

■ Escape

The issue of escape has been around almost since the time that the mass media were invented. Many parents and educators were worried that young people would much prefer to spend time in the media world instead of the real world. Social critics have painted bleak pictures of mesmerized children attending to various forms of media: radio, movies, TV, video games, and net surfing. In the future, this concern might have more validity since the media realities that are available are becoming more and more lifelike. Home theaters that duplicate the theater experience are already on the market. Big-screen HDTV sets with stereo sound and interactive features are also available. Manufacturers of video games are experimenting with ways to make their displays three-dimensional. And who knows what advances will be made in the virtual reality area? What happens when it's far more fun to be in some media-generated reality than in real life? In fact, virtual reality simulations raise the question, What exactly is "real" life anyway? Will large numbers of us abandon socially relevant pursuits for a romp in the media world?

And what happens farther down the road? In William Gibson's 1984 novel *Neuromancer*, people plug computer chips, called "stims," directly into their brains. Stims provide experiences for all the senses, usually preprogrammed, but there is also the possibility of becoming a "rider," traveling through the world computer matrix (which bears an eerie resemblance to the Internet) or even shifting yourself into another person's reality and experiencing the world as the other person experiences it. Could this be the ultimate media experience? Alternate realities hardwired into the cerebral cortex? You decide.

■ MAIN POINTS

- Surveys and experiments are the two main quantitative techniques used to study the effects of mass communication.

- Media can serve as socialization forces when they are the primary sources of information about a topic and that information is presented in a consistent manner.

- Media can cultivate false perceptions of reality among some heavy users.

- TV ads directed at children can influence attitudes and perceptions about certain products.

- The media can set the priority of certain issues for the public.

- TV viewing does little to help academic skills.

- TV violence shows a small but persistent correlation with antisocial behavior among heavy viewers.

- Experiments have shown that TV can produce prosocial behavior, but little evidence of this effect has been found in surveys.

- Television has had little effect on voter turnout. The media are more effective in reinforcing or crystallizing a person's voting choice. TV has had significant impact on the conduct of politicians and political campaigns.

- Exposure to pornography has been linked to feelings of sexual callousness.

- The main topics of research concerning the Internet are its effects on the usage of other media, the relationship between social isolation and online media use, and the new phenomenon of Internet addiction.

- Future concern about the effects of mass communications have implications in the areas of privacy, isolation, and escape.

■ QUESTIONS FOR REVIEW

1. What are the two main methods that social scientists use to investigate media effects?

2. What gets cultivated in a cultivation analysis?

3. Summarize the catharsis versus stimulation debate. What viewpoint does research evidence favor?

4. What is the difference between the public's agenda and the media's agenda?

5. How do the media influence the voting choices of the audience?

■ QUESTIONS FOR CRITICAL THINKING

1. Why is it difficult to establish the effects of mass communication?

2. Young children are not the only ones who go through a socialization period. College students have to be socialized as well. What were the main socialization agencies that prepared you to fit into college life? How important were the media?

3. How are college students portrayed on prime-time TV? Do these portrayals perpetuate any stereotypes?

4. Why has the debate over media violence gone on so long? Will scientists ever amass enough evidence to satisfy everybody? Why or why not?

5. What sorts of research projects should be developed to study the social impact of the Internet?

■ KEY TERMS

survey (p. 482)
panel study (p. 482)
experiment (p. 483)
field experiment (p. 483)
agencies of socialization (p. 483)
cultivation analysis (p. 487)

mainstreaming (p. 489)
resonance (p. 489)
agenda-setting effect (p. 492)
framing (p. 493)
agenda building (p. 493)
catharsis theory (p. 500)

stimulation theory (p. 500)
prosocial behavior (p. 503)
reinforcement (p. 507)
crystallization (p. 507)
Internet addiction (p. 511)

■ SUGGESTIONS FOR FURTHER READING

Bryant, Jennings, and Dolf Zillmann. *Media Effects*. Hillsdale, NJ: Erlbaum, 1994.

Comstock, George, and Erica Scharrer. *Television: What's On, Who's Watching, and What It Means*. New York: Academic Press, 1999.

Harris, Richard. *A Cognitive Psychology of Mass Communication*. Hillsdale, NJ: Erlbaum, 1999.

Heibert, Ray. *Impact of Mass Media*. New York: Longman, 1995.

Jeffres, Leo, and Richard Perloff. *Mass Media Effects*. Prospect Heights, IL: Waveland Press, 1997.

Lowery, Shearon, and Melvin DeFleur. *Milestones in Mass Communication Research*. New York: Longman, 1994.

National Television Study. Thousand Oaks, CA: Sage, 1997.

Reeves, Byron. *The Media Equation: How People Treat Computers, Television and New Media Like Real People and Places*. Stanford, CA: Center for the Study of Language, 1996.

Van Evra, Judith. *Television and Child Development*. Hillsdale, NJ: Erlbaum, 1990.

Zillmann, Dolf. *Media, Children and the Family*. Hillsdale, NJ: Erlbaum, 1994.

■ SURFING THE INTERNET

In addition to websites, several newsgroups and listservs are useful to those interested in mass media effects. The listings that follow represent only a small sample.

www.aejmc-mcs.org
Home page of the Mass Communication and Society division of the Association for Education in Journalism and Mass Communication. Contains a link to various news groups.

www.gsu.edu/~wwwcom/content
Site devoted to content analysis of communication messages. Contains summaries of studies of media content, some of which deal with violence and stereotyping.

http://tvnews.vanderbilt.edu
Home page of the Vanderbilt University Television News Archive. Researchers can examine abstracts of network news programs dating back to 1968.

www.uiowa.edu/~commstud/resources
Contains links to resources in all areas of mass media effects.

Glossary

acculturation   In a media context, the tendency of reporters or other media professionals to adopt the ideas and attitudes of the groups they cover or with which they have a great deal of contact.

advertising agency   A company that handles both the creative and the business side of an advertising campaign for its clients.

agencies of socialization   The various people or organizations that contribute to the socialization of an individual.

agency   Organization that handles basic needs of advertisers.

agenda building   The ways the media decide what is newsworthy.

agenda-setting effect   The influence of the mass media created by emphasizing certain topics, thus causing people to perceive those same issues as important.

alphabet   A group of letters used to symbolize each of the sounds that make up a word.

AM   Amplitude modulation of radio waves.

Arbitron   The professional research organization that measures radio audiences.

Audit Bureau of Circulations (ABC)   An organization formed by advertisers and publishers in 1914 to establish ground rules for counting circulation data.

authoritarian theory   The prevailing belief that a ruling elite should guide the intellectually inferior masses.

banner ads   Type of advertising found on web pages.

best-seller list   Ranking of best-selling books based on retail sales.

beware surveillance   A media function that occurs when the media inform the public of short-term, long-term, or chronic threats.

Billboard   The sound-recording industry trade publication that tabulates record popularity.

block booking   A policy of major film studios that required theater owners to show several of a studio's low-quality films before they could receive the same studio's top-quality films.

broadband   Increased bandwidth for Internet connections, which speeds up downloads.

browsers   Type of software that lets individuals search for content on the World Wide Web.

business-to-business advertising   Advertising directed not at the general public but at other businesses.

campaign   In advertising, a large number of ads that stress the same theme and appear over a specified length of time.

carriage fee   Fee paid by cable systems to carry a cable network.

categorical imperative   Ethical principle that states people should behave as they would wish all others to behave.

catharsis   A release of pent-up emotion or energy.

catharsis theory   A theory that suggests viewing aggression will purge the viewer's aggressive feelings.

cease-and-desist order   A Federal Trade Commission order notifying an advertiser that a certain practice violates the law; failure to comply with a cease-and-desist order can result in fines being levied against the advertiser.

channel   The pathway by which a message travels from sender to receiver.

circulation   The total number of copies of a publication delivered to newsstands, vending machines, and subscribers.

clock hour   Radio format that specifies every element of the program.

commercial television   Television programs broadcast by local stations whose income is derived from selling time on their facilities to advertisers.

Communications Act of 1934   Act of Congress creating the Federal Communications Commission.

communist theory   Theory of the press that holds the media should promote the goals of the ruling political party.

comprehensive layout   The finished model of a print ad.

computer-assisted reporting (CAR)   Skills involved in using the Internet to aid reporting.

concept testing   A type of feedback in which a one- or two-paragraph description for a new series is presented to a sample of viewers for their reactions.

consent order Federal Trade Commission order in which the advertiser agrees to halt a certain advertising practice without admitting any violation of the law.

consequence The importance or weightiness of a news story.

consumer advertising Advertising directed at the general public.

controlled circulation A type of circulation in which publications are sent free or distributed to a select readership, such as airline passengers or motel guests.

convergence The blending of communication technologies.

conversational currency Topic material presented by the media that provides a common ground for social conversations.

copy Headlines and message in an ad.

creative boutique Advertising organization that specializes in the creative side of advertising.

credibility The trust that the audience holds for media that perform surveillance functions.

critical/cultural approach Analytical technique that examines power relationships in society and focuses on meanings people find in texts.

crystallization The sharpening and elaboration of a vaguely held attitude or predisposition.

cultivation analysis An area of research that examines whether television and other media encourage perceptions of reality that are more consistent with media portrayals than with actuality.

culture Common values, behaviors, attitudes, and beliefs that bind a society together.

cycle In all-news radio, the amount of time that elapses before the program order is repeated.

decoding The activity in the communication process by which physical messages are translated into a form that has eventual meaning for the receiver.

defamation The act of harming the reputation of another by publishing false information.

demo A demonstration tape used to sell a musical performer or group.

developmental journalism Type of journalism, practiced by many Third World countries, that stresses national goals and economic development.

developmental theory The assumption that government uses media to further national, economic, and social goals.

digital technology A system that encodes information—sound, text, data, video—into a series of on and off pulses that are usually denoted as zeros and ones.

digital television (DTV) Television signals consisting of binary signals that allow for improved picture quality.

digital videodisk (DVD) A disk that stores audio, movies, video, and graphics in digital format that is compatible with DVD players and home computers.

direct action An ad that contains a direct response item (such as a toll-free number) that allows advertisers to see results quickly.

direct broadcast satellite (DBS) A system in which a home TV set receives a signal directly from an orbiting satellite.

disintermediation The process of delivering a product or service directly to the consumer.

distribution system The actual cables that deliver the signals to subscribers.

distributors Sector of media industry that takes products from manufacturers and delivers them to retailers.

double feature Practice started by theaters in the 1930s of showing two feature films on the same bill.

dummy Rough version of a magazine that's used for planning how final version will look.

dysfunction Consequence that is undesirable from the point of view of the welfare of society.

e-book Digital version of a book, which can be read by using a computer or a special reader.

editorial policies Guidelines the print media follow to persuade the public on certain issues or to achieve specific goals.

electronic news gathering (ENG) Producing and airing field reports using small, lightweight portable TV equipment.

e-mail Electronic messages sent from computer to computer.

encoding The activity in the communication process by which thoughts and ideas from the source are translated into a form that may be perceived by the senses.

Equal Opportunities rule Part of the Communications Act of 1934; Section 315 allows bona fide candidates for public office to gain access to a broadcast medium during political campaigns.

evaluation Research done to measure the effectiveness of an advertising or a public relations campaign.

experiment A research technique that stresses controlled conditions and manipulates variables.

Fairness Doctrine Now defunct FCC doctrine that required broadcast stations to provide various points of view on a controversial issue.

Federal Communications Commission (FCC) A regulatory agency, composed of five individuals appointed by the president, whose responsibilities include broadcast and wire regulation.

feedback The responses of the receiver that shape and alter subsequent messages from the source.

field experiment An experiment that is conducted in a natural setting as opposed to a laboratory.

First Amendment The first amendment of the Bill of Rights, stating that Congress shall make no law abridging the freedom of speech, or of the press.

FM Frequency modulation of radio waves.

focus group A group of 10 to 15 people led by a moderator that discusses predetermined topics.

format Consistent programming designed to appeal to a certain segment of the audience.

format wheel Visual aid that helps radio programmers plan what events happen during a given time period.

formative research Advertising research done before developing a campaign.

framing The general way a news medium treats a topic.

franchise An exclusive right to operate a business in a given territory.

Freedom of Information Act (FOIA) Law stating that every federal executive-branch agency must publish instructions on what methods a member of the public should follow to get information.

free-link exchange Web advertising technique in which one company exchanges free ad space with another.

free marketplace of ideas Press philosophy that endorses the free flow of information.

full-service agency An ad agency that handles all phases of advertising for its clients.

functional approach A methodology that holds something is best understood by examining how it is used.

gag rules Judicial orders that restrict trial participants from giving information to the media or that restrain media coverage of events that occur in court.

gatekeepers Individuals who decide whether a given message will be distributed by a mass medium.

golden mean Ethical principle that states moderation is the key to virtue.

gramophone A "talking machine" patented in 1887 by Emile Berliner that utilized a disk instead of a cylinder.

graphophone A recording device similar to the phonograph, but utilizing a wax cylinder rather than tinfoil.

hard news Timely stories with significance for many people.

head end The antenna and related equipment of the cable system that receives and processes distant television signals so that they can be sent to subscribers' homes.

heavy metal Counterculture musical trend of the 1960s–1970s, characterized by a vaguely threatening style and heavy use of amplification and electronic equipment.

hegemony Dominance of one entity over another.

Hicklin rule A long-standing obscenity standard based upon whether a book or other item contains isolated passages that might deprave or corrupt the mind of the most susceptible person.

house drop The section of the cable that connects the feeder cable to the subscriber's TV set.

human interest News value that emphasizes the emotional, bizarre, offbeat, or uplifting nature of a news story.

hypertext Digital navigational tool that links one electronic document to another.

IBOC (in-band, on-channel) Digital radio broadcasting system that is also compatible with current analog radio.

ideology Particular set of beliefs or ideas.

independents Radio or TV stations unaffiliated with any network.

indirect action ad Advertisement that works over the long run to build a company's image.

information gathering Phase of a public relations campaign where pertinent data are collected.

injunction A court order that requires an individual to do something or to stop doing something.

instrumental surveillance A media function that occurs when the media transmit information that is useful and helpful in everyday life.

Internet addiction Condition in which a person spends too much time on the Internet, cannot control his or her Internet use, and neglects social responsibilities to spend time online.

interpersonal communication A method of communication in which one person (or group) interacts with another person (or group) without the aid of a mechanical device.

investigative reports   News reporting that requires extraordinary efforts to gather information about matters of public importance.

jazz   A form of popular music that emerged during the Roaring Twenties and was noted for its spontaneity and disdain of convention.

jazz journalism   Journalism of the Roaring Twenties that was characterized by a lively style and a richly illustrated tabloid format.

joint-operating agreement (JOA)   An agreement, intended to preserve editorial competition, in which two newspapers merge their business and printing operations but maintain separate newsrooms.

joint venture   Method of movie financing in which several companies pool resources to finance films.

Kinetoscope   The first practical motion picture camera and viewing device, developed by William Dickson in 1889.

libel   Written defamation that tends to injure a person's reputation or good name or that diminishes the esteem, respect, or goodwill due a person.

libel per quod   Written material that becomes libelous under certain circumstances.

libel per se   Falsely written accusations (such as labeling a person a "thief" or a "swindler") that automatically constitute libel.

libertarian theory   The assumption that all human beings are rational decision makers and that governments exist to serve the individual.

limited partnership   Method of movie financing in which a number of investors put up a specified amount of money for a film.

linkage   The ability of the mass media to join different elements of society that are not directly connected by interpersonal channels.

machine-assisted interpersonal communication   A method of communication involving one or more persons and a mechanical device (or devices) with one or more receivers.

macroanalysis   A sociological perspective that considers the functions performed by a system (e.g., mass media) for the entire society.

magazine   Printed publication that contains an assortment of materials that appears on a regular basis.

mainstreaming   In cultivation analysis, the tendency of differences to disappear among heavy-TV-viewing people, apparently because of cultural and social factors.

management by objectives (MBO)   Management technique that sets observable, measurable goals for an organization to achieve.

marketing   Developing, pricing, distributing, and promoting an idea, a good, or a service.

mass communication   The process by which a complex organization, with the aid of one or more machines, produces and transmits public messages that are directed at large, heterogeneous, and scattered audiences.

mass media   The channels and the institutions of mass communication.

meaning   The interpretation an audience makes of text.

media buying service   An organization that specializes in buying media time to resell to advertisers.

Mediamark Research Inc. (MRI)   Company that measures magazine readership.

media vehicle   A single component of a mass medium, for example, a newspaper or TV network.

message   The actual physical product in the communication process that the source encodes.

message research   Pretesting messages in an ad campaign.

microanalysis   A sociological perspective that considers the functions performed by a system (e.g., mass media) for the individual.

modem   Device that allows computers to communicate via phone lines.

Motion Picture Patents Company (MPPC)   An organization formed by the nine leading film and film equipment manufacturers in 1908 for the purpose of controlling the motion picture industry.

MP3   Digital method of encoding sound files on the Internet.

MPAA rating system   The G, PG, PG-13, R, NC-17 rating system for movies administered by the Motion Picture Association of America.

muckrakers   Term coined by Theodore Roosevelt to describe the reform movement undertaken by leading magazines in the 1890s; corrupt practices of business and government were exposed to the general public by crusading members of the press.

national advertiser   Advertiser who sells a product all across the country.

National Public Radio (NPR)   A noncommercial U.S. radio network.

network   An organization composed of interconnecting broadcasting stations that cuts costs by airing the same programs.

newsgroups   Section of the Internet devoted to message boards that are organized according to topic.

newshole   The amount of space available each day in a newspaper for news.

nickelodeon   A popular name for the many penny arcades and amusement centers that emerged around the beginning of the 20th century and specialized in recordings and film.

noise   In communication, anything that interferes with the delivery of a message.

noncommercial television   Television programs broadcast by those stations whose income is derived from sources other than the sale of advertising time.

nonduplication rule   FCC rule passed in 1965, stating that an AM-FM combination may not duplicate its AM content on its FM channel for more than 50 percent of the time.

observational learning   A form of education in which individuals learn by observing the actions of others.

ombudsperson   An individual in a media organization assigned to handle complaints from audience members.

one-stops   Individuals who sell records to retail stores and jukebox operators who are not in a position to buy directly from the record company.

operating policies   Guidelines that cover the everyday problems and situations that crop up during the operation of a media organization.

paid circulation   A type of circulation in which the reader must purchase a magazine through a subscription or at a newsstand.

panel study   A research method in which data are collected from the same individuals at different points in time.

paradigm   A model used for analysis.

parasocial relationship   A situation whereby audience members develop a sense of kinship or friendship with media personalities.

pass-along audience   That portion of a magazine's total audience composed of individuals who pick up copies of a magazine while at the doctor's office, at work, while traveling, and so on.

payola   Bribes of gifts and money paid to DJs by record companies in order to gain favorable airplay for their releases.

pay-per-view (PPV)   A system that allows cable TV subscribers to pay a one-time fee to view one specific program or movie.

penny press   The mass-appeal press of the early 19th century.

persistence of vision   Quality of the human eye that enables it to retain an image for a split second after the image has disappeared.

phi phenomenon   Tendency of the human perceptual system to perceive continuous motion between two stationary points of light that blink on and off; basis for the illusion of motion in motion pictures.

phonograph   A "talking machine" developed by Thomas Edison in the late 1870s; the hand-cranked device preserved sound on a tinfoil-wrapped cylinder.

photojournalism   Journalism in which written text is secondary to photographs in news stories.

pickup   A technique of financing a motion picture.

pilot   The first episode of a projected television series.

pilot testing   A process that involves showing a sample audience an entire episode of a show and recording their reactions.

policy book   At radio and TV stations, a book that spells out philosophy and standards of operation and identifies practices that are encouraged or discouraged.

political press   Newspapers and magazines of the 1790–1820 era that specialized in publishing partisan political articles.

polysemic   Having many meanings.

portal   The first page a person sees when opening an Internet browser.

positioning   In advertising, stressing the unique selling point of a product or service to differentiate it from the competition.

primary audience   That portion of a magazine's total audience made up of subscribers or those who buy it at the newsstand.

primary demand ad   Advertisement that promotes a specific product category, such as milk.

Prime-Time Access Rule   Rule adopted in 1970 intended to expand program diversity by barring network programs from the 7:30–8:00 P.M. (E.S.T.) time slot.

printing on demand   One-at-a-time printing of books that exist in a digital database.

prior restraint   An attempt by the government to censor the press by restraining it from publishing or broadcasting material.

prominence   News value that stresses the importance of the person involved in the event.

prosocial behavior   A general term used by researchers to describe behaviors that are judged desirable or worthwhile under the circumstances.

protocol   A common language accepted by computer programmers.

proximity   News value based on the location of a news event.

Public Broadcasting Act of 1967   Congressional act that established the Public Broadcasting Service.

publicity   The placing of stories in the mass media.

public journalism   The philosophy that newspapers should try to solve civic problems as well as report the news.

publics   The various audience served by public relations.

publishers   Segment of the print media industry responsible for the creation of content.

rack jobbers   Individuals who service record racks located in variety and large department stores by choosing the records to be sold in each location.

Radio Act of 1927   Congressional act establishing the Federal Radio Commission, a regulatory body that would issue broadcasting licenses and organize operating times and frequencies.

rate base   Number of buyers guaranteed by a magazine and used to compute advertising rates.

rating   The ratio of listeners to a particular radio station to all people in the market; the ratio of viewers of a particular TV program to the number of households in the market equipped with TV.

receiver   The target of the message in the communication process.

reinforcement   Support of existing attitudes and opinions by certain messages.

resonance   In cultivation analysis, the situation in which a respondent's life experiences are reinforced by what is seen on TV, thus reinforcing the effect of TV content.

retail (local) advertiser   Business that has customers in only one trading area.

retailers   Segment of the media industry responsible for selling media products to the consumer.

revenue sharing   Process by which video stores share movie rental fees with movie companies.

rough layout   Early version of a print ad.

satellite news gathering (SNG)   Using specially equipped vans and trucks to transmit live stories from any location via satellite.

Sedition Act   Act of Congress passed in the late 1790s that made it a crime to write anything "false, scandalous or malicious" about the U.S. government or Congress; it was used to curb press criticism of government policies.

selective demand ad   Ad that stresses a particular brand.

self-determination   Ethical principle that states that human beings deserve respect for their decisions.

share of the audience   The ratio of listeners to a particular radio station to the total number of listeners in the market; the ratio of the number of households watching a particular TV program to the number of households watching TV at that time.

shield laws   Legislation that defines the rights of a reporter to protect sources.

slander   Spoken defamation. (In many states, if a defamatory statement is broadcast, it is considered libel, even though technically the words are not written. Libel is considered more harmful and usually carries more serious penalties than does slander.)

sliding scale   An arrangement between a motion picture exhibitor and a distributor that details how much box office revenue will be kept by the movie theater.

social responsibility theory   The belief that the press has a responsibility to preserve democracy by properly informing the public and by responding to society's needs.

social utility   The media function that addresses an individual's need to affiliate with family, friends, and others in society.

socialization   The ways an individual comes to adopt the behavior and values of a group.

soft news   Features that rely on human interest for their news value.

source   Person who initiates communication.

spam   The electronic equivalent of junk mail.

status conferral   A process by which media attention bestows a degree of prominence on certain issues or individuals.

stimulation theory   A theory that suggests viewing violence will actually stimulate an individual to behave more violently.

storyboard   A series of drawings depicting the key scenes in a TV ad.

strategic planning   Management technique that sets long-range, general goals.

streaming video   Method of sending TV over the Internet.

subsidiary rights   Rights given by a publisher to others, allowing them to reproduce certain content.

surveillance   The news and information function of the mass media.

survey   A technique of gathering data that typically uses a questionnaire.

tabloid   A heavily illustrated publication usually half the size of a normal newspaper page.

tactical planning   Management technique that sets short-range, specific goals.

target audience   In advertising, the segment of the population for whom the product or service has an appeal.

technological determinism   The theory that contends technology drives historical change.

Telecommunications Act of 1996   Major revision of U.S. communication laws that affected broadcasting, cable, and telephone industries.

text   Object of analysis in the critical/cultural approach.

timeliness   News value that stresses when an event occurred.

time shifting   Recording programs and playing them back at times other than when they were aired.

tracking studies   Study that examines how ads perform during or after a campaign.

trespass   Illegal entry onto another's property.

UHF   The ultra-high-frequency band of the electromagnetic spectrum; channels 14 through 69 on the TV set.

underground press   A type of specialized reporting that emerged in the mid- to late 1960s, with emphasis on politically liberal news and opinion, and cultural topics such as music, art, and film.

uses-and-gratifications model   A model proposing that audience members have certain needs or drives that are satisfied by using both nonmedia and media sources.

utility   Ethical principle that stresses the greatest good for the greatest number.

Variety   The entertainment industry trade publication.

V-Chip   A device installed in a TV set that restricts the reception of violent or objectionable material.

veil of ignorance   Ethical principle that argues that everyone should be treated equally.

VHF   The very-high-frequency band of the electromagnetic spectrum; channels 2 through 13 on the TV set.

web page   A hypertext page contained within a website.

website   A set of hypertext pages linked to each other that contain information about a common topic.

World Wide Web (WWW)   A network of information sources that uses hypertext to link one piece of information to another.

yellow journalism   Sensationalized journalism, appearing during the 1890s, noted for its emphasis on sex, murder, popularized medicine, pseudoscience, self-promotion, and human-interest stories.

zoned edition   Newspaper that has special sections for specific geographic areas.

Index